ALEXANDER I

ALEXANDER I

THE TSAR WHO DEFEATED NAPOLEON

Marie-Pierre Rey

TRANSLATED BY SUSAN EMANUEL

NIU
PRESS

DeKalb, IL

© 2012 by Northern Illinois University Press
Published by the Northern Illinois University Press, DeKalb, Illinois 60115
Manufactured in the United States using acid-free paper.
All Rights Reserved
Design by Shaun Allshouse

First published in French as *Alexander Ier* by © Éditions Flammarion, 2009

Library of Congress Cataloging-in-Publication Data
Rey, Marie Pierre.
[Alexandre Ier. English]
Alexander I : the tsar who defeated Napoleon / Marie Pierre Rey ; translated by Susan
Emanuel.
pages ; cm
Includes bibliographical references and index.
ISBN 978 0 87580 466 8 (cloth) — ISBN 978 1 60909 065 4 (electronic)
1. Alexander I, Emperor of Russia, 1777–1825. 2. Emperors—Russia—Biography. 3. Rus-
sia—History—Alexander I, 1801–1825. I. Emanuel, Susan, translator. II. Title. III. Title:
Alexander the First.
DK191.R4913 2012
947'.072092 dc23
[B]
2012030680

This book was published with the generous financial support of the Centre national du
livre (Paris, France). Publié avec le soutien du Centre national du livre (Paris, France).
Financial assistance was also kindly provided by the Fondation Napoléon (Paris) and the
University of Paris I Panthéon Sorbonne.

Contents

Acknowledgments

The writing of a life is a passionate intellectual adventure, the pitfalls of which may arouse doubts and speculations (and sometimes discouragement), so arduous is the task. I wish here to render amicable and sincere homage to those who supported me as I pursued this project. My gratitude goes first to my French editor, Hélène Fiamma, whose benevolent and confident help and the well-considered advice she always offered me have been extremely precious over the course of these six years of work.

I would also like to thank the directors and curators of the archives and libraries who lent me their assistance: Sergei Mironenko, director of GARF, and Larissa Rogovaia and Elena Shirkova, archivists; Mikhail Ryzhenkov, director of RGADA; Christina Grafinger, curator at the Vatican Library and Archives; Mireille Pastoureau, curator at the Library of the Institut de France; Geneviève Chesneau, of the Library of the Chevalier de Cessole; as well as the staffs of the Imperial Library of St. Petersburg, the British Library, the Bibliothèque Nationale de France, and the Archives of the French Ministry of Foreign Affairs. Anne Maitre, curator of the Gagarin and Saint Georges archives deposited at ENS-LSH in Lyon, and Father René Marichal, formerly in charge of these collections, gave me constant help in the exploration of these valuable documents. I thank them warmly.

During the course of writing, I could count on the meticulous, attentive, and exacting readings by my friends Christine Moreau and Jean-Pierre Minaudier: the manuscript owes substantial improvements to them, and I am extremely grateful. My gratitude also goes to Korine Amacher who let me benefit from her solid knowledge of the reign of Alexander the First.

As concerns the American edition of the work, I want to thank the publishers, Northern Illinois University Press, and in particular its director, Alex Schwartz, who received the manuscript with enthusiasm, and editor Amy Farranto for the constant care she brought to preparing the text. My gratitude also goes to my translator, Susan Emanuel, as well as to the French institutions that have financially supported the translation of the book and made its English-language edition possible: the Centre national du livre, the Fondation Napoléon, and the Université Paris I Panthéon Sorbonne. My gratitude is immense.

Finally, this biography would not have seen the light of day or been accomplished without the unwavering support of my family, so the book is naturally dedicated to them.

Author's Note

During the tsarist period, the Russian Empire lived at the rhythm of the Julian calendar, which in the eighteenth century was eleven days behind the Gregorian calendar used in the rest of Europe (and twelve days behind in the nineteenth century). To avoid resorting systematically to giving double dates, I have chosen to use the latter (Gregorian) dating system, except where the abbreviation (O.S.)—Old Style—indicates the use of the Julian calendar. Place-names (towns, villages, regions) are given their current appellations.

Introduction

In the history of the Russian Empire, Tsar Alexander occupies a singular place. Rare are the major political figures that have aroused such discussion and contradictory verdicts among their contemporaries. A "heavenly angel"[1] in the eyes of Empress Elizabeth, his wife, endowed with a "fine mind" and "perfect equanimity in his humor, a quality very rare and precious in a sovereign, whose source lay in the goodness of his soul"[2] for the Countess of Choiseul-Gouffier, Alexander was only a "crowned Hamlet" for Herzen, a "Talma[3] of the North," a "Greek of the Lower Empire, fake as a coin" and "stubborn as a mule"[4] for Napoleon.

If those close to him[5] saw him as sincere, he was (in the astute and provocative judgment of the Swede Lagerbielke) a monument of duplicity: "In politics, fine as a pinpoint, sharp as a razor, and false as sea foam."[6] Possessing an "excellent heart, but perhaps a little weak,"[7] in the eyes of the Austrian military envoy, Stutterheim, posted to St. Petersburg, he was by contrast described by the Marquis of Caulaincourt as a man of character: "He is thought to be weak but that is a mistake. He can undoubtedly bear many adversities and hide his displeasure [...] but he will not go beyond the circle he has traced for himself, which is made of iron and will not be stretched."[8]

Beyond their antinomies, these contradictory perceptions attest to one indisputable fact: whether he was the object of adulation or rancor, whether he crystallized hopes and desires or vexations, Alexander I remained (despite a reign of almost 25 years) an elusive person, "an inscrutable sphinx to the tomb,"[9] even an enigma. And his sudden death, occurring in disturbing circumstances in 1825 when he was only 48, added to the mystery, feeding extravagant rumors and dividing his contemporaries.[10]

Enigmatic in his lifetime, Alexander has remained so for posterity—and this is no less the paradox of his character—since the many historical studies of the tsar have not forged a uniform image of him. Quite the contrary.

In the nineteenth century, several biographers stressed contrasting judgments of him and their need to use them in order to explain the contradictions of his reign.[11] At the beginning of the twentieth century, the magisterial work devoted to him by Grand Duke Nicholas Mikhailovich insisted on his irresolute character,[12] whereas a book written shortly afterward by the Polish historian K. Waliszewski stressed his duplicity and his taste for dissimulation.[13] Thus, both of them contributed to the dark legend of

Alexander I. And for many tsarist historians, it was the tsar's childhood[14]—the difficult years when, idolized by his grandmother Catherine II, he was cut off from his parents, the future Paul I and his wife, Maria Feodorovna—that lay at the source of his so-called "duplicity" and at the origin of his vacillating character.

More recently, the historians (from the interwar period up to today) who have taken an interest in Alexander I have also created contrasting portraits that usually rely on biased interpretations and peremptory verdicts. In fact, while most of them do agree in stressing the secretive, even disguised, nature of Alexander—whom historians perceive as a "northern sphinx,"[15] an "enigmatic tsar,"[16] "mystical,"[17] or even as "a will o' the wisp"[18]—their verdicts become more polemical when politics enters the matter. He was a "prince of illusions"[19] for Daria Olivier, an "ideological tsar"[20] for Pierre Rain, and even a banal autocrat for Michael Klimenko,[21] whereas for Allen McConnell he was a "paternalist reformer."[22] The Russian historian Vladimir Fedorov calls him a hard and secretive man, "republican in his words but autocratic in his deeds,"[23] and Alexander Sakharov[24] sees him as man of extreme complexity, torn apart and almost paralyzed by his own contradictions.

In this context, to undertake a new biography of Alexander I might seem to be an impossible task, given that any coherence in the subject is hard to establish. But at the same time, the crucial importance of Alexander's reign for Russian history and the changes of stature and status that the country underwent in those 25 years invite the historian to take up the biographical challenge.[25]

In fact, Russia knew major changes during Alexander's reign. On the domestic level, reforms of liberal inspiration were initially undertaken, notably the reorganization of the central administration and the creation of several universities, while by contrast the second half of the reign saw the establishment of the terrible military colonies of Count Arakcheev. In foreign affairs, conducting a very active expansionist policy, the Russian Empire managed to incorporate Finland and then Bessarabia, to extend toward the Caucasus, and to make a foothold on the American continent, whereas at the same time, amidst armed conflicts and hostile periods of peace, Russia assumed a predominant place in the concert of European nations. It was also under Alexander's reign that tsarist Russia underwent the most tragic experience in its history, marked by the invasion of the Napoleonic armies and the burning of Moscow, its sacred capital, in 1812. In each of these episodes, Alexander's role—his choices, his perceptions—was determining, due as much to the autocratic nature of imperial power as to the complex personality of the emperor.

It is in order to better apprehend and comprehend this crucial 25 years that I have chosen to recount Alexander I's life, relying on the existing voluminous bibliography and exploiting significant bodies of documents in the archives. In the course of my reading, it appeared to me that many of the books devoted to Emperor Alexander merely updated preexisting works, which themselves merely recycled previous writing, without drawing on direct archive sources. This excessive confidence in prior writings has contributed to reproducing and amplifying certain assertions, even pontifications, on the personality and reign of Alexander without their pertinence ever being analyzed or contested. To avoid falling into this trap, it was essential to go back to direct documentary and contemporary sources.

To do so, I first went to the archives of the Imperial Russian State, meaning first to the personal papers of the Romanovs—including those of Alexander I[26]—and to the very precious stores of the Manuscript Collection in the library of the Winter Palace. These papers contain documents written in either French (the majority) or Russian. I have also consulted the diplomatic archives of several European states—French, Polish, Vatican—and I enriched the reading of these public documents by consulting private archives emanating from great noble families of Russia, Poland, and Italy, as well as by consulting ecclesiastical sources, including the Jesuit archives.[27]

These documents were usefully illuminated by taking into account the abundant and often specifically pertinent correspondence, reminiscences, and memoirs written by those close to Alexander—his grandmother, Catherine II, his wife Elizabeth, his various tutors, as well as statesmen, military commanders, diplomats, courtiers, artists, and men and women of letters who came to court and to serve him, or else to oppose and fight him. Despite their polyphonic contrasts, even contradictions, these sources helped me to grasp the personality of Alexander, to draw out certain aspects of his reign little explored until now—for example, the key role played by his republican-minded tutor, his relations with his mother, and the eclecticism of his religious convictions—as well as to present entirely new material on his duel with Napoleon, his European dream, and his desire for the fusion between the churches of East and West.

Finally, it appeared essential to let the reader hear the voice of Alexander, that is to say, to rely as much as possible on his private and public writings and on his precious correspondence.[28] By turns serious and light-hearted, spontaneous and restrained, intimate and public, this rich correspondence allowed me to unveil more of the tsar's mystery and to shed light on this strange judgment delivered by Napoleon in exile in Saint Helena:

The Emperor of Russia is a man infinitely superior to all that: he has spirit, grace, and education; he is easily seductive, but he should not be trusted: he is without candor, a true Greek of the Lower Empire. [...] Perhaps also he was trying to mystify me, for he is subtle, false, and adroit; he could go far. If I die here, he will be my true heir in Europe.[29]

ALEXANDER I

Prologue

The Murder of Paul I: March 23, 1801

In the early morning of March 24, 1801, for his first official outing as emperor, Alexander I, then aged 23, offered the courtiers gathered in the Winter Palace the strange image of a haggard man devastated with grief:

> The new emperor walked forward slowly, his knees seemed to be bent, his hair in disarray, his eyes swollen with tears; he stared straight in front of him, seldom inclining his head as if in greeting; his whole attitude and aspect were those of a man laid low by pain and broken by the disaster that had overcome him.[1]

This suffering and sadness were accompanied by deep remorse. Returning to Russia in the spring of 1801 after having been exiled by Paul I, the Polish prince Adam Czartoryski, a childhood friend of Alexander, said he was told by the new sovereign:

> "If you had been here," he added, "nothing of this would have happened to me; having you close to me, I never would have been entrained in this way." Then he spoke to me of the death of his father with a painful expression and inexpressible remorse.[2] [...] "I must suffer; how can I stop suffering? This cannot change." Sometimes when the conversation returned to this sad subject, Emperor Alexander still often repeated to me the details of the plan he had formed to establish his father in St. Michael's Castle and then procure for him (as much as possible) the enjoyment of the imperial residences in the country. "St. Michael's Castle was his favorite residence. He would have had the whole winter garden at his disposal for walks and horse-rides."[3]

Why this feeling of guilt? What happened during the night of March 23–24, 1801?

The tragedy that unfolded in the sinister Michael Palace, where the imperial family had been in residence barely a month, was so confused and disordered that accounts of it diverge and even contradict each other. Since we cannot be certain about the exact circumstances of Paul's death,[4] we can only reconstruct the general outlines of the scenario.

Around one o'clock in the morning, abruptly woken up by a group of tipsy officers who had managed to penetrate his apartments without the knowledge of his bodyguards and valet, Emperor Paul had only time to take refuge behind a folding screen. Quickly flushed out of his paltry hiding place, the frightened tsar tried to oppose the intruders by refusing energetically the abdication they were ordering him to accept. Furious at this refusal, the officers manhandled the tsar and under cover of the room's darkness, they strangled him before one of them delivered the final blow. In a document written in 1826, based on the testimony that the conspirators had given a few years after Paul's death, the Count of Langeron, a French emigrant who had gone into Russian service, wrote:

> The assassins had neither a cord nor a towel to strangle him. Karyatkin, I am told, gave his scarf, and this was how Paul perished: it is not known who should be given the horrible honor of his cruel end; all the conspirators participated, but it seems that Prince Yashvil and Katarinov were most responsible for this frightful crime. It appears that Nikolay Zubov, a species of butcher, cruel and emboldened by the wine he had gulped, punched him in the face, and since he grasped in his hand a gold snuffbox, one of its sharp edges wounded the emperor under his left eye.[5]

Confusion and ambiguity dominate the account given of these events by the emperor's younger son Constantine.

> I suspected nothing—I was sleeping as one sleeps at age twenty. Platon Zubov [Catherine's last favorite and one of the main instigators of the plot], drunkenly entered the room making a lot of noise (already an hour had passed since my father ceased existence), and threw back my covering and said insolently, "Get up and get going to Emperor Alexander, he's waiting for you." You may imagine how astonished—and even frightened—I was. I looked at Zubov, I was still half asleep and thought I was dreaming. Platon pulled me by the arm to make me get up; I pulled on trousers and boots and followed him mechanically, taking the precaution of bringing my Polish saber, [...] I came to my brother's antechamber; I saw a crowd of noisy and overheated officers, and Uvarov drunk like them and sitting on a marble table, legs dangling. I

entered my brother's living room, I found him lying on a canapé and weeping, as well as the Empress Elizabeth; only then did I learn of the assassination of my father, *I was so stunned by this news that I thought at first it was a plot from outside against all of us.*[6]

Yet even if confusion and disorder were a factor in the execution of this coup, the plot was not enacted in an improvised way. On the contrary, it was the outcome of a carefully conceived machination, prepared long before Paul was killed.

Back in 1798–1799, the Russian court was full of rumors of assassination, and in the tsar's immediate entourage an opposition started to build around Count Nikita Petrovich Panin. Vice Chancellor and nephew of Catherine II's former chancellor, a childhood friend of Paul's, Panin professed liberal and Anglophile convictions that he shared with Admiral Ribas, the Zubov brothers, and their sister Olga Zherebtsova, at the time the mistress of the British ambassador, Lord Whitworth. Deeply worried at the way the regime was evolving, which they perceived as increasingly despotic and dangerously Anglophobe, the little group that met frequently at Olga's gradually came up with a plan to depose the tsar, without bloodshed, in favor of his son Alexander, who would be proclaimed regent. So it was a matter of implementing a peaceful palace revolution. But the plan remained vague. In the spring of 1800, the Zubov brothers and their sister, who had served Catherine II and thus incarnated in Paul's eyes a past period that he hated, were sent away from St. Petersburg; shortly afterward, Lord Whitworth, victim of a crisis in Russo-British relations, was also forced to leave the country. From that date, the plot appeared compromised, but Panin did not give up, as signaled in a barely covert way in the letter addressed to him by the British lord on the eve of his departure.

> Think of me, as I will think often of you. The last wish I make is to exhort you to courage, patience, resignation. *Think how much depends on you in these critical circumstances. As long as you are devoted to the cause, I will not lose all hope.*[7]

It was also at this moment that Panin began approaching Alexander. During a secret meeting at the baths, he tried (without managing to obtain) the tsarevich's tacit consent for his plan. In parallel he began the material preparation with the financial support of Lord Whitworth. In fact, the British archives attest to the fact that in May 1800, the Lord borrowed and spent the sum of 40,000 rubles "necessary for the accomplishment of my mission"—

and "in accord with His Majesty's secret services," he later said.[8] In his meticulous article devoted to the affair,[9] the historian James Kenney concludes that most of this sum was devoted to bribing individuals close to Paul; thus Kutaisov, his barber and confidant, was given a stipend to persuade the emperor to bring the Zubovs back to St. Petersburg. From the British archives it appears that the Foreign Office was not the direct commissioner of the murder, but that the British secret services, informed of what was being set in motion, gave full initiative to Whitworth. Returning to London in May 1800, almost ten months before the plot was put into effect, he could not be accused of anything.

In November 1800 Panin was disgraced and in turn forced to leave St. Petersburg; it was now Count Peter Pahlen, a distant cousin of Panin and governor-general of St. Petersburg, who, increasingly opposed to Paul's anti-British policy, would ensure the practical organization of the plot, aided by generous funds from Britain put at his disposal by Panin.

Skillfully, Pahlen began to work on the army, in particular the regiments of the Imperial Guard, by distilling for several months any remarks and criticisms of the tsar's despotism and arbitrary use of power.[10] Then he methodically organized the coup:

> I wanted to be seconded by people more solid than this body of whippersnappers;[11] I wanted to rely on friends whose energy and courage were known to me. I wanted to use the Zubovs and Bennigsen, but how to get them back to Petersburg? They were disgraced and exiled and I had no pretext for having their exile lifted.[12]

Using his credit with the emperor and the funds that Panin paid him to bribe Kutaisov and others, Pahlen tore from Paul I an amnesty that allowed several hundred banished officers to come back to the capital. From among these humiliated discontents the count would recruit his accomplices, around 60 persons, including General Bennigsen, the three Zubov brothers, General Talyzin (commander of the Preobrazhensky Regiment), General Uvarov (commander of the Horseguards) and the Georgian Prince Yashvil. Pahlen, although valued by Paul (who in February 1801 named him Director of Postal Administration and two days later President of the Foreign Affairs Council), remained faithful to the plan he had set himself. To succeed, he had to obtain, if not the support of the Grand Duke Alexander, then at least his tacit approval. He soon applied himself to this task, while promising Alexander that his father's life would be spared:

For more than six months, my projects had settled on the necessity of toppling Emperor Paul from the throne, but it appeared impossible (and indeed it was) to manage without having the consent and even the cooperation of Grand Duke Alexander—or at least without warning him. I sounded him on this subject, at first lightly and vaguely, contenting myself with throwing out a few words on the dangers of his father's character. Alexander listened to me, sighing and not responding.

This is not what I wanted and so I decided to break the ice and say openly and frankly what appeared to me indispensable to do. At first Alexander seemed revolted by my plan; he told me he did not dissimulate either the tsar's dangers to the empire or to himself, but he was resigned to suffer everything and determined to undertake nothing against his father. I was not discouraged and renewed my attempts, making him feel the indispensable necessity of a change, which each day a new mad act made even more indispensable. By dint of flattering him or frightening him about his own future, by presenting the alternative of the throne or a dungeon and possible death, I managed to shake his filial piety and even to make him decide upon a denouement whose urgency he could not conceal.

But I owe it to the truth to say that Grand Duke Alexander did not consent to anything before having required my most sacred word that no attempt would be made on the life of his father; I gave it, I was not so deprived of commonsense as to commit myself internally to an impossible thing, but it was necessary to calm the scruples of my future sovereign and so I flattered his intentions, sure that they could not be fulfilled. I knew perfectly well that a revolution had to be achieved or else not undertaken, and that if Paul did not cease to exist, then the doors of his prison would soon be open, the most frightful reaction would take place, and the blood of innocents as well as the guilty would soon inundate the capital and the provinces. The Emperor had become suspicious about my contact with Grand Duke Alexander. We were aware of this; I could not appear with this young prince, we did not dare to speak to each other for a long while, despite the relations our places gave us. So it was by means of notes (imprudent and dangerous but necessary) that we communicated our thoughts and the arrangements to be made; these notes were sent via Count Panin: the Grand Duke Alexander answered in notes that Panin transmitted to me. We read them, we answered and burned them on the spot.[13]

Now sure of Alexander's approval, Pahlen envisaged proceeding at the end of March, but circumstances obliged him to bring this forward. On March

19, at seven in the morning, he was summoned by the emperor, who had just learned of a plot against him and that Pahlen was the instigator. Demonstrating his presence of mind and sangfroid, Pahlen replied with aplomb that he was indeed implicated in the conspiracy but only in order to control and thwart it when the time came. Pahlen gave Paul I a list of the conspirators, adding the names of grand dukes Alexander and Constantine and that of the Empress Maria Feodorovna. Reassured of the intentions of the governor-general and of his personal loyalty, Paul then signed arrest orders aimed at the three "conspirators" and gave them to Pahlen to use when the latter judged it appropriate. Armed with these documents, Pahlen now informed Alexander of the imminent threat hanging over him and his family and thus convinced him that it was time to act. Alexander set the date of the night of March 23 to 24, since the guard outside the castle would be the third battalion of the Semenovsky Regiment, "of which he was more sure than the two others."[14] Once again he exhorted Pahlen to spare his father's life.

Henceforth things happened fast. On the evening of the twenty-third, Paul was newly suspicious and put Alexander and Constantine under arrest in their rooms and forbade them to leave the castle; meanwhile the conspirators met at 11 p.m. in the apartment of General Talyzin in a wing of the Preobrazhensky barracks; an hour later, they marched to St. Michael's Castle whose heavy walls, moats, and drawbridges seemed memories of bygone days. The first group was led by Pahlen, the second by Bennigsen and Platon Zubov. Since Pahlen voluntarily hung back to avoid playing even a minor role at the key moment, it was Bennigsen and Zubov who were the first into the tsar's apartment and so would take direct responsibility for Paul's death.

No longer doubting the deed's favorable outcome, Pahlen quickly took over management of operations, worried about the attitude of the troops, many of whom were deeply attached to Paul. It was he who announced the sinister news to Alexander, and when the young man burst into tears, he thrust him forward with "That's enough of being a child. Go reign. Come show yourself to the guards!"[15] before taking him to appear before the regiments assembled in the interior courtyard of the castle.

Thus the new emperor made his first public declaration. Stating that his father had died of an attack of apoplexy, he asserted his will to pursue the work of his grandmother. And so in the early morning of the twenty-fourth, it was under the auspices of Catherine II that the young Alexander chose to inaugurate his reign.

* * *

Several biographers of Alexander have taken an interest in his implication in the plot that cost Paul I his life; their conclusions diverge. For some, who refer to Pahlen's testimony, Alexander's involvement was essentially passive: the tsarevich did not wish for his father's death but only his deposition. For others, Paul would never have abdicated voluntarily because the nature of his autocratic power received from God prevented any renunciation of the throne. Moreover, he benefited from wide popularity within the army, and hence a deadly outcome was inevitable,[16] of which deep inside himself Alexander must have been perfectly aware.[17] Still today it is difficult to settle this debate: certainly the facts that Alexander feared for his life and that the erring ways of his father gradually fixed in him the idea that it was his moral and political responsibility to seize the throne by force cannot be doubted, which would lay full responsibility upon him. However, it is impossible to establish whether Alexander sincerely hoped his father's life would be saved, or whether he tried to convince himself in order to exonerate his own culpability.

Whatever the case and the degree of involvement, it should be stressed that a deep feeling of guilt would not cease to haunt Alexander until the end of his days. His wife Elizabeth felt this on the night of the tragedy, when she wrote to her mother: "The Grand Duke Alexander, today an emperor, was absolutely devastated by the death of his father, by the way in which he died; his sensitive soul will always remain torn apart."[18]

Time would never manage to assuage the feeling of an irreparable wrong committed: parricide and tsaricide, two sins in the sight of God. Whether sanctioned consciously or unconsciously, the memory would remain an open wound in Alexander forever. The very breadth of this guilt and its durable impact on the emperor's behavior invite the historian to wonder precisely about his motives during the drama of March 23, 1801: why and how did this 23-year-old prince, gentle and timid, who confessed many years later that he was "always embarrassed to appear in public,"[19] ultimately decide (or was he cajoled?) to assume the role of a parricide and "a crowned Hamlet"?[20] Were ambition, taste for power, cynicism, or hatred at work? Or should we take into account a bundle of circumstances that are more complex and subtle? At least part of the answer is to be sought in the childhood and adolescence of Alexander.

PART ONE

THE CHILDHOOD AND
YOUTH OF AN EMPEROR,
1777–1801

CHAPTER 1

Monsieur Alexander and Catherine the Great

Do you know Monsieur Alexander? Do you often go to Versailles? Do you know the assistants to the assistants of Monsieur Alexander? At least you know Monsieur Alexander as the subject of *The Ingenu*. But I bet you do not know him at all, at least the one I am speaking about. It is not Alexander the Great but a very small Alexander who has just been born, the twelfth of this month at ten forty-five in the morning. This is to say that the Grand Duchess has just given birth to a son who, in honor of Saint Alexander Nevsky, has received the formal name of Alexander, and whom I call Monsieur Alexander because he partakes of life without fail; in time, his assistants will have assistants. This is the prophecy and gossip of grandmothers. […] My God, what will become of this child? […] I console myself with reading Bayle and the father of Tristram Shandy, who was of the opinion that one's name influences the person: a proud one and he is illustrious. […] Family models also have some effect, what do you think? The choice is sometimes embarrassing. But examples have nothing to do with it: to believe the venerable evangelist Pastor Wagner, it is nature that does it all, but where do you find that? Is it at the bottom of the bag of a good constitution? […] It is a shame that fairies are out of fashion; they could give you a child who has all that you could wish; me, I would have given them fine presents and would have whispered in their ears: Ladies, give him what is natural, a tiny bit of nature, and experience will gradually do the rest. Adieu. Take care.[1]

On December 25, 1777 (by our calendar), with these playful words, Empress Catherine II announced to the German Baron Grimm the coming into the world of her first grandson. Friedrich Melchior Grimm lived in Paris and penned a "literary correspondence" paper that he disseminated in fifteen copies solely to monarchs and princes who desired to be up to date with Parisian cultural life. Concerned to promote her image as an enlightened monarch, Catherine was a subscriber.[2] In 1775 Grimm had gone to St. Petersburg on the tsarina's invitation; upon his return with a stipend from the empress, he kept up a correspondence with her. This regular correspondence, pursued over the course of 20 years and very varied in themes and topics (Grimm was a confidant, an informer, a cultural agent), is a precious source for grasping the psychology and intimate life of Catherine II. This letter sharing the news of Alexander's birth attests to her joy as well as her worry: "My God, what will become of this child?"

On December 23, 200 cannon shots boomed from the Peter and Paul Citadel and the Admiralty; a Te Deum was celebrated in the palace chapel. Eight days later the child was baptized in the great chapel of the Winter Palace by Father Ivan Panfilov, the empress's confessor. Paul had chosen the first name of his son in honor of Alexander Nevsky, the patron saint of St. Petersburg. Catherine as godmother had persuaded Emperor Joseph II of Austria and the king of Prussia, Frederick II, to act as godfathers, although they were not present at the christening. For the empress, nothing was too solemn or too prestigious to salute the birth of the future emperor of All the Russias, whose reign, she thought, could not help being an extension of her own.

At Alexander's birth, Catherine was 48 years old. She had reigned since July 9, 1762, the date of the military coup that led to the deposition and assassination of Tsar Peter III, her husband—and that raised her, a former minor German princess called Sophia of Anhalt-Zerbst, to the imperial throne. In that reign of 15 years, Catherine had contributed to a significant assertion of Russian power and to major changes on the domestic level, but an assessment in 1777 would be mixed. Although she wanted to be an enlightened sovereign, Catherine remained no less attached to her autocratic power—from which she distanced even her own son.

The Russian Empire in 1777: Power and Modernization

Starting in 1762, Catherine associated her actions with the legacy of Peter the Great, asserting her desire to pursue a foreign policy of intense diplomatic and military activity and a domestic policy of reform and modernization.

On the diplomatic level she had her heart set on ensuring for the Russian

Empire a choice place in European affairs. To her mind it should participate in the concert of nations on a par with England, France, Austria, and Prussia—and even try to become predominant on the continent. To do so, Catherine entrusted to Nikita Panin, the head of the College of Foreign Affairs, the direction of Russian diplomacy. With the support of William Pitt, the British prime minister, Panin went on to promote and apply the "Northern system," meaning a union of Russia, Prussia, England, and Denmark directed against the union of the Bourbons, made up of the Catholic states of France, Spain, and Austria.

This Northern policy was largely explained by Catherine's expansionist aims: desirous to extend the southern frontiers of Russia to the Black Sea, to the detriment of an Ottoman Empire already allied with France, she needed solid support on the international scene. Armed with the Northern system, Russia began in 1768 an armed conflict with the Turkish Sublime Porte. Six years later, in 1774, this conflict led to the signing of the advantageous Treaty of Kutchuk-Kainardji that gave Russia major territorial gains, authorizing a Russian hold on the northern shores of the Black Sea and the annexation of the port of Kerch and declaring the khanate of Crimea independent of the Ottomans. Moreover, the treaty gave the Russian Empire significant economic advantages: its merchant ships acquired the right of free circulation in the Black Sea and the straits. Finally, on the political level, while the provinces of Moldavia and Wallachia still remained Ottoman possessions, Russia obtained the right to oversee the situation of Christians living in the Turkish Empire. This last proviso was fundamental: it effectively conferred on the Russian state immense international prestige as protector of Christian peoples who were held "prisoners in an ungodly land."

Russian expansionism in Europe also took place at the expense of Poland: it was a matter of profiting from the weakening of a state undergoing decomposition in order to expropriate lands that had formerly been part of Kievan Russia. In 1772 the first division (of three) made by Austria, Prussia, and Russia resulted in amputating from Poland a third of both its territory and its population. Russia acquired the regions of Polotsk, Vitebsk, and Mogilev, as well as part of Lithuania—representing a total of 1.3 million persons and 85,000 square kilometers, which substantially enlarged imperial territory.

While these territorial aggrandizements demonstrated the growing influence of Russia, they did not suffice to make it a great power—hence the efforts at political and economic modernization that the empress undertook from the beginning of her reign.

* * *

This undertaking would not be easy on any count. Confronted with successive traumas like the Mongol yoke, the terror of Ivan IV's reign, and the religious schism[3] of the 1660s, Russia had remained outside the great currents of thought—the Renaissance, humanism, and the Reformation—that had enriched Europe. Thus it remained a "pariah" figure on the European cultural scene. Moreover, the structure of Russian society was gripped by profound anachronisms. With its docile service nobility, little inclined to take any initiative, and its often uneducated clergy, incapable of playing the role of cultural transmission that the clergy performed in Western Europe, and finally, its subjugated and illiterate peasant mass, Russian society in the middle of the eighteenth century appeared quite refractory to any progress.

Aware of the breadth of the difficulties, Catherine tried to promote the modernization to which she aspired by resorting to measures that were less coercive than incentivizing. Of course, as under the reign of Peter the Great, it was still up to the autocratic state, incarnated by an empress attached to her prerogatives, to lead the reforms that would enable political, social, economic, and cultural modernization. In 1764, to launch a vast reform of current legislation, Catherine wrote and published Instruction for the Legislative Commission (Nakaz) that tried to frame the future work of a legal commission. In this long text, inspired by Montesquieu's Spirit of the Laws and Beccaria's Treatises of Penalties and Punishments, which she shamelessly plagiarized, she pronounced on very concrete issues, for example calling for the suppression of torture. But despite these initial ambitions, the outcome of the commission was disappointing: charged to reflect on reforms to current legislation, it would meet only from 1767 to 1768 and yield no concrete results. On the other hand, the reform of provincial administration was more successful; launched between 1764 and 1775, it managed to establish a more uniform and effective organization that was more concerned with the well-being of the empire's subjects. Similarly, the Charter of the Gentry that she decreed in April 1785 aimed to strengthen the nobility's rights, while seeking to make it the privileged actor in a limited form of political modernization. Exempt from taxes and any corporal punishment, nobles were free to enter or not into state service, and they were authorized to elect provincial assemblies that had the right to present their requests to the governors. In parallel, Catherine took inspiration from the writings of liberal English economists in order to foster private initiative and free trade. In October 1762, a ukase (that is, an imperial decree) lifted monopolies on industrial and commercial activities, now authorizing any individual, with the exception of the inhabitants of Moscow and St. Petersburg, to become "entrepreneurs" and to allow millions of state peasants[4] to produce textiles, leather, and pottery. Wanting to obtain quick success in this enterprise, the empress again called on the expertise of competent Europeans, whom she attracted to Russia by paying them generously. For example British Admiral Knowles was invited to participate in modernizing the Russian fleet. But interestingly, this call upon European expertise was not limited to elites, since the imperial state also facilitated a massive migration of free peasants from central Europe. Drawn by fiscal, financial, and legal opportunities that were particularly advantageous, several thousand Germans came to colonize the Volga basin and to turn the fertile lands of southern Russia into the future wheat granary of the empire.

Finally, in order to give Russia the cultural influence that ought to belong to her, the tsarina tried to open up her empire to Europe: culturally, artistically, and intellectually. To promote the influence of the Enlightenment in Russia, she facilitated the dissemination of ideas from the western part of the continent. In 1768 she created a special fund to translate into Russian the literary and scientific works of western Europe; she fostered the establishment in Russia of European artists like Quarenghi, Falconet, and the Scottish architect Charles Cameron, who was asked to familiarize Russia with art of neoclassical inspiration and to oversee the architectural renovation of St. Petersburg.

This cultural and intellectual openness to Europe was also manifested in the empress's behavior: she liked to write (apart from her memoirs, we have several historical essays and plays) and maintained a correspondence with Diderot, Voltaire, and (as we have seen) Baron Grimm. However, we should not mistake the significance of these literary exchanges: they testify both to her sincere openness to Enlightenment Europe, but also to her desire to make a striking demonstration of the European-ness of Russia and to give the image of a modern and cultivated monarch who had broken with the "barbarous" heritage of the preceding centuries. It was her concern for her own image that explains her spectacular and generous gesture to Diderot, purchasing his library, while leaving him the right to enjoy it until his death.

In 1777 Catherine had been continuing the enterprise of Peter the Great for 15 years, striving to foster the emergence of a more modern Russia, better administered and more tolerant, influenced by the spirit of the Enlightenment. But we should not exaggerate the scope of the changes she brought about, since any assessment would reveal her attachment to an autocratic regime and her refusal to concede the least share of her power, particularly to her son Paul.

Autocratic Power Undivided

In the decade from 1760 to 1770, the Russian state had been open to the ideas of the Encyclopedia of Diderot and d'Alembert, but by 1777 its political influence remained still very limited—the autocratic foundation of the state remained unchallenged. In fact the legislative reforms initially encouraged by Catherine quickly got bogged down, as with the Legislative Commission. Moreover, the few explosions of popular discontent that did flare up, or any attack that sought to shake off autocratic rule, were repressed in a systematic and brutal manner.

In 1770 the country was struck by plague: in the spring of 1771, it reached Moscow and killed almost 400 people per day at the start of the summer. The inability of power to contain the epidemic (which would kill almost 130,000 in Moscow alone) aroused the population's anger and soon its insurrection. Far from trying to temporize, Catherine charged Gregory Orlov with restoring order through force. This would be achieved in September, while the epidemic began to recede the following month.

Similarly, Catherine proved harsh during the revolt fomented and directed after 1772 by Emilian Pugachev, a Cossack from the Don. Then aged 20, Pugachev claimed to be Tsar Peter III (whom Catherine had had deposed and killed) and posed as the representative of legitimate power while she was a "usurper"; for more than two years, he defied the empress by raising an army of Cossacks, fleeing serfs, and workers from the Urals. Calling for the restoration of a more just monarchy and the abolition of serfdom, he seriously threatened the foundations of the empire. But, betrayed by those close to him in September 1774, Pugachev was finally handed over, and his atrocious execution (he was decapitated in a Moscow square in January 1775), as well as the severe repression in the Urals, testify to the pitiless nature of a regime that was not respectful of the humanist values and practices advocated by the Enlightenment.

Any openness of mind to enlightened Europe had not shaken the social order, either. Catherine had tried at the start to promote reconsideration of serfdom, but the ferocious hostility of the nobility to any change in the condition of serfs and the conviction that Russia was not yet ripe for a reform of such scope had quickly dissuaded her. Between 1762 and 1777, the conditions of the subject peasants continued to deteriorate. This situation aroused speculation on the part of Grand Duke Paul, who was held at a distance by his mother and had difficult relations with her.

* * *

Paul had been born in October 1754, under the reign of his great aunt Elizabeth I,[5] when the Grand Duke Peter, nephew of Elizabeth and heir to the throne, and Grand Duchess Catherine had been married for nine years. Rumors affirmed that the child was not Peter's[6] but likely that of Sergey Saltykov, the Grand Duke's chamberlain; Elizabeth, who wanted to ensure the dynasty's survival, closed her eyes to the affair and celebrated the birth of the future emperor with magnificent parties and masked balls at court. From the infant's first hours, she took him from his parents to supervise his education herself. Peter and Catherine were authorized to see their son only 40 days after his birth, and they would only see him four times during the first six months of his life.

The infancy of Paul was overseen by numerous nurses, maids, and governesses. After 1760 Elizabeth confided the supervision of his education to Count Nikita Panin, promoted to his principal tutor. Endowed with various teachers of renown, Paul learned Holy Scripture, Russian, French, German, history, geography, arithmetic, and physics; he proved over the years an able student who did not apply himself. Elizabeth wanted to familiarize him with the exercise of power, obliging him to attend audiences of foreign ambassadors; Paul was rarely permitted to play with children his own age. He had no friends apart from Alexander Kurakin, Count Panin's nephew, and Andrey Razumovsky,[7] and met his parents only once a week.

Little Paul was "handsome—so handsome that when one saw in the gallery of Count Stroganov Paul's portrait at age seven in the grand costume of the order, alongside that of Emperor Alexander at the same age and in the same costume, strangers often asked why Count Stroganov had two copies of the same portrait."[8] But in 1764–1765 the child fell victim to smallpox, which left his face blistered and marked by scars. His humor tightened as a result: now phases of despondency alternated with crises of agitation and anger.

On January 5, 1762, the death of Elizabeth made Grand Duke Peter the new emperor. Peter from the start adopted popular measures, among them the abolition of the secret chancellery (the feared secret police), a reduction in the salt tax, and permission granted to Old Believers who had been exiled by his aunt to come back to Moscow and freely practice their faith. Peter secularized the goods of monasteries, turning thousands of serfs who had been harshly treated in them into peasants of the state with better prospects. But while he was ambitious on the social level, Peter III proved maladroit, even provocative, with respect to the army. A Germanophile, he undertook negotiations to put an end to the Russo-Prussian war and he announced his intention to restore conquered territories—just when the victorious Russian army was marching through eastern Prussia. Even more seriously, he envisaged, with the support of Frederick II of Prussia, a war against Denmark aiming to recover Schleswig, a former possession of his native Holstein. On June 22, 1762, the signature of a diplomatic and military alliance with Prussia brought the army's discontent to a paroxysm.

It was in this tense climate that Catherine, concerned for her future and for Paul's survival (Peter had never been concerned with someone he knew not to be his own son and did not mention him in the proclamation when he ascended the throne), decided to resort to a military coup. Far from being content with a regency, as Count Panin had hoped when he supported her enterprise, Catherine chose to exercise fully her new power and to have herself crowned, by which the Church gave her legitimacy. On July 9, 1762, after the coup, Paul swore fidelity to the new empress, who made him her heir that day; nevertheless, the intimated little boy of seven, who held himself straight in the Kazan Cathedral where the ceremony took place, would never know maternal tenderness, growing up far from the empress.

* * *

Paul resided four kilometers from Tsarskoye Selo (and 27 kilometers south of St. Petersburg). Two mornings a week, he visited his mother, accompanied by Count Panin.[9] Week after week, the encounters were alike: while the child wanted to please his mother and arouse her tenderness, Catherine was cold and distant, distrustful of the one who could someday be the instrument of a plot to get rid of her. In Secret Memories of Russia, Colonel Charles Philibert Masson, a future poet who lived in Russia from 1787 to 1797[10] and eventually became secretary to the Grand Duke Alexander, gave an extremely severe verdict on Catherine's behavior toward her son:

> From infancy he showed qualities that she stifled by her bad treatment; he had spirit, activity, a penchant for science, sentiments of order and justice: everything has perished for want of development. She has morally killed her son—after long deliberating whether she should actually get rid of him. Her hatred of him is the single proof that he is the son of Peter III, and this proof is weighty. She could not bear him, holding him far from her, surrounding him with spies. While her favorites (who were eventually younger than him) were

governing Russia and swimming in wealth, he lived retired, insignificant, and lacking in what was necessary.[11]

Yet Paul still remained destined for the throne of Russia, and it was for this purpose that Catherine continued to perfect his education. From the age of fourteen, he was taught politics, which left him cold, and military matters, about which he was passionate, to the regret of Count Panin, who wanted to see his pupil take an interest in managing the state. For his eighteenth birthday, on October 1, 1772, Catherine offered him the post of admiral of the Russian navy and made him colonel of a cavalry regiment.[12] But contrary to Panin's expectations she did not give Paul any portion of her power and even feared the young man's popularity. Perceived as "Russian" while Catherine was perceived as foreign, Paul began in fact to crystallize the hopes of writers critical of Catherine's regime and closer to Panin, like Fonvizin and Sumarokov, as well as those in military circles. In 1772 a first attempt at a military conspiracy was formed around Paul, and a year later a new embryonic plot was formed; both were uncovered and these attempts fed the empress's growing distrust of her son.[13]

At the same time, to ensure the solidity and durability of the dynasty, Catherine decided to marry Paul off. After long consultations and negotiations that began in 1768, her choice was finally Wilhelmina, daughter of the Landgrave of Hesse-Darmstadt. On October 10, 1773, Paul married the young princess, who had converted to Orthodoxy under the name Natalia Alexeievna.

At this date, Paul was happy in his marriage but very shocked by the scope of Pugachev's revolt, and he began to take an interest in political questions and wanted to act for the good of the state. In 1774, with the help of Count Panin and the latter's brother, Field Marshal Peter Panin, who even envisaged a plot to bring Paul to power,[14] the young man wrote a text titled Reflections on the State in General—at the very moment when Catherine was finishing her reform of provincial administration. From the start Paul asserted in his memorandum ideas that ran counter to Catherine's practices. He declared himself in favor of an imperial government that with the guidance of the senate (whose power would be strengthened) might evolve toward constitutionality, as well as in favor of peace and domestic development. In Paul's eyes, the empire should end the interminable wars that were exhausting it, and in future it should conduct only defensive wars. To this end fortresses should be built along the borders; their command and organization should be confided to local troops, who would defend them all the better since they would be defending their own soil. The army should be composed of volunteers, recruited as a priority among the sons of soldiers. The rights and duties of soldiers would be governed by precise regulations, and regiments would be subject to irreproachable discipline and order. A text that soon resonated as a critique of both Catherine's absolutism and the ruinous political expansionism that she was conducting, in contempt of the living conditions of her people, was scarcely reassuring to the empress. And while she continued to shower Prince Potemkin (her lover since 1774) with political prerogatives, honors, and presents, Catherine continued to keep her son outside the circles of power.

Isolated, treated with disdain by his mother, Paul soon suffered a new personal tragedy when on April 15, 1776, Natalia died in childbirth. Hoping to remarry him as soon as possible, even though he was inconsolable, Catherine resorted to the cynical (even cruel) strategy of revealing to him, with letters in support, that Natalia had been the mistress of Paul's childhood friend, Count Andrey Razumovsky. Painfully attacked in domains of both love and friendship, Paul shortly afterward agreed in the presence of Frederick of Prussia to marry (on October 7, 1776) the young princess Sophie Dorothea of Württemberg, converted and baptized under the name of Maria Feodorovna. But Paul had difficulty recovering from a trauma that left him depressed and full of bitterness, while Catherine was proclaiming more and more openly her contempt for someone she considered both dangerous to her and intellectually limited.

In December 1777 when "Monsieur Alexander" was born of the union between Paul and Maria Feodorovna, all the ingredients for a political and familial battle were in place. It was in this tense climate that the childhood of the grand duke was going to unfold.

CHAPTER 2

"The Monarch-in-Training"

From Alexander's infancy—although she had suffered from having been deprived by Empress Elizabeth of her own son, Paul, from birth—Catherine withdrew him from the grand ducal couple on the pretext that Maria Feodorovna and Paul were too young (he was 23 and his wife 18) to be capable of taking care of a future emperor's well-being and education.

The break was not as radical as the one that had separated Catherine from her son, since Alexander did maintain ties with his parents. He visited them from time to time, and as soon as he was old enough, he wrote to them. Childish and rather terse, Alexander's letters[1] (which until 1790–1792[2] were written under the gaze of—and even dictated by—his tutors) lack warmth and spontaneity, but their very existence contributed to maintain a small flame of filial love. Moreover, Catherine II proved generous with the young couple: upon Alexander's birth, she offered them a comfortable allowance and a domain of 400 hectares to construct a residential palace to suit their taste. This would be the Pavlovsk Castle, to the design and decoration of which Maria would devote immense energy. Nevertheless, deprived of their son, the parents of Alexander could only be silent and powerless witnesses of a childhood exclusively controlled by Catherine to suit her own values and humors.

Grandmother and Grandson

From his first months, Alexander occupied a major place in the preoccupations and time of Catherine II, and over the years the person whom she called "the Monarch-in-Training"[3] became the almost exclusive object of her tenderness and marvel.

Buoyed by the theories of Rousseau and Pestalozzi that she had read (and continued to read)[4] in order to play her role of grandmother, Catherine was keen to dictate the principles of childhood education that were to be put into practice with Alexander. She gave her grandson a Russian governess, Sophie Benckendorff, and a British maid, Prascovie Gessler; at the empress's express demand, they accustomed the baby to sleep with the windows open, not in a crib but in a small iron bed protected by a balustrade and stuffed with austere leather cushions. Each morning, in a room whose temperature was never above 16 or 17 degrees Celsius, he was given a cold bath or shower. Catherine wanted him raised "in the old style," in a spartan manner, in order to make him tougher, although Maria Feodorovna was worried by these methods.

The empress went so far as to design Alexander's wardrobe, and here she showed great modernity. In a letter to Grimm, she described proudly the practical and comfortable outfit she had invented for her grandson, even accompanying the description with a little sketch.

> But since you speak of Monsieur Alexander [...] here is how he has been dressed since he was six months: all is sewed together so it can be put on fast and fastened behind with four or five little hooks; on the edge of the costume is a fringe and this suits perfectly. The King of Sweden and the Prince of Prussia have asked for and obtained the pattern [...]. There is no tying up and he is almost unaware of being dressed: his arms and legs are simultaneously inserted into his costume and it is finished—a bit of genius on my part.[5]

Day after day, week after week, Catherine observed, supervised, and commented in detail on the toddler's physical and intellectual development. She scrutinized the smallest progress, and in her correspondence with Grimm she surprisingly recounted the slightest change with fulsome details, addressing someone more comfortable with political and literary issues than with arcane matters of child psychology! Her tenderness for Alexander did not cease to grow: she happily cultivated the art of being a grandmother while boasting—we recognize her egocentric nature—of exercising a strong influence on the child and making what she wanted of him. At the end of May 1779, when Alexander was 18 months old, she wrote:

> But do you know that in speaking about Monsieur Alexander you are taking me at my weakest? I told you he was a prince who was doing well, but presently it is quite another matter: he begins to show a singular intelligence for a child of this age: I delight in him, and this kid would spend his life with me if they let him. He is steady in his humor because he is doing well, and this humor consists of being always gay, welcoming, considerate, fearing nothing,

and lovely as love. This child delights everybody, and in particular me; I can do with him what I want; he walks on his own; when he is growing teeth, even the pain does not change his humor; he shows the pain he feels by laughing and frolicking. He understands everything that is said to him; by signs and sounds, he has formed a very intelligible language of his own. The gayest music is what pleases him most. Paisiello will tell you what role he plays in the concerts that he arranges and sometimes de-ranges in his fashion, and how he comes to beg them to play any sort of air that pleases him, after which he thanks them in his fashion.[6]

Over the months, Alexander occupied a growing place in Catherine's schedule; there were daily rites in the relationship between the grandmother and her grandson.

I have already said, and I repeat, that I delight in this kid. Each day we discover new things: of each toy we make ten or twelve others, and one of us develops his genius even more. It is extraordinary how industrious we have become. [...] Mother Nature has made us robust and intelligent, everybody exclaims at the miracle of *grandmamma,* and we continue to play together. After dinner my kid comes to me as often as he wants, and he spends three or four hours a day in my room, often without my paying attention to him. If he gets bored, he goes away, but this rarely happens.[7]

On May 8, 1779, Maria Feodorovna gave birth to a second son, whom Catherine decided to name Constantine, a choice that would soon resonate as a geopolitical manifesto, reflecting the imperial desire to place her second grandson on the throne of Constantinople. Now the two boys would be raised together, entrusted to the same nurses and same maids. But Catherine kept a special affection for the elder and continued to educate him herself, according to methods she invented and put into practice. In July 1779 she undertook to teach him the letters of the alphabet and ten months later, in May 1780, she composed a little ABC primer for him, accompanied by short maxims:

It begins by telling him that he is a kid born naked, like a hand that knows nothing, that all kids are born like that, that by birth all men are equal,[8] that by studying they differ infinitely from each other; then from one maxim to another,[9] strung like pearls, we go from one thing to another. I have only two goals: to open his mind to the impression of things, and to raise the soul by training the heart. My ABC is full of plates, but all of it striking and directed to the goal. Everybody, papa and mama included, says that this is good.[10]

At the same time, still under the influence of Rousseau's theories, Catherine deeply wanted to awaken her grandsons to manual and physical activities that were in harmony with nature; from the age of three or four, Alexander and Constantine were by turns metamorphosed into gardeners, butchers, and carpenters.[11]

During the first years Catherine's influence on her grandchildren was all the greater and more exclusive because for more than a year (September 1781 to November 1782), at the demand of the empress, Paul and Maria traveled incognito (under the names of "Count and Countess of the North") throughout Europe. Their journey was modeled on the Grand Tour that any Russian aristocrat of the second half of the eighteenth century who was concerned to perfect his cultural and political knowledge was supposed to take across European soil. In their absence and then when they returned, Catherine watched over the primary education of her grandsons, while continuing to govern her whole empire just as energetically. In 1783, pushed by her favorite and chamberlain, Prince Potemkin, she engaged in a new showdown with the Ottoman Empire that led to the de facto annexation of the Crimea and allowed Russia to control both shores of the Sea of Azov. Was she not dreaming of offering the throne of Constantinople to little Constantine?

* * *

In July 1783 Maria gave birth to her first daughter, Alexandra, nicknamed Alexandrine. To salute this birth, Catherine II again proved very generous, offering the young parents the Gatchina Palace that she had just bought from the heirs of her former favorite Gregory Orlov. But this time, she was not concerned to take the baby girl from her parents; like her five sisters,[12] Alexandra would be raised by her father and mother. For Catherine the fate of her granddaughters was of relatively little interest, as she frankly expressed in a letter to Grimm in August 1783:

> To tell you the truth, I love boys infinitely more than girls. Mine are perfectly doing well, running and jumping, adroit and nimble, resolutely rowing with oars and steering marvelously on canals where there is a foot of water, and God knows what all they do: they read, write, sketch, dance, all of their own will.[13]

Still supervising the formal education given to the grand dukes, Catherine soon wanted them to receive structured and systematic knowledge: faithful to her methodical spirit and her desire to manage everything, she drew up an education plan largely inspired by the writings of Locke and Rousseau.

She finished her child-rearing manual in March 1784[14] and sent it as "instructions composed for the governor Nicholas Saltykov,"[15] the person now promoted to "grand master" of the grand dukes, who was charged with watching over their physical and intellectual development.

Written in Russian and organized into thematic chapters, the plan deals successively with health and dress (chapter 1), the need and means for inciting children to do good (chapter 2), the virtues and Christian values that must be inculcated in them (chapter 3), good manners (chapter 4), and their use in relations with adults and in society (chapter 5), disciplines to teach them and learning methods to be utilized (chapter 6), before she decrees rules to which children should conform in relations with their various minders, teachers, and tutors.

Catherine brought to the preparation of this text meticulous care, and she "legislated," prescribed, or proscribed regarding the smallest details of daily life. The chapter devoted to health care and nourishment is particularly representative. As regards dress: "Whatever the season, not overly warm clothing, the chest should not be compromised. Clothes as simple and light as possible." As for food, the empress prescribed simple and frugal nourishment:

> Without spices or fermenting roots and without too much salt. When Their Highnesses want to eat between dinner and supper, they should be given a piece of bread. Wine is prohibited, unless on a doctor's order. In summer, one may serve for lunch (or else between dinner and supper): cherries, strawberries, gooseberries, apples, and ripe pears. They should not be asked to eat or drink when they do not feel the need. They should not drink when they are sweating or warmed up.

Lingering over hygiene in the life of the grand dukes, Catherine insisted on the need to aerate their apartments "in winter at least twice during the day by opening the fan-windows," by leaving the children "in the open air, winter and summer, at least as long as this does not harm their health," by avoiding as much as possible "that in winter they keep near the fire," by ensuring that "their apartments will only be heated to sixteen or seventeen degrees Celsius." They should "sleep on mattresses, not on duvets, and under light bed coverings, in summer simple Persians lined with a bed-sheet, quilted in winter. They will sleep with head uncovered and as long as they want, since sleep does children good, but since it is healthy to get up early,

Their Highnesses will be habituated to go to bed early. After age seven, 8 or 9 hours of sleep appear to suffice."

Finally, the Young Highnesses should be encouraged to play or to study but "never to remain idle. If they are not studying or playing, they should be conversed with as befitting their age and their intelligence, and in order to augment their knowledge."

In this first chapter we find a synthesis between the spartan model of endurance and frugality, which Catherine had been trying to put into practice from the birth of Alexander, and more modern pedagogic prescriptions: thus the importance she gives to play, "for movement develops children's physiques and intellectual capacities," and to sleep.

Chapters 2 and 3 then deal with the conduct of children and the moral traits that should be encouraged—or on the contrary should be reproved. Affability, leniency, honesty, and the taste for justice—including in games and pleasantries—should be advocated, whereas "pride, impudence, presumption, and dissimulation are unbearable" and therefore to be punished.

Christian virtue and "true knowledge of God, the Creator of the visible and the invisible, on which our happiness depends, to the love of which we owe all the good that we possess, which merits our whole admiration by our deeds and prayers, as the most perfect Being" are the essential qualities that should be taught by "the high priest of Saint-Sophia, Samborski." But the grand dukes should also be taught "absolute obedience toward Us and Our imperial power. What is ordered by grandmother must be executed without question; what she has prohibited must not be done in any way; may it seem to them as impossible to infringe as to change the weather according to their will." The aim is clear: on the model of all other subjects of the Russian Empire, the young grand dukes should prove themselves obedient, loyal, and faithful.

In their games and distractions they will be forbidden to lie and to cheat and "to torment or kill inoffensive animals such as birds, butterflies, flies, dogs, cats, any more than to damage something intentionally; on the contrary, they must be habituated to care for the dog, bird, squirrel or any other animal that belongs to them, and even for potted flowers, by watering them. As soon as something that belongs to them no longer attracts their attention, it will be taken away, since everything in life demands care." Finally, there should be removed "from the eyes and ears of Their Highnesses any bad or vicious example"; everybody is forbidden from pronouncing in front of them "vulgar, indecent, or hurtful words"; and they should develop courtesy toward others.

Having thus proclaimed instructions of an essentially moral character, the empress in chapter 4 (titled "Instructions concerning knowledge to be acquired") comes to properly pedagogic considerations. The purpose of study and the duty assigned to tutors "is to teach their students courtesy, healthy notions of things, proper conduct for every occasion, principles of virtue, obedience to Us, respect for their father and mother, love of truth, benevolence toward humankind, leniency to their kin." Then Catherine pronounces the methods she is promoting.

Lessons should never last longer than a half hour "since it is difficult for children to apply themselves" and lessons will be interrupted before they start to get bored. No constraint will be exercised on the boys to make them study; no reproach will be made to them in the course of learning, but they will be showered with praise when they obtain good results. Tutors should be patient and of equanimity, for "fear does not teach. One cannot make education enter a soul obsessed with fear, any more than one can write on a sheet of paper that trembles." As an enlightened monarch of the eighteenth century, Catherine believed in the virtue of pedagogy and not in constraint.

Moreover, the children will be taught foreign languages, including French, German, and ancient Greek, but it is important that "above all they will not forget the language of their native country; so they should be spoken to and read to in Russian, and care taken that they become perfect masters of their mother tongue." This point is very interesting: while she seems open to the West, Catherine remains no less attached to giving her grandsons an education anchored in Russianness. While mathematics, geography, astronomy, and history will be taught, the children should in their daily use of time devote several hours to their knowledge of Russia. This will be done concretely on the basis of geographical and geological cards that will allow them to discover its territory, resources, bodies of water, population, and so forth. Finally, they will be encouraged to engage in physical activities like horse riding, swimming, acrobatics, fencing, archery, and wrestling and to perform manual work if they want to. But there will be no music or poetry, which are considered to be useless.

The education of the two young grand dukes as advocated by Catherine II in her plan of study as written for General Saltykov aimed to make them virtuous Christians, obedient to imperial power, cultivated and open to the external world, but very informed about Russian realities and of irreproachable morality. This program appears particularly ambitious, calling for the implementation of a specific organization of learning and the inculcation of significant capacities. In her March 1784 letter to Grimm announcing that she has composed "a fine instruction for the educations of Messieurs Alexander and Constantine, which I will send as soon as I have a presentable translation," the empress confides that she expects much from an educational model that takes into account the precocious qualities demonstrated by the elder of her grandchildren:

> M. Laharpe will be one of those placed close to Monsieur Alexander with the express order to speak to him in French; another will speak to him in German; he already speaks English. [...] In everything—height, strength, intelligence, amiability, and knowledge—he is well above his age. In my opinion he will become an excellent personage, provided that the *second-rate ones* [her son and daughter-in-law] do not slow me down in his progress.[16]

But what was Alexander really like? Were Catherine's aspirations satisfied? Were the promises of the plan fulfilled?

Alexander's Education and Training

In 1783–1784 Alexander and Constantine had reached the ages of six and five respectively. To achieve her ambitious plan, Catherine replaced the nurses and maids who had surrounded the little boys since their births with exclusively male personnel. In March 1784 Count Nicholas Saltykov, field marshal and minister of war, was named "grand master": he took charge of directing all the staff assigned to the boys' education. He was seconded by General Protasov, individual tutor to Alexander, and by Baron Osten-Sacken, tutor to Constantine. Alongside these three men, several teachers, of whom some were famous, were appointed to provide specific subjects. Charles François Philibert Masson taught mathematics and Georg-Wolfgang Kraft taught physics. The author Mikhail Muravyov[17] was in charge of Russian history and literature, and the explorer Pallas covered geography and the natural sciences. Finally, the children also received lessons in German, a class in French taught by the Swiss tutor Laharpe, and classes in English given by the archpriest Andrey Samborski, who had lived 14 years in London as chaplain to the Russian legation and had married an Englishwoman and so was in a position to teach them the language of Shakespeare as well as scripture.

According to several contemporaries, not all the mentors chosen by Catherine to educate the grand dukes were up to the tasks assigned them. Charles Masson, then part of the team, later delivered severe and ironic verdicts on his colleagues and on the personal responsibility of the empress for the vagaries in the education of the two boys:

Catherine composed an education plan for her grandsons, as she had composed instructions for the legislation of her peoples. Derived from Locke and Rousseau, [...] this plan does honor to her mind; if the plan had been followed, then Alexander and Constantine would certainly have been the best raised princes in Europe. [...] But as we saw with the code, once the laws were drawn up, they were left to a committee of ignoramuses, bigots, and buffoons, which fortunately never gathered. Similarly, the education of the young princes was entrusted to people who were barely able to read the plan whose spirit and letter they were supposed to follow. The only rule that they managed to understand was this (apparently because it was negative): the young grand dukes will not be taught either poetry or music, because it would take too long for them to become skillful. They tried to extend this rule to all the sciences.[18]

In fact, General Saltykov aroused contrasting but uniformly severe judgments on the part of his contemporaries. While Masson asserts with some contempt that the general's role was almost non-existent—"His main occupation was to keep them from strong winds and to keep their chests uncongested"[19]— Saltykov was described by Countess Golovina[20] as a servile courtier who had a harmful influence on Alexander's character development:

His tutor Count Saltykov, a clever, scheming and treacherous man, constantly dictated behavior that would destroy openness of character and replace it with continual study of his own words and actions. Count Saltykov wanted to reconcile the favor of the Empress and that of her son, and so he involved the young Grand Duke in continual deception.[21]

And Prince Adam Czartoryski stressed the hypocritical good manners used by the old courtier and his role as intercessor between Catherine and her son Paul:

Count Nicholas Saltykov [...] supervised the education of the two grand dukes. Small in stature, with a huge head, grimacing and nervous, and a state of health that demanded constant attention, [...] he passed as the most astute courtier in Russia. [...] The count was not only the channel by which messages and admonitions from Empress Catherine passed to the young grand dukes, but it was he who carried the word each time Catherine had something to say to Grand Duke Paul, and he omitted or softened what was sometimes disagreeable or overly severe in the orders or reproaches the Empress sent to her son. He did the same with the answers he carried back, he kept back half the things he had been told and modified the rest such that both sides were satisfied with being reciprocally explained to each other, as much as circumstances allowed. This ruse as intermediary meant he alone knew the truth and he refrained from speaking it. Perhaps there was merit in filling this role, but it has to be recognized that a man with the bearing and character of the Count was scarcely suitable for directing the education of the young heir of an empire, nor could he have a salutary impression on his character.[22]

Whatever the case, beyond these unflattering portraits, it should be stressed that despite his moral deficiencies and incompetence in education, Saltykov knew how to surround the two children with affection. And Alexander remained grateful for this affection to the point that in 1818 when Saltykov died, the emperor attended the burial of his old governor and accompanied his coffin on foot to the cemetery.

Severe about Saltykov, Masson was equally so about Protasov, whom he considered insignificant and weak in character, in a manner both comical and crude:

> Protasov, governor of the elder, would have been more in place if he had been named apothecary. He came each day to make a report to Saltykov of the most insipid details, especially of the number of stools the prince had produced. Blinkered, mysterious, bigoted and pusillanimous, he was not wicked, but he made himself ridiculous in the eyes of everybody, except his pupil's, who noticed only his attachment to him and acknowledged his gratitude, whereas according to malign courtiers General Protasov merited only contempt.[23]

On the other hand, most of the teachers were men of talent: in his memoirs, Masson pays homage to the pedagogic qualities of Kraft, Pallas, and Laharpe. But he also stresses that these teachers had only limited latitude and remained, with respect to decency and morality, under the strict control, even censorship, of Saltykov and Protasov, as he relates in this amusing anecdote.

> The famous Pallas gave them a botany class in the gardens near Pavlovsk. The explanation of the Linnaean system about the sexes of flowers and their propagation gave the young people their first ideas about that of humans, and led to a flood of questions both very pleasant and naïve. This alarmed their governors: Pallas was told to avoid details about pistils and stamens, and the botany course was halted.[24]

Masson also salutes Samborski's humanity, which he judged open and tolerant. But to Masson, the priest, who wore neither a beard nor religious vestments, appeared to be an original, more preoccupied with spreading his expertise in agronomy than with teaching the Orthodox faith to the young grand dukes. In fact, Samborski gave them only the superficial rudiments of a religious education, to the point that while Alexander was henceforth pleased to follow the Orthodox liturgy and to observe its rites, he neither read nor knew scripture, and as he would admit much later, he was not a sincere believer.

> Catherine was full of prudence and spirit, she was a great woman and her memory will live forever in the history of Russia. But relative to that part of the education that develops true piety in the heart, we were at the court in St. Petersburg at the same point as in everything else: much exterior practice, but the holy essence of Christianity was hidden from us.[25]

Throughout these years of study, unlike Constantine who was pugnacious and rebellious and made life difficult for his governors whom he did not hesitate to slap or bite, Alexander proved a rather assiduous student, full of the desire to learn:

> Kraft spoke one day of the hypotheses of certain philosophers on the nature of light, and said that Newton had thought that it was a constant emanation from the sun. Alexander, then aged twelve, responded: "I don't think so, for if it were, the sun would become smaller every day." This objection, made with as much naïveté as spirit, had in fact been the strongest one offered to the great Newton. It proved the sagacity of the young Grand Duke.[26]

At Catherine's express request, the children were raised in modesty, if not prudery: the empress stressed this principle forcefully in her instructions to Saltykov, even if it was thwarted by the slackness of her own morals and those of her courtiers. But it is far from the principle to the reality, and on this point the testimony of Masson is again both precious and funny:

> Catherine had required that her grandsons be kept in perfect ignorance of the mysteries of love, reserving such instruction for herself and intending to have them initiated when she wanted to marry them; but a pleasant event aborted this plan. One day, a greyhound belonging to the princes mated with a female in their presence; they observed curiously this maneuver and demanded an explanation. General Protasov, quite frightened, tried in vain to separate the

dogs, and we know what physical obstacle prevents this. So the princes had time to examine things, and Alexander responded to his governor who assured him that the dogs were fighting: "Oh, no! No! You can't fool me. I see that they are marrying." This was a thunderclap for Protasov, who was responsible for the prince's innocence. He came trembling to tell Count Saltykov that the cat was out of the bag. They conferred and precautions were taken so the princes did not go to entertain the grandmother with what they had seen. She would have been outraged to see her plan fail.[27]

Thanks to these witnesses, we may measure to what point the daily life of the grand dukes as much as their intellectual and psychological development, starting in 1784, were punctuated by the permanent contact they had with governors and tutors appointed by Catherine. It was a disparate group, since in the intimate circle of the grand dukes there coexisted well-tempered characters and less courageous men, scholars with established reputations and notoriously ignorant courtiers. The motivations that guided Catherine in such choices were confused, to say the least. But starting in the second half of 1784, these disparities assumed less importance. From that date, Frédéric-César de Laharpe, initially the French teacher, rose to the rank of principal governor of their imperial Highnesses, which substantially changed the situation.

* * *

Nobody in Alexander's life would have such great importance as the Swiss Frédéric-César de Laharpe.[28] In May 1797, two years after the latter had to leave Russia, Alexander addressed to his mother-in-law, the Princess of Baden, who was then on the verge of meeting her son-in-law's former tutor, a letter that illuminates the gratitude and affection that he felt toward Laharpe:

> I am writing to you, dear Mama, via Mr. de La Harpe, my tutor whom I recommend to you as my intimate friend and as a man to whom I owe everything except life itself. He was with me from the age of seven, he is a man of intact integrity and probity with uncommon enlightenment and knowledge. I must admit that he alone never flattered me and his advice was not founded on his personal interest but really sprang from the attachment he always felt for me. My gratitude to him knows no bounds. Finally, as I have said, he is a man to whom I owe everything.[29]

Many years later, when he was on the point of acquiring his title as liberator of Europe and was at the height of his power, Alexander introduced his former tutor to the King of Prussia and his sons, and again he paid him homage in Langres in 1814 by asserting: "Everything that I know, and perhaps all that I am worth, I owe to M. Laharpe."[30]

Born in April 1754 in Rolle,[31] a large village in the Vaud canton, Laharpe was the son of a former Swiss military man coming from the minor nobility. He pursued his studies at the high school in Rolle, during which he became passionate about ancient history,[32] then completed his secondary studies at the seminary of Haldenstein, before studying mathematics and philosophy in Geneva and then law in Tubingen. Received as a doctor in law at the age of 20, he was soon established as a lawyer, staying alternately in Berne in the winter and the rest of the time in Rolle. But this peaceful life bored him, and the aristocratic spirit of the Vaud, quite removed from the Genevan democratic spirit, bothered his republican convictions. He soon left the bar and envisaged going to fight in North America. Then he was approached by Baron Grimm, who proposed in 1782 that he play the mentor and accompany to Italy for a year the young Count Yakov Lanskoy (younger brother of Catherine's favorite) and his cousin. Laharpe immediately accepted a mission in which he found the unexpected opportunity to "travel over beautiful Italy, the object of my desire."[33] Beyond the intellectual, artistic, and financial attraction of the trip, the episode proved decisive in Laharpe's life, since he acquitted his task so well—"the good conduct, the wisdom and fine mind of Sir Laharpe have so well captivated those present and those absent,"[34] the empress wrote about him—that Catherine II invited him to bring young Lanskoy to St. Petersburg and pay a visit. At the end of 1782, the two men arrived in the capital, and barely a year later, in March 1784, the young Swiss gentleman was chosen by the empress to teach French to the elder of her grandsons. But quickly the ambitious and enterprising Laharpe aspired to nobler and more important posts.

Desirous to leave the relative anonymity of the other tutors to the grand dukes, he wrote (only three months after his nomination as French teacher) a pedagogic memorandum addressed to Catherine through the intermediary of Count Saltykov. Very ably and perhaps obsequiously, the text takes inspiration from the educational plan just concocted by the empress, to convince her to give the education of the future emperor greater unity and coherence—and suggesting that the author of the memo would himself be able to accomplish this arduous task. Seduced by the intelligence and ambition of the project, Catherine II recorded that "the person who composed this appears assuredly capable of teaching more than just the

French language,"[35] and from mid-September, she made Laharpe the principal tutor of the grand dukes.

For more than ten years, on a daily basis, Laharpe designed the ensemble of courses dispensed by the various tutors, including Masson, Pallas, Samborski, and Kraft, while delivering his own teaching. But this task was not always easy, as he recognized in his autobiographical account; Laharpe was well aware of his youth and inexperience: "Raised in solitude, completely foreign to high society, having lived more with books and fantastic beings than with real men, I had to spend a dozen years at the court without directors and without advisors."[36]

Moreover, he was a convinced republican. He would adopt the cause of the French Revolution and expect much from it for the future of Switzerland, at the very time when Catherine was renouncing the values of tolerance and openness advocated during the first half of her reign and when she began to engage in a repressive policy toward the ideas of freedom and national sovereignty carried by the French Revolution. After 1789–1790 she closed the Masonic lodges, and several writers who (on the model of Alexander Radishchev) had been denouncing in their writing both absolutism and the cruelty of serfdom were arrested and imprisoned. But Laharpe did not remain inactive in Russia. In 1790–1791, he wrote more than 60 pamphlets calling on his compatriots from the Vaud canton to quit the tutelage of Berne in order to join the republic of Geneva. But in the autumn of 1791, these writings destined for his compatriots earned him a denunciation to Catherine by authorities in Berne who had intercepted them. Summoned before the Empress to explain these pamphlets, he wrote a letter that both reaffirmed his democratic sentiments as a Swiss citizen but denied forcefully that he had ever disseminated his ideas to the two boys. Convinced of the tutor's loyalty, the empress attached no more importance to this affair: "All she required of me was to remain apart from the affairs of Switzerland as long as I remained in her service," recalled Laharpe in his Memoirs.[37]

However, a year and a half later, the affair opened up again and a cabal was formed at court. For the Prince of Nassau-Siegen and Count Esterhazy, whose wife was from Berne, and for several French emigrants[38] who had been chased out by the French Revolution and taken refuge in St. Petersburg, the education of the grand dukes could not be confided to a republican without some danger. The cabal destabilized Laharpe, who suffered from its harassment; on the occasion of the recent engagement of Alexander, when the officers in his service received promotions in grade and financial compensation, only Laharpe obtained no gratification at all.

He envisaged quitting Russia, but at the end of June 1793, a new conversation with Catherine II renewed her confidence in him and convinced him to remain. "Monsieur, you may be a Jacobin, a Republican, anything you want; I believe you are an honest man, and that is enough for me. Remain with my grandchildren, keep my confidence in them, and give them your care with accustomed zeal."[39]

To these difficulties linked to Laharpe's democratic convictions were added the nasty remarks and vexations that on a daily basis he suffered from a court that was increasingly hostile to events in France and from whom the excesses of the Jacobin Terror had removed any taste for Enlightenment philosophy. Sometimes Laharpe slumped into discouragement: "When I was with my students, few weeks passed without my being tempted to abandon everything, with so many obstacles, chicanery, and disgust heaped on my path; but calm regained me when, forgetting my surroundings, I looked toward the future and fixed my sights on the goal to which my labors were devoted," he wrote many years later, in February 1810, to his friend Stapfer.[40] But his passion for teaching, his growing affection for Alexander and the evolution of his personal life—Laharpe married a woman from St. Petersburg and thanks to this found himself better integrated into Russian society—all convinced him to remain at his post and to meet the challenge he had set himself: to inculcate in Alexander not only knowledge but principles and moral qualities, to shape the future emperor such that he would reign for the good of his people.

As he explained in the memorandum sent to Catherine in June 1784,[41] for him it was not a matter of turning the future emperor into an erudite man, a specialist to be recognized in some field (physics, mathematics, or philosophy) but rather an "honest man" and an "enlightened citizen" capable of exercising his critical mind and thereby best performing his functions as emperor. From this standpoint, Laharpe belonged to the lineage of the writings of Bishop Fénelon, who back in the seventeenth century had given credence to the idea that any monarch should as a child be inculcated with a quality education and high moral principles so that once he ascends the throne, he will become an exemplary sovereign. But, at the same time, the tutor's use of the concept of "enlightened citizen" attests to the fact that he was also a man of the Enlightenment, passionately attached to the ideals of democracy and the republic, and very influenced by the thinking of Rousseau and his Discourse on the Origin of Inequality.

In August 1785, in a letter addressed to his friend Jean Marc Louis Favre, Laharpe recounts the nature of his teaching. Mentioning the history course he was giving the young men,

[I] insisted in a republican way on equality, and after having shown the earliest chiefs dressed in a tiger or lion skin and seated on a stone instead of a throne and living in a cabin covered with tree branches, I showed the same men ceasing to believe themselves the equals of others, having become kings not by divine mandate but by the grace of God who made men such that the one who is strongest, most adroit, and most spiritual and the most able thinks he has a decisive right to rise above his peers and always profits from the situation whenever their negligence and patience allows him to do so peacefully. I pronounced to my student this hard-to-digest doctrine and applied myself to making him feel and to firmly convincing him that all men are born equal, and that the hereditary power of some was a matter of pure accident.[42]

The idea is quite clear: while he defended himself to Catherine II from the accusation of distilling "subversive" ideas to his pupils, he could not prevent these theses from being present in his teaching.

Among the subjects he taught Laharpe gave crucial importance to history, particularly Roman history. To transmit it in a living way, he drew examples able to nourish moral reflection that would be useful to the future monarch. Strong ideas stand out from his curriculum: each man, including the sovereign, should respect the laws;[43] tyranny and the oppression of one man by another are to be condemned; "it is always dangerous to reduce men to despair;" a good prince should be prudent and temperate in his behavior; he should work for the good of his people and never descend into laziness and idleness; he should not resort to torture. Here, Laharpe left ancient history in order to indulge in a digression on the Calas case of the eighteenth century, the death by torture of a Protestant merchant falsely accused of killing his own son. Laharpe explained the affair at length to his students as a demonstration of the involvement of Enlightenment philosophers in favor of Calas's posthumous exoneration. Thus he writes in his notes as an aside to his Roman history course:

The legal assassination of the virtuous Calas in that century by one of the premier courts of France finally awakened public attention by exciting the indignation of all honest men. The immortal Montesquieu and Voltaire in France, Beccaria in Italy, and several other philosophers and orators employed eloquence equal to the importance and grandeur of their subject, and their generous efforts were successful in several countries where torture and barbaric punishment were abolished.[44]

One of the key ideas in Laharpe's teaching was that the monarchical claim of divine right was an illusion, imposed by individual men to justify the extent of their power. He wrote in his notes:

> Would it not be exceptionally absurd to believe that the Creator of these countless suns that shine above our heads has given some individuals, often weaker than others, the right to dispose by whim of all other creatures? How can we think that Caligula, Nero, Borgia, Philippe II, Genghis, Louis XI— these monsters born for the shame and misery of humanity—could be the envoys or representative of the Great Being?[45]

And Laharpe called on his pupils to promote laws and a constitution for the greater happiness of all: "Everywhere that the sovereign is merely the first magistrate of the nation, the first servant of the state, and the father of his people, he has kept power by means of the law and the love of his subjects much better than by citadels and soldiers."[46]

Concerned with the quality of his teaching, Laharpe read much and drew the sources of the learning he transmitted from the best works of his time: thus Gibbon's Decline and Fall of the Roman Empire was chosen as the text for Roman history.[47] To give flesh and depth to his teaching of ancient history, Laharpe had students read the great authors of antiquity in French translation; to lead them to take an interest in the Middle Ages, he gave them extracts from the works of Joinville and Geoffroy de Villehardouin. So he was concerned with access to original sources as much as with conveying a taste for living details; in this he proved a modern teacher, anxious to seduce his audience and bring them to wonder deeply about the facts and their significance.

Although history occupied a predominant place in Laharpe's teaching, literature was also very present. His course in literature for the year 1786[48] attests to the wealth and diversity of an education that—again in a very modern way—alternated the study of ancient authors (Seneca, Cicero, Titus Livy, Sallustus) with that of modern writers (Molière, Corneille, Racine, La Bruyère) or was devoted to contemporary philosophers (Montesquieu and Voltaire in the foreground). For each, he would give a biographical summary, a thematic commentary, and a detailed study of one work.

Alongside history and literature Laharpe gave rudiments of a geography that would complement the lessons from Pallas. As a doctor of law and a former lawyer, he taught law to his young pupils, insisting on the nature of law and on the obligation to respect it to ensure good governance.[49] On the other hand, physics and mathematics continued to be taught respectively by Kraft and Masson and at a very honorable level. In 1790, at the age of twelve, Alexander mastered all arithmetical operations with and without fractions and decimals and could resolve equations of the first degree, and he was starting to learn logarithms.[50]

Seconded by Saltykov and Protasov, Laharpe also watched over the child's moral and social education. In Catherine's opinion, Alexander was growing up in a harmonious way. In September 1787, when he was getting ready to celebrate his tenth birthday, the empress was insisting on his good looks, amiability, and seduction (traits that recur in the recorded observations of her contemporaries):

> Monsieur Alexander is in body, as in heart and mind, a person of rare beauty, goodness, and understanding: he is lively and composed, prompt and thoughtful, has profound ideas and yet singular ease in everything he does, so that one could say that he has done that all his life; he is tall and strong for his age, and nimble and agile on top of it. In a word, this boy reconciles a number of contradictions, which makes him singularly loved by those surrounding him. Those of his age easily share his opinions and willingly follow him. I fear only one danger for him: that of women, for he will be chased, and it is impossible this will not happen, for he is a figure that sets everyone alight; moreover he does not know he is handsome and until now has not made much of his looks. (You will understand why we do not make him more aware of the fact.) And he is very educated for his age: he speaks four languages, is familiar with the history of all countries, he reads willingly, is never idle; all the amusements of his age please him and are to his taste. If I speak to him seriously, he pays attention, listens and responds with equal comfort. If I make him play blind man's bluff, he enjoys it. Everybody is equally happy with him, and me also.[51]

In light of Laharpe's course notes and the reports he regularly sent to Count Saltykov and even the empress, the knowledge dispensed by Laharpe over the years 1784 to 1795 appears very broad. Moreover, in line with Catherine the Great's instructions, Laharpe taught calmly, rarely punishing the grand dukes. While he often deplored that Constantine, scatterbrained and barely interested in studying despite his lively mind, was content with superficial learning, he complained little about Alexander, whom he perceived as a serious and attentive student. However, around the age of 12 or 13, the future emperor tended to become lazier and more negligent in his work. This led Laharpe to increase his reprimands and to oblige Alexander to perform self-criticism in a regular diary that he kept at the request of his tutor. In 1790 the child wrote: "Instead of encouraging myself and redoubling my efforts to profit from the years of study that remain to me, each day I become more nonchalant, apply myself less and am more incapable, and each day I am approaching my peers who stupidly think they are perfections just because they are princes. At thirteen, I am as much like a child as at eight, and the more I advance in age, the more I approach zero. What will I become? Nothing, by all appearances." Or else: "I, the undersigned, have lied to cover my laziness and get out of trouble, by claiming not to have a moment to execute what was assigned to me two days ago, whereas my brother did the same things and in the same interval of time. On the contrary, I have gallivanted about, chatted, and behaved since the beginning of the week as a man devoid of emulation and insensible to shame and to reproach."[52]

* * *

What can we conclude from this education, from its methods and content? By all the evidence, Laharpe undertook to transmit to his students by modern methods (and using encouragement rather than constraint), making use of original sources rather than school textbooks, a great breadth of knowledge, nourished by references taken from Greco-Roman antiquity, from French classicism of the seventeenth century, and from the contemporary thought of Enlightenment philosophy. These references all had the goal of leading the future sovereign to a virtuous practice of power, with respect for morality and the law, and maybe even respect for a constitution that might eventually be adopted in the name of equality among men. And from this standpoint Laharpe's instruction served a dual function, both educational and political. But this educational model presented limits, even defects, which some contemporaries hastened to note. For example, the fabulist Krylov wrote Education of the Lion Cub, in which an eagle (representing Laharpe) undertakes the education of a lion cub (Alexander); while the instruction allows the future king of animals to know everything about the needs and way of life of birds, at the same time the little lion proves completely ignorant of the needs of his fellow creatures, to whom he promises to teach the art of making nests as soon as he is on the throne. The moral of the fable leaps out: any teaching illustrated by references other than to national ones is doomed to failure. This objection is important, since in fact Laharpe was not familiar with Russian history and literature and did not feel capable of teaching them; thus, his instruction sinned by the small importance it granted to the national situation. This was also the verdict of the historian

Kliuchevski, for whom Alexander was being fed on "political and moral dogmas" and a whole "kaleidoscope of heroic images and political ideals" in which Russia, in its "past and unattractive present," was left out of account.[53] But, at the same time, might not openness to other horizons constitute an advantage in the game of someone who was to put the international stage in his line of sight?

Later, some[54] objected that Laharpe's teaching, too dense and too abstract, could only result in sowing confusion in two childish minds that were incapable of understanding the notions presented to them. Here again, the criticism is important. Yet, if we refer to the tutor's course notes, we perceive that Laharpe distrusted abstract learning and used specific examples and references to make his teaching concrete and accessible.

However, Laharpe's education did not, in fact, fulfill the ambitious mission he set himself; in practice, it would remain incomplete, if not abortive. Many of the ideas he tackled were only superficially "absorbed" by Alexander, who later admitted he was incapable of mastering them. This semi-failure was less the responsibility of the devoted tutor than of Catherine because, starting in 1792–1793, the empress constantly subjected the adolescent to all sorts of court obligations and imposed on him concerns and an adult lifestyle that, even before the departure of Laharpe, contributed to alienating the disciple from his master.

CHAPTER 3

A Grand Duke Torn Between Greater and Lesser Courts

> Paul had no influence or authority over the education of his sons. He was obliged to ask Saltykov for permission to see them, or to win over their chamber valets in order to know what was happening around them. During the summer, they had permission once or twice a week to go spend one or two hours with their parents.[1]

Masson testifies in this passage from his *Secret Memoirs on Russia* to the fact that Catherine the Great's whims ruled the education of her grandsons. For entire years she kept them from Paul and his wife Maria Feodorovna. Throughout his childhood Alexander's daily life was very unequally divided between the worlds of his grandmother and of his parents.

Life Split between Grandmother and Parents

The childhood of the future emperor unfolded in the almost exclusive shadow of his grandmother; the time he spent in the company of his parents was almost stolen. As their correspondence attests, Maria Feodorovna and her son constantly invented stratagems to try to meet face to face in private. Yet, the influence over him of Paul and Maria Feodorovna was far from negligible. By discovering in their company aspects and conversations quite different from those he observed at the Great Court, Alexander was confronted with two opposite models, each totally contrasting with the other.

At the Winter Palace, at Tsarskoye Selo (25 kilometers south of St. Petersburg), or the Tauride Palace, "Monsieur Alexander" witnessed as a privileged observer the spectacle of a great court wholly occupied with celebrating—in luxury, pomp, and magnificence—the power and glory of Catherine the Great. He rubbed shoulders with obsequious and servile courtiers, devoted servants, artists, and writers of great talent. Even though after 1790–1791 the era no longer belonged to the Enlightenment, he found there a certain freedom of expression and thought. He could enjoy the manifest affection of his grandmother, her equanimity of humor, and her attentive care, the warm and mischievous presence of his brother Constantine, and the patient attention of his tutors. However, behind this amiable facade he also sensed the breadth of the corruption afflicting the court and the country. Behind the play of anodyne words, jokes, and gallantry, he divined the licentiousness in which Catherine indulged in the company of lovers whose age tended to approach scandalously close to her grandsons': in 1796 Platon Zubov, the last of the dozen official and hired lovers who succeeded each other in the bed and heart of the empress during the 34 years of her reign, was only three years older than Alexander.

At the Great Court, Alexander dressed in French style—velvet frock coat, silk stockings, and ribboned shoes; he applauded enthusiastically at theatre plays, concerts, and parties given in the parks of the castles or on the banks of the Neva River, in the company of young nobles. Some of these young aristocrats, older than he, began to figure among his close friends: Victor Kochubey, Paul Stroganov, and then after 1795 the Polish prince Adam Czartoryski. As for his parents, Alexander saw them rarely at the Great Court. Paul was permitted to attend only twice a week to hear the reports drawn up by his mother's ministers; he dined with her on Sundays. Maria Feodorovna preferred to welcome her son at Pavlovsk or Gatchina, where she felt freer than under the gaze of the courtiers.

The passage of time did not bring Grand Duke Paul any closer to Catherine. Admittedly, Paul had renounced his liberal and constitutional ideas, and he shared the absolutist conceptions of his mother on domestic policy. But on the diplomatic level, he remained deeply pacifist and always condemned the expansionist policy she was conducting against Poland and the Ottoman Empire;[2] in his eyes it was costly and was detracting from the country's domestic development. These divergences exacerbated Catherine's distrust of her son and her wish to keep him removed from Alexander. Relegated to his domain of Gatchina, starting in August 1783, he spent the summer and autumn months there, living in Pavlovsk the rest of the year. Over the years Paul bore this situation imposed on him with increasing difficulty, as he confided in 1784 in a letter addressed to a major dignitary:

I am thirty years old and I have nothing to do. [...] My serenity, I assure you, does not depend on the circumstances that surround me; rather it is based on my clear conscience and the conviction that there are virtues that are not dependent on any earthly power, and it is toward them that I must tend. This helps console me in the many troubled periods [...], this teaches me patience, which many interpret as a sign of my gloomy character. As regards my behavior, you know that I try to make it coincide with my moral concepts and that I can do nothing against my conscience.[3]

In fact, although "hated and despised by his mother, humiliated by the favorites, ridiculed by the courtiers, living alone and forgotten under a brilliant and sumptuous reign," Paul "kept regular and austere habits amidst the corruption and disorder of his mother's court."[4] There was no question of libertine living in his entourage. Both out of love for Maria Feodorovna, who watched over him tenderly, and out of revulsion at his mother's immorality and licentious behavior, he made every effort to respect morality and propriety. In 1785 he did begin an idyll with the young maid of honor Catherine Nelidova, but this relationship remained platonic: the conjugal life led by the grand ducal couple was a decisive break with the amorous and sensual effusions of Catherine II.

At Gatchina as at Pavlovsk, Paul and his wife led a rather modest existence that contrasted, too, with the opulence of the empress's way of living. This restraint is explained by Paul's simple tastes but also by financial motives: Paul and his wife had to support the needs of their family and the costly upkeep of their two castles. Paul even had to take out loans from several of his in-laws. So he felt a growing sense of frustration toward Catherine, who refused to increase his pension—no doubt out of fear that he would be tempted to support a bigger army—even when she was showering her favorite with extravagant gifts. In 1789, when the Count of Ségur came to say good-bye to the Grand Duke before returning to France, he received the confidences of an increasingly exasperated Paul:

He talked to me almost exclusively and for several hours, of his supposed grievances against the Empress and Prince Potemkin, the disagreeableness of his position; the fear that people had of him, and the sad fate that was being prepared for him by a Court accustomed to wanting (and able to bear) only the reign of women.[5]

Bitter about his future, Paul nevertheless reigned as absolute and despotic master over Gatchina, which he used as an entrenched camp and a model estate.

In 1783 his troops consisted only of two squadrons of 30 men each; thirteen years later, on the eve of his ascension, Paul kept 2,399 men divided into four infantry battalions, a company of chasseurs, four regiments of cavalry (gendarmes, dragoons, hussars, and Cossacks) and an artillery of twelve cannons (foot and horse), all commanded by 19 command officers and 109 senior officers.[6] At Gatchina Paul, who rose at four every morning for the first parade, could give himself over to his passion for military things. All his men wore uniforms—short jackets, gloves to the elbows, very high boots— that closely resembled those of the Prussian Army, and under his direction they performed incessant maneuvers and parades in iron discipline; imperfect execution was punished with beatings and cruelty.

The whole estate, peasants as well as soldiers, lived at a military pace. In this martial world he had constructed Paul seemed in full bloom, desiring to transmit to his children, whom he treated as soldiers and adults, the values of discipline, courage, endurance, and outstripping oneself—quite different values from those on display at Catherine's court. Paul's severity was moderated by the extreme attention he paid to the well-being of his men: over one decade, he founded a hospital, a school, and an orphanage for the children of soldiers, set up a church open to both Catholic and Lutheran worship, though favoring the Orthodox faith. He encouraged the creation of factories making glass, porcelain, and textiles. Moreover, in Gatchina the social order counted for little: minor nobles of the impoverished class, men rising from the ranks, even the dregs of the regular army could earn, by their bravery and total fidelity to the Grand Duke, Paul's confidence, his esteem—and promotion. This was the case with the young Alexis Arakcheev. From the minor nobility, but poor to the point of having only a single pair of riding breeches that he washed every night, Arakcheev entered the cadet school at age thirteen[7] as an artillery student and distinguished himself by his great capacity for work, his sense of discipline, and his excellent scholastic results.[8] He arrived in Gatchina as a lieutenant in September 1792; one month later he was made captain and had the privilege of dining at the Grand Duke's table.[9] In 1796 he was named colonel, promoted to the role of inspector and leader of the infantry battalion, and shortly afterward assumed command of Paul's army.[10]

Alexander was quickly seduced by the way of life at Gatchina. Booted and strapped into their Prussian uniforms, he and his brother participated in maneuvers once a week in the summer.[11] The two boys appreciated the frank and direct sociability of the soldiers, the cult of order, the ties of virile camaraderie, and the physical activity, all of which were lacking at the Great Court. They were happy to share the masculine world of their father.

Their tasks as corporals, their bodily fatigue, the need to avoid inspection by their grandmother when they came back exhausted from exercises, in accoutrements that had to be taken off, and even the jokes of their father, of whom they were afraid, all made this career attractive. It had no relation with the career the Petersburg public and Catherine herself would want them to pursue.[12]

However, repeated exposure to the cannon fire of Gatchina soon resulted in Alexander's deafness in the left ear. Detected in the spring of 1784, this infirmity deeply affected the empress,[13] and according to Count Rostopchin, it began to affect Alexander's character: "What made the Grand Duke disagreeable in society was his deafness; you had to speak very loudly since he heard nothing in one ear."[14] The court doctors did not hesitate to use an electrical treatment that prevented Alexander from becoming totally deaf and improved his condition somewhat,[15] without restoring his full auditory faculty.

Then a real complicity united Paul and his sons, and several witnesses report it: The young grand dukes believed deep in their hearts, and actually they were, more part of the so-called Gatchina army than the Russian Army. Gatchina was Paul's favorite castle, as his autumn residence where, more removed from Petersburg, with less restraint he could indulge in his fads. The grand dukes were sorry not to be able to go, but even so they could adopt the appearance of Paul's troopers and speak of what was happening in his little army, saying "That's our manner, in the Gatchina manner."[16]

After the spring of 1795, Alexander and Constantine began to go to Gatchina or Pavlovsk four or five times a week to participate in the summer military exercises supervised by the Grand Duke. They were prodded by Laharpe, who, while he did not share Paul's values, still wished to see the adolescents express their filial love and become closer to their father. The following year, the rhythm of exercises accelerated: in June and July the two boys participated daily in maneuvers, from six in the morning to one o'clock in the afternoon. "This summer, I can truly say that I did my military service," Alexander wrote to Laharpe with some pride.[17]

At Gatchina as at Pavlovsk, when discipline became too harsh or their father too severe, the grand dukes could count on the goodness and generosity of their mother, who brought them unfailing support and interceded in their favor. It often happened that Maria Feodorovna, who detested conflict and lived serenely, surrounded by her daughters, composed excuses on behalf of her sons:

Constantine (I have tried to imitate your style),

"I dare protest before our God, my dear Father, that I did not come last evening after supper to your antechamber because I thought I was dismissed by you, and having done the same thing last Sunday, to come would contravene the order. The reproach you gave me and my brother makes us both very unhappy. We have not merited it and at the cost of our blood we will prove, my dear papa, that all our education has been based on our sacred duties to you. Please receive at your feet your son, who with the most profound respect..."[18]

The changeable moods of Paul and his growing hatred of Catherine II did have an effect on the relations he had with his sons; the Grand Duke often oscillated between tenderness and anger—and even disdain—toward Alexander and Constantine, whom he perceived as Catherine's allies. But Maria Feodorovna was keen to maintain strong ties with her sons, despite the interdictions imposed by Catherine's strictness and Paul's bizarre behavior. The letters[19] she exchanged in 1792–1793 with Alexander while at the Tauride Palace attest to the profound affection and complicity that united them. This trait, relatively neglected by the historians, appears very important to me. Alexander always felt toward his mother the gratitude, affection, and trust that were durably woven over the course of these difficult years. And this very strong relationship largely explains the role and prerogatives that she would exercise at the court well after Alexander's marriage and his accession to the imperial throne. This is a subject to which we will return.

From an early age, then, Alexander lived in a dual world: this duality of place and people as models of values and behavior laid the groundwork for an uncomfortable if not destabilizing situation and no doubt led the child to feel, if not distrust, then at least reservations about those around him. Did it push him, as several historians have asserted,[20] to practice duplicity and to raise it to a consummate art? This thesis appears excessive to me. Of course, being torn between two worlds, each of which tried to attract him away from the other, Alexander was constrained from early on, out of prudence or fear, to adapt and compromise, to hedge. But this necessity was related to a survival instinct and only marginally affected the adolescent's character. Far from indulging in the least cynicism, Alexander appears as a young man who was reserved in social relations but capable of great sincerity and voluble as soon as he felt confidence in himself, as the letters he addressed to his mother and close friends and his conversations with Laharpe bear witness. Starting in 1792–1793, though, Alexander's universe underwent new changes, due to decisions made by Catherine the Great regarding his future.

Alexander's Marriage

In 1790, when Alexander was only 13 years old, Catherine was already planning her grandson's engagement. She carefully considered a plan, confided it to Grimm, and in November 1790 sent Nicholas Rumyantsev to Karlsruhe to examine and judge the two daughters of the hereditary Prince of Baden, Charles Louis and his wife, Amalie-Friederike of Hesse-Darmstadt. Louisa Maria Augusta was aged eleven,[21] and Friederike Dorothea was two years younger. Satisfied with Rumyantsev's report, the empress decided in 1792 to have the two little German princesses conveyed to St. Petersburg, intending to make one of them the future spouse of her grandson. On October 31 (O.S.), 1792, she wrote in an explicit way to Grimm:

> We are expecting this evening the two Baden princesses: one is thirteen and the other eleven. You must suspect that here we do not marry so young; that is not the present purpose, but rather provision for the future. While waiting, they will accustom themselves to us and see our uses and customs. As for our man, he does not think of that; he is in the innocence of his heart, and this is a diabolic trick I am playing on him, for I am leading him into temptation.[22]

The first encounter between Louisa and Alexander took place on November 14: the two adolescents, very intimidated, exchanged only a few words. But in the days that followed a real closeness arose between them, which allowed Catherine to accomplish her plan. In January 1793, with the agreement of an Alexander more and more conquered by the young girl, she sent the margrave a letter asking for his consent for the marriage between Louisa and her grandson. With the consent quickly obtained, Alexander was authorized by his grandmother to kiss the girl for the first time on the occasion of Easter; on June 2, 1793, Louisa converted to the Orthodox faith and was baptized under the name Elizabeth Alexeievna. The next day the engagement was celebrated, after sumptuous preparations:

> They started by arranging that part of the Winter Palace that lies at the corner of the Neva and the Admiralty, placing priceless mirrors and hangings there. The bedchamber became a model of elegance and magnificence. The hangings were of white cloth from Lyon with borders embroidered with large roses; the columns of the alcove, the doors and glass wainscoting, pink in color, were mounted in gilded bas-reliefs with white cameos that, applied on these transparent masses, gave them the air of floating on the wave of an

atmosphere more extensive than the chamber [...].

The baptism of the princess and the engagement took place on the twentieth and twenty-first of May.[23] In the chapel of the palace, she made her confession of faith in a loud voice. She was beautiful as an angel. Her dress was pink, embroidered with large white roses with a white skirt embroidered with roses of the same species, but in pink, not one diamond, and her lovely blond hair was floating down—like Psyche! [...] The Grand Duke, whose childish hairstyle had been changed, wore a suit of silver brocade embroidered with silver. [...] It was a fine spectacle to see this great Empress mounting a platform with the lovely couple to present them to God and to the nation. Me, I cried copiously.[24]

A few weeks later, on October 9, Catherine had the marriage of the two adolescents celebrated in the church of St. Savior of the Transfiguration. The church bells rang for three days and the festival lasted for two weeks, culminating on October 22 in sumptuous fireworks over the tsarina's private meadow.

Catherine's rush to hold the engagement and then marriage of Alexander is explained largely by psychological factors: Alexander had reached puberty at the age of 12, and when the grand duke reached 14, General Protasov had noted "in both his statements and in his nocturnal dreams, strong physical desires that grew in the course of his frequent conversations with pretty women."[25] Thus Catherine charged a lady of the court with initiating her grandson "in the mysteries of all the transports engendered by sensual delight,"[26] and she decided to marry him quickly in order to channel his impulses and desires. To this motive should be added political aims: starting in 1793, as her hostility to Paul grew, her design to transmit imperial power to her grandson grew stronger. So, by a precocious marriage, she was ensuring the durability of her dynasty.

Catherine's choice appeared judicious, and observers present at court heaped praise on Elizabeth's extraordinary beauty, her charm, and modesty. The young girl had received a brilliant education at the Baden court: she spoke and wrote French and German,[27] had studied history, geography, philosophy, French and German literature, and thanks to the geographical proximity of the Baden principality with France, she was au fait with all the cultural novelties coming from Paris.

During her stay in Russia, the French portrait painter Elisabeth Vigée-Lebrun met Elizabeth at Tsarskoye Selo a few months after the marriage. Right away, she was smitten with the young princess:

She was seventeen at most. Her facial traits were fine and regular, in a perfect oval; her delicate skin was not animated but of a pallor in harmony with the expression on her face, whose sweetness was angelic; her blond hair floated around her neck and forehead. She was dressed in a white tunic, attached by a belt knotted casually around a small and supple waist like that of a nymph. I cried to myself: "She is Psyche!"[28]

This uncommon beauty was combined with great vivacity of mind. Despite her young age and her inexperience at the Russian court, she had character, convictions, and firm opinions that she expressed most particularly in her correspondence with her mother, the Margravine of Baden. And it is to her that we owe the most precise physical and psychological portrait of Alexander as an adolescent:

Very tall and well-formed, especially the legs and feet well turned, although the feet are a little big; light brown hair, blue eyes, not very big but not small either; very pretty teeth, charming skin color, straight nose, rather handsome.

A few months later, in January 1793, she made a more critical judgment of her fiancé:

You ask me if the Grand Duke *truly* pleases me. Yes, Mama, he pleases me. For some time he has pleased me like mad, but presently, now that I begin to know him (not that he loses by being known, on the contrary), one notices little nothings, truly nothings, which are not to my taste and have destroyed the excessive way in which I loved him. I still love him very much, but in another way. These little-nothings are not in his character, for on that side surely I believe there is nothing to reproach, but in the manners, in something exterior.[29]

Although deprived of the company of her relatives—her sister Friederike Dorothea remained in St. Petersburg only until the wedding and then went home—Elizabeth was not timid. It was she who took the initiative of declaring her sentiments to the Grand Duke[30] and who in the summer of 1793 sent him little notes written in halting Russian, alternating with passionate letters written in a fluent French, like this one in August written from the Tauride Palace:

You tell me I have the happiness of a certain person in my hand. Ah, if this is true, his happiness is assured forever. I will love him, he will be my best friend

my whole life—unless there is heavenly punishment. It is he who taught me
not to rely on myself too much, he is right and I admit it. He holds my life's
happiness in his hands. It is certain to make me forever unhappy if ever he
stops loving me. I will bear *everything* except that. But it is to think badly of
him to even have such an idea. He loves me tenderly. I love him too and this
causes my happiness. Farewell, my darling. Have these sentiments, this is my
great desire. Of me you can be certain that I love you beyond words.

Goodbye, my friend.—Elizabeth.[31]

On his side, Alexander also wrote very short love notes that he accompanied
sometimes with sketches, like a little horse's head, badly drawn with pencil
on paper, and carefully folded into four in a little envelope.[32]

While the two adolescents seemed to find great happiness in their nascent idyll, very quickly difficulties arose due to the increasingly stifling atmosphere of Catherine's court.

To watch over the young couple to whom she had given sumptuous apartments and a small court, the empress had appointed Count Golovin as the
Grand Duke's Hofmeister, and the Countess Shuvalova as Elizabeth's. Hated
as much by Paul as by Alexander, the latter employed herself, on Catherine's orders, with limiting contact and meetings between Alexander and
his parents. Several letters exchanged between Alexander and his mother
in 1793–1794 mention the ruses to which Maria Feodorovna and her son
resorted in order to meet without the knowledge of the redoubtable countess who monitored the visits by the young couple. Alexander often regretted
not being able to meet his parents "in total freedom." In a letter dated the
end of 1792, he complains that the countess "has already gossiped about our
going as seldom as possible to Papa's" and hopes that "since I am going today
to my sister Olga's, you will make a little visit there so I may speak to you
at ease."[33] In the autumn of 1793, he inveighs against "this cursed countess"
who "has done us so much evil, for she is still partly the reason why we do
not enter your apartments and they always dismiss us at the door."[34] A few
months later he congratulates himself on reaching "an accommodation with
the countess […] that will procure us the happiness of seeing each at least
on the same footing as previously, for how it has been during these two last
occasions has pained my heart more than you can imagine."[35] In the autumn
of 1794, he expressed in a letter to his mother the sadness and weariness he
felt at being permanently separated from her.[36]

Deprived of the presence of Paul and Maria Feodorovna, the young couple found themselves increasingly exposed to court intrigues. Platon Zubov,
the nominal favorite of Catherine II, got it into his head to seduce the well-

behaved Elizabeth and acted with little discretion. She remained above re-proach but found herself in a very embarrassing position with the empress, whose reaction she feared.

At the same time, when the exciting spring love of the first months had passed, Alexander and Elizabeth, inexperienced and barely nubile, had difficulty transforming their real affection for each other into an actual conjugal relationship. At the end of 1793 or the very beginning of 1794,[37] Alexander admitted this embarrassment to his mother, in modest circumlocutions:

> You ask me, my dear Mama, if my little Lisa is pregnant. No, not yet, for the thing is not accomplished. It must be agreed that we are big children and very maladroit ones, since we take all the trouble imaginable to do so but we do not succeed.[38]

In the following months, this situation was not remedied. The immature Alexander preferred to spend his time in the company of young noblemen of his age or with his valets, shied away from his wife, and committed pranks of doubtful taste. More than once, General Protasov despaired in his letters to Count Vorontsov, admitting in May 1794:

> My annoyances are much greater than you think. My former student begins to get carried away, and if this continues, goodbye to peace. He has favorites who flatter him, he is getting accustomed (without realizing it and in the greatest innocence) to the taste of liquor, and the habit is a bad thing. Overall he does nothing worthy, and I often have scenes with him [...]. He is spoiled in every sense.[39]

And in June:

> This dear student is thoroughly spoiled. Apart from the scenes that I noted previously [...], yesterday he had a fine one atop the figurehead column in the middle of the pond. Monseigneur took it into his head to walk around the edge as if he were walking on a wide board, afterward he jumped through an opening where the stair was, and when his wife and I objected, he gave us paltry and childish excuses for jumping again.
>
> I do not need to comment on this, but to give you an idea of his way of life, I will tell you he has invited me to a pleasure party tomorrow, for the mating of his English mare with Rostopchin's stallion, adding that Rostopchin had assured him that he would be very interested in seeing the movements of the two horses during this act. Judge from this, my dear count, whether I should accept the invitation.[40]

Alexander was neglecting his wife while she, deprived of the company of her sister, who had returned to Karlsruhe, was feeling more and more alone. Lacking affection and without a moral compass, Elizabeth was not long in losing her head and throwing herself into an amorous friendship—distinctly ambiguous—with Countess Varvara Golovina. During the second half of the year 1794, the very beautiful wife of the court marshal, aged 29, became the young wife's intimate, and they shared readings, discussions, and promenades. If this lively and reciprocal friendship seems to have been—at least at first—encouraged by Alexander, it seems likely that he was, out of naïveté or indifference, not really aware of the measure or nature of such an attachment, which, as Elizabeth acknowledged covertly in letters to the countess, attested to a social prohibition. And she lied to Alexander when she spoke to him about the relationship. In December 1794, in a particularly exalted letter, Elizabeth writes to Varvara:

> I love you so much and I will love you despite the whole world. Moreover, they cannot *forbid* me from loving you and I am even in some fashion authorized *by someone else*[41] who has the right (just as much if not more) to order me to love you. You understand me, I hope.[42]

This lends credence to the idea of Alexander's complacency. But in the spring of 1795,[43] the most cryptic and the most heretical letter that Elizabeth wrote to the countess appears to exonerate Alexander from any complicity:

> Oh, my dear, the 30ths. How long they will take to come back! My God, all the sensations that merely the memory of these sweet moments brings back to me! The grand duke who has read your letter has just asked me for an explanation. I partly told him. And thinking of this happy 30th of May turns me upside down. You may imagine, I hope, how dear the date of the day when I gave myself totally to you shall remain to me.[44]

The letters to the Countess Golovina, sensual and inflamed, abruptly stop in the autumn of 1795, and lacking sources, it is difficult to know why. In the following years this relationship appears to be calmer; Countess Golovina remained a close friend and confidante of Elizabeth, and her interesting *Souvenirs*[45] were written with the latter's approval.

At the same time court obligations involved Alexander and Elizabeth in an incessant whirlwind of activities, as frivolous as they were vain. Writing to her mother, the young woman recurrently states that her time is consumed with parties, balls, concerts, and various entertainments. At the start of 1794, supported in this project by his grandmother, Alexander launched into the construction of a marionette theater, whose puppets, some months later, would offer the court a ballet called Dido.[46] And consequently, the young Grand Duke neglected his studies more and more.

Of course, he defended himself in his letters to Maria Feodorovna; his weekly schedule continued, at least on paper, to grant a predominant place to the teaching of Laharpe, whom he saw four mornings a week, the rest of the time being devoted to other disciplines, notably religion and the study of fortifications. In reality, the student was less assiduous and used excuses about the most banal impediments, as attested by this little note he sent at the start of 1794:

> My dear Monsieur de Laharpe, I ask a million pardons; I am obliged again today to cancel our engagement. I hope that you will excuse this, for it comes from the fact that my wife is not well and she was obliged to take medicine. I beg to see you another time! I count even more on your indulgence because you are also a married man, and consequently know the care that must be taken over one's wife.[47]

This lack of studiousness did not escape those close to the Grand Duke. In May 1794 a letter written at Tsarskoye Selo that General Protasov addressed to Count Vorontsov complains of growing laziness:

> We arrived here on the 13th. Our two young people are very happy to do nothing, and consequently they did not do much in town either. Idleness, laziness, sloth and an indifference to all serious things on the part of our dear Grand Duke are at their height.[48]

Alexander's frivolity was largely encouraged by Catherine herself. In the autumn of 1793, the empress became convinced that her grandson's education was finished and the presence of Laharpe was now useless. Doomed from this point on, Laharpe managed to benefit from a reprieve thanks to Saltykov's intervention,[49] but this was merely a postponement, and a year later, on October 23 (O.S.), 1794, Laharpe was officially dismissed, given the title of colonel, travel expenses of a thousand ducats, a salary corresponding to his grade, and a pension. This news was a tragedy for Alexander, who, in a moving letter to his mother, expressed his deep distress and sorrow:

> I am on the eve of losing M. de La Harpe, who will soon receive his dismissal and will leave. This causes me grief all the greater in that I see him also, I

dare say so, annoyed to quit me. I have done everything in the world to bring a remedy: I spoke to Count Saltykov who told me that the Empress wanted to dismiss him upon my marriage and that it is only because of his petitions that he was kept on, but that now after having recompensed him she wants to dismiss him, and all that is due to the old story on the subject of his correspondence with his parents that was discovered and that Esterhazy interpreted badly and made a Jacobin of him.

I cannot tell you what pain this gives me; this was a true friend I had, who surely did not spoil me and to whom I owe everything that I know. He promised to prepare me a plan of studies so that I should continue. This loss is terrible for me; only your acts of kindness, my dear and good Mama, might soften my grief. I dare hope for them by trying to make myself worthy.

Adieu, dear and good Mama, I kiss your hands tenderly.[50]

In April 1795, tormented by the idea of leaving his student for good, Laharpe composed the Instructions that he gave him at his departure. The text abounds with practical and material advice: he should get up early and not go to bed late, so as to be able to study in the morning; it is best to awaken at a fixed hour and to devote little time to his toilette. Then he mentions Alexander's environment at the court and puts him on his guard by stressing that "there are only two persons with whom your eminent situation permits you to live on a footing of familiarity: the companion who is your happiness, and your brother who was your childhood friend. Tighten with all your strength the ties that unite you with these two persons and who must assure you long enjoyment of domestic happiness."[51]

Finally, he insisted on the qualities the future emperor should demonstrate in his government:

> I have often told you this before and I will end here. The only friend that never flatters is a good judiciary, and it is only by the light of such a torch that you will distinguish the deeds and merit that you will one day employ. May you by this means be made invulnerable, and may your generous and human heart, led by a just and enlightened mind, make you worthy of the eminent post to which you will be called for the service of a great people.[52]

This text, which reflects values dear to Laharpe (the notion of a "just and enlightened mind" is no doubt the key to his 11 years of teaching), also testifies to the tutor's worry at leaving an adolescent who seemed to him vulnerable, isolated, and no doubt not yet firm in his moral principles and habits. In response to this letter, Alexander sent him on the day of his departure in

May 1795 his portrait and Elizabeth's in a frame surrounded by diamonds, accompanied by a short letter of farewell full of affection, gratitude, and sorrow.[53] By losing Laharpe, Alexander lost not only a tutor and a man he could trust but still more a man whose moral landmarks and strict conscience had served him as a compass. More and more exposed to the traps of the court, and always confronted by the antagonism between his grandmother and his father, Alexander now had to confront alone the tensions and political gambles during the end of Catherine II's reign.

Faced with Catherine's Political Aims

Laharpe's departure reinforced the already noticeable changes after the grand duke's marriage. The formerly studious and structured way of life that kept Alexander on the margins of the court gave way to practices and behaviors that aimed to place him in the orbit of power. For by giving him his own court, very fine apartments, and a generous pension, Catherine was evidently trying to inculcate in her grandson her own taste for the pomp and magnificence of autocratic power. But at the same time—and this is another paradox in the empress's attitude—she delegated to Alexander no political responsibility whatever and in no way prepared him to execute the high office that she would transmit to him. Instead, she confined him to a life of performance and futile pleasures.

> After Laharpe left him, and after he was given an individual court and some persons of merit were dismissed, he was even more badly surrounded and a more idle prince. He spent his days in tête-à-tête with his young wife, his valets, or in the company of his grandmother. He lived more indolently and more obscurely than the heir of a sultan inside the harems of a seraglio.[54]

According to Masson, whose judgment on the end of Catherine's reign is pitiless, Alexander seems to have been caught by laziness, futility, and idleness—the three court maladies against which the devoted Laharpe had repeatedly warned his student—all in a period of barely a few months. Yet this criticism appears excessive, for the young man was aware of the distractions multiplying around him and tried (for what it was worth) to remain faithful to the line of conduct set by his tutor. In February 1796 he wrote to Laharpe:

> For me, I have reformed myself. I get up early and work in the morning according to the plan you know. This was starting to go well, I was becoming

very sedentary in the study, but an obstacle arose. They wanted me to take morning walks from ten to eleven. Here is already an interruption, but still I do what it is possible to do. At this moment there is another one: festivals on the occasion of the marriage of the second son of the heir to the throne, but that will end soon and Lent is approaching. We are going to the countryside and I will go back to reading and studying more than ever. I find myself strong in my regime, I feel marvelous, I am gay most of the time, despite my troubles, and quite happy with my wife and my sister-in-law.[55]

In fact, from then on, Alexander opted for a way of life that he subsequently never quit: he got up early, spent little time on his toilette, and lunched frugally; in a general way, he ate and drank with moderation, while appreciating fine cuisine. But it was difficult to impose on himself a rigorous discipline when all around him the mood was in favor of distraction and partying. Thus, it is not certain that Alexander was long able to resist the court example, and no doubt in his letter to Laharpe he tends to draw a flattering picture; he may have deluded himself about his constancy and application to studies. But the fact that he tried to keep a semblance of organization and regularity in his daily life and that he tried to continue his learning on his own, attests that Laharpe's virtuous influence upon the young man remained potent.

Moreover, while he did read and study less than previously, to the point that he paid attention to Elizabeth's advice about his reading, and although the lifestyle imposed by Catherine tended to doom him to the fatuousness of court life, his horizons gradually widened, and he began to take an interest in politics. Alexander cultivated very strong friendships with a small number of young people who came from old noble families that had long been close to power, who were cultivated and open minded, attracted to the Enlightenment spirit and to liberal ideas.

At the heart of this group was Viktor Kochubey, born in 1768 of Tartar origin, nephew of the chancellor and Minister of Foreign Affairs (Alexander Bezborodko), who had been frequenting Alexander since 1792 and therefore was his oldest friend. In 1784, at the age of 16, Kochubey was sent as an auxiliary diplomat in the Russian embassy to Sweden. He profited by taking courses at the University of Stockholm and wrote an essay devoted to the rights of man. During his stay in Europe, extending from 1788 to 1792, he studied political science in London and then philosophy in Paris and began to emulate liberalism. In July 1792 his uncle, worried about the harmful effect that long months spent in revolutionary France might have on the young man's career, recalled him to St. Petersburg. A few months later, at the age of 24, Kochubey was named by Catherine to the prestigious post of Russian ambassador to the Ottoman court in Constantinople.

Count Paul Stroganov was the youngest of Alexander's friends. Born in Paris in 1772, Paul was the only son of the wealthiest dignitary of the age, Count Alexander Stroganov. A patron of the arts and a great collector,[56] an independent mind and a Freemason, Count Alexander was incapable of evaluating his fortune precisely and was ignorant about the exact number of his serfs. He had raised his son to worship the Enlightenment and liberalism, and he encouraged him to go to Europe in 1790. Alongside his tutor, the Republican mathematician Charles-Gilbert Romme, Paul went first to Switzerland, where he met the Genevan jurist Louis Dumont, a close friend of Jeremy Bentham, then to France. There he frequented the Jacobin Club under the name of Paul Otcher (a pseudonym he took from the name of one of his father's estates in the province of Perm); he became its librarian, took as mistress the Revolutionary courtesan Théroigne de Méricourt, and even wore the Phrygian red bonnet! But the scandal of his love affairs and his radical convictions reached the ears of Catherine II. In 1791 Paul Stroganov was abruptly brought back to Russia at the express demand of the empress; furious, she admonished the old count for his paternal irresponsibility and condemned Paul to internal exile on family lands near Moscow. In 1796 the ban was lifted, and Paul quickly entered the circle of Alexander's favorite friends.

That same year, Adam Czartoryski was 26. Handsome, elegant, cultivated, and intelligent, the young Pole came from an old princely family. After the 1795 Polish uprising against Russian rule led by Kosciuszko, which was brutally put down by Russian troops, he was sent by his parents to St. Petersburg with his brother Constantine in order to obtain, as reward for their allegiance, the lifting of the confiscation of his family's enormous wealth. Alexander was fascinated by his thorough education in the spirit of the Enlightenment, the cultivated milieu in which he grew up before his arrival in Russia—he had relationships with Herder and Goethe and had stayed in England where he studied British political organization, in Scotland where he met the philosopher David Hume, in Germany, and in France. In addition, he had an aura of bravura, since in 1794 he had taken up arms against Russia under the flag of Kosciuszko, veteran of the American War of Independence. In the spring of 1796, as Prince Czartoryski himself stressed in his memoirs, he became an intimate friend of the grand duke[57]—before seducing Elizabeth and becoming, no doubt at the end of 1796 or the beginning of 1797, her close friend and then her lover.

The fourth and older member of the little group was a cousin of Paul Stroganov, who as son of a sister of Count Alexander, had been raised by his uncle. Born in 1761, Nikolay Novosiltsev had served in the Russian army during the wars against Sweden in 1788 to 1790 and had then held several posts within the College of Foreign Affairs. He figured as a man of letters who knew the law, economics, and diplomacy of the age; wielding an elegant pen, he was also characterized, unlike the sober Alexander, by an epicurean-ism and a noted taste for alcohol.

In the course of the meetings and conversations of this group of young men, the young Grand Duke revealed a sharpened critical mind that broke with the naïveté of his former judgments.

* * *

In fact, from 1793 the evolution of the Polish question and the role played by Catherine had aroused negative commentary from the young Grand Duke. After 20 years of the status quo, Poland had suffered in 1793 a second division that allowed the Russian Empire to take a portion of White Russia (the region of Minsk) and the western Ukraine.[58] In March 1794 a national uprising led by Kosciuszko (who had prestige from the American Revolu-tion), was rapidly defeated by Russian and Prussian troops and resulted only in a new partition. In October 1795 the Russian Empire obtained the rest of Lithuania, as well as the duchy of Courlandia[59] in Latvia, previously dis-puted between Russia and Poland.

This new dismemberment aroused Alexander's disapproval, and in a let-ter to his mother, he disavowed Catherine's choices. But, still very young (he was only 17 then), he summoned moral and religious considerations that were still vague. Politics as yet had no place in his approach:

> You ask me, dear Mama, what I think of Polish affairs, and I am groaning, but I have always thought like you—as you remember—that they cannot end well. The Supreme Being who is just cannot suffer an injustice, and sooner or later it will be punished. I dare say that, because I am certain that nobody but you and my wife will see this letter.[60]

On the other hand, things were different a year later: Alexander was now ca-pable of elaborating critical judgments about Catherine's policies, this time not only in the name of morality and religion, but in the name of politics and by reference to Enlightenment ideals. Recounting a conversation he had had with the grand duke in the spring of 1796, Adam Czartoryski wrote:

Then he told me that he in no way shared the ideas and doctrines of the cabinet at Court; that he was far from approving the policy and conduct of his grandmother, that he condemned her principles, that he wished well for Poland and its glorious struggle, that he had deplored its fall, that Kosciuszko was in his eyes a great man by his virtues and by the cause he was defending, which was that of humanity and justice. He admitted to me he detested despotism everywhere and however it was exercised, that he loved freedom, which was equally due to all men, that he took the liveliest interest in the French Revolution, that while disapproving of its terrible abuses, he wished for the success of the Republic and rejoiced over it.[61]

Similarly, in a letter sent in May 1796 to Viktor Kochubey (who was then in Italy), Alexander established in outline a parallel critique of the domestic state of his country and the expansionist policy of Catherine II. She had just taken advantage of the third partition of Poland, sealed at the end of 1795, and three years after the signing of the Treaty of Jassy that pushed back the borders of the Ottoman Empire for the benefit of Russia, she had just founded the military and commercial port of Odessa. He wrote: "Our affairs are in incredible disorder, we are pillaging on all sides; all our departments are badly administered; everywhere order seems banished, and the Empire only increases its territory."[62]

Thus, by 1796 far from being content with the futile life in which Catherine tried to confine him, Alexander was henceforth sensitive to politics. Focused on the good of the state and the well-being of its people, Laharpe's precepts seemed to be bearing their first fruits. But these reflections did not find any application, and the audience for them did not exceed the circle of Alexander's close friends: the young man was kept out of political affairs—even the plan that concerned him most directly.

＊ ＊ ＊

As early as 1791, Catherine began to think about making Alexander her direct successor, thus depriving Paul of his right to mount the throne. On October 30, 1793, she summoned Laharpe to share her intentions, mentioning to him "the future elevation" of Alexander and soliciting his help to convince Alexander to rally to this plan. But Laharpe, out of a legitimist spirit as much as out of prudence, pretended not to understand what was expected of him, refusing de facto to help the empress enact her resolve:

My conversation[63] with the Empress lasted two hours; we spoke of all possible things and from time to time the Empress hazarded by speaking a few words on the future of Russia, and omitting nothing to make me understand the true purpose of the interview, but without directly stating it. Having divined her intentions, I made every effort to prevent the Empress from disclosing her designs, and at the same time to allay any suspicion on her part that I had penetrated her secret. Happily I succeeded at both. But the two hours I spent in this moral torture are among the most difficult of my life, and their memory poisoned the rest of my stay in Russia.

Although the interview finished in a charming manner, I thereafter fled the society of the Court as much as possible, for I feared a repetition of these discussions, and the second time it would not have been possible to get out of the affair as easily as the first. Catherine twice reproached me, but finally when she saw that I was recalcitrant and that I came to Court only to occupy myself with my pupils, she must have been convinced that I was not disposed to play the role she was urging on me.[64]

Laharpe preferred not to get involved in this dangerous project: "If this secret had been discovered, all the responsibility would have fallen on the defenseless foreigner," he lucidly wrote in his *Memoirs*. A year later, in 1794, when Alexander had just married, Catherine mentioned the plan again, this time to her closest advisors, advancing Paul's "incompetence" and his incapacity to ensure the grandeur of the imperial state. But she encountered reservations and especially the opposition of Musin-Pushkin, who saw in this illegitimate plan a source of destabilization and potential political disorder. The issue of the succession was now set aside for a while, although Catherine did not give up on her plan. Having found no support from Alexander's tutor or her advisors, Catherine turned to her own family. On July 7, 1796, when Maria Feodorovna had just given birth to a third son called Nikolay,[65] and she found herself alone with Catherine at the Tsarskoye Selo palace, the empress tried to convince her daughter-in-law, whom she knew was very close to Alexander, to push Paul to renounce the throne. The testimony of Grand Duchess Anna, one of Maria Feodorovna's daughters, who later became queen of the Netherlands, attests to this imperial pressure:

> I since learned, from my husband's mouth, that after the decease of my brother Emperor Alexander, when he hurried to Russia to share my family's sorrow, that my mother went back to this distant past. In one of her effusive

moments, she recounted to [my husband] that while she had just given birth to my brother Nicholas, Empress Catherine gave her a paper which raised the matter of requiring my father to renounce his rights to the Crown in favor of my brother Alexander, insisting that my mother sign this paper as a token of her adherence to this deed, which the Empress wanted to obtain. My mother felt justly indignant and refused to sign it.

Empress Catherine was very irritated, and the coldness that she showed [Mother] was the consequence of seeing her project thwarted.[66]

Maria Feodorovna's refusal to sanction her project did not discourage the empress, who finally decided to broach it with the interested party himself. On September 16 (O.S.), 1796, Catherine confided in Alexander her intention to see him succeed her on the throne and informed him that for this purpose she had undertaken to write a manifesto, and soon she gave him a copy. Less flattered by the plan than worried about the responsibilities that would become his, Alexander's answer remained vague; he said nothing of the resolution he had already formed.

> September 24 (O.S.), 1796
> Your Imperial Majesty!
> Never will I be able to express my gratitude for the confidence with which Your Majesty has honored me, and the goodness with which She has deigned to write in her own hand something to serve as explanation of other papers. I hope Your Majesty will see, by my zeal to merit her precious acts of goodness, that I sense the whole cost. Truly I will never be able to pay even with my blood for what She has deigned and still wants to do for me.
> These papers confirm all the reflections that Your Majesty wanted to communicate, which, if it is permitted to me to say so, cannot be more just.
> It is by laying once more at the feet of Your Imperial Majesty the sentiments of keenest gratitude that I take the liberty of being with the deepest respect and most inviolable attachment
> Of Your Imperial Majesty the very humble and very submissive subject and grandson,
> Alexander.[67]

Thus, in the autumn of 1796, Alexander's loyalist intentions were already firmly decided, and it is not by chance that he also addressed his father as "Majesty"; in his eyes, Paul should reign upon Catherine's death and he would not usurp imperial power.

Two key factors explain Alexander's attitude at this time. First, we must stress the nature of the education he had received and, once again, the role of Laharpe. Raised—even if formally—in absolute respect for family ties and educated in the hatred of tyranny, violence, and coups, the young Alexander could not, at barely 19 years of age, dream of himself as a usurper, even less so because in 1796 his filial love was very deep. The second crucial point is that, while Alexander felt interest in politics and he was apt to articulate critical judgments on the state of his country, as we saw above, he did not yet feel capable of remedying the evils from which the empire suffered. Paralyzed by a profound lack of self-confidence, he was not moved by any political ambition. In February 1796, in a letter addressed to Laharpe that he had Viktor Kochubey convey to his mother-in-law, the Margravine of Baden, for her to transmit to his tutor, he expressed the clear desire to "get out of his charge"[68] as soon as possible. On May 22, 1796, in a letter to Kochubey, he confessed—and this is an important text—his inability to respond to the challenge that the exercise of power constitutes and his aspiration to lead a simple and retired life, far from the turpitudes and corruption of a court he execrated:

> Yes, my dear friend, I repeat, I am in no way satisfied with my position, it is much too brilliant for my character, which loves only tranquility and peace. The Court is not a habitation made for me; I suffer each time that I must perform there and it makes my blood boil when I see the baseness almost always committed to acquire some distinction for which I would not have given three pennies. I feel unhappy to be obliged to be in society with people I would not want to have as servants, and who here enjoy the prime places— such as P. Zubov, M. Passeck, Father Bariatinsky, the two Saltykovs, Miatlev, and a host of others who do not merit being named, who are as low as their inferiors and who crawl before the one they fear. Finally, my dear friend, I do not feel myself made for the place that I occupy at this moment and that I have sworn to renounce, one way or another. There, my dear friend, is the great secret that I have so long delayed to communicate to you.[69]

Later on, after having mentioned the disastrous state in which Russia found herself, Alexander adds:

> How can a single man manage to govern it and even correct its abuses? This would be absolutely impossible not only for a man of ordinary abilities like me, but even for a genius, and I have always had the principle that it is better not to be entrusted with a job than to fulfill it badly; it is according to this

principle that I took the resolution of which I spoke above.

My plan is that once I have renounced this scabrous place (I cannot set the date of such a renunciation), I will go settle with my wife on the banks of the Rhine, where I will live peacefully as a simple individual, making my happiness consist of the company of my friends and the study of nature. You will mock me; you will say that this is a chimerical plan: you are free to say that, but wait for the event and afterward I will allow you to judge. I know that you will blame me, but I cannot do otherwise, for a quiet conscience is my first rule, and it will never be quiet if I were to undertake something beyond my strength.[70]

This text is of crucial importance on the political level: in the spring of 1796, Alexander had already declared his conviction and would not change, despite the pressure from his grandmother, who felt her end approaching. But it is also precious because it reveals Alexander's personality. At 19, the "monarch-in-waiting," the one educated to reign without ever having been allowed to actually exercise power, in fact perceived himself as an ordinary man, with simple and modest tastes, a man incapable of rivaling the historical heroes described by Laharpe and therefore incapable of assuming the colossal task implied by the good government of the Russian Empire. Twice, in February and May 1796, Alexander affirmed that he did not feel up to the role for which he was destined, and that, convinced of his inadequacies, he had decided to abdicate and to retire to the banks of the Rhine. This meant on German territory, and perhaps we should see this trope as a fluctuation in his own identity: in 1796 Alexander did not feel himself truly "Russian."

Whatever the case, his admission also reveals the flimsiness of Catherine II's education: despite her affection and permanent attention, she had not succeeded in transmitting to Alexander her passion for power. It also reveals the partial failure of Laharpe's educational model: of course, this teaching had given Alexander reference points and moral imperatives that broke with the corrupt and lying practices of Catherine's court, and it also familiarized him with a certain number of political notions—liberty, equality, and justice—that would serve him after 1796 as an analytical grid for judging the Russian situation. But at the same time the historical references with which he was fed, both overwhelming by the exemplary values they put into play and inoperative on the political level because too distant and abstract, contributed to awakening doubts in him, even complexes, about his own competence. Raised to rule and to impose his will, Alexander at 19 was an adolescent unsure of himself and frightened by power.

On November 16, 1796, Catherine II, victim of a heart attack, plunged into a coma that lasted 22 hours. That very day, informed of his mother's critical state, Paul left Gatchina to go to her bedside and watch over her until her death, which came in the early hours of November 17. Paul then asked Platon Zubov for all his mother's personal papers and, having found Catherine's will by which she transferred the throne to Alexander, he burned it. For his part, Alexander said nothing about the provisions made in his favor by his grandmother. The reign of Paul I could begin.

CHAPTER 4

The Tsarevich at Paul I's Court

1796–1801

For many decades Paul I has been an unloved figure: historians paid little attention to him[1]—and were quite severe in their judgment of him. Unanimously described as an angry and capricious despot, affected by a paranoia that grew apace, he was said to have few coherent thoughts other than his hatred of Catherine II and his desire to obliterate her memory and deeds. Detested and feared by his contemporaries, who became increasingly worried by the erratic course of his reign, Paul seemed a character that belonged to an absurdist and grotesque novel.[2] He was someone who met a tragic fate—and quite deserved it.

Today, this monochrome representation has been somewhat challenged, and a more nuanced interpretation is appearing. Without denying the many excesses and inconsistencies of his reign, current historiography[3] tends to show that Paul was not acting in an impulsive and disorganized way but rather was pursuing objectives based on a political vision. And because this vision ran counter to the interests of certain elites, they were led to the plot to get rid of the emperor; through their writings and testimony after Paul's reign, they then elaborated a black legend designed to justify his murder.

This current rereading is interesting: first, because it gives more strength to Paul's character, but also because it tends implicitly toward a fresh hypothesis about the conditions under which Alexander came to power. Far from being a tragic episode made necessary by Paul's insanity, the assassination of the emperor may find its true origin in a prosaic conspiracy deriving from realpolitik. What was Alexander's precise role in the course of the months preceding the murder? What motivations could have pushed the grand duke to acquiesce in the plot? To try to see more clearly, we must look not only at Paul's reign properly speaking but also at the life that the tsarevich led at his father's court and at the interior journey that in barely five years transformed an adolescent of 19—unsure of himself, full of filial love, and without any noticeable taste for power—into a man who had decided to ascend to the throne and who, while wanting to spare his father's life, sought to depose him.

The End of the "Reign of Women"

Arriving on the throne in November 1796 and crowned the following April, Paul quickly tried to get rid of both the symbols and actions that were his mother's heritage. From the night when the empress was sinking in her coma, he hurried to destroy the personal papers of Catherine II. When assured of the full legitimacy of his power, he quickly asserted his desire for radical changes.

From the start, there would be no more "reign of women";[4] the era would belong not to his mother's decadent fascination for immoral pleasures, frivolous beauty, and French fashions but to the cult of order and virility, inspired by the shades of Frederick the Great of Prussia. Paul immediately ordered the detested palace of Tsarskoye Selo closed down, and he moved to the Winter Palace, while continuing to spend the summer and autumn months at Gatchina or Pavlovsk. Barely proclaimed emperor, he launched into drawing up persnickety decrees (ukases) that aimed to reform what he considered the degenerate manners of the capital. From now on, nobles should eat in a frugal manner at one o'clock; a curfew would be set at ten p.m., and the main streets of St. Petersburg would be closed by barriers at night, only accessible to doctors and midwives; officers would be authorized to circulate only in open carriages or on horseback; finally, clothing should obey precise rules; everything that might recall French influence—now perceived as subversive—was forbidden.

> He banned going out in tailcoats; one could not appear outside one's home except in the dress of one's social station, sword at one's side, and wearing decorations if one had them. Round hats, trousers, folded-down boots, and cordon shoes—all that was severely and immediately prohibited, such that the necessary time and pecuniary means were insufficient for passive obedience. Some people were forced to stay hidden at home, while others appeared as best they could: small round hats were transformed by means of pins into three-cornered hats, tail-coats had their turned-down collars removed and pockets added, trousers were hitched up at front and secured at the knees, hair was cut in the round, covered with powder and a queue was attached at the back.[5]

In the following months and years the restrictive measures only increased. By means of decrees, the emperor undertook to remodel everything, clothing as well as customs and language, buildings as well as landscapes. In February 1799 the waltz was banned; a few weeks later it was forbidden to "wear quiffs of hair that hung down on the forehead," women could not "wear multicolored ribbons on the shoulders as men do and nobody should wear loops that fell too low." Jabots and side whiskers were also banned; calm should preside everywhere; children were no longer permitted to go out in the streets without being accompanied—and coachmen and postilions no longer had the right to call loudly to their horses en route![6]

These measures were matched with more substantial rules concerning censorship. In February 1797 a first ukase forbade reading and disseminating most French works; words of French origin (like citizen, club, society, and revolution—even when concerning the stars!) were now to be chopped out. In May 1798 censorship offices were established in all Russian ports in order to inspect all imported written documents. In April 1800 a new decree purely and simply banned the import of any foreign music score and any foreign book. Finally, the tsar forbade all young aristocrats from pursuing their studies abroad. Of course, all these measures exasperated the educated elites.

Paul's activism was not limited to the manners or reading matter of his subjects. In a sort of frenzy, the man who had become emperor at the age of 43 manifested an obsession to make up for lost time, and he lashed out on all fronts. This desire to quickly conduct the changes he wanted to impose on the country led Paul into a veritable legislative and regulatory fever, as witnessed by the flurry of manifestos, ukases, and regulations that were adopted: 2,179 over 1,586 days of a reign lasting from November 1796 to March 1801—or only half as many as during the three full decades of Catherine's reign![7]

Lacking symbols of his own and in quest of legitimacy, the person who had been the adulterous child rejected by his mother and who felt a need to publicly assert his lineage would erase the "ignominy"[8] of 1762. Doing so in a rather macabre way, he had Peter III's body exhumed from the Alexander Nevsky Monastery, the pantheon of the imperial crown, and had the coffin exhibited at the Winter Palace alongside that of Catherine II, before ordering both bodies to be reburied in the Peter and Paul Fortress. Later, in the spring of 1797, a few weeks after his coronation, he promulgated a text on the modes of succession to the throne: the rule of masculine primogeniture would now prevail. No more grand duchesses could accede, except in cases where the masculine branch was extinct.

During the first weeks of his reign, Paul undertook to liberate almost all those prisoners whom his mother had locked up for political or religious reasons. On the first day he had the writer and publisher Nikolay Novikov removed from the Schlusselburg Fortress; then he signed a ukase freeing Radishchev from the Ilimsk penal colony but putting him into domestic exile, and soon he released all the imprisoned followers of Saint Martin. Faithful to the Polish-loving convictions that he had several times expressed in front of Catherine II, he visited General Kosciuszko in November, liberated him, and granted him a pension that counted as political and moral compensation for the suffering endured by the Polish patriot. But Paul did not commit himself to find a political remedy for the Polish tragedy.

Paul's pacifism, already apparent in his 1774 memorandum, which broke with Catherine's bellicose activism, was concretely manifested in his foreign policy. The emperor recalled the army sent by Catherine on a campaign against the Persians in the Caucasus, and he refused to send an expeditionary force she had promised to assist the British and Austrians in their war against Revolutionary France—not out of sympathy for the latter, which he execrated, but out of hatred for war.

His distrust of the nobility and his desire to possess absolute power over all his subjects—as he told the Swedish ambassador, "Nobody is great in Russia except the person I am talking to, and then only for the time I do so"[9]—pushed him to force nobles to serve the state and to restrict the privileges conceded by Catherine II. Without abrogating the Charter of Nobility she had promulgated in 1785, he suppressed some of its guarantees. Nobles were now subject to occasional taxes and could be banished to Siberia or subjected to corporal punishment.

Finally, Paul tried to fight the corruption and laxity that riddled both government administration and the army. He reasserted central authority by requiring sharper submission from regional governors who had been too free for his taste, and he laid out a drastic reform of the military.

Prepared by Lieutenant-General Rostopchin, the strict new regulations (which got lost in details of alignment and spacing between men on parade and on the march) were published for the cavalry and infantry in 1796 and in 1797 for the navy. Strongly inspired by the Prussian model elaborated by Frederick the Great, the regulations quickly aroused disapproval from most of the high-ranking officers. Suvorov bravely informed Paul: "Russians have always beat the Prussians, so why do we want to copy them?"—which in February 1797 earned the brilliant general a sacking from the army for "insolence."[10] In exchange for a substantial increase in the number of soldiers and officers, Paul required all regiments, including those of the Guard (until then having the lightest obligations) to perform full-time service under iron discipline, and he acquired the means to verify that his orders were respected by creating an inspection corps.

These measures designed to restore order to the army might seem justified: upon his arrival on the throne, Paul realized that some regiments existed only on paper and that desertion was a common phenomenon. But the brutal methods to which the tsar resorted (in three years, 7 field marshals, 300 generals, and more than 2,000 officers were dismissed),[11] on top of the extreme centralization of decision making (the emperor alone could grant leave longer than 24 days, military power was concentrated in his hands, seconded by a chancellery and all staff officers suppressed),[12] aroused malaise and even anger within the army. Moreover, by imposing new uniforms that closely resembled those of the Prussians and were not comfortable,[13] by exposing officers to disciplinary punishment[14] and by granting more rapid promotion to soldiers from the Ukraine or Germano-Baltic regions who had emerged from the Gatchina army, Paul clumsily offended the patriotic feelings of Russian officers,[15] particularly the Guards regiments, who were already livid at losing many of their service privileges.

His deep and sincere religious sentiments led him to want to improve the condition of the peasants, but he tackled this, as the Russian historian Alexander Sakharov has correctly underlined, with a patrimonial (even paternalist) approach,[16] rather than an economic one. In the manifesto issued for his coronation on Orthodox Easter Day, he pronounced that it would henceforth be forbidden for peasants to work on Sundays and religious holidays and that the compulsory work owed to landowners would be limited to three days a week.[17] Later, a ukase banned the selling of peasants without also selling the lands on which they worked. But at the same time—and this is another example of his contradictions—Paul sadly adopted a practice of Catherine II by distributing almost 100,000 serfs to his favorites upon his accession.[18]

To help his reforming task, he promoted some of Peter III's old advisors and leaned especially on his "Gatchina men," to whom he gave increased powers. From the end of 1796, Alexey Arakcheev, newly promoted general, was made military commander of St. Petersburg.

This frenzy of action was combined with a flurry of trips whose purpose was to enable him to know the country better and to remedy the evils that undermined it. In the spring of 1797, the emperor and his two elder sons, accompanied by Arakcheev (just made a baron and decorated with the Great Cross of the Saint Alexander Nevsky Order, he was more than ever the tsar's prime advisor) visited Moscow, Smolensk, Mogilev, Minsk, Vilno,

Grodno, Riga, and Narva. Alexander gave a very concrete account of this voyage to his mother back in Gatchina in almost daily letters, which are precious documents for the historian. He gives his impressions of the trip, the regions traversed, the cities visited, and the landscapes; he sketches amused commentaries on the sometimes rudimentary comforts that awaited them at many stops or else praises the high quality of the welcome and food that were offered.[19] For the first time in his life, the young man took the true measure of the geographical and human diversity of the Russian Empire.

A year later, the emperor was again on the road, still accompanied by Alexander and Constantine, but this time going to Novgorod, Tver, Moscow, Vladimir, and Nizhni-Novgorod. In the course of these two trips, Paul met representatives from all levels of society and criticized and punished those whom he found guilty of abuses; but by doing so harshly and pitilessly, he sowed terror among subjects accustomed until then to living far from the scrutiny of power.[20] And he began to worry Alexander by his fits of anger and violence.

Indeed, impulsive and impatient in his concern to reform, Paul resorted to force and arbitrary power as he tried to establish a more militarized style of government. Distrusting the old noble families who had been in favor under Catherine II, he did not hesitate to send them away, even to condemn them to exile and to confiscate their goods, often on futile or imaginary pretexts.

> He began by exiling not the guiltiest, for nobody dreamed they were that, but the coldest, the most assiduous and prostrate [nobles]. Exile put a damper on the others; there were more banishments and new apprehensions and soon general consternation on all sides, and permanent suspicions, such that at the end of three years, there was no longer in St. Petersburg a man or a family left in the posts that Empress Catherine had put them before she died.[21]

The historian Nathan Eidelman has provided very interesting figures on the scope and nature of the court cases dealt with during Paul's reign.[22] In four and a half years, 721 civil cases were judged (during Catherine's long reign the total was 863), and of these 721 cases almost half (44%) incriminated nobles, of whom most were imprisoned or exiled.[23] This shows to what extent under Paul the impunity of the nobility was just a memory.

Thus, although the first measures Paul adopted might have augured a reign able to fix some of the crying abuses and dysfunctions inherited from Catherine, very quickly arbitrary rule raised to a style of governing made the sovereign unpopular. Of course, he remained appreciated by humbler people, in particular by peasants and rank-and-file soldiers, to whom he brought greater welfare, but he was hated by the elites, particularly by those at court. Forced to submit, they regarded him as a despot and all the more dangerous in that he was unpredictable. Alexander did not escape this feeling of fear and insecurity any more than did other courtiers.

Alexander at Paul's Court

From the beginning of Paul's reign, Alexander's situation was ambivalent. On the material and financial plane, his position had gotten perceptibly worse:

> Grand Duke Alexander saw from the first year how his fate was different from that of the Emperor under the same conditions. He was paid an income of 500,000 rubles and Madame the Grand Duchess a pension of 150,000 rubles, but apart from lodging, nothing was provided for him. He had his own court, his table, his stables—but it was up to him to pay for them.[24]

But things were better on the political level: unlike Catherine, who had so long held him away from power, Paul, as soon as he was proclaimed emperor, confided important posts to his two older sons, and in particular to Alexander. These provisions flattered the grand dukes and strengthened their filial love and seemed to attest to Paul's desire to make a clean slate of the suspicion and rancor inherited from Catherine's reign. From this point of view, the reign began in a climate of peace, even tacit reconciliation. Alexander was named colonel of the Semenovsky Regiment, then raised to the post of First Military Governor of St. Petersburg, leader of the Semenovsky Regimental Guards, member of the Senate, Inspector of Cavalry and Infantry in the divisions of St. Petersburg and Finland, before becoming at the start of 1798 president of the Senate's military department. Still, the young man did not take long to realize that these titles, as brilliant as they might be, in reality conferred on him neither autonomy nor power. Placed by his father under the constant surveillance of Arakcheev, Alexander was reduced to the status of a child deprived of any freedom. From the start of the reign, each morning he had to scrupulously account for his activities to the emperor, from whose arbitrary rule he suffered like any other subject. And he was afraid of his father, who treated him often as incapable and an imbecile and showered him with humiliating reprimands and reproaches.

He was leader of the second Guard regiment, Inspector-General of the Army, leader of the War and Navy Offices, director of the empire's police, he presided over the Senate—all that would constitute a complete prime minister, but nobody took note of his apparent authority nor his good favor. He could not hire or dismiss anybody, or even sign his name without an express order that he was not even free to go and request. Pupil and victim of the Gatchina men, he was treated by them not as a leader, not as the son of an emperor, but as a student who is by turns taken up and then neglected.[25]

Often, he managed to escape his father's anger only by the intercession of Arakcheev, who played the role of buffer and helped him without Paul's knowledge. Instead of Alexander, it was the favorite who occupied himself on a daily basis with the training of the men of the Semenovsky and it was often he who wrote the reports that Alexander was supposed to address twice a day to his father on the general state of the garrison, population movements, and the arrival or departure of any foreign or provincial traveler.[26] This devotion was obviously of capital importance. Forged in this trying period when Alexander felt particularly vulnerable, the relationship of complete confidence that slowly was established between the tsarevich and the young general gave rise to a lasting and mutual feeling of gratitude.

More and more exhausted by repeated military exercises,[27] subject to a father who obliged him as president of the Senate's military department to sign acts (particularly condemnations) of which he personally disapproved, Alexander was permanently subject to Paul's caprices, in an atmosphere that became burdensome after only a few months. In one of her letters to her mother, dated 1797, Elizabeth wrote:

It is always something to have the honor of not seeing the Emperor. In truth, mama, this man is *widerwärtig* [repugnant] to me, to hear him alone spoken of, and his society is even more so; anyone who says in front of him something that has the misfortune to displease His Majesty may expect to receive a coarse rebuke. I assure you that except for a few affiliates, most of the public detests him. People even say that the peasants start to talk about him. What were the abuses I detailed last year? Now they are double, and there are cruelties under the very eyes of the Emperor. Imagine, mama, once he had an officer beaten who was in charge of provisioning his kitchen because the boiled meat was bad; he had him beaten in front of him and even chose a very strong cane. He was put under arrest; my husband told [the Tsar] he was innocent and another was at fault, and he answered: "It's all the same, they will sort it out together." Oh, mama, it is painful and frightful to see daily injustices and brutalities, to see people made miserable (how many does he have on his conscience?) and to have to make a semblance of respecting and esteeming such a man. Tell me, mama, if that is not being a martyr, to have to court such a man! I am the most respectful daughter-in-law, but really not fond of him at all; moreover, it is all the same to him if he is loved, provided he is feared—he said so himself. And his will is generally fulfilled; he is feared and hated—at least by everyone in Petersburg. He is sometimes likeable and affectionate when he wants to be, but his humor is more changeable than a weathervane.[28]

This dolorous atmosphere and the abuses that Alexander witnessed, as well as the repeated vexations of which he was victim, all tended to reinforce his conviction that the style of government chosen by his father was not in the interests of the country. And while in 1796 Alexander in his letters to Kochubey had not projected himself into the role of sovereign, after the spring of 1797, his increasingly virulent criticism of the tyranny exercised by Paul was now accompanied by reflections on his own conception of power and the means by which he intended to exercise it "when his turn came." Henceforth, he could no longer remain a critical spectator of the increasingly dysfunctional court; now he would become the main actor in the changes to be conducted.

* * *

In the letter he wrote to Laharpe in October 1797—it was given by Nikolay Novosiltsev[29] (traveling to Paris) straight into the hands of his former tutor—Alexander asserted:

My father in ascending the throne wanted to reform everything. His beginning was rather brilliant, it is true, but the rest has not lived up to it. Everything is turned upside down at once, and this has merely increased the already great confusion that reigned. The military takes up almost all his time, and in parades. For the rest, there is no plan being followed. Today something is ordered that will be countermanded in a month: representations from others are never tolerated except when the evil is already done. Finally, to put it in a nutshell, the welfare of the state counts for nothing in the regulation of affairs; there is only absolute power, which does everything wrong in all directions. It is impossible for me to enumerate all the madness that has been committed. [...] My poor fatherland is in an unspeakable state: the farmers are vexed, commerce injured, personal freedom and well being annihilated. This is the picture of Russia, and you may judge what my heart suffers. Myself employed in military minutia, wasting all my time in the duties of a junior officer, not having a moment to give to my studies, which were my favorite occupation before the change—I have become the unhappiest being.

You know about my ideas leaning to expatriation. At this moment, I no longer see how to execute them; the unfortunate situation of my fatherland has turned my ideas to another side. I thought that if ever my turn came to reign, instead of leaving the country, I would do much better to work to make my country free and thereby preserve it, than in future serve as a plaything for the insane.[30]

This major change was largely motivated by Alexander's personal evolution; it is also explained by the support brought to his political thinking by his circle of close friends. In April 1797, even as the ceremonies of Paul's coronation were unfolding, Alexander gathered in Moscow his friends Adam Czartoryski, Paul Stroganov, and Nikolay Novosiltsev[31] in order to confide his desire to promote fundamental political reforms once he was emperor himself. From this date the four men adopted the habit of meeting daily, discreetly, at the home of Count Alexander Stroganov, who held a reputedly liberal salon. In the margins of the salon discussions, and in secret meetings, the foursome freely tackled many key subjects, as illustrated by the remainder of the letter Alexander sent to Laharpe:

This has given me a thousand thoughts that have showed me that this would be the best kind of revolution, taking effect through legal powers, which would cease to exist as soon as the constitution was achieved and the nation had representatives.

This is my idea. I communicated it to enlightened persons who, for their part, had long thought the same thing. We are only four: Monsieur Novosiltsev, Count Paul Stroganov, Prince Adam Czartoryski, my aide-de-camp and a rare young man, and myself. [...] On the other hand, once my turn comes, it will be necessary to work, little by little, to achieve a national representation that will be directed to make a free constitution, after which my power will cease absolutely, and if Providence seconds our work, I will retire to some spot and I will live content and happy in seeing and enjoying the happiness of my country. This is my idea, my dear friend.

Ah, I would be happy if I could have had you by my side in these times! What services you could render us! But this is an idea I dare not indulge. [...] May heaven enable us to reach the goal of making Russia free, and guarantee it against the attacks of despotism and tyranny! This is my sole wish, and I willingly sacrifice all my effort, and my life, to this goal that is so dear to me.[32]

This letter is of crucial importance, not only because, for the first time since 1796, Alexander seems to be reconciled to the prospect of one day mounting the throne but also because the scope of the reforms to which he aspires, with the adoption of a constitution in the foreground, attests that he has decided to make his reign the instrument of a political revolution.

In this letter Alexander does not mention Victor Kochubey. The young ambassador to Constantinople[33] knew nothing yet of these early discussions, but when recalled to Petersburg in 1798 to be named vice-chancellor, he immediately joined the group and contributed to the general thinking. However, while the circle's activity was intense—Novosiltsev made a synthesis of their thoughts in many notes and drafts—it did not last. Paul became increasingly suspicious of them and the young men had to disperse. In September 1797 Novosiltsev, suspected by Paul of liberal tendencies, left Russia for England; in August 1799 Kochubey resigned from his post as vice-chancellor, and after his marriage in November, he undertook a long journey with his bride to Europe and settled in Dresden, Germany at the start of 1801. Adam Czartoryski, already dismissed by Paul for his liberal ideas, was abruptly forced to leave Russia as ambassador to the court of Sardinia on May 30, 1799, after having been threatened with deportation to Siberia. In fact, that day Elizabeth gave birth to a little girl, Maria, whose resemblance to the Polish prince caused chatter at court and triggered Paul's anger. Of fragile health, the infant died on August 8, 1800, plunging Elizabeth into great grief.[34]

These successive departures—only Paul Stroganov still managed to remain in Alexander's entourage—isolated the heir to the throne. But he pursued thinking about his reform plans. An extract from his personal diary, titled "Thoughts at various times on all sorts of subjects touching the public good," written sometime between June 1798 and November 1800, clearly testifies to this intense intellectual activity and his desire to abolish serfdom:

> Nothing could be more humiliating and inhuman than the sale of human beings and so it is absolutely necessary to start by promulgating an edict that will forbid it forever. To the shame of Russia, slavery still exists here. It would be superfluous, I think, to explain why it is desirable that it be ended. However, it has to be recognized that this is very difficult and dangerous to achieve, especially if it is undertaken abruptly. I often reflect on the means of obtaining this and I have not found anything but this:
>
> First, publication of the above-mentioned edict.
>
> Second, publication of an edict that will allow all sorts of people to buy land, even with villages, but on condition that the peasants of these villages

are not obliged to pay rent except on the land they inhabit, and that in the event they are not satisfied, they are free to go wherever they want. [...]

Third, after a while [...] it will already be possible to publish a third edict that will oblige all nobles to purchase lands and villages only under these conditions. [...] The Government should set an example by conferring on peasants of the Crown the status of free peasants. [...]

Shame, that powerful weapon residing everywhere that honor exists, will largely help to incline many to follow this example. Thus Russia will gradually free itself from these rags of servitude that have clothed it until now. [...]

All this will be doubly useful: first, the slaves that we once were will become free beings, and second, social conditions will gradually become more equal, and then classes will disappear.[35]

Although deprived of his close circle and harassed by the military activities in which he was forced to participate, Alexander nevertheless managed in 1798–1799 to formulate critical judgments about the current state of the Russian Empire, but now he did so as a future political decision maker.

At the same time his personal situation became more critical as the state of his father's mental health deteriorated. Of course, the emperor was not falling into madness properly speaking,[36] but he was overcome with obsessions, and even growing paranoia; he became more and more suspicious of his sons and even of Maria Feodorovna, accusing them repeatedly of fomenting plots. In his Secret Memoirs on Russia during the Reigns of Catherine II and Paul I, Masson reports that "one day, seeing his wife talking softly near a chimney with Prince Kurakin, he entered in a fury: 'Madame, you want to make friends and are preparing to play the role of Catherine, but know that you will not find in me a Peter III.'"[37] It was also in 1799 that Eugen of Württemberg, nephew of Maria Feodorovna, then aged thirteen, was called to the Russian court by Paul to be observed and perhaps raised by the emperor to the rank of future heir.[38] And so, while Alexander was ripening in politics but feeling increasingly under threat, Paul's political decisions began to crystallize as a serious opposition to him.

Growing Opposition

Two key factors, the emperor's religious policy and his foreign policy, seem to have played determining roles in this crystallization. Starting in 1799–1800, Paul was exasperating the dignitaries of the Orthodox Church.

The Society of Jesus had been present in the Russian Empire since 1772, date of the first division of Poland and the territorial annexation that followed; it had been briefly suppressed by Pope Clement XIV in 1773 but had maintained itself in the Russian Empire, benefiting from the protection of Catherine II, who saw the order as an instrument for promoting quality secondary education in Russia, as well as an advantage for her Polish policy.[39] In this context the Jesuits had developed and sowed missions along the Volga River, on the banks of the Black Sea, the Caspian Sea, the Caucasus, and Siberia. But what had been an act of tolerance inspired by Catherine's well-understood interests turned under Paul into a demonstration of assertive sympathy. In 1800 the Society of Jesus was given authorization to found a college in St. Petersburg, as well as a seminary in Vilno (Vilnius) on Catholic land. Then in March 1801, in response to a request by the vicar of the Jesuits in Russia, the Pole François-Xavier Kareu, and with the personal support of the tsar, Pope Pius VII published the brief Catholicae Fidei, which legitimized the existence of the society in the Russian Empire.[40] Perceived by the hierarchy of the Orthodox Church and by nationalist elites as an unbearable attack on both the prestige of the official church and "Russianness," these measures provoked irritation from a court that was already disgusted by the immense reputation enjoyed by an Austrian called Gabriel Gruber with Paul. An engineer, chemist, specialist in naval architecture, the vice-vicar of the Jesuits in Russia was the only person in the emperor's entourage to be able to present himself without being announced in advance. His frequent spiritual discussions with Paul upset Russians who held strictly Orthodox convictions. The emperor would even go so far as to ask Gruber to prepare a text aiming to unite the Churches of East and West. Completed and handed to the tsar on March 22, 1801—the day of his death—this text, which could have been extremely important for the history of Christianity by helping redefine relations between the Catholic and Orthodox churches, remained on the imperial desk, never brought to Paul's knowledge.

Benevolent toward the Jesuits, Paul also favored the Knights of Malta. Here again, he seemed to be following Catherine II, who had established links with this order shortly after the French Revolution expelled it from France. But what had resulted from interested tolerance under Catherine—bringing support to a persecuted Catholic order—under Paul appeared as the result of personal preference, in which the tsar's fascination for knightly orders was in conflict with his hatred of impious France and the "Republican plague."[41] This commitment to the Knights soon led him to spectacular gestures that seemed incomprehensible—if not insulting—in the eyes of the Orthodox Church and its dignitaries. In August 1798, anxious to amplify his support of the order—when the French had just captured the island of Malta and forced out all the religious orders—the emperor welcomed them to Russia, declaring himself Grand Master of the order and protector of the island, regardless of the fact that the Knights of Malta recognized the pope as head of the church. For Paul, the struggle against revolutionary France required a rapprochement between the Christian churches, and even a form of ecumenism. His position was a sacrilege to the Orthodox, and it accentuated Paul's unpopularity among the traditional elites.

To the discontent aroused by his religious policy were soon added tensions over the diplomatic strategy Paul adopted in 1799. After an initial period of withdrawal from international affairs at the end of 1796 to 1798, Paul took an increasingly activist position on the foreign scene, which again recalled the political choices made by Catherine II.

In December 1800, after negotiations started the previous year with the ruler of Georgia, Georgi XII, he signed a manifesto of "union" between Russia and the Christian kingdom of Kartl-Kakhetia that placed this part of eastern Georgia, under threat from the Persians, under Russian protection, with a design to quickly annex it. Similarly, the emperor was anxious to enlarge the empire's borders toward the north Pacific. Until 1799 Russian expansion into Alaska had remained spontaneous, arising almost exclusively from private initiatives by trappers and adventurous merchants. But after 1799 Paul decided to give his official and active support to the private Russo-American Company, to which he gave a charter guaranteeing for 20 years its monopoly on the exploitation of territories situated beyond the fifty-fifth parallel, with an exclusive right to hunting and mining in that region.

Finally, although he had at first sought to preserve Russia's neutrality, the emperor felt constrained to intervene in European affairs in 1797–1798. Here again he was following imperatives defended by Catherine. On the political and ideological levels Paul saw the successes of Revolutionary (and then Napoleonic) France as a threatening adventure, likely to put in danger the social order on which autocratic Russia rested. On the geopolitical level Bonaparte's expansionism that aimed at the Mediterranean Sea if a potential alliance with the Ottoman Empire could be achieved appeared to Paul as a challenge to the prerogatives that Russia had seized since the Kutchuk-Kainardji treaty in 1774. In this worrying context he opted for measures that were both symbolic and military.

First he asserted in a public and official way his support for the French monarchists. As part of his "anti-republican crusade," in 1797 he invited the Prince de Condé and his army to place themselves under his protection: no fewer than 5,000 men, 200 generals, and several thousand exiled families gathered on imperial soil. Condé took an oath of allegiance to the emperor of Russia and was made grand commander of the Order of Malta; his army, equipped and reconstituted into five regiments, was established in

Volhynia.[42] Similarly, Paul invited the future Louis XVIII to take refuge in Russia, offering him as residence the Mitava Castle, where the heir to the French throne settled with his court in exile.[43] But Paul was not content with symbolic gestures to manifest his repudiation of how Europe was evolving.

Advised by his minister Bezborodko, he soon undertook a political offensive, partly by entering into the Second Coalition against France that united England, Austria, Naples, Portugal, and the Ottoman Empire, and partly by offering the sultan Russian protection against France. In December 1798 this Russian proposal led to a treaty by which the two empires mutually guaranteed their territorial possessions. Paul soon made a military demonstration of his anti-French commitment: in the winter of 1798–1799, a Russo-Turkish flotilla under the command of Admiral Ushakov began to operate with success in the eastern Mediterranean and managed to chase the French armies out of the Ionian islands. A few months later, in 1800, these islands were organized into a republic placed under Ottoman tutelage but in fact occupied by Russian troops. Their unprecedented military presence in this geographic region was very satisfying for the Russians, which caused Bezborodko to comment ironically:

> We had to wait for the arrival of monsters like the French to witness a spectacle that I would never have believed I would see in my lifetime: an alliance with the Porte and the passage of our navy through the Straits.[44]

At the same time Russian armies led by Suvorov (recalled by the emperor from his forced exile at the request of the Austrian Archduke Franz) conducted in Italy ferocious and victorious battles against the French; the particularly hard battle of Novi took place in August 1799. For the first time in its history, Russia appeared on the international scene as a Mediterranean power.

However, Paul's foreign policy ceased being rational and became confused, due to the evolution of the international situation and the growing influence on the emperor of the Anglophobe party. It was this abrupt switch, which baffled the pro-British party at court, that precipitated the conspiracy.

In April 1799 Bezborodko's death resulted in the nomination of two vice-chancellors at the head of the College of Foreign Affairs: the chamberlain Count Rostopchin, and Nikita Panin, nephew of Catherine II's old advisor. However, these two men did not share the same views on foreign policy. Like the Russian ambassador to London, Simon Vorontsov, Panin was partial to an Anglo-Russian alliance, while Rostopchin supported a rapprochement with France. Starting at the end of 1799, because he was disappointed with the behavior of his allies and was yielding to the influence of Rostopchin and

Suvorov (who had been defeated in Zurich in September), Paul seemed to be reconsidering his participation in the Second Coalition.

In effect, while Russian troops had not spared any effort in the Italian campaigns, the Russian-Austrian alliance was not long in vacillating over its first victories. Quickly, the subjects of contention between the two powers multiplied,[45] pushing Paul to break in October 1799 the pact formed seven years earlier by Catherine. Meanwhile, relations between Britain and Russia deteriorated because London did not appreciate seeing the emperor of Russia proclaim himself "Protector of Malta" and make advances in the Mediterranean, a zone where Great Britain thought it had privileged rights. Thus Russia found itself isolated again on the international scene. In this context, Bonaparte's coup d'état (18th Brumaire) introduced a new factor to which Paul was sensitive: Bonaparte's power was set to last and that reality had to be dealt with. The tsar asserted:

> A change is taking place in France, and we have to await the outcome with patience, without exhausting ourselves [...] I am full of respect for the First Consul and his military talent. [...] He acts—he is a man with whom one can deal.[46]

Consequently, in March 1800 Russia officially quit the Second Coalition, and on the eighteenth, the emperor announced to Ambassador Lord Whitworth that he had requested his recall to London. Between the start of March and the end of May—when the ambassador had to leave Russian territory—Lord Whitworth and Vice-Chancellor Panin tried in vain to reverse this new course of Russian diplomacy. The departure of the ambassador was followed by a de facto suspension of relations between Britain and Russia. In October 1800, after the British seized Malta and unleashed the tsar's anger, Rostopchin submitted to Paul an ambitious diplomatic plan. On the one hand, an alliance with France would in time allow Russia to impose a division of the Ottoman Empire and to retake Constantinople and the straits; it would eventually result in "the fusion of the thrones of Peter [the Great] and Constantine."[47] On the other hand, an alliance with Prussia and Austria and a policy of armed neutrality against England, if circumstances permitted, could lead to open conflict. Paul acquiesced and was soon in a showdown with England. In October 1800, in reprisal for the taking of Malta, British merchant ships were captured and sequestered in Russian ports, and their crews (1,043 people in all) were arrested and sent to various towns and districts.

These incidents, manifestations of a major crisis between Britain and Russia, were perceived in Paris as favorable signals; the First Consul's reaction was not long in coming. Weeks later, Paul received a letter from Bonaparte proposing an alliance that the emperor accepted with enthusiasm in January 1801. Anxious to show his goodwill, Paul expelled from imperial territory all the French émigrés, including the future Louis XVIII; he asked his chancellery to accelerate preparations for war against England and ordered the chief of the Cossack army of the Don to organize an expedition against the British army in India.

It was precisely this diplomatic switch of sides and these anti-British decisions that were adopted in urgency that served as catalyst for the plot fomented by Panin. For the vice-chancellor, the new pro-French course of Russian diplomacy was inconceivable in and of itself; Paul's bellicose actions and the rush with which he involved Russia in a very hazardous military expedition in India demonstrated the "madness" of the tsar and fully justified carrying out the plot that had been in gestation for several months. Far from being the machinations of a handful of nobles to get rid of the intolerable and bizarre actions of a despot, the plot now assumed the dimensions of an act to save the nation's health and maybe even tinged the conspiracy with the spirit of sacrifice.

Alexander—already hostile to the political evolution of the regime and concerned to remedy it, undermined by threats against himself, and raised by Laharpe to worship the tyrannicide heroes of ancient Rome—was extremely receptive to these notions. Thus it is at the intersection of political and psychological predicaments that we must situate the tsarevich's tacit agreement to the plot. But very quickly the cruel execution of a man in his nightshirt driven to hide behind a screen replaced a heroic gesture with a brutal reality whose memory, as traumatic as it was demeaning, would hang over the new emperor forever.

PART TWO

THE PROMISING REIGN

A Spirit of Reform, 1801–1807

CHAPTER 5

Reformist Attempts

After the death of Paul I, the accession of Alexander to the imperial throne launched an explosion of jubilation and optimism in both St. Petersburg and Moscow. The new sovereign's youth, his charm, and the liberal education he had received all appeared to be favorable omens. Both court elites and educated public opinion thought that this auspicious reign could only bring better days. Reflecting a widespread feeling, poet and statesman Gavrila Derzhavin proclaimed his relief in verse:

> The raucous north wind has ceased to shout
> The terrible frightening eye has closed.[1]

Young Countess Edling, newly settled in St. Petersburg with her parents (she would later become a lady-in-waiting to Elizabeth) also remembered:

> A new century and a new reign had both begun. That of Paul I, somber and uncouth for Russia, had just ended in the most terrible catastrophe. Honest men, while deploring the crime, felt their hearts open to joy and hope. Everyone hurried to leave the enforced isolation in which we had lived, asking only to forget the past and to salute a new era with transports of joy.[2]

No voice in Russia was raised to denounce the plot of which Paul had been the victim, although a few acid comments emanated from foreign observers: Madame de Staël wrote ironically that "in Russia the government is a despotism mitigated by strangulation,"[3] while on the occasion of Alexander's coronation on September 27, 1801, in the Cathedral of the Dormition in the Kremlin, Count Golovkin reported:

> The French police of Vienna seized a letter from Madame de Noisseville, an émigrée who had remained in Russia, to Count O'Donnell, chamberlain to

the Emperor of Austria. In it was found this daring phrase (worthy of Tacitus) that the Tuileries was pleased to spread: "I have seen the young prince walking to the cathedral, preceded by the assassins of his ancestor, surrounded by those of his father, and by all appearances, followed by his own."[4]

The general benevolence toward the new sovereign appeared all the more justified because the empire had many so many dysfunctions to remedy.

The Russian Empire in 1801

At the start of the nineteenth century, despite the assertion of its stature as a great power on the international stage[5] and the industrial progress achieved under the reigns of Peter the Great and then Catherine the Great[6]— for example, Russia became world leader in the production of cast iron—the empire was held back by a daunting range of archaic impediments.

On the political level, whereas in western Europe the time was ripe for the assertion of the inalienable rights of the individual, the Russian Empire was still characterized by the all-powerfulness of an emperor who was considered a monarch by divine right and who could govern the state as he liked and impose his will on all his subjects. The emperor incarnated the sole source of right and justice, and he exercised his power through an extremely centralized[7] administrative apparatus, which was in turn relayed by a corrupt local bureaucracy—despite the efforts made by Peter the Great and then Catherine II to fight against these scourges.

Imperial power was exercised over a society that remained extremely compartmentalized, although it was in full demographic expansion. The population was growing spectacularly—from 32 million in 1795 to 34 million in 1801 and to 41.7 million in 1811[8]—in part due to territorial expansion, yet Russian society at the start of the nineteenth century remained largely rural—only 4 percent were city dwellers. Society was characterized by a very imbalanced division into hermetically sealed orders:[9] nobility, clergy, merchants, free peasants, and serfs. At Alexander's ascension, almost 225,000 nobles counted for 0.6 percent of the total population;[10] 215,000 were men of the church; 119,000 were merchants, to whom should be added 15,000 higher officers and as many civil servants, for a total of 590,000 persons representing 1.73 percent of the population. The remaining were largely illiterate peasants numbering a bit more than 33 million. They included 13 million state peasants working for the emperor on his rural domains or in manufacturing, in particular the metal factories of the Urals, but the majority of them were serfs—more than 20 million of them—possessed by property owners.[11] To these owners (who had complete authority over them), serfs owed compulsory labor (by those who worked the land) or a tax in money (from those who worked in industry or as artisans). In the regions of agricultural production with rich soil like the "black lands" of the center, the Ukraine, Byelorussia, and the Volga, compulsory labor often meant working four or five full days a week, if not sometimes seven, despite the recommendation[12] pronounced by Paul in 1797 limiting the corvée to three days. The living conditions of peasants were very hard. Treated as cattle, worked to the bone, under pressure economically and financially, peasants suffered their fate with religious fatalism but revolted regularly: in 1801, 32 of 42 regional governments in the empire were touched by peasant rebellions[13] that aroused among landowners the agonizing specter of a new revolt like Pugachev's.

Although constituting a single order, the nobility of the empire was extremely heterogeneous: in 1797, 83.5 percent of nobles owned fewer than 100 serfs, while 1.5 percent of nobles possessed more than a thousand of them, and this fraction alone counted for more than a third of the peasant population subjected to serfdom.[14] Moreover, nobles had an ambiguous relation to power. We recall that, in her desire to modernize the country economically, Catherine II had sought to make the nobility the prime mover in this development. Accordingly, she freed it from the obligation to serve the state and sent it back to its estates. In parallel, from a concern to rationalize and make the administration more efficient, the empress had given a greater role to representatives of the nobility and even granted some autonomy in the management of local affairs.[15] Pushed by the state to move in the direction of growing liberty, the aristocratic elites had started to benefit at the local level from responsibilities that were administrative and social, if not political. Thus many charitable works and philanthropic associations were created. Benefiting from the intellectual freedom supported by Catherine at least until 1790–1791 (in 1783 the state monopoly on printing had been abolished and private publishing began), the nobility had contributed to the development of intellectual societies, salons, and Masonic lodges. These various sites were propitious for the circulation of ideas and in barely a few years had fostered the emergence of an embryonic civil society. But there was an inherent paradox that Alexander inherited at the start of the nineteenth century: the imperial desire to structure Russian society into quite distinct orders with rights and duties to the state in fact derived from edicts issued by the sovereign (like the Charters of the Nobility and of Towns promulgated in 1785)[16] and thereby contributed to anchoring Russian society in a paternalist mold that was unpropitious for private initiative and dynamism, and more and more anachronistic. Moreover, by sowing terror and arbitrary rule and by weakening elites, Paul's reign had further undermined the nobility: exposed to the tsar's hare-brained schemes and his anger when they did try to play a public role, the nobles had a tendency to withdraw in on themselves at the very moment when a new wave of censorship, rigid and omnipresent, once again prevented any creativity.

Frozen on the political level as well as on the social, the Russian Empire appeared quite hemmed in by enclaves. Thanks to three centuries of continuous expansion,[17] the empire had great ethnic, religious, and cultural diversity. When Alexander came to power, the Eastern Slavs—then considered "Russian" in the wider sense of the term and today divided into Russians, Ukrainians, and Byelorussians—formed 83 percent of the tsar's subjects, but they were very much in the minority on the banks of the Baltic Sea, in Poland, and in the middle valley of the Volga, where Slavs were faced with peoples who spoke Finnish and Hungarian languages, with peoples like the Balts and Turks, with German speakers (including the Jews) and Polish speakers. However, the percentage of each of these peoples other than Russians in relation to the whole population was never more than three percent. Orthodox believers (about 80 percent of the population, on a par with the percentage of Russians) included a majority of Ukrainians (a minority of them adhered to the Uniate Church that used Orthodox liturgy but was subject to papal authority in Rome), a portion of the Byelorussians, and some other peoples like the Chuvash,[18] Mordavians, and Maris,[19] who had all been Christianized in the seventeenth century. But other faiths were also represented: Catholicism accounted for a little more than 10 percent of the total population and was well implanted among the Poles, Lithuanians, some of the Byelorussians, and the Balts; Lutheranism (5 percent of the total) was in the majority in the Baltic provinces and among the German peoples of the empire; Islam (4 percent) was the religion of the Tatars of the Volga, the Tatars of the Crimea, and Bashkirs; and finally Judaism (2.5 percent) was present in the western part of the empire. There were also more isolated minority religious groups. At the start of the nineteenth century, by the annexation of a portion of Armenia,[20] the Russian Empire had integrated Christians belonging to the Monophysite Gregorian Church, while in Siberia, Kalmuks and Buriats had remained faithful to Lamaism since the seventeenth century. Lastly, there were also even some remnants of paganism in Siberia and in the general peasantry.

This cultural, religious, and ethnic diversity did not help the empire's cohesion, especially because communication was still limited. Here, too, the country suffered from patent backwardness: more than 100,000 villages and market towns and 583 cities were barely linked to each other by roads that were mediocre at best and river routes that were not navigable throughout the whole year. Centers of population remained very isolated. The first steamboat made its appearance on the Neva only in 1815, and the first railroad line did not begin operating until 1837. Moreover, on the level of trade and commerce, Russia played only a modest role: in 1801 its share of world trade was only 3.7 percent.[21] Thus, on the territorial level, as well as socially and economically, the empire was split into enclaves.

Faced with this backwardness, the elites of the nobility remained rather passive, out of fear that any challenge to the social order might hurt their own privileges, particularly any challenge to the system of serfdom, which assured their existence and their status. Yet among them some personalities who had rallied to Enlightenment ideals or who had been influenced by liberalism were hoping for reforms: they aspired to a political evolution toward a parliamentary system, with greater freedom for the nobility vis-à-vis the tsar's power, as well as for economic and social changes—including an eventual reform of serfdom. They were well aware that serfdom was deplorable on the moral plane and inefficient on the economic plane.

Within this very narrow liberal elite, some great aristocrats were very close to the court: Vice-Chancellor Panin, the Zubov brothers, and Count Pahlen were all Anglophiles who had been involved in the plot against Paul. There were also writers of more modest origins who had made some of the first critiques of the empire: Novikov played a role in the dissemination of Enlightenment ideas, the young Karamzin was a supporter of a constitutional government, and Radishchev wrote The Voyage from St. Petersburg to Moscow (1790), which was the first attack on serfdom and peasant backwardness. As we saw, he had been imprisoned by Catherine and then condemned to internal exile by Paul. When Alexander reached the throne, the expectations of this enlightened elite were all the greater because the young sovereign had since 1796–1797 made himself a critical observer of the empire and of its political regime. By his behavior and the first measures he adopted, he incarnated the very idea of reform.

A New Style

From the first weeks of his reign, while remaining personally haunted by the tragedy of his father's assassination, Alexander separated himself from Paul on all levels. Just as much as the former emperor had created terror in his entourage, so the new one seduced everyone with his charm, ease, and charisma, to which the emissary from Napoleon to the Court of St. Petersburg would later testify:

> Nature had done much for him [...] and it would have been difficult to find a model so perfect and so gracious. [...] He spoke French in all its purity, with no foreign accent, and always employed lofty expressions. As there was no affectation in his speech, one could easily infer that it was the result of careful education.[22]

From the start Alexander adopted a lifestyle radically different from that of Paul and his predecessors. Upon his arrival on the throne on March 24, he ordered his mother to leave the St. Michael Palace and to come back to the Winter Palace. He also granted her the privileged status of Dowager Empress, giving her prerogatives and prestige that were unprecedented in Russian history. Henceforth she became a powerful actor in the new Imperial Russia, on both the symbolic and political levels. As stressed by Marie Martin in her biography of Maria Feodorovna, this new situation was established to the detriment of Alexander's wife, Elizabeth. Indeed, in most official ceremonies Alexander gave his arm to his mother while Elizabeth followed them on her own; the years that followed would officially confirm this hierarchy. Dining seating plans mentioned in the journal of the maitre d'hôtel, published for St. Petersburg in 1806, specify the place of each member of the imperial family at the table:

> The Empress [Maria Feodorovna] was found to the right of Alexander when he was present, meaning in the place of honor. The Grand Duchess Catherine, aged eighteen, sat to her brother's left, or in the second place of protocol. Elizabeth sat close to her mother-in-law. Another detail: when the writings of the period speak of the Empress, without any other precision, they are almost equally referring to Maria Feodorovna and to Elizabeth.[23]

At the same period, in his report addressed to Talleyrand, then the Minister of Foreign Affairs, French Ambassador Savary confirms Maria Feodorovna's power and the scope of her prerogatives:

> The protocol favors the Mother Empress. All the external honors and all the salutations are directed to her. In public ceremonies, Maria Feodorovna often takes the Emperor's arm; Empress Elizabeth walks behind her, and alone. I saw the troops bearing arms and the Tsar on horseback waiting for his mother, who

had not yet arrived. No favor in Russia is granted and no nomination made unless one goes to render homage to her and kisses her hand to thank her. But nobody says anything to Empress Elizabeth; that is not the practice. The great of St. Petersburg are careful not to let two weeks go by without making an appearance before the Dowager Empress. Elizabeth almost never goes there, but the Emperor dines there three times a week, and often sleeps there.[24]

Alexander also paid substantial income to his mother, which allowed her to maintain a veritable parallel court, more brilliant than that of the emperor, and to direct with an iron hand a large network of charitable organizations and educational institutions whose role would be crucial throughout Alexander's reign.

Several historians have seen in the unprecedented status of Maria Feodorovna the concern of Alexander to "render back" to his mother the status of empress that the death of Paul had prematurely removed. While this explanation cannot be excluded, it seems important also to stress the deep, frank, and sincere affection that united son and mother, the breadth of the trust that the young man placed in Maria Feodorovna, and the need Alexander felt to carry out a tacit division of roles: to his mother the imperial luster and to himself simplicity and proximity to his subjects. Alexander Mikhailovsky-Danilevsky (later the tsar's aide-de-camp and then a historian of the wars of 1812) very quickly detected the humanity—quite unprecedented in the Russian Empire—in Alexander's conduct.

His predecessors had been enclosed like Asiatic monarchs in the narrow confines of their palaces; the people only saw them on solemn occasions, surrounded by the pomp and splendor of supreme power. [...] After Peter the Great, Alexander was the first to reject etiquette as an archaic custom and to appear among the people as a private person. With his wife, he made impromptu visits to balls and soirées given by certain great lords. [...] He travelled in ordinary carriages that were distinguishable from others only by their extraordinary cleanliness. He walked alone around the city. [...] For the first time, his subjects could recognize and love the man who lay inside the external appearances.[25]

This taste for simplicity and for a form of proximity with his subjects, contrasting as much with the military confinement in which Paul had lived as it did with the magnificent lifestyle led by Catherine, no doubt relates to the lessons received from Laharpe. For the tutor ancient virtue implied, if not a form of asceticism, then at least simplicity, sobriety, and temperance. But it is also explained by Alexander's desire to escape the shackles of a court that he had distrusted and despised since childhood. Finally, in a more secret way, the circumstances by which the young emperor had reached the throne lay at the origin of a melancholy, even depressive, sadness:

> A sort of melancholy spread over the beginning of his reign that contrasted with the sparkle they wanted to give the coronation festivities.
>
> The young and handsome couple who were going to be crowned did not appear to be happy. [...] The coronation festivities were for Alexander a source of redoubled sadness. [...] He had bouts of devastation, to the point that they feared for his reason. [...] I strove to soften the bitterness of the reproaches he constantly made to himself. I tried to reconcile him to himself, for the sake of the great task that lay before him. [...] My exhortations only imperfectly obtained their effect, but they did manage to engage him to take enough control of himself so that the public could not read too much into his soul. But the gnawing worm would always remain.[26]

Alexander's taste for simplicity and asceticism seduced part of the court and his close entourage, who saw this return to the simplicity of manners of Peter the Great as a noticeable affirmation of a break with a lofty conception of the Russian monarchy inherited from Catherine and Paul. But it was not understood in this way by everybody, far from it, and several of those closest to him reproached him for it. Coming back to St. Petersburg in 1801, Laharpe wrote to him in August to warn him against too much simplicity. Paradoxically, the person who had inculcated a frank aversion to luxury and pomp seemed to be counseling a more nuanced position.

> First, it seems to me that for you the highest importance is to *play the emperor*,[27] both when you appear in public and when you deal with men to whom you have entrusted some department. I am not a blind panegyrist of etiquette, but when the Head of a nation presents himself, speaks, or acts as such, he should (in the picturesque expression of Demosthenes) be clothed in the dignity of his country. Your nation has been long accustomed, especially in the interior of the Empire, to attach much importance to this, and I believe it has need of it. Your youth, Sire, commands you perhaps all the more imperiously not to relax on this point.[28]

Similarly, Maria Feodorovna often complained to him about this simplicity. In her eyes, by adopting a spartan way of life that was much too simple for subjects accustomed to being dazzled by a sovereign whose power proceeded from divine will, the emperor was devaluing symbolically and politically the function entrusted to him. In 1806 she wrote a long letter in which she posed the relationship between the tsar's behavior, the symbolic system of power, and the nature of his duty:

> You ascended the throne at the age of twenty-three. At this time of life, one captures love, interest, and tenderness, but respect is only obtained with age, especially when, like you, dear Alexander, one is not surrounded with the prestige of any grandeur. You have abolished it all, differing on this point completely from your Grandmother's way of thinking, who wanted to give the public, by the frame of grandeur with which she surrounded even the youngest of your sisters, a motive for respecting herself. On the contrary, from your advent you have abolished in your person any glow that in the eyes of the vulgar would mark your grandeur, and in many respects you have placed yourself at the level of others. [...] The great feast days now have no other ceremony than ordinary Sundays in the time of the departed Empress; and on ordinary Sundays, the Court is deserted and the Great do not frequent it. When the people know that their Sovereign and his family are at church and they see the Great promenading in the streets [...], then the comparison with the past comes to mind and is disadvantageous to the Sovereign, for it proves a lack of eagerness by the public to see him and shows there is less religion among our Great, who abstain from the duties prescribed by the Church. These reflections diminish respect for the Sovereign, respect for our Great, and perhaps even have a harmful influence on the people's religion. [...]
>
> Finally, all this magic of grandeur that once impressed the public no longer exists. On top of that, neither the Great nor the public are flattered by the Sovereign; decorations, not even being presented from your hands, are less esteemed and prized (although perhaps still desired) because the rewards cannot be compared either in their allure or magnificence to those once granted by the late Empress and late Emperor. You conclude that as both motives of amour-propre and interest no longer exist, then you should, you alone, dear Alexander, by your virtue and by dint of great and fine qualities and good actions, captivate the sentiments and support once enjoyed by Sovereigns who employed and benefited from all the advantages of Sovereignty. We live as individuals in ease and wealth—but not in the style suitable for crowned heads. [...] A complaint that people have against you, dear Alexander, is of not esteeming and grasping your place as emperor, having set aside all the apparatus of grandeur.[29]

The simplicity of Alexander I did not escape foreigners posted to the court, either. The ambassador from the King of Sardinia, who arrived in May 1803,

Joseph de Maistre, a counter-Enlightenment philosopher, mentions in one of his first dispatches that "the emperor often goes out alone and without servants,"[30] that he wears neither jewels nor rings nor a watch,[31] that he often walks without an escort, and requires of subjects whom he meets outside merely a respectful salute: no need to kneel nor even halt when he passes. But the diplomat deplores also the fact that Alexander's good qualities are not appreciated sufficiently in Russia, and he attributes this situation to the absence of maturity in the Russian people:

> When the emperor meets someone he knows on the Quai,[32] he does not require that person to leave the carriage to salute him, just a wave suffices. Unfortunately this simplicity that might be suitable in southern countries where people know how to appreciate majesty without pomp does not produce the same impression in Russia. Personal respect is very weakened. Such a virtue cannot be appreciated by such a people. However, one must salute his great love of men and of his duties.[33]

While at his ascension the new sovereign experienced phases of melancholy, he did not live in despondency, nor did he live as a recluse. By his side the young Empress Elizabeth radiated beauty and charm. The Minister of Saxony, Rosenweig, wrote fervently of her:

> It is difficult to render all the Empress's charms: features of extreme fineness and regularity, a Greek profile, large blue eyes, and hair deliciously blonde. Her person radiates elegance and majesty and her movement is quite aerial. In short, she is no doubt one of the most beautiful women in the world.[34]

And Nikita Panin used similar language in a letter he sent to his wife in April 1801:

> I passed through the Great Court, and meeting by chance Their Imperial Majesties who were going to prayer, I was presented to the young empress when I was least expecting it. She is embellished and changed totally in her manners. A tone of ease and full of dignity has replaced that excessive timidity that formerly prevented her from taking advantage of the means she has for presenting herself at court.[35]

Still, Elizabeth's discreet nature was not long in coming to the fore; the young woman quickly accustomed herself to the simplicity demanded by Alexander and to the prerogatives that the emperor granted to his mother, although they were at her own expense. Meanwhile, despite Elizabeth's human qualities—her attention to others, her modesty, her culture and curious mind—the shared trials did not bring the young couple closer together. Was this perhaps because the presence of the person who was by his side the night of the parricide might have reminded Alexander constantly of his own guilt? Or perhaps because Elizabeth was smitten with Prince Czartoryski and had been unfaithful to her husband? Whatever the case, by 1801 their marriage was already just a facade.

Admittedly, Elizabeth assumed with charm and intelligence her duties at court; admittedly, Alexander always demonstrated affection for her in public, thus presenting the appearance of a harmonious marriage. But in reality, their relations had been strained since 1796, and they deteriorated even more between 1800 and 1801. Alexander had many ephemeral liaisons: Madame Phillis, a French lyric singer, was succeeded by a French actress, Madame Chevallier, before the emperor became smitten with several ladies at the court whose husbands, obliged to be accommodating, turned a blind eye. In parallel, Alexander maintained a relation that was quite ambiguous with his young sister Catherine; for whole years he addressed passionate and equivocal letters to her. In September 1805 he wrote to her characteristically:

> If you are a madwoman, at least you are the most delicious one who ever existed. I declare that you have conquered me totally and that I am mad for you. Do you hear? Adieu, Bissiamovna [his pet name for her], *I adore you.*[36]

And the next month:

> What is happening to the dear nose that I find so much pleasure in flattening and kissing? I do fear it is hardening during this eternity that we are separated! Oh, what a temptation I have to come in the place of a messenger to give you a kiss and afterward return to my post![37]

Four days later:

> Seeing myself loved by you is indispensable to my happiness, for you are one of the prettiest creatures in the world. Adieu, dear madwoman of my soul, *I adore you, provided that you do not despise me.*[38]

During the Carnival festivities in March 1801, Alexander fell under the charm of Maria Naryshkina, who attracted him less by her intelligence (reputedly mediocre) than by her extraordinary Raphaelite beauty (Wiegel said this beauty seemed impossible, almost supernatural), her gaiety, and her love of life. Daughter of the Polish Prince Antoine-Stanislas Chetvertinski, Maria was born in February 1779; in 1794, at the age of fifteen, she was named *demoiselle d'honneur* to Catherine II before marrying in the following year Prince Dimitri Naryshkin, one of the richest lords in the time of Catherine II. She then became one of the most visible women at court, and her marriage was celebrated in a poem by Gavrila Derzhavin entitled "The Establishment of the Newly Married." It was also to her that Derzhavin addressed the epistle *Aspasia*. But the marriage soon proved to be a mismatch and turned into a fiasco: Naryshkin, indifferent to his wife's beauty, rapidly adopted the role of indulgent husband, and in 1801 Maria was the mistress of Count Zubov before becoming two years later the mistress of the emperor—as we shall see later.

* * *

If by affirming his preference for simplicity Alexander distinguished himself from the lifestyle of both Paul and Catherine II, the young sovereign did not break completely with the values and habits that had been inculcated in him since childhood. From his grandmother he inherited a pronounced taste for the pleasures of conversation, lively exchanges in salons, and a love of the theater.

> He was very fond of the French theater, and even our actors; he treated them with a benevolence that they sometimes abused by a familiarity that was in bad taste, which would have shocked a monarch who was less good and less indulgent than he.[39]

Alexander particularly appreciated the comedies and classical tragedies of the seventeenth century, as well as Russian works belonging to this vein. He was attuned to the talent of the playwright Vladislas Ozerov (1770–1816). A career soldier who had become a major general (he left the army in 1808), Ozerov wrote five plays—The Death of Oleg (1798), Oedipus in Athens (1804), Fingal (1805), Dmitri Donskoy (1807), and Polyxenes (1809)—that seduced Alexander and were very successful among the elites of St. Petersburg. Often inspired by historical themes, these plays showed the interior anguish of souls—like the work of Racine, of whom Ozerov was a great admirer—and earned him the reputation as the founder of Russian tragedy.[40] On the other hand Alexander liked poetry much less, although it was in vogue in Russia at the start of the nineteenth century.

He also loved balls and parties given in his honor by great figures at court; rarely going to bed before three o'clock in the morning, he reproached himself in French and undoubtedly recalled the warning from Laharpe about time wasted in useless distractions:

> You are sleeping, miserable wretch, and a load of affairs await you. You are neglecting your duty and give yourself to sleep and to pleasure, and unfortunates are suffering while you are wallowing on your mattresses. For shame! You do not have the courage to overcome the idleness that has always been your prerogative. Get up, shake off the yoke of your own weakness, become again a man and citizen useful to your country.[41]

In parallel, he had inherited from Paul a pronounced taste for military exercises, reviews, and maneuvers (for "parade-mania," in Prince Czartoryski's expression), as well as an obsessive concern for detail and order that would turn into a mania as the years passed.

So, while affirming a new way of living from the first weeks of his accession to the throne, Alexander was also rapidly adopting an ensemble of measures on both domestic and foreign levels.

Measures of Symbolic and Political Scope

A manifesto issued on the morning Alexander ascended the throne, written by Trochtchinkski, Catherine's former crown prosecutor, stressed the heritage of her reign:

> We, in receiving the inheritance of the Imperial Throne of all the Russias, receive at the same time the obligation to govern the nation that God has entrusted to Us according to the laws and according to the heart of Our Very August Grandmother who reposes in God, the Empress Catherine the Second, whose memory will be eternally dear to Us as to the whole country, with the hope of bringing Russia to the summit of its glory and offering indestructible happiness to all our faithful subjects by following her wise intentions.[42]

Yet this faithfulness to the work of Catherine II should not be overestimated: although we may detect many undeniable elements of continuity, Alexander as a critical observer of his grandmother's practices, especially those from the twilight of her reign, aspired on a certain number of points to distinguish himself from this heritage, as he did from that of Paul I.

On March 11 the new sovereign moved from the St. Michael Palace to live in the Winter Palace, like Catherine II before him. Concerned to break with the excesses of Paul's reign, he began by lifting the clothing restrictions: French-style round hats, coattails, and English-style waistcoats were again permitted; the Russian uniform was restored to the Army; a number of freedoms confiscated by Paul were reestablished. On April 3 Alexander restored the freedom to travel, adopting a ukase on "the free movement of persons who are returning to Russia or leaving it."[43] On April 12 he authorized the domestic printing of works of foreign literature and abrogated the decree of April 1800 that had banned the import of foreign books and music; as in the time of Catherine, private printing was again authorized and censorship was considerably relaxed; henceforth, each Russian could freely subscribe to foreign newspapers and reviews. The results of this relaxation were quickly felt: whereas in 1800 there were only a thousand books printed in Russia, this number had quadrupled by 1807.

Meanwhile, loudly proclaiming his desire to abolish the repressive dimension of Paul's regime, Alexander proclaimed an amnesty on all those who had left the empire to flee tyranny. He recalled from exile 12,000 civilian and military victims who had been disgraced by his father: for example, the radical writer Radishchev, who had been liberated from Siberia but forced to live in exile in the province of Kaluga, and the lieutenant colonel of artillery, Ermolov, once banished to Kostroma. He also freed all political prisoners who were held in the Peter and Paul Fortress. Similarly, from the outset he freed all religious sectarians who had been condemned and imprisoned by his predecessors. Flagellants, castrates, and dukhobory (the millenarian "spirit fighters") were now authorized to move freely and without surveillance from local authorities. After decades of persecution, the Old Believers now had the right to build their own churches and to have their own cemeteries.

On April 14 Alexander issued a manifesto that dissolved the "secret expedition," i.e., the political police. He asserted his desire to end such abuses of power: he wanted to act in conformity with the law. This proclamation is fundamental: beginning in the first weeks, it introduced references to the law (directly inspired by principles taught by Laharpe)[44] and to rights as supreme principles, thereby inaugurating a "legalist" as well as a "reformist" reign. To give this proclamation concrete effect in a humanitarian spirit that might recall the principles of Catherine II in the Nakaz (legal code) as well as Laharpe's course (in particular his digression on the Calas Affair[45]), the monarch in April put an end to public hangings, and then in September he abolished torture.

On April 14, despite his deep distrust of the nobility, he reestablished the full validity of the 1785 Charter, restoring prerogatives that Paul had suspended. Henceforth, nobles were no longer subject to obligatory service; they had the right to possess villages of serfs; they were free of any personal tax, had the right to travel and serve freely abroad, and could name their representatives to local and regional bodies. Finally, they were not liable to any form of corporal punishment.[46] Similarly, in June, Alexander exempted members of the clergy and deacons from any corporal punishment in cases where they were guilty of crimes.

Still on the political plane, he announced on April 17 the creation of a permanent council of high dignitaries. He organized it into four distinct sections charged with managing, respectively, the national economy, foreign and commercial affairs, military and naval affairs, and civil and religious affairs. On June 17 he created a commission to prepare a legal code, presided over by the formerly proscribed Radishchev, demonstrating his commitment to establishing a state based on the rule of law. The same day, he called on members of the senate to present him with a report on the cause of this institution's decline, on its rights and duties. Shortly before mid-June, Alexander gave Alexander Vorontsov the task of drawing up a text similar to the French Declaration of the Rights of Man and the Citizen. Called "Charter Addressed to the Russian People,"[47] it was to be promulgated in time for the coronation festivities. Like the French document, the charter, whose first draft came by the end of June, proclaimed freedom of thought, expression, and worship for all the empire's subjects and guaranteed to the nobility full freedom to circulate both inside and outside the borders; with respect to justice, it advanced the rights mentioned in British habeas corpus law and in Catherine's Nakaz: any individual had the right to personal security, he was presumed innocent as long as his guilt was not proven, his imprisonment or confiscation of his goods was only possible once his guilt had been established by verdict. But, on the other hand, the text remained silent on the thorny question of serfdom. However, this silence did not prevent the emperor on June 9, 1801, in his first (modest) decision touching the question of peasants, from banning announcements of sales of serfs without land. During the coronation festivities in September, flouting a tradition he considered infamous, he made no gifts of state peasants.

Thus, in barely a few weeks Alexander adopted key measures that demonstrated his will to break with Paul's arbitrary and repressive practices and to install in Russia a regime based on the law. Important changes were rapidly formulated for the domestic scene. Meanwhile, decisions just as novel were adopted in the realm of diplomacy.

Soon expressing his desire to end the risky and bellicose policy of his father, Alexander began by annulling the expedition that was supposed to fight the British in India; a few days later, he gave up the title of Grand Master of the Order of Malta. In June 1801 the Russian government, now under the influence of the pro-English party—key roles were played by the Vorontsov brothers, Alexander and Simon,[48] experienced senior officials of Catherine's reign—signed a commercial agreement with England that soothed the relations that had been strained during Paul's short reign, which also prefigured the signature of a bilateral statement of understanding. Diplomatic relations with Austria were reestablished, while a policy of appeasement with France was conducted. In October 1801 a peace treaty was concluded, which was accompanied by a secret convention with France.[49] So Alexander expressed everywhere his desire for peace, shared with the new sovereign by Vice-Chancellor Kochubey, now in charge of foreign affairs. In his memoirs Prince Adam Czartoryski recalled the positions defended by Kochubey:

> Count Kochubey had adopted a system that he thought entirely in accord with the opinions and views of the Emperor, and at the same time in accord with his own sentiments. It was to stand back from the affairs of Europe, to stay uninvolved as much as possible, to be on good terms with the whole world, in order to be able to devote his time and attention to domestic improvements. This was indeed the advice and desire of the emperor and that of his intimates, but nobody adopted it with more conviction and supported it with more insistence, nobody decided to follow it with such unshakeable constancy, as Count Kochubey. He said "Russia is sufficiently large and powerful by its extent, its population, and its position; it has nothing to fear from any side, provided that it leaves others alone. It is overly involved in too many affairs that do not concern it directly; nothing could happen in Europe without it claiming to take part; it waged useless and costly wars. In its happy situation, the Emperor can remain at peace with the whole world and devote himself to domestic reforms without fearing that anybody would dare disturb him in his noble and salutary work. It is within that Russia can make immense conquests by establishing order, economy, and justice in all parts of the vast Empire, by making agriculture, commerce, and industry flourish."[50]

Thus, nonengagement in European affairs is largely explained by Alexander's desire to ensure the peace that he needed to advance his reforms.

In a few weeks ambitious and courageous sets of measures on both the internal and external levels, which aimed to prepare for the establishment of a legal Russian state, were adopted. But beginning in July 1801, we observe a certain amount of tension arising: the "Charter Addressed to the Russian People" was not promulgated, and Alexander's distrust of the senators, though he had encouraged them to reflect on the future of their institution, started to grow.

In their name, in August, Count Zavadovski presented the tsar with a plan that, first, would grant the senate preeminence over the prosecutor general; instituted by Peter the Great, this official dignitary had the power to confirm the senate's decrees, and he had served as interface between tsar and senators, which gave him extended powers. Moreover, now elevating the senate, the plan would give it the right to propose taxes, plus the right to petition and make "remonstrances" in cases where an imperial decree might be "contrary to texts previously published, or unclear, or else harmful."[51] But quickly the tsar asserted that any constitutional reform would only come from him alone.[52] So in September 1802 a decree made the senate the most important body in the regime after the emperor and granted it the right of remonstrance but did not satisfy any of its other requests.

According to the historian Allen McConnell,[53] these first liberal measures were supposedly imposed on Alexander, who was perhaps terrorized by Count Pahlen, then at the height of his power and a resolute partisan of a constitutional regime in the English style. Once Pahlen was got rid of—he was exiled to Courland in June 1801—McConnell says, Alexander gave up on more radical measures out of a concern to conserve his autocratic power in all his prerogatives.

This thesis has the merit of underlining a point long neglected by historians: the dominant place occupied by Pahlen in the antechamber of imperial power in the three months following the killing of Paul. Indeed, his key position was stressed by many contemporary witnesses. In his memoirs Czartoryski attests to the fact that, under cover of sustaining the young emperor, Pahlen in fact dictated what lines to follow.[54] For his part, General Duroc stressed in a dispatch sent to Bonaparte in May 1801 that "M. de Pahlen is always at the head of affairs and appears to have a great influence,"[55] while Simon Vorontsov in a letter to Novosiltsev the same month was worried that "the Sovereign is in their hands. He may not have the will or security to oppose what this terrible cabal wants."[56] The personage of Pahlen was omnipresent: named military governor of St. Petersburg before Paul's death, he became by the end of March a member of the College of Foreign Affairs and of the Council of State, and the civil administrator of the Baltic provinces, as well as of the province of St. Petersburg from June onward.

Thus Pahlen's power between March 24 and June 29 is a well-established fact—to the point that, despite the support of the procurator-general,

Bekleshov, and of Maria Feodorovna and her entourage,[57] Alexander delayed more than three months before the dismissal and condemnation to internal exile of the person who had organized the plot, whom he would not forgive for the death of his father. In August the person who first conceived of the general deed, Nikita Panin, suffered the same fate. Then it was the turn of those who had executed it: Major-General Yashvil and Colonel Tatarinov were also condemned to domestic exile, while Platon Zubov was obliged to leave the imperial territory at the start of 1802. Yet the consequences of these successive disgraces should not be overestimated: first, because although it was well-known that Pahlen was favorable to an evolution toward a constitutional regime, no document suggests that he exercised pressure on Alexander in this direction; second, because in the measures that Alexander did adopt, a clear continuity can be observed between those that preceded the fall of Pahlen and those that followed it. The preparation of the "Charter Addressed to the Russian People" was pursued until the end of June; it was subject to commentary from Alexander's close collaborators in mid-August; the emperor submitted it himself for the approval of the permanent council on September 21—a few days before his coronation— before he decided to make a volte-face and to renounce its promulgation. Thirdly, according to the opinion of those close to him, Alexander's sincere attachment to political reform was wholehearted in 1801. As a consequence, if changes can be perceived after the month of June that would be made concrete in the months and years that followed, this shift seems less related to the fall of Pahlen (properly speaking) than to the rise in power of other groups in the imperial entourage.

The Tsar, His Advisors, and the Work of Reform

While Pahlen still exercised a dominant influence on political affairs, Alexander dearly wanted to gather a small group of trustworthy friends, who would in fact constitute a "secret committee," in order to help him in his reforming task.

From the month of March, he recalled to St. Petersburg those whom Paul had forced out for their "suspicious characters." Adam Czartoryski arrived in mid-March, joined a few weeks later by Novosiltsev and Kochubey. Kochubey wrote in April from Dresden, which he was on the verge of leaving to come back to Russia, a letter to Simon Vorontsov that revealed the state of mind of Alexander's friends:

I am leaving because I think I owe something to Grand Duke Alexander; I am leaving because I think that all honest men must gather around him and make every effort to heal the infinite wounds inflicted by his father upon the country.[58]

Awaiting the arrival of his friends in St. Petersburg, Alexander summoned Paul Stroganov for a conversation in which he confirmed his reforming intentions in May. However, the method to be followed was not yet decided: this was the main subject of their discussion. For the count, it was crucial to start to work on reorganizing the administration before coming around to the key question of a constitution. For Alexander, it was indeed proper to privilege administrative reform but without forgetting the establishment of a constitution whose purpose was both to set up a legal state and to guarantee citizens' rights in a durable way. To conduct this ambitious planning, Stroganov proposed a committee be set up; the emperor agreed,[59] and several weeks later, after the return of Czartoryski, Novosiltsev, and Kochubey, a "non-official"[60] or "intimate" committee was created, which Alexander facetiously called "my Committee of Public Safety."

This structure benefited from no official status, and it functioned in parallel with the state apparatus, in the shadows and in great freedom. It met regularly from July 5, 1801, to May 17, 1802, then after a pause of a year and a half, resumed work and continued to meet (at least until September 1805).[61] As we saw above, after August 1801 Kochubey was named vice-chancellor, and his functions as head of Russian diplomacy meant that he could no longer participate in the committee except at a distance in time and space.

In his memoirs Czartoryski devoted fascinating pages to the informal functioning of the committee, its secret nature, and the role it played in Alexander's reform plans. Czartoryski says that Alexander "had understood the often insurmountable obstacles that even the most elementary reforms would encounter in Russia. But he was anxious to prove to his circle that he still held to his former opinions despite the change in his position. However, they should not be revealed, and even less, be flaunted before a public that was so little prepared to appreciate them, and which would have considered them with both surprise and apprehension."[62]

Aware of the scope of the reforms that he wanted to undertake and the difficulties that he would unfailingly confront, the emperor chose to work in secret in order to work more freely. In a "summary of the fundamental principles of the organization of a Committee to cooperate in the government's reform work" that he submitted to the emperor in May 1801, Paul

Stroganov insisted, too, on the need to act in secret so as not to compromise the success of the enterprise.

> One might suggest in principle that the search for the state of the public mind cannot give exact results unless much secrecy accompanies the deliberations about government.
>
> It is secrecy alone that may overcome the reservations that would inevitably arise without that precaution.
>
> Before going farther, we can suggest here that secrecy should be one of the fundamental bases of the organization of this association.[63]

That said, the method followed—meeting on the sly, the fact of working in parallel with existing state structures—also attests to the Romanesque character of the enterprise, even Alexander's taste for mystery, if not transgression.

> We had the privilege of coming to dine with the emperor without a prior invitation; our confabs took place two or three times a week. After coffee and a moment of conversation, the emperor would withdraw and while the other guests departed, we four affiliates entered by a corridor into a small *cabinet de toilette* that directly led to the interior chambers of Their Majesties, where the emperor entered from his side. There various reform plans were discussed. There was no subject that was not up for discussion; each brought his ideas, sometimes his work or information he had gathered on what was happening in the current government situation and the abuses that had been noticed. The Emperor fully disclosed his thoughts and his true sentiments.[64]

Two or three times a week, therefore, the group met in the emperor's private apartments, generally after dinner,[65] and the most fundamental subjects were tackled without taboos or reservations. This was particularly true at the session of November 30, 1801, when they dealt with the issue of serfdom. Novosiltsev feared the demoralization that this reform might produce in the Russian nobility, but Stroganov responded by enunciating a judgment that was brusque but speaks volumes about the radical tenor of discussions in the intimate committee:

> What are the principles that might bring about dangerous fermentations? Who are the parties or individuals that are discontented? What elements? It is the people and the nobility. What is the nobility that these gentlemen appear to fear? What is it composed of? What is its state of mind? Our nobility is

composed of a quantity of people who became gentlemen only by service, who have received no education, and all of whose ideas are concerned with seeing nothing above the power of the emperor.

Not right, not justice—nothing can give them the idea of the slightest resistance! It is the most ignorant class, the most villainous one, whose mind is the stupidest.[66]

Throughout its existence, the nonofficial committee produced very animated discussions, even disputes, as attested by the letter of apology sent by Paul Stroganov to his sovereign:

I must, Sire, make an apology for the vivacity with which I got carried away yesterday in the discussion that occupied us; I know that you are indulgent—sometimes too much—but I know that what I did is bad, and that what should characterize the propriety of actions is quite contrary to mine. Thus, if you have the goodness not to condemn me, I must do so myself, and have you know that I find my vivacity very reprehensible. I should not profit from the benefit of your indulgence by not noting the impropriety of my conduct.[67]

But Alexander was concerned to maintain total freedom of thought and expression within the group, and so he was indulgent toward the count:

My dear friend, I think you have become completely crazy! How is it possible to note this and to accuse you of a thing that is the best proof of your regard for me and of your love for the public good? Know that I have never misunderstood you and that while disagreeing with you, I pay justice to the feelings that animate you. For goodness sake, no more of these explanations that do not suit the friendship that unites us. What would not be appropriate for us in public may quite find its place when we are alone, and the greatest proof of friendship that you can give me is to scold me when necessary, when I merit it. Adieu, my dear friend. To you for life,—Alexander.[68]

These working sessions, nourished by preparatory notes composed by Paul Stroganov at the request of the emperor, frequently tackled questions of reforming the state on a constitutional basis, as well as reforming the administration. The members of the little group all remained attached to the goals set by Alexander as far back as 1797, but over the weeks their positions became more and more cautious, which illustrates the difficulty of the enterprise. Moreover, the monarch's intensions were not always very clear.

If the various members of the nonofficial committee always agreed in thinking that reforms were indispensable and all of them pushed the emperor to move in this direction, they were rarely unanimous as concerns their concrete positions. Stroganov took positions that were the most openly constitutionalist; by contrast, Novosiltsev and Kochubey were more circumspect, if not pusillanimous: they supported less the establishment of freedoms and individual rights than the institution of a state of law as guarantee of the good functioning of institutions. They thus approached Alexander's personal views. During the session of August 3, 1801, Novosiltsev declared himself hostile to the principle of the individual's judicial security, although it was mentioned in the first draft of the charter.[69] Then, when it came to the role and prerogatives to grant the senate, Novosiltsev, who was very pessimistic about the political intelligence of the senators, disapproved of any increase in that institution's powers as liable to tie the sovereign's hands. As for Czartoryski, he delivered a tirade against a senate "composed of men who for the most part were incompetent and without energy, selected for their insignificance,"[70] while Stroganov stated violent contempt not only for the senators, but more generally for the nobility—from which the senators came for the most part.

These positions for various reasons tended to push the emperor to moderation by making him aware of the scope of the obstacles along the road, and they converged somewhat paradoxically with the views of Laharpe. Two months after ascending the throne, in May 1801, in answer to a letter on this occasion from his former tutor, Alexander responded to his mentor, who had meanwhile become a member of the Helvetian Directory, in a moving letter full of the affectionate gratitude he still felt:

> The first moment of true pleasure I have felt since finding myself at the head of the affairs of my unhappy country was what I felt when I received your letter, my dear and true friend. [...]
>   I will try to make myself worthy of having been your student and I will glory in this all my life. It was only due to obeying a strict order [from Paul] that I stopped writing to you, without ceasing to think of you and of the time we spent together. It would be sweet to hope it might come back, and it would make me happy. Here I submit absolutely to you and your domestic situation, for there are no others who could ever oppose this. But one favor that I ask of you is to write to me from time to time and give me your advice, which will be so salutary in a post like mine, which I have undertaken only to be useful to my country and to preserve it from new evils. If only you could be here to guide me with your experience and to save me from the traps to which I am exposed by my youth, and perhaps also by my ignorance of the blackness of

perverted souls! One judges so often according to oneself; desiring the good, one flatters oneself that others have the same intentions, until experience comes along to prove the contrary. Then one is disillusioned, but perhaps too late, and the evil is done. My dear friend, this is why an enlightened and experienced friend is the greatest treasure that one may have.

My occupations prevent me from writing to you more. I end by telling you that what gives me most difficulty and work is to reconcile individual interests and hatreds, and to make everybody cooperate for the single goal of generally being useful.

Adieu, my dear friend. Your friendship will be my consolation in my difficulties. Tell your wife a thousand things from me and receive the compliments of mine. If I can be useful to you, make use of me and tell me what I can do.[71]

Encouraged by a letter hinting at a return to Russia (although the tsar did not formally ask him[72]), Laharpe set off. Despite difficulties—Panin detested him as a "French agent" and unbeknownst to Alexander refused to grant him the passport he needed to enter Russia—Laharpe reached St. Petersburg in August 1801, having decided to support the young sovereign in his reforming enterprise. But the person whose teaching had inspired Alexander to issue decrees to end public hangings and to abolish torture and who was in the eyes of court conservatives and even of certain liberals a "dangerous man"[73] (in Panin's words) due to his democratic ideals and his so-called "Bonaparto-philia," was no longer the radical republican he had been in 1796–1797. More circumspect about the benefits of republican government, he had also changed his views about the future of Russia. For him, due to its size and its political immaturity, the empire should tend only in the long term toward a constitutional monarchy in the British style, while in the medium term it should take inspiration from the Prussian model of an enlightened monarchy. Moreover, the allegation that he favored Bonaparte was unfounded: Laharpe met Bonaparte only once (in Malmaison in 1800); his inclination toward a rapprochement between France and Russia is explained strictly by geopolitical considerations and not out of any sympathy for the First Consul.

Laharpe was not appreciated among those close to Alexander, perhaps because his positions were judged as being too moderate and too idealistic, or because of his age, and no doubt because of his lower social status (from the minor nobility, and a foreigner to boot). They had a tendency to treat him with condescension, if not contempt. The former tutor would never be admitted to the committee's sessions; in the eyes of Prince Czartoryski, his influence on the tsar was insignificant:

> De La Harpe was then about forty-something. [...] He appeared to us (and I say *us*, because we all made the same judgment), much below his reputation and the high idea that the Emperor had formed of him. He was of that generation of men fed by illusions at the end of the 18th century, who thought that their doctrine—a new philosopher's stone, a new universal remedy—explained everything, and that sacramental phrases would suffice to make various difficulties disappear in practice. [...] The Emperor, without perhaps admitting it to himself, felt the high opinion he held of his so-called governor diminish, but he still sought reasons to show his skill to us. [...] The fact is that M. de La Harpe's stay in Petersburg at the start of the Emperor's reign was very insignificant, and he had little or no influence on the reforms that Alexander later accomplished.[74]

Yet this is too severe: if in fact Laharpe was not associated with the working group, he did continue until his departure in the autumn of 1802 to have the emperor's ear. The two men saw each other almost every day, either at court or more discreetly at Laharpe's house (the former tutor was living with his father-in-law in the Quai des Anglais), which the sovereign visited in the evening, incognito, outside protocol and convention. They frequently exchanged short notes and long memoranda, with Laharpe endeavoring throughout his stay to gratify the young sovereign with advice of all kinds. If Alexander sometimes made a little fun of his old teacher, whose behavior seemed to him old-fashioned and whose longer notes sometimes irritated him, the young monarch remained attached to the civic values and morality dispensed by Laharpe and even listened to a certain number of ideas defended by the Swiss, for example on schools and the educational system.[75] In a general way he was sensitive to the prudence for which his old tutor was calling. In several letters he sent to Alexander even before his arrival in St. Petersburg, Laharpe insisted on the need to develop education as a priority and only then to turn to reform of the justice system and the legal code,[76] but not to rush things. "Make haste slowly,"[77] wrote Laharpe in a letter dated April 1801: "All this requires time,"[78] he said in October. For if Laharpe advocated reform, he was at the same time quite aware that it would not fail to encounter the marked hostility of a certain number of social categories, with the nobility in the front rank.

> Reform is necessary, but it will have against it all those who have profited, do profit, or hope to profit from abuses, in particular: 1) all high authorities, 2) all the nobility with few exceptions, 3) the great majority of the bourgeoisie that in its circle of activity has assumed the habit of domination and lacks

enlightenment, 4) almost all men of a mature age, whose habits run in the opposite direction and who change with difficulty. [...] Reform has in its favor: 1) Alexander I, who sees in absolute power only the laws that his country has given him, as a means to procure civil liberty for the Russian people, 2) a few nobles more enlightened than others, having the generosity and warmth that are the privilege of youth, of which mature age has too often deprived others, 3) a portion of the bourgeoisie, not knowing too much about what it desires, 4) a few men of letters without influence, 5) perhaps also the subaltern officers and simple soldiers.[79]

This advice about caution corresponds to a number of warnings from members of the secret committee as well as to analysis of some senators, hostile to any challenge to autocratic power and any evolution toward a constitution. Simon Vorontsov, a high dignitary from the reign of Catherine II, wrote in a characteristic way:

> As for what you tell me of the Emperor's desire to diminish his own authority, this means a change in the constitution of the state, it means giving new laws to thirty million habitants. So, when it is not a matter of changing the constitution of a single little republic like Geneva or Lucca, it would take years to weigh this change before executing it, if one wants to avoid troubles and great misfortune. But to make such essential changes in the vastest Empire in the world, in a population of more than thirty million, in an unprepared, ignorant, and corrupt nation, and at a time when the fermentation of minds is universal on the whole continent, is—I do not say risky—but unfailingly to bring trouble, if not the fall of the throne and the dissolution of the empire.[80]

So it is this bundle of appeals to prudence, reinforcing Alexander's own doubts, more than the fall of Pahlen, that explains the evolution we witness after June–July 1801.

* * *

What can we conclude from the first months of the reign of Alexander I? Clearly, from his accession, the young emperor had his heart set on announcing, by his style of living and by his adoption of political measures with strong symbolic significance, his concern to put a stop to the arbitrary rule of Paul and to set the country on the path to reform. In fact, in a few weeks, a new edifice began to take shape in Russia. However, despite the constitutional convictions that he manifested to his close advisors, the tsar was nevertheless shaken by the pessimism that reigned within the little group, by the counsel of prudence from Laharpe, by his own distrust of a nobility that did not seem mature enough to bear the idea of reform. As of that summer, a hardening seemed to appear. In this evolution and in Alexander's hesitations, certain historians see an illustration of his so-called duplicity, while others blame his supposedly irresolute character or his attachment to a superficial liberalism, behind which lurked his taste for absolute power. In reality, it seems that in the summer of 1801 the sovereign's hesitations merely reflected his awareness of the high stakes in establishing a government of law and the fear—quite legitimate for an emperor of 23—of assuming this project.

CHAPTER 6

Reforming Program
1801–1805

In the spirit of the rulings adopted by the emperor in the spring of 1801, the four years that followed led to intense reform activity on the political, economic, and social fronts. Some modest decisions were to disappoint the expectations of the liberal Anglophiles and the more radical members of the secret committee, yet they were not anodyne: in many domains what was adopted between 1801 and 1805 contributed to outline new administrative practices and to foster the takeoff (timid but real) of a civil society.

Political Changes: Limited But Significant

In the wake of their first working sessions in the summer of 1801, the members of the secret committee continued to reflect on reform, successfully pushing the emperor to persevere in this direction. As Adam Czartoryski recalled:

> Although these meetings for a while merely passed the time in endless discussions without any practical result, it is true to say that there was no domestic improvement, no useful reform, attempted or achieved, during Alexander's reign that was not born in these confabs.[1]

The variety of subjects they touched upon demonstrates this; the group remained active until the end of 1802, when the increasing constraints of foreign policy led Alexander to disperse the group for a while and to postpone his reforming activity until later. In the course of their working sessions, the members recurrently returned to the great issues of the day: How to promote the rule of law without dangerously weakening imperial power? How to establish a legal state in a country devoid of any political culture? How to advance the reform of serfdom without challenging the existing order and without undermining the whole political and social edifice? Finding convincing answers to these key questions proved all the more difficult because the inner circle suffered from a lack of legitimacy. This little group that was calling for the establishment of a legally based state resulted only from the tsar's will—and some would say, his whim—which earned him ferocious criticism from the court and high administration. Moreover, while the committee was studying crucial questions to be solved, while it was drawing the emperor's attention to the need to tackle them in a methodical and gradual manner, Alexander was also taking the brunt of the conservative influence of the existing government machinery:

> The true government—the Senate and Ministers—continued to administer the country and to conduct affairs as it wished. It sufficed for the Emperor to leave the particular room where our meetings took place for him to fall back under the influence of old ministers, and so none of the decisions we had taken inside our unofficial committee could be implemented.[2]

Probably these conservative influences explain, at least in part, the modesty of those reforms that were ultimately undertaken. One should also mention (as does the Russian historian Alexander Sakharov) the emperor's firm conviction that, while indispensable, the desired reforms were liable to harm prerogatives that overall suited him quite well. Some historians also mention the fear that Alexander may have felt at the idea of arousing a wave of hostility likely to lead to his assassination, remembering the examples of his father and his grandfather.[3] These various considerations cannot be eliminated despite the fact that no surviving document confirms the supposed fear of a plot. In any case, it is worth noting that any projects undertaken by the secret committee between 1801 and 1805 came up against the problem of what method to follow. How to concretely tackle a profound reform of the political and social system when the intermediaries on which such reforms had to rely were lacking? This crucial question did not stop haunting the members of the group and they were unable to answer it. For if political reform might find possible support from within the nobility, particularly from the senatorial party that was favorable to any change likely to make the senate the foundation of a legally based state, it was also doomed to be opposed by the nobility, the most traditional social stratum of Russian society and also the least favorable to any reform of the social order, especially of serfdom. This was the major problem, if not the impasse. Laharpe tried to bring some elements of a solution to this difficulty. In his individual meetings with the sovereign, he insisted repeatedly on the narrowness of the possible relays of reform—a minority of educated nobles, a portion of the nascent bourgeoisie, some thinkers "without influence"—and he stressed the need to undertake reform in a gradual fashion and to set concrete and modest objectives—at least until imperial action was able to find wider intermediaries thanks to progress in education.

Consequently, due to the committee's hesitations, to Laharpe's advice, as well as to the tsar's cautious nature (as Stroganov often deplored, he did not always expound clear thoughts to the committee),[4] the decisions adopted during the period from 1801 to 1805 seem limited and modest. Yet they remain emblematic of Alexander's will to pursue a reforming program.

Despite Stroganov's call for the proclamation of a constitution establishing a strict separation of powers (for him the foundation of any legal state), no constitutional text was adopted in the period. The tsar stuck to simple reform of the central administration. Instituted in April 1801, two and a half months before the fall of Pahlen, the Permanent Council included eight to ten members, who were joined by a minister, depending on the issue being dealt with. Its function was to examine state affairs and to prepare a reform of the administration. Until its disappearance in 1810, it was an important consultative body: it would be directly associated with restoring the Charter of the Nobility, as well as with dissolving the "secret expedition"; in some cases where it expressed a different opinion from the emperor's, it did manage to prevail. For example, back in January 1801, Paul I had hurriedly ratified an act of union between Russia and the kingdom of Kartl-Kakhetia, determined to use it to annex the region. Alexander proved hostile to pursuing such an annexation, although the Permanent Council was favorable to it. In August the secret committee took up the subject in turn: Novosiltsev and Stroganov were against annexation. But the following month, yielding to the view of the Permanent Council, Alexander issued a manifesto confirming the annexation of the kingdom.[5]

Prepared by Novosiltsev, a manifesto to reform the senate was adopted in September 1802.[6] As supreme judicial body the Senate was now divided into functional departments in order to be more effective and rapid in its judgments. Any case not decided at the departmental level would be brought before the senate's General Council, which would set the nature and scale of punishment, with no possible appeal. However, while the prerogatives of this body were now clarified, they remained strictly limited to the judicial sphere and were not extended to the political field. Unlike the aspirations outlined in the text of July 1801,[7] the reformed senate was not transformed into a House of Lords with legislative powers in the British style.

In line with that July 1801 senatorial document, several projects that emanated from liberals who were more or less close to power did quickly see the light of day. Thus came a plan defended by Paul Stroganov, who (despite his distrust of the nobility) intended to increase the powers of the senate and so transform it into a master institution in charge of applying any future constitutional law. Likewise, Count Mordvinov's project (presented in May 1802 to the Permanent Council) to make the senate a political body of which only a portion of the members would be elected rather than appointed by the sovereign (specifically two senators per province[8]), would be a first step toward a representative monarchy. Discussed by the secret committee, these various projects did not always win support: again, in May 1802, the arguments advanced by Alexander's personal advisors remained the same. Taking account of the mentality and retrograde behavior of the nobility, there could be no question at present of entrusting it with the least parcel of power by means of a reformed senate. In essence the nobility would be incapable of making good use of power. A year later, although the manifesto of September 1802 had given the senate a "right of remonstrance" (article 9, the right to attract the monarch's attention to the necessary coherence of all laws with each other), Senator Severin Potocki asked for an audience with the tsar. At the head of a delegation of senators, he argued that the text adopted in December 1802 by the minister of war with the approval of the emperor[9] did not respect existing legal provisions. Alexander's response was swift: in March 1803 he declared that the right of remonstrance would only apply to laws already edicted in the past and not to future laws. Thus two years after Alexander became tsar, the dream of certain liberals—to see the senate gain influence and power and then be transformed into a political body—was over. From this date power remained concentrated in the hands of an autocratic monarch.

While the 1802 manifesto affected only peripherally the structure of the senate, it did have a noticeable impact on administrative reform by creating new ministries.

The old ministerial colleges founded by Peter the Great were now replaced by eight new hierarchical and centralized ministries: Foreign Affairs, Army, Navy, Domestic Affairs, Finances, Justice, Commerce, and Public Education. Three of the old colleges (War, Admiralty, and Foreign Affairs) remained but were placed under the authority of the new ministries.[10] At the head of each ministry was a minister named by the emperor (seconded by an assistant and a secretary) who became "the sole master in his jurisdiction."[11] Each ministry would include a chancellery, a vice-minister, and several departments directed by heads; on a daily basis they reported to the minister about current situations and aided him in taking decisions. All ministers were by right members of the Permanent Council.

In principle, the senate possessed a supervisory power over the executive bodies of the state,[12] including the ministers, but in practice the latter referred directly to the emperor, which of course weakened the potential power of the senate. Ministers worked in close collaboration with the emperor; they could propose new laws and amendments to existing ones. Every year each minister was to present the emperor with a written overview of activity; this report would then be transmitted to the senate, which could demand explanations or clarifications. In reality, the fact that ministers often came from the senate further diminished the latter's freedom of action, thereby contributing (in the expression of the historian John Ledonne) to the emergence of a veritable "ministerial despotism"[13]—a trend that the emperor encouraged.

While the ministers did appear before the emperor each day to report on current affairs, there was no cooperation between one ministry and another. In principle, the Council of Ministers was supposed to have responsibility for the whole and "to act as a general staff for the commander-in-chief, the autocrat."[14] This was the wish of Czartoryski, who, in the working session of the close circle in February 1802, had stressed the idea of cohesion and collective ministerial responsibility:

> In choosing ministers, it should be decided to put in only people whose way of thinking would be uniform, so that they formed a perfect unity, so that the foolishness of one would be attributable to the others, and so they would all be responsible for the same mistake. Such an administration, set in motion by this single force and directed by a good system, would bring Russia in short order to a high degree of prosperity. At present His Majesty agrees that the disunity of ministers is singularly harmful to the Empire, since one of them pulls in one direction and someone else in another, and in the middle it is the state that suffers.[15]

Alexander did institute a committee of ministers that was supposed to gather ministers into teams around a precise agenda, but he did not make this committee a systematic instrument of government and was often content to summon one minister or another, reserving the right to decide alone on interministerial conflicts. However, the role of the committee of ministers was not negligible: while the Permanent Council quickly faded away, the committee of ministers would continue to meet (if not regularly, then at least frequently) to deal with political questions. Alexander presided over a number of meetings, 20 of 23 that were held in the autumn of 1802; the following year the tsar attended all 42 meetings and then in 1804, 26 of 31 meetings.[16] Lastly, when in 1805 he was forced to leave his capital to join his army on campaign, it was the committee of ministers that managed political affairs in his absence, proceeding to a majority vote of those present for any urgent decision. This situation was exceptional: the committee of ministers had never functioned in a systematic way, and each minister's direct contact with the sovereign remained the norm. But this bilateral way of functioning was criticized by the inner circle, who saw it as a source of inefficiency. Stroganov complained:

> The Emperor has adopted the working method of concerning himself every day successively with all the ministers; they each enter at set hours and report on their respective affairs; the Emperor gives his decisions, and that is how the work gets done. This method has several disadvantages. [...] In never gathering together all the ministers to summarize all the work being done, by not making them a single group and thereby coordinating all parties, the whole is lost from sight and ministers forget the ensemble that ought to be formed by all the parties. Each in his own way only works on his own part and subordinates to it all the others.[17]

By contrast, in a letter to Laharpe from November 1802, Alexander spoke of his great satisfaction, stressing his personal responsibility in the new organization:

> The measure we often spoke of together [the creation of ministries] is in full activity. The ministries are organized and have been going rather well for more than a month. Business has acquired much greater clarity and method, and I know who to get after if something goes wrong.[18]

In fact, the ministers chosen by Alexander did not form a solid team—far from it. There were young reformers, close to or emanating from the inner circle, as well as conservative dignitaries who were little inclined to reforms or change. Czartoryski, Novosiltsev, and Stroganov obtained respectively the posts of vice-ministers of foreign affairs, justice, and internal affairs, while Viktor Kochubey became minister of the interior, a post he kept continuously until 1812. Mikhail Muravyov, vice-minister of education, shared the reforming views of the younger men; as for the navy, Admiral Mordvinov was reputed to be a liberal and an Anglophile. But at the same time Alexander gave the justice post to the poet Derzhavin; reputedly very conservative, the latter never stopped complaining about the "French and Polish constitutional spirit" with which Alexander's entourage was "stuffed." Similarly, most of the heads of ministerial departments, often former dignitaries from Catherine's reign, were characterized by conservative positions and averse to any change. Therefore, barely four months after the creation of the ministries, there was disillusionment within the secret committee. "There is no group; the ministers detest each other and bicker, and the agreement so necessary to an administration has never existed for an instant," complained Kochubey to Vorontsov[19] in a letter of January 1803—a few months after the ministries were created. The same day Novosiltsev echoed him:

> You are perhaps curious to know how our ministries are going? Not as well as could be desired: little unity, little harmony; some have too much activity, others not enough; some isolate themselves and think only of their own party, others meddle in everything and obliquely control everything.[20]

Consequently, while the creation of the ministries made the state administration more efficient, they remained very compartmentalized and the role of the Committee of Ministers remained modest. Moreover, political reform did not go beyond administrative and functional improvements. Thus, in the period from 1801 to 1805, there was no evolution toward the constitution of a really homogeneous government. Power remained autocratic and centralized—despite Alexander's marked interest in the idea of federalism and the corresponding concessions he made in regional administration.

Upon his arrival in power, thanks to the trips he had once taken with his father, the young sovereign was well aware of the territorial immensity and national, cultural, and religious diversity of his empire, as he was au fait with the realities of a regional administration beset by corruption and indifference.[21] He often mentioned these issues to Laharpe; in a letter of July 1803, he said he wanted to approach Thomas Jefferson[22] to ask the American president how federalism in the young United States of America worked. And he did write a letter to President Jefferson in August 1805, expressing his admiration for the United States and the "free and wise constitution that ensures the happiness of each and all,"[23] and affirming his interest in this model because it combined federalism and constitutionalism. A year later, in April 1806, Jefferson wrote to Lovett Harris, U.S. consul in St. Petersburg: "The Emperor manifested a wish to know our constitution. Consequently I have chosen the two best studies we possess on the subject and beg you to find a place for them in his library."[24]

But here again, Alexander acted prudently, even overcautiously, by beginning with a modest reform of regional administration. Now the governor at the head of a province would refer directly to the sovereign for all questions relating to his authority, while the provincial council composed of local functionaries (for tax revenue, commerce, justice, police, etc.) would send its reports to various ministries. This organization tended to give regional governments increased powers and better-qualified staff. As Marc Raeff stresses:

> This same governor now had the means to direct and supervise the affairs of his province with the help of experienced men, under the supervision of specialized and competent ministries. A certain amount of administrative decentralization became possible, greater latitude might be left to local initiative and local autonomy, which was indispensable to oil the gears and thereby make management more flexible.[25]

Without giving up the rule of administrative unity among provinces, Alexander also soon introduced some flexibility into the management of non-Russian territories of the empire. The Nystadt Peace of 1721 had granted the Baltic provinces the privilege of autonomous administration, and the tsar did not challenge this privilege or seek to interfere in Baltic affairs. The annexation of the kingdom of Kartl-Kakhetia—which, as we saw, took place after much hesitation—was accompanied by the abolition of the Georgian monarchy, but the status of the Georgian Orthodox Church was respected,[26] and Georgian nobles could integrate into the Table of Ranks in order to obtain titles of Russian nobility and to participate in the management of local affairs.

Finally, out of a concern to promote religious toleration in his reign—when at the time he was personally rather indifferent to the Orthodox religion, which he perceived as producing obscurantism—Alexander wanted to improve the conditions of Jews in the empire.[27] In November 1802 he created a special commission, the Committee for the Organization of Jewish Life, on which sat Czartoryski, Potocki, Valerian Zubov, and Derzhavin. Representatives from the Jewish community were invited to make their demands heard before this commission, and in 1804 it published regulations that, without questioning the discriminatory measures under which Jews suffered (since Catherine's reign, they had been confined to living in the western regions, could not purchase land, and were subject to heavy taxes), did try to ameliorate their situation somewhat. Admittedly, they could still not acquire land[28] and the wine trade was forbidden to them, but the "Territory of Residence" was enlarged to the regions of Astrakhan and the Caucasus, and the taxes they paid were lightened. Moreover, in order to foster the assimilation of Jews—many spoke German, which accentuated their isolation—the regulations authorized Jewish children to freely enter schools, colleges, and universities belonging to the state, while also authorizing the foundation of Jewish schools. These various measures provided a much more comprehensive and liberal situation for Jewish subjects than in the past.

Thus, in a few years Alexander had tried to improve the way that central and regional administrations functioned, while demonstrating some flexibility in his approach to the territorial and cultural specificities of the empire. Therefore, these political reforms, even if they were not able to concretely manifest Alexander's constitutional and federalist ideas, were nevertheless significant. But on the economic and social levels, progress was more limited.

Draft Reforms

In 1796–1797 Alexander had expressed his deep distaste for serfdom; from his arrival in power, he frequently raised this issue with members of the secret committee and with Laharpe. But the concrete changes he put into effect from 1801 to 1805 were very limited.

Early on, as his private correspondence and his diary show, Alexander was convinced of the need to improve the condition of the peasantry; the persistence of serfdom was for him both a moral and an economic anomaly.[29] But how to envisage ending serfdom without compromising the status of the nobility and thereby unleashing its hostility or without challenging the social order and the very foundations of the political regime in Russia? Of course, as we have already noted, the tsar had no particular esteem or sympathy for the Russian nobility; when the secret committee met in July 1801 he confessed to his close friends that he had agreed only reluctantly to reestablish the Charter of the Nobility, so much did aristocratic privileges seem to him both unmerited and unjustified. The inner circle echoed Alexander's aversion to the nobility; however, the monarch had to deal with what he despised.

In the summer of 1801, Platon Zubov, who had not yet been removed from the inner circle, prepared at Alexander's request a plan for reforming serfdom. Without going so far as to advocate a complete overhaul, he made many daring proposals. For example, he suggested authorizing nobles to free (in return for financial compensation from the state) those of their serfs who, living near them in town, might become artisans and thus figure in the registers of the soslovija (i.e., the states) as citizens. Given that about 8 percent of the town population (or almost 190,000 people)[30] was composed of serfs, this proposal was significant. Zubov also proposed banning any sale of serfs without lands and setting up precise rules for serfs (who were financially able) to buy back their freedom. Debated before the secret committee in the month of August, Zubov's plan to liberate town serfs was rejected as too costly for imperial finances.

At the end of 1801, a new memorandum, this one written by Admiral Mordvinov, proposed extending to merchants, artisans, and peasants who were attached to the crown the right to acquire lands, secured or not with serfs. For the admiral this would begin to challenge the exclusive privileges of the nobility and to foster the takeoff of a new type of farming that used free and salaried peasants. Eventually this type would prove more profitable than estates functioning with serfs, which would gradually lead landowners to accept the liberation of their peasants. In November 1801 both this plan and Zubov's were discussed by the inner circle. There were differences of opinion: Novosiltsev was favorable to enlarging the right to acquire land to social categories other than the nobility but hostile to the idea of banning nobles from selling their serfs without land, out of fear of violent opposition. His viewpoint was shared by Laharpe, who for his part advised Alexander to advance on the question of serfdom "slowly and above all without the least attack on property rights."[31] Kochubey and Czartoryski were favorable to both measures but stressed that they would affect only a tiny proportion of serfs, and so the overall problem of serfdom would remain. Stroganov, the most radical of the group, reasserted that there was no reason to worry about the nobility, which was cowardly, without character, and not at all dangerous. There was much more to fear from the anger of serfs mistreated by their owners:

> In our country at all times it is the peasant class that has taken part in all the troubles that have occurred; it is never the nobility that has rebelled, and if the government has something to fear and some party to watch, it is really the class of serfs and not any others.[32]

But he did not convince the tsar, who preferred to partially adopt Mordvinov's plan. On December 24, 1801 (the emperor's birthday), a ukase authorized all social categories to buy land without serfs, which meant that the functional monopoly of the nobility was lifted, although it kept the privilege of owning serfs. But none of the measures advocated by Zubov was accepted by Alexander. A year later, in November 1802, a new plan was presented by Count Sergey Rumyantsev, son of Field Marshall Rumyantsev, who had once studied law at Leyden University and was known for his liberal and philanthropic ideas. He suggested authorizing owners to liberate their serfs, individually or by whole villages, giving them each a plot of land. In both cases liberation would be compensated by a sum of money fixed by the owners themselves. Seduced by the idea—in this scheme, the nobles would not be damaged and the state would not have to bear the cost of freeing the serfs[33]—Alexander adopted in February 1803 a "law on free farmers" that transformed serfs into free farmers as soon as they managed to buy themselves back—and were authorized by their owners to do so.

Still, although the 1803 law gave hope to serfs, its impact remained very limited. Between 1803 and 1825, 47,153 male serfs[34] were affected, mostly in the early years: 20,747 between 1804 and 1808; 10,508 between 1809 and 1813; 4,696 between 1814 and 1818; 10,057 between 1819 and 1823; and 1,145 between 1824 and 1825. Almost a third of the serfs (13,371) were freed by the will of a single owner, Prince Alexander Nikolaievich Golitsyn, for the total sum of 5,424,618 rubles (an average of 406 rubles per peasant).[35] In this case—quite singular given the number of serfs involved—the total sum owed by the peasants was advanced by the imperial treasury, and the peasants had to reimburse the state. In the majority of the 47,153 cases, however, the serfs paid a portion of their ransom at the time of their liberation and the other part in installments, by prior agreement.

Alexander also adopted a decree forbidding the publication in the Moscow and St. Petersburg newspapers of announcements of the sale of serfs without land. Finally, inaugurating an approach he would apply in other circumstances, the sovereign used more advanced measures on the periphery of his empire, making the Baltic provinces (Estonia, Latvia, and Courland) an "experimental laboratory" for the reform of serfdom. Hoping (as he told the secret committee) that the "provinces will furnish an example to the rest of the empire,"[36] the emperor pushed the diets of Estonia and Latvia to adopt texts to give peasants a legal status. In July 1802 the Estonian diet gave peasants who respected their feudal obligations "a hereditary and perpetual usufruct" over land they cultivated, and it also set up local tribunals; two years later the Latvian diet adopted these provisions and added others: the law now set the nature and scope of taxes and work details owed by peasants.[37]

Yet the implemented reforms remained well below the initial expectations. But they were an important stage on the path to abolition: first, because for the first time since the establishment of serfdom, imperial power publicly expressed its desire to challenge an institution it considered no longer acceptable; second, because within the governing elites the idea of a reform (if not abolition) of serfdom, as carried in the projects of Zubov, Mordvinov, and Rumyantsev, was also making headway.

While the issue of serfdom monopolized Alexander's attention and that of his advisors, other social and economic topics were also broached. To the sovereign, who was reviving the voluntarist approach of Peter the Great and Catherine II, it was up to the state to foster initiative and entrepreneurship.

From the start Alexander wanted to promote the colonization of lands to the south. For this purpose between 1803 and 1805 he encouraged by fiscal measures the settling in southern Russia and Ukraine of almost 5,000 colonists—Germans and Czechs in the lead. Founded in 1795 and exempted from customs duties, the city of Odessa (starting in 1803) was administered by the Duke of Richelieu, a French émigré who had gone into the Russian imperial service and was named by the sovereign to this post. In 1805 he became governor general of New Russia. This choice proved judicious: in a few years the duke managed to make Odessa a city enjoying full expansion. By 1805 it had 15,000 inhabitants and took fourth place among cities, after St. Petersburg, Moscow, and Warsaw; its commercial port was very dynamic, responsible for a major portion of cereal exports. At the end of the 1790s, before the foundation of Odessa, ports of the Black Sea had exported only two to three percent of Russian wheat; by 1802 Odessa accounted for 17 percent of the total.

After 1805–1806 the colonization of the south, still encouraged by the imperial state, called less on foreign colonists than on crown peasants who came from regional governments with relatively high population density and where land was not fertile enough to feed rural communities, as was the case in the northeast.

Again out of a concern to foster the free circulation of goods and merchandise and to stimulate commerce, Alexander emphasized progress in internal navigation. In the wake of Peter the Great, who had dreamed of uniting by means of canals the Baltic Sea, the White Sea, the Caspian Sea, and the Black Sea, Alexander launched major public works. Started back in 1711, the construction of the Vyshniy-Volochok Canal to link the Volga and the Neva rivers and the Caspian and the Baltic seas was pursued throughout his reign and was finished in 1818. Envisaged by Peter I, the Tikhvin Canal, dug during Alexander's reign, allowed the linking of Tikhvina, a tributary of the Ladoga, with the Volga. The Maria Canal, whose construction started in 1799 and ended in 1808, united the two navigable rivers in the upper part of their courses: the Kovja, a tributary of the White Lake and the Vytegra, a tributary of Lake Onega. Finally the North Canal, begun under Catherine II's reign, was finished in 1820, forming a junction between the White Sea and the Caspian Sea. The monarch also favored mercantile trade by decreeing all Black Sea ports free of customs duties. Finally, in 1805, he ordered the construction of a canal within the walls of St. Petersburg. Finished in 1822, it circumscribed the city to the south and allowed merchant ships of various sizes to load and unload merchandise more easily. Thus, like Peter the Great and Catherine II, Emperor Alexander was concerned to develop transport and communication infrastructure, aware of the crucial role they played in development. However, at the start of his reign, it was to education that the emulator of Laharpe gave priority.

* * *

As a disciple of the Enlightenment and of Laharpe, Alexander gave major importance to education as the means for individual improvement and eventually for collective progress. When it had become better educated, open-, and critical-minded, Russian society would be better prepared to understand and to defend the idea of reform incarnated by the sovereign. For Alexander as for Laharpe, public education therefore represented a crucial investment for the future of the country, all the more so since the emperor was very critical of the system in force when he ascended the throne. In January 1802 he sent Laharpe a report once presented to Paul I by the Imperial Commission of Schools, with a devastating note:

> My dear, I attach the unsatisfactory memorandum[38] I told you about. I doubt that you can get much out of it, but at least it will give you an idea of the current uselessness of an institution that is so important for the nation.[39]

With this radical realization, he began as soon as he was in power to make major changes.

The reform of September 1802 led to the founding of a Ministry of Public Education initially entrusted to Count Zavadovski, an aged and inactive veteran who had led the school commission under Catherine II. As of January 1803 the ministry included a "General Office of Schools" that became the actual decision-making body. Directed by Basil Karazin (1773–1842) and including some close friends of the emperor like Czartoryski, it came in fact to direct the ministry, as Alexander admitted explicitly to Laharpe in a letter of July 1803:

Your regrets about the nomination of Zavadowsky as minister of public education would dissipate if you knew about the organization of his ministry. He is nobody. A council composed of Muravyov, Klinger, Czartoryski, Novossitzoff, etc. governs everything. Every paper is worked on by them. The frequency of my relations with the latter two prevents the minister from posing the least obstacle to the good we are trying to do. We have made him as easy-going as possible, a real sheep; he is nobody and has only been put in the ministry so he cannot cry that he was excluded from it.[40]

Accordingly, in November 1804 the General Office published a "Status of Schools" that was inspired by both Czartoryski's thinking in his memo of 1802 on school matters (in turn taken from the teaching model developed by Condorcet in France in 1792)[41] and by a memorandum written by Laharpe in March 1802.[42]

The empire would be divided into six huge education districts that would each eventually have a university. The head of each district, the trustee of the university, would exercise authority and supervise all the gymnasia (secondary schools) of the provinces situated in the district. At the provincial level the director of the gymnasium had the task of supervising all the schools in the local districts. At the level of each local district, a supervisor was charged with taking care of parish schools. In the Baltic provinces teaching would be in German, while in Russian-speaking regions it would be in Russian. Parish schools would deliver one year's instruction; and district schools two years' instruction; and provincial schools four years. In parish schools priority would be given to reading, writing, arithmetic, religion, and morality, as well as to notions of hygiene and agriculture. District schools would stress religion, law, the Russian language, history, geography, mathematics, physics, the natural sciences, technology, and drawing. Children destined for provincial schools would also receive the rudiments of Latin and German. Finally, provincial schools would teach mathematics, physics, technology, the natural sciences, ethics, law, political economy, history, geography, Latin, German, French, and drawing. (Note the important place given to teaching religion in parish and district schools and its absence from the secondary curriculum: for members of the General Office influenced by German idealism, the teaching of religion in the lower grades would give children solid moral guidelines.[43]) As in Condorcet's plan, teaching would be open to girls as well as boys and would be free of charge, with books freely supplied to poor children. But in reality education under Alexander's reign would remain the privilege of boys. Moreover, for lack of finance, of competent teachers, and of Russian textbooks, many schools planned for the countryside never saw the light of day.

University education was also reformed. Moscow University had been founded in 1755, and it was simply reorganized and provided with new regulations in November 1804. Four faculties were created: political and moral sciences, mathematics and physics, medicine, and letters. While university organization remained traditional—based on the medieval model—it aspired to train not only competent civil servants but also the engineers and specialists that the country still lacked. Under the authority of the university, several libraries, scholarships for poor students, a classical lycée, and a pedagogic institute were created. Moreover, now endowed with a printing press, Moscow University was also able to publish ambitious scientific works. In parallel, new universities were opened in Vilnius[44] and in Tartu in 1803, where the courses were given respectively in Polish and in German. A year later, in 1804, the universities of Kharkov and Kazan were opened. Finally, the pedagogic institute in St. Petersburg, shut in 1801, was reopened and formed the nucleus of the university that was officially created in 1819.

In these various universities that educated a few hundred students at a time, the teaching body was composed of Russian and foreign professors giving a variety of courses. (In 1804 Moscow University had eleven professors from Germany.) While giving an important place to traditional subjects—theology, scripture, Russian civil and criminal law—university education gave a good share to the exact sciences and to disciplines from western Europe: Roman law, diplomacy, and even political economy.

Both illustrious names and Alexander's friends figured among the first trustees of the universities: Muravyov, the vice-minister and a former tutor to the emperor, was the first trustee of Moscow University; Novosiltsev was trustee of St. Petersburg University from 1804 to 1810, and Prince Czartoryski trustee of Vilnius University from 1804 to 1824. This demonstrates the interest the tsar took in the universities. But the creation of these institutions often required the overcoming of difficulties, as illustrated by Kharkov. Alexander approved the project as personally presented by Karazin in 1801, but the university did not see the light of day until January 1805, due to financial and administrative vagaries. However, Alexander's investment in university development was irrefutable: each year the state gave the universities a budget higher than the whole budget that Catherine II had devoted to education.

Under Alexander's reign students remained few in number, but by their friendship and social networks—they often formed clubs—as well as by the journals and newspapers they published, they contributed to forming the dynamic embryo of an enlightened society.

In parallel to the establishment of a denser grid of public schools, the monarch encouraged the foundation of "modern lycées," meaning colleges at an intermediate level between gymnasia and universities, often privately financed, usually offering scientific and technical education. The first was created in Yaroslav; financed by Demidov, a rich entrepreneur from Ural, it was approved by Alexander in January 1805 and opened its doors under the name of the Demidov School of Law. The same year an institute of history and philology was founded in Nezhin (Ukraine), thanks to the financial support of Prince Bezborodko. And in 1811 a third lycée—the most famous one—opened in Tsarskoye Selo, welcoming children from the regime's aristocratic elite; it included Pushkin among its first students.

Overall, there was real educational development under Alexander's reign: in 1801, on the eve of reform, there were only 334 schools in the Russian Empire, including 241 primary schools and 93 secondary schools serving 21,533 pupils in all, from a population of 34 million, or a schooling rate of 0.06 percent. By 1825 the number of primary schools had risen to 370, and there were 600 secondary schools and lycées, representing a total of 69,629 pupils,[45] for a population now estimated at 53 million, or a rate of 0.13 percent. The breeding ground for young people trained in these higher and secondary establishments would play a key role during Alexander's reign, not only on the economic and social levels, as they went on to become the civil servants and specialists the country needed; on a cultural level, the lycées would educate the great names of art and literature during the reign, as well as supply the audience for those artists and writers.

Meanwhile, the emperor wanted to open Russia up to Europe, to integrate it into the intellectual and cultural exchanges of the era. This is why he adopted in 1804 an extremely liberal censorship code, the most liberal one of the nineteenth century, and encouraged Russian students to spend time abroad, particularly in Germany. Each year, two students from each of the universities on imperial territory could pursue their studies in western Europe at the state's expense. The tsar also commissioned the translation into Russian of certain literary, philosophical, and political works that seemed to him likely to foster this openness: Adam Smith's On the Wealth of Nations was published in Russian in 1804. However, this receptiveness to European culture was not to be to the detriment of the Russian patrimony. In 1814 the Imperial Public Library opened in the center of St. Petersburg at the corner of the Nevsky Prospect. By 1838 it had almost 42,700 volumes and more than 17,000 manuscripts.[46]

The consequences of this intellectual and cultural openness were not long in coming: between 1801 and 1825 there was an explosion in the number of publishing houses (55 were created in 1813) and periodicals: reviews, almanacs, newspapers multiplied in just a few years. The lifespan of these publications was sometimes brief, but they still managed to stimulate, in away unprecedented in Russia, the circulation of ideas, values, and tastes. In a few years, under the influence of the Free Society of Lovers of Literature, Sciences and Arts, several magazines in various formats came out: in 1804 the Northern Messenger and in 1805 Russian Belles-Lettres. Individual initiatives were behind other new magazines: the Messenger of Europe was founded in 1802 by Nikolay Karamzin and the Russian Messenger by Sergey Glinka in 1808.

Concerned to open up to Europe while fostering the development of a certain kind of Russianness, the tsar also had an urge to renovate and embellish St. Petersburg, to make it one of the most beautiful capitals in Europe. From the start he distanced himself from the baroque, if not rococo, style that had been in fashion under Catherine. Steeped in Greek and Latin references thanks to Laharpe, he asserted a marked taste for neoclassicism. So it was in this direction that the architects of his day, mostly Russians and no longer western Europeans, would work, inventing a "Russian Empire" style of Palladian inspiration that was frequently considered to be a "Romantic classicism."[47] In the course of the years 1801 to 1825, forms were purified, and geometry and symmetry were rediscovered;[48] the majestic and monumental constructions also featured political symbols.

During the first years of his reign, Alexander launched major rebuilding at the Admiralty. Symbol of St. Petersburg's strategic and military role, it was renovated starting in 1805, under the direction of Andrey Zakharov, then professor of architecture at the Imperial Academy of Beaux-Arts. But the architect died in 1811, and it was Andrey Voronikhin, a talented architect and a serf freed by Count Alexander Stroganov,[49] who took charge of the construction. When the work was completed in 1823, the result lived up to imperial aspirations: the facade of the main building of the Admiralty was 415 meters long, decorated with sumptuous bas-reliefs, the central tower bore 28 statues and four monumental sculptures that represented Pyrrhus, Achilles, Ajax, and Alexander the Great, proclaiming a symbolic continuity between ancient Greece and the Russian empire. Finally, on the summit of the building stood the admiralty arrow, 72 meters high, which became an essential landmark on the Petersburg horizon. But Alexander (like his father before him) was not content with erecting only secular buildings: in 1801 on Paul I's initiative, construction of the Kazan Cathedral had been undertaken by Andrey Voronikhin, and Alexander pursued the work until it was finished ten years later. Inspired by the basilicas of St. Peter and Sta. Maria Maggiore in Rome, the cathedral opened in an elegant semi-circle onto the famous Nevsky Prospect. From the first years of its consecration, it became the pantheon of the saints and heroes of the Russian nation.

Thus, in the course of the years from 1801 to 1825, change was in the air and the reforming intentions of the sovereign were to be seen in many domains. However, the concrete decisions were modest if not disappointing, not up to the height of initial hopes, for Alexander's constitutionalist and reformist dream quickly ran up against a harsh reality: the absence of any relays and support within Russian society. So, from 1802–1803 onward, the sovereign was pushed to opt for caution and very gradual reform.

A Young Emperor Searching for Himself

Paul I had banned Freemasonry everywhere, but in 1802 the new emperor authorized it once more. This benevolence was partly based on tolerance, comparable to what he observed among various religious sensibilities. But this tolerance mutated into positive attraction. We lack the sources to be precise about Alexander's feelings about Freemasonry, but we do know that many of his close friends (all those in the inner circle), ministers, and advisers were Freemasons and that he himself was undoubtedly initiated in 1803–1804 by Rodion Koshelev. Significantly older than the tsar (he was then 55), a great connoisseur of German mystic philosophy and of Louis-Claude de Saint-Martin, Koshelev occupied the post of chamberlain at the imperial court, which meant he was in charge of the general security of the emperor, the court, and the palace, which enabled him to reside at the Winter Palace and to share a number of philosophical and spiritual discussions with Alexander, entering gradually into "intimacy with the tsar."[50] Introduced by Koshelev to a Russian Freemasonry of liberal and deist inspiration (distinct from the western European variety that was usually atheistic and republican), Alexander took his place within the lodge of the Preobrazhensky Regiment. Later on, the emperor himself founded a Masonic lodge with Koshelev and Alexander Golitsyn, nicknamed "Three in One," where the ideal of Masonic fraternity would try to cohabit with his own messianic spirituality—a subject to which we will return.

Simple and open in his relations with others, Alexander (like his grandmother) appreciated salon wit and conversations where he could shine, particularly among women, whom he seduced as much with his culture as with his sense of presence. In her memoirs Countess Edling insists on the emperor's taste for the company of the finer sex, whom he regarded with "an interest and chivalric respect full of grace and goodness."[51] Amiable and gallant, Alexander despite his partial deafness and the slight myopia that obliged him to use a lorgnette (that he often lost), pleased many people. In April 1801 General Duroc, the aide-de-camp of Bonaparte who was sent to the court of St. Petersburg, attested to Alexander's seductiveness to his entourage and the court: "The emperor combined a handsome and agreeable physique with gentleness and honesty; he appeared to have good principles and education; he had a taste for the military."[52]

A seducer, Alexander had many affairs. But although some liaisons lasted, most of these were passing fancies and often platonic, based on sophisticated banter in the style of Marivaux inherited from eighteenth-century France, and they had little consequence—at least until the second half of 1803, when Maria Naryshkina, whom he had loved unrequitedly since 1801, became his mistress. Then began a liaison that would last more than ten years.

> Gallant toward all women, his heart loved only one of them, and he loved her with constancy until the time when she herself broke a link that she could never appreciate. Madame Naryshkina, whose ideal beauty was found only in the pictures of Raphael, had captivated the emperor.[53]

This pretty testimony from Countess Edling, a lady of honor to the empress and hence not likely to be indulgent toward Elizabeth's rival, is precious for the historian. Archive sources fail to take account of Alexander's passionate love affair; at most we find a few documents dealing with the children of the beautiful Polish woman: daily reports from James Wylie in April 1824 on the illness of the young Sophie Naryshkina[54] and some awkward notes[55] written by her children. The emperor was always very discrete, even proper, toward the woman who was his sole passion. He never mentioned her in his letters to his mother, Maria Feodorovna; this silence, surprising when one knows the intimacy between mother and son, is perhaps suspicious. (In fact, we know that Nicholas I would destroy many letters exchanged between his brother and his mother.) On the other hand, Maria Naryshkina and her children were more present in the frequent letters Alexander sent to his sister Catherine. They are mentioned in an evasive way but always with tenderness and propriety; thus the monarch gives news about their health, although he never speaks about his wife Elizabeth. A single reminiscence from Alexander allows us to glimpse the durable passion that united him to Maria Naryshkina, his lack of any guilt toward Elizabeth, and his indifference to her feelings. Many years after the rupture with his mistress, he let escape in a confidence to Countess Edling:

> I am guilty, but not as much as one might think. When unfortunate circumstances troubled my domestic happiness, I attached myself, it is true, to another woman; but I imagined, wrongly no doubt (and I feel it only too much now), that the appearances that united us, my wife and I, were without our participation, and so we were free before God, although joined in the eyes of men. My rank obliged me to respect these appearances, but I thought I could dispose of my own heart, and for fifteen years it was faithful to Madame Naryshkina. I do not have any seduction to reproach myself for. I can say truthfully that the idea of dragging someone to act against her conscience has always horrified me. She found herself in the same situation as me and fell into the same error. We simply imagined we had nothing to reproach ourselves for.[56]

By her marriage and her immense fortune, Maria Naryshkina occupied a privileged position at court; her liaison with the emperor only reinforced it. Always dressed in white, wearing no finery or jewels, Maria displayed a wise and reserved allure, like Madame Récamier in France, that contrasted with the extravagant costumes and insolent luxury of the aristocratic women who surrounded her. As owners of a castle in Florence, a villa in Fiesole, a palace in St. Petersburg (on the Fontanka), and a summer residence on Krestovski Island (located quite close to Alexander's summer residence on Kammeny Island), the Naryshkin couple led a grand life, giving resplendent parties whose gaiety and good taste entranced their contemporaries. However, while Maria drowned herself in partying, she behaved throughout her liaison with the emperor with great discretion, never participating in intrigues or imposing her views on a political level. In this she disappointed those who hoped that, due to her origins, she would serve the Polish cause. As for Alexander, he proved always very discrete, concerned not to expose to the public eye his second home and his children. Two little Elizabeths, born in 1803 and 1804, both died at an early age, as did Zenaide, born in 1810; surviving were Sophie (born in 1808) and a boy Emmanuel (born in 1814). So the sovereign had founded a second family, and it was as an affectionate father that he behaved with his illegitimate children.[57] He led a conjugal life, going to Maria Naryshkina's every day and spending the evenings there. In the archives of the Hermitage Palace is a short note in English, studiously written in big letters by little Sophie (then aged five), that attests to the tender feelings:

My dear papa,
    I am very sorry that you hurt yourself. I hope you will soon be well for I long to see you.
    I think of you every day. I send you my love and a kiss.
    Your little affectionate Sophy [58]

Later, even when fickle Maria was deceiving him (and it is not certain that little Emmanuel was really Alexander's son), the emperor wanted to ensure in a generous and permanent way the material and financial future of his illegitimate children. One month after Emmanuel's birth in 1814, Alexander sent a letter to her husband, Dimitri Naryshkin, that was unambiguous:

> Taking a sincere interest in the well-being of your family, I have decreed in conformity with your desires the following provisions: 1) All the goods and property left upon your death will be divided between the brother Emmanuel and his sisters Marina [Naryshkin's older daughter] and Sophie, according to the law. 2) Consequently there will be an estimate of the property given to Emmanuel and Sophie, and the equivalent amount will be paid to your older daughter Marina by my office. [...] If I cannot in my lifetime myself execute these provisions, I charge my heirs with fulfilling this obligation so dear to my heart.[59]

But while Alexander felt no remorse, this radiant and happy family life proved particularly painful for the childless Elizabeth.

Officially, appearances were saved, and the tsar continued to proclaim tenderness and respect for Elizabeth. But the simplicity of the life they led at court—the emperor and his family only appeared in regalia on festival days and Sundays, returning from mass and taking dinner inside their apartments, away from courtiers—and Alexander's lack of interest in ceremonies and splendor kept Elizabeth very isolated, on the margins not only of power and honors but also of the simplest family pleasures. No doubt she carried her own share of responsibility. In her memoirs, a former lady of honor drew a severe portrait of Elizabeth, implicitly exonerating Alexander from any fault.

> A burning and passionate imagination was combined in her with a cold heart incapable of true affection. These few words explain her story: the nobility of her sentiments, the loftiness of her ideas, the virtuous penchants, and a ravishing face all made her the idol of the crowd—without her being able to bring back her husband. But the praise that flattered her pride could not suffice to

make her happy, and it was only at the end of her life that this princess finally recognized that the affection that alone embellishes existence is won only by giving affection.[60]

Whatever the case, Elizabeth resigned herself as best she could to the existence of the other household, but with no children of her own she found it difficult to bear the repeated pregnancies of Maria Naryshkina. They reminded her of her own maternity, particularly since she had lost a daughter in August 1800. In a letter to her mother (dated June 1804), Elizabeth evoked the suffering caused by the two successive births of the little girls who were the fruit of Alexander's extramarital relationship:

> You have probably not yet received our letters, for Amelia says she told you of the confinement of that Lady,[61] who gave birth to a girl. They say she thinks she is pregnant again; I don't know if this is true, but I will no longer have the goodness to care as I did the first time. Did I tell you, dear Mama, that the first time, she (madame had the impudence to tell me of her first pregnancy, which was so little advanced that I would not have been aware of it, at a ball, and the thing was not as notorious as it is now. I spoke to her as to any other when I asked for news of her health) she told me that she was not well, "since I think I am pregnant." Don't you think, Mama, this was the height of effrontery? She knew very well that I was not ignorant of how she got pregnant. I do not know what will happen and how it will end, but I do know that I will not alter either my character or my health for a creature who is not worth it, for if I have not become misanthropic and hypochondriac, there is some happiness.[62]

A few months later, in December 1804, Elizabeth announced to her mother that the newborn was dead like the previous baby girl. This was an opportunity for the empress to speak obliquely of her jealousy of Maria Naryshkina at the same time as of her own distress, diminished by the solicitude shown by Maria Feodorovna:

> I do not know if Amelia has written to you of an event that has struck me, and would make me believe in a just Providence, if I did not already. It is the death of that baby, whose existence and birth had caused me so much pain. It really seems that Providence does not want to suffer an illegitimate child in this family. It was in August that this death occurred, and I felt sorry for the emperor from the bottom of my heart because he was keenly and deeply afflicted for almost a week, but the mother consoled herself quickly,

because without that he would not be consoled either. Moreover, she lost another child last winter—and danced three weeks later. The friendship that I showed on that occasion, without effort (for she is and will always be in my heart on his account), and the way I shared in his pain earned me almost tenderness on his part, but for two weeks only. Moreover, he is very good for me when we are together, but these moments are neither long nor frequent. As for my manner toward him, Mama, I cannot give you better testimony than to convey the opinion of his mother, who certainly must be more partial than any other woman, who constantly tells me that she finds me perfectly good for him. She says she has a great desire to see him entirely back with me, and I cannot believe she is not sincere, judging from the really loving advice that she gives me.[63]

Despite everything, despite the praise she always received from observers at court, the young empress, then aged 25, suffered terribly from not being a mother. In 1802 she did return to Adam Czartoryski, who had come back to Russia at Alexander's request, but their liaison remained sterile—to Elizabeth's great distress.

In the course of 1803, Elizabeth met at court a handsome captain of the Guard, then aged 23, Alexis Okhotnikov. She started to be interested in him, and he fell under the charm of the empress, but their mutual passion was only declared at the end of 1805 or the start of 1806.[64] Elizabeth then broke off with Adam Czartoryski and became this young man's mistress, but this ardent love affair ended tragically. In October, leaving a St. Petersburg theater, Okhotnikov was stabbed by an unknown person. After having seen Elizabeth several times come to his bedside incognito, he died of his wounds in January 1807. Constantine was no doubt the one who ordered the murder without his older brother's knowledge: for him, this passion was all the more degrading because the empress had become pregnant by the captain, and so it was an unbearable insult to the prestige of a brother to whom he professed immense affection. So while Okhotnikov was dying in prolonged agony, Elizabeth gave birth in November 1806 to a daughter, also given the name Elizabeth. This birth, which everyone in the imperial family knew was illegitimate (Alexander had confided to his mother and those close to him that he had not had sexual relations with Elizabeth for several years), was received coldly. However, appearances were maintained at court since the birth was greeted with an official announcement. Deeply affected by the death of Okhotnikov, Elizabeth focused all her tenderness and love on the baby girl. However, in May 1808, eighteen months after her birth, little Lisinka died of a dental abscess, leaving her mother brokenhearted. In a few short years Elizabeth's life had tipped into tragedy, at the very moment that Alexander on his side was enjoying marital and family happiness.

The years from 1801 to 1805 were thus dense years in the life of Emperor Alexander. Placed politically and socially under the aegis of reform, they brought about modest but concrete reforms, emblematic of a desire for change. On the personal level they were dominated by a love affair that, outside the ties of marriage, gave the sovereign a full but discrete family life. But they were also marked by intense diplomatic turmoil: the international context was becoming increasingly uncertain and arousing growing worries.

CHAPTER 7

On the International Stage

1801–1805

Confirming his first declarations in 1801, Alexander I made himself the herald of a pacifist European policy—at least until 1804–1805. For the tsar, the moment belonged to domestic reforms and to a lesser extent to territorial advances toward the south. But this neutrality could not resist the rising power of Napoleonic ambitions, and from 1804–1805 the tsar launched into political and ideological combat (as well as diplomatic struggle) against Napoleon.

Pacifist in Europe, Expansionist to the South

Between 1801 and 1804 Alexander I wanted to be a resolute partisan of a cautious and pacifist policy in Europe. Viktor Kochubey, his vice-minister of foreign affairs, thought the same: Russia should hold herself apart from conflicts in which in the past she had got imprudently and expensively involved. Rather than going astray on the international stage, it was necessary to engage in major interior reforms. However, this credo did not prevent the tsar from observing with a sharply critical mind the political evolution of France and the diplomatic evolution of Europe.

From his accession Alexander wished to reestablish peaceful relations with all countries of Europe—in particular with Britain and France. He declared himself ready, if necessary, to serve as mediator between the two warring powers. But this facade of neutrality did not prevent the emperor from expressing preferences: in his instructions in July 1801 to Count Morkov, his new minister plenipotentiary departing for Paris, Alexander specified that "it is with the courts of Vienna, London, and Berlin that the general interest, as well as that of my empire, brings me to desire a solid union."[1] The statement was unambiguous.

On June 17 the tsar signed a maritime convention with Britain, prepared at the instigation of the Anglophiles at court, Count Panin and Ambassador Simon Vorontsov. With two separate articles and another secret one, it constituted a de facto peace treaty, achieved at the cost of mutual concessions.[2] Russia renounced any attempt to reinforce the Second League of Armed Maritime Neutrality founded by Paul I in 1800 with Prussia, Denmark, and Sweden. Nevertheless, Britain did not manage to entice Russia alongside it into a war against France, despite the pressure exerted in July 1801 by Panin, who thought the interests of the two countries were convergent: British maritime and commercial power was not a danger to Russia, whereas the despotism and ambitions of France represented a great threat to all of Europe.[3] He wrote in a memorandum to the tsar in July 1801 that "political and commercial relations between our Court and that of London are based on a perfect identity of interests, and the impossibility that they might clash as long as both follow healthy policies."[4] But Alexander chose not to go further, in order to keep his hands free. He did not share Panin's Anglophilia; influenced by the Enlightenment and his French education, he felt no particular attraction to the British political model.[5] In 1801 it was reasons of state that dictated this rapprochement, and he had to remain cautious.

In parallel, the new sovereign tried to establish relations of trust with Austria. In September 1801 Count Razumovsky was named ambassador to Vienna and was supposed to obtain for Russia a cooperation with Austria over German matters—preserving the interests of small German states from any foreign ambition, whether French or Austrian—as well as Turkish affairs, to ensure the territorial integrity of the Ottoman Empire.

Finally, while he did not wish to go so far as the alliance to which Paul aspired at the end of his reign, the tsar sought peace with France too. In April 1801 Alexander granted a pleasant interview with Duroc, the aide-de-camp sent by the First Consul to the court of St. Petersburg, conveying these views:

> I have always desired to see France and Russia united; they are two great and powerful nations that have given each other proof of esteem; they should agree to put a stop to the small divisions on the continent. [...] I would very much like to speak directly with the First Consul, whose loyal character is well-known to me.[6]

In the course of this meeting, the tsar called for the reestablishment of peace in Europe; for this purpose, he proved understanding about the occupation of Egypt by the French armies, but he also reasserted, due to treaties and commitments previously made by Russia, his position as "protector" of the kings of Sardinia and Naples. In the July 1801 instructions to his envoy Morkov, who was heading for Paris, the tsar said he was favorable to peace with France, which he saw as a pledge for the restoration of peace to Europe.[7] But his instructions were very clear on this point: there would be no question of concluding a rapprochement at any price whatever, nor of appearing to admit any weakness. He wrote with an assurance and firmness surprising on the part of a young man who had just arrived on the throne and had little experience on the diplomatic level:

> If the First Consul of the French republic continues to make the maintenance and firmness of his power depend on the discord and troubles that agitate Europe [...], if he lets himself be carried away by the torrent of revolution, if he trusts in fortune alone, then war might be prolonged. [...] In this order of things, if my concern for the reestablishment of general tranquility is only feebly endorsed, then the negotiator in charge of my interests in France should confine himself to observing the march of the government and chatting to pass the time until more propitious circumstances allow the use of more effective means.[8]

In this spirit a peace treaty was signed between France and Russia on October 8, 1801, followed two days later by a secret convention. Article 1 of the agreement reestablished "normal" diplomatic relations on the model of relations prior to 1789. Each party promised to grant no support, military or financial, to internal or external enemies of the other. Russia recognized French territorial acquisitions, and France agreed to pay the King of Sardinia compensation in exchange for his possessions lost in Piedmont. The accord guaranteed the independence of the Ionian islands, forbidding any foreign power from keeping troops there. The French army would withdraw from the Kingdom of Naples as soon as the fate of Egypt was decided; the latter's neutrality would be recognized and guaranteed by the two powers; Russia would try to obtain from Great Britain and the Ottoman Empire their recognition of this neutrality. Finally, the two countries declared themselves in favor of cooperation on the matter of what territorial compensation to grant to German principalities that had lost possessions on the left bank of the Rhine.

But signing this agreement changed nothing about the order of imperial priorities: for Alexander I the entente with Britain was prime. In October he did refuse a military alliance proposed by Britain, judging it premature. But an Anglo-Russian rapprochement remained his goal, as he stressed in a letter to Ambassador Vorontsov in November 1801. Alexander authorized him to inform the British government of the tenor of the accord concluded with Paris, including if necessary its "secret" clauses—which speaks volumes about the emperor's double game—and he stressed his intention not to engage further in special relations with France:

> I leave to your judgment whether to communicate to the British minister the acts that were concluded in Paris, either entirely or in part, thereby showing them my frankness and securing their assurance that the secret conditions will not be revealed. I think it is necessary on this occasion to communicate (for your information alone) that I absolutely do not intend to enter with the French government into any ulterior plan whatever, and that Talleyrand's reference to some ulterior entente in his meetings with Count Morcoff could only relate [...] to concerted measures relative to German affairs.[9]

Thus, throughout 1801 the tsar felt a distrust toward Bonaparte's France that pushed him to get closer to legitimist European monarchs—even while he remained attached to his liberal convictions—and to diversity his interlocutors. From this perspective Alexander decided to visit the King of Prussia, Frederick-Wilhelm, and Queen Louise, sticking to the planned trip despite the signing on March 25, 1802, of the Peace of Amiens between France and England.

At the tsar's initiative plans for the visit were formed at the end of 1801 and were warmly welcomed by the royal couple, who hoped in fact to sound out Alexander and if possible obtain his support on the current issue between France and Russia, i.e., German reparations. The emperor's goals were less precise: it was a matter of diversifying Russia's diplomatic contacts and asserting sympathy, mixed with the admiration that (like his father and grandfather) he felt for Prussia and the Prussians. However, the plan for a private trip met opposition from Czartoryski and Kochubey, who saw it as an unwise diplomatic choice. In December 1801, in a letter to Simon Vorontsov, Kochubey expressed his alarm at Alexander's pro-Prussian sentiments and the parallel diplomacy to which the tsar was resorting:

> I saw him on this occasion—as on so many others—briefed in the most favorable manner on the King of Prussia personally and on his ministers. I discovered that this prince had written individual letters to the emperor, of which [our] ministry here had no knowledge. This correspondence, and even more so the approaches by the hereditary Prince of Mecklenburg, the Duke of Holstein, and all this family of ministers we had seen in Pavlovsk, had left (I believe) deep traces that are undoubtedly harmful to an impartial system that, in my opinion, is most suitable for us.[10]

The plan for the trip also ran up against repeated warnings from Maria Feodorovna; although of German origin, she feared that this initiative, reminding the Russian court of the blindly pro-Prussian commitments of Peter III and then Paul I, would arouse visceral reactions within the army, even suspicions of a plot. But Alexander ignored the criticism: he was determined to carry out this trip, and in fact its diplomatic consequences would prove important—to Kochubey's great regret, as shown in his correspondence. When the tsar was on the point of leaving in June 1802, Kochubey had just sent to Simon Vorontsov a dispatch in which his discontent wrestled with his desire to clear himself of any responsibility in the affair:

> I hope, my dear friend, to have no need to assure you that I had no part in such an impolitic initiative, and it was not up to me to prevent it. It seems that the emperor, without saying anything to anybody, had last year promised the King of Prussia to meet him somewhere on the border, and everything was arranged through the hereditary prince of Mecklenburg, his brother-in-law, a sot of the first order. Three weeks ago, summoned to Court, I was told by the emperor of this trip and ordered to get ready to travel. I was then (and I am still) very angry. Who will imagine that two sovereigns are going to review a few regiments? At bottom that is what it will be, but who will imagine that a minister of foreign affairs had no knowledge of this jaunt? Yet this is only too true. Whatever the case, I am accompanying the emperor.[11]

En route, accompanied by Kochubey, Novosiltsev, and Grand Marshal Count Tolstoy, Alexander stopped at Narva, then at Tartu, where he visited the university, before staying two days in Riga, where he was warmly welcomed by the population of Lithuania. And on June 10, after nine days of traveling, the tsar made his entry into Memel.

* * *

Received with luster and sympathy by the royal couple, the young sovereign was soon caught up in a whirlwind of receptions, parades, parties, and balls given in his honor for almost a week. At the Prussian court everybody judged him to be as handsome as he was considerate and kind; Queen Louise, then age 26, was soon captivated by his charm. In return he was conquered by the queen's beauty, culture, and intelligence, but the relationship remained platonic despite the temptations offered to the seductive Russian tsar, as he admitted to Czartoryski:

> After one of the interviews with the Prussian Court, the emperor, who was smitten elsewhere at the time, told me he had been seriously alarmed by the arrangement of rooms that communicated with his own and that at night he locked himself in so nobody came in to surprise him and induce him into dangerous temptations that he wanted to avoid. He even declared this forthrightly to the two princesses[12] with more frankness than gallantry and courtesy.[13]

Remaining within suitable limits, the relationship formed between Louise and Alexander coincided with the cordial sentiments that were quickly established between the tsar and Frederick-Wilhelm. In only a few days close ties were sealed, placing Prussia under the "protective" wing of Russia.

In his memoirs Czartoryski strongly criticizes Alexander for his attitude, reproaching him for having in the name of chivalric chimeras committed Russian diplomacy to a direction that was not in accord with its interests. According to him, it was a harebrained idea shared neither by Russian diplomats nor by Prussian ones.

> Relations with Prussia were all personal between the two sovereigns, and there was scarcely any sympathy between the cabinets. And the opinion of [our] army and [our] salons was no more favorable to Prussia: its equivocal conduct, its flat submission to France, and the acquisitions that this submission had secured it, were badly viewed by the Russians, who did not spare their sarcasm. Yet the emperor was faithful to his friendship with the king and the high opinion he had formed of the Prussian army.[14]

However, this negative verdict should be moderated. If after 1802 the Prussian component assumed a significant weight in Russian foreign policy, this was due to the imperial desire to guarantee in principle a balance among states, as much as to Alexander's feelings for Queen Louise or his fascination with Prussia's grand past. Moreover, if sympathy for Prussia pushed the tsar to take a close interest in German compensations, he did not forget the interests of the smaller German states with which he had many familial ties. His grandfather was born Duke of Holstein-Gottorp, his grandmother Catherine II was called Sophia Frederica Augusta of Anhalt-Zerbst, his mother was Sophie-Dorothea de Württemberg, he had married Louise of Baden and his brother Constantine a princess of Saxe-Coburg-Saalfeld. All this explained the personal interest Alexander had in the issue of compensations for Germany and the diplomatic effort he exerted for this purpose. In June 1802 the Russian sovereign asked his ambassador in Paris to prepare a bilateral convention on territorial changes to be planned for Germany; in August he pleaded during discussions held in the German sovereigns' diet in favor of the interests of Prussia and of the small German states so dear to him—and he managed to be effective. During the meeting of the imperial deputation in March 1803, a plan for territorial reparations was officially presented by France and Russia. Adopted by the diet a month later, this text was confirmed by Emperor Franz of Austria in May 1803. It gave several substantial advantages to Prussia: dispossessed of 127,000 subjects on the left bank of the Rhine, it recuperated more than 500,000 elsewhere; and as regards the Grand Duchy of Baden, after having lost 30,000 subjects, it obtained almost 30,000 others, gaining the towns of Heidelberg (with its prestigious old university) and Mannheim.

So, on German issues the Franco-Russian rapprochement achieved concrete results that, without affecting Russia's vital interests, brought it some diplomatic advantages. On the one hand, Alexander was able to advance the interests of German principalities, and on the other hand, for little expense he had demonstrated his loyalty with regard to France. But at the end of 1802, the French refusal to take account of Russian intercession in favor of the king of Piedmont-Sardinia was a first source of tension between the two powers, pushing Russia gradually along the path to an alliance with England. Alexander I, still attached to peace, profited from the interval to reorganize the administration of foreign affairs.

In September 1802 the creation of a new Ministry of Foreign Affairs was accompanied by the dismissal of Victor Kochubey, whose attachment to the principle of Russian diplomatic neutrality was increasingly out of phase with Alexander's perspective, and the appointment of the very Anglophile Count Alexander Vorontsov (1741–1805). He was undeniably an experienced diplomat: he had been successively chargé d'affaires in Austria (1761–1762), minister plenipotentiary in England (1764–1768) and then Holland; he had participated in the negotiation and signing of agreements with France (1786), with the king of Naples and the king of Portugal (1787), and with Sweden (1790); finally, he had negotiated the Treaty of Jassy with the Ottoman Empire (1791), before being dismissed in 1792. At his side Prince Czartoryski was promoted to vice-minister.

The same day, on September 20, a second decree confirmed the existence of the Colleges of War, Admiralty, and Foreign Affairs. In its first years the latter college tended to keep a number of its prerogatives, to the detriment of the corresponding ministry, remaining the body where the empire's foreign policy was elaborated and executed. Moreover, the fact that Vorontsov recruited within the college the experienced civil servants he needed to move the new chancellery forward only accentuated the primacy of the college over the Ministry of Foreign Affairs, further confusing the boundaries between the old and the new structures.[15] But the authority of the ministry was gradually asserted; its new chancellery was composed of four departments or "expeditions": the first managed Asian affairs; the second, Ottoman affairs, the mission to Constantinople, and commercial issues; the third, the Russian diplomats and chargé d'affaires in posts abroad; and the fourth, relations with representatives from foreign countries who were posted in Russia. The division of these various responsibilities into distinct departments aimed to ensure a clearer and more rational working of the ministry.

With the agreement of Alexander I, Vorontsov recruited as diplomats both foreigners and non-Russian speaking subjects of the empire whom he judged to be best qualified: French émigrés brought to Russian soil by the tumult of the Revolution, as well as German aristocrats from the Baltic provinces like Count Lieven (future ambassador to London) and Count Stackelberg (who would be sent to Vienna). An old tradition—one that was now more widespread than under the reign of Catherine II—this recruitment of non-Russian speakers did not fail to arouse criticism from a Russian nobility that felt itself dispossessed of its rights, as well as doubts about the capacity of western Europeans to understand and serve the interests of the Russian Empire.

In early 1804 a sick Vorontsov left Foreign Affairs, and the post of minister then fell to Prince Czartoryski—to the annoyance of a certain number of diplomats, courtiers, and some close to Alexander, including his mother, who were either worried or furious to see responsibility for all Russian diplomacy incumbent on a Pole, although he was a subject of the Russian Empire. But battling winds and tides, Alexander imposed his choice and would keep Czartoryski in his post until June 1806, when he would be dismissed due to his opposition to the rapprochement with Prussia and to the entry of Russia into the new coalition.

In parallel with the reorganization of the administration of foreign affairs, Alexander began to study restructuring the army, its organization, and how it worked. Wanting to introduce reforms, he called upon Arakcheev.

In April 1803, three years after having been exiled to his estates by Paul I, Arakcheev received a message from Alexander, calling him back to St. Petersburg. Arakcheev obeyed and arrived in the capital in May, to be named inspector general of artillery and commander of the artillery battalion of the Guard; the tsar gave him carte blanche to reorganize and reinforce the artillery. Arakcheev applied himself to the task, beginning by inspecting over several months the regiments of the imperial army, which then included 446,000 men. From his observations he concluded that it would be desirable to separate artillery from infantry and give artillery its own chain of command and its own resources, and that it should cease being considered as simply support for the infantry. From this perspective he founded artillery schools for officers and troops and created a magazine, the Artillery Review, whose purpose was to arouse an esprit de corps among gunners. However, this reform aroused criticism from infantry officers, and as we shall see, during the first engagements against Bonaparte, it was not yet fully operational.[16]

The reorganization of Foreign Affairs and the beginnings of restructuring the army unfolded as Alexander (still a pacifist in European issues) led a much more aggressive policy in the south.

At his accession, as we remember, the tsar was not in favor of the annexation of the kingdom of Kartl-Kakhetia that had begun under Paul's reign. And he only gradually rallied to the arguments of those within the Permanent Council who defended it. But once this decision was ratified, Alexander engaged in an expansionist policy in the Caucasus, extending the authority of the Russian Empire over small independent states to the west and situated on the border of the Black Sea, using the establishment of political protectorates that would lead after varying periods to pure and simple annexations. Thus, in 1803 the principality of Mingrelia, a year later the kingdom of Imereti, and then the principality of Guria passed successively under Russian control.

The object of imperial covetousness was, of course, the innumerable natural resources of the Caucasus—in addition to the mines, there were silk and the madder of the Transcaucasus, the cotton of eastern Armenia—and the ambition to increase the volume of Russian exports to the Ottoman Empire and Persia. But it was also a matter of taking into account the strategic role of the Caucasus as a "buffer zone" against the Ottomans and Persians.

Establishing Russia in the Caucasus soon translated into tangible advantages: whereas in 1802 the countries of Asia represented only 3.3 percent of Russian exports, this rose to 30 percent in 1827, testifying to the growing role played by this region in imperial commerce. But it soon also posed problems on the domestic and foreign levels.

In the case of the ancient kingdom of Kartl-Kakhetia, the choice of annexation implied setting up a Russian administration staffed by Russian civil servants that referred largely to Georgian laws and customs. But once in place this administration made clumsy missteps and humiliated the Georgian nobility, which was now dispossessed of any power. By 1802 this aroused serious anti-Russian ferment. In response, Alexander named

General Tsitsianov as commander general of the Caucasus; the descendant of a Georgian prince who had supported Russia, he appeared to the tsar as a providential man: nominating a general to this post was significant of Alexander's will to quickly integrate the Caucasus into the empire. So, the sovereign expected much from Tsitsianov and his knowledge of Georgia. But Tsitsianov quickly made himself the violent champion of an authoritarian order, someone who despised the indigenous people. In a short time his methods resulted in a Georgian revolt that burst out in 1804; two years later, when Tsitsianov mounted an offensive against Persia destined to seize the principality of Baku, he was brutally assassinated there.

Thus Russian settlement in the Transcaucasus appeared particularly fragile, even more so because it also ran up against international obstacles: it contravened both the interests of the shah of Persia, dispossessed by the Russians of his territories, and the interests of the Ottoman Empire, traditionally attached to the same region. In 1806, at the height of the conflict between Russians and Ottomans, the Imeretians,[17] hostile to Russian tutelage, made common cause with the Ottomans. At the start of Alexander's reign, expansionism into the Transcaucasus was proving a difficult process on both military and diplomatic levels.

The scope of the obstacles and the military and human cost of this engagement convinced Alexander that he should stand apart from the European theater in order to avoid having to fight on several fronts. But French schemes ended up trumping this guiding principle.

Throughout the years from 1801 to 1803, Alexander tried to be pacifist, but this did not prevent him from becoming increasingly critical of the First Consul, as the topics of dissension between France and Russia kept multiplying. In a letter sent to Laharpe in July 1803, which says a lot about his own state of mind and the strength of his liberal convictions, the young emperor vividly deplored the "treachery" of Bonaparte and his evolution toward a form of power that was increasingly personal and "tyrannical":

> Like you, dear friend, I have reconsidered my opinion of the first consul. Since becoming Consul for Life, the veil has fallen and things have gone from bad to worse. He began by depriving himself of the finest glory reserved for a human that it remained for him to gather: proving that he was working without any selfish interest, solely for the happiness and glory of his country and faithful to the constitution to which he himself swore, to relinquish after ten years the power he held in his hands. Instead of that, he has preferred to mimic [royal] courts while violating his country's constitution. Now he is one of the most infamous tyrants that history has produced.[18]

In 1803 the tsar and Vorontsov were still trying to stall, avoiding any confrontation with Bonaparte, while showing increased Russian interest in European affairs. In July 1803 d'Oubril, the Russian chargé d'affaires in Paris, expressed to Bonaparte's foreign minister Talleyrand the tsar's desire to reestablish peace in Europe and to guarantee it by respecting the equality among states.

> Far from wanting to rekindle the fire of war on the continent, His Majesty's heart's desire would be to make it cease everywhere, but he also wishes that the French government, since it declares it has the same wish, would leave at rest those who have the strongest desire not to take part. His Majesty's sole desire is for peace to be reborn in Europe, for nobody to try to arrogate any supremacy at all, and for the French government also to recognize the equality of states that are less strong but just as independent as it is. Russia, one cannot repeat enough, has no desire or interest in making war. It is the force of circumstances that will dictate the position it will take.[19]

However, the emperor's attachment to peace whatever the cost in the name of national interest was arousing critical reactions and even anguish. Joseph de Maistre, ambassador of Sardinia in St. Petersburg, wrote testily in May 1803:

> Russia, assuming a more threatening attitude and raising its voice, could easily have restored some kind of equilibrium to Europe, but just try to put such ideas into a head stuffed by la Harpe! The emperor of Russia has only two thoughts, "peace and the economy."[20]

The meeting between d'Oubril and Talleyrand having got no reaction from the French, the tsar was confirmed in this negative opinion of Bonaparte, though he did not opt for an aggressive policy toward France. His priority always remained neutrality in European affairs in order to have room to maneuver in his policy of southern expansion. But this preference could not resist either the evolution in Balkan affairs or the scandal provoked in Russia (as everywhere in Europe) by the kidnapping by French dragoons of the Duke d'Enghien (the last Bourbon survivor of the House of Condé) and his execution.

In July 1802 a peace treaty between France and the Ottoman Empire had been signed that caused worry among Russian diplomats because since 1799 the Turks had been tied by an alliance that guaranteed Russian ships free access to the Dardanelles and Bosphorus straits. At the same time the concentration of French troops in Italy, ready to intervene in the Balkan provinces of the Ottoman Empire, and more generally France's new interest in the region, both thwarted Russian diplomacy; for several decades Russia had considered the region a zone of privileged influence. Russian reaction came soon: although the 1801 agreement with France had stated that the Ionian Islands would be free of all foreign troops, in the month of August, with the active support of Kochubey (who in February had declared himself in favor), 1,600 troops were sent from Odessa to make the islands a Russian military base. By autumn 1804 there were almost 11,000 Russian soldiers and 16 warships in the archipelago, and a military advisor for their defense was set up in Corfu at Alexander's request.[21] These measures show the tsar's singular strategy: he wanted to make the strategically important islands a symbolic space where Russian domination would prove infinitely more lenient than French domination, as well as a laboratory for experimenting with a constitution. It was this dual plan that lay behind the preparation in 1803 of a constitution, drafted by the viceroy of the islands, Count Mocenigo, and then refined in St. Petersburg by a German jurist from Latvia, Baron Gustav Rosenkampf. It created an Ionian senate of 17 members holding executive power and initiating laws, a chamber of representatives that would vote on those laws, and a college of three censors supervising respect for (and application of) this constitution. These three bodies were elected by peer assemblies, including not only the hereditary landed aristocracy but also the upper bourgeoisie and senior figures in commerce, industry, arts, and sciences. This achievement is what must have led the tsar later to tell Napoleon that in this region he had helped to create "a qualified constitutional nobility" while preserving the hereditary aristocracy.[22]

At the same time French intrigues in the Balkans caused intense discussions in the emperor's entourage.[23] Alexander Vorontsov took a position in a report presented in November 1803: the French advances in Italy and the Balkans were direct threats to Russian interests because they aimed in time to dismember the Ottoman Empire for France's benefit.[24] Czartoryski's analysis was subtler: he was not so vehemently alarmed about the danger from France but suggested a rapprochement with England with a view to an alliance.[25] Thus, Russia began envisaging a war against France in the winter of 1803–1804. In March 1804 Czartoryski confirmed in writing to Vorontsov that Alexander I was ready to enter into a struggle against Napoleon as soon as circumstances required it, while calling for consultations with England on the Balkan issues and still hoping to avoid war.[26]

In this tense context the kidnapping of the Duke d'Enghien in March 1804 in Baden, a German territory particularly dear to the tsar's family (the empress was born Louisa of Baden), and then his summary execution back in France caused grief and anger at the Russian court as soon as it was learned. For the monarch and those around him, it was an intolerable provocation. In a dispatch to his sovereign in April, Joseph de Maistre wrote:

> Indignation is at its height. The good empresses cried over it. Grand Duke [Constantine] is furious and his Imperial Majesty no less deeply affected. The French legation is no longer received or spoken to. [...] The emperor is in mourning and notice of a seven-day mourning has been sent to the whole diplomatic corps. Today there is a service in the Catholic Church. [...] I have never seen such emphatic public opinion.[27]

For Alexander, French violation of the neutrality of Baden and its contempt for international law demonstrated, if there was still need, how dangerous Bonaparte's power was, and he took the incident as a personal affront that convinced him of the need to oppose the First Consul, whatever the cost. On April 17 a meeting of the council of state gathered around the tsar:[28] all its members plus the Count of Morkov, General Budberg, and Prince Czartoryski (de facto minister of foreign affairs since Vorontsov had retired for health reasons). At seven p.m. Czartoryski opened the meeting with a text he had prepared overnight at the tsar's request:[29]

> His Imperial Majesty, indignant over an infraction as glaring as possible against what the equity and law of nations can prescribe as most obligatory, feels repugnance at keeping relations any longer with a government that knows neither brake nor duty of any kind, and which, stained by an atrocious assassination, can now be regarded only as a brigands' lair.[30]

Alexander wanted to break off diplomatic relations with France: Russia would now quit the uncomfortable position of mediator it had occupied until now and from which it had gained nothing: England continued to occupy Malta, Bonaparte had refused any compensation to the king of Piedmont Sardinia, and France had not ceased growing in power and influence in the Balkans, the Near East, Italy, and Germany. The majority of those present at the council, including Kochubey and Czartoryski, spoke in a single voice and encouraged the sovereign to make a political alliance against France with England, Austria, and Prussia. But a few called for moderation, like Rumyantsev (minister of commerce) and Zavadovski (education); they considered that Russia should not get mixed up in German affairs and that the death of the duke, as reprehensible as it was, did not contravene Russian interests.[31] These different viewpoints led

Alexander to a more nuanced position: he gave up the idea of breaking off diplomatic relations and upon this advice simply marked his discontent publicly. He also sent to the Imperial Diet a solemn protest against the violation of Baden territory, while the tone of letters exchanged between Russian and French diplomats grew increasingly sharp. By the intermediary of his representative in Paris, d'Oubril, Alexander demanded that the freedom and security of Germany be assured and again demanded the evacuation of the kingdom of Naples and compensation for the kingdom of Piedmont Sardinia. At the same time the tsar opened negotiations with Emperor Franz of Austria; in April 1804 the latter declared himself ready to supply an army of 200,000 men in case of conflict with Napoleon, but Alexander preferred a defensive alliance. He still hoped to avoid war, although the international situation was deteriorating constantly. Not only were the Russian demands not accepted by French diplomats, but a stinging note sent on May 16, 1804, by Talleyrand (French minister of foreign relations) to d'Oubril added still more dissension. After stressing that "the First Consul does not meddle in parties or opinions that might divide Russia, therefore His Majesty the Emperor has no right to meddle in parties and opinions that might divide France," Talleyrand perfidiously remarked that "the complaint that Russia raises today leads to wondering whether, when England was contemplating the assassination of Paul I, if it had been known that the authors of plots were found a league from the border, someone would not have been in a hurry to have them seized."[32] His provocative sally was to make the tsar deeply and lastingly resentful of both Talleyrand and Napoleon. Then d'Oubril got the order to leave Paris with all the staff of the Russian legation, and General Hédouville, who had become persona non grata at the Russian court, went back to France at Napoleon's request. Soon the only person left in St. Petersburg was a simple chargé d'affaires, Rayneval, to deal with current issues.

Before his departure d'Oubril tried again to avoid war by sending an ultimatum to Talleyrand on July 21. But while on Napoleon's order Talleyrand was procrastinating, France was making military preparations. The French minister only sent his "negative" response to d'Oubril on August 28; at the same time he expressed his consummate contempt for Russian diplomats, as attested by a note to French representatives abroad on August 2:

> There is perhaps no court as devoid of able men as that of Russia. M. de Morkov is an eagle there. The Vorontsovs are well-known for being all English. [...] They are no longer Russians; for a long time this British faction has sought to sell the national interests of Russia to the cabinet in London.[33]

D'Oubril left his post in Paris in August 1804, but Russia did not immediately embark on a war with France. The tsar was now convinced that Russia could no longer stand apart from European issues and should therefore oppose Napoleon's ambitions. For him it was crucial to make a military entente against the French emperor, but this alliance had to be given an ideological dimension, by pledging to an ambitious plan for Europe. This was the source of the diplomatic mission on which he sent Novosiltsev in September 1804, when Rayneval in turn left St. Petersburg.

Commitment against Napoleon

In 1803, when he was still only a personal advisor for diplomatic affairs, Prince Adam Czartoryski (at the tsar's request) wrote with the aid of his Italian secretary, the former abbot Piatoli,[34] a long Memorandum on the political system that Russia ought to follow, which would be completed in 1804 by an Article for the arrangement of affairs in Europe after a successful war.[35]

Calling on Russia to conduct a policy that was "generous and great" for "the general good of nations," Czartoryski first proposed ending the Napoleonic expansionism judged to be intolerable and doing so by committing Russia to a military alliance with England. However, once the enemy was defeated, Russia should not remain there but consolidate this alliance by setting up a European system based on new foundations. Under the leadership of Russia and England, this new system should make peace in Europe its prime goal and should seek to manage international relations by resorting to reasoned arguments and by refusing the "state of nature"[36] that currently dominated. For Czartoryski it was a matter of transferring onto the international scale the Enlightenment values of reason, openness, and tolerance.

This new system would be inscribed—the second important idea in the memorandum—in a European space that Czartoryski suggested be modeled on two key principles: liberalism and (an unprecedented) respect for nationalities. Behind this adherence to the principle of nationalities, perceived as a prime factor in the reconstructed system, lay no doubt the patriotic sentiment of a Polish prince in the face of the painful disappearance of his country over three successive divisions at the end of the eighteenth century. But we should also detect the influence of some philosophers, including Herder. Like him, Czartoryski saw nations as organic groups "with their own ways of seeing and feeling"[37] that should under no circumstance suffer from foreign domination, which is "contrary to the balance of things."[38]

These two principles led to defining the European system as an ensemble of liberal states, organized into republics or constitutional monarchies that respected the principle of nationality. From this perspective states could take the form of either nation-states (the case of France but also Switzerland or ideally Poland) or else federal states (he envisaged the creation of federations in northern Italy and in Germany). Finally Czartoryski mentioned the case of the Ottoman Empire: if it crumbled, then distinct states should be fostered but united in a federation "on which Russia might have a decisive and legal influence by means of the title of emperor or else 'protector of the Slavs and of the Orient' that would be given to His Imperial Majesty."[39]

These texts—and the master idea that underlay them of establishing a Russian-British alliance—caught the tsar's interest. When in August 1804 the fall of the British minister Addington led to Pitt's becoming prime minister, it seemed a propitious occasion for a rapprochement, and Alexander took the decision to send to London a secret emissary, his personal friend Count Novosiltsev. Unknown to Simon Vorontsov, his ambassador in post whom he suspected of being blinded by his Anglophilia, the tsar gave Novosiltsev the mission of negotiating secretly with the new prime minister toward a rapprochement that was not just limited to anti-Napoleonic tactics but might evolve toward an ambitious program to reconstruct Europe. To explain his objectives, Alexander gave Novosiltsev his Secret Instructions[40] on the eve of his departure (September 11, 1804 [O.S.]).

* * *

From the start—and this is crucial—the tsar was making his project part of a major ideological struggle that was to be won against Napoleon. For him, Napoleonic propaganda had cleverly manipulated for its own benefit certain principles and ideas that now had to be reappropriated. Thus Alexander asserted:

> The most powerful weapon the French have used until the present and with which they still threaten all countries, is the universal opinion they have been able to spread that their cause is that of liberty and the prosperity of peoples. It would be shameful for humanity if such a fine cause had to be considered as specific to a government that in no way merits being its defender. It would be dangerous for all states to leave any longer to the French the marked advantage of keeping up this appearance. The good of humanity, the true interest of

legal authorities, and the success of an enterprise that the two powers[41] would propose must require that they tear from the French this formidable weapon, appropriate it, and use it against them.[42]

The stakes being established, the tsar said he was favorable to an alliance between Britain and Russia that might have "a really useful and benevolent goal,"[43] and in his Instructions he details his conception.

On the political level he begins by mentioning the cases of countries subject to French tutelage and says he is favorable to the reestablishment of the king of Sardinia on this throne—provided that Russia and England jointly agree to exhort the king to "give his people a free and wise constitution"; he wants to guarantee the existence and political organization of Switzerland and Holland, stressing that this should be done out of respect for the national will.[44]

The French case then inspires a very long development: first, it would be unthinkable to reestablish in France any divine-right monarchy:

> Finding it repugnant to make humanity go backward, I would like for the two governments to agree between them that, far from claiming to re-establish, in a country that must be freed from the yoke of Bonaparte, some other abuses and a state of things that minds that have tasted forms of independence could not bear, we will on the contrary try to assure them of freedom founded on veritable bases.[45]

This point shows Alexander's political sense. For him, neither the memory of the French Revolution nor what Napoleon had achieved could be obscured. But his advocacy—surprising in someone who had inherited four years before an autocratic regime of divine right—does not derive from simple opportunism. For a disciple of Laharpe, if it was a matter of taking account of the heritage of the French Revolution and of beating Napoleon on his own ideological ground, then it mattered even more to remodel the European continent according to some principles to which he was attached.

Underlining that the coalition powers "desire nothing other than liberating France from the despotism under which it is groaning and giving her free choice of the government she wants to have,"[46] he declared himself in favor of the institution in France of a constitutional monarchy—if that was the wish of the French.[47] He then enlarged his statements to other European countries, launching into a veritable plea in favor of regimes that respected "the sacred rights of humanity," telling Novosiltsev:

> This is neither the place nor the moment to trace the various forms of government that might be established in these various countries. I leave you complete latitude to deal with the English minister on this important objective. The principles no doubt should be the same everywhere, and above all [we] must agree on this point. Everywhere they should be based on the sacred rights of humanity, producing the order that is its necessary consequence; everywhere the same spirit of wisdom and benevolence should guide institutions. But the application of the same principles might vary from place to place, and the two powers, in order to agree on this, will find the means to procure just, impartial, and detailed facts about each place—which should be trustworthy.[48]

This dense passage reflects Alexander's deep attachment to Enlightenment ideas and illustrates his desire to distinguish himself from Napoleonic practices. By proposing to associate people with the choice of their government, he rejects the Napoleonic method that imposed his model by force of arms. One might naturally object that at the very moment when the tsar was making himself the herald of constitutional and liberal ideas, he remained at the head of an empire that he governed as an autocrat—and that he had refused to grant the Charter to the Russian People. But in his eyes this apparent contradiction was not actually a clash: Russia was simply not yet mature enough for a representative and liberal regime.

On a more geopolitical level the Secret Instructions were even more innovative: they advanced the concept of a European federation.[49] In Alexander's conception it should be built upon respect for human rights and on principles formalized in a "treaty that would become the basis for reciprocal relations of European states." Thus he wrote in lyrical style:

> It is not a dream of perpetual peace that is being realized, but rather this can be approached with more correspondence to the results it augurs, if in the treaty that would terminate the general war we would manage to fix (based on clear and precise principles) some prescriptions for the rights of peoples. Why not include the positive rights of nations, ensure the privilege of neutrality, and insert the obligation to never begin a war unless mediation by a third party has been exhausted, in a way we could highlight respective complaints and try to resolve them? It is on similar principles that one might proceed to general peace and give birth to a league whose stipulations would form, so to speak, a new code of law among peoples, which when sanctioned by the majority of the states of Europe would painlessly become the immutable rule of governments, particularly since those who wanted to infringe that code would bring down on themselves the forces of the new union.[50]

This passage seems important to me. First, it reflects the moral dimension of the combat in which the tsar was engaging. Alexander was in fact proposing to all of Europe a geopolitical system that would vanquish the Napoleonic system precisely because it would respect the rights of nation and the rights of peoples. This points to a radical change of perspective, if not a mental and political revolution. Until the end of the eighteenth century, Russian leaders have been permanently obliged to demonstrate their quest for "European-ness" and to submit to the "European model." After 1804 not only was Alexander not trying to demonstrate that his empire was European (which appeared evident to him), but the tsar of Russia was now capable of proposing to Europe an overall political project. This is how far Russian power had come in a few years.

As striking is the modernity of Alexander's European project. His concept was of a peace league of European nations in which recourse to mediation and negotiation would be systematic, where each would respect a certain number of common political values. Later in the document is the timid allusion to the constitution of a military force that would unite the forces of various nations adhering to the league. All this suggests a visionary approach that prefigures the attempts that would take place during the twentieth century.

On top of these principled geopolitical considerations came more concrete ideas. Alexander first insists on the need to establish the new states inside their natural geographic limits,[51] to make sure they are composed of "homogenous peoples." Here we find not only ideas pronounced by Czartoryski but also the influence of the thinking of Joseph de Maistre, who in his Political Memorandum on Italy and the Houses of Austria and Savoy (the second half of 1804) insisted on the need to constrain France to return to its ancient territorial limits without annihilating it, which would be contrary to the European (which for him meant "Christian") order. This text circulated among those close to the tsar and was then read by Alexander himself. In fact, by the end of 1804, de Maistre was frequenting Kochubey and Czartoryski; in January 1805 the diplomat noted that his memorandum was communicated to the tsar "by a friendly hand outside official channels."[52]

Once European states were formed in this way, then a "natural equilibrium" would have to be sought, and for that, alongside the existing great powers, "second order states" would have to be created to serve as counterweight. The notions of equilibrium and counterpower have importance in Alexander's analysis: it is from this perspective that we must regard his position in favor of the constitution of a federation of German principalities independent of Austria and Prussia:

It is evident that the existence of too many small states will not accord with the goal being proposed, since having no intrinsic strength, they will serve only as bait and means to ambition, without being of any utility to the general good. We cannot remedy this disadvantage except by gathering them into larger states or else by forming federating unions among the small ones. The need to encircle France and to form counterweights to Austria and Prussia demands that these considerations should not be forgotten relative to Italy, and principally with regard to Germany.[53]

Thus, on the political as well as the geopolitical levels, the tsar of Russia laid out in his Instructions to Novosiltsev an ambitious project for reconstructing Europe. However, this project would receive a lukewarm reception in London.

* * *

Arriving in London at the start of November 1804, the tsar's secret emissary stayed until February 1805. For these three months Novosiltsev tried to convince the British authorities of the interest and pertinence of Alexander's projects. In his memoirs Prince Czartoryski gives a harsh verdict of this mission, making Novosiltsev largely responsible for its failure.

> M. de Novosiltzow found M. Pitt very little prepared to listen to our proposals, and solely preoccupied with his own point of view on the affairs of Europe. [Ambassador] Count Simon, in his admiration of the narrow system of the English cabinet, was always ready to combat the modifications we wanted to introduce. Either due to the difficulties that resulted from this state of affairs, or for other motives, M. Novosiltzow did not acquit himself in a suitable way of this important mission, which required much prudence and reserve but also great firmness in following the instructions that he had been given. He barely stammered the conditions to which we attached the greatest importance, he did not mention the name of Poland, and made no mention of the precarious state of Europe, caused by the iniquities that had to be redressed.[54]

What really happened? At the start of his mission, Novosiltsev had been optimistic, convinced that he would reach success in a short period of time. Three weeks after his arrival, he wrote in a report to the tsar (dated December 4) that he thought "very easy to obtain the consent of the English minister to all the principles that Your Very Gracious Majesty counts on adopting as the basis for directing this new alliance."[55] Meanwhile, in St. Petersburg the tsar continued to grant crucial importance to this mission, as attested in the letter Czartoryski sent to the emissary on December 9:

> We need you to give us good news. This expectation is the only thing in which our Master still has the same interest. He always repeats: "We will see what Novosiltsov sends us; we have to wait for his news." In a word, it is up to you to lift our spirits. If the English have—I will not say generous and exalted senti-ments—any common sense, they will necessarily have to lend themselves to everything and share our ideas, for otherwise it will not work and the emperor will do only what he is absolutely forced to, and against his feelings.[56]

But Novosiltsev ran up against the distrust of the British prime minister, who suspected the Russian Empire of imperialist aims on the Ottoman Em-pire and who therefore refused to discuss any plan for dismemberment or a protectorate that would turn to the advantage of Russia. Even more, No-vosiltsev ran up against the skepticism expressed by Pitt for any Russian project for a European system.

Indeed, Pitt did share part of the geopolitical analysis. In the interview he granted Ambassador Vorontsov in December 1804, for example, he af-firmed the need "to surround a France reintegrated into its former frontiers with great and powerful states"; like Alexander, he wanted to achieve this by the creation of a federation of Italian states.[57]

Similarly, judging that Napoleon "has annihilated the rights of peoples," the British prime minister declared himself in favor of this right being guar-anteed by an "association of states" that would be under the protection of Russia and England. However, Pitt was not ready to go so far as signing a peace treaty imposing on member states any precise rules of conduct. In his meeting of December 25 with Novosiltsev, he was dubious about a league, stressing that "the nation that feels offended and at the same time sufficiently strong, will always be little inclined to conform to the decision of a third power."[58] Therefore he merely gave vague acquiescence to the idea of de-fining "the prescription of international conduct in an exact and positive manner in the form of a new code of international law,"[59] but without stating anything about the content of this code. This distrust largely compromised the "European security" part of Alexander's project, which resulted in only a relatively classic military alliance.

A first version of the convention was elaborated at the end of January 1805, and a Russian-Swedish treaty of military alliance was also conclud-ed. The final text of the British-Russian convention, written by Novosiltsev and taking Pitt's positions into account, was signed on April 11, 1805, in St. Petersburg by the British ambassador at the Russian court. But despite the triumphalism proclaimed by Novosiltsev, the content was disappointing in relation to the initial project. In exchange for 115,000 soldiers that Russia promised to launch into the struggle against Napoleon, Britain promised to finance the war effort to the tune of 1,250,000 pounds sterling for each hundred thousand Russian or Austrian soldiers involved in the conflict and to participate in the war with naval and land forces. Moreover, conforming to Russian wishes, several secret clauses did lay out the geopolitical reconstruction of Europe, foreseeing the return of France to its former frontiers, the reestablishment of the independence of states occupied by Napoleon, and territorial compensation for Prussia and Austria. But the other elements in Alexander's project were carefully eluded or postponed: for the British prime minister the time was ripe for realpolitik, not for utopia.

At the same time, in March 1805, Napoleon proclaimed himself king of Italy, and Genoa and Lucca were annexed by France. More and more worried, the emperor of Austria rallied to the Russian/British alliance, with a promise from Alexander to increase his effective troops: now it was not 115,000 but 180,000 troops that the tsar agreed to throw into the war against Napoleon. On June 4, 1805, in Vienna, a military plan of action was adopted by the three powers that set the number of combatants that Austria and Russia should engage (250,000 and 180,000 respectively) plus 100,000 Prussians, 16,000 Swedes, 16,000 Danes, 35,000 Germans from various principalities and provinces, 20,000 Neapolitans and 5,000 British—for a total of almost 622,000 men. On August 9 a treaty of alliance was signed by the Austrian ambassador to St. Petersburg, Count Stadion, but in August Prussia chose to remain outside the alliance that was taking shape and to proclaim its neutrality in the coming conflict; the king did not want Russia to be too strong and was distrustful of Russian aims over Prussian Poland. These hesitations did not prevent the diplomatic and military network from being woven. In September 1805 an alliance was approved between Russia and the Kingdom of Two Sicilies, and in October a treaty was sealed between Britain and Sweden. That autumn the third coalition against Napoleon was in place and war was already on the way. Alexander mourned the demise of his pacifist aims.

PART THREE

THE NAPOLEONIC WARS
1805–1815

CHAPTER 8

From the First Military Fiascos to the Tilsit Agreements

1805–1807

The years from 1805 to 1807 were particularly intense in the European theater. But while Alexander spared no effort either on the military or diplomatic level, success eluded him: in less than two years, one of the pillars of the third coalition had to sign the "humiliating" Peace of Tilsit, arousing among his entourage a combination of incomprehension, disapproval, and anger, ending a particularly difficult period in his life.

From the Third Coalition to the Austerlitz Disaster

After having solemnly passed in review the regiments of his Guard on the eve of their departure on campaign (August 22), Alexander announced his intention to join the theater of operations. For him, a sovereign should be close to his army. On September 21, after long meditation in Our Lady of Kazan Cathedral, the emperor left the capital accompanied by Counts Tolstoy, Lieven, and Volkonsky (the latter were generals and aides-de-camp) and his faithful advisors, Czartoryski, Stroganov, and Novosiltsev.

After eight days' travel toward the western frontier of the empire, Alexander halted for two weeks at Pulawy, the family estate of the Czartoryskis, situated on the Vistula River, in Austrian Poland. Meanwhile, two Russian armies headed west: one of 50,000 men (later assigned to Mikhail Kutuzov) was to gather on the southwest frontier to meet up with the Austrian troops; the other of 90,000 men commanded by General Michelson was supposed to go to the border with Prussian Pomerania and prepare if necessary to invade Prussia.

Back in St. Petersburg the court was split. Several of the Anglophiles close to the tsar were proving patriotic and bellicose, including some of the central administrators and diplomats in post across Europe: Vorontsov in London, Razumovsky in Vienna, Tatishchev in Naples, and Italinski in Constantinople. Even the placid Elizabeth got carried away by her visceral love for Russia in a letter to her mother:

> At present, mama, I admit that I feel strongly in my entrails for Russia, which, whatever pleasure I would have at re-seeing Germany [...], I would be desolate to leave Russia forever. And if by some imaginary circumstance, I found myself isolated and mistress of choosing where to live it is to Russia that I would go.[1]

On the other hand, others—out of Francophilia (as with Count Rostopchin) or else the desire to preserve Russia's diplomatic and military independence (the argument of ministers such as those for trade (Rumyantsev), education (Zavadovski), and justice (Lopukhin)—were hostile to the involvement. Prince Kurakin, a member of the permanent council, shared this view: the vital interests of the empire were not being threatened, and Russia should remain outside the conflict that was on the horizon. For everyone, anyway, the war to come was still a distant abstraction that was not injuring either the French presence or cultural prestige in Russia. In November 1805, Stephan Zhiharev, a young Moscow civil servant wrote in his journal, noting an astonishing paradox.

> And while we are combating the French abroad, the French here stage various comedies and entertain Moscow as if nothing was happening. Never has the French theater seen so many spectators as gathered for the soirée organized for the benefit of Madame Sérigny and Monsieur Rose. It is true that the theater is not very large, but it was full; they performed the comedy in three acts called *Conjectures or the Makers of News*.[2]

At Pulawy the parties, balls, and receptions multiplied, rumors flew around, buoyed by the amiable attitude of the sovereign. Polish dignitaries thought they had won him around to the idea dear to Czartoryski that once victory over Napoleon was achieved, Russia would be able to proclaim and guarantee (under its protection) the independence of Poland. But in reality, cultivating a certain ambiguity, Alexander made no real promises. He had several irons in the fire.

Meanwhile, the international crisis was beginning in Germany. At the start of October, 20,000 French soldiers left Hanover (occupied by Napoleon)[3] in the direction of the Danube, violating Prussian neutrality by crossing the territory of Anspach; the tsar announced his intention to leave Pulawy to go to Berlin without stopping at Warsaw. Polish patriots interpreted this declaration as the death knell of their hopes: how could the emperor, leaving for Berlin to try to form an alliance, still be working to establish a state that Prussia did not want? Everybody in Pulawy bitterly deplored what seemed a cruel volte-face, if not a betrayal. In reality, as of September and unbeknownst to Prince Czartoryski, Alexander had sent to Berlin his aide-de-camp Prince Peter Dolgoruki to secretly negotiate with the king of Prussia. The latter was hesitant at first, preferring to keep his distance from France as well as from Russia and Great Britain, to the point that Dolgoruki sent pessimistic dispatches back to the emperor. But the violation of Anspach abruptly changed the situation: on October 4, furious that the neutrality of Prussia had been flouted even when relations between France and Prussia were supposed to be excellent, Frederick-Wilhelm III authorized Russian troops to cross his territory and announced his intention to rejoin the coalition. It was this decision that motivated Alexander's reaction: for the tsar, Prussia was the keystone of the arrangement for linking up the allied troops and therefore the king's new moves should be encouraged.

Alexander I arrived in Berlin on October 13 and was warmly received. But soon the first military reversals occurred. The next day Austrian troops were attacked on the Danube and defeated; on the nineteenth General Mack, trapped in Ulm, capitulated with his 32,000 men, which allowed the Grande Armée to advance across German territory. In this threatening context an agreement between Russia and Prussia became an absolute priority. On November 3 in Potsdam, diplomats Hardenberg and Haugwitz for Prussia and Czartoryski, Alopeus, and Dolgoruki for Russia wrote a treaty[4] providing for a one-month ultimatum; Prussia, the so-called mediator between members of the third coalition and France, would demand that the latter renounce some of its German conquests (which Napoleon would find unacceptable) or else Prussia would engage in the conflict with 180,000 men. In exchange for this Prussian support, Alexander I agreed in a secret article to recognize Prussia's right to annex Hanover. This article was a violation of the agreement between Russia and Great Britain concluded in St. Petersburg on April 11, 1805, which had called for Hanover's independence, but for Alexander that was the price of Prussia's support. And to better secure his privileged tie to the Hohenzollern dynasty, on the initiative of Queen Louise and in her presence, Tsar Alexander and King Frederick-Wilhelm took an oath by torchlight on the night of November 3 in front of the tomb of the great Frederick II.

The sudden capitulation of General Mack, when Kutuzov was still 270 kilometers from Ulm, compromised any idea of a military junction and devastated the initial plans of the coalition partners. Appointed general in command of allied forces, Kutuzov was immediately confronted with a dilemma: as supreme commander of the armies against Napoleon, he should defend Vienna, threatened by the progress of the Grande Armée, but as a Russian general, he must spare his own army as best he could.[5] On October 25, suspecting that the Austrian army that had begun a fighting retreat from Vienna was contemplating an armistice, he decided to withdraw to Enns, covered by the rearguard of Bagration, and then to Durenstein,[6] where on November 10–11 he attacked unsuccessfully the troops of General Mortier. He reached Olmütz shortly afterward and found there, apart from the still-intact Austrian troops (about 15,000 men), his emperor, for Alexander had arrived the previous week. But the atmosphere was more than morose: "I was astonished like all the other generals at the coldness and mournful silence with which our troops received the emperor,"[7] wrote Langeron, a French general who was in the service of Russia. This was because these troops—poorly equipped, shod, and fed—had been confronted with the greatest material difficulties. Lacking everything, the Russian army was undisciplined, on top of which relations between Russian and Austrian soldiers were execrable. The understanding between the two allies appeared very fragile.

Meanwhile, in the background diplomatic dealings were underway: Napoleon's initiative was to Alexander, while Prussia's was toward the new emperor of the French.

* * *

For Napoleon—as he expressed clearly in a letter to the emperor of Austria on November 8—the tsar was blinded by his advisors' preference for Britain so he had to be convinced of France's peaceful intentions. Thus, Napoleon sent to Olmütz his aide-de-camp Savary to meet the Russian emperor and at the same time discreetly gather information about the state and size of the coalition forces. On November 27 Savary gave the tsar a letter from Napoleon in which the French emperor displayed his courtesy and amiability. But Savary was received coldly at Russian headquarters.

Awaiting the tsar's response, Savary chatted both amiably and skillfully with the officers who were heedlessly trusting, if not irresponsible. Relating the episode, a bulletin of the Grande Armée (dated December 3, 1805) did not fail to denounce the naïveté and incompetence of Alexander's staff:

It was easy for [Savary] to understand, after the conversation that he had for three days with thirty-some whippersnappers who under various titles surrounded the emperor of Russia that presumption, imprudence, and thoughtlessness reigned in the military decision-making, as they had reigned in the political.[8]

On November 27 the emissary left the headquarters with a letter handwritten by Alexander. Addressed to "the head of the French government" (a minimal formula that implicitly refused the title of emperor), the tsar's letter was cold in tone and devoid of any desire for rapprochement:

I have received with gratitude the letter of which General Savary was the bearer and I hasten to express all my thanks for it. I have no other desire than to see peace in Europe reestablished with loyalty and on equitable bases. I wish at the same time to have the occasion to be able to be personally agreeable to you. Please receive this assurance, as well as my highest regards.[9]

The same day, Alexander at the head of his troops, having in effect removed General Kutuzov from supreme command, gave the order to seek combat against the French. The next day, near Wischau, a first engagement between the French and the allied Austrians and Russians (in superior numbers) turned to the advantage of the latter. For the young tsar leading his troops with spirit and courage on the field of battle, the success seemed a good omen for the campaign operations.

In parallel with the diplomatic dealings between France and Russia, discussions were ongoing between Prussia and France. On November 28 in Brünn, the Prussian emissary, Haugwitz, a former minister of foreign affairs, met Napoleon and gave him a letter from the Prussian king written in Potsdam at the end of October. But now there was no question of an ultimatum: Haugwitz, less bellicose than Hardenberg, really aspired to make a deal with France to avoid war. Prussia was indeed the weak link in the coalition.

The next day, Savary was once again in Olmütz to convince Alexander to accept a meeting with Napoleon. But the tsar, perhaps carried away by his first military success, preferred to send Prince Dolgoruki to the French camp. A long-standing Anglophile and a partisan of pursuing the war, the young prince arrogantly addressed Napoleon, who was indignant in a letter to the elector of Württemberg about the behavior of the Russian emissary:

I had a conversation with this whippersnapper in which he spoke to me as one would speak to a *boyard* who was being sent to Siberia. [...] This young man was excessively arrogant and he must have taken my extreme moderation as a mark of great terror.[10]

Yet, the French emperor tried to temporize, astonished at the tsar's bellicose attitude, but the meeting deteriorated. Napoleon's annoyance reached its height when Dolgoruki, having stressed that Russia was expecting no territorial advantage from its engagement in the conflict and was intervening only to defend the independence of European states against French ambitions, added provocatively that peace could only be envisaged if Napoleon renounced the kingdom of Italy, the left bank of the Rhine, and Belgium and evacuated Vienna. Such demands amounted to a refusal to negotiate, and henceforth Napoleon was convinced that war with Russia was inevitable. On November 30, shortly before Austerlitz, he confided to Talleyrand and reaffirmed his sympathy (somewhat condescending) for the young tsar:

> Tomorrow there will probably be a very serious battle with the Russians; I have done much to avoid it, for it is blood spilled uselessly. I had correspondence with the emperor of Russia and all I am left with is that he is a brave and worthy man led astray by those around him, who are sold to the English—to the point that they want to force me to give Genoa to the King of Sardinia and to renounce Belgium![11]

And his letter to the elector of Württemberg (December 5) was along the same lines, affirming that the tsar was of a good nature and filled with great qualities, but "was surrounded by twenty-some rascals who are leading him to misery."[12]

Dolgoruki had just returned from his mission and given Alexander an optimistic report. He thought the French troops feared a military engagement because the superior coalition numbers (90,000 faced with 70,000 French soldiers) were crushing: "Our success is beyond doubt," he wrote in his report. "It suffices to go forward and our enemies will retreat like they retreated at Wischau."[13] Unfortunately for Alexander I, nobody could be less clairvoyant.

＊ ＊ ＊

Over several weeks before Austerlitz,[14] there reigned in the Russian headquarters a strange atmosphere that combined excitement, an appetite for glory, and total recklessness. Surrounded by young swaggerers who were totally inexperienced, who all dreamed of beating Napoleon, Alexander was eager for battle and despised the old generals. Langeron's harsh judgment was explicit:

He had little regard for them, received them rarely, spoke to them little and reserved all his favors for five or six young favorites who were his adjutants, (Lieven,
Volkonsky, Gagarin, Dolgoruki). He gave himself over to a familiarity with them
that was humiliating for the old generals, who saw their bearing and manners
ridiculed by all these children whose influence extended to everything.[15]

Farther on, he wrote about General Kutuzov: "The young men who surrounded the emperor made fun of Kutuzov and called him 'General Lam-
bin'—he was without power and respect."[16] For them, as for Alexander, old
General Kutuzov, known for his taste for pretty women and his propensity
to drink, blind in one eye, corpulent, and slow to mount a horse, was past
his prime. His extreme caution—he refused to lead offensive actions against
Napoleon—was an admission of cowardice. Only Adam Czartoryski in
the entourage of Alexander, did not support the warlike enthusiasm of the
young officers, and the fact that the emperor had taken the head of the coalition troops appeared to him to be dangerous, but the Polish prince, whose
relations with Alexander were strained since he had gone to Berlin, was also
being marginalized. So Alexander did not heed either the firm injunctions
from Czartoryski, who advised him to yield command to a military man,
or from Kutuzov's reserves, who wanted to delay engagement and wait for
reinforcements. In Alexander's favor, it should be stressed that Kutuzov did
not express his reservations strongly; the old courtier, of boundless devotion
to the young tsar, bent to all his desires.

On the night of December 1, the Austrian general Weyrother convened
a war council in which he presented his arrangement for the battle to come.
Speaking in German, his exposition was translated to the Russian officers,
who got lost in the names of villages and landmarks;[17] Kutuzov was sighing
and appeared to doze. Only Langeron dared challenge a plan that he considered complicated and hazardous. Convinced that Napoleon was weakened,
Weyrother aimed to attack the French troops from the plateau of Pratzen; he
would descend toward the plain where most of the French army was located,
outflank it from the right, and enclose it in Brünn. But Napoleon had antici-
pated this maneuver and would use the enemy plan to deliver the decisive
battle he was seeking. He willingly withdrew his right flank and retrenched
in a village behind the frozen marshes.

At 7:30 a.m. on the second of December, the coalition forces amassed
on the Pratzen began to descend on their left to attack the French right
flank and take the whole army from the side. Doing so, they presented their
own flank during the maneuver, and then at 8:30 the French center led
by Soult attacked the Pratzen, which was already in confusion due to the

movement. As the fog dissipated, the sun revealed the French attack, and Kutuzov understood the danger. Around 9:00, to remedy the abandonment of the heights of the Pratzen, he gave the order to his army (including the imperial Guard) to regain the top of the plateau. But the tsar had arrived on the spot along with the emperor of Austria, their generals, aides-de-camp, and advisors; he criticized this decision, demanding that the troops assault the French, addressing General Kutuzov in the familiar form: "Mikhail Ilarionich, why aren't you advancing? We are not on maneuvers in Tsaritsyno where the parade does not commence until all the regiments are there." Kutuzov defended himself but complied: "Sire, if I do not start, it is precisely because we are not on the field of Tsaritsyno. But if you order it . . ."[18]

The order proved catastrophic: the engagement was immediately disastrous for the Russian troops. They were submerged in a French assault that soon took the Pratzen plateau. The French installed their artillery and from there fired cannons down on their adversaries, whose lines below were dislocated. At 11:00 the signal for retreat was given but would only be executed two hours later, transforming the defeat into a rout. Many soldiers would die frozen in the Satchan pond in crevasses opened up by the French bombardment:

> The water, penetrating through crevasses soon surged over the ice and we saw thousands of Russians,[19] as well as their horses, cannons, and chariots, slowly sink into the chasm! It was a horribly majestic spectacle that I will never forget! In an instant the surface of the pond was covered with every thrashing thing that could not swim: men and horses struggled amidst the ice and water.[20]

Kutuzov was lightly wounded. The tsar, jostled by his fleeing troops and desperate at the scope of the defeat and trembling with fever, broke down in tears at the foot of a tree. He owed his survival only to the vigilance of his equerry Ené and his courier Prokhnitski, as well as the intervention of his doctor, James Wylie, who took it upon himself to administer a few drops of opium in wine to knock him out and allow him to escape for several hours from the nightmare of Austerlitz. But when he awoke, the tsar of Russia now had to face the disastrous consequences of the defeat.

Aftermath of Austerlitz to the Friedland Defeat

The defeat at Austerlitz, in which the tsar took a direct share because he assumed command of military operations, took a very heavy toll. First, on the human level: the allies lost 35,000 killed or missing (25–28,000 Russians and 6,000 Austrians),[21] as opposed to only 9,000 for the Grande Armée. On the diplomatic level the emperor of Austria made an armistice with Napoleon on December 4, by which Russian troops had to leave Austrian territory immediately, and later that month Austria signed the Treaty of Presburg, which marked the end of the Third Coalition. Despite the advice of Talleyrand, who was unsuccessfully trying to moderate "Napoleon's destructive plans,"[22] the French emperor (no doubt carried away by his successes) imposed very harsh conditions on Austria, which was thrown out of northern Italy and forced to concede Venetia, Istria, and Dalmatia and to accept the creation of the principality of Lucca and Piombino, which then fell into the Bonaparte family's pockets. On German land Austria had to cede its possessions in Bavaria, Baden, and Württemberg. Austria came out of the conflict very weakened. Demographically, it lost 4 million of the 24 million inhabitants that made up the country in 1805; financially, it was subject to heavy war reparations of 50 million florins; and symbolically, Franz I had to give up his title of emperor of the German Holy Empire, which disappeared the following August. As Talleyrand had foreseen from the start, these harsh conditions incited in Austria a desire for revenge and in the long term could not guarantee a lasting peace. But in the short term Austria was wiped out of the war.

On December 5 Alexander met his former ally at Holitsch, then set off for St. Petersburg, having sent a message to the king of Prussia stating that he was ready to support Prussia with all his forces. But Frederick-Wilhelm III had little confidence in the promises of Alexander or in his ability to keep them, and so he preferred to negotiate with Napoleon. In the king's name, in Schönbrunn, Haugwitz signed a treaty of alliance (both defensive and offensive) with France on December 15, which granted Hanover to Prussia, while the Prussian enclaves of Ansbach, Cleves, and Neufchatel went to France. From this date—although the king had not yet ratified the treaty—the Third Coalition was dissolved.

On December 8 Alexander arrived in St. Petersburg at four in the morning, going directly to the Kazan Cathedral and then reviewing his troops in front of the Winter Palace. People and courtiers were joyful, for the tsar had come back alive from the theater of operations, and everybody saluted his return, convinced that responsibility for the disaster fell on the Austrians, who were suspected of treachery. In the evening Alexander gave a large party in the palace, at which he decorated Kutuzov with the Order of St. Vladimir, naming him governor of Kiev, an honorary but distant post that removed the old general from Alexander's sight; his presence alone was a living reproach. But the truth about the campaign was soon known, as Novosiltsev wrote in a letter to Stroganov in January 1806:

You know that when we separated, you left us very concerned about how we would appear in St. Petersburg. The worry and shame of appearing there increased as we approached the capital. Imagine our astonishment when we learned that the emperor was received with an enthusiasm that cannot be described, that he entered amid unprecedented acclamations, that the whole good town was in heaven over the distinguished way our army had behaved in the recent affair; that it was composed only of heroes […] that our army was said to ask for nothing more than to begin again right after the battle, but that the Austrians did not want to, and that to prevent us, they made an armistice without our knowledge; and finally these Austrians were the real traitors who sold out to France, and that we only lost the battle because they had communicated the plans to the French and their whole army suddenly went over to the French. There had to be victims and guilty ones: so Count Razumovski [ambassador in Vienna] who had not sounded out public opinion enough in committing the court of Vienna to declare itself against the French! He merited nothing less than to be ignominiously fired; […]. You may easily imagine that all the tales like this could not be believed for very long; people from the army kept arriving and setting the public straight. Everybody soon knew how things actually happened, what the real cause of our defeat was, and how we behaved afterward. So after our arrival, the emperor fell in public opinion in an alarming way. Nobody spoke any more of treason, but now all the misfortune was attributed to him alone.[23]

In fact, once the truth was known, Alexander I faced severe criticism from his advisors, his ministers, and his own family. Prince Czartoryski was particularly vehement, reproaching him first for having contributed to the disaster by his useless presence on the battlefield:

Instead of continually going to the advance posts, or later exposing yourself in front of the columns, where the presence of Your Majesty, far from helping, if I may speak the truth, only upset and hindered the generals, it would have been better to remain more distant from the army, to let it march forward without accompanying all of its movements, but rather use all your care, Sire, all your time and all your faculties to occupy yourself without sparing any means of making the whole thing proceed, not blocking any administrative branch of your empire, reorganize Austria, […]. But how was it possible to attend to so many difficult and important objects, since days were taken up with other occupations of little utility, and which also exhausted your time and energy? But by accustoming the soldiers to your presence without any useful goal, Your Majesty has weakened the charm that was attached to it. Your Majesty's presence had no advantage at Austerlitz; it was precisely at the place you were located that the rout was immediate and complete. Your Majesty had his share of that chaos and ought to have hastily got away from something to which you should never have been exposed. At Holitz your departure, Sire, which was only a consequence of your arrival, if I dare say so, was little calculated to the circumstances of the moment and increased the sense of a panicky retreat and general demoralization.[24]

Then, on a more political level Czartoryski was critical of Alexander's orientation as still partisan to an alliance with Prussia. In March 1806 Alexander wrote to Frederick-Wilhelm III that union between Prussia and Russia appeared all the more indispensable. However, Prussia, after having played a double game and trying to negotiate secretly with both Napoleon and with England over recognition of its rights over Hanover, had just concluded a peace treaty with France! Consequently, Czartoryski expressed in the same letter his profound disagreement, enjoining Alexander to stop taking account of Prussian interests at the expense of Russia's. To give strength to his arguments, he sent the emperor a "Memorandum on Relations between Russia and Prussia,"[25] written around January 1806, in which he tried to revise Russia's diplomatic orientation. In another note in April, he pleaded once more for an ambitious Polish policy that would result in reconstituting a kingdom of Poland under the aegis of the tsar. But Alexander continued to privilege the Prussian alliance, as much out of sympathy for the sovereign as out of conviction (because he saw Prussia as the cornerstone of his strategy against Napoleon); thus he could not call for the annexation of Prussian Poland. So he answered Czartoryski with a flat rejection: "You want a discussion, I am ready to grant one, but I cannot prevent myself telling you that it won't serve any purpose, since our starting points are so diametrically opposed."[26] The old intellectual and political complicity of the two friends had disappeared.

Meanwhile, Alexander was undergoing severe admonitions from his mother. Long silent, Maria Feodorovna came out of reserve in the spring of 1806, and in a long letter written on April 30, she gave a very critical reading of the international situation, reproaching her son for having imprudently launched into a war against Napoleon, for not having been able to surround himself with competent and experienced senior officers, and finally, for having dangerously weakened the country's position. There is no doubt that both Maria Feodorovna's forthright (even brutal) reproaches and her pessimism about the current diplomatic and political situation were widely shared at court:

It is said that the existence of Russia is in danger, it has lost its influence and esteem, it no longer counts in the balance of Europe, its allies are lost. Austria has made the most shameful peace in the face of our armies, so to speak; Naples had to be abandoned by our troops and is subjugated by France; finally, our troops have had to retreat everywhere; we were lured and then deceived by Prussia and betrayed by Austria. The glory of our armies has suffered the most regrettable failure; the prestige of invincibility acquired under the reign of the dead Empress and sustained in the reign of the departed emperor by Suvorov is destroyed, and never has a lost battle had so many grievous consequences. Our soldier is no longer what he once was, he has no confidence in his officers and generals. The military spirit has changed. In a word, the army is disorganized, and in this state of affairs, Russia is threatened with a new war. [...] In this urgent peril, what are we doing, what measures are we taking? Our armies are on the borders, fortunately, but who is designing the plan of operation? The young military men who surrounded the emperor are devoted and attached to him, but do they have the knowledge and necessary experience for a job that demands veteran elders, who have the confidence of the nation and who have paid with their persons? Where are they? There is not one among all those who surround the emperor who enjoys this political confidence. He saw in the battle of Austerlitz that memory alone does not suffice, we need a reasoned plan, discussed with all the possible *sangfroid* of experience, that calculates for both success and for the possibility of a reversal, so that in the unfortunate case, people do not lose their heads. The emperor has proved his finest personal value, but the profession of war must be studied in the great school of experience; one has to consult people who have been through it. Why does he not surround himself with these old veterans, whose name alone would quell the clamor? [...] The situation of England makes its friendship useful only on the sea, but if the fight begins, we alone will support it on the continent.[27]

Finally there were insistent rumors, whispered softly by those who saw in the failure of Austerlitz, or in the genius of Napoleon, or in the atrocious military organization in the coalition camp, just the expression of God's anger against the son who murdered his father.

Despite these reproaches and insinuations and his isolation, Alexander stubbornly persisted in his diplomatic choices, in the pro-Prussian stance that he was the only one to promote. The sole master of his foreign policy in 1805–1806, the tsar was far from resembling the waverer depicted by some historians but rather appeared sure of his choices, even pigheaded, justifying Napoleon's judgment that he was like a mule! And so he relaunched negotiations with Prussia—although that country was henceforth allied with France.

* * *

In fact, on February 15, 1806, Prussia had signed in Paris a treaty that confirmed the provisions agreed to in December on territorial exchange but added three new conditions: Prussia had to cede the fortified town of Wesel to France, close its ports to British ships, and declare war on England. On March 5 the king of Prussia ratified the agreement and explained this ratification to Alexander; in a letter to the tsar, he confessed to having been forced to this "extreme measure in order not to lose everything."[28] But signing this treaty put Prussia on bad terms with England and Sweden, and of course, defeated Austria was no longer part of the coalition. This meant that by March 1806 Napoleonic diplomacy had managed to isolate Britain and Russia in their anti-French determination. But Alexander I did not give up, sending the Duke of Brunswick, commander in chief of the Prussian armies, on March 7, a memorandum in which he offered Prussia a military alliance that would be the basis of a future anti-Napoleon coalition. But again Prussia played a double game: the Duke of Brunswick did accept the principle of an alliance with Russia, but in parallel on March 27 the Prussian minister of foreign affairs confirmed his intention to occupy Hanover and to close Prussian ports to British maritime ships—which took place the very next day. As a reprisal, Britain closed its ports to Prussian ships on April 5 and declared war on Prussia on May 11. The next day Sweden announced that it had joined the blockade of Prussia.

Despite this difficult context—the members of the former coalition were now openly opposed to each other—the tsar remained omnipresent on the international scene. On May 13 he offered to mediate in Anglo-Prussian and Swedish-Prussian conflicts, pursuing in parallel secret negotiations with Prussia for a defensive military alliance. For Alexander it was crucial to try to bring the new enemies back together, both for diplomatic reasons (Prussia was still the pivot of his strategy) and for economic reasons. At the start of May, an alarming report written by Minister of Commerce Rumyantsev stressed the need to end the maritime war between the British and the Prussians that was hurting Russia's Baltic trade.[29] In July 1806 the Confederation of the Rhine was created under French protection, giving France dominant weight in German affairs, which made teeth grind in Berlin. The king's entourage was increasingly irritated with Napoleon and hence increasingly in favor of rapprochement with Russia. France, who had not consulted Prussia about this creation and was planning to deprive it of Hanover to give instead to England, tried to mollify the king of Prussia by suggesting that he form a confederation of northern German states, of which his country would be the motor. But Berlin judged this unrealistic, and now the choice of alliance was made. On July 1 Frederick-Wilhelm agreed to sign a secret declaration that was reinforced by another secret text signed by Alexander on July 24. The documents reactivated the 1800 treaty: Prussia promised not to place itself alongside France in the event of a conflict over Austria or the Ottoman Empire, to seek peace with England, and to participate in preparations for a new coalition against France. In exchange, Russia would guarantee the independence and territorial integrity of Prussia. Thus in barely a few weeks, the tenacious tsar had managed to put an end to Russia's diplomatic isolation and to make the new rapprochement with Prussia concrete.

Czartoryski continued to disapprove of this direction, and on July 8 he was dismissed by the tsar, who put in his place as head of foreign affairs Baron Andre Budberg. This infantry general of German and Baltic origin was an experienced diplomat—he had been ambassador in Stockholm from 1796 to 1801—but above all he had been a resolute partisan of the war against Napoleon. This was why he had been chosen, although he would keep the post only a year, being dismissed in September 1807, ostensibly for health reasons.

The forced departure of Czartoryski displeased Stroganov and Novosiltsev, the members of the old inner circle. Anglophiles, they deplored Alexander's preference for Prussia, but the two friends were powerless to change his mind. Meanwhile, Alexander proceeded to some changes in the diplomatic apparatus: for example, in Vienna the tsar named one of his trusted men, Count Alopeus, whom he thought would work for an agreement with Austria.

At the same time, relations between France and Russia had become peculiar, to say the least. In the spring of 1806, with the French consul in St. Petersburg assuring Alexander that Napoleon was favorable to talks with Russia, the tsar sent d'Oubril to Paris as "agent for prisoners of war," charged with an exchange of prisoners from Austerlitz. Arriving in Paris on July 8, the emissary lingered there, seduced by Napoleon and Talleyrand, and on July 20, although he had no plenipotentiary power, he signed an imprudent "treaty of peace and friendship."[30] This text obliged the tsar to renounce any plan of war against France, without the latter granting sufficient concessions over Russian interests in the Ottoman Empire or in Germany. Thus as soon as he returned to St. Petersburg, d'Oubril was disavowed by the emperor and sent into exile on his estates. With ratification of the treaty abandoned, Russia could prepare for war: Alexander created a war council that began to reflect on ways of strengthening the country's defenses. The tsar was convinced of an imminent confrontation.

Yet it was Prussia and not Russia that provided the spark to ignite the conflict. On October 1 the king sent Napoleon an ultimatum, demanding the dissolution of the Confederation of the Rhine and the withdrawal of French troops beyond the Rhine. The response was swift: six days later the Grande Armée invaded Prussian territory. On October 14, in two battles, one at Jena led by Napoleon, where the old Duke of Brunswick was killed, and one in Auerstaedt led by General Davout, the Prussian army was annihilated. In the face of the French advance that captured all the fortresses in the kingdom and occupied the capital, Frederick-Wilhelm was forced to leave Berlin and flee with his wife Louise eastward, first to Grauden on the Vistula, then to Königsberg, and then Memel.

Swift and irreversible, the Prussian defeat took the tsar by surprise and aroused great worry in St. Petersburg. When Frederick-Wilhelm called on his ally for aid, many (starting with Maria Feodorovna) advised Alexander not to intervene for various reasons: the trauma of Austerlitz was still too fresh and the Prussian army too weak (it had only 14,000 men), and the Russian army was even less ready to confront again the invincible Grande Armée because a portion of its troops was at the same time engaged in a war against the Ottoman Empire. But Alexander ignored these warnings and on October 26, 1806, announced in a solemn manifesto the start of a new war against France.

＊ ＊ ＊

To lead the conflict against Napoleon, still traumatized by what happened at Austerlitz, the tsar chose to make General Bennigsen, not Kutuzov, the generalissimo of the Russian army. Originally from Hanover, Bennigsen had served Catherine II and been one of the conspirators who had caused the death of Paul I. But he was a very talented and experienced commander—and that was enough for Alexander. A month later the tsar ordered the Orthodox Church to excommunicate Napoleon: he wanted the country, particularly its elites, to be warned about the despotism incarnated by the French emperor in order to be able to resist his seduction. Napoleon's aura as a military genius continued to daunt the Russians. To reach his ends, the tsar decided to resort to any weapon, using arguments as mendacious as they were detestable. Throughout 1806 an announcement from the Holy Synod, read out in all the Russian churches on Sundays and religious holidays, accused Napoleon, the "beast of the Apocalypse," of wanting the end of the Orthodox Church—out of sympathy for the Jews. For the first time since the start of his struggle against Napoleon, Alexander resorted to anti-Semitic arguments[31] in order to arouse in the population a nationalist as well as religious fervor. And for the first time in Russian history, anti-Semitism became a political weapon.

Anti-Napoleonic caricatures and pamphlets were published in the press to incite elites to support the tsar; former Francophiles now figured among the most ardent despisers of the French. Among them, Count Rostopchin composed in French[32] in the spring of 1807 a comedy called The Living Dead, in which "extravagant partisans of French fashion" are held up to public obloquy for the purpose of arousing patriotic enthusiasm in Moscow. In March 1807, under the chivalric pseudonym of Bogatyrev,[33] he wrote a particularly virulent pamphlet in Russian:

> See what these damned people have done these last twenty years! They have annihilated, burned, devastated everything! They have trodden on the laws, soiled the temples, killed their tsar—and what a tsar! A real father! They have cut off heads like cabbages; all of them wanted to rule, sometimes one and sometimes another of these brigands. They imagined that this would mean equality and liberty, and yet nobody dared open his mouth or show the end of his nose. As for their justice, it was worse than Shemiakin's [a famous Russian bandit]. Good God, what a people, these French! They are not worth a kopek! Our misfortune is that our youth read Faublas [knightly tales] and not history, otherwise they would have seen that each French head contains a windmill, a hospital, and a madhouse![34]

The mobilization also included economic and financial dimensions. Wealthy individuals, towns, and religious orders were asked to support the national war effort. From this standpoint, 1806 was a dress rehearsal for 1812.

Deciding to follow at close hand the operations on the ground, the tsar went to join his army. He stopped first at Jelgava[35] in Courland, where he met the Count of Lille, as the Bourbon heir was known. Alexander promised the future Louis XVIII to aid him to recover the French throne, while (significantly) saying he was hostile to a full restoration of the old French monarchical order. As he had already stated in his instructions to Novosiltsev in 1804, the achievements of the French Revolution and the empire could not be struck off by the pen of the new king.[36] He then went to Palanga,[37] a border town on the Baltic coast, where he met the king of Prussia, before going with him to Memel, where Queen Louise was waiting for them. Friendship between Russia and Prussia was once again celebrated by an alliance between tsar and king signed in April 1807 at Bennigsen's headquarters at Bartenstein—however, it was still not unanimously accepted within the Russian army. Despite the mobilization and the resources being thrown in by Russia (120,000 men and 486 cannons, alongside 14,000 Prussian men and 92 cannons), the new campaign against Napoleon quickly turned into a catastrophe.

Hostilities began on December 23, 1806, in Russian Poland and eastern Prussia. The coalition forces lacked supplies, forage, and munitions. After an assault that forced Bennigsen to retreat to Pultusk on December 26, and then the indecisive battle of Eylau—fought in a glacial blizzard[38] on February 7–8—that even Napoleon himself called carnage (losses were estimated at 26,000 on the Russian side and 20,000 on the French), the disaster culminated in the battle of Friedland on June 14, 1807, the anniversary of the battle of Marengo, where Bonaparte had beaten the Austrians in 1800. This sounded the death knell of Russian hopes. With 12,000 dead or wounded, almost 10,000 taken prisoner (while the French lost only 1,645 killed and 8,000 wounded), the Russian army suffered a veritable catastrophe that forced the tsar, then present in the village of Olita on the Russian border where he had come to inspect the reserve troops, to engage in peace talks that had to be premised on a diplomatic and strategic revolution.

From the Tilsit Meeting to the Alliance with Napoleon

Since 1805, in reversal after reversal, Alexander had not ceased being confronted by Napoleon's military superiority. Despite his deep conviction that the French emperor was a threat to Europe that Russia had to oppose, the disasters of 1807 forced him to a painful diplomatic reorientation, which he resolved to take despite himself and almost shamefully, one might say. For the first time since 1804, he did not keep his Prussian ally informed about his approaches to the French; later he would admit to Prince Kurakin, one of the diplomats present to help him at Tilsit when he met Bonaparte, how painful for him was the change in course dictated by circumstances.

Admittedly, from a strictly military standpoint, the tsar, as Bennigsen suggested, could have pursued the war by bringing his army back beyond the Niemen River, even to the Dvina, where it could be reconstructed; the empire's territory and resources were not yet in peril, even if the war had taken a heavy toll on the state budget. But at court, the defeats suffered in an already unpopular war (we remember Maria Feodorovna's warnings) seemed incomprehensible, and so anger and calls for peace became more urgent, particularly on the part of Grand Duke Constantine, who had witnessed the disaster at Friedland.

* * *

At the same time, Russia had to face a second front: in August 1806 the Ottoman Empire, supported by France,[39] had provoked the tsar by deposing the leaders of the principalities of Moldavia and Walachia and by closing the straits to Russian war ships, in breach of the treaties concluded in 1774 and 1792. This violation led the Russian army to strike back by invading both principalities in November 1806. In return, the Ottoman Empire declared war on Russia, obliging her even when she was in difficulty in central Europe, to keep a part of her army in the Caucasus. On June 15, when the tsar was absent, a crisis meeting was organized by Grand Duke Constantine in St. Petersburg; taking part were Kurakin, Czartoryski, Novosiltsev, Budberg, and other high dignitaries. The participants were almost unanimously in favor of peace negotiations[40] with France, and only Budberg still wanted to pursue the war. The defeat of Prussia, the neutrality of Austria that left Russia alone against France, evidently the fact that Britain was in no hurry to support her, and the existence of a second front with the Ottoman Empire were all unfavorable elements that inclined everyone to peace. Informed of the conclusions of this meeting, the tsar resolved to ask France for an armistice; two days after the catastrophe of Friedland, on June 16, he authorized Bennigsen to start peace talks and announced his intentions to send Prince Dimitri Lobanov Rostovski as his deputy in the armistice negotiations.

* * *

Dimitri Lobanov Rostovski, a direct descendant of Prince Rurik, founder of Kievan Russia, belonged to one of the oldest noble families and had served under Catherine II. He left immediately for Tilsit, in eastern Prussia, to meet Napoleon, accompanied by Prince Kurakin, the former ambassador to Vienna. The latter was also an experienced aristocrat, who had served under Catherine II; he was close to Maria Feodorovna and kept her regularly informed[41] (without Alexander's knowledge) of the negotiations. For Alexander the time no longer belonged to young diplomats like Dolgoruki or d'Oubril, but rather to the old guard, and there was a significant change in perspective. Lobanov Rostovski was supposed to engage in talks "to put an end to the blood-letting" and to conclude an armistice without engaging precisely in peace talks, because the tsar feared that the latter would cost him heavy losses of territory. But at Tilsit the French emperor received Prince Lobanov Rostovski amiably, to the latter's great surprise. Far from wanting to amputate the least parcel of land from Russia, Napoleon called for peace and even an alliance. For him, more than ever, the main enemy was England. Thus, on June 17 Napoleon sent General Duroc to contact Bennigsen about a peace process.

Relieved and reassured about Napoleon's intentions, and thus encouraged to purse negotiations, the tsar reacted rapidly to this proposal. In the instructions he sent to Lobanov Rostovski the following week, he insisted on the need for immediate and direct negotiations between the two sovereigns.

> You will express to emperor Napoleon how sensitive I am to all he has said to me via you, and how much I desire that a close union between our two nations may repair the past evils. You will tell him that this union between France and Russia was constantly the object of my desires and that I carry the conviction that it alone may ensure the world's happiness and tranquility. An entirely new system should replace that one that has existed up to now, and I flatter myself that Emperor Napoleon and I will understand each other easily, provided that we deal with each other without intermediaries. A lasting peace can be concluded between us in a few days.[42]

In response, Napoleon (by the intermediary of his faithful Berthier) repeated that he wished not only to conclude a peace treaty but also to form a real alliance with Russia. Two days after signing the armistice, the letters of ratification were exchanged on the night of June 23–24, and the first meeting between the two emperors was set for June 25. As an anonymous Parisian poet wrote:

> On a raft
> I saw two masters of the world
> On a raft
> I saw peace, I saw war
> And the fate of all Europe
> On a raft.
> I wager that England
> Would fear an entire fleet
> Less than this raft.[43]

A lot has been written about the Tilsit meeting, including popular songs and poems like this one. The event has been subject to many and divergent interpretations due to its impact on Franco-Russian relations and on the future of the European continent. For some, the division of Europe performed there to the detriment of England and Prussia illustrates an understanding between two sovereigns who were equally ambitious and immoral. For others, Alexander was subjugated by Napoleon and had to suffer the ascendancy of a victor who could dictate his conditions. For still others, Tilsit was only a comedy played by two peerless actors: "Declarations of friendship, handshakes, embraces, fantastic projects for shared conquests,—everything was just the postponement of hate," wrote Chateaubriand in a brilliant and murderous sally.[44]

The difficulty posed for a historian concerned to understand what really happened in Tilsit is also due to the fact that despite the decorum and theatricality that surrounded an event that was skillfully staged, the reality of the meetings itself was lost to gazes and commentaries: "From the banks of the river, one could see the two sovereigns get onto the raft, enter by the two ends of the pavilion, embrace—and that was all. The rest was out of sight,"[45] recalled General Paulin, present in Napoleon's squadron, in his memoirs. Although few direct sources deal with Tilsit, the event quickly stimulated a variety of commentaries. In 1812, when a new war was approaching, both the Russians and the French indulged in a reconstruction of this pivotal event, aiming to justify their conduct at the time, and later Napoleon would offer his own interpretation in Las Cases's Memorial of Saint Helena. Thus, Tilsit as a historical fact of prime importance was quickly raised to the status of myth—which complicates the historian's task However, it is crucial to try to see it clearly, and once again the Russian archives, particularly the personal correspondence of Alexander offer us evidence for a fresh interpretation that includes how events unfolded, as well as the motivations, intentions, and goals of the tsar.

On June 25 the first meeting took place, a tête-à-tête for two hours, between the two emperors on a raft floating in the middle of the Niemen River. For the occasion Napoleon was dressed in the uniform of his guards, hung with a cord of the Legion of Honor; he came first onto the raft, came to meet the tsar who had just disembarked and gave him an accolade; then the two men disappeared inside a pavilion decorated with their respective coats of arms. What views were exchanged at this secret meeting?

According to Napoleon (as he recalled in his letter to Alexander on July 1, 1812), Alexander had at first proclaimed an anti-British determination, declaring that he detested the English as much as the French did and that he would be "his second against England." Having thus put his interlocutor in the best frame of mind,[46] Alexander said he wanted "to plead the cause of an unfortunate ally,"[47] and obtained the right for the king of Prussia, excluded by the French from this first meeting, to be able to attend the second, planned for the next day, again aboard the raft. But this concession was purely formal because Frederick Wilhelm, openly despised by Napoleon, had to be content with witnessing the second meeting without being able to play the slightest role. The French emperor did not want defeated Prussia to participate in the dialogue between France and Russia.

During their first meeting the two sovereigns observed each other, each trying to discern the other's personality, in a duel of barbed but veiled remarks. The Russian wanted to obtain an honorable peace, the Frenchman wanted to seal a trustworthy alliance. Napoleon wanted Alexander to recognize the legitimacy of his titles and conquests in western and central Europe, to accept the dismemberment of Prussia, and to support him actively in his struggle against England. Meanwhile Alexander hoped to sign a peace treaty without lost territory, save the Prussian monarchy, and obtain free movement in relations with the Turks, without committing himself too far to an alliance.[48] For almost two weeks Napoleon and Alexander had frequent conversations, while their diplomatic advisors worked frantically to prepare texts. The sovereigns' conversations bore on strategic and geopolitical topics, but also on political matters. Alexander, as a worthy pupil of Laharpe, proclaimed his liberal positions, which surprised the French emperor. Later, on St. Helena, Napoleon would confide to Las Cases:

> Still, he was not without real or feigned ideology; this would be the remains of his education and his tutor. Will anyone ever believe, said the emperor, what I debated with him: he argued to me that heredity was an abuse of sovereignty, and I had to spend more than an hour and use all my eloquence and my logic to prove to him that this heredity was the refuge and happiness of peoples.[49]

Alexander never gave a public commentary other than a purely diplomatic report on the Tilsit meetings. Still, several years later (1813), he returned in detail to his meeting with Napoleon in a conversation with Countess Edling:

> The emperor expanded warmly on this enigmatic character and told me of the study he made during the meetings at Tilsit. In this conversation, where there were no constraints, I saw how mistaken people were in supposing that Alexander had illusions about Napoleon. Obliged to recognize the superiority of genius, he accepted with good grace the great man's advances, without ever

letting himself be dazzled by false confidence. [...] The emperor, in speaking of Napoleon, could not defend himself from a certain irritation, but never so far as to utter a bitter or unmeasured expression. This moderation was quite rare at a time when one never heard the name Napoleon pronounced without some epithet resembling a curse. The emperor continued the conversation on this interesting subject and expressed himself as follows: "The current period reminds me of everything this extraordinary man told me at Tilsit on the fortunes of war. We talked for a long time, for he liked to show me his superiority and spoke complacently, letting himself go in imaginative sallies. He told me one day: 'War is not as difficult an art as people imagine, and frankly it would be often embarrassing to say how one battle or another was won. The fact is that one got afraid last, and that is the whole secret, for there is no general who does not doubt the outcome of the combat and it is a matter of hiding this fear as long as possible. It is only by this means that one's enemy is intimidated, and then success is not in doubt.' I listened to everything he was pleased to tell me with profound attention, having decided to profit from this assertion in the next occasion."[50]

For these two weeks the two sovereigns showered each other with kind gestures and compliments, and the seduction seems to have been mutual. In a famous letter to Josephine, Napoleon confided to his spouse: "My dear, I have just seen emperor Alexander and I am very pleased with him, he is a very handsome, good and young emperor. He is more intelligent than it is commonly thought."[51]

Later he concludes frankly that "if Alexander were a woman, I would make him my lover."[52] For the tsar's part, he says he was impressed by the "genius" and charm of the emperor and listens with apparent admiration to Napoleon shine in their conversations. But if he gave the appearance of appreciating the mind of the French emperor and applauding his sparkling chat, if he flattered him, Alexander remained lucid and aware of the important stakes at play in Tilsit and of his own vulnerability. The negotiations had been imposed by circumstance and did not change his diplomatic priorities in any way. Far from being dazzled by the alliance that was on the verge of being concluded, he remained viscerally hostile to the one who continued to call himself in private correspondence "Bonaparte" or "the Corsican." On June 7, 1807, when Alexander was still in Weimar, on the point of setting off for Tilsit, he wrote to his sister Catherine something that reflects his state of mind: "Bonaparte claims that I am only an idiot. He who laughs last laughs best! And I put all my hope in God."[53]

For Alexander, the usurper who had betrayed the ideals of the French Revolution and the Enlightenment and who for personal motives had thrown Europe into the torment of war, was a tyrant who had to be beaten as soon as circumstances allowed. However, he did not underestimate either Napoleon's genius or political skill. Four days after his first meeting with the French emperor, he sent a letter to his sister Catherine in which he reported with excitement but with clear eyes about the extraordinary event he had just experienced:

> God has saved us: instead of sacrifices, we get out of the struggle with a kind of luster. But what do you think of all these events? Me, spending my days with Bonaparte, to be whole hours in tête-à-tête with him! I ask you if all that seems a little like a dream! It is past midnight and he has only just left. Oh, I wish you could have invisibly witnessed all that happened. Adieu, dear friend, I write to you rarely but on my honor I have not a moment to breathe![54]

A few weeks later, in one of the letters sent to his mother while still in Tilsit, again there was no question of succumbing to a Napoleonic mirage. On the contrary, the young tsar proved perspicacious, even cynical, wagering on the vanity of the French emperor and on his own capacity to play on it.

Prince Kurakin echoes the tsar's analysis in a letter to Empress Maria Feodorovna expressing his relief that, given the scope of the Russian defeat, there had been an unhoped-for recovery of the situation.

> Amid the anguish caused by our political situation, after the recent disasters of our army, from the cruelest worries we are now transported by the greatest joy. God was watching over Russia, over the person and glory of the emperor your son! Blood will no longer flow, the calamities that afflicted humanity and Europe as a whole will cease. Russia will have only to regret the brave troops she has lost, but their bravery has acquired a new glory and in recovering her tranquility she keeps all her power and all her borders. [...] Your Majesty will deign to agree that nothing happier could have happened to us. Heaven has granted us a blessing and favor in the most critical period in which Russia has ever been found! Abandoned or not at all supported by our allies, we had to assume alone the burden of a war that we could only do with the effective help of England and Austria. We lacked money, provisions, arms; our troops, after the losses they had suffered, could only be revived at the expense of our population and still, new recruits would not have first replaced our old soldiers. We had before us, on our borders, a victorious enemy with three times the strength of ours, who had only to take a step forward to enter our Polish

provinces where insurrection was smoldering and which were ready to receive it and rise up. What did we have to oppose it? The debris of a great army discouraged by all that the generals had made it suffer; total disorganization in our means and resources; no hope of success and no utility whatever in the sacrifices to which we could have stubbornly stuck! This picture, exactly true, where nothing is partial or exaggerated, suffices to make us feel how happy we are to finally exit advantageously from this painful and dangerous struggle in which we were engaged. I cannot doubt that Your Majesty shares my conviction about this.[55]

In what respect did Russia leave advantageously from the struggle?

On July 7, 1807, the Treaty of Tilsit[56] was signed between France and Russia; two days later, a second treaty was concluded between France and Prussia. Negotiated by Princes Lobanov Rostovski and Kurakin on the Russian side and by Talleyrand, the Prince of Benevent, and the minister of foreign affairs on the French side, the treaty was really composed of two different documents: a treaty of peace and friendship that included 30 open articles and seven secret ones, and a treaty of offensive and defensive alliance with nine articles, all secret.

While, to the great relief of Russian negotiators, Russia had to concede no parcel of imperial territory, Alexander nevertheless did have to evacuate the river mouth in Dalmatia and the Ionian Islands that had been occupied by Russian troops,[57] as well as the principalities of Moldavia and Walachia that he had just taken from the Ottomans. In parallel, the tsar did not manage to defend effectively the interests of Prussia, which paid a high price for the new Franco-Russian entente. In effect, Prussia lost most of its former Polish possessions, to the benefit of the king of Saxony, and all its lands situated to the west of the Elba, to the benefit of a new kingdom of Westphalia, which Napoleon had set up for his brother Jerome. The formerly Prussian part of Poland was henceforth the Grand Duchy of Warsaw. Alexander had refused to annex to Russia the Polish land extending to the Niemen and Vistula, and so this new entity would be governed by the king of Saxony, a docile vassal of France.[58] All of these amputations represented half of Prussia's population (5 million out of 10 million) and a third of its area, so badly mutilated was the country after Tilsit. Moreover, it had to suffer occupation by French troops until it had paid war reparations imposed by the victor. Still, the efforts made by Alexander I in favor of his ally were not completely in vain: as article 4 of the treaty stated, Napoleon "out of regard for his Majesty the Emperor of all the Russias, and wanting to prove his sincere desire to unite the two nations by ties of trust and inalienable friendship,"[59] agreed to restore to Frederick Wilhelm the boundaries that pertained in 1722, which meant Pomerania, Silesia, and part of Brandenburg. The city of Danzig was declared free on the model of Hamburg and placed under the protectorate of Prussia and Saxony; the territory of Byalistok was taken away from Prussia and fell into the Russian lap; finally, some Prussian land east of the Elba was confiscated under the treaty and given to Westphalia. Although not as effective as hoped, Russian help was not negligible: on June 30 King Frederick Wilhelm expressed his gratitude to his ambassador in Vienna:

> Emperor Alexander sincerely shared my excruciating position and took it upon himself to plead my cause. I must render him the honor that he gave me on this occasion with the most touching proofs of his personal friendship and his participation in the fate of my monarchy.[60]

Obliged to ratify these major territorial changes, Alexander had to accept a certain number of more political clauses: he had to recognize the Confederation of the Rhine and the new kingdom of Westphalia; he had to recognize Napoleon's older brother (Joseph) as king of Naples (heretofore Russia had been allied with a Bourbon king on that throne), to accept French mediation in the war against the Ottoman Empire, and finally, to engage in an alliance both offensive and defensive against England. Indeed, the secret alliance called for the two allies to make common cause either on land or sea against their enemies; in particular, Russia promised to act in concert with France against England in the event the latter refused Russia's offer of mediation. Finally, Russia was obliged to participate actively in the continental blockade, which meant the closing of all Russian ports to British ships and to imports from England.

In the course of negotiations, two other topics were raised: the Polish question, temporarily solved by the creation of the duchy of Warsaw, and the Ottoman question, more complex and a source of dissension between France and Russia. Napoleon had vigorously asserted his refusal to cede Constantinople to Russia ("Constantinople is the world's empire!"[61] he exclaimed), but he had also implied (at Alexander's insistence but not in writing) that he was not opposed to a future settlement between the two empires of the Ottoman question, which Alexander hastened to interpret as a blank check written to him.

The balance sheet of the Tilsit treaties appears deeply ambivalent on the Russian side. Admittedly, Alexander had saved the peace, and without ceding any part of imperial land, two crucial points for him. He had saved his Prussian ally and avoided its worst fate, a protectorship of the kingdom of

Prussia. And by accepting the principles of zones of influence dictated by Napoleon, he had raised the geopolitical status of the Russian Empire. But he had to recognize French hegemony in central Europe and accept evacuating the Balkan principalities—without getting any acknowledged legitimacy for Russia to supervise Turkish affairs (except verbally), and he had to promise to enter into an alliance that made England the new enemy of the Russian Empire, thereby contravening years of bilateral friendship.

On July 9 the two sovereigns separated, promising to send each other new representatives to ensure the maintenance of the dialogue, and Alexander returned to his capital.

But while the tsar was rather relieved at the results obtained in the course of difficult negotiations undertaken as the vanquished party, he ran up against an open revolt at home. His closest friends and advisors (Czartoryski had called the Tilsit agreements "disastrous"[62]), the court, and the elites were all furious at the defeat and reproached him for the courtesies exchanged with Napoleon and the immoral alliance just concluded with the "Beast of the Apocalypse." For them, the tsar had only bowed before the French emperor, and the many concessions he had made proved his inability to defend the interests of Russia; they only augured growing submission to France. The court buzzed with rumors of plots, and for the first time since the accession of Alexander to the throne in March 1801, the threat was serious.

CHAPTER 9

The Time of the French Alliance

1807–1812

While the Russian popular imagination was soon carried away by the drama on the raft in a direction favorable to Alexander—the rumor circulated that good Tsar Alexander profited from the meeting on the Niemen to baptize the Antichrist—by contrast, within the elites and the army, the Peace of Tilsit aroused such criticism that imperial power seemed threatened. Despite this turmoil, the autocratic tsar, inflexible and deaf to all reproaches, remained faithful to his new line. In effect, he imposed the French alliance on the country, as in 1805 he had imposed the Prussian alliance.

Yet, despite the dismay that it ignited among the court Anglophiles, this diplomatic change did not constitute a disavowal of Alexander's convictions. Throughout the years from 1807 to 1812, he would proclaim his goodwill toward Napoleon and his desire to respect the spirit and the letter of the alliance. But he was already convinced that it could not last, given that it was imposed by circumstances. Sooner or later, the struggle against Napoleon would resume, for which French expansionism was responsible. The Peace of Tilsit was thus only a pause in the military confrontation, a breathing space from which the most advantage should be drawn, diplomatically and geopolitically. Here, far from appearing to be vacillating or hesitant, Alexander on the contrary demonstrated his maturity, if not his political cynicism. He remained attached to a conception of a European balance of power that condemned French hegemonic tendencies, and he continued to proclaim his stubborn faithfulness to Prussia: in August 1807, upon his return to Russia, he publicly affirmed his disagreement with Napoleon's proposals at Tilsit that aimed to increase Russian territory at the expense of "our ally."[1] This shows how reluctantly he had entered into the French alliance. But he would respect his commitments despite the incomprehension and anger that his decisions induced among his close entourage within the court.

The Peace of Tilsit and Its Consequences

Upon his return to St. Petersburg, the tsar found he had unleashed an explosion of blame. The atmosphere was tense: a palpable and worried mood pervaded the diplomats in post in St. Petersburg. Count of Stedingk, the Swedish ambassador, wrote to his king in October 1807:

> Discontent with the emperor is increasing and the statements heard everywhere are frightening. The emperor's loyal servants and friends are in despair, but there is nobody who knows how to remedy the evil and who has the courage to make him recognize the great danger in which he finds himself. They say they see no cure, that the emperor is obstinate in his opinion, that he is not ignorant of the bad opinion, but that he attributes it to foreign causes, to the millions the English throw around to make partisans (which is entirely false and something that Savary alleges), and that he wants only the good of his subjects, and so has nothing to fear from them. However, it is too true that in particular societies and even in public assemblies, people often entertain the thought of a change of reign, and forget their duty to the point of saying that the whole masculine line of the reigning family should be proscribed.[2]

As regards our court observer Joseph de Maistre, he was even more explicit in his correspondence with his master, the king of Sardinia: "To get out of this perilous situation, many people see only the Asiatic remedy,"[3] meaning, of course, the assassination of the tsar, and his replacement by Maria Feodorovna or Catherine Pavlovna. In fact, anchored in positions viscerally hostile to the alliance with France, mother and daughter encouraged the cabal, to the point of arousing the anger of Empress Elizabeth, livid at this moral betrayal. At the beginning of September 1807, she wrote to her mother, speaking of Maria Feodorovna, who in her castle in Pavlovsk was leading the revolt:

> The empress, who as a mother should support and defend the interests of her son, instead out of carelessness or *amour-propre,* (and certainly for no other reason, for she is incapable of bad intentions), has managed to resemble the leader of a revolt. All the malcontents, who are numerous, rally around her, praising her to the skies, and never has her court been so large,

never has she attracted so many people to Pavlovsk as this year. I cannot tell you how indignant this makes me. At a time like this, when she is aware of how bitter the public feels toward the emperor, at this moment she attracts, honors, and flatters those who shout the loudest! I do not know why, but I cannot find this conduct praiseworthy, especially from a mother. [...] They say the Grand Duke Constantine, when his brother's back is turned, shouts like the others about what has happened and still happens. [...] Finally, I assure you there are moments when this good emperor, who is the best person in the whole family, appears to me *verrathen und verkauf* [betrayed and sold] by his own family.[4]

Isolated in his stubbornness in supporting the French alliance, the emperor was not helped in his task by Napoleon's decisions, either. After the Tilsit meetings he chose to send to the Russian court his faithful Savary, not as ambassador, but as "officer-general attached to the person of the emperor."[5] No choice could have been more disastrous; everyone in St. Petersburg knew that the person who commanded the imperial police in 1804 had played a key role in the kidnapping of the Duke d'Enghien—and hence in his death. Making the best of it, Alexander proved amiable to the newcomer, but the court, seeing this selection as a provocation that showed the French emperor's contempt, unanimously shunned him. Barely arrived, Savary seemed a pariah. The welcome interview granted by Maria Feodorovna to the new French ambassador lasted fifty seconds!

Of course, the court included a few Francophiles like Count Rumyantsev, promoted to minister of foreign affairs in place of Budberg at the end of 1807.6 An experienced diplomat trained in the school of Catherine II, Rumyantsev had been previously in charge of foreign trade and now performed both functions.[7] But the Francophiles' task was hard, so set was the court in its radical opposition, sharpened by the shocking presence of Savary. Elizabeth herself was "embarrassed" (a euphemism) by the presence of the Duke of Rovigo (the title Napoleon gave to Savary) in St. Petersburg. In a letter to Rumyantsev in October 1807, the empress did not conceal her unease:

I have just received a letter from the emperor in which he tells me I must invite General Savary to dine at least twice in the space of ten days; having failed out of ignorance to do what he desires, I hastened to repair this fault today. Do me the pleasure, Count, if that is possible, of coming to me today, for I admit that I am embarrassed by the obligation the emperor is imposing on me.[8]

Barely settled in St. Petersburg, General Savary perceived the rebellious tendencies at court, and he confided to the emperor that he was worried about "the consequences [...] this license might have in a country where palace revolutions were only too common."[9] But Alexander himself was well aware of the danger he was in: since mid-January 1807, to better discern the mood of the court and the elites and to try as much as possible to prevent difficulties, he had set up a "Committee for General Security" whose reports, increasingly alarming, also attest to the scope of the discontent. Yet Alexander kept his head down, declaring to the French emissary: "Oh, by God, I know it, I see it, but what do you want me to do against the destiny that leads me to this dangerous situation?"[10] But, at the same time, he resorted to taking protection from Count Arakcheev, to whom he granted extraordinary powers. In December 1807 an imperial decree assimilated all the orders given by Arakcheev to orders personally signed by the emperor;[11] some weeks later, the count was promoted to the rank of minister of war. "Like a guard dog with his obtuse ferocity and unconditional loyalty,"[12] Arakcheev, in whom Alexander had total confidence, was thus tacitly charged with watching over the son as he had previously watched over Paul.

The choice of the French alliance, taken despite criticism and risk, also separated the tsar from his Anglophile friends within the former inner circle. Guilty of having in concert with the British ambassador spread a pamphlet of British inspiration titled "Reflections on the Peace of Tilsit," Novosiltsev and Czartoryski were asked to leave Russia, while Kochubey had to give up his portfolio as interior minister. All three were relieved of their responsibilities; the sovereign thought that the new policy should be carried out by new men who were less marked by their pro-English commitments. For Alexander the price paid for the French alliance was thus very high on the political as well as the psychological and affective levels.

In November 1807, perhaps because the personality and past of Savary scarcely suited the St. Petersburg court, Napoleon replaced him with Armand de Caulaincourt, while Alexander sent to Paris Count Tolstoy as emissary. Initially the tsar wanted to make Kurakin, one of the two Tilsit negotiators, his representative in the French capital, but the latter, saying he was too old, declined the offer. In reality, his refusal is largely explained by his ties to Maria Feodorovna, "the rabid Napoleonophobe."

Arriving in St. Petersburg in December 1807, Caulaincourt did his best to be amiable but did not manage to soften the court, which remained set in its hostility to the French emperor and to his representative, who (despite himself) had been mixed up in the murder of the Duke d'Enghien.[13] Courtiers were sarcastic about Caulaincourt. In a dispatch to Sardinia, Joseph de Maistre echoed many others with his biting irony:

> I am much amused in considering Caulaincourt. He is well-born and boasts about it; he represents a sovereign who makes the world tremble; he has six or seven hundred thousand in rent; he is foremost everywhere. But he has the common air underneath the embroidery; he is stiff as if he had marionette strings in his joints. Everybody thinks he is like Ninette[14] at Court."[15]

Yet, on December 8 Alexander received him like "an old friend," putting at his disposal the sumptuous Volkonsky Palace on the banks of the Neva, "whose splendors eclipse by far the elegant and comfortable Thélusson mansion Napoleon had just bought from Murat to make it the Paris residence of Alexander's representative. [The Volkonsky] was the finest mansion in St. Petersburg and without argument the finest building after the palace of Grand Duke Constantine."[16] That very evening, the French ambassador witnessed a performance at the Winter Palace, sitting in the same row as the imperial family despite court grumbling. Yet little by little, thanks to the wealth Caulaincourt deployed (to the point of indebtedness), the magnificence of the receptions he organized, and the quality of his table, but still more to his tenacity to please and to convince people of his sincere interest in Russia, he managed over the months to rally a great part of the court, with the notable exception of Maria Feodorovna and those close to her, unshakably Francophobes.

Meanwhile in Paris, the task of Count Tolstoy appeared easier, since he chose to serve the alliance with France by serving his tsar faithfully. When appointing him, Alexander had been sufficiently explicit, declaring: "Remember one thing, it is not a diplomat I need, but a brave and honest soldier, and that is just what you are."[17] But his Prussophile convictions and his mistrust of Napoleon quickly took the upper hand. From his first meeting with the emperor, Tolstoy made many criticisms of the person he continued to call "Bonaparte," correctly pointing to the essential problem:

> Bonaparte's views of us are evident. He wants to make us an Asiatic power, push us back into our ancient borders. [...] As for Constantinople, he is trying to remove our troops in order to be the master there by proposing we throw one part of our army against Sweden and use the other on distant campaigns, in Persia, the Indies.[18]

But this lucid critique of the French emperor would push Alexander during his meeting at Erfurt with Napoleon in October 1808 to replace Tolstoy[19] with Kurakin as better able to represent him.

At the same time, Franco-Russian relations were proving complex and more strained than the elaborate demonstrations of friendship at Tilsit would have augured. Stumbling blocks soon appeared. Admittedly, promises of fidelity to the alliance had been given by Russia; on November 6, having failed in its mediation of peace between France and England, the tsarist government broke off its relations with Britain in accord with those Tilsit commitments. But deep divergences on the Ottoman and Polish issues still separated the allies.

Relying on the verbal guarantees given by Napoleon at Tilsit, Alexander charged Count Tolstoy in Paris with arranging a diplomatic act to ratify the surrender of the provinces of Moldavia and Walachia to the Russian Empire; we recall that Russia had occupied them during its military campaign against the Ottoman Empire. But in response, for the price of its "benevolence" in this affair, France demanded territorial compensation, specifically a new enlargement of the Grand Duchy of Warsaw. This would strengthen a state already placed under French influence, and it appeared to the Russians as a dangerous security threat—hence the categorical refusal of Russian diplomacy and the resultant impasse in negotiations. In February 1808 Napoleon tried to restart the dynamic of the alliance by proposing "a campaign against the pearl of the British Crown, India"; he implied that as a counterpart to Russian participation in this campaign, he would be ready for concessions on the Ottoman question. For Napoleon it was a matter of obtaining at whatever cost Russian support against England, and so the Indian expedition might adequately seal this commitment. For this purpose he proposed to the tsar a new bilateral meeting in order to determine together the details of the coming campaign.

Skeptical at first, Alexander ended up supporting the idea; on March 13, 1808, in a letter to Napoleon,[20] he accepted both the principle of Russian participation in a campaign against India and the idea of a new meeting, on the express condition that France would take into account a certain number of Russian demands. The same day, receiving Caulaincourt, the tsar reaffirmed his priorities: in the event of the two allies' sharing the Ottoman Empire, Constantinople and the three European provinces (Bessarabia, Moldavia, Walachia) would be annexed by Russia and the straits would be put under Russian control. A few weeks later, in a new meeting, Alexander declared very explicitly about Constantinople:

Geography wants me to have it, because if it belonged to another, I would no longer be master at home. Nor is it inconvenient for others (the emperor will admit) for me to have the key to the door of my house.[21]

But these declarations remained without effect: discussions in March between Caulaincourt and Rumyantsev led to nothing concrete. French diplomats thought they could not grant Russia a blank signature on the Ottoman issue. Napoleon also proposed another currency of exchange: in a letter to the tsar in February, he suggested a Russian advance toward the Baltic Sea, in the direction of Finland, which was then a possession of Sweden, ally of England. For the French emperor it was a matter of offering Russia some territorial compensation that would in no way harm his own interests and would permit anchoring Russia more solidly in the French camp.

Armed with this support, Alexander a few days later began the conquest of Finland, without even having formally declared war on Sweden. Fifty thousand combatants were thrown into battle, and on March 2 the fall of Helsinki resulted in the siege of Sveaborg. Isolated by ice, the fortress, which could not receive reinforcement by sea, was forced to capitulate in May, which temporarily halted hostilities.

Meanwhile, the Polish question remained another thorn of contention between the Tilsit allies. For Napoleon, Poland should in time be restored, and this restoration should take place under the aegis and protective wing of France, while for the tsar, a reconstituted Poland, if transformed into a bastion of French interests, could only represent an unacceptable threat to Russia, on both the security level and for its own territorial integrity. A new Poland might then aspire to reconstitute the old Polish-Lithuanian kingdom to the detriment of the Russian Empire.

Thus, in September 1808 as the tsar was getting ready to leave for Erfurt, none of the bones of contention that divided the allies had been resolved. For many in Russia, the meeting to which Alexander I had imprudently consented was a mistake, so much did St. Petersburg view the alliance as a fool's game. Moreover, by then Napoleon had freed himself of any political and moral restraints: he had kidnapped the pope, he had deposed the Spanish sovereign and led him into a trap in Bayonne. Russia was afraid for the personal safety of the tsar. On August 25 Maria Feodorovna wrote to dissuade Alexander from going to Erfurt. She was very worried for his life and reasserted her hostility for any new demonstration of Franco-Russian "friendship," for which Russia and its tsar might have to pay the costs.

You are the only person in the world who believes this approach can prevent evil and allow happiness and peace to be reborn. My Alexander, it is not so, you are fooling yourself in a criminal way; what you are doing to prevent misfortunes will bring them fully down on our heads. Bonaparte knew how to tear from you in Tilsit the promise of breaking with the English, making war with Sweden, and even this unfortunate meeting, and since the past shapes the terms for the future, this meeting will tear from you new bloody measures, carnage, and will entail the ruin of your country and finally your own. You will consent to act against Austria, against all Bonaparte's enemies. You will come to share his views, you will act for him, thereby destroying yourself, for is it not evident that by weakening the forms of power that resist Bonaparte, you will exhaust yourself and you will increase the mass of forces that he will deploy someday against us?[22]

But once again, despite the admonitions and criticism, Alexander stuck his ground. He thought he had to feign once more to believe in the alliance to gain time; far from being the dupe, the victim, or the plaything of Napoleon, the tsar appeared deeply determined, and in his answer to his mother, written the same day, he delivered a very pertinent geopolitical analysis:

The moment chosen for this meeting is such that it imposes on me the duty not to evade it. Our interests have forced us in recent times to conclude a tight alliance with France; we will do everything to prove the sincerity and nobility of our way of acting. [...] France has to believe that her political interest can be allied with that of Russia; as soon as she does not have this belief, she will see in Russia no more than an enemy that it will be in her interest to try to destroy. [...] Was it not in Russia's interest to get along with this fearful colossus, with the sole truly dangerous enemy that Russia can have? We will see his fall calmly, if such is the will of Providence; and it is more than plausible that the nations of Europe, tired of the evils they have so long suffered, will not even dream of beginning a struggle against Russia out of vengeance, just because she was allied with Napoleon at a time when each of them aspired only to that. [...] If Providence has decreed the fall of this colossal state, I doubt that it can be sudden, but even in this case, it would be wiser to await this fall and only then to take measures. This is my opinion. [...] How else could Russia conserve her union with France except by sharing its views for a while and proving that she can remain so without seeming to distrust her intentions and plans?

In my political behavior, I can only follow the inclinations of my conscience, of my main convictions—my desire, that has never quit me, of being useful to my country. This, dear Mother, is what I judge to be my duty in answering your letter. I admit that it is painful for me to see, when I have only the interests of Russia in sight, that the sentiments that are the true force of my actions may be so misunderstood.[23]

In September 1808 Alexander set off for Erfurt, accompanied by a modest retinue. Apart from his brother Constantine, the emperor brought two avowed Francophiles, Vice-Minister Mikhail Speranski and Chancellor Rumyantsev, Count Tolstoy, Prince (and minister) Alexander Golitsyn, and Princes Trubetskoy, Volkonsky, and Gagarin, who were his aides-de-camp. On the way, always faithful to his Prussian friendships, Alexander made a stop at Königsberg to meet the king and queen, who in unison with their prime minister, Baron von Stein, exhorted him to take the lead of a new anti-French coalition. But for Alexander the hour scarcely lent itself to a military engagement: the Russian army was undergoing a restructuring and was already fighting on the Ottoman front. In Erfurt he would again have to perform his role of friendship and play his part in the Napoleonic game, while waiting for a better chance.

* * *

As in Tilsit, luster, pomp, and profusions of friendship were displayed on both sides. Alexander arrived in the town on September 25 in the evening, but only on the twenty-seventh did the official meeting of the two retinues take place, at some distance from Erfurt. Napoleon came on horseback and met the Russian sovereign. Barely out of his carriage, Alexander was presented with a magnificent grey mount, Eclipse, covered with a white bearskin. After kissing each other "fraternally," the two sovereigns (Alexander in a green general's uniform and Napoleon in the uniform of the chasseur guard) entered on horseback into the town of Erfurt, a small peaceful village that had not been predestined to receive guests of this rank:

> A tranquil village of bourgeois and officials, Erfurt did not have a taste for grandeur and its disposition did not lend itself to its new fortune. Its tortuous streets, badly paved and unlit at night, and its irregular squares seemed unsuitable for the deployment of retinues and the movement of troops. Its narrow houses, with sharp gables and picturesque facades, where the art of the sixteenth century had sculpted delicate ornaments, may have sufficed to house the intimate luxury of an opulent bourgeoisie, but could not answer the necessities or grand requirements of the court.[24]

The town dressed up for the occasion in its finery to show itself worthy of the honor conferred on it; apart from the two sovereigns and their staffs, Erfurt welcomed several German princes (the kings of Bavaria, Saxony, Württemberg, Prince Wilhelm of Prussia), writers (including Goethe), and artists, including the famous actor Talma who gave in Weimar on October 6 a very fine and triumphant interpretation of Brutus in The Death of Caesar, a tragedy by Voltaire. Meetings lasted until October14, and as at Tilsit, personal meetings and working sessions alternated with public occasions. Regiments were reviewed, there were dances, parties, hunts (including a great stag hunt in the Forest of Ettersberg near Weimar), and past victories were commemorated. On October 14 (the anniversary of his victory of Jena), Napoleon took his ally on a tour of the battlefield that had seen the routing of the Prussian army. We may easily understand what it must have cost Alexander to keep a good countenance despite this provocation. Finally, every evening at 7:00 p.m., at Napoleon's invitation, the French theater company performed before "an orchestra of kings"[25] and of German princes and aristocrats, the plays of Corneille, Racine, and Voltaire. The operation of seduction conducted by the French emperor was at its zenith: Napoleon wanted to celebrate in the greatest pomp his power—as well as this Franco-Russian alliance he needed so much. For in fact, the stakes were high: bogged down in Spanish and Portuguese campaigns, the French emperor wanted to secure from his ally real support in his struggle against Austria and England. He was open about this in his instructions to Talleyrand, who for a year had no longer been minister of foreign relations (he resigned upon returning from Tilsit) but who was brought to Erfurt to take part in negotiations:

> We are going to Erfurt. I wish to come back free to do in Spain what I want; I want to be sure that Austria will be worried and contained, and I do not want to be committed in any precise way with Russia as concerns affairs in the Levant. Prepare me an agreement that contents Emperor Alexander, that is above all directed against England, and over which I can be at my ease about the rest. [...] Make your arrangements to leave; you must be at Erfurt a day or two ahead of me. You will find the means to see Emperor Alexander often. You know him well, you will speak to him in the language that suits him. You will tell him that, given how useful our alliance can be for men, one recognizes the will of Providence. [...] I will help you! Prestige will not be lacking.[26]

But Napoleon's plan—which cynically wagered on Alexander's naïveté— stumbled against a more complex situation because behind the ostentatious demonstrations of friendship, the political exchanges were tense. Very soon

Napoleon realized that his "ally" had become much less malleable than the vanquished party of Tilsit had been. He complained bitterly to Caulaincourt: "Your emperor Alexander is stubborn as a mule. He is deaf to things that he does not want to hear. This devilish affair of Spain is costing me dear."[27] Arguing with Alexander, he even threw a comical scene:[28] angry, he threw his hat on the ground and stamped on it, while the tsar replied with a calm smile: "You are violent, and I am stubborn. With me, anger gains nothing. Let us talk and be reasonable, or I am leaving."

If Napoleon was irritated with negotiations to the point of losing his sang-froid (or feigning to lose it), this was because Alexander refused to cede to most of his demands. Admittedly, the tsar recognized the legitimacy of French conquests in Italy and Spain (but he was pertinently aware that the French positions in Spain were fragile, to say the least), and he reasserted his fidelity to the continental blockade despite its high financial and economic cost.[29] But he balked at engaging alongside Napoleon in demanding the disarmament of Austria, and he merely promised, in case Austria recommenced hostilities, to commit to any new conflict an army of 150,000 men. Indeed, Alexander would never participate in the annihilation of Austria. Apart from the fact that this would be incompatible with his conception of the balance of powers, it might allow the Polish territories of Austria to emancipate themselves, to be joined to the duchy of Warsaw, and thus form a Poland under French influence, which would be still more powerful and more threatening.

At the same time, while Napoleon was still counting on the tsar's active engagement against England (in exchange for France's recognition of the legitimacy of the annexation of Finland), Alexander remained vague. To secure his agreement, Napoleon said he was ready to accept new Russian conquests at the expense of Sweden, but Alexander did not wish to extend his territory in the direction of the North Sea. Lacking chips to bargain with, the tsar's commitments to Napoleon remained limited: on the one hand, Alexander condescended to a common diplomatic approach in the form of a letter to the king of England, proposing peace talks on the basis of uti possidetis. And on October 12 he signed a theoretically secret agreement[30] (valid for ten years) that reaffirmed the Tilsit commitments and stated that the concrete modes of military operations against England would be fixed during a forthcoming meeting between the two sovereigns. This final meeting, which was to take place later in the year, would never happen—and the outcome of their agreement would remain practically nil.

On his side, while Alexander hoped to convince Napoleon to withdraw his troops from Prussia, this demand aroused a hostile reaction, and so the tsar had to settle for two minor concessions: reduction of the war reparations owed by Prussia (from 140 to 120 million francs), and extension of the duration of its payment (from a year and a half to three years). Despite this reversal that complicated his relations with the king and queen of Prussia, Alexander obtained something at Erfurt that was crucial with respect to his own court, apart from the recognition of the conquest of Finland: the legitimacy of the acquisition by Russia of the principalities of Walachia and Moldavia. Indeed, article 5 announced that the "high contracting parties are committed to regarding as an absolute condition of peace with England that they will recognize Finland, Walachia and Moldavia as part of the Empire of Russia."[31] So strengthened by this French assurance, Alexander would resume military hostilities against the Ottoman Empire in April 1809 in order to ensure the definitive possession of the Danube principalities.

Throughout the eighteen days of the Erfurt conference, Alexander proved pugnacious, and overall he won his wager, drawing the best outcome from the Napoleonic game. In this result we should see the effect of the tsar's personality, the expression of his desire to stand up to "Bonaparte" and to obtain at whatever cost from this new meeting the precious wins able to pacify minds in Russia. He was clear-sighted about a character who no longer fascinated him. But we must also detect the intervention of an external element: the support that Talleyrand was giving the tsar from the wings. Talleyrand had been at Erfurt from September 24, and it was he who received Alexander at his arrival the next day. Talleyrand was staying close to the tsar's residence, and the two men saw each other almost every evening at the home of the sister of Queen Louise of Prussia, the princess of Thurn and Taxis. And in private Talleyrand told the Russian emperor things that are surprising, coming from someone who was supposed to be representing the interests of France:

> Sire, what are you doing here? It is up to you to save Europe and you will not manage unless you stand up to Napoleon. The French people are civilized, but their sovereign is not; the sovereign of Russia is civilized, but his people are not. Thus it is up to the sovereign of Russia to be the ally of the French people. [...] The Rhine, the Alps, and the Pyrenees were the conquests of France; the rest is the conquest of Napoleon and France has no attachment to it.[32]

Talleyrand went even farther. He asserted to the tsar that "the plan for a war in the Indies and the sharing of the Ottoman Empire are only phantoms produced on a stage to draw the attention of Russia away until Spanish affairs are arranged,"[33] and in parallel he pushed Alexander to do everything to reassure Austria of his peaceful intentions. Henceforth, the French emissary was playing a double game: fearful of Napoleon's megalomania but incapable of arresting his crazy course, Talleyrand chose to betray the French emperor in order to remain faithful to his own idea of French interests. The confidence established between the tsar and the diplomat was such that Alexander did not hesitate to show him the final plan of the secret agreement; the emissary "took advantage of it to persuade the tsar to attenuate and dilute, to the point of insignificance, the articles regarding Austria."[34] Talleyrand's biographer relevantly stresses the singular nature of the Erfurt negotiations: "The history of this treaty is unique in the annals of diplomacy. Talleyrand 'played a hand' on both sides, French and Russian, even though he was not present as an official minister."[35]

Similarly, when on October 12 Napoleon confided to Talleyrand his intention to divorce Josephine (with whom he still had no child) and to ask in marriage one of the tsar's sisters, in order to further secure the Franco-Russian alliance and give his empire an heir, the French diplomat, who was hostile to the plan ("I admit I was frightened for Europe of one more alliance between Russia and France,"[36] Talleyrand wrote in his memoirs) quickly passed this information on to Alexander. The latter immediately shared Talleyrand's reservations and—a sign of the complicity that now linked them—confided the riposte he had decided to use to sabotage any marriage proposal. Talleyrand wrote:

> All the art I thought I needed with Emperor Alexander was unnecessary. At the first word, he understood me—and precisely as I wished to be understood: "If it was only a matter of me," he said to me, "I would willingly give my consent, but it is not only mine that must be had, because my mother has kept over his daughters a power that I must not contest. I might try to give her guidance, and it is probable that she would follow, but I don't dare answer for it. All this, inspired by true friendship, should satisfy emperor Napoleon."[37]

The diplomatic positions defended by Talleyrand were in fact mixed up with his selfish interests: at Erfurt, he obtained from Alexander for his nephew Edmond of Périgord, the hand of the very rich Princess Dorothea of Courland—just when the girl, aged only sixteen, was on the point of getting engaged to Adam Czartoryski! And after Erfurt it was in hard currency that Talleyrand would sell his services to the tsar.[38]

* * *

Upon his return from Erfurt, Alexander, fearing that Napoleon would indeed ask for his sister Catherine in marriage, decided to prevent this union. Although not beautiful, the young woman, then aged twenty-one, was imaginative and sensual; she breathed intelligence and a lively mind. The mistress of General Bagration, she was seductive to those around her, including her own brother (as we have seen). Having decided to prevent any diplomatic embarrassment (even though the French emperor had not officially formulated any demand), Alexander hurried with the agreement of the person concerned and of Maria Feodorovna to marry "Cathau" to Prince George of Oldenburg, the younger son of Peter of Oldenburg and Frederika of Württemberg. The young man came from a princely family but had little money. So, in order to assure the couple an income worthy of the sumptuous lifestyle of his beloved sister, the tsar named his brother-in-law governor of the rich region of Tver. Alexander saw to it that the French alliance sealed at Tilsit and then at Erfurt would not be strengthened by any family tie that would later be liable to hinder his European policy.

Slow Deterioration of Bilateral Relations

Back in St. Petersburg Alexander did not play the role of a docile ally, for he conducted on all fronts an active diplomacy that soon annoyed the French. In January 1809 he received with a warm pomp the Prussian sovereigns who were visiting Russia; for 24 days, without regard for his French "ally," he gave ostentatious demonstrations of his attachment to the cause of the Hohenzollerns. He showered the king with warmth and bestowed on Queen Louise sumptuous gifts (a gold toiletry set, fine Persian and Turkish shawls, and lace gowns). Furious at these manifestations that flouted the spirit of Erfurt, Caulaincourt lost his civility to the point of a rude remark, as reported by Joseph de Maistre in a letter to his minister:

> My pen is hardly able to render the speech that the ambassador of France made at the home of Princess Dolgoruki, but it is absolutely necessary to let you know this word. The ambassador said bluntly: "There is no mystery about this trip; the queen of Prussia is coming to have sex with emperor Alexander." This is exactly what he said, but I do not know enough French to lend to such a horror the name it deserves.[39]

This accusation was not only vulgar but unfounded: the fond relationship between Alexander and Louise remained platonic. We should see the demonstrations of friendship toward the Prussian sovereigns merely as a reflection of Alexander's real compassion, crosscut with his own guilt: in fact, since Tilsit he had carried like a cross his participation in the dismembering of Prussia. The Prussian monarchs, despite the warm welcome they had received, were bitter about their situation, and on the eve of her departure from St. Petersburg, in a premonition of her coming death,[40] Louise wrote in her diary: "I bring back from these brilliant parties only fatigue and pain. I return as I came. [...] Henceforth, nothing will dazzle me any more: my kingdom is no longer of this world."[41]

Shortly after the Hohenzollern stay in Russia, it was the turn of the Austrian prince Schwarzenberg to pay a visit to St. Petersburg. Charged with announcing to Alexander that Austria had decided as part of a future coalition to resume hostilities with France, the emissary from Vienna had the task of obtaining from the tsar the neutrality of Russia in the war to come. Little desiring to be dragged into a conflict that he thought premature, the tsar hesitated for several weeks before opting for a compromise solution. During the audience granted to Schwarzenberg (in a secret document) he committed to guarantee de facto Russia's neutrality, while specifying that in accord with the letter of the Erfurt agreement, Russia would have to declare war on Austria.

While in the winter and spring of 1809 the Austrian question preoccupied the tsar, his mind was especially on the war with Sweden. Having recommenced in the winter of 1808, the conflict went to the advantage of the 35,000 men led by Bagration, faced with 20,000 Swedish and Finnish soldiers. The outcome of an attack on Stockholm at the start of 1809 was the Swedish surrender; then the tsar went to Finland to witness the opening of the Finnish national diet at Porvoo on March 15, before concluding the Peace of Hamina a few months later. This gave Russia the Aland Islands and made Finland a grand duchy that was integrally a part of the Russian Empire. Alexander was enthusiastic:

> This peace is perfect and absolutely the one I wanted. I cannot thank the Supreme Being enough. The entire concession of Finland with the Aland Islands, the adhesion to the continental system, the closing of ports to England, and finally the peace with the allies of Russia: all settled without intermediaries. There is enough to sing a fine *Te Deum Laudamus*—so our Te Deum in St. Isaac Cathedral tomorrow, with its military pomp, will not be sneezed at![42]

This strategic advantage to the northwest strengthened the hegemony of the empire over the Baltic seas and culminated the work of Peter the Great by anchoring Russia in northern Europe. However, this conquest aroused the disapproval of Laharpe (who saw it as the expression of a guilty and costly expansionism liable to turn the tsar away from domestic reforms);[43] nor did it dazzle the emperor. Admittedly, Russian military prestige was burnished and some luster restored to imperial troops in want of glory, but Alexander was not intoxicated by his success—still less because in the weeks following his stay in Finland, the European theater was becoming worrying.

By mid-April, the Austro-French war was at its height; Napoleon demanded via Caulaincourt the military support from Russia that had been promised at Erfurt. But he would not get it. While Alexander did mass along the border with Austria some 70,000 men under the command of Prince Golitsyn, he knowingly delayed their movement. The marching order (promised to Napoleon for April 27) was not given until May 18, and once the Russian troops were en route, they advanced very slowly to the border, which they crossed while carefully avoiding meeting the enemy on the terrain. Meanwhile, the Grande Armée had progressed to the point of occupying Vienna as soon as May 13 and inflicting on Emperor Franz I at Wagram a severe defeat on July 6 that obliged him to sue for peace. Despite victories that in fact made Russia's military involvement superfluous, Napoleon was furious with Alexander and no longer believed in the viability of the alliance. On June 2, 1809, the foreign affairs minister, Champagny, wrote to Caulaincourt:

> Mr. Ambassador, the Emperor does not want me to hide from you that the recent circumstances have made him lose much confidence in the alliance with Russia, and that they are for him a sign of the bad faith of this government. One never pretended to protect the ambassador of a power on which war is declared! Six weeks passed, and the Russian army made no move, and the Austrian army occupied the grand duchy like one of its provinces. […] The Emperor's heart is wounded; because of that he no longer writes to Emperor Alexander; he cannot express a trust he no longer feels. He says nothing; he does not complain; he holds his displeasure within himself, but he no longer values the alliance with Russia. […] The 40,000 men that Russia should have sent to the grand duchy would have been a real service, and would at least have maintained some illusion about a phantom alliance.

Consequently, Champagny concluded by enjoining Caulaincourt to stick purely to a game of appearances:

> Let the Court of Russia be always as content with you as you appear to be with her; even though the Emperor no longer believes in the Russian alliance, it is all the more important to him that this belief of which he himself is disabused be shared by the rest of Europe.[44]

Henceforth, distrust was mutual; the following months were nothing but a succession of misunderstandings, disagreements, and outrages that made the march to war increasingly inexorable.

* * *

On October 14, 1809, the Treaty of Vienna inflicted on Austria heavy territorial losses in Galicia, in the Salzburg region, and in the Illyrian provinces. As a recompense for the pseudo-participation by Russia in the war (Napoleon wanted to save appearances), it was granted the Galician district of Tarnopol, but it also paid a price for its passivity: it was forced to ratify the shift of the lands taken from Austria to the duchy of Warsaw, which was substantially enlarged, to the great displeasure of Alexander, who did not want to see on the borders of Russia an "independent" Poland under French tutelage; moreover, nationalist public opinion was furious at Russia's losing influence over the Polish question. Mentioning the toxic reaction of aristocrats at court the day after the treaty was signed, a worried Caulaincourt wrote to his minister that "he had not yet seen ferment at this level and of this scope." Then he reported the aggressive and contemptuous remarks about Alexander in the capital's salons:

> They say the emperor is good but stupid, and Rumyantsev an imbecile, they never know how to take sides. Making war, they had only to start by seizing Galicia, and the Poles would never come to dispute it. The emperor should be made a monk and maintain peace at the monastery; Naryshkina should be made a nun to service the chaplain and gardener, especially if they were Polish [we recall the tsar's mistress was of Polish origin]. As for Rumyantsev, he should be made a merchant of kvass.[45]

This gossip shows that even many of the educated public found the tsar's European policy incomprehensible.

In this context, in January 1810, Rumyantsev and Caulaincourt met in St. Petersburg to draft a bilateral agreement on the Polish question. Its first article stated that "the Kingdom of Poland will never be re-established" and article 5 banned any new territorial enlargement of the duchy of Warsaw. Five days later Caulaincourt informed the tsar of Napoleon's intention to divorce Josephine and his wish to marry Princess Anna Pavlovna; in exchange for this demand in marriage, valid for only 48 hours, he offered Alexander I the chance to work for a mutual understanding over the Polish question.

Alexander said he was honored—but asked for a delay of ten days before giving his answer because, he said, under Paul's testament, Maria Feodorovna kept full power over the marriages of her daughters, and therefore she had to be consulted. To Caulaincourt's great concern, when the deadline passed, there was no response from the Romanovs. It was only on February 3 that the tsar, "rallying to the opinion" expressed by Maria Feodorovna (in fact they had shared the same view since the start) announced to the diplomat that Anna, then aged 14, could not marry the French emperor until two years had passed. This "diplomatic" answer actually masked the Romanovs' visceral opposition to this marriage: young Anna would never marry the illegitimate "Bonaparte" and find herself banned from all the great courts of Europe, with an uncertain and dangerous future. Meanwhile, though, Napoleon had engaged unbeknownst to many of his diplomats (including Caulaincourt) in negotiations with Franz I of Austria and had already obtained the hand of Archduchess Marie Louise. Sent on February 7 and received in St. Petersburg on February 23, the dispatch announcing the imperial marriage was a real snub for the tsar.

For Napoleon the Russian procrastination and the subsequent marriage refusal attested, yet again, to the failure of the alliance; thus he reneged on his Polish promises and the Polish plan drafted at the end of December. On February 6 he wrote to Champagny to disavow his minister and his ambassador in St. Petersburg:

> I cannot say that the kingdom of Poland will never be reestablished, for that would mean saying that if one day the Lithuanians, or other circumstances, wanted to re-establish it, I would be obliged to send troops to oppose this. This is contrary to my dignity. [...] My goal is to pacify Russia and to attain this, an article will suffice in the following terms: Emperor Napoleon promises to never give aid or assistance to any power or any internal uprising that might happen to try to reestablish the kingdom of Poland.[46]

This declaration is interesting: it attests to a Napoleonic conception of Poland that rested on historical and not just linguistic facts, which could therefore only worry the Russians.

Thus, in February a new text was prepared; however it would not be ratified by Napoleon, and in the course of 1810, while diplomats endeavored to save the peace, the military men were already preparing for war, as grievances accumulated on both sides.

For two months, the tsar delegated to Paris an ambassador extraordinaire, Prince Alexey Kurakin (Alexander Kurakin's brother), to try once more to make progress on the Polish issue. But he met with a flat refusal, and when he took leave of Napoleon in August 1810, the war was already looming in the latter's mind as well as in his statements.

∗ ∗ ∗

Further subjects of contention accumulated, starting with a trade war. While the continental blockade of Britain was increasingly hindering Russian foreign trade and weakening the empire's economy,[47] Napoleon showed no sign of understanding his ally's dilemma. He rightly reproached the tsar for his ill-will in carrying out the blockade but made even more demands: in 1810 the French emperor published a new tariff forbidding the importation into France of any colonial goods on board either French or neutral ships, and he asked his ally to do the same. But on December 30, 1810, Alexander refused to comply, considering that the measure would do additional damage to the Russian economy, and he adopted a ukase that, pointing at the fall of the ruble, prohibited the entry by land of merchandise coming from France—silk goods in particular—and opened all Russian ports to neutral vessels, introducing a serious breach in the blockade.

A month later a new subject of tension arose, this time over the Swedish question. Whereas geographically and geopolitically Russia considered Sweden as one of its primary zones of interest, his French ally had kept Alexander out of the deal that led to the elevation of Bernadotte to the Swedish throne. Another subject of contention was that Napoleon decided to annex the Hanseatic towns and the duchy of Oldenburg, on the grounds that the duchy had become a "warehouse for contraband British merchandise" that had to be annexed to ensure the blockade. This act aroused the fury of both tsar and the court because of the kinship between the duchy and the imperial family.[48] To pacify Alexander, Napoleon proposed to pay off the Duke of Oldenburg by offering him Erfurt; but this bargain was judged odious by both the duke and the tsar and was refused. So, on March 13, 1811, Alexander expressed to Napoleon in restrained but clear terms the scope of his resentment as well as his determination not to yield to his "ally's" demands:

> Neither my sentiments nor my policy has changed; I desire only the maintenance and consolidation of our alliance. Is it not permitted to suppose that it is Your Majesty who has changed in regard to me? Your Majesty accuses me of having protested against the Oldenburg affair, but how could I not? A little corner of land possessed by the one individual who belongs to my

family, who has performed all the formalities required of him, a member of the confederation, and therefore under the protection of Your Majesty, and whose possessions are guaranteed by an article of the Treaty of Tilsit, finds himself dispossessed—and without Your Majesty saying a word beforehand!

Of what importance could this piece of land have for France and how could this process prove to Europe Your Majesty's friendship for me? All the letters written from everywhere at this time prove that it was seen as a desire by Your Majesty to hurt us. [...] You suppose that my ukase on the tariff is directed against France. I must combat this opinion as gratuitous and unjust. [...] [The ukase] has two goals: first, by prohibiting most severely British commerce, it grants some facilities to American commerce as the only sea transport that Russia may use to export products too bulky to go by land; second, it restrains as much as possible the importation by land as more disadvantageous for our balance of trade. [...] I think I may rightly say that Russia has observed the Treaty of Tilsit more scrupulously than France. [...] The Erfurt agreement assures me of the possession of Moldavia and Walachia, and so I am entirely in order. As for the conquest of Finland, it was not in my policy, and Your Majesty should remember that I only undertook the war against Sweden as a consequence of your continental system. The success of my arms won me the possession of Finland. [...] But if Your Majesty cites the advantages that Russia has drawn from her alliance with France, may I not cite those drawn by France and the many unions she has formed in parts of Italy, in northern Germany, Holland, etc.? [...] Coveting nothing from my neighbors, loving France—what interest would I have in wanting war? Russia has no need of conquests and perhaps already has too much land. The superior genius for war that I recognize in Your Majesty leaves me no illusion about the difficulty of the struggle that might occur between us. [...] Moreover, my pride is attached to the union with France. Having established it as a policy of principle for Russia, having had to combat for a long time old opinions that were against it, it is not reasonable to suppose I now have a desire to destroy my work and make war on Your Majesty. And if you desire this as little as I do, very certainly it will not happen. [...] [But if war must break out] I will know how to fight and sell my existence very dearly.[49]

In March 1811 the tension reached its height, and the gears of war were set in motion, even if the tsar still tried to avoid confrontation. However, in the eyes of some historians, neither the Polish question nor the issue of the duchy of Oldenburg was of a nature to trigger a confrontation between France and Russia. For them, the vital interests of Russia were not threatened. In fact, given the coming patriotic war's scope and cost (human as well as economic and social), they feel justified in wondering whether Alexander had engaged himself, imprudently or not, in a conflict he could have avoided. But the archive sources and materials I have consulted do not show that the tsar was guilty of thoughtlessness or imprudence. Admittedly, there is no doubt that Alexander reacted instinctively as well as politically in the Oldenburg affair, but that incident was merely superimposed on a set of disagreements and contentions that had built up. And if we remember that it is only reluctantly (and braving the opposition of those close to him) that Alexander I had entered into the Tilsit alliance, then it is clear that after 1810–1811 he was almost relieved to end the playacting he had performed for many long months. The hour had now come to have a fight with the "tyrant," the usurper who in contempt of all practice continued to use force or intimidation to modify the map of Europe to suit himself, putting into peril the security of all powers, and foremost the Russian Empire. For Alexander, the French game in the Balkans and the territorial aggrandizement that Napoleon had granted the Grand Duchy of Warsaw without consulting his ally, were intolerable threats to the interests and security of Russia.

Since 1810 the tsar had been urgently reorganizing his army and had set up in Paris a precious information service to give him data of great value about the state and structure of the French forces.[50] However, all his confidential remarks made in this period demonstrate that he feared the shock of the war to come and was well aware of his daunting task.

❊ ❊ ❊

At the end of 1810 and the start of 1811, the tsar entertained a plan to conduct an offensive war on German and Polish territory—which would spare Russian land—with the support of Polish patriots to whom he was ready to promise the reestablishment of a kingdom of Poland under Russian authority before the start of military operations against France. In two letters dated January 1810 and February 1811[51] to Prince Czartoryski (then in his estate in Pulawy), Alexander declared himself in favor of a "union of all the lands that formerly comprised Poland, including Russian provinces except for White Russia." He proposed that this reconstituted kingdom would be "forever united with Russia and the emperor would henceforth carry the title of 'Emperor of Russia and King of Poland.'" Finally, he invited Czartoryski to sound out discreetly the leaders of the Polish nation and army on their intentions, specifying that "as long as I cannot be sure of Polish cooperation, I have decided not to start the war with France." He went on: "If the

Poles back me up, success cannot be doubted because it is founded not on a hope of counterbalancing the talents of Napoleon but solely on the lack for forces in which he will find himself, combined with the exasperation that ferments against him throughout Germany."[52]

But Alexander absolutely had to know the intentions and mood of the inhabitants of the duchy of Warsaw. Hence his questions: What would be their attitude in the event of a war between France and Russia? Would they be prepared to follow the tsar if he promised them political status and rights? To give more weight to his plan, the tsar calculated precisely in his first letter the forces that could be mustered: 100,000 Russians, 50,000 Poles (if they chose the Russian side), 50,000 Prussians, 30,000 Danes—i.e., 230,000 men who might be rapidly deployed and reinforced by 100,000 more Russians; faced (in Alexander's view) for the time being with only 60,000 French spread over Germany, Holland, and eastern France, 30,000 Saxons, 30,000 Bavarians, 20,000 soldiers from Württemberg and 15,000 from Westphalia—or 155,000 in all. But this estimate of French forces might be reduced because if the Polish rallied to the Russians, then the German troops might be tempted to do the same, which would reduce the Grande Armée to its French base.[53]

On January 18 Adam Czartoryski replied that the Poles would only rally to Russia if the tsar promised to respect a certain number of conditions: the May 1791 constitution had to be restored, all Polish lands unified, and the new state had to have access to the sea. But he expressed doubts about the feasibility of the plan: he stressed the confidence the Poles had placed and continued to place in Napoleon, and he was doubtful about the attitude of German troops. In his reply Alexander reasserted that he was in favor of a sovereign Poland with a national army, but he still refused to give Byelorussia and the lands east of the Dnieper and Dvina Rivers to any new Polish entity. In a general way, he was aware of the difficulties and stakes:

> It is beyond doubt that Napoleon is trying to provoke Russia to break with him, hoping that I will make the mistake of being the aggressor. In the current circumstances, this would be a mistake that I am decided not to commit. Everything changes if the Poles want to unite with me. Strengthened by the 50,000 men that I would owe them, by the 50,000 Prussians who then might without risk join in the same way, and by the moral revolution in Europe which will be the necessary result, I might get as far as the Oder without encountering opposition. [...] As long as I cannot be sure of cooperation with the Poles, I have decided to not begin war with France.[54]

But he still remained attached to his plan. For this purpose he approached the king of Prussia and in October 1811 ordered the commanders of Russian troops stationed on the western border to prepare to go on campaign. Russia, he announced to them, was liable to start a sudden offensive.[55] However, ultimately, the king of Prussia's reservations and those of Czartoryski won out over Alexander's bellicose intentions. In April 1812 he wrote to his Polish friend:

> Your preceding letters have left me too little hope of success to authorize me to act, and I could not so reasonably resolve unless I had some probability of success. Thus I must resign myself to see what happens and to not provoke by my actions a struggle whose importance and dangers I appreciate, though without believing that I can escape it.[56]

By this date the tsar had given up his plan for an offensive war. But while he had long been hesitating over the path to take, as of the spring of 1811, the Russian Empire was also preparing a defensive war whose first manifestations— building fortresses, installing regiments—were visible in Russian Poland and aroused Napoleon's anger against Caulaincourt, who was called back to Paris. Judged by Napoleon as guilty of having succumbed to Russian propaganda— "Alexander wants to make war against me! You are the dupe of Alexander and the Russians! You speak like a Russian! You have become Russian!"[57] Napoleon rebuked him when he returned—and of having been inattentive to the preparations begun by the imperial army in Poland, Caulaincourt was in May replaced by General Lauriston, whose room for maneuver would prove nonexistent. While Caulaincourt did remain an indefatigable partisan of the alliance, as a lucid observer in September 1810, he composed a judicious portrait of Alexander in a letter to the French minister of foreign affairs.

> With respect to this prince, it seems to me he is not judged for what he is. He is thought weak, but that is a mistake. No doubt, he can bear much contrariness and hide his discontent, but this is because his goal is the general peace, and he hopes to reach it without violent crisis. But this facility of character is circumscribed: he will not go beyond the circle he has traced; this circle is made of iron and will not bend because deep down at the bottom of this character of benevolence, frankness, and natural loyalty as well as elevated sentiments and principles, there is an acquired sovereign dissimulation, which marks a stubbornness that nothing can vanquish. The talent of a government and of anyone who deals with him must therefore be to divine this limit, for the emperor will never exceed it.[58]

On the day of Caulaincourt's departure, as a mark of his esteem, Alexander gave him both the Order of St. Andrew and a magnificent lacquer box with a lid decorated with a miniature portrait of himself.

Napoleon, for his misfortune and that of his empire, took no notice of his ambassador's warnings. In June 1811 in his chateau in St. Cloud, he spoke privately with Caulaincourt for almost seven hours. During the interview Napoleon complained several times that the Russian alliance had been of no use in his anti-British strategy, that Russia was sabotaging the continental blockade, and that, taking into account the many bones of contention, war had become unavoidable. Caulaincourt tried to temporize, to convince him of the need to pursue the alliance, but Napoleon would have none of it. On August 15, trying to intimidate the tsar by proclaiming his aggressiveness and his condescension toward him, Napoleon during a diplomatic meeting launched into an insulting and public diatribe against Russian ambassador Kurakin that says much about the deteriorating relations between the two supposed allies:

> You have just been beaten near Rustschuk because you lacked troops and you lacked them because you withdrew five divisions from your Danube army to transport them to Poland. [...] I am not so stupid as to accept that it was Oldenburg that concerns you—one does not fight for Oldenburg. I clearly see that it is about Poland; I am starting to believe that you want to take it away. Well, no, you will not have one village, not one windmill of the grand duchy. Even if your armies were camped on the heights of Montmartre, I would not give you one inch of Warsaw territory! I do not know if I will beat you, but we will fight. I have 800,000 men, and each year I will have 250,000 more. You are counting on allies. Where are they? Austria, from whom you have stolen 200,000 souls in Galicia? Prussia, from whom you have taken Bialystok? Sweden, which you have mutilated by taking Finland from it? All these grievances will not be forgotten, you will have all of Europe against you! [...] You resemble a hare that has received a bullet in the head and that turns and turns without knowing what direction to go.[59]

Far from being intimidated, Alexander wove his own web: in February 1811, despite the insult over the marriage of Marie Louise, he renewed contact with Austria. He received (discreetly, at the home of Count Tolstoy) General Saint-Julien, the Austrian envoy, and told him he wanted to avoid any conflict to come, while declaring firmly:

> Your sovereign knows that since my peace with France I have applied myself in particular to avoiding anything that could cause a new explosion. Nevertheless,

recent events might well lead to war. I will avoid it as long as possible, but if the dignity of my empire requires it, and if I am forced to, then I will draw my saber. [...] I have 200,000 men assembled on those of my borders that might be threatened—and behind them 130,000 more. I desire that your sovereign be informed of how I could oppose an enemy. But I am far from proposing any transaction to your court, knowing very well Austria's situation.[60]

In March he sent the Austrian emperor a secret letter asking him to remain neutral in the event of a future war between Russia and France; for the price of this neutrality, he offered to help him to recover his former Italian and Balkan possessions. But without closing the door on any negotiations, Franz's answer remained evasive.[61]

At this date the tsar still hoped to benefit from Austrian support. But Alexander would be disappointed: on March 14 Austria signed a treaty in Paris that set up an alliance with France and called for Austria to bring a contingent of 30,000 men in case of conflict. But Alexander did not give up. After another meeting with Saint-Julien on April 7, he obtained from Chancellor Metternich an oral and secret agreement guaranteeing that Austria would only participate weakly and pro forma in the coming war,[62] in violation of the agreement just concluded with France. Meanwhile Alexander approached Bernadotte of Sweden, who, furious with the fact that in January 1812 Napoleon had occupied Swedish Pomerania to strengthen the blockade, agreed to sign a treaty of alliance that guaranteed Swedish neutrality in exchange for putting at the disposal of Sweden 35,000 Russian soldiers to help it to conquer Norway. Wanting to have as much freedom of movement as possible, Alexander tried also to conclude a quick peace with the Ottoman Empire, which would be accomplished in May 1812. Finally, diplomatic contacts with Britain were secretly revived.

This shows that diplomatic activity was at its most furious when, on June 24, 1812, the Grande Armée—composed of 20 nations and 12 languages, totaling almost 450,000 men—abruptly invaded Russian territory.

CHAPTER 10

Between Domestic Reforms and Military Preparations

1807–1812

The years from 1807 to 1812 were also of major importance on a domestic level. Upon the return to peacetime, Alexander could again devote himself to the work of reform begun in 1801 that the upheavals and subsequent military engagements had abruptly frozen after 1805. But as we have seen, the fragile and ambiguous peace of Tilsit and of Erfurt left little respite: on one hand, because its negative impact was quickly felt on Russian economy and development, and on the other hand, because starting in 1810 military consultations and preparations took the upper hand, gradually tearing the tsar away from his domestic preoccupations.

The Hour of Reform

When peace was restored, Alexander revived his work from 1801 to 1804 and again asserted his desire to reform the empire's administration to make it more effective and just. He devoted all his energy to these issues in the years from 1807 to 1811—despite his personal suffering. In July 1810 he lost his little Zinaide, born of his liaison with Maria Naryshkina "and with her, a part of the happiness I enjoyed in this world."[1]

To help him in this reforming task, he chose the support not of his old friends from the inner circle (who had fallen into disfavor since Tilsit), but rather the help of Mikhail Speransky, a "new man."

Between 1801 and 1805 the tsar tried to rationalize the central administration by creating ministries in September 1802 and officially fixing the responsibilities of ministers and of their departments. But while making central administration more effective, reform also had a tendency to accentuate the compartmentalization of ministries and the absence of any coordination among them. Moreover, some key sectors continued to evade the newly installed central administration. In 1808 the Ministry of Internal Affairs, which was concerned with policy and security as well as public health, did manage to eliminate an epidemic of the plague by resorting to draconian quarantine measures, but the same year it proved incapable of ensuring the provision of foodstuffs in the zones most affected by disastrous harvests. Worse, no other ministry was able to supplement this deficit, since there was no ministry of agriculture.[2] In 1807–1808, while peace was restored, there remained a lot to do, both concerning the responsibilities and functioning of ministries as well as their relations with regional and local administrations. Finally, while even before coming to the throne Alexander had expressed his intention to reform the regime by orienting it to a constitutional monarchy, by 1807 no concrete progress had been made in this direction.

The years from 1803 to 1807 were a period of reflection and maturation: in 1803, as we recall, a constitution had been granted to the Ionian Islands.[3] Prepared by Gustav Rosenkampf, this constitution was intended by Alexander to serve as an experiment—and perhaps a model—for the Russian Empire. In 1804 the tsar had confided to Baron Rosenkampf that he desired to grant his subjects civic rights, as well as participation in political affairs.[4] But the jurist's deliberations resulted in the publication of merely a short brochure (written in German) presenting "fragments of a constitution but in no order, with lacunae and omissions like the agrarian question."[5] So by 1807 the idea of a constitutional reform still remained in suspension. In this context, at the end of 1808 Alexander charged Mikhail Speransky with working on a reform likely to change deeply the political structure of the whole empire.

Born in 1772 in a small village situated in the Vladimir province, the son of a priest, Speransky had been educated at the Vladimir seminary, then at Alexander Nevsky seminary in St. Petersburg, where he graduated in 1791; after 1792 he taught theology there, before being named director in 1795. In 1797 he entered the civil service. He in no way resembled Alexander's old friends in the inner circle. Of extremely modest origins, Speransky owed his extraordinary social ascension to his superior intelligence, his grasp of the interest of the state, and his devotion to work. Speaking fluent French, English, and Russian, reading Greek and Latin, imbued with classical humanism while being open to the contemporary world, Speransky had been supported by Prince Kurakin and entered the imperial chancellery in 1801 as assistant to Dimitri Troshchinsky to draft laws; he was assigned the following year to the new Ministry of Internal Affairs. As secretary of state there, he soon became the right-hand man of Kochubey, preparing for him many contributions to the secret committee. The two men were linked by mutual esteem and friendship; later, Speransky's daughter would marry Kochubey's nephew,[6] thus entering into one of the richest and most illustrious families of Russia.[7]

Working in the shadow of Kochubey, Speransky got close to the members of the secret committee and was soon noticed by the tsar. In 1803 he was promoted head of the sole department of the Ministry of Internal Affairs, making him de facto vice-minister, and a year later, when the ministry was split into three "expeditions,"[8] he became head of the second, in charge of state management. In this post he began to reflect on reforming the state and wrote synopses for the tsar's attention, such as Reflections on the Structure of the Imperial State or his Note on the Judicial Organization and Public Offices in Russia, and even a little work titled On the Spirit of Government. In the course of 1808, after the Peace of Tilsit, Speransky grew in the tsar's favor: when Novosiltsev left Russia and Kochubey began to lose his influence, he was named "reporter of affairs of the highest importance" to Alexander, becoming his principal assistant. The tsar took him to Erfurt and presented him to Napoleon and to Talleyrand. Speransky had frequent conversations with the French minister, whom he pleased with his uncommon intelligence; Napoleon appreciated him too and even offered him a gold snuffbox with his effigy entirely surrounded by diamonds.[9] On their return to St. Petersburg, Alexander appointed Speransky vice-minister of Justice (in place of Novosiltsev) and gave him the mission of preparing a legal code designed to introduce new political practices.

Speransky soon got down to this task, fully in accord with Alexander's ideas and objectives. As Speransky stressed in a letter he sent to the tsar during his later exile in Perm, it was indeed within the framework of an intense collaboration between the two men—the fruit of shared reading and conversations[10]—that the plan of 1809 saw the light of day.

For the monarch as well as for Speransky, whose qualities as administrator were allied with unequalled analytic capacities,[11] Russia was a European country presenting no specificity able to explain the political backwardness in which it found itself. Therefore, it should engage as quickly as possible in structural reforms that would bring it closer to the European model.[12] A man of culture, a connoisseur of the writings of Montesquieu and of the Italian Enlightenment jurist Beccaria, of the thinking of Jeremy Bentham (with whom he was in correspondence), and of Dumont (whom he would meet),[13]

Speransky wished to implement a system that was liberal in inspiration and tinged with ethical and spiritual references. He wanted to guarantee a certain number of freedoms to individuals, to legally ensure the protection of the people against the excesses or weakness of bureaucracy, all leading to a political life that would be both just and moral. But there was no question of installing in Russia a constitutional government like the American or French ones (the latter on the model of the Year VIII Constitution) that might be liable to dispossess the sovereign of his prerogatives; the sovereign should remain the inspirer and master builder of which reforms to promote. Eventually, such reforms would indeed facilitate the establishment of a monarchical regime that was both "tempered" by, and consolidated under, the law.

With this structure in mind, Speransky went to work, and by November 1809 he gave his achievement to the emperor in the form of three documents: a long report titled Introduction to the Code of State Laws, a Brief Summary on the Formation of the State, and a General Overview of All Reforms and Their Chronology. Meanwhile, he was active on other fronts. In December 1808 he revised two decrees that Alexander rapidly adopted: the first one, in April 1809, was titled "On Court Ranks"[14] and obliged nobles to serve in the army or administration in order to advance their careers; in August the second established an examination system for admission to the civil service and also banned the appointment to any rank above college assessor (the eighth rank of the Civil Table of Ranks)[15] of anyone lacking a university diploma. This latter measure was designed to combat incompetence and inefficiency in the bureaucracy and to facilitate the social ascension of educated commoners—but it was badly received by the nobility, which started to feel its prerogatives under attack.

Speransky's reform agenda, particularly his long report introducing the legal code, was ambitious: in the vice-minister's opinion, "the general goal of reform consists of decreeing and instituting an autocratic government based on an infallible law."[16] Henceforth, supreme power would be limited by a national system of representation that would be founded on property rights (not just on the rights of the nobility), and this power would be expressed in legislative, judicial, and administrative domains. For Speransky, it was crucial not only to apply the concept of national representation, but indeed to integrate into this representation a range of social categories of those who owned property (the bourgeoisie and rich free peasants) wider than the nobility alone, whose political and social conservatism he feared (as did Alexander).

Moreover, in the lineage of liberal ideas inherited from the French Enlightenment, Speransky's plan tried to create a separation of powers:

legislative power would reside with a state duma; an independent judicial power should be entrusted to the senate; and executive power, which would be responsible to legislative authority, would be incarnated by the ministries. The state duma would be the keystone of the arrangement, the body that would limit imperial power. No law could be adopted without its agreement; it would enjoy the right to oversee ministerial executive bodies; ministers would be responsible to it; and it would have the right of remonstrance.

In this new political architecture, the emperor would keep major powers: he would control the executive power by appointing ministers and heads of regional and local administration; he alone would decide on war and peace; he could resort to ordinances that would give him the partial right to initiate laws—but, importantly, he would have no judicial power anymore. To assist him, he would have a Council of State that would ensure communication between the three structures (duma, senate, ministries) and himself. Named by the emperor, members of this council would deal with the most important affairs of state. No law could be adopted without the joint agreement of the Council of State and the duma, which would amount to a sharing of legislative power.

Once the central level was in place, this tripartite structure would be reproduced throughout the empire. Provincial governments[17] would be subdivided into districts,[18] which would be subdivided into communes.[19] Everywhere, at governmental as well as regional and communal levels, there would be administrations, dumas, and tribunals. However, this uniformity would leave some regional specificities untouched: in zones populated with nonnatives—like Siberia, the Caucasus, and in the region of the Don—regions[20] would have increased autonomy. This point must be stressed: in accepting a diversity of status that was linked to a diversity among peoples, Speransky's scheme took into account the empire's multinational character.

Fundamental rights would be recognized among a population that would henceforth be divided into three categories: the nobility, property owners who were not nobles (like merchants and businessmen), and non-owning workers (serfs, state peasants). All individuals would benefit from civil rights,[21] there would be no punishment without a hearing—but only the first two social categories could participate in political life via a property-based right to vote.

In addition to his description of institutions to build, Speransky's plan included a precise timetable: on January 1, 1810, the Council of State should hold its first meeting; in the course of that month the new ministries of finance and treasury would be created, followed in February by the police; on May 1, an imperial manifesto would convene an assembly that would be in charge of officially adopting the new legal code, the assembly would be transformed into the state duma on August 15, and would begin to meet on September 1, 1810. Speransky definitely intended to be a methodical, rigorous, and rapid reformer!

Along with this heavy task, Speransky tackled in a more peripheral way a reform of the seminaries, which reveals the scope of his interests. He increased the share of generalist education in the curriculum—including history and ancient languages—and suppressed corporal punishment. His plan was to make these seminaries the training grounds for the small and medium local bureaucracy.

Finally, he was charged by the emperor with reflecting on the nature of the administration to be set up in Finland. In April 1808 an imperial manifesto had annexed Finland, and this decision was ratified a year later by the peace of Hamina in September 1809. So the establishment of a new administrative and political architecture was a matter of urgency. The annexation of Finland by the Russian Empire put an end to a situation that was 600 years old. Since the Middle Ages Finland had in fact been an integral part of the kingdom of Sweden, and its elites spoke Swedish. But, as a result of the deals made at Tilsit and Erfurt, in 1808–1809, it suffered a brutal invasion by Russia, then an annexation that made the Finnish elites very worried about the tsar's political objectives.

To take the measure of the local situation, Alexander and Speransky went to Finland; in the shadows Speransky again began an immense project to orchestrate imperial goals in that country. In February 1809 Alexander convened in Porvoo the Finnish estates—nobility, clergy, bourgeoisie, free peasantry (there was no serfdom in Finland)—which were constituted into a diet. On March 27, 1809, he declared to it, in a speech prepared by Speransky: "I have promised to maintain your constitution, your fundamental laws—and your gathering here guarantees my promise. This meeting will be a landmark in your political existence."[22] And he ended by saying (arousing the enthusiasm of the Finns): "Henceforth Finland will have its place among the nations."[23]

* * *

Historians have wondered about the meaning of the tsar's benevolent policy with respect to Finland. Some have insisted on military factors; others point to political considerations. It is certain that Alexander demonstrated pragmatism in his approach to the Finnish question: it was indeed less costly to rely on local elites rather than resort to Russian military force to secure imperial authority and Russian bureaucracy to administer the region.[24] But, as a former student of Laharpe, he was also trying to use Finland (as previously he had used the Ionian Islands and later "his" Poland) as an experimental laboratory in order to spread through the Russian Empire ideas from the Enlightenment and constitutionalism—to which he remained attached. In 1811, while he was on the point of attaching to an autonomous Finland not only the territory acquired by Russia at the Peace of Abbo in 1743 but also the Vyborg government acquired by Peter the Great (this would be done in December), he told General Armfelt, about the political rights he had granted to Finland:

> I swear that these forms please me more than the exercise of arbitrary power that has no other basis than my will, and which presupposes a principle of perfection in the sovereign—which is not present, alas, in all of humanity. Here, I cannot be wrong unless I want to be. [Here] all the lights are offered to me; there I am surrounded only by uncertainty and (almost always) the habits that have taken the place of laws. You will see how I think about that where there is a means of effecting a change in my States, since I am going incessantly to unite old Finland with your region and give it the same constitution and the same forms of freedom.[25]

In fact, the mode of governing Finland conceived in St. Petersburg in 1809 by Alexander I and Speransky appears as a compromise between some traits inherited from the Swedish administration and some innovations stamped with the Enlightenment seal.

The new structure would maintain the privileges of the estates, which had been established in their current form in the eighteenth century. The tsar touched neither the administration of provinces nor of rural areas; he did not challenge previously acquired municipal autonomy. He also retained the rights of the Lutheran Church, dispensed Finland from supplying military recruits, and authorized it to keep a small army.[26] Finally, Finland kept its own customs, its bank, and its currency. Its privileged economic relations with Sweden were maintained and guaranteed by the peace of Hamina.[27] Far from trying to wipe a slate clean of the practices inherited from the period of Swedish domination, the tsar was concerned to inscribe the new Russian domination within a historical continuum by respecting the sociopolitical rights that had been acquired. In parallel (and this is crucial), without asserting himself as a constitutional monarch, Alexander tried to manage Finland within respect for the existing law in force; for example, he would not raise taxes without having obtained the diet's approval in advance. So, in fact, he was introducing into

Finland a certain measure of national representation and constitutionalism—innovations without precedent in Russia. Still, we should not overestimate the scope of the concessions: while the respect for laws would be real, the role of the diet would remain symbolic. It was not reconvened until 1863!

To manage Finland, Alexander gave it a properly Finnish administration, and in this he distinguished himself from the Swedish heritage: there was no question of trying to "Russify" either administration or society. To lead this administration he set up in Turku a council of government composed of a dozen representatives of the estates, which would be renamed in 1816 the "Imperial Senate of Finland," and then in 1819 transferred its seat to Helsinki, the new capital. However, the presidency of the governmental council was granted to a Russian, given the title of governor-general and commander in chief of the Russian armies. For this post, Alexander chose in April 1809 General Mikhail Barclay de Tolly. This was not a fortuitous choice: aged 47, faithful soldier of the tsar, of Scottish origin and a Lutheran by faith—his family had come to Lithuania in the seventeenth century—Barclay was considered by Alexander to have liberal principles[28] and thus was particularly able to incarnate the spirit of openness and toleration necessary for the office of president of the Finnish Council. The dozen members of the council, divided into two sections (economic and legislative) were designated by the emperor for a fixed period, and their nomination did not depend on the estates, which were, however, to be represented on the council. Half the seats were reserved for the nobility and the other half for commoners, a system that allowed the Finns as a whole to take part in their administration by enlarging the national base to all social categories. This was a preoccupation dear to Speransky. Finally, back in St. Petersburg Alexander named a Finn to the post of Russian secretary of state to assist in Finnish matters, to adapt the affairs prepared by Russian ministers to Finnish legislation, and to transmit to Finland the imperial desiderata in matters of legislation.

These benevolent arrangements, which combined elements from the Swedish period with some innovations, soon secured significant political and social peace for the empire. We may call the Finnish policy of Alexander and Speransky a success. However, the results were clearly less convincing as regards the general reform of 1809.

* * *

Upon reading the elaborate text prepared by Speransky, Alexander reacted positively, judging it both useful and satisfactory. On December 31

(O.S.), 1809, in accordance with Speransky's timetable, he invited 35 senators to gather the next day at 8:30 in the morning in one of the halls of the
Shepelev Palace, where at 9:00 he gave a speech that solemnly inaugurated
the work of the Council of State and publicly confirmed his will to give
the country a civil code.[29] But the creation of this council and the plan as
a whole, which had been kept secret from public opinion until the meeting
that January 1, immediately encountered vigorous opposition.

First, even from within Alexander's family entourage there was opposition. Today the archives of the Russian Federation have conserved a text
little known by historians: the commentaries of Maria Feodorovna written
in December 1809 in St. Petersburg in response to the document Alexander gave her for comment. This text is doubly interesting: First, because it
attests once again to the immense confidence that, despite their frequent
disagreements, continued to unite mother and son. While his marriage was
collapsing and his passion for Maria Naryshkina was undergoing highs and
lows (after 1809 they were unfaithful to each other, and the tsar had many
passing affairs, including with a maid of honor to his sister Grand Duchess
Catherine), his mother was an essential source of support and a key marker.
Secondly, the document is important because Maria Feodorovna's perspicacious analysis expresses doubts connected to a peculiarity of the Russian
Empire that no reformer could sweep away:

> The principle upon which the plan to give a particular body the right to delib-
> erate and to propose new laws is based, seems eminently respectable, just, and
> well developed. But in a monarchic state like Russia, which has not known
> until now any other source of laws and new orders than the Sovereign's will,
> by announcing so authentically a principle that seems—if not to remove this
> power from the Sovereign, then at least to limit it—it appears essential, in
> order not to offend and alter the general idea that the [illegible] has formed
> of the Sovereign's authority, which appears so necessary in such a vast state
> where civilization is not yet generally widespread, therefore it appears essen-
> tial, I say, that the nation remains persuaded that the emperor is not depriving
> himself of the power to dictate law when required by circumstances. In guar-
> anteeing this opinion, it appears to me before God that this order of things,
> surveyed with vigilance and firmness, should lead to good.[30]

So for Maria Feodorovna (as for some members of the inner circle back in
1802–1803) the emperor, if he took into account the political immaturity in
which Russia was mired, could not give up his legislative omnipotence.

At the same time, Speransky's plan also encountered more instinctive and less reasoned opposition from a part of the administrative apparatus, starting with Arakcheev. On December 24 (O.S.), Arakcheev, who was irritated at having been kept ignorant of a plan he could only disapprove of, since it challenged the autocratic system, abruptly resigned from his duties as minister of war and inspector-general of infantry and artillery. He withdrew to his estate in Gruzino, from which he sent an ambiguous letter to his sovereign:

> Your very gracious Majesty!
>
> For fifteen years I have enjoyed your goodness, of which the papers [the plan] I received today are new testimony. […] I read them all before I left and I would never dare to understand them otherwise than by relating my own knowledge and strength to the rationale of these wise provisions.
>
> Your Majesty! You know the limits of the education I received in my youth; to my misfortune, it was confined to textbooks given to me, which is why, at my age today, I feel I am nothing more than a good officer who can only watch over the scrupulous application of our military profession. […]
>
> Today, to apply your wise provisions requires a man who has had a complete education in general matters. Only such a man would be useful in this important corporation that includes the military state, the foremost in the Empire.
>
> I am incapable of assuming this task, Majesty. […] Do not be angry with a man who has lived fifty years without flattery, but instead relieve him of this charge.[31]

This letter does not refer to the political reform or the creation of the Council of State, but Alexander was not fooled by this omission, as illustrated by his vigorous and irritated response to his war minister:

> To what should I attribute your intention to quit the office you occupy? […] All those who have read the regulations of the new council have found it useful for the good of the Empire. But you, from whom I expected the most help, you who have so often repeated that apart from your love of country, your sole motive was your personal attachment to me, you alone, despite these sentiments and forgetting the good of the Empire, you make haste to abandon the part that was entrusted to you—and at a time when your conscience cannot ignore how necessary and irreplaceable you are. […]
>
> But allow me to leave aside the title I bear and speak to you as a man to whom I am personally attached and to whom I have demonstrated this attachment on every occasion. What effect will your departure produce on the

public at a time when a reform so useful and agreeable to all will be installed in the government? This will certainly be for you the worse effect. [...]

At a time when I should be expecting ardent and zealous help from all honest people who are attached to their country, you alone leave me, and preferring your personal vanity, supposedly wounded for the sake of the Empire, you are really harming your reputation this time.

At our next interview, you will tell me decidedly if I can still see in you the same Count Arakcheev, on whose attachment I can firmly count, or if I will have to choose a new minister of War.[32]

But Arakcheev firmly refused, and the tsar, not wanting to deprive himself of a collaborator whose devotion he rightly appreciated, ended up by appointing him (with his accord) president of the new department of military affairs at the Council of State, making Barclay de Tolly, until then governor-general of Finland, his new minister of war. And to seal their reconciliation, Alexander went so far as to offer Arakcheev at the New Year a magnificent sleigh drawn by a pair of superb horses.[33]

* * *

Finally, there were some opponents who saw any reform that was liable to challenge autocratic power as a danger to the throne. This was the case for Joseph de Maistre and still more for the writer Nikolay Karamzin. At the start of 1811, at the request of Alexander's sister Catherine Pavlovna, whose fief of Tver was one of the bastions of the conservative opposition, Karamzin delivered in the form of "A Memo on Ancient and Modern Russia,"[34] a philosophical and historical reflection on the destiny of Russia, as well as a blistering attack on reforms that he saw as an illegitimate challenge to the autocratic principle.

Faced with these many forms of opposition, the tsar did not yield. The new Council of State was indeed in place—its presidency was given to Chancellor Count Rumyantsev—and far from Speransky's reputation falling, in the following months his reforming activity was strengthened. In February 1810 Speransky was behind an imperial manifesto that instituted a reform aiming to clean up the state of public finances. At this time, the treasury was in a bad state. Even before the wars of 1805–1807, the budget was not balanced; in 1804 state revenues did not exceed 95.5 million rubles while expenses were around 109 million. War significantly aggravated the situation: in 1807 fiscal revenue was 121 million rubles and expenses 170 million. Two years later the situation had become alarming: revenue reached only 127 million and expenses rose to 278 million![35] Faced with this crisis due to the rise in military expenditure and the drop in revenue linked to the decline in foreign trade, Speransky opted for drastic measures: he put an end to the issue of paper assignats, while keeping them on the state's debt books; he proceeded to sell some imperial real estate to improve the treasury's liquidity; he raised taxes as a whole and temporarily introduced a tax on the income of nobles, based on a self-evaluation of this income. These measures aimed to increase resources to allow the state to balance its budget.[36] And, in fact, by 1812 revenue was close to 300 million rubles.[37] But the measures also aroused growing discontent among the nobles and increased the number of Speransky's enemies. Some months later, the manifesto of August 1810 (and that of July 1811) reorganized the ministries, reaffirming the authority of the minister over his department and defining the nature of relations between ministries and other higher administrative bodies—i.e., the senate, Council of Ministers, and Council of State.

Speransky increased his portfolios: secretary of state, vice-minister of justice, director of the Commission to Prepare Laws and the Commission for Finnish Affairs, author of the financial reform, chancellor of the University of Turku—he had more offices and power than ever. A veritable workhorse, ambitious out of a concern to reform the empire and lead it toward more efficiency and justice, Speransky attracted enmities—of which he was well aware. In February 1811 he confided to the tsar, complaining humorously of "having been in just one year by turns a Martinist,[38] a Freemason,[39] a defender of liberty, a persecutor of serfdom—and ending as a passionate Illuminato."[40] And even though his probity was not in doubt, he would soon be accused of being paid by France through the intermediary of Caulaincourt.

Throughout 1810 and 1811 Alexander paid no attention to the attacks on his minister, yet while being seduced by the ambitious and complex agenda, he hesitated to put it into effect. Some historians have seen these hesitations, or even turnarounds, as a new manifestation of the supposedly vacillating nature of the tsar, even of his duplicity and his instinctive fondness for the autocratic regime he had inherited from Catherine and from Paul. Others attribute his hesitations to his fear of hostile reactions from the nobility.[41] However, neither of these views seems supported by any evidence. Admittedly, Alexander was always hesitant by nature, "too weak to govern and too strong to be governed," as Speransky would recklessly declare. Admittedly, by 1810, confronted with the realities of power since 1801, he no longer showed the idealism that characterized his advent. But he did remain desirous to promote a liberalization of the Russian political system, as witnessed by the trust with which he honored Speransky. However, the perennial question of how to apply reforms still stumped him: how to accept giving up part of his prerogatives when the so-called educated classes appeared stuck in their conservatism and incapable of thinking of reform? On what forces and abilities should he lean to apply reform at the top and relay it out to the provinces? These crucial questions, remaining unanswered, put a brake on Alexander's reforming will, already thwarted by the inertia, if not opposition, of a portion of senior dignitaries. Consequently, the 1809 plan resulted in measures that were modest in effect.

Reform did lead to defining in a clearer and more rigorous way the responsibilities and functions of the ministries; but contrary to the reformers' wishes, ministers remained responsible to the emperor and not to the Council of State. The state duma did not see the light of day, and the plan for a civil code was postponed indefinitely.[42] Only the Council of State began to function but in a quite different way from what Speransky had projected. While initially it was supposed to be a body "charged with supervising the activities of ministries and elaborating all the great law projects at the imperial level,"[43] it became in reality a key body in the governmental structure for the execution of imperial desires—without possessing any legislative initiative. Composed of four departments (laws, economy, civil affairs, and military affairs) and a plenary assembly, the Council of State was throughout Alexander's reign made up of members appointed for life by the emperor, a large majority of whom[44] came from the high landowning nobility and more than a third of whom had the title of prince or count. All came from the first three classes of the Table of Ranks; almost two-thirds of them had served in the army, not in civil administration; and they were largely Orthodox. Their average age was 56 years and three months. This data[45] delineates a milieu that was homogeneous but relatively little inclined to the spirit of reform. Herein lies the whole ambiguity of the choices made by Alexander: while deploring the conservatism of the aristocracy, it was on that group that he relied to make the council work, putting an end to Speransky's hope of seeing the sphere of responsibilities open up to wider social categories. That said, did the tsar between 1810 and 1825 have any real possibility of relying on other social groups? That can legitimately be doubted.

Suffering from the tsar's procrastinations, the implementation of the 1809 plan also suffered from the deterioration in relations with France and the increasingly Francophobe mood that overwhelmed the Russian elites. After 1811–1812, while clouds accumulated on the international scene and the blockade against England took an increasingly negative impact on the Russian economy, it was time for military preparations—and so there was even less scope for reform.

The Russian Empire on a War Footing

As of 1808–1809, and even more from 1811, Alexander was worried about and convinced of the unavoidable dimension of the coming conflict. In November 1811, in a letter to his sister Catherine, he deplored the evolution of the situation:

> Never have I led such a dog's life. Often in the week I get out of bed to sit at my desk and I leave it only to eat a morsel alone, and then go back until I go to bed. [...] You say I am lazy not to come see you—ah, if only I could. [...] We are on continual alert: all circumstances are so thorny, things so tense, that hostilities may commence at any moment. It is impossible to leave my center of administration and activity. I have to wait for a more propitious moment, or else war will definitely prevent me from coming.[46]

A few days later, in January 1812, he wrote her that he kept himself "more a sentinel than ever, but the horizon is increasingly dark."[47] In this menacing situation he had to try to plan the defense of the empire as best he could.

As we have seen, at first the tsar dreamed of leading an offensive war but then ran up against the procrastination of the king of Prussia as well as the doubts about Polish cooperation expressed by Prince Czartoryski. So eventually Alexander decided on a firmly defensive war. But if he hesitated over the turn that military operations would take, starting in 1808 he expressed his desire to give the empire a more effective and better-structured army. In 1801 the young tsar had already undertaken to reform the army, following proposals from a military commission charged with examining the troop situation and their reorganization. The measures adopted tended to significantly augment military personnel, including in peacetime. While in 1801 the Russian army had included 446,000 men, this total rose to 475,000 in 1805. The infantry still remained the pillar of the Russian army, but the cavalry, and especially the artillery, provided with more efficient weapons, saw their role strengthened. With a company of engineers, the Russian army gained technical skill and know-how. But this first wave of reforms, undertaken in peacetime, no longer sufficed as war approached. We saw that in January 1808 Alexander named Arakcheev to the posts of minister of war and inspector-general of the infantry and artillery. Perceived as narrow-minded and ignorant by many courtiers—including Joseph de Maistre—in a few months Arakcheev began to reinstill strict discipline within the army, he fought corruption and the irresponsibility of officers by pitiless measures, and he worked to improve the provisioning of food and munitions. In parallel, a maniac for order and cleanliness like Alexander himself, Arak-cheev transformed his estate at Gruzino into a colony of "peasant-soldiers" that charmed the tsar all the more because it reminded him of the impec-cable order at Gatchina. After the visit he made in 1809, Alexander wrote his sister Catherine of the admiration he felt for Gruzino, and he began to dream of having an army composed of peasant-soldiers who would be well fed, well disciplined, and wholly devoted to the mother country. But in Janu-ary 1810 the appointment of Barclay de Tolly to the war ministry changed the situation: there was no question of a utopia of peasant-soldiers in the short term; there were urgent and pragmatic measures that the new minis-ter, helped by Prince Peter Volkonsky as director of the supply corps, had to implement.

In February–March 1810 the minister proposed a plan to reinforce the western border and to make the Dvina-Dnieper the principal line of de-fense. Moreover, to protect Finland from any potential attack from Swe-den, Barclay proposed installing two divisions and two fortresses, one in the northern part of Finland and the other on the Aland Islands.[48] A few months later, in August 1810, Barclay de Tolly enjoined the tsar and Foreign Affairs Minister Rumyantsev to make peace with the Ottoman Empire as quickly as possible, in order to redeploy the forces from the southern theater to the western border, which stretched almost 1100 verstes from the Baltic to Ukraine.[49] Sensitive to this argument, Alexander made the Peace of Bu-charest in May 1812.

In parallel, continuing the actions of Arakcheev and with his support, Barclay de Tolly worked to improve the army numerically and qualitatively. In October Arakcheev submitted to the Council of the Empire a plan titled "On the matter of military recruitment." Despite the extreme length of mili-tary service—25 years even in peacetime—Arakcheev worried in his report about the insufficiency of reserve troops in the regular army and its high rate of unfit men. He estimated that ten percent of the men were incapa-ble of adapting to the military regime and pace—and he worried about the need to remedy these deficiencies as fast as possible. Armed with this report, which supported his own analysis, Barclay de Tolly proceeded to increase troop strength. Between September 1810 and March 1812, in three succes-sive enrollment campaigns, he increased the proportions of recruits among the population. Whereas an imperial ukase of September 1810 recruited one man in 700, that of 1811 enrolled one per 500, and in March 1812 two per 500.[50] He also forced regiments to conduct more frequent mobilization exercises, increased the level and frequency of training, had storehouses built to stock munitions and grain, and launched into the consolidation of the western frontier. Aware that Russia would be alone against Napoleon and could count only on its own resources—this was a leitmotif that ran through several of his reports to the tsar—Barclay de Tolly was concerned to increase the army's efficiency. And very quickly, in terms of strength, equipment and training, the measures took effect. In 1811 Alexander had 225,000 armed and equipped men divided into small units between the Dvina and the Dnieper. A year later, on the eve of the war, the Russian army, without counting Cossack troops, was composed of three armies structured into a dozen infantry corps and five cavalry corps, each corps constituting "a vast autonomous unit on the French model,"[51] or in all 380,000 foot soldiers, 62,000 cavalry, 43,500 gunners, and 4,500 engineers. Yet the fortification of the border took longer to achieve, and when the Grande Armée invaded imperial territory in June 1812, it was still not finished, making Barclay de Tolly's efforts fruitless.

Reorganizing the Russian army at the price of some tensions—Barclay's leadership encountered a rebellious protest from some generals who were not inclined to accept the authority of a German-speaking Russian, moreover a Lutheran—Barclay engaged also, with Alexander's full support, in the intense activity of information gathering and espionage.

In December 1810, even before the signing of the secret military agreement, friendly relations with the king of Prussia took the form of secret cooperation between the war ministries of the two countries. Maps of Germany, Holland, and central Europe, very detailed topographically ("the quintessence of the secret map collections possessed by the Prussian depository"[52]), were secretly sent to Barclay de Tolly in Berlin by Count Lieven, Russian ambassador in Berlin. In parallel, Barclay had recourse in Paris to the information services of a Cossack colonel, Alexander Chernyshev. An aide-de-camp to the tsar, whom he served as courier between St. Petersburg and Paris, aged 30, Chernyshev was a distinguished dancer and a seducer. In his memoirs Laure d'Abrantès expounded wittily on the success he had with the women at court during a ball at the Tuileries:

> They looked at each other like wild cats when the Northern Lovelace appeared among them. [...] Everything about him, even his attire, that waspish way of being enclosed in his suit, his hat with its plume, and hair thrown in big tufts, and that Tartar face, his almost perpendicular eyes—everything was of an original and curious type.[53]

In 1806 the Russian chargé d'affaires d'Oubril had made the acquaintance of someone called "Michel," a French functionary in the military transport office of the war ministry. For pay, Michel transmitted copies of reports he wrote for his ministry. Later, the deterioration of relations between France and Russia made Michel's information even more precious. Becoming worried about his fate, Michel tried to step back. But it was too late: the victim of blackmail by the Russians, Michel was obliged to deal with Chernyshev, to whom he had to supply complete and detailed information on the French army. Until February 1812, when he was arrested with three accomplices before being tried and condemned to death for "high treason" and then guillotined in April,[54] he had enabled the Russian headquarters to be informed, precisely and frequently, about "situation notebooks," i.e., bimonthly reports (transmitted by Ambassador Kurakin without knowing their content) on the resources, strength, and position of Grande Armée regiments.

This military espionage was backed up by political espionage. In 1808 Alexander I charged Speransky with setting up an information service in Paris, unbeknownst to the diplomatic corps. At its center was Count Nesselrode,[55] the recipient in Paris of all correspondence to Russia and charged with forwarding it secretly to Speransky. And Talleyrand, again in return for pay, sent Nesselrode secret reports on the state of France. In these epistolary exchanges all parties used code names: according to circumstances, Talleyrand was called "my cousin Henry," or "handsome Leander"; Fouché (the police minister) was "Natasha" or "the president"; the tsar became "Louise." These letters are today in the Nesselrode archives; they had no military or logistic interest, but they did enable Alexander to grasp the mood of the country and better understand the balance of power on France. They were grimly converted into cash by Talleyrand; he was already being paid in "trade licenses with England" but did not hesitate to become greedy, exposing himself to the tsar's irritation. On September 15, 1810, he wrote to Alexander that he "needed fifteen hundred thousand francs" and that:

> It is important I have them by November. While a simple thing in itself, I must take precautions in the choice of means to procure them. If Your Majesty finds that in addressing myself to you, I have only rendered homage to your generous qualities [...], then I beg you to write to M. Bentham that he gives M. Labinski, his consul in Paris, a note of credit for the sum to him, Bentham, in Frankfurt.[56]

But the tsar firmly refused.

Through these two espionage networks, one can measure how in 1808 (and again after 1810) Alexander I had an almost obsessive concern to know as much as possible about Napoleon, to figure him out in order to detect his resources, his capabilities, and his possible weaknesses. The tsar had not been fascinated by the emperor for a long time, but he remained very impressed by him: Alexander's behavior reveals his desire to take the exact measure of his potential adversary. Meanwhile, while he continued to talk of a defensive position, affirming long and loudly that he would not start the war and would never take the initiative in a conflict, Alexander undertook to prepare public opinion and to galvanize its patriotic sentiments by making pledges to the conservative and French-hating elites.

* * *

From 1804 Alexander expressed the conviction that the war to conduct against Napoleon would be a war of ideas as much as of men and that the support of the people, in an engagement whose violence and breadth was fearful to him, would therefore be crucial. This conviction had been more or less consciously reaffirmed in 1805–1806 when he chose to turn Napoleon into an anti-Christ to fight. But in 1812, after the French alliances of Tilsit and Erfurt had confounded the reference points, to the disgust of those who hated the French, Alexander more than ever had to ensure the support of public opinion and quell the doubts, and even virulent criticism, that swirled around him. The atmosphere at court remained tense, and rumors of plots resurfaced. In his dispatch to his king, the envoy from the Stockholm court wrote in April 1812:

> Even now, Your Majesty will hardly understand how far freedom of speech goes in so despotic a country as this. The more the storm threatens, the more they doubt the skill of the one who is steering. The Emperor, who is informed about everything, cannot fail to know how much he has ceased to have the trust of his nation. There must even exist a party in favor of the Grand Duchess Catherine, wife of Prince Oldenburg, at the head of which, they say, is Count Rostopchin. [...] With the facility of this nation to lend itself to revolutions, its penchant for being governed by women, it would not be astonishing if someone profited from the current crisis to carry out a change.[57]

The tsar endured increasingly open attacks; he was reproached for his alliance with France, for his inopportune choices that were said to reflect his inability "to steer," for the weight of the blockade that, imposed by Napoleon to asphyxiate England, was impoverishing Russia by the day.

On the eve of the blockade's implementation, it was to England that Russia exported the greater part of its primary materials, including iron, hemp, wood, linen, wheat, potassium, and wax; England alone absorbed more than half of Russian foreign trade.[58] Moreover, before the execution of the blockade, most Russian exports—particularly wheat—were transported to western Europe by ships usually flying the British flag. In 1804 from the port of St. Petersburg (through which 49 percent of exports and 43 percent of imports by sea transited), British ships brought 63 percent of the merchandise, and Russian ships only 35 percent.[59] The blockade pronounced by Alexander on November 21, 1807, two days after breaking off relations with the British, but enforced only from spring 1808, interrupted these flows—without Russian traders and industrialists being able to find other suppliers. In 1808 the volume of exports of Russian goods circulating from the Baltic seaports was three times lower than in 1806.[60] This disruption entailed an economic and financial crisis: in a few months, the ruble assignat lost half its value, the slump in agricultural products depressed the imperial treasury as never before, and the deficit grew from 126 million rubles in 1808 to 157 million a year later.[61] The energetic financial measures taken by Speransky improved the situation a little—in 1810 the deficit was only 77 million62—but the situation remained worrying, and public discontent was at its height. It was therefore time for Alexander to show his determination to safeguard Russian interests and to give the signals that the public was expecting. In December 1810, as mentioned, an imperial ukase partially lifted the blockade and imposed customs duties on French luxury goods. In the spring of 1812, the tsar adopted political decisions that aimed to prepare the people for the idea of a war that Alexander did not doubt would be major. In April 1812 he wrote to Adam Czartoryski:

> Rupture with France appears inevitable. Napoleon's goal is to annihilate, or at least bring down, the last power that remains on its feet in Europe, and to achieve this, he is advancing demands that are inadmissible and incompatible with the honor of Russia.
>
> 1) He wants all commerce with neutral countries to be interrupted. This would deprive us of the only one that remains.
>
> 2) At the same time, he demands that, lacking any means of exporting our own products, we put up no hindrance to the import of French luxury goods, which we have prohibited, being not rich enough to pay for them.
>
> Since I cannot consent to such proposals, it is probable that war will follow, despite everything Russia has done to avoid it. It will make waves of blood flow, and this poor humanity will again be sacrificed to the insatiable ambition of a man who was created, it seems, for its misery.[63]

In March 1812, wanting to win over anti-French opinion, Alexander named Count Rostopchin governor-general of Moscow: as we have seen, he was close to Catherine Pavlovna and had written virulent pamphlets against the French, so his appointment appeared highly symbolic. A few days later, the emperor resolved to sacrifice Speransky on the altar of patriotism.

In the evening of March 29, Speransky was summoned to the tsar, and after a two-hour private chat that left him deeply distressed, he was accused of treason for the benefit of Napoleon and arrested. The accusations were wholly fabricated by the police minister Balashov and obviously unfounded, but Speransky was hated by the conservative elites for his Francophilia and admiration for Napoleon. And he had been imprudent: in correspondence intercepted by Balashov's agents, he had several times denigrated the emperor, reproaching him in an ironic and disrespectful manner for his softness, hesitations, and finally his inability to govern. Just as imprudently, Speransky had also kept to himself, without the knowledge of Alexander to whom it was destined, an encrypted message from Nesselrode. Deeply upset by this treachery (if not political, then at least moral), Alexander chose to sacrifice Speransky. Deprived of all his goods, Speransky was that very evening exiled and led under escort to Nizhni-Novgorod; his main collaborator, Magnitsky, suffered the same fate. Officially the two men were accused of plotting again the security of the state and ought to have been prosecuted; Speransky's fall was perceived by court elites as a victory over the French and caused general joy. But, although furious with Speransky for his moral fault, Alexander was also ill at ease, for deep down he knew very well that this man of integrity could not have been guilty of any collusion with France. The next day Alexander declared to Golitsyn: "If someone cuts off your arm, no doubt you would shout and cry in pain; last night I was deprived of Speransky and he was my right arm. [...] You will examine [his] papers but you will find nothing; he was not a traitor."[64] He tried to justify himself to Novosiltsev: "He is really guilty only toward me alone, guilty of having paid back my confidence and my friendship with the blackest and most abominable ingratitude."[65]

In this context Alexander ultimately opted for an intermediary sanction: Speransky was exiled, but the punishment was both light in relation to the gravity of the crimes of which he was accused and severe in relation to the reality of the errors he had committed. In fact, the official decree of this condemnation was not issued. Speransky was not stripped of his decorations or his title as count (acquired through service), and his trial never took place. Another sign of the attachment and esteem Alexander bore him was that he was "pardoned" by the emperor after four years of exile and became governor of Penza and then in 1819 governor-general of Siberia.

After this sacrifice of his right-hand man, Alexander did not stop working to galvanize the population; he was worried about Napoleon's power but aware of his own assets. In the letter to Czartoryski of April 1812, he insisted on the combative and confident state of mind in which Russians had decided to tackle the coming conflict:

> I will only recall the immense extent of the terrain that the Russian armies have behind them into which to withdraw and not let themselves be broken, and the difficulties that will augment for Napoleon in becoming so distant from his resources. If the war starts, we here are resolute not to put down arms. The military resources that have been gathered are very large: public spirit is excellent, differing essentially from what you witnessed the first two times. There is no longer this conceit that made us despise the enemy. On the contrary, we appreciate his force, we think that reversals are very possible, but despite that we have decided to support the honor of the empire at all costs.[66]

A few days later, on April 26, Alexander I was in Vilnius, in the middle of his soldiers. The danger was imminent and the time had come for holy union behind the tsar.

CHAPTER 11

1812

The Duel of the Emperors

The huge bibliography devoted to the Napoleonic campaigns and in particular to the war of 1812 makes one dizzy: no fewer than 5,000 books and almost 10,000 articles were published in Russian between 1812 and 1912,[1] with almost as many in all the other European languages! While in the course of the twentieth century Soviet historians seemed to slow down and turn away from this field,[2] the West has taken over, through research centers and societies of Napoleonic studies. This speaks to the enduring fascination with the subject of the French invasion of Russia. Here I cannot relate in detail the history of the campaign—a whole volume would not suffice, and other historians have done so with talent[3]—but rather I want to give an account of the major phases, before turning to the analyses, perceptions, and behavior of Alexander at the time of the cataclysm that shook the Russian Empire.

The Campaign of 1812

In the merciless duel[4] in which Napoleon and Alexander were engaged in 1812, everything opposed them to each other: rhetoric, ideology, objectives, means, and strategy. Apart from the terrible shock of throwing 600,000 men into combat, there was a confrontation between two wills, two consciences, two conceptions of power, and two world views. Often concerned not to ruin the image of Napoleon as a genius at strategy, French historians have had a tendency to incriminate the coldness and harshness of the climate and the extraordinary valor of the Russian troops rather than to pinpoint Napoleon's errors.[5] But if, in fact, "the general winter" did not facilitate the invader's task, it was more the errors of judgment committed by the French emperor—his excessiveness and his conviction that victory would be swift, which pushed him to neglect the climatic obstacles as well as distances—and his inability to understand the mind and personality of his adversary and to discern his psychology, that caused his failure.

At the head of the Grande Armée, Napoleon decided to invade the Russian Empire in June 1812 because he suspected the Russian army was at the point of moving onto the offensive (based on the scope of the forces disposed along the western frontier). The French emperor was counting on a rapid war, which he expected to win thanks to one decisive battle. After Austerlitz and Friedland, he intended to inscribe into the collective imagination yet another stunning victory that would force Alexander I to capitulate, push him back east once and for all, and allow France to have a free hand in Europe. Yet, those close to Napoleon had not stopped warning him about this reckless plan; Cambacérès, Fouché, Prince Jerome, and Caulaincourt had all tried to dissuade him from undertaking a campaign that appeared foolhardy—one that presupposed a long stretching of the communications lines—as well as illegitimate. But Napoleon would not listen: he wanted at all costs to conduct this campaign to end Russian resistance and to marginalize England for good.

While at the start of the conflict the tsar had not yet completely decided the strategy to follow, by all the evidence he had resolved to oppose the invader's plans. Alexander did not underestimate this invasion: in March 1812, receiving an Englishman, Rector Parrot, at the Winter Palace, Alexander confessed frankly his anguish in anticipation of the coming war, as well as his determination to concede nothing to Napoleon:

> The terrible struggle will decide the fate of my empire and I do not hope to triumph over the genius and strength of my enemy. But I will surely not make a shameful peace, and I would rather bury myself under the ruins of the empire. If heaven has ordered that to happen, speak of me to posterity. You know my heart.[6]

In the same period, receiving John Quincy Adams, who was visiting St. Petersburg, he sadly confided his disillusionment: "Here comes this war that I have done everything to avoid."[7] But while the looming war appeared daunting, the tsar decided to face the invader, confident in his people, as in the immensity of the Russian climate. In 1811 his confidences to Caulaincourt were reported by the latter in a private conversation with Napoleon:

While paying justice to your military talents, he often told me that his country was big, and your genius might give you many advantages over his generals, but that […] they have the margin to cede you land and that if you get far from France and supplies, this would already mean successfully combating you. Your Majesty will be obliged to come back to France and then all the advantages will be on the Russian side: the winter, the iron climate, and more than all that, the stance and loudly proclaimed will of Emperor Alexander to prolong the struggle and not to be so weak, like so many other sovereigns, as to sign peace in his capital.[8]

And Caulaincourt insisted on what the tsar had been saying:

If Emperor Napoleon makes war on me, it is possible, even probable, that he will beat us if we accept combat, but that will not bring him peace. The Spanish were often beaten and they are neither vanquished nor subjugated. However, they are not so far from Paris as we are. They have neither our climate nor our resources. I will not be the first to draw my sword, but I will be the last to put it back in its sheath. If the fortune of war should run against me, I would rather withdraw to Kamchatka [in Siberia] than cede provinces and in my capital sign treaties that are merely ceasefires. The Frenchman is brave, but long privations and a bad climate will wear him out and discourage him. Our climate, our winter will make the war for us. Miracle feats only take place for you where your emperor is, and he cannot be everywhere and far from Paris for years.[9]

This declaration is obviously very interesting: it shows that almost a year before the invasion, Alexander had already understood that any direct contact with the enemy risked being fatal and that the salvation of the empire might be found in this refusal to fight because the climate, that hostile milieu, would work in Russia's favor. This strong intuition would prove particularly well founded. And the declaration also says a lot about the tsar's view of Napoleon: aware of his charisma and his capacity to multiply "miracle feats," Alexander was also astonishingly lucid about the fragility of that kind of power, which unlike his own (part of the age-old history of Russia), rested only on the personality of the emperor.

When Alexander and members of his staff met at Vilnius, Barclay de Tolly and Phül, a Prussian officer who had the tsar's ear, had similar thoughts, and their arguments persuaded Alexander even more because he had a traumatic memory of the "decisive battles" of Austerlitz and Friedland. Phül wanted to let the Grande Armée proceed as far as a fortified camp—his choice was the camp of Drissa on the Dvina River—where the first Russian army would frontally attack the enemy, backed up by the second army that would attack laterally.[10] Barclay de Tolly also subscribed to this plan: he was of the opinion that it would be best to avoid any direct engagement with the enemy and to withdraw further and further back, to oblige the enemy to advance and thereby to weaken. But inside the emperor's entourage, some generals—the impetuous Bagration and the young Ermolov (the future conqueror of the Caucasus)—did not share this analysis. Despite Barclay's brilliant military deeds (which meant he could not be accused of cowardice), the minister's plan, if it consisted of fleeing before the enemy, was not morally acceptable to them. Thus, on the eve of the invasion, while Russian strategy tended to reject the idea of a decisive battle, this was not definitively decreed nor even unanimously accepted.

* * *

On the evening of June 23, in the magnificent property belonging to the Bennigsens situated near Vilnius, at Zakret, close to an estate that the emperor himself had just acquired, Alexander attended a ball given in his honor. The guests present there were captivated by the emperor, who was dressed on this occasion in the blue-lined and lapelled uniform of the Semenovsky Regiment. At age 35 Alexander was still a very handsome man: despite his deafness and incipient baldness, with his blue eyes and light brown hair always carefully dressed, his light skin and the light lavender scent on his face and hands, he showed immense charm:

> If he spoke to men of distinguished rank, it was with much dignity and affability at the same time; if to persons in his retinue, with an air of almost familiar kindness; if to women of a certain age, with deference; to young people with infinite grace and refinement, seductive with an expressive face.[11]

While Alexander was dining in the garden, General Balashov suddenly approached to tell him in a low voice that the Grande Armée, with a total of 448,000[12] men, had crossed the Niemen. Contrary to the assertions of a certain number of tsarist and then Soviet historians, a declaration of war had indeed been sent by Napoleon to the Russian government, as well as to other European governments,[13] but the tsar had not yet been informed. Therefore, the surprise effect was total. Not letting his emotions appear, Alexander immediately excused himself and went to join his staff.

Several hours before the invasion, Napoleon had the following text proclaimed to his troops, from which one may infer his motivations and objectives:

Soldiers!

The second war of Poland has begun. The first ended in Friedland and Tilsit: in Tilsit, Russia swore eternal alliance with France and war with England. Today she has violated her oaths. She does not want to give any explanation of her strange conduct until the French eagles have gone back over the Rhine, thereby leaving our allies to her discretion. Russia is driven by her fate. Her destiny should be carried out. Does she think we are degenerates? That we are no longer the soldiers of Austerlitz? She places us between dishonor and war. Our choice cannot be doubted, let us march forward! Let us pass the Niemen! Let us take war onto their territory. The second war of Poland will be glorious for French armies, like the first. But peace that we will conclude will bring us its guarantee, and put an end to the imperious influence that Russia has for fifty years exercised over the affairs of Europe.[14]

For Napoleon, the war that he was on the verge of unleashing was intended to turn Russia away from Europe for the exclusive benefit of France. His declaration saluted the glory of the French armies but not the twenty nations that composed the Grande Armée, and he said not a word about the possible reestablishment of a Polish state. At the hour of the impending titanic clash, Napoleon thus proclaimed a very French-centered position that must have disappointed his allies. When difficulties and then reversals subsequently occurred, this multinational army would lack reference points and find itself destabilized in the face of a Russian army whose national spirit, by contrast, would be strengthened by its trials.

Meanwhile, in the face of this invasion of unprecedented scope—all the Grande Armée's soldiers would take four days and nights to cross the Niemen River—and once the first shock was over, Alexander and the Russians quickly revived. On the advice of Rumyantsev, he made a final attempt at reconciliation: he asked Balashov to send Napoleon a letter enjoining him to end the conflict, but when the letter arrived, it was refused. Meanwhile, the tsar wrote (aided by his new secretary Admiral Shishkov) an imperial ukase in solemn style that was aimed at both troops and public opinion. Invoking the help of "the Almighty, witness and avenger of the truth," he asserted his determination not to lay down arms "as long as a single armed enemy soldier remains in my empire," and he concluded with a phrase both laconic and striking: "I am with you. God is against the aggressor." In the duel of two emperors, words would play an immense role, as we shall see.

The front line of all three Russian armies was concentrated along the western border. The first western army was directed by war minister and infantry general Barclay de Tolly; initially based at Vilnius, it comprised 120,210 men stretched in a cordon along the Niemen, from the mouth of the river to the bend in Grodno. The second, under the command of infantry general Prince Bagration, was garrisoned at Bialystok, with 49,423 men, slightly to the south between the Niemen and the Bug. Finally, the third so-called observation army was directed by the cavalry general Tormasov and composed of 44,180 men based in Dubno in Volhynia. Behind, in the second line, came two reserve corps of almost 100,000 men, to which should be added a Finnish corps of 57,526 men, the army of the Danube, and troops detached from inside the empire, about 108,000 men. Finally, if we add to this total the troops from the Caucasus and the Crimea, Cossack troops, and military administration, a total of 716,000 men were mustered as Russian land forces.[15]

But this army suffered from some structural problems: first, the command lacked cohesion. While Barclay as minister of war was, according to the hierarchy, superior to Bagration and Tormasov, in fact things were otherwise, for Bagration's prestige, his experience and military competence, plus his ties with the imperial family (he had been the lover of Grand Duchess Catherine) were such that he felt able to contest certain orders and do as he wanted, to the minister's great displeasure: "Sire," Barclay wrote to Alexander, "it is extremely disagreeable that Prince Bagration, instead of immediately executing the orders of Your Majesty, wastes time in futile discussions that he shares with Platov, confusing the head of this poor general, who is already not very intelligent and moreover lacks any education."[16]

On top of that, Barclay de Tolly had to deal with the military advisors who surrounded Alexander I; each tended to give his advice at the risk of sowing even more confusion, which provoked the ironic assessment made by Napoleon to Balashov: "While Phül proposes, Armfeld contradicts, Bennigsen examines, and Barclay, on whom the execution rests, does not know what to conclude."[17] Finally, based on a system of conscription that enrolled adolescents who had been torn from their families and rural communities to be placed for 25 years under the authority of officers who were often contemptuous and cruel and subjected them to absurd levels of iron discipline, the Russian army partook of a feudal and coercive regime[18] that was a priori unpropitious for a sense of sacrifice. However, despite the difficulties and trials the cohesion of the Russian army remained strong, and there were few cases of desertion, with no comparison to the situation in the Grande Armée. It is precisely in the archaic nature of the Russian army, which bore so many elements of weakness, that we must seek the key to this cohesion: for a peasant drafted for 25 years, year after year, the regiment took the place of the family and became a total community, a collective reference with which he identified and without which he could not imagine living—hence his ardor to defend it against all fate's blows.[19]

So, in the night of June 23–24, Napoleon crossed the Niemen, and with his advance guard he headed toward Vilnius where he could threaten both Moscow and St. Petersburg. The 80 miles that separate Kaunas from Vilnius were covered in three days, and on June 28 Napoleon was ready to enter the city. But meanwhile Barclay had ordered his troops to evacuate Vilnius, (after having blown up bridges and warehouses); reaching the fortified camp of Drissa, he ordered Bagration's army to withdraw to Minsk. On June 27, at three o'clock in the morning, Alexander and his staff left Vilnius, abandoning the city to the Grande Armée, which entered it the next day. A majority of the population were Poles who welcomed enthusiastically this army that they thought had come to liberate them.[20] And, in fact, from Napoleon's establishment in the city, where he would remain almost 18 days, he hurried to make his mark by installing a provisional government of Lithuania, dividing the region into departments, and setting up a military administration that lasted until December 1812.[21] But according to Napoleon's Grand Equerry, Armand de Caulaincourt, the French emperor was not satisfied:

> He was astonished that they could have given up Vilna[22] without a fight and that they took their decision in enough time to escape. The lost hope of a grand battle before Vilna was for him a real disappointment. He would take vengeance by shouting about the cowardice of his adversaries, who were playing his game by dishonoring themselves in the eyes of the brave Poles; who had yielded the country and Polish fortunes to him without having done the honor of fighting for them.[23]

Moreover, this first "conquest" by Napoleon was already proving costly: while the troops were bivouacked close to the city, a violent snow- and hailstorm that beat for several hours over the region caused the deaths of hundreds of soldiers and of 8,000 horses. Bread was lacking and cases of dysentery increasing, and already the number of marauders was estimated at 30,000.[24]

Meanwhile, on the Russian side, the fall of Vilnius angered several generals, including Bagration, who would have preferred to give battle to prevent it. But this disapproval did not change Barclay's determination to avoid a frontal confrontation. The following weeks saw the same tactic: at the head of the first army, Barclay took the route to Drissa where he arrived on July 21, but in the opinion of several experts, including the Prussian colonel Von Clausewitz,[25] Colonel Michaud (an officer from Nice who had passed into the tsar's service), and in the opinion of Barclay and Bennigsen, the Drissa camp was insufficiently protected. As Bennigsen put it:

> More than 2,000 men had worked for six months on these defensive works and they were called a second Gibraltar. You can imagine my surprise when I found it the worst, most disadvantageous position I ever saw chosen to receive a battle that might decide the outcome of the campaign—and perhaps of the State![26]

And so Barclay de Tolly decided to abandon Drissa and head to Vitebsk where he hoped to achieve the junction with Bagration's troops.

Meanwhile, following suggestions coming from Arakcheev, Balashov, and Shishkov, as well as his sister Catherine's insistent advice, Alexander decided to leave the theater of operations. For those close to him, the tsar's power was by nature sacred and should not be exposed to the misfortunes of battle. So, while keeping the title of commander in chief of the Russian armies, Alexander handed over to Barclay the responsibility for his army. Leaving it, he solemnly told him: "Good-bye, general, good-bye again. I entrust you my army: do not forget that I have no other. May this thought never forsake you."[27] Then he left for Moscow in order to raise new recruits. And in a week, no fewer than 80,000 new men joined up.

Napoleon had grasped the meaning of the Russian maneuver and wanted to prevent the junction of the troops so he tried to beat Barclay to Vitebsk in order to overwhelm him and then trap him. On July 25–26 he reached the Russian rearguard at Ostrovno, near Vitebsk, and hoped to have the much-anticipated decisive battle. But Barclay de Tolly, who had not yet managed to join Bagration's army, chose to withdraw in the direction of Smolensk in order to effect the junction of the armies farther east. On July 28, the Grand Armée entered a deserted Vitebsk without having obtained the decisive victory—postponed again.

On August 2 the armies of Barclay and Bagration finally effected their union under the walls of Smolensk and decided to go onto the offensive. Four days later, Barclay de Tolly engaged in a first cavalry assault that opposed the French general Murat's troops to those of Count Osterman: the battle turned to the advantage of the Russians, but the two Russian armies chose to fall back toward Smolensk on the Dnieper. This gave rise to an irritated letter from Bagration to Arakcheev, written during the retreat march:

It is really not my fault. They started to stretch me like catgut along the whole line. The enemy entered without having fired a shot and we began to withdraw, I know not what we are supposed to have done wrong. You will not persuade anyone either in Russia or in the army that we were not betrayed; I cannot defend all of Russia alone. The first army should retire immediately and march to Vilna at all costs, but that is just what is feared. I am surrounded by the enemy and I could not tell you in advance where I will then find myself. What God wants to happen will happen, but I will not sleep unless my strength betrays me, for I have not felt well for several days. I pray you insistently to advance on the enemy, otherwise things will end badly, as much on the enemy's side as on ours: one does not joke with national feelings and the Russians are not made to flee. We have become worse than the Prussians. I will find a breach to escape, naturally with losses. But shame on you. You have a fortified camp behind you, open flanks, weak enemy corps in front of you—it is your duty to attack. My rearguard fights every day and I cannot withdraw to either Minsk or on the Wyeyka River because of the bad roads and the swamps. I have not a moment of respite, I am not thinking of myself. As God is my witness, I ask only to do what I can.[28]

On August 16–17, while the Grande Armée was approaching Smolensk, combat began in the suburbs. Violent and fierce, it caused 12,000 killed or wounded on the Russian side and 10,000 among the assailants and was ended by an order to retreat given by Barclay de Tolly. Judging the balance of forces to be to his disadvantage (80,000 Russians to 120,000 invaders), Barclay de Tolly gave this order after having burned the warehouses and bridges over the Dnieper. But this new retreat provoked the open anger of other generals. In a rage Bagration wrote to Ermolov: "I am ashamed to wear the uniform. What an imbecile. Minister Barclay is running away. I admit that this disgusts me so much I'll go crazy."[29] In a letter to Rostopchin, he let his hatred burst forth with oaths against "this bastard, this riffraff, this damned Barclay."[30]

The Russian retreat allowed Napoleon to enter a deserted and devastated Smolensk: of the 2,250 houses in the town, only 350 remained standing. But the taking of the town did not mark a decisive victory. In addition, the Grande Armée was confronted with increasing difficulties: badly fed men were weak; the heat beating down on the area provoked epidemics and a rise in mortality. At this date Napoleon was hesitating between two strategies:[31] either to pause long enough to help the Grande Armée get back on its feet or else to continue the offensive to Moscow, 300 miles away, to seek the decisive victory there. For him, it was inconceivable that the Russian armies would abandon their holy capital without a battle. In addition, because Moscow as the economic capital of the country was a great river junction, and rivers were the only means of transport in Russia, it appeared crucial to hold Moscow in order to hold the tsar. If deprived of its provision of raw materials, St. Petersburg, which was well defended on a military level, would be gradually asphyxiated and Alexander would be forced to negotiate. For the historian Andrey Ratchinski, the choice of Moscow is also explained by more symbolic objectives: in his conquest of the world, Napoleon aimed to consecrate his work by having himself crowned emperor in the Kremlin after conquering Moscow, "the third Rome." This assertion is interesting because it illustrates the ideological and symbolic dimension of Napoleon's plan, showing how much the war of 1812 was a war of ideas, as much as of men. But the sources cited by this historian are allusive and sparse, leaving room for doubt. Whatever the truth of this hypothesis, after having granted his army a week's rest, Napoleon started off for the sacred city.

Meanwhile, the Russian army was undergoing an acute crisis: French proclamations that were disseminated in the provinces of Vitebsk and then Smolensk promised freedom to the peasants and had provoked violent disturbances. Nobles had been assassinated and their property looted, which made the centers of power fear a new "Pugachevs-china,"[32] drastic social destabilization.[33] Moreover, on the specifically military level, Barclay de Tolly's strategy was being increasingly contested. Within the general staff rumors flew about "foreigners" guilty of treason, while troop morale was declining during this interminable withdrawal that had already given the enemy a portion of imperial territory.

* * *

Because Barclay de Tolly was the target of increasingly sharp criticism, the emperor began to doubt his choice (Alexander did not forget that despite his qualities as a man and soldier, Barclay had not managed to federate the Russian army around himself), and so the emperor made a crucial decision. He decided to convene an "Extraordinary Committee" composed of Count Saltykov (the president of the Council of State), Prince Lopukhin, Count Kochubey, Arakcheev, and Balashov, in order to remove Barclay de Tolly from his role as commander in chief and to find a successor for him. In a letter to Catherine written in St. Petersburg in August 1812, Alexander explains why the committee's choice settled on General Kutuzov:

Here I find spirits lower than in Moscow and in the inner part of the country and a great ferocity against the Minister of War which, I much admit, is due to the irresolution of his conduct and the disorder with which he looks after his duties. The tiff between him and Bagration has aggravated it to such an extent that I was forced, after explaining things to a small special committee I named for this purpose, to nominate a commander-in-chief for all the armies. After serious deliberation, we decided on Kutusoff as being the oldest and thereby giving Bennigsen the possibility of serving under him, for they are linked by friendship, too. In general, Kutusoff is in great favor among the public, here and in Moscow.[34]

This decision was not easy to take: Alexander appreciated Barclay's personal qualities, his courage, simplicity, and uprightness. And he detested Kutuzov. Apart from the fact that the sight of the old general reminded him of the fiasco of Austerlitz, he had only contempt for Kutuzov's dissolute character and manners. Aged 67, blind in one eye, obese, and almost impotent, Kutuzov was known for his laziness, his obsequiousness, his taste for luxury—even on campaign, he ate his meals off silver service—and his sexual appetite. A rumor claimed that two very young girls disguised as Cossacks accompanied him throughout operations. Far from the heroic and mythic picture of him that Tolstoy gave in War and Peace, Kutuzov aroused the disapproval, if not revulsion, of many contemporaries. Langeron has left a severe description:

One could not be wittier than Kutuzov but one could not have a less forceful character, one could not be smarter and more cunning, and one could possess no fewer real talents and more immorality. A prodigious memory, well educated, rare amiability, friendly and interesting conversation, a good nature (a bit superficial in truth, but agreeable to all who wanted to be duped by it)—these are the charms of Kutuzov. Great violence and the crudeness of a peasant when he got carried away or when he did not have to fear the person he was addressing; a baseness toward individuals whom he thought in favor, carried to the most groveling level, insurmountable idleness, apathy that extended to everything; a formidable egotism, villainous and disgusting *libertinage,* no delicacy about the means of making or getting money—these are the drawbacks of the same man.[35]

But the old soldier, who had just been unanimously elected head of the militias of St. Petersburg and Moscow, enjoyed within both army and public opinion great popularity due to his glorious military deeds. Charismatic, experienced, and courageous, Kutuzov was able to cement the army better than the unfortunate Barclay had done. Moreover, because he was Russian, he appeared better able to incarnate the patriotic war that would now unfold, no longer in the Lithuanian provinces, but in the heart of Russian territory. However—and this is not the least paradox of the situation—Kutuzov's nomination as head of the general staff brought only minor changes to a strategy that remained essentially unchanged.

* * *

Kutuzov was named commander in chief in order to retake the offensive and inflict on the enemy the defeat that would force it to withdraw and in order to galvanize both troops and the civilian population. This change in perspective was quickly translated into action. On September 7, when Russian troops had for two days been very close to the village of Borodino situated 90 miles from Moscow, a battle began. Proving particularly murderous—42,000 wounded and dead (including Bagration) out of 112,000 soldiers on the Russian side and 28,000 missing out of 130,000 combatants in the Grande Armée—the Battle of Borodino left Napoleon's troops (led by Generals Ney, Davout, Grouchy, and Poniatowsky) as masters of the battlefield. But this unconvincing victory did not modify the balance of forces, and as a follow-up to this assault, Napoleon aspired to finally deliver a decisive battle in Moscow. However, on September 13, 1812, in the village of Fili, the Russian general staff held a war council, and after having consulted the participants, Kutuzov took the decision to cede Moscow without fighting. In the night troops evacuated the city, followed by hundreds of thousands of inhabitants, who, overtaken by panic, fled in barouches, carriages, by harness, or on foot. Of a population of almost 300,000 residents, only 6,200 civilians (2.3 percent of the population)[36] and 20,000 wounded soldiers who had been abandoned to their fate remained in the city when the French entered. The next afternoon, September 14, it was into a dead city that Napoleon made his entrance; the officers of the Grande Armée felt incredulity and fright at the sight of such a strange and incomprehensible spectacle:

> In good order, without saying a word, we walk along the long lonely streets, with house shutters closed, the roll of drums resonating in deaf echoes. In vain we try to show on our faces a serenity that is quite far from our hearts. It

seems to us that something quite extraordinary is going to happen. Moscow appears to us like an immense cadaver; it is the kingdom of silence, a fairy city where the buildings and houses have been built for the enchantment of us alone! And now I think of the impression produced on a traveler made pensive by the ruins of Pompeii or Herculaneum. But here the impression is still more sepulchral.[37]

While the 130,000 men who entered Moscow—the rest of the troops (already very diminished in number) were straggling along hundreds of miles—aspired only to be fed and to be allowed to sleep, suddenly a gigantic fire burst out in several points of the city on the night of September 15–16. The majority of houses, churches, and storerooms were made of wood, and because the water pumps had been evacuated from the city by the governor-general, Count Rostopchin, the fire quickly spread and would last three days.

Count Rostopchin always denied in his memoirs having been the source of the fire. But on September 13 he had declared to Prince Eugen of Württemberg: "If I am asked, I will not hesitate to say 'Burn the capital rather than deliver it to the enemy!' That is the opinion of Count Rostopchin. But the governor of the city has the mission to watch over its safety and he could not give this advice."[38] There is little doubt about his responsibility for the fire. Moreover, in her later memoirs Natalia Rostopchin, the count's daughter and sister of the Countess of Ségur, would attest that, in the night of September 13–14, during a secret meeting that took place at her father's domicile, the chief of police, Balashov, and several of his assistants received from the governor-general, her father, precise instructions about which buildings were to be burned.

The capture of the sacred city, followed by its burning (which was soon attributed by Russian propaganda to the "barbarian invaders"), gave rise to confusion and anger everywhere, particularly since the fall of Moscow, like that of Smolensk before it, was accompanied by sacrilegious acts—the Grande Armée housed its horses in the churches—and by violence against the civilian population. For many Russians the abandonment of Moscow was a culpable action—for some, even a sin for which the tsar would be accountable before God; but if such criticism arose among the elites, more generally the tragedy helped to cement the Russians, transforming the conflict into a patriotic war that provided a foundation for Russian nationalism. A veritable political and social cohesion suddenly emerged; for some perspicacious witnesses, the fall of Moscow marked an irreversible turning point in the war. On September 25 Count Paul Stroganov wrote to his wife:

Admittedly, the occupation of Moscow by the enemy is frightful, yet if it is possible to set aside the sad spectacle of our ancient prostituted capital being despoiled by the monster that occupies it, and to consider this calamity from the abstract military point of view, one could draw consoling conclusions. I believe that this success, far from being favorable to him, has put him in difficulties of which he was previously unaware. This is worth expanding, and this is how I explain it: this man believed firmly and persuaded his whole army, thanks to this illusion, that all the fatigues that he had showered on them until that day were going to end, that Moscow was the final goal, that it was in Moscow they would find peace and abundance, that from Moscow he would leave, strengthened to subjugate that part of Europe that still resisted him. He managed to arrive in Moscow, but there he only found heaps of ash, fire, and debris—the whole lit by our own hands. Nobody spoke to him of peace; like a father who would rather kill his daughter than see her dishonored, we annihilated Moscow at the moment when we could no longer defend it. He was scarcely used to such receptions in the other capitals of Europe—even Spain was more amiable—and here he is terribly disappointed.[39]

In fact, the Grande Armée was in a state of exhaustion: the deficient chain of supply no long allowed the soldiers to be fed properly, and they were weakened by interminable marches and felt discouraged at "taking" deserted towns where they could not find food. There were early signs of indiscipline: a burned Moscow was quickly prey to pillagers and marauders. The general mood was for giving up. This degradation in his army pushed Napoleon to solicit peace. In vain: Alexander refused any kind of talk. On the night of October 18, sowing panic among sleeping soldiers, Cossack troops went onto the offensive against 25,000 of Murat's men who were bivouacking near the village of Vinkovo, and the losses were heavy on the French side. The next morning Napoleon still planned to restart the offensive by leaving Moscow, heading south and taking the warehouses of Kaluga. But five days later the hard battle of Maloyaroslavetz—the little town changed hands eight times, with a loss of 6,000 killed and wounded on the French side and 7,000 on the Russian—would, in fact, decide the fate of the war. The Grande Armée, with 130,000 soldiers, was only a shadow of itself, while the imperial army, perked up thanks to the arrival in Volhynia of the Danube army led by Chichagov and the Finnish corps led by Wittgenstein, had a total of 144,000 combatants, who managed to block Napoleon's progress to the south. Napoleon was forced to sound the retreat and take the route back to Smolensk, "an itinerary in which requisitions and pillaging had emptied the reserves and whetted the local population's desire for revenge."[40]

After the end of October, due to snowfalls that became heavier, and still more after mid-November,[41] due to the extreme cold that set in, the forced march retreat of the Grande Armée was made an ordeal. On top of this, on its way back, the Grande Armée suffered from the incessant harassment by regiments of the regular army (regular means all the army except for the cossaks) and Cossack detachments, as well as from attacks by armed peasants trying to chase the impious invader out as fast as possible. During this retreat, the passage of Berezina—a small river situated along the town of Borissov, 45 miles northeast of Minsk—lasting from November 26 to 29, was an episode both heroic and painful. The Russian armies had burned the only bridge over the river, which was full of blocks of ice but was not deeply frozen and could not be crossed. And so, for long hours the 400 bridge builders of General Eblé, most of whom would die of cold and exhaustion in the course of this trial, worked in icy water to construct two temporary bridges. When they were finished on the afternoon of the twenty-sixth, the crossing for the next two and a half days allowed 60,000 combatants to escape; but despite its heroic nature, the episode left a bitter taste. On November 29, having given the order to burn the new bridges to avoid the Russians' pursuing the Grande Armée, Eblé had to leave behind him almost 20,000 more soldiers and civilians, who, too exhausted to walk and cross the bridges in time, were abandoned to the Russians. Those who escaped with the Grande Armée recrossed the Niemen on December 13, which marked the end of the Russian campaign. For the Russians and their emperor this was the date of liberation.

But the toll of this war was frightfully high. On top of the material destruction of cities, towns, and villages that had been entirely burned or ravaged, there were colossal human casualties. Of the 600,000 Grande Armée combatants (the 448,000 men who crossed the Niemen in June 1812 had been joined in the course of the campaign by almost 150,000 more), barely more than 10 percent came back to France. Soldiers had been exposed to terrible suffering. In a letter to his brother Joseph, dated December 21 and written from Vilnius, Xavier de Maistre recounted with horror the scenes he had witnessed:

> I cannot give you an idea of the route I have taken. The cadavers of French obstructed the road that from Moscow to the borders (about 800 verstes) appears to be a continuous battlefield. When we approached villages, most of them burned, the spectacle became even more awful. The bodies were in heaps, and in several places where the unfortunate soldiers had gathered in houses, they were burned inside them without having the strength to come

out. I saw houses where more than fifty bodies lay together, and among them, three or four men were still living, stripped to their shirts, in minus 15 C degrees[42] of cold. One of them said to me: "Monsieur, get me out of here or kill me, my name is Normand de Flageac, I am an officer like you." It was not in my power to help him. We gave him clothes, but there was no means of saving him and we had to leave him in that horrible place. [...] From all sides and on all roads we met miserable men who were wandering around, dying of hunger and cold; their large number meant that one could not always gather them in time, and they mostly died on the way to the depots. I saw none without thinking of that infernal man who led them to this excess of misfortune.[43]

And in his correspondence to his king, Joseph de Maistre (the former's brother) wrote in turn:

The state of the French cannot be expressed; it is said about them things that resemble the siege of Jerusalem. They are said to have eaten human flesh. Someone asserted that he saw a man being roasted; all the stories, both written and oral, agree that Frenchmen were seen lying on the carcass of a horse to devour it with their teeth. Here is another sure thing: someone took as prisoner a veteran soldier wearing broken chevrons on his sleeve, the mark of long and distinguished service, and who had done all Bonaparte's campaigns, including in Egypt. For several days he had lived on a little dead flesh, and for two or three days since then, he had eaten nothing at all.[44]

As regards the Russian army as a whole, it suffered heavy losses, around 400,000 men: this was the scope of a cataclysm that aroused in Alexander a moral and spiritual crisis of great intensity, followed by a "rebirth."

Alexander during the Patriotic War

The idea of the coming war had not ceased to haunt the tsar since 1809–1810, and he was well aware of his adversary's advantages. Since 1802–1803, he had been no longer "seduced" by the First Consul, and we remember the acerbic statement he made about Napoleon on the eve of Tilsit. "Napoleon takes me for a fool, but he who laughs last laughs best." But at the same time Alexander recognized the exceptional charisma of his enemy, his magnetism and intelligence, which soon led him to reflect on the unparalleled courage and tenacity that he would have to show to triumph over this extraordinary adversary. And naturally it was into this relentless combat that he launched himself in June 1812.

From the first hours of the invasion, while he was still in Vilnius, he adopted a ukase countersigned by Barclay de Tolly that reaffirmed his faith and trust in God. Meanwhile he decided very pragmatically to increase the strength of the regular army by resorting to using the forestry guards of the western provinces.[45] A few days later, on July 18, when accompanying the troops of the first army, he found himself in the fortified camp of Drissa and issued a manifesto. Mixing religious inspiration with patriotic sentiments, the text referred to mythic and historical references:

> The enemy has penetrated our territory and continues to bear arms inside Russia, hoping by force and temptations to overthrow the tranquility of our Great State. He has in mind the bad intention of destroying our glory and prosperity. With a heart full of malice and a mouth full of flattery, he is bringing chains and eternal fetters for Russia. We have asked God to help us to oppose him with our troops, but we cannot and should not hide from our subjects that the forces of the enemy are numerous and that we have to gather other troops to form a second front that will defend the homes, women, and children of each and all of us. We have already called on Moscow, our first capital, but today we are calling on all our faithful subjects, on all orders and estates both religious and civil, inviting them, by their unanimous and general uprising, to cooperate against the designs and expectations of the enemy. May he find at every step the faithful sons of Russia who will strike him by all their means and with all their strength, without listening to any of his malice, any of his lies. May he encounter in each noble a Pozharsky,[46] in each cleric a Palitsyn,[47] in each bourgeois a Minine.[48] Nobility, in all times you have been the savior of the country. Holy Synod and Clergy! By your ardent prayers you have always summoned Grace down upon the head of Russia. Russian people! Brave descendants of the brave Slavs! You have more than once broken the teeth of lions and tigers that were attacking you. Unite! With the cross in your hearts and weapons in your hands, no human force will be able to vanquish you.[49]

He also called for the constitution of popular militias designed to assist the regular army. The energy he deployed so prodigiously was accompanied by a sort of existential anguish, due to his extreme lucidity about the responsibilities incumbent on him. In 1814 he confirmed to the Countess of Choiseul-Gouffier: "One has to be in my place to have any idea of the responsibility of a sovereign and of what I am feeling, thinking that one day I must account to God for the life of each of my soldiers."[50] We saw that in

July 1812, yielding to the injunctions of those close to him and his military advisors, Alexander resolved to leave the front, but it was to go to Moscow in order to galvanize the population and to work to cement the people around their tsar, their faith, and their endangered country. Alexander feared that Napoleon, as the spiritual son of the French Revolution, would bring (as he already had to Prussia and Warsaw) his share of "temptations"—he used exactly this word in his manifesto of July 18—and might even destabilize the empire by promising the peasants that he would abolish serfdom. And, in fact, Napoleonic proclamations spread in the provinces of Vitebsk and Smolensk did arouse violent disturbances, although it is not easy for the historian to grasp what was due to French influence and what arose from a tradition of jacquerie[51] that was anchored in Russia itself. Consequently, to stop the process, Alexander had to resist the invader with words as well as actions, skillfully combining religious and nationalist themes to convince the population that the Napoleonic invasion was not the consequence of errors committed by the tsar but rather the fruit of the insatiable lust for power of a tyrant who had nothing to do with the good of the people. On the road to Moscow, Alexander halted at Smolensk, where the town's nobility had raised and equipped 20,000 militiamen in his honor. In this small provincial village Alexander was overcome with dizziness for the first time. He now incarnated the national spirit; nascent public opinion, which on many occasions had murmured if not complained about him and had rarely understood him, had finally lined up behind "its" tsar.

He arrived in Moscow on July 23 in the evening and soon ignited an intense patriotic fervor. On July 24 in the morning, the tsar attended a blessing in the Cathedral of the Dormition in the Kremlin. Three days later, he met the deputies of the nobility and merchants of Moscow who displayed their patriotism and offered him respectively 3 and 10 million rubles, which validated his faith in the people and its determination to fight.

Returning to St. Petersburg after a week's stay in Moscow, he continued his intense propaganda activity, trying constantly to convince people and to justify his stance. On August 4 an imperial ukase raised new troops, and on August 13 a new manifesto forcefully asserted:

> French troops have broken through the frontiers of our empire. The most perfidious aggression has been my punishment for my strict observance of the alliance. To keep the peace, I exhausted all means that conformed to the dignity of my throne and were useful for my people—but I obtained no result. Emperor Napoleon had firmly in mind a plan to destroy Russia. The most moderate proposals remained unanswered. The unexpected invasion has clearly

revealed the falseness of the kindly affirmations and promises professed even a short while ago. This is why nothing remains but to brandish weapons and put myself in the hands of Providence to find the means to fight force with force. My hope lies in the zeal of my people and the bravery of my troops. Threatened within their own homes, they will defend them with firmness and valor. Providence will bless our just action. The defense of the homeland, the maintenance of our independence, and the honor of our people have obliged us to go to war. I will not lay down arms as long as a single soldier in arms is still present in my empire.[52]

Disseminated by newspapers and pamphlets, these various imperial edicts were backed up by tracts from Count Rostopchin. Written in a more brutal (and even offensive) style and posted in the streets of Moscow, they aimed to solder the people behind the tsar by sharpening hatred of the invader. All this patriotic propaganda was echoed in the press: the journal *The Son of the Fatherland* played a major role among elites throughout the conflict, as did the visual arts—pictures by Kiprensky dramatized heroic fighters like the young Peter Olenin—which also participated in the patriotic effort.

Equally concerned to counter the French propaganda spread by the bulletins of the Grande Armée and posters addressed to the inhabitants of occupied towns, Alexander set up a mobile printing press in the theater of operations, charged with diffusing among the non-French soldiers of the Grande Armée proclamations inciting them to abandon the fight.

However, despite the fears expressed by Alexander and despite Napoleon's first actions during his entry into Vitebsk, then Smolensk, the latter gave up pushing peasants to revolt; in the territories occupied by the Grande Armée, serfdom was not in fact abolished.[53] This reluctance aroused, and still arouses, many questions among historians. Is it explained by Napoleon's desire to spare his enemy and not destabilize his empire in order to continue to negotiate with him? Or out of a concern not to destabilize his own supply lines? Or does it express, as the Russian historian Vladlen Sirotkin asserts, a contempt tinged with fear of the Russian peasants, the muzhiki, who were perceived as unpredictable and dangerous barbarians? The answer is not clear. Whatever the case, reassured in the loyalty of the peasantry, Alexander consented to the creation of peasant militias, who during the Grande Armée's retreat played a key role in continually harassing the routed troops.

In parallel to his engagement on the domestic front, the emperor also conducted intense diplomatic activity. He reestablished peace with England in August and confirmed that henceforth no restriction would affect the circulation of ships and commercial exchanges. In mid-August he met

Bernadotte in Turku and obtained from Sweden the promise to guarantee the inviolability of Finland; this was a major advance: Alexander was now free to bring the Finnish corps to the western front.

* * *

Alexander's commitment was total and merciless, but he was not isolated: the whole imperial family was mobilized in the war effort. Grand Duke Constantine, very active in the general staff, took part in all military decisions. Elizabeth had proclaimed from the start of the conflict a determination and patriotism that ceded nothing to Alexander's. In a letter written on the same day the Borodino battle was taking place, August 26 (O.S.), 1812, she wrote to her mother with an honorable clairvoyance:

> I am sure that you are badly informed in Germany about what is happening here. Perhaps they have tried to make you believe we have fled to Siberia, whereas we have not left Petersburg. We are prepared for everything, in truth, apart from negotiations. The more Napoleon advances, the less he must believe in a possible peace. This is the unanimous feeling of the emperor and the whole nation in all classes, and thank heaven, there exists the most perfect harmony in that respect. This is what Napoleon did not expect: he got that wrong, like many other things. Each step he takes in this immense Russia makes him approach the abyss. We will see how he bears the winter![54]

Two days later, in a new letter to the margrave of Baden, the empress saluted the patriotic spirit that had overwhelmed the country, turning into derision the supposed French "civilization" faced with Russian "barbarity," and she reaffirmed that Alexander would not make a pact with the enemy:

> Daily you must see and hear (as we do) enough proofs of patriotism and devotion and the heroic bravery in all military and civil ranks so as not to think them exaggerated. Ah! This brave nation shows what it is, and what those who understand it have known for a long time, despite stubbornly treating it as barbarian. However, the barbarians of the north and the bigots of the south of Europe are those who now resist the supposedly *civilized nation* the most,[55] and they are far from being reduced to nothing.
>
> From the moment Napoleon crossed our borders, it was as if an electric spark extended over all Russia, and if the immensity of its extent had allowed everyone at the same moment to be informed in all corners of the Empire, it would have raised a cry of indignation so terrible that it would have been

heard at the end of the universe. As Napoleon advanced, this feeling increased. Old men who had lost almost everything said: "We will find the means to live! Anything is preferable to a shameful peace." Women who had all their kin in the army still regarded the dangers they were running as secondary and they feared only peace. A peace that would be the death knell of Russia cannot be made, fortunately: the emperor cannot conceive of the idea, and even if he wanted to, he could not. This is the fine heroism of our position![56]

Still, the unanimity that surrounded Alexander was severely tested with the burning of Moscow. On September 15, prostrated by the terrible news, Catherine wrote to her brother of her distress, offering help and enjoining him to continue the fight:

Moscow is taken, there are inexplicable things. Do not forget your resolution: no peace and you have the hope of recovering your honor. If you are in pain, do not forget your friends who are ready to fly to you, and only too happy if they might be of some help, so make use of them.

But my dear, no peace, and even if you were at Kazan, no peace.[57]

But this catastrophe in no way affected Alexander's determination, as he says in a brief note written back to Catherine:

Yesterday morning, my dear, I received your sad letter of the 3rd. There are things it is impossible to conceive. But be persuaded that my resolution to fight is more unshakeable than ever; I would prefer to cease to be what I am than to compromise with the monster that performs the misfortune of the world.[58]

However, in the following days Catherine, under the influence of criticism starting to arise, was more severe. She sent her brother a letter in which she echoed the harsh reproach to which the abandoning of Moscow gave rise in a court that was really unpredictable:

The taking of Moscow has raised the exasperation of spirits to a pitch; discontent is at its highest point, and no consideration is shown for your person. [...] You are loudly accused of your empire's misfortune, of general and particular ruin, and of having lost the country's honor and your own. It is not just one class but all of them are united in decrying you. [...] One of the principal accusations concerns failing to keep your word about Moscow, which expected you with impatience, and the neglect in which you left it. You seem to have betrayed it. [...] I leave you to judge the situation of a country where the leader is despised; there is nothing that people are not ready to do to recover honor, but in the desire to sacrifice everything for the fatherland, people say, "where will this lead, when everybody is massacred, ruined by the ineptness of the leaders?" The idea of peace, fortunately, is not general; far from it, for the feeling of shame that follows the loss of Moscow gives birth to the desire for vengeance. People complain about you loudly. [...] Save your honor that is under attack. Your presence can bring spirits back; neglect no available means.[59]

Harshly criticized for having abandoned the holy city without a fight, Alexander found himself also under pressure from Constantine, Maria Feodorovna, and Rumyantsev, who did implore him to accept peace talks with Napoleon. And yet again, at a key moment, the emperor found at his sides only his wife to support him. But he remained unshakable. In a very fine long letter written to Catherine on September 7, he justifies his choices:

After having sacrificed the utility of my personal amour-propre by leaving the army because it was claimed that I was harmful to it, that I was depriving the generals of any responsibility, that I inspired no trust in the troops, that the reverses imputed to me were more annoying than those imputed to my generals, then judge for yourself, my good friend, how painful it must be for me to hear that my honor is under attack, when I only did what people wanted me to in leaving the army when I had no other desire than to stay there. I was firmly resolved to return to it before the appointment of Kutuzov, which I renounced only after this nomination, in part by the memory of what the courtesan character of this man had produced in Austerlitz, and in part by following your own advice and that of several others of the same opinion as you. [...]

At present, let us examine whether I could have come to Moscow? As soon as it was made a principle that my presence in the army would do more harm than good, when the army was approaching Moscow after its retreat from Smolensk, could I decently be in Moscow? Although I could never have thought Moscow might be abandoned in such an unworthy way, yet I did have to say to myself that if after one or two lost battles such a thing could happen, then what role could I have played and would I have to come to Moscow to pack my baggage with the others?

Then he says he is wounded by the lack of trust emanating from his own family at such a difficult moment for him. He confesses the breadth of the task that faces him against a talented aggressor, and he insists once more on his will to stand firm:

As for me, dear one, all I can answer for is my heart and my intentions and my zeal for everything that can tend to the good and to the utility of my fatherland, according to my best convictions. As for talent, perhaps I lack some, but it is not provided; it is a blessing of nature and nobody has ever procured it. Seconded as badly as I am, lacking instruments on all sides, directing so enormous a machine in a terrible crisis and against an infernal antagonist who possesses the most horrible wickedness joined to the most eminent talent and is helped by all the forces of Europe as a whole, and by a mass of talented men who have been trained for twenty years in war and revolution, one would be obliged to agree, if one is fair, that it is not astonishing that I feel reversals. [...] You will recall that often I foresaw this in talking with you; the very loss of two capitals was believed to be possible, and it is perseverance alone that was considered to be the remedy for the evils of this cruel period. Far from discouraging me despite all the setbacks I have suffered, I am resolved more than ever to persevere in the struggle, and all my care goes to this goal. It is with frankness I admit to you that being misunderstood by the public or by a mass of beings who know me poorly or not at all, is a lesser pain for me than that of being similarly treated by the small number of those to whom I have devoted all my affections and who I hope would know me deeply. But even if this pain was added to all those others I bear, I protest before God that I would not accuse them and would see in this only the common fate of unfortunate beings, that of being abandoned.[60]

The events of October and November proved the tsar to be right: Napoleon's debacle silenced his critics and put a halo around Alexander of unequalled prestige. But the scope of the doubts that had gripped him throughout these crucial months, the isolation from which he suffered, and the criticism heaped on him gradually led him closer to God, as he discovered in himself a vibrant and sincere faith.

* * *

For whole years Alexander had remained indifferent to faith and religious questions. Of course, he had been educated with respect for and the practice of Orthodox precepts, but in reality his faith belonged to a vague deism inherited from the Enlightenment. In his meetings with Abbot Eylert in 1818, the tsar would describe the superficiality of his religious practice, and he would impute it to the education he had received from Catherine II:

Catherine was full of caution and spirit, she was a great woman, and her memory lives forever in the history of Russia. But as regards this part of an education that develops real piety of the heart, we at the Court of St. Petersburg were at almost the same point as everywhere else: lots of words, but little meaning; lots of external practices, but the holy essence of Christianity was hidden from us. I felt the emptiness in my soul and a vague presentiment accompanied me. I came, I went, I gave myself distractions.[61]

In his private correspondence he often spoke (as did Enlightenment men) of "the Supreme Being." Moreover, his initiation into Freemasonry[62] tended to remove him a little more from the Orthodox religion. But from 1812, while the threat of war was insistent, Alexander rediscovered both pious practice and the great religious texts. However, at this moment his "return to the altar" was more a political act than a specifically religious one. Faced with a foreign enemy that was in the majority Catholic, it was a matter of proclaiming his attachment to Russian identity and to Orthodoxy, confounded into the same entity. However, after June 1812 and the traumas of the invasion, his doubts and anguish were combined in a painful "Way of the Cross" that led to God. For in fact this desperate struggle of unequal strength against an enemy whose superior intelligence he was the first to recognize, was for him a struggle against Evil, over whom he could not triumph alone. If he managed to beat Napoleon this was because he had been elected and supported by God. In his conversations with Abbot Eylert he would declare:

> In the end, the burning of Moscow illuminated my soul, and the judgment of God on the frozen battlefield filled my heart with a warmth of faith that it had never felt before. From this moment, I learned to know God as Holy Scripture has revealed him. Henceforth I learned to understand—and I understand now—His will and His law, and the decision to devote my person and my reign only to Him and to His glory, matured and was fortified in me. Since that time, I have become another man: to the deliverance of Europe from ruin, I owe my own salvation and my deliverance.
>
> Only since Christianity has become for me more important than everything else, only since the faith in the Redeemer has manifested its force in me—and I thank God for it—his peace has entered into my soul. [...] Ah, I did not arrive there all of a sudden; believe me, the road led me there through many other struggles and many doubts.[63]

The burning of Moscow was the turning point of his existence. Several witnesses, like Countess Edling and Alexander Golitsyn, as well as Alexander's own words attest in unison to the intensity of this spiritual revolution. On the eve of Napoleon's invasion, Alexander had rediscovered the New Testament, but until the taking of Moscow, his interest in sacred writings did not have primordial importance. By contrast, after the burning of the sacred city, his sharpening awareness that the end of the world was possible brought him closer to the Apocalypse, the Book of Revelation that he so admired, as he confided to Golitsyn: "There, my dear brother, there are only wounds and lumps."[64]

From now on, books of piety and the Bible became his preferred reading, and he meditated, prayed, and withdrew into himself, drawing from them the serenity and peace that the political situation refused him. At the end of 1812, when Napoleon left Russian territory, it was a profoundly transformed Alexander that rose from the ashes and rubble left by the Grande Armée. Animated by this sincere (though still vague) faith, he would lead his troops right to Paris, armed with a plan to make the European continent a place of peace and fraternity.

CHAPTER 12

A European Tsar

1813–1815

At the end of 1812, the debacle and then retreat of the Grande Armée marked the end of the French occupation. Russia had triumphed over its invader, and the whole country celebrated the political courage of the leader who, in his stubbornness in pursuing the combat and refusing any compromise with Napoleon, enabled the empire to emerge as uncontested victor. At this time and more than ever, Alexander I was indeed the tsar of all the Russias, a tsar united with his people in an affinity that was both political as well as moral and religious. It was not by chance that the senate proposed conferring on him the title "blessed." Imbued by a vibrant faith that led him to see God's hand in the Russian victory, evoking the pitiful end of the Napoleonic army, he wrote to his friend Alexander Golitsyn that "the Lord was marching before us. It is He who vanquished our enemies."[1] He did not stop thanking Providence for the crucial help; on the commemorative medal struck in honor of the victory, he had engraved the motto "Non nobis, sed nomine tuo, Domine," (Psalm 113: "Blessed be the name of the Lord"), and he tried to establish a close link between patriotic faith and religious faith throughout the empire. In 1811, when war was imminent, Our Lady of Kazan Cathedral in St. Petersburg had received a miraculous icon that was popularly believed to have sustained Ivan the Terrible in his conquest of the city of Kazan and then in 1612 delivered the country from the Polish invasion. Now that the new conflict was over, in this same cathedral Alexander chose to celebrate the heroes of the patriotic war. In 1813 he exhibited there more than a hundred flags and imperial eagles taken from the soldiers of the old guard of Napoleon,[2] and he had the remains of Marshal Kutuzov (who had died abruptly in April) transferred there as a symbol of the national resistance to the invader. But while proclaiming loudly and long his gratitude to God, his faith in his people, and his attachment to his empire, Alexander at the end of 1812 did not think he had yet finished with Napoleon.

Entering Paris!

At the end of 1812, Alexander was convinced that the fight should be pursued, that the interest of Europe required new military engagements.

At the same time, Madame de Staël, the French writer and political theorist, was visiting Russia and met the tsar. His confidences during their conversation, shortly before the emperor left for Kalisch,[3] usefully illuminate for historians his psychology and objectives at the time. Madame de Staël recalled:

> I finally saw this monarch, absolute by law as by custom and yet so moderate by inclination. […] What first struck me about him was an expression of goodness and dignity such that the two qualities appeared inseparable and seemed to be a single one. I was also touched by the noble simplicity with which he tackled the great interests of Europe, from the first phrases that he addressed to me. I have always considered as a sign of mediocrity that fear of dealing with serious matters inspired in many of Europe's sovereigns: they are afraid to pronounce words that have any real meaning. Emperor Alexander, on the contrary, talked with me as a British statesman would; they put strength in themselves and not in the barriers that might surround them. Emperor Alexander, whom Napoleon had tried to make misunderstood, is a clever man who is remarkably educated, and I do not believe that in his empire a minister would be found who is stronger than he as regards judgment and leadership. […] Alexander gives and withdraws his trust with greatest reflection. His youth and his exterior advantages alone, at the beginning of his reign, could have made people suspicious of his lack of thought but he is serious as only a man who has known misfortune can be. Alexander expressed his regrets at not being a great captain; I replied to this noble modesty that a sovereign was rarer than a general, and that to sustain the public spirit of his nation by his example was to win the most important of battles, and the foremost of this kind that was won. The Emperor spoke to me with enthusiasm of his nation and all that it was capable of becoming. He expressed the desire, which everybody knows about him, of improving the condition of a peasantry that was still subject to slavery. "Sire," I said, "your character is a constitution for your empire and your conscience is its guarantee." "Even if those things were so," he

answered, "I would always be merely a happy accident." Fine words, perhaps the first of this kind that an absolute monarch ever pronounced![4]

Madame de Staël's portrait is interesting on more than one count. It attests once again to Alexander's charm, his modesty tinged with religious humility, and his melancholy—"I would always be merely a happy accident"—but also his determination as regards European matters and his political projects. At the end of 1812, the tsar was convinced that Napoleon was still a danger. In his eyes the French emperor had not been annihilated—Alexander was aggrieved at Kutuzov for having, out of nonchalance or the desire to spare Russian blood, let Napoleon escape during the Berezina River crossing—and he estimated that consequently Napoleon would not remain as he stood. Sooner or later the French emperor would reconstitute his army and take the offensive again; moreover, the greatest uncertainty hovered on the international plane, in particular over the Polish issue. Two birds could be killed with one stone: push French troops back beyond the Rhine to guarantee the security of the Russian Empire[5] and definitely liberate Europe from the French tyrant in order to reestablish it on new values. In the November 1812 ukase he sent to Count Rostopchin, Alexander stresses that the sacrifices made by the people of Moscow had enabled the triumph over the enemy and asserted forcefully, "Russia, by the harm it has suffered, has bought its tranquility and the glory of being the savior of Europe."[6] Similarly, in December from Vilnius where he rejoined his army as supreme commander again, he declared to his fighters: "You have saved not just Russia but all of Europe,"[7] thus encompassing the War of 1812 in a much larger perspective than strictly the defense of Russian land.

Geopolitical and ideological imperatives thus converged to push him to take the offensive. But once again this plan ran up against solid objections from his sister Catherine and his mother (both influenced by Karamzin), by his general staff (Kutuzov in the forefront) and by his government, men like Razumovsky and Shishkov. Their arguments were primarily of a political nature: these new campaigns would spill more Russian blood; while the country was no longer directly threatened, the people would not understand why he had to fight again, and it could imperil the fine unity forged earlier that year. But there were also geopolitical arguments: on the one hand, "the complete fall of Napoleon would strengthen England, which will draw all the benefits,"[8] and on the other, the true interests of Russia were not in Europe but in the Ottoman Empire and in Asia, so imperial diplomacy should be oriented in that direction. Finally, in the event the offensive was decided upon, in order to be successful, it would have to wait at least until the reserve troops were ready. But none of these objections convinced the sovereign, and on January 13, 1813, Russian troops placed under his command and Kutuzov's crossed the Niemen and penetrated Prussian territory.

At that moment Prussia was still allied with France, at least formally, but this alliance was coming undone. On December 30 General Johann Yorck, commander of a Prussian auxiliary corps based in Tauroggen, had concluded under his own authority with Russian General Dibich, a neutrality agreement that let the Russian troops into Prussia without resistance. Meanwhile, Alexander wrote to Frederick-Wilhelm III to propose Russian aid in the reestablishment of Prussia's status and its borders; on February 22 he sent all Germans as well as other peoples fighting alongside Napoleon a generous proclamation designed to counter the Napoleonic mirage: "Profiting from victory, we extend a helping hand to oppressed peoples."[9]

The king of Prussia quickly replied favorably to Alexander's offer. While France had just refused to recognize the neutrality of Silesia and to pay Prussia an indemnity of 94 million francs for supplies delivered to the Grande Armée in 1812, the king decided to embark on a military alliance with Russia. Concluded on February 28, 1813, at Kalisch, where Alexander and his general staff were located and reinforced by the Breslau convention signed on March 7, the bilateral alliance called for 150,000 Russians and 80,000 Prussians to be mobilized against France, and it banned any separate peace. The same day as this convention Prussia declared war on France, and in April the new alliance received the financial support of two million pounds sterling from Great Britain. But the new alliance's military debut was not impressive: although part of the Grande Armée was stuck in Spain and although, in order to compensate for the gigantic losses in the Russian campaign, Napoleon had to resort to veterans and to hastily trained young soldiers, the French emperor had two successive victories (Lützen on May 2 and Bautzen on May 20). Kutuzov's death occurred on April 28, and his replacement by General Ludwig Wittgenstein (who did not manage to galvanize his troops) contributed to these reversals for the Russo-Prussian armies. Stunned by these defeats, Wittgenstein asked to be relieved of his post, and Alexander decided to recall Barclay de Tolly as commander in chief. Now leading the fight on foreign territory and directing a multinational army, in 1813 Barclay's Lithuanian origins were no longer a handicap but an advantage.

At the end of May, given the intervention of Austria allied with France since Marie Louise had married Napoleon, the Russo-Prussians solicited an armistice whose principle Napoleon accepted: on both sides, there was a desire to gain some time to reorganize troops. After difficult negotiations, conducted on the Russian side by the young Count Nesselrode, on the Prussian side by General Kleist, and on the French side by Armand de Caulaincourt, the cease-fire was concluded on June 4, to last for six weeks hence, but then prolonged until August 10, which proved crucial for the coalition. In this interval the Austrian government switched to the Russo-Prussian side. It had long hesitated because Metternich distrusted Russian ambitions in Poland and the Balkans, and he was on record as favorable to maintaining a France able to serve as counterweight; thus he aspired to find a diplomatic solution to the conflict that might enable the Napoleonic dynasty to be maintained. As Joseph de Maistre stressed with caustic wit: "Austria has delivered a princess and wanted, now that the shame was drunk (in the common expression) to maintain at least this mixed blood on the throne of France whose possession might accommodate many things."[10] But Napoleon's refusal to accept Austria's mediation and to negotiate a peace acceptable to all, the French defeat at the hands of Wellington at Vitoria in Spain, and finally the machinations of Grand Duchess Catherine, who in Bohemia maneuvered Metternich at her brother's request to bring him to the common cause,[11] all convinced the chancellor to rejoin the new coalition in gestation. On June 27, 1813, at Alexander's headquarters in Reichenbach, the Russian, Austrian, and Prussian governments signed an alliance treaty that set three objectives: restoring Prussia and Austria's possessions, giving German states their independence, and dissolving the duchy of Warsaw. Armed with this document, Austria declared war on France on August 12, but once again, the coalition's first engagements (which aligned 484,000 men against 280,000 Napoleonic soldiers) were failures, and on August 26 and 27 the allies suffered a new defeat, losing 30,000 men by trying in vain to retake Dresden from Napoleon.[12] In the allied ranks immense worry undermined the brand-new coalition: deeply alarmed by the breadth of the defeats, Frederick-Wilhelm III and Emperor Franz I envisaged abandoning the fight, and only Alexander, although shaken by the successive fiascos, did not give up. His determination paid off: on August 30 in Kulm, faced with 32,000 soldiers of the French marshal Vandamme (who was captured in the battle), the 54,000 coalition soldiers led by Barclay de Tolly were victorious. Encouraged by this success, the three powers signed the Treaty of Töplitz on September 9, 1813. On the military level they promised to each supply 150,000 men and (of course) to refuse any separate peace. On the political level they said they were favorable to the restoration of the independent German states, to the dissolution of the Rhine Confederation, and to negotiations over the future of the duchy of Warsaw. Shortly after, Bernadotte, who feared losing the throne of Sweden, in turn joined the coalition, which now was assured numerical superiority: 490,000 men might now face the 440,000 that Napoleon would be able to muster.[13]

Each of the two parties aspired to a decisive battle, and it took place in Leipzig from October 16 to 19, 1813. At the start of the engagement, the battle opposed 220,000 coalition soldiers and 175,000 Napoleonic, but from the first day the losses were heavy (40,000 killed or wounded among the former and 30,000 among the Grande Armée). To make up these losses, reinforcements arrived during the night of the seventeenth—15,000 for the French and 110,000 for the allies. The figures speak for themselves; the balance swung to the coalition. Led by Prince Schwarzenberg, the "battle of nations," which cost the lives of 65,000 men of the Grande Armée[14] and 54,000 within the coalition, signaled the end of the French presence in Germany. This was a dual success for the tsar: by beginning to push the French back to the Rhine, he had achieved his first objective, assuring the security of the empire's borders; and by taking part in operations (he himself directed a Cossack attack on French cavalrymen), Alexander got rid of the traumatic memory of Austerlitz. Still, far from attributing to himself the merit of this success, he again saw the intervention of Providence in his favor, as shown by his letter to Golitsyn on October 21 (O.S.):

> Almighty God has granted us a striking victory over the famous Napoleon, after a battle of four days under the walls of Leipzig. The Supreme Being[15] has proved that before Him nothing is strong, nothing is great here below except what He wants to raise. Twenty-seven generals, almost 300 cannon and 37,000 prisoners are the results of these memorable days! And here we are at two days march from Frankfurt![16]

After his decisive victory, the coalition paradoxically gave signs of deep differences. Neither the Austrians nor the Prussians envisaged launching military operations on French territory, while for the tsar the need to finish with Napoleon demanded that he pursue the combat there. Alexander's stubbornness finally overcame these hesitations, since the Austrians and Prussians did not want to let the Russian troops enter France alone and draw the benefits of this final stage in the struggle against Napoleon. Moreover, the coalition powers were being greatly assisted by the British government that in February 1814 delegated its foreign affairs secretary, Viscount Lord Castlereagh, to the allied powers in order to bring them new financial support and to push them to continue the offensive.

On the eve of the campaign in France, the tsar addressed a solemn proclamation to his soldiers: despite the suffering of his army and his people and in order to serve his image as much as his convictions, he preached moderation and Christian charity as regards the French enemy. Doing so, he already delivered a key to his future behavior in France, i.e., his desire to give both public and elite opinion in Europe the image of a Russian nation that was "policed," meaning civilized, far from the barbarity that had been caricatured by Napoleon's propaganda throughout the conflict:

> Warriors! Your valor has led you from the banks of the Oka to the banks of the Rhine. […] Penetrating into the interior of our empire, the enemy that we fight today caused great disasters; but a terrible punishment has fallen on his head. […] The wrath of God has burst on our enemies. […] Let us not imitate them; forget what they have done to us. Let us carry into France, not resentment and vengeance, but a hand held out in peace. The glory of the Russian is to vanquish the enemy that attacks him, and to treat the disarmed enemy as a brother. Our revered faith teaches us, by the very mouth of God, to love our enemies, to do good to those who hate us. Warriors! I am convinced that by the moderation of your conduct in this enemy land that we are going to enter, you will know how to vanquish as much by the grandeur of soul as by the force of arms, and that by uniting to the valor of the warrior the humanity of the Christian, you will put the seal on your great actions, by conserving the renown that they have acquired for you as a valiant and policed nation. I am also persuaded that your generals will neglect no means to maintain the spotless honor of our arms.[17]

Between December 21, 1813, and January 1, 1814, the coalition troops crossed the Rhine from Coblenz to Basel. But the campaign in France began with new French victories: in the first weeks the Napoleonic armies, although weak in numbers, had a dozen victories in the first 14 engagements. This bespeaks how much French resistance in the face of the invaders was courageous and desperate in its turn. The unexpected scope of this resistance soon caused doubts within the uneasy coalition. Both Frederick-Wilhelm II and Franz I, fearing that war might trigger in France a resurgence of the revolution and combative spirit of Valmy[18] (on January 31, 1814, Napoleon called for a general mobilization of the French people), said they were ready to negotiate. Once again, Alexander's obstinate refusal to accept any compromise with the enemy and Castlereagh's intervention made them change their minds. The British minister pushed for the allies to sign the protocol of Langres, which called for the return of France to its 1792 borders. In March at Chaumont yet another treaty strengthened the coalition with a new defensive alliance for a duration of 20 years; again, there was no question of negotiations or a separate peace. Each signatory country had to supply a contingent of at least 150,000 men for the anti-Napoleon struggle. A series of victories garnered during March would decide Napoleon's fate; the last negotiations failed, and Paris capitulated on March 30. On April 6, the emperor of the French abdicated, and on April 11 he signed the Treaty of Fontainebleau, which exiled him to the island of Elba. The armistice was signed on April 23.

Alexander I proved generous, both with respect to the defeated emperor and his relatives; in effect, he was able to impose on his allies, who were demanding more severity, conditions that were relatively merciful. Apart from being ceded the island of Elba, of which he was now the sovereign, Napoleon was given an annual pension of two million francs and the right to keep a guard of five hundred men. Josephine was authorized to keep her title of empress, with significant financial support since she obtained a pension of a million francs and was authorized to keep the ownership of all her property. Hortense, separated from Louis Bonaparte, received 400,000 francs to support herself and her children (including the future Napoleon III). This magnanimity toward the defeated might seem surprising, given how long and how bitter the struggle between the two emperors had been. In reality, it can be understood only if one takes into account not only the political and diplomatic codes then in use but also the psychological and religious evolution of Alexander I.

* * *

Throughout 1813 Alexander on campaign had bolstered his faith by contact with close friends in whom he confided, as well as with simple soldiers. In a letter to Rodion Koshelev on February 6, written in Polotsk, he talked about his faith and his trust in God:

> Address your prayers to the Supreme Being, to our Savior, and to the Holy Spirit that emanates from them, for them to guide me, making me firm in the sole path that leads to Salvation, and give me the faculties necessary to achieve my public task, by making my country happy, but not in the vulgar sense. It is in the advancing of the true reign of Jesus Christ that I place all my glory.[19]

In February he wrote to Golitsyn, minister of worship and head of the Holy Synod, that he accepted "with pleasure a place among members of the Biblic Society,"[20] in order to increase his knowledge of the Holy Book. But he was also more sensitive to the spirituality of humble people, which he saw as the expression of the most authentic faith and the reflection of Russian identity. On March 10, while at the head of his armies proceeding west, the emperor wrote to Golitsyn:

> You already know of the occupation of Berlin. Glory to the Almighty!
>
> I do my prayers, and many soldiers with me. We listen to prayers together. Our divine service goes admirably. I have succeeded in what I desired and our regimental musicians sing so well as not to yield to the Court cantors. This mass of people praying together with fervor and unction is truly edifying, and my heart is fully warmed.[21]

A few days later, on March 13, he continued: "I have just said my prayers. I have never said them with the feeling I had this time."[22]

On April 29, when he had just entered Dresden, where he celebrated Russian Easter amid his troops, a wave of spiritual emotion overcame him as a new military trial awaited him:

> A thousand thanks, my dear friend, for your letter on Easter. It is from the bottom of my heart that I respond: "In truth he is arisen!" And Praise God that this not be a vain expression!
>
> It is Saturday after mass that we have made our entry into Dresden, and at midnight we have sung the Easter hymn on the banks of the Elba. It would be difficult for me to express to you the emotion that penetrated me thinking about all that has happened in the last year, and where Divine Providence has led us.
>
> Yet alongside these sensations of pleasure and gratitude toward our Savior, we are preparing with submission for a difficult ordeal.[23]

This new faith, far from being limited to the private sphere, would rapidly influence the tsar's diplomatic plans. In the manifesto he proclaimed on March 12, 1813, in Kalisch, Alexander was enjoying hoping for a new era when international treaties would be respected "with that religious faith, that sacred inviolability which the consideration, strength, and conservation of empires depend on,"[24] thus echoing what he had declared in December 1812 to the Countess of Choiseul-Gouffier:

> Why, the emperor said, would do not all the sovereigns and nations of Europe agree among themselves to love and live as brothers, by helping each other in their reciprocal needs? Trade would become the general good of this great so-

ciety whose members, no doubt, would have different religions, but the spirit of tolerance would unite all faiths. I believe it little matters to the Almighty whether he is invoked in Greek or in Latin, provided that we fulfill all our duties to Him and we satisfy those duties of honest men. It is not always long prayers that touch the most.[25]

From the end of 1812, we can pinpoint the origin of the Holy Alliance project; it is with this mentality that the tsar would make his entry into Paris.

On the night of March 30, 1814, the Paris police chief and the mayor of the city went to Bondy, where the headquarters of the allied armies was located, to negotiate the capitulation of Paris. In his first declaration to the representatives of the French authorities, Alexander I took care to distinguish between the guilt of Napoleon and the innocence of the French people. And doing so, he delivered a skillful political lesson:

> The fortunes of war have led me here; your emperor who was my ally deceived me three times. He came to the heart of my country and brought evils whose traces will last a long time. A just defense has brought me here, and I am far from wanting to render to France the evils I have received from her. I am fair, I know that it was not the sin of the French. The French are my friends, I want to prove to them that I came to render good for evil. Napoleon is my sole enemy.[26]

In the spirit of this declaration, Alexander promised to protect the city, to billet there only elite troops as troops of occupation, to maintain the Parisian national guard of 40,000 men in arms. He exhorted the French to adopt a government "that gives you rest and gives it to Europe."[27] From his entry into the French capital, then, he displayed extraordinary moderation, while the Russian empire with its 55 million inhabitants and the most numerous army in Europe, was then extremely powerful.

The next day at 10:00 in the morning, under an unpropitious sky, Alexander entered Paris at the head of the allied armies. He rode his grey mare Eclipse that Napoleon had given him at Erfurt, with the king of Prussia on his left and General Schwarzenberg on his right, representing the emperor of Austria. For almost five hours, coalition troops paraded before the inhabitants of the capital, astounded at the sight of regiments of Cossacks with their sheepskins and lances and Bashkir soldiers armed with bows and arrows. Through his youth, charm, and benevolence, the tsar immediately conquered the jubilant crowd, who pressed to admire the victor as he passed:

Despite the regularity and delicacy of his features, the freshness of his complexion, his beauty was less striking at first sight than was his air of benevolence that captivated all hearts; from the first movement he inspired trust. His noble height, elevated and majestic, often gracefully bowing as in the pose of ancient statues, was portending portliness, but he was perfectly well made. He had a lively and spiritual look with sky-blue eyes; he was a little short-sighted, but his eyes smiled, if one may use that expression about his gentle gaze. His nose was straight and well formed, his mouth small and attractive; his whole round figure as well as his profile much recalled that of his beautiful and august mother.[28]

His benevolent attitude baffled those, like the French poet Chateaubriand, who were expecting a cruel and deserved punishment of the enemy who had subjected his people to so much suffering and territorial sacking.

> The emperor of Russia and the king of Prussia were at the head of their troops. I saw them parade along the boulevards. I felt stupefied and overwhelmed, as if they had torn the name of Frenchman from me to substitute a number by which I would be known in the mines of Siberia, at the same time I felt my exasperation grow against the man whose glory had reduced us to this shame.
>
> However, this first invasion by the allies remains unparalleled in the annals of the world: order, peace and moderation reigned everywhere; the shops reopened; the Russian soldiers of the guard, six feet tall, were piloted through the streets by small French rascals who made fun of them, like puppets and masks in a carnival. The vanquished could be taken for the victors, who trembled with their success and seemed to excuse themselves for it.[29]

Alexander immediately named General Osten-Sacken as governor of Paris, with three local commanders (Goltz, Herzogenberg, and Rochechouart, a French émigré in Russia's service). The same day, around 3 p.m., when the troop parade was finished, he had published in the name of the three allied powers a very explicit declaration:

> The armies of the allied powers have occupied the capital of France. The allied sovereigns welcome the greeting of the French nation. They declare that if the conditions of peace had to contain the strongest guarantees when it came to chaining up the ambition of Buonaparte,[30] the conditions should be more favorable when, by a return to wise government, France itself will offer the assurance of this rest.
>
> Consequently the sovereigns proclaim:

That they will no longer deal with Napoleon Bonaparte, nor with any of his family;

That they respect the integrity of ancient France such as it existed under its legitimate kings; they may even do more because they still profess the principle that for the happiness of Europe, France must be great and strong;

That they will recognize and guarantee the constitution that the French nation will adopt. They thereby invite the Senate to designate a provisional government that will be able to answer the needs of the administration and prepare a constitution that suits the French people.

The intentions I have just expressed are shared with all the allied powers.[31]

This first public declaration by Alexander in Paris is to be stressed on several counts. It shows his intransigence with respect to Napoleon, his pacific concern toward the French nation, and his attachment to a monarchical power that he perceives as the only legitimate one. But he also wants France to remain strong in order to serve as counterweight to balance British power and Austrian power. On this point he had not forgotten the geopolitical arguments that Kutuzov had put to him. Moreover, aware that the experience and memory of the French Revolution could not be totally obliterated, he solemnly reaffirmed his support for the idea of the establishment of a constitutional regime in France. Here again, the principal of balance of power was essential in Alexander's thinking.

This point—to which we shall return—is of great importance, and it does contradict a theme of Soviet historiography, which saw Alexander's campaign of 1813–1814 as the expression of his supposed desire to reestablish a conservative monarchy in France. In reality, this interpretation is an anachronistic view of this period that is supported only by the way in which Russian diplomacy evolved after 1818, but it does not take into account the objectives that the emperor was pursuing in 1813–1814. At this time, what was most important to him was to set up in France a political regime that would respond to the wishes of the French people, that would take account of their history and their collective memory, and that would, through its stability and moderation, guarantee peace in Europe. In Alexander's eyes—as he constantly explained in a clear and instructive way to his interlocutors—the fate of France and that of Europe were linked to each other, and so they should be treated with balance and moderation. The tsar's viewpoint seemed perfectly rational, and this clarity was underlined by Chancellor Metternich: "I found the emperor of Russia's views very reasonable," he wrote to Emperor Franz I when he had just arrived in Paris. "He talks much less nonsense than I would have believed."[32]

In any case, in the short term, for Parisians forced to undergo foreign occupation, the tsar's declaration appeared rather reassuring. And the Russian sovereign's stay in the French capital, where he proved to be alternately magnanimous and seductive, only confirmed this favorable first impression.

The "Liberating Tsar" and "Benefactor" of Europe

Alexander's Parisian sojourn is known to us from many French sources: writers who rushed into the capital's salons to salute the victor included Madame de Staël, Benjamin Constant, Chateaubriand, and the Countess of Boigne. All of them wrote about their presentation to the tsar and sketched lively portraits of him. But to grasp the details of this sojourn and its atmosphere, two sources are particularly precious. The first comes from the tsar's aide-de-camp, Lieutenant General Alexander Mikhailovsky-Danilevsky. A brave fighter—he was seriously wounded at the Battle of Borodino—he was a refined and cultivated man: he had studied at the University of Göttingen; he spoke German and French, as well as Russian; and he knew Latin. Subsequently becoming a confidant of the tsar, he was asked by the latter to write the official history of the campaign of Russia, becoming the first historian of the war of 1812, about which he gathered abundant documentation.[33] From 1808 to 1839, he wrote in Russian a diary[34] that was precise and detailed as regards the activities of the tsar while he was in France. In December 1814 Mikhailovsky-Danilevsky put his diary aside to write in French a small brochure of memories titled Reflections on the Years 1812, 1813, and 1814 as They Touch Me, which was to be published after his death. Thus, both brochure and diary are particularly interesting. The second source is an anonymous brochure published in Paris in 1815 under the title Alexandrana, or Sallies and Remarkable Words of Alexander I. Written by someone on his general staff, either a Russian or a Frenchman who went into his service, the work celebrates the tsar's glory, while reporting many anecdotes and interesting details of his stay in France.

Upon his arrival in Paris, Alexander did not wish to stay in the imperial Tuileries chateau and wanted to reside in the Elysée Palace, but Talleyrand dissuaded him for security reasons. The building would be listened to, offering risks of an attack, and so Talleyrand pressed him to stay at his own home; Alexander ended up accepting. Thus it was at Talleyrand's home in rue Saint-Florentin that a first grand political conference took place, drawing monarchs and dignitaries. In the course of this meeting to deal with France's political future, participants decided to reestablish the house of

Bourbon on the throne. In the interim, 64 senators would designate a provisional government, of which Talleyrand was named president. That very day Alexander freed 1,500 soldiers who had been taken prisoner during the campaign in France. That evening at the invitation of the master of ceremonies, Talleyrand, he attended at the Opéra a great party given in his honor. Singers and actors celebrated the glory of the new hero with "bad couplets,"[35] singing on the air of the song Le Roi Henri:

Vive Alexandre!	Long live Alexander!
Vive ce roi des rois	Long live the king of kings!
Sans rien prétendre,	This victorious commander
Sans nous dicter de lois	No harsh conditions brings.
	Laying no commands on us,
Ce prince auguste	This prince in whom we trust
A ce triple renom	Has three claims to renown:
De héros, de juste,	He's a hero, he is just,
De nous rendre un Bourbon.[36]	He gives the Bourbons back a crown.[37]

While sensitive to this flattery, as maladroit as it was, the "king of kings" was not exhilarated by his success. His generosity and leniency were eminently sincere and in accord with his faith, but their manifestation also aimed to reassure both elite and public opinion that Russia, despite the hostile propaganda in the Grande Armée's bulletins, was indeed part of Europe, at the very heart of the European civilization that had been perverted by Napoleonic tyranny but that was now being regenerated.

Aware that the coalition armies, who had suffered so much from the French invasion, might be tempted to execute reprisals against the population—in April and May, while Russian troops advanced into France, there had been looting[38]—Alexander demanded irreproachable conduct from his officers and his soldiers, prescribing punishment up to the death penalty for those who behaved badly. He also forbade them from attending entertainments during Holy Week, since the Orthodox should be respectful of religious customs. These requirements were quickly crowned with success. Whereas, on the eve of the coalition invasion, the simple mention of the word "Cossack" was synonymous with the ultimate in barbarism and aroused terror in a population that had been swayed by Napoleonic propaganda, the reality proved quite different and soon opened the eyes of the French. Admittedly, for many Parisians, the bivouacking of Cossacks on the Champs-Elysées—the officers had billets in private homes but not the troops—was an exotic spectacle:

It was a singular sight for our eyes and minds to see these inhabitants of the Don peacefully following their ways and customs in the heart of Paris. They had no tents or shelter of any kind; three or four horses were attached to each tree and their horsemen sat near them on the ground, talking together in soft voices and harmonious accents. Most of them sewed, they fixed their rags or fitted and prepared new ones, repaired their shoes and horse harnesses, or fashioned for their use their share of the booty from previous days. Yet they were regular Cossacks of the guard and since they were rarely used as scouts, they were less fortunate in the looting than their brothers, the irregular Cossacks.

Their uniform was very pretty: large blue pantaloons, a dalmatic tunic, also blue, padded on the chest and tightly cinched at the waist by a large belt of shiny black leather, with buckles and ornaments in bright copper that held their weapons. This semi-Oriental costume and their bizarre attitude on horseback (where they were totally upright, the height of the saddle meant they did not bend their knees) made them objects of great curiosity to the passers-by of Paris. They let themselves be approached easily, especially by women, and children who were willingly put up on their shoulders.[39]

In his valuable study of the French occupation in 1814, Jacques Hantraye claims that "during the invasion, regional inhabitants who had been still spared felt doubts about the poor reputation of the Cossacks. But a police report of January 1814 noted that the Parisian bourgeoisie said 'they were nasty only in the gazettes.'"[40]

The young Victor Hugo, then aged 12, similarly wrote many years later that "the Cossack ogres were lambs."[41] And Jacques Hantraye comments: "In 1815, there were no recorded incidents imputed to the troops of Alexander, unlike what was attributed to the Prussians."[42] Thus, from the first months of the occupation of France by coalition troops, Russia's image, forged through the forced contacts that were established between civilians and military personnel, evolved in a very favorable way. On the model of their emperor, the Russian troops were the embodiment of dignity and gentleness—of the "civilization" to which both peoples were similarly attached. From this standpoint, with respect to collective representations and imagery, Alexander in barely a few weeks fully attained his objective.

On April 10, Easter Day,[43] proclaiming a will for ecumenical peace, Alexander had celebrated on the Place de la Concorde a solemn thanksgiving service by seven Orthodox ministers assisted by chaplains of the imperial chapel. A Te Deum resounded in the same place where Louis XVI had been guillotined. For the tsar, the instant was full of immense spiritual emotion:

> It was a solemn moment for my heart, moving and terrible. I told myself, and so, by the unfathomable will of Providence, I brought my Orthodox warriors from the depth of their cold Nordic country here, in order to see them raising toward the Lord our common prayers in the capital of these foreigners who recently, were attacking Russia, at the very place where the royal victim succumbed to popular fury. […] One might say that the sons of the North celebrated the funeral of the King of France. The Tsar of Russia prayed according to the Orthodox rites, along with his people, and thus purified the bloodstained square. […] Our spiritual triumph has fully reached its goal. I was even amused to see the French marshals and generals jostle each other to be able to kiss the Russian cross![44]

The last remark indicates Alexander's clarity; despite his vigorous religious faith, at the top of his glory the tsar still remains capable of irony, both toward himself and others.

Publicly expressing the sincerity of his religious faith, Alexander did not lead a reclusive life in Paris—far from it. He invited the king of Prussia and the emperor of Austria to dinner and entertained them with sumptuous meals. He showed up at salons in the capital, where he polished his image as a cultivated, spiritual, and modest man. He visited the monuments of French culture and history. On May 11 he went to Versailles, visiting the chateau accompanied by his brothers Nicholas and Mikhail and by the king of Prussia and his sons. In front of the statue at the Place Vendôme, forged from the bronze of cannons taken from the Russian and Austrian armies at Austerlitz, which represented Napoleon as Caesar, he quipped, "If I were placed so high, I would fear getting dizzy,"[45] while taking measures to protect the effigy from the anger of the royalists. At his request the statue of the emperor was taken down and put under cover, temporarily replaced by a white flag. French royalists had asked him to debaptize the bridge named after Austerlitz, but he elegantly replied that "it is enough that people know that Emperor Alexander passed by there with his armies."[46] Visiting the Tuileries Palace, he stopped at the hall of peace and humorously asked his guides, "What use was this room to Buonaparte?"[47]

During his stay, among the many French intellectuals he met, the tsar received Abbot Sicard and invited him to dine, out of filial tenderness as much as out of sympathy for the man. Sicard was director of the Institute for the Deaf and Dumb of France and well known to Maria Feodorovna, who admired his work and had invited to St. Petersburg one of his disciples to establish similar teaching in Russia. In homage to his work, Sicard had been decorated by the tsar with the Order of St. Vladimir, but Napoleon had forbidden him to wear it;[48] Alexander's visit thus allowed him to establish direct contact with this humanist. Finally, the most astonishing aspect of his stay in Paris was that Alexander went frequently to meet Empress Josephine or to see her daughter, Hortense. The small group dined, listened to music, and picnicked in the park (to the understandable distress of the Bourbons, who were furious at this open mark of sympathy with the family of the fallen emperor). But these singular moments had a tragic outcome: by the end of May, Josephine died after catching cold during a promenade in the company of Alexander I.

The prestige and aura of the Russian monarch were such that he was constantly solicited by individuals coming to ask him to intercede in their favor to obtain some favor or position. A general of the Grande Armée went as far as to beg for his intervention for a decoration from the future king as a reward for his deeds of bravery—against the Russians! This shows how Alexander's presence in Paris tended to blur elementary markers. On arrival, the sovereign who had just been emotionally reunited with Laharpe, asked him to serve as special secretary and to answer in his name the flood of such requests. But Laharpe's goodwill did not suffice; so the tsar was soon forced to have Nesselrode publish a note in which he stated that "His Imperial Majesty has come to France to help bring back peace and happiness, but he has the self-imposed rule of not exerting any influence on all that relates to the execution of laws and rules of French public administration. Consequently, all persons who might have requests to make are invited to address the responsible authorities of the provisional government."[49]

Taken up by his social activities, Alexander still remained active on the political level, expressing firm convictions on the future of France.

* * *

From his first public declaration (March 31), as mentioned above, he had stressed the need to promote a strong and moderate France that had a constitution. Two days later, speaking to the senate, the tsar reasserted his attachment to liberalism: "I am the friend of the French people; it is just and it is wise to give France liberal institutions that relate to current enlightenment; my allies and I are here only to protect the freedom of your decisions."[50] In the following weeks, he asked the Count of Provence (the future Louis XVIII, who had not yet returned to France) to grant a constitution, which irritated the monarch, who was angry at this interference in French affairs.

In 1813 a correspondence was established between the two men, although no trust was born from it. Alexander felt contempt for the Bourbons, whom he personally considered unworthy of regaining the throne of France; the future king was irritated by the tsar's treatment of him and by what he thought of as the unjustified concessions that Alexander wanted to impose on him. The Russian emperor's open contempt can be detected in his correspondence with the future Louis XVIII; he repeatedly addressed him as "Monsieur le Comte," while the heir to the French throne called him "Monsieur my Brother and Cousin." It was only after the letter of April 17, 1814, that Alexander decided to use the expected phrase "Monsieur my Brother." In the same letter he announced that he was sending his minister Pozzo di Borgo to him. Insisting, in a way that could only irritate Louis, on the legitimacy that he had acquired by his engagement in the struggle against Napoleon, he preached again in favor of a liberal regime:[^51]

> In the meantime, if my enterprises in this holy and stubborn war have been of some utility in Your Majesty's cause, if I have thereby acquired the right to his friendship and trust, then he will listen with some interest to General Pozzo di Borgo. [...] There is no doubt that the Kingdom of France expects its happiness and regeneration from Your Majesty, but it is no less true that there exists a general will. Your Majesty will subjugate all hearts if he shows liberal ideas that tend to maintain and strengthen the organic institutions of France.[^51]

During his first audience with the king of France, Pozzo di Borgo stressed in his turn the need for Louis to set up a constitution, for "it is only on this condition that he can ensure for his government the authority and force necessary to pacify minds in France and the security of domestic order."[^52] In the king's immediate entourage some did understand the tsar's viewpoint very clearly. For example, Chateaubriand in his Memoires d'outre-tombe pointed out that "the head of two supreme authorities, doubly autocratic by sword and by religion, he alone of all the sovereigns of Europe had understood that France at the age of civilization it had reached could only be governed thanks to a free constitution."[^53] Louis XVIII finally rallied to the tsar's viewpoint and ended up conceding the need for political rights and granting a constitutional charter. But relations between Alexander and the Bourbons remained difficult: their attachment to the white cockade (where Alexander thought the French army should keep the tricolor cockade),[^54] their desire to maintain ancient etiquette, and their rigid behavior all exasperated Alexander very much, as attested by the Countess of Boigne in an astonishing anecdote. The tsar thought highly of Caulaincourt (the Duke of Vicenza) and tried to end the ostracism of which Louis XVIII made him the victim (he was blamed for involvement in the death of the Duke d'Enghien by inviting the Count d'Artois[^55] to dine with him). But the attempted rapprochement turned into a fiasco and made Alexander even more bitter toward the Bourbons:

> [Back in his rooms the emperor] gave a diatribe on the ingratitude of people for whom a kingdom had been re-conquered at the price of his blood, while their own was spared and who did not know how to yield on a simple question of etiquette. When he had calmed down, he was told that perhaps [D'Artois] felt […] it was not a matter of etiquette but of feeling, since he believed that the Duke of Vicence was guilty in the [Enghien] affair. "I told him no." [answered the emperor] […] [It was pointed out that] one might excuse his [D'Artois's] repugnance by remembering that the Duke d'Enghien was his close relative. The Emperor halted his pacing. "His relative… his relative… his repugnance." Then he stopped and looked at his interlocutors; "I eat every day with Owarow!" A bomb falling in their midst would not have had more effect. After a moment of stupor, the Emperor resumed pacing and spoke of other things. […] General Owarow was supposed to have strangled Emperor Paul[56] with his two enormous thumbs, and Alexander was shocked to see our princes refuse to make their susceptibilities yield to politics, when he had made much more poignant sacrifices for the sake of politics.[57]

Afterward, things went from bad to worse: when he arrived in Compiègne in April 1814, Louis XVIII received Alexander, who had come to plead for keeping the tricolor cockade and to enjoin him to be careful with "the past twenty-five years of glory."[58] Louis treated him with coldness and condescension; seated in a large armchair, he only offered the tsar a simple chair to sit on, which enraged the latter.

Still, it was thanks to Alexander's influence as much as to British diplomacy (equally anxious for balance), and to Talleyrand's know-how as plenipotentiary to the new king, that France was relatively spared in the first treaty of Paris, signed on May 30, 1814.

Indeed, France kept the borders it had possessed in January 1792. Thus, it kept Avignon and a large part of Savoy and Mulhouse but had to give back the left bank of the Rhine and territories annexed by Napoleon in Italy, Holland, and Switzerland. It did not have to pay any war reparations, and England was forced to give France back all its colonies except for Tobago and St. Lucia in the Caribbean, an island in the Indian Ocean, and Malta. On the political level it was decided to convene a congress in Vienna to settle the remaining European issues. The treaty also carried secret clauses that ceded Venetia to Austria and the port of Genoa to the kingdom of Sardinia. In May 1814, then, thanks to Alexander's benevolent intervention, France was able to limit the scope of its losses.

After the signing of the treaty (and almost two months after his arrival in the French capital), Alexander left Paris with ambivalent feelings. Admittedly, he had fully succeeded in his enterprise of captivating public opinion and obtaining the approval of the elites; he had pushed for the adoption of the constitutional charter in the name of the balance of power (an ideal he shared with British diplomacy); and he had allowed France to emerge relatively unscathed from its defeats. But he still felt bitter, disappointed by the ingratitude of the reigning dynasty. And a similar disappointment soon arose in his relations with the British monarchy.

At the end of May 1814, the tsar went to London with his secretaries of state Nesselrode and Kapodistrias in order to consolidate political contacts formed in the course of the anti-Napoleonic period. As in Paris, if not more so, his arrival had been expected "with impatience and passionate enthusiasm"[59] and aroused extraordinary infatuation:

> The effect of his presence was very remarkable: it produced a striking impression, and when one adds to this natural gift, the halo of glory that then surrounded him, one understands the prodigious enthusiasm that he excited in England. Frenetic demonstrations broke out in the streets, in the City, in the theaters. For the fifteen days he remained in London, I can say without exaggeration that there were never less than 10,000 persons stationed around the park and the street where his hotel was located. Traffic was entirely interrupted at certain hours of the day, he could take a walk at ease only once and had to go out clandestinely through the mews.[60]

As in Paris, the tsar was showered with honors: Oxford University made him a doctor in civil law, and many poems and songs were dedicated to him—but again, his head was not turned.

His spiritual quest, which he pursued in London, brought him many conversations and spiritual exercises in an open-minded and ecumenical approach. He met members of the London Biblic Society and attended a Quaker meeting. Impressed by the approach of the Society of Friends to religious matters, he invited three of them (William Allen, Stephen Grellet, and John Wilkinson) to visit him the next day at his hotel to continue their spiritual conversation. Allen recalled:

> About prayer he declared that he entirely shared the Friends' point of view, that it was an internal and spiritual matter. He declared that he himself

prayed every day. [...] He remarked that divine prayer did not consist of exterior ceremonies or a repetition of words that miscreants and hypocrites might easily adopt, but of a submission of the spirit before God.[61]

Meanwhile, still seeking a subtler reading and interpretation of the Bible, he began a correspondence with Madame de Krüdener, a pietist of Lithuanian origin whose mystical renown had spread across Europe.

But in London the popular enthusiasm was not shared by the ruling elites. Minister Castlereagh was worried about a popularity that seemed politically dangerous; in the public festivities that punctuated the tsar's stay, he arranged for Alexander to be "accompanied by other victors," specifically the king of Prussia and General Blücher, in order that "he would not be the sole object of admiration,"[62] as Castlereagh stated in a letter to the prime minister. The court did not spend much effort on the tsar; the Countess of Lieven, wife of Alexander's ambassador to London, noted that during the imperial stay of two weeks, the regent gave only two "grand dinners and two soirees" in his honor. So we may conclude that the British government held itself back.

This quite British mistrust of the extreme feelings that the tsar aroused was reinforced by the behavior of Grand Duchess Catherine. Recently widowed by George d'Oldenburg, she settled in London to be closer to her brother, but her incessant intrigues and her haughtiness were inimical to the prince regent, and by association they discredited the tsar, too. It should also be noted that in a very undiplomatic way Alexander reserved his attentions for the Whig Party, which was in opposition, and this preference annoyed the ruling Tories, without winning him any sympathy from the liberals. In Britain there was a total misunderstanding. "He is a vain man, an imbecile,"[63] said Lord Grey in an uninspired and unjustified judgment.

The Congress of 1815 and the Holy Alliance

After his stay in western Europe, Alexander returned for a few weeks to more familiar lands. He left London for Portsmouth on June 22, embarked at Dover for Calais, and traversed Holland to rejoin Elizabeth, who was with her relatives in Baden. He spent several days there with friends, including Laharpe, who had made the trip. There, a delegation of four Russian dignitaries came to meet him and to offer him in the name of the senate and Holy Synod the title of "Blessed by God," and a monument to be erected to his glory. Alexander declined both proposals: his victory was the work of God and not his own, and it was not fitting to salute his success other than by prayers to God. Shortly after, he asked the governor of St. Petersburg to cancel all the celebrations planned in honor of his forthcoming return: the Russian blood spilt in the ordeal should not occasion festivities. Upon his arrival in St. Petersburg on July 25, it was with the greatest discretion—without fanfare or a parade—that he went to the Kazan Cathedral to praise God.

While a month's stay in his capital should have allowed Alexander to recover peace and serenity, it proved rather painful. In his absence, Maria Naryshkina, who had fallen in love with Prince Gagarin, decided to break with the tsar, as she abruptly informed him when he got back. Without giving him the main reason for the breakup, Maria gave moral and political motives, and Alexander seems to have acquiesced. In a letter to his sister Catherine in the summer of 1814[64] (a pencil draft in which not all words are legible), Alexander mentions the arguments given by Maria and movingly speaks of his distress at the rupture with his longtime mistress:

> You suppose me happy within an adored and united marriage [i.e., household] with her with whom I hoped to spend the rest of my life. Alas, we saw each other, but only to experience most cruelly the pain that separates us forever. I found her suffering, but physical suffering was only the consequence of her moral suffering.
>
> Since the great events that have just happened, her desire to see me had become totally unbearable since people think she is the obstacle to a rapprochement with my wife. [...] I love her too much to make her act against her conviction. She says she does not want my nation to have a wrong to reproach me for, and so the happiness of fourteen years of union[65] will be sacrificed to our duties. I am about to depart for Vienna, and consequently am on the eve of a separation that, if not eternal, still breaks forever the relationship in which I put my life's happiness.[66]

The tsar's grief was immense and the shock difficult to bear, given the strength of the relationship that since 1803 had given him the home he had never been able to build with Elizabeth. After all this time his love remained, if not whole, then at least preeminent, and the break affected him deeply. Three years later, in a letter to a friend, the tsar would express himself in a less gentle way about his former mistress; maybe by this time he had learned more about her real motive:

> I cannot delay telling you about the arrival of Madame de Naryshkine. I hope you know my present state well enough not to have the least worry on my

account. Even if I were still a social man there would be no merit in my remaining totally immune to this person, after all she has done.[67]

Whatever the case, Alexander's return to Russian land was only a stopover, and two months later he was en route for Austria, where he would participate in the Congress of Vienna. He halted in Pulawy at the Czartoryski family estate, where he had a long conversation with Prince Adam and Novosiltsev about the future of Poland. He arrived in Vienna on September 25.

* * *

The Congress of Vienna was a key event for the diplomacy of the nineteenth century, and there is an immense bibliography devoted to it. Everything about it was outsized: its duration (it sat from November 1814 to March 1815), the vertiginous number of states present or represented (216 states, including two emperors, five kings, and 209 principalities, or almost 20,000 people, if you include diplomatic staff, servants, spies, and demi-mondaines),[68] the importance of its decisions (it redrew the map of Europe), and its finally dramatic coup, since it was during the Congress of Vienna that Napoleon launched what would become his Hundred Days (March 1 to June 18). With its official sessions, its consultations, salons, asides, receptions, reversals, and celebrations on the margins of the political discussions, the Congress of Vienna also inaugurated the era of modern professional diplomacy. So we should not be surprised if several contemporary diplomats have been interested in this event and written books and articles about it.[69] Finally, bringing together a number of princes and princesses and aristocrats of all ranks, the Congress, amid the festivals and concerts (Beethoven conducted his Seventh Symphony there), was a venue for much merrymaking, many intellectual exchanges—and romances.

For example, it was in Vienna that Grand Duchess Catherine made a conquest of Prince Wilhelm of Württemberg, who would become her second husband. And during the Congress Elizabeth (who had broken up with the Polish prince when having an affair with Okhotnikov) saw Adam Czartoryski again; at age 45 he forgave her for the infidelity, and they fell in love with each other again. In the GARF archives lies Elizabeth's draft of a moving letter (dated February 13, 1815)[70] that tells us much about the empress's feeling for him. She complains of the destiny that forces her "to sacrifice to the legal order the true happiness of her life, in separating her from the being who[m] she had been accustomed during the fourteen best years of her existence to regard as another self." On March 8, when Elizabeth was to leave Vienna the same day, Czartoryski begged her to divorce Alexander and marry him; out of loyalty he informed Alexander of his request for marriage. But Alexander was hostile to the plan, less out of attachment to Elizabeth than for reasons of state: while difficult negotiations were opening in Vienna about the future of Poland, the divorce and remarriage of the empress of Russia with a Polish prince known for his commitment to reestablishing the Polish state, would not be accepted by Russian public opinion and would risk compromising the current Russo-Polish rapprochement. This argument ultimately convinced the dutiful Elizabeth to renounce her own happiness, and in November 1815 she went back to St. Petersburg for good. After having traversed a deep crisis and envisaging retiring to a convent or even ending her life, she decided by the end of 1815 or the beginning of 1816 to remain in Russia, "to suffer in silence," and to "submit herself entirely to the will of Providence."[71]

Meanwhile, while working frantically on diplomatic affairs, Alexander was flitting about, having affairs, for example with the Duchess of Sagan (who shortly before had been the mistress of Metternich!) and Princess Bagration, plus platonic flirtations with the Princess of Auersperg, the Countess of Szechenyi, and the Countess de Sabran. This behavior did not suit the tsar's mystical predilections but may be explained by the crisis in his own private life. He had been devastated by the rupture with Maria Naryshkina and tried to forget the beautiful Polish woman in a frenzy of seduction.

* * *

The purpose of the Congress of Vienna, a crucial diplomatic event, was to redesign the European map by undoing most of the changes born of the French Revolution and empire, for the sake of implementing two other principles: the security of the European continent and its balance. It relied on the work by a statistical commission that "translated imperturbably into numbers of people the indications given of the envisaged exchanges of territories, and traded souls for souls, a thousand acres for a thousand acres, quantitatively and without worrying about national sentiments."[72]

In this task the agreement was general among the victors: the Congress validated the provisions of the first treaty of Paris of May 1814 that had been ferociously negotiated by Talleyrand and Alexander, and it created a new confederation composed of 39 German states endowed with a federal diet to sit in Frankfurt. But disagreements soon arose among the allies: Austria and Prussia each aspired to assert their hegemony in Germany; Prussia and England were opposed over Saxony; Austria and England contested Russian claims over Poland.

Alexander I was the only monarch to take a direct part in the work of the Congress. Given the stakes, he relied on the help of Prince Razumovsky, his former ambassador to Vienna, on Count Stockelberg, the current ambassador, and Count Nesselrode, de facto minister of foreign affairs before becoming so officially, Baron Anstett, and two diplomatic advisors, Pozzo di Borgo (a Corsican who was notoriously anti-Napoleon), and Kapodistrias, the former state secretary of the Ionian Islands, who had gone into Russia's service when they were acquired by France in 1807. Three of these men were foreigners, like the diplomatic corps as a whole, which was hardly "Russian." Mikhailovsky-Danilevsky recorded in his diary:

> Russia presents the unique example of a country whose diplomatic corps is composed in large part of foreigners. Some of them do not even know our language, some have seen of Russia only the city of St. Petersburg. In consulting a directory, I noted that out of 37 civil servants employed by Russia in its various embassies, there were only 16 bearing Russian names. [...] Does this not testify to the true grandeur of a country, so sure of its strength that it is completely indifferent about who represents it outside![73]

But others within the court did not share this optimistic view: the situation began to arouse grumbling within the Russian nobility, which felt itself dispossessed of its rights. It doubted the capacity of western Europeans to be able to understand and serve the interests of the Russian Empire—a subject to which we shall return.

During his stay in Vienna, Alexander alternated between lunches with those close to him—his sisters Catherine and Marie, Laharpe—and state dinners to which he invited the crowned heads who were participating in the congress, taking care to provide his guests with refined cuisine. When he invited Emperor Franz I to lunch, he had his French cooks prepare traditional Austrian dishes but did not depart from his preference for a certain Burgundy wine, the only one that he drank and that he had brought to the caves of St. Petersburg three times a week.[74] He also had frequent working talks with his state secretaries, as well as with Laharpe and Czartoryski on the Polish question.

* * *

In 1814 nothing seemed to force or even predispose the tsar to the least indulgence on the Polish question. The defiance of the Polish elites in response to the hand extended by the tsar in 1811, the active participation of 100,000 Polish soldiers in the Grande Armée, and the atrocities that Russian memoirists imputed to them during the invasion of 1812[75]—all strengthened the deep bone of contention between Russians and Poles. However, unlike those agitated by the topic, Alexander treated the question with moderation: in January 1813 he had assured a worried Czartoryski that vengeance was a sentiment he did not feel[76]—and he did not take long to prove it. In February 1813, when he was in Vilnius, he published a manifesto granting amnesty to the Poles for their engagement on Napoleon's side and liberated Polish war prisoners.[77] In May 1814, in a solemn letter to the patriot leader Kosciusz-ko—we remember that he was the subject of a disagreement between Catherine, her son, and her grandson—Alexander informed him of his plan to reconstitute a Polish entity, asking the old hero to help him in this enterprise. At the same time, Czartoryski, supported by Kochubey—once more in the tsar's favor and since March 1812 president of the economic department of the Council of State—as well as by Novosiltsev, tirelessly defended the Polish case to the emperor. For Czartoryski, the salvation of Poland and its future required an agreement between Russia and Poland that would guarantee the existence of a country that would be independent but dynastically linked to Russia, with its recomposed territories ruled by a constitutional monarch.

* * *

Alexander partially rallied to this plan. During a conversation in September 1814 with Czartoryski and Novosiltsev, the tsar appeared to accept the integration of the western provinces of the empire into a new Polish entity,[78] but in fact, to Czartoryski's great regret, he still hesitated about an issue that was extremely sensitive in Russian opinion.

When the Congress opened, Alexander demanded that the Grand Duchy of Warsaw, which had been aggrandized thanks to territories taken from Prussia and Austria during the partition, form a state of which he would be the sovereign, a sort of buffer state that would ensure Russian security. To plead his cause among the other powers, the tsar insisted on the breadth of the sacrifices to which he had consented during the war, demanding "just" compensation and stressing the need for Russia to make its western border secure by means of this new state. But he also resorted to a threat: "I conquered the Duchy," he declared to the Congress, "and I have 480,000 soldiers to defend it."[79] In exchange for concessions to be made by Austria and Prussia, he proposed giving Austria Lombardy, Venetia, the Tyrol, the region of Salzburg and Dalmatia, while Prussia would obtain a part of Saxony, with the remainder going to Weimar and Coburg. But these proposals appeared tantamount to a hegemonic ambition: British diplomats led by Castlereagh and then by Wellington (after mid-February 1815) did not believe in the fiction of an independent Polish state[80] and saw these demands only as a means for Russia to increase her power. Other states, including Austria, took the British side and advocated either the reconstitution of a completely independent Poland or else a new partition. There were fierce and tense debates throughout September and October.

Wanting to reassume the diplomatic offensive, Alexander sent to the Austrian, British, and Prussian delegates a new treaty proposal, presented by Nesselrode by the end of December: the text called for giving the Poznan region to Prussia and Tarnopol to Austria, and it made Krakow and Thorn free cities. All the rest of the duchy of Warsaw would go to Russia, which reserved the right to establish a constitution there. Free trade would be created throughout Polish lands, and the Polish subjects of Austria and Prussia would have national institutions. But this new proposal was opposed by the former coalition partners; the Austrians were particularly hostile to national institutions within territories under Habsburg rule. Skillfully and cynically manipulated by Talleyrand, who saw it as an opportunity to bring France into the international game, this opposition resulted in the signature on January 3, 1815, of a secret defensive alliance between France, Austria, and Britain—against Russia and Prussia. Telling Louis XVIII of this achievement, Talleyrand wrote proudly: "The coalition is dissolved—and forever."[81] But Napoleon's landing on March 1, 1815, suddenly changed the whole situation. Alexander's lively letter to his mother is worth quoting at length:

> An unexpected event, dear Mama, that will astonish you as much as it has us, has just given a different direction to all ideas. [...] The Bourbons not only did not take precautions to prevent [Napoleon] from leaving his island, but the pretenders to the empire of the seas, the English, who had with Napoleon a Colonel Campbell, did not know how to choose for this important mission an individual able to fulfill it or to furnish him with the necessary vessels. In the end, Napoleon left his Island of Elba on February 26—but not alone! Embarking with all his men, two battalions and two hundred cavalrymen

with some artillery, were 1,200 men in all!!! They left on two feluccas and two corsair boats that he had on the island to protect against Barbary pirates. His guards were insouciant and clumsy enough not to perceive his escape until the next day. As far as we can tell, he remained in sight the whole day, headed toward the southern coast of France. Calm weather prevented the English and French ships from pursuing him. Here it is generally supposed that this was only a feint, that he was actually headed toward Naples. I did not share this assumption and I thought from the outset that he would go to the south of France, probably having support there. Finally, we received the news from Genoa that he did disembark in Cannes, near Antibes, on March 1. He tried to take the castle by surprise but failed, the fortress having been shut up by the commander. Then he marched with his troops toward Grasse several leagues from there, and his destination appeared to be Grenoble, where the French government was gathering a corps to act against Murat in the Kingdom of Naples. At first sight, the appearance of an execrated individual who was the scourge of the human race with such a small troop, right in the middle of a country that had been liberated from his slavery and most of whom were against him, a country that was governed by his mortal enemies, perhaps did not seem important for the outcome, which might have announced his total destruction as well as that of his adjutants. But when one reflects about the clumsiness of the new government when it had to capture minds and above all to galvanize them for all that could be cajoled from the army, when one thinks of the number of Napoleon's partisans who remained in this army, then this surprising appearance is right to produce the grimmest thoughts. As with the beginning, everything depended on the turn taken by events. If the government had managed to send against Napoleon as few as three regiments, but whose colonels did their duty, with enough hold over their troops to make them obey, then in all likelihood this man would be destroyed. But if instead Napoleon managed to take a few donjons and use them for support, thus swelling his little army, if only to 20 or 20 thousand men, very probably he would march with it on Paris. In this case, I doubt that the Bourbons would have enough hold to find another army to oppose him, and with a fight between the two becoming impossible, it is very probable that Napoleon would take Paris and re-assume the reins of government. From the moment he again became the emperor of the French as in the past, we, if we did not want to succumb again one by one to his rule, would be forced to recommence our struggle more vigorously than ever, to prevent him from seizing more [...]. I admit, Mama, that this prospect is devastating. After having seen Napoleon in all his glory, and admired his clarity and a fall so complete as my first example, and the second no less striking of having seen

him in the abyss, to see him again on the throne of France—how not to infer
that men's wisdom is only folly, and that which is great and solid is solely what
God achieves! Yet my conviction that this evil genius would end up one way
or another brought down and destroyed, this conviction does not leave me, I
base it on the words of our Holy Religion, provided that we take it to the end
as is prescribed for us. Also, dear Mama, I proposed more energetic measures.
[…] A mass of 850,000 would be ready to combat and crush the evil genius
if he tried to exercise his wicked empire even briefly. Yet this apparatus,
imposing and reassuring as any human thing can be, did not prevent me from
thinking first of you, dear Mama, and of all the pain you are going to feel at
the very idea of a new struggle. […]

Finally, let us put ourselves in the hands of the Almighty with resignation
and without complaining, and try our best to fulfill his Supreme Will. That
is the only goal that we should have in sight. I did not stop to take [illegible]
about my person, which will take place tomorrow, to be able to leave as soon
as my engagements were done. The overly long duration of the Congress at
least had the advantage that we were all together when this singular news
arrived, and consequently all measures could be taken in concert. This event
also has the other advantage that it will accelerate the termination of the
Congress. […]

Here is a very long letter, dear Mama, that I end by asking you to put your entire
trust in God alone and telling you that our first duty is to obey his Holy Will.[82]

This missive to his mother, both pragmatic and inspired, was how Alexander
reacted to the news of Napoleon's invasion. First of all, this hastily written letter demonstrates his perceptiveness about the situation and the stakes. There
is no doubt he thought that the Bourbon government, which had not rallied
public opinion, would not be able to oppose an emperor who could still count
on many partisans on French soil. Hence the necessity to act quickly, to reorganize forces that could fight the despot, while counting on God's help.

In fact, after having landed on French soil in March 1815, Napoleon did
reassume leadership of his country once Louis XVIII had fled. Soon the
secret treaty between the French, Austrian, and British states (opposed by
Prussia and even more so by Russia), came out, with a copy enabling the
tsar to point a finger at his allies' treachery. But this revelation, while it made
Alexander angry and bitter, did not change anything about the direction
he had chosen. Napoleon remained the enemy to beat; the coalition had to
be summoned again, and the preparation of the final text of the Congress
of Vienna was accelerated so it could be signed on June 9, 1815. The flight
of the eagle was rather short: the Hundred Days ended on June 18 with the

catastrophic Battle of Waterloo, in which Russia did not participate. Four days later Napoleon I signed his second abdication, and this was now the true end of his venture.

At the end of June, Alexander was again in Paris to negotiate the second treaty of Paris, which would be concluded on November 20. This time he stayed at the Elysée Palace as the guest of Louis XVIII, where he played the generous master of ceremonies. He wrote to Chef Antonin Carême, then in the service of Talleyrand, putting him in a requisitioning situation to "design and direct a banquet to take place on September 10 at the 'Plaine de Vertus'"[83] after reviewing the troops. There were no fewer than three grand banquets for 300 people, which Carême consummately directed at the head of a brigade of 35 cooks, although his heart was not in it. "I never did anything as beautiful; anger made me a genius,"[84] later wrote the chef known for his attachment to Napoleon.

Meanwhile, negotiations proved harder than the year before. The British and especially the Prussian emissaries (Blücher the keenest of all) wanted to impose pitiless conditions on France. In September, worried about this fierceness, Louis XVIII asked Alexander to intervene in France's favor, and in order to give a pledge of his goodwill, the tsar named to foreign affairs the Duke of Richelieu; governor of Odessa for twelve years, the latter enjoyed the trust and personal esteem of the tsar. And in fact Alexander did manage to limit the territorial losses: it was on his insistence that France kept Alsace, Lorraine, the Franche-Comté, and Burgundy, on which Prussia had designs. It was also thanks to him that the conditions of the foreign occupation of France were softened. Alexander's intervention is again explained by his concern for an equilibrium in the face of Great Britain, Prussia, and Austria, and it was saluted by the French themselves. The Count of Molé, a great figure in the Bourbon Restoration, wrote in his memoirs:

> In 1815, Russia defended against everybody—I will not say just the interests but the very existence of our unfortunate homeland. If France is still France, it is thanks to three men whose names it should never forget: Alexander and his two ministers, Kapodistrias and Pozzo de Borgo. England, Prussia, and Austria only wanted to weaken us. On the contrary Russia had every interest in our remaining a power of the first order.[85]

The Russian sovereign brought unfailing support to Louis XVIII, who this time knew he was beholden, and Franco-Russian relations became firmer on the geopolitical level. But Alexander still left Paris full of bitterness toward the coalition. He wrote to Catherine on October 13:

> Dear and good friend, here I am outside this horrid Paris! In fact I see around me only a desire to grow fat from France and the desire to give in to the passion of vengeance that I detest above all.[86]

For, despite Russian support, the second Paris treaty was disastrous for France, which was reduced to its 1790 borders. It could keep Avignon and the Comtat Venaissin, Montbelliard, and Mulhouse, but it lost the duchy of Bouillon and the fortresses of Philippeville and Marienburg to Holland, Sarrelouis and Sarrebruck to Prussia, Landau to Bavaria, the Gex region to Switzerland, and a large part of Savoy to Piedmont. As regards its colonies, the loss of St. Lucia, Tobago, and Malta were confirmed. And financial sanctions were added to the territorial losses: France had to pay 700 million francs (the coalition had initially demanded 800 million but lowered the amount at Alexander's insistence), of which 137 million were to be devoted to erecting fortresses to keep an eye on the French border. It had to suffer five years of military occupation (and not seven as initially requested by the coalition, which once again yielded to Alexander) in its northern and eastern border zones—which it had to finance entirely (150,000 men). So the Hundred Days episode cost it a lot, in land and money as well as politically, despite efforts made by Talleyrand, the Duke of Richelieu, and Louis XVIII. The same day (November 20, 1815) the four allies solemnly renewed the pact concluded at Chaumont. France remained a pariah on the international scene.

Meanwhile, the Polish question was finally settled, thanks to a compromise. A friendship treaty between Russia, Austria, and Prussia (May 1815), made by Prince Razumovsky and ratified by Alexander six days later, sealed the fate of Poland, for most of its decisions were incorporated in the final act of Vienna. In relation to his initial ambitions, the tsar accepted major concessions: he kept the major part of the Warsaw duchy, which allowed him to control Warsaw and the central basin of the Vistula; he obtained the right to use the title of king of Poland, but he had to cede northwest regions (including Poznan and Kalisch, or about 810,000 inhabitants) to Prussia and Western Galicia (meaning Tarnopol with 400,000 subjects) to Austria.[87] Cracow became a free city. The treaty recognized that, despite the new territorial arrangements, the Polish nation now constituted a single historical identity, but without its eastern part. Its article 5 stated the right of Poles to benefit from national and representative institutions—this key idea would be reprised in article 1 of the Congress of Vienna's final act, which made provision for free trade between the various Polish regions. So the international community had thus consented (on Alexander's insistence) to put the rights of the Poles to benefit from representative government into a diplomatic text.

On both subjects—French borders and the status of Poland—the positions defended by the tsar demonstrate a dual concern: to defend Russia's geopolitical and security interests and to serve the liberal and constitutional ideas to which he was attached. He had pushed the Bourbons to adopt the charter and had put into the treaty the right of Poles to have representative institutions. In homage to Laharpe, he also contributed to the establishment of an independent and neutral Swiss confederation, enlarged by cantons from the republic of Geneva and by the principalities of Neuchatel and Valais.

* * *

To ensure the application of this second Paris treaty, the coalition powers intended to maintain the Quadruple Alliance formed in Chaumont and to do so by future meetings on a frequent and regular basis. But for Alexander this commitment was not sufficient; they had to profit from current circumstances—the fall of Napoleon and the presence of the allies at the same congress—to elaborate a new system of international relations based on spiritual and moral foundations.

Back in January 1814 Alexander had confided in a note to his state secretary Kapodistrias his diplomatic grand design: with the help of Providence he aspired to construct a general alliance to ensure a lasting peace in Europe. He was thus returning to two major goals already formulated in 1804 when he wrote to Prime Minister Pitt: to reach an equitable regulatory system that would both respect the identity of each nation and guarantee the peace of Europe by means of a grand alliance to prevent conflicts. But now this plan was strongly tinged with strong religious connotations. We recall the references to God and to Providence in his meeting with the Countess of Choiseul-Gouffier in December 1812, quoted above.

In a note of December 1814 addressed to the plenipotentiaries of the other allied states who were in Vienna, Alexander proposed that a reform of the Quadruple Alliance be undertaken on the new foundation of "immutable principles of the Christian religion."[88] The proposal is very important: it shows that for Alexander I in 1815 liberalism, constitutionalism, and attachment to Christianity were mutually compatible. But the plan remained very general; so the interlocutors of the Russian sovereign, believing it was a purely formal declaration of intention, did not follow up. Alexander renewed his attack in the following months. He offered the Austrian emperor and the Prussian king a "holy alliance" that would consider that the three states—Catholic,

Protestant, and Orthodox—belonged to the same family, the "Christian nation," and would stress the need to promote fraternal relations among them in accordance with the principle of Christian charity. With this radically new religious reference, the peaceful community that the tsar had dreamed of back in 1804 henceforth became increasingly a moral and spiritual one.

Barely launched, the text caused a sensation. It ran up against the skepticism of the British, who saw it as a "piece of sublime mysticism and nonsense,"[89] against the irony of Metternich, who denounced "philanthropic aspirations disguised under the mantle of religion,"[90] and the hostility of the pope, who was not inclined to foster ecumenical temptations. But the then-dominant position of Russia on the European scene obliged the Austrian and Prussian governments to make concessions, and on September 26 Franz I and Frederick-Wilhelm III agreed "in the name of the Very Holy and Indivisible Trinity" to sign the "Holy Alliance"—having obtained amendments. The text's preamble inscribes the document within a Christian paradigm that was intended to serve as the basis for any diplomatic action.

> Their Majesties the emperor of Austria, the king of Prussia, and the emperor of Russia, after the great events that have marked Europe in the course of the past years, and principally the good deeds it has pleased Providence to spread over states whose governments have placed their confidence and their hope in it alone, having acquired the conviction that it is necessary to found the paths of powers in their mutual relations on the sublime truths taught us by the eternal religion of the Saving Lord:
>
> We solemnly declare that the present act has the goal of manifesting to the Universe their unshakeable determination to govern their conduct, either in the administration of their respective states or in their political relations with any other government, by the precepts of this holy religion, by the precepts of justice, charity, and peace.[91]

With this framework established, article 1 asserted that "in conformity with the words of Holy Scripture that commands all men to regard each other as brothers," the three monarchs were to consider each other as "compatriots," ready to help in any circumstance, and to conduct themselves as "fathers of family" with respect to their subjects and their armies "to protect religion peace, and justice." The second article repeated these themes, insisting on the need for the three governments of the signatory monarchs "to consider themselves all as members of the same Christian nation," "delegated by Providence to govern three branches of the same family," "confessing that the Christian nation, of which they and their peoples are part, has no other lord than He to whom power belongs, for in Him alone is found all the treasures of love, science, and infinite wisdom, that is to say, in God, our divine Savior Jesus Christ, the Almighty Word of Life." The third and final article stated that the Holy Alliance was ready to welcome "all powers that want solemnly to accept the sacred principles that are proclaimed in the present act."

The spiritual tone of the text, its style full of mystical effusion, has given credence to the idea that the Baroness de Krüdener had played a key role in composing it. In fact, the Swedenborgian mystic had been maintaining a spiritual correspondence with Alexander since 1814, and she had visited him during his stay in the German town of Heilbronn in May 1815; she was in Paris during his second stay. She was very much enjoyed the favor—if not the infatuation—of the Russian sovereign, whose spiritual quest had led him into the web of her sermons; she thought him "chosen." Three days before his first meeting with Madame de Krüdener, he wrote to Catherine, herself on the verge of meeting the pietist.

> Tell her that my affection for her is eternal, that despite all the ways it could be analyzed, it is so pure, so much a tributary of the admiration that my soul bears her soul, that it is impossible to disfigure it. Virginie[92] knows that I have never asked anything of her, so why should she be angry with me? May she leave me my worship of her, it makes no demand on her, and is identified with my existence.[93]

Here we may detect the excessive (and hardly Christian) nature of the cult the tsar was devoting to this singular mystic.

Other sources confirm this influence. The Countess de Boigne, who frequented her in Paris, described the Baroness de Krüdener, then aged about 50, as thin and pale, with sunken eyes and "straight grey hair parted over her forehead," dressed in black, living in a fine apartment on the Faubourg-Saint-Honoré run with extreme austerity:

> The mirrors, decorations, and ornaments of all kinds, the furniture were all covered with grey cloth; even the clocks were shrouded so you could see only the face. The garden extended to the Champs-Elysees, and this was how Emperor Alexander lodged at the place, went to visit Madame de Krüdener at all hours of the day and night.[94]

She had skillfully benefited from her immense credit with the tsar.

> Countess[95] de Krüdener did not tell me how she has reached intimacy with the emperor, but she did manage it. She had invented for him a new form of adulation. He was blasé about those that represented him as the first potentate on earth, the Agamemnon of kings, etc., so she did not speak to him of his worldly power, but of the mystical power of his prayers. The purity of his soul lent then a force that no other mortal could attain, for nobody had resisted so many seductions. And by surmounting them, he showed himself the most virtuous of men and consequently the more powerful with God. It was with the aid of this skillful flattery that she led him to do her bidding. She had him pray for her, for himself, for Russia, for France. She had him fast, give alms, impose privations on himself, renounce all his tastes. She obtained everything from him in the hope of increasing his credit in heaven.[96]

The Countess de Boigne insinuated that the many concessions obtained by Alexander for France's benefit had in fact been dictated by Madame de Krüdener, herself under the influence of Talleyrand. The latter had been in disfavor with Alexander since the revelation by Napoleon of the secret treaty directed against Russia, and thus he had recourse to an intermediary. While this hypothesis cannot be supported by sources, this testimony still illustrates in a striking way that Alexander was then a man under the influence, profoundly marked by German pietism and the mystical transports of the Baroness de Krüdener. But nevertheless, he was the sole drafter of the Holy Alliance text. Alexander Stourdza, the tsar's personal secretary, latter confided that he was "the first to copy and retouch the Act of Holy Alliance, written wholly in pencil by the emperor's hand."[97]

On the diplomatic plane the Holy Alliance seemed to be a success since between 1815 and 1817 it was adhered to by Austria, Prussia, France, Spain, Piedmont, Sicily, Holland, Denmark, Saxony, Bavaria, Württemberg, and Portugal, and then Switzerland and small German states. Only the British government—which still declared it accepted its principles—and the Holy See (hostile to a text that it saw (with reason) as affirmation of a Christian ecumenism that contravened the all-powerfulness of Catholicism and as a contestation of its temporal power (it had not been proposed to place it at the head of the Holy Alliance)), would refuse to join the other signatories. The Ottoman Empire denounced the treaty as propitious to a new crusade. However, in reality, two serious reservations stood out. On the one hand, the text signed in September had been expurgated by Chancellor Metternich of everything that could be considered subversive. For example, he considered the allusion to "the fraternity of subjects" among the three initial states as too liberal. And while article 1 in Alexander's formulation stated, "In conformity with the words of Holy Scripture that ordered all men to regard each other as brothers, the subjects of the three contracting states will remain united by the ties of true fraternity," the text actually adopted said, "In conformity with the words of Holy Scripture that ordered all men to regard each other as brother, the three contracting monarchs will remain united by the ties of a veritable and indissoluble fraternity."[98]

This revision imposed on the tsar paved the way for a conservative application of the text. Moreover, many of the signatories seemed to rally to the idealism professed by Alexander in foreign policy, but this support was only opportunism of pure facade that changed nothing about their practices.

By contrast, Alexander's sincere attachment to this text cannot be doubted. He often referred to it in his correspondence, considering it as the crowning achievement of the Congress of Vienna and by ukase had the original text (not the one expurgated by Metternich) read aloud every year on the anniversary of its signature in all the churches of the empire. He indeed aspired to make the Holy Alliance the high point of his foreign policy. But this generous plan soon ran up against an international reality that was less and less favorable to it.

PART FOUR

AN INCREASINGLY CONSERVATIVE REIGN, 1815–1825

CHAPTER 13

Mystic Exaltation, Reformist Aspiration, and Conservative Practice

1815–1820

After four years marked by the omnipresence of military and diplomatic issues, Alexander I gave priority back to the domestic scene. From the end of 1812, the tsar confided to several of his interlocutors, including Madame de Staël, his desire to remedy the condition of the peasants[1] and after so many years of hesitation to finally make happy his "beloved Russian nation." In 1814 he told Countess Edling, "Yes, I love my nation, despite the fact that I have not yet done much for her; I especially love this fine people! Although I do not show the people the predilection I bear, my affection can be guessed, and I am convinced that they count on mine. A great task to fulfill remains for me: to give liberty to a people who have so well merited it. I have no illusions about the difficulty attached to this great issue, but believe me, I could not die peacefully if I did not manage to resolve it before my death."[2]

In fact, the people's expectations were great. Devastated by the conflict, the country still lacked the most elementary infrastructure—before the war, no paved road linked Moscow to St. Petersburg—and would have to be reconstructed, if not constructed. Many saw in this work an opportunity to build a Russia that was more just and more fraternal—like the Holy Alliance—and more modern. Humble people, particularly the peasants who had paid such a heavy price for victory, hoped in a confused way for better tomorrows that could bring them emancipation. And among the officers who had accompanied the tsar as far as Paris, many in the course of their travels through western Europe, had taken the measure of the Russian Empire's backwardness—political, economic, and material. Returning to their native soil, they had decided to work for the common good. These expectations were of an

almost millenarian nature—after the suffering and the triumph over the Antichrist, it was time for redemption, but was the monarch capable of grasping
and fulfilling such hopes?

A Tsar Transformed

Alexander returned to Russia haloed by his successes: public opinion was
ready to celebrate publicly his triumph over Napoleon. Yet his return was
discreet and austere; known for his taste for parades and perfectly executed
military maneuvers, the emperor in fact celebrated his success over the "hy-
dra" by prayers and praise to God. There was no national festival to com-
mune collectively over the memory of the ordeals undergone. This behavior
as well as the monarch's long absence—he had gone on military campaign in
1813 and then been long delayed in Paris and Vienna—were surprising and
even disturbing to people whose hopes born of the war were so immense.

Upon his return to Russian land, Alexander was unanimously saluted as the
savior of Russia. The title "blessed" with which the senate wanted to honor him
testifies to the fervor surrounding the monarch, which was very real among
the people (in 1816 Moscow gave him a warm welcome amid the building
works). But very soon among the elites the criticism began mounting, and the
sacred union that had been observed in 1812 began to fray. The responsibility
of Alexander for this evolution is not negligible: the emperor had completely
internalized his combat against Napoleon, and once victory was achieved, he
had difficulty making the patriotic war an object of national pride, a memorial reference to weld together the nation and its tsar. Admittedly, in August
of 1814, he published a ukase honoring the valor and courage of the Russian
people, announcing domestic reforms, and expressing his desire to improve
the existence of the social classes that had participated in the war effort. And
he did try to apply his success to the urban space: in 1817, the first stone was
laid in Moscow for a church to be built in memory of the dead of the 1812 war;
an arch of triumph celebrating the victory over Napoleon was erected on the
square of the Winter Palace in St. Petersburg during its restoration by Carlo
Rossi and Vasily Stasov. But in general, the great deeds of the war were only
sparingly commemorated: no statue nor monument recalled any campaign of
1813–1814, however costly in Russian lives—even while Alexander ordered
celebrated in Russian churches every year the Holy Alliance anniversary.

Barely comprehensible, Alexander's behavior with respect to his triumph,
both personal and national, was even more the subject of criticism with respect to his foreign policy. For many court dignitaries the high cost of the

war and the sacrifices seemed to justify a more offensive diplomacy on the emperor's part, one that would be less generous to France and especially to Poland, widely perceived as guilty of having supported Napoleon. Shortly after the signing of the second treaty of Paris, Count Vorontsov wrote bitterly to his son Mikhail:

> It appears they are more concerned with the advantages of others than with the well being of our own country. At the very least, we could have obtained for all those sacrifices, especially from Prussia (which has grown enormously), the city of Memel in order to have a natural border by the Niemen. But we were occupied only with Poland, which remains without any link to Russia but attached to her only through the person of Alexander, against whose successors Poland will make war every time we are occupied by some other embarrassing war. All this makes one weep.[3]

To this incomprehension about Alexander's diplomatic choices were added suspicions about the many diplomats of foreign origin who had gone into the service of Russia; they were accused at best of incompetence and at worst of deliberately sabotaging national interests. Alexander defended himself against this double accusation, stressing the devotion of the foreign diplomats and the incapacity of the Russians themselves. As early as 1806 he had retorted:

> If I do not choose to resort to the help of foreigners who are well known and whose talents are proven, then the number of capable men, already very limited, will be even more reduced. [...] What would Peter have done if he had not employed foreigners? At the same time, I feel that it is bad. [...] But how can one arrest the course of events until our nationals are at the top?[4]

This did not prevent accusations being leveled at foreigners, as well as at subjects of the Russian Empire who were not themselves Russian. Combined with the tsar's long absence and his personal participation in the endeavors of the Congress of Vienna, the idea grew in public opinion that the emperor cared more about European questions than the future of his own country, that because he was wholly preoccupied with the destiny of Europe, Alexander had already turned away from Russia.

This sentiment was exacerbated in 1814–1815 because during the tsar's absence in Vienna, it was the redoubtable Arakcheev who stood in for the emperor. Placed at the head of Alexander's secretariat in 1812, in August 1814 promoted to liaison between the work of the Committee of Ministers and the emperor,[5] then raised in December 1815 to the post of supervisor of that work, Arakcheev was gaining in power month by month. He acquitted himself seriously, devoted to the tasks that the tsar gave him. He never overstepped his role, taking care to remain the zealous executor of the imperial will. But the man was frightening: his stubbornness, his cruelty, his narrowness of mind, his political conservatism, and his customary acts of violence were all well known. For many Russians at court and foreign observers, Arakcheev incarnated an autocracy at its zenith, which ill suited the liberal spirit proclaimed by Alexander.

However, this allegation does not do justice to the tsar's own efforts. Even when far away, Alexander continued to administer the empire and to take important decisions. Even while the war was still going on, he was engaged in lifting Moscow from the rubble and reconstructing it as quickly as possible under attentive state control and according to town-planning and aesthetic rules. From the end of 1812, he ordered emergency financial aid for the most deprived Muscovites; in May 1813 he set up a construction commission to which he assigned three main objectives: to reconstruct houses and shops that had been destroyed, to conceive a development plan for a "new" city, and to embellish the city with architecture of neoclassical style,[6] designed to celebrate imperial power.[7] Very involved in the project to restore the city, Alexander insisted on the need to give Moscow new monuments, symbols of its renaissance after the catastrophe. Thus Red Square was entirely redesigned—embellished with new neoclassical buildings housing shops, it would welcome in February 1818 a statue dedicated to Minin and Pozharski[8] that commemorated Russian resistance to the Polish invasion of 1612. As for Theater Square—larger than the Place de la Concorde in Paris or St. Peter's Square in Rome[9]—it would serve as the setting for the new Bolshoi Theater.[10] Only a few years after the cataclysm of 1812, by way of thumbing its nose at Napoleon, Moscow had become one of the most beautiful cities in Europe, the only capital in the "Empire" style.

But while the sacred union forged in the ordeals of 1812 seemed to augur a new union between the monarch and his people, in reality a much more ambiguous relationship set in. But Alexander was not aware of this ambiguity, wholly engaged as he was by his faith in God and in the miracle of revelation that had taken place.

* * *

The year 1812 had changed the tsar's life, had brought him to God, but as he confided in 1818 to Abbot Eylert, this path was not without many struggles and doubts. From his return to Russia until around 1820, he did not cease pursuing his quest through reading and the spiritual exercises to which he was devoted, plus meetings with spiritual advisors. The influence of the illuminism and pietism of the Baroness de Krüdener was patent, at least until 1816. But other influences can be detected, above all, that of Alexander Golitsyn, who had been named in 1803 ("against his conscience and ideas"[11]) the procurator of the Holy Synod. As a deist and functionally anti-clerical, he was leading a very dissolute life. Then he gradually converted to reading the Bible—to the point of becoming the person who in 1812 initiated the tsar to meditation on holy scripture. Fed by references to German mysticism, an amateur of the kabbalah and gnosticism, an adept of the ideas of Saint-Martin, who called each believer to form an "interior church,"[12] Alexander Golitsyn preached an individual faith that had few ties to the rites and dogmas of the Orthodox Church. While he was not officially the tsar's confessor, he was de facto his spiritual director. In July 1820 or 1821, he wrote to him: "Continue, Sire, to follow the path of Jesus Christ, he will pull you and deliver you to Himself, and He will communicate to you His gifts, and then Himself. Such are my wishes and prayers for your spiritual journey."[13]

I should also cite the influence of Rodion Koshelev, who, as we recall, had initiated Alexander into Freemasonry. Alongside Golitsyn he now helped the tsar discover the other spiritual thinkers of his age—Lavater, Swedenborg, Eckartshausen, Jung-Stilling—as well as the Quakers and Moravian Brothers, pietists who were well established in the Baltic provinces and who preached a form of spiritual egalitarianism among Christians and the reading of the Bible in vernacular languages,[14] and with whom Koshelev had developed a correspondence.[15] By the end of the 1810s or in the spring of 1821 at the very latest, the three men had formed a lodge called "Three-One," directed by Golitsyn, where they performed regular spiritual exercises and made commentaries on holy scripture. The GARF archives contain many short notes sent in 1821 by Tsar Alexander to Golitsyn in order to confirm or postpone their meetings for sacred readings and discussions of scripture. They were systematically signed with the phrase "Devotedly in Our Lord."[16] Alongside Golitsyn and Koshelev, others played roles in the tsar's religious practice. He had turned away from Baroness de Krüdener, who had moved to St. Petersburg in 1818 and whom he expelled from the empire in 1822, so weary was he of her sermons and repeated demands for money and her appeals for the cause of Greek independence. But meanwhile he found a new prophetess: the Russian Catherina Tatarova had a circle of ecclesiastics and laity who commented on scripture and prayed together, meditated, and even experimented with hypnosis.

He was also reading a great deal: holy books, works of piety, the great Christian writers. This heterogeneous reading is surprising for an Orthodox sovereign because the authors were largely Catholic. Among his correspondence with his sister Catherine figures a curious and interesting text titled "On Mystical Literature"[17] that Alexander wrote during 1812 about various theological doctrines of his day. He begins by recalling the distinction between an external religion that is politically necessary and the interior one:

> The policy of sovereigns has transformed this mysterious doctrine[18] into the one common religion of nations. But in promoting worship, policy could not manifest the mysteries. Consequently, even now as always, there is an external Church and an Internal Church.
>
> The doctrinal foundation is the same for both—the Bible—but in the former one knows only the letter, while in the latter the meaning is taught.
>
> There is countless literature for the external Church, whose systematic exposition is called Theology.
>
> There is also considerable (but not as prodigious) for the internal Church, the ensemble of which is called mysterious or mystical Theology. We should not understand this as referring to any single system (for there is no exact or systematic exposition of this kind of theology) but as applying to all writing in general that belongs to this genre, known under different denominations such as *Spiritual, Theosophical,* or *Ascetic Works,* etc.

Then he went on to commentaries on the books he had read and contemplated, establishing a scale of values. Fundamentally, and thus at the foot of the ladder, he mentions works by Jakob Böhme (translated by Saint-Martin), Swedenborg, Saint-Martin, Jung-Stilling; then he goes on to St. Augustine's *Confessions,* Malebranche's treatise *Search after Truth,*[19] the works of Eckartshausen, and the spiritual writings of Fénelon as more important. His ultimate preference is for the writings of Saints Francis de Sales and Teresa of Avila, and Thomas à Kempis's *Imitation of Christ,* which are all considered as "pure unalloyed gold." Finally, he finishes his paper by underlining how essential it is to read the Bible, especially the four Gospels.

These various influences and the very personality of Alexander brought forth a sincere piety, founded on assiduous Bible reading and individual prayer—but the tsar was not attached to the public rites, to the great regret of the Orthodox hierarchy. He was capable of praying with the same fervor in an Orthodox church or a Protestant one, or in a Catholic chapel. In 1819, welcoming to St. Petersburg the Quakers William Allen and Stephen Grellet, he took communion and prayed with them, demonstrating great emotion. Later, Grellet would attest that the tsar's face was "bathed in tears"[20] at the end of the service; and Allen would recall the tsar telling him, "When I am with you and am like you who love the Savior, then I can breathe."[21]

This eclectic and even liberal conception of religion, which resembles the political principles dear to him, was a fundamental feature of Alexander's faith. For him, believing was an individual act, founded on an active approach that makes it incumbent on each person to start from his own reflections on the Bible and to construct his personal faith. In his 1818 conversation with Abbot Eylert, he said he was in favor of each person's reading the Bible "in his own language" and the need to disseminate scripture in the vernacular, without commentary:

> Holy books should be disseminated as they were given to us. Commentaries have the disadvantage of more or less substituting for the text the ideas of the person who interprets it to suit his system. Not everybody will accept these ideas. It should be the affair of every Christian, whatever communion he belongs to, to freely let the sacred Code act upon him in its whole impact; this action can only be beneficial and stimulating, as one might expect from a divine book, the Book of Books. Its action on each person will be different, but this is precisely what is grand and extraordinary about it; it makes of each individual what it is possible to make of him due to his particular nature.[22]

Then he becomes explicit about the link between faith and political activity:

> Unity in variety, is that not the great point at which one must arrive in order to make Churches and States prosper? This principle of unity in variety, we perceive everywhere outside, and similarly in the history of nations, except that one should not take as a measure the short space of time in which we live. It is to the centuries and tens of centuries that one has to look when one wants to judge the result of a great struggle between opposing and hostile forces. Contradictions, lies, vain commentaries—all these offspring of time and partisan spirit, will be resolved by time. Truth remains. But the action of truth is slow: it often takes centuries to be accepted; nevertheless it pierces and there is no way of hermetically sealing it up, as some people would like to do with Holy Scripture. Do not the sun's rays pierce? Those who live in its clarity are the children of light.[23]

Thus this "unity in variety" is willed by God and should guide both religious and political practices. This enables us to better understand the project of the Holy Alliance: it was precisely aimed in the long term at inspiring unity in geopolitical variety. Alexander would often return to this theme of a duality that haunted him. Witness a conversation with Joseph de Maistre, as reported by the latter in a dispatch to his king in February 1816.[24] The concept of the Holy Alliance appeared to many to be enigmatic (if not confused), and so Maistre asked the tsar if the Holy Alliance's goal was to make "a fusion of all communions, such that each sovereign could no longer exclusively defend his own." Alexander categorically denied this:

> Not at all! Not at all! On the contrary! Each sovereign invariably remains attached to his particular religion. You can see this clearly, since of the three sovereigns who signed it, the Austrian emperor was Catholic, the Prussian king a Protestant, and me Greek. The King of France who is Catholic gave me a copy of the Convention signed and even written in his hand. [...] Let us start by attacking non-belief; this is the great evil we should be concerned with. Let us practice the Gospel—that is the main point. I do believe that all communions will one day be united; I hold this as certain, but the moment has not yet come.[25]

This strong resonance of the spiritual quickly affected the tsar's religious policy in his empire. At the invitation of Golitsyn who had helped found it in 1813, he joined the Biblical Society as an ordinary member (not wanting to be its leader) and financed its work with an initial donation of 25,000 rubles and an annual subsidy of 10,000. The Society's main objective (as was happening at the same time in western Europe) was to translate the Bible into the vernacular, in order for believers to have direct access to it. (We recall Alexander's ambition formulated with Abbot Eylert.) This meticulous work was entrusted to a group of serious and devoted translators. But the initiative soon encountered criticism from conservatives; grouped around Admiral Shishkov, they made themselves the defenders of the Slavonic Church, for they thought that reading and teaching sacred texts in the vernacular was a sacrilege. In 1818, despite this opposition, the Spiritual Academy of St. Petersburg led by Archimandrite Philaret finished the translation into modern Russian of the New Testament, and by the end of that year the Society had published 371,000 copies in 79 editions in the 25 languages and dialects in use on imperial territory.

But Alexander's incursion into religious affairs did not stop there. Despite his conviction that the exterior and interior churches could have nothing in common, he took measures, halfway between the religious and the political, that illustrate his gradual slide to conservatism and intolerance.

One of the very first concerned the Jesuits. As we have seen, they had been long protected by Catherine II, by Paul, and by Alexander himself due to their important role in secondary education. In December 1815 the tsar adopted a ukase that suddenly chased them out of St. Petersburg, forbade them entering Moscow, and obliged them to leave for Polotsk in Polish territory; their pupils were sent back to their families. Contemporaries wondered about this decision, and for some Catholics (Joseph de Maistre and several ecclesiastics)[26] it was explained by the refusal of the Jesuit fathers to grant the absolution demanded by Maria Naryshkina, a Catholic, after her rupture with the tsar. But although in December 1815, more than a year after that event, Alexander was still very attached to his former mistress, this explanation is not believable, and direct sources are lacking to support it. More fundamentally, this disgrace seems to me to result from a set of circumstances that were unfavorable for the Jesuits: a wave of conversions to Catholicism being observed in Russian high society (particularly among women), and then that of Alexander Golitsyn, the nephew of the homonymous minister of religion, who became so angry that he began to attack the Jesuits. Maybe the disgrace was even more due to the refusal of the general who headed the Jesuit order in Russia to participate in the Biblical Society.[27] Then there was the pope's condemnation of the Holy Alliance—all of which contributed to quickening the disgrace of the Jesuits. In 1820, newly targeted, they were abruptly forced to leave imperial territory. Made official by a ukase in March, the expulsion of the Jesuits proceeded smoothly:

> The trip of 750 of them across Russian land was paid for; their admission to Austria facilitated, where most of them were able to stop in Galicia at the Tarnopol College, which the government in Vienna gave them. Others pushed onto Italy, where the order was starting to recover the favor of the Holy See, and others went as far as China.[28]

But the eviction produced turmoil among Catholics present at the St. Petersburg court, and it made Joseph de Maistre want to leave. Very affected by a decision that shocked his religious convictions, the diplomat obtained from his king a recall to Sardinia.

* * *

At the end of 1816, profiting from the fact that Razumovsky, minister of public education, was about to retire, Alexander reorganized this department by combining it with religious affairs. The Holy Synod disappeared. Directed by Golitsyn, the new ministry was to look after all religions and was organized into four sections: Orthodox Russians and Old Believers,[29] Roman and Uniate Catholics, Protestants and Sectarians, and non-Christians. This interesting structure lasted until the ministry was dissolved in 1824, and it says a lot about Alexander's religious nonconformism. By creating four sections, he explicitly recognized the empire's religious diversity, and by associating the Orthodox and schismatics in a single department, he was trying to weaken the prerogatives of the Orthodox Church and to call into question its status as the official church. However, his benevolence toward the Old Believers, tolerated since the reign of Catherine II, will not last: in 1825 they will be placed under the surveillance of a secret committee directed by the metropolitan of Novgorod and the archbishop of Tver, who were in charge of ensuring their respect for the law and for local institutions. Furthermore, a hardening toward and a distrust of the schismatics were back on the agenda in 1820.

The creation of a dual ministry that established a structural link between religion and education, as well hiring committed believers to administer the department charged with educational matters—Alexander appointed as head V. Popov, one of the secretaries of the Biblical Society—led to rapid changes on the pedagogic level.

Henceforth, all education would be inspired by scripture. Armed with this principle, the minister vigorously took Russian universities in hand, a campaign conducted by Mikhail Magnitsky. Coming from a noble but poor family, a Freemason, Magnitsky had been Speransky's right-hand man, and in 1812 he had paid dearly for his faithfulness to his minister by being sent into exile. Given an amnesty and named vice-governor of the province of Voronezh in 1816, he became governor of Simbirsk a year later and had subsequently been evolving toward conservative positions—in this, he was similar to Golitsyn and Arakcheev. It was he who orchestrated the clampdown on the universities: he wanted to stamp out European ideas, particularly German ones, which were corrupting Russia, and to return to a national education that celebrated God and the Russian identity. This program decreed, Magnitsky spent six days in 1819 inspecting the University of Kazan. The freedom and atheism that reigned there so shocked him that he asked Alexander to close the establishment immediately. The emperor refused to take such a drastic measure, but named Magnitsky as inspector of the Kazan school district, giving him every latitude to haul the university into line. Twelve professors, or more than half the teaching body, were fired; the library was purged of suspect titles like Machiavelli, Voltaire, Rousseau, and

Kant; subjects like geology (considered incompatible with Biblical teaching) were forbidden and others, like mathematics and philosophy, were placed under strict surveillance. From Kazan the crackdown was extended to other universities. In St. Petersburg the rector, who was close to Magnitsky, led the charge against the teaching body, accused of professing ideas contrary to scripture, and he dismissed four people. These measures aroused perplexity and then anger among students, who soon deserted the new sites of clerical propaganda; in a few months, there were only 40 left at the University of St. Petersburg, 50 at Kazan—less than a third of previous undergraduates. In parallel, secondary school curricula were also revised: potentially subversive subjects like philosophy and applied sciences (political economy, technology) were reduced if not suppressed, while subjects like history, ancient languages, and geography were favored. At the level of district schools, courses in natural history and technology were replaced by daily lectures on the New Testament.

In addition, under the joint influence of Arakcheev and Golitsyn, both concerned with purging the harmful influences of liberal and atheistic ideas among youth, censorship hardened, and young writers soon paid the price—foremost Pushkin. Born in 1799 of a well-educated father of the old nobility and a mother who was descended from the African Abraham Hannibal, who had been godson and comrade-in-arms of Peter the Great, the young Alexander Pushkin received French culture from his parents. At the age of 12, he entered the Imperial Lycée of Tsarskoye Selo and began to write verses he declaimed before his fellow pupils. In January 1815, he composed a poem that earned him the enthusiastic encouragement of the poet Zhukovsky and opened the doors of the Arzamas Literary Society, where he could meet the greatest writers of his time. Leaving the lycée in 1817, he settled with his parents in St. Petersburg on the Fontanka Canal and was introduced into salons and literary societies, including the Green Lamp, founded in 1819 and of liberal inspiration, where he became an assiduous member. In 1820 he completed his first great poem, Ruslan and Ludmila. Inspired by a medieval novel adopted by Russian folklore, the poem belonged to the Romantic movement, which took inspiration from historical subjects to affirm the cruelty of individual destinies, while keeping classical rhythms and versification. The young writer proclaimed his liberal convictions, indefatigably calling for political liberty. In his Ode to Freedom in 1819, he pronounced in favor of a constitutional monarchy, and in The Village, composed the same year, he hoped that people would one day be "free of all oppression" and that "enlightened freedom" would reign in Russia. These texts (especially the violent epigram he aimed in 1817 against Arakcheev) finally provoked Alexander's anger. On May 6, 1820, at the age of 21, Pushkin was exiled, first in Ekaterinoslav, then in Bessarabia, which had been recently annexed to the Russian Empire.[30] The conservative hardening was therefore patent with respect to intellectuals and artists who were too enamored of liberty.

* * *

Seized by his new faith, desiring to submit entirely to "the decrees of Providence,"[31] while still maintaining that he wanted to make the happiness of his people, Alexander was also questioning his power and gripped by the idea of abdication.

In fact, we observe a clear correlation between the consolidation of his faith, strengthened by various ordeals, and the doubts that assailed him as emperor. Admittedly, as we may recall, the idea of abdicating figured back in 1796 in a letter to Viktor Kochubey, but since he had ascended the throne in 1801, there was no question of this. However, at the end of 812, at the moment when he found faith, this temptation returned. In Vilnius, in his conversation with Countess Choiseul-Gouffier, he confided in the midst of his indisputable triumph, "No, the throne is not my vocation, and if I could honorably change my condition, I would do so gladly."[32]

Five years after, in September 1817, when he came to confess to a monk at the Monastery of Grottoes in Kiev, he told his aide-de-camp Mikhailovsky-Danilevsky that any monarch "should remain at his post as long as his physical strength allows. As concerns myself, I feel perfectly well at present, but in ten or fifteen years when I am fifty...."[33]

It was in 1819, this time with family members and on two successive occasions, that Alexander mentioned the plan that still haunted him. In the summer, in his residence at Krasnoe Selo, during a dinner in the presence of the Grand Duke Nicholas and his wife Alexandra Feodorovna, Alexander confided openly his desire to leave power, as his youngest brother's wife remembered:

> One day after emperor Alexander had dined with us, he sat between us and chatted casually, but suddenly changed the subject and became serious, in the following terms telling us "that he had been satisfied this morning at the way his brother acquitted himself of his military command, that he was doubly happy to see Nicholas fulfill his duties well, since one day a great weight would rest on him, that he regarded him as his replacement, and much earlier than could be presumed, since it would happen while he was still alive." We were

seated like two statues, eyes wide open, dumbfounded. The emperor continued "You seem surprised, but know that my brother Constantine was never concerned about the throne and is more than ever determined to renounce it formally by passing his rights of succession to his brother Nicholas and his descendants. For myself, I am decided to leave my functions and to retire from the world. More than ever Europe needs young sovereigns with all their energetic strength; for me, I am no longer what I was, and I believe it is my duty to retire before it is too late; I believe that the King of Prussia will do the same, and put Fritz in his place."

Seeing us about to sob, he tried to console and reassure us, saying that this would not happen soon, that years would pass before he put his plan to execution, and then he left us alone—you can imagine in what state. Never had the shadow of such an idea come into our heads, not even in our dreams.

We felt as if struck by lightning: the future appeared to us somber and as if closed to happiness! This was a memorable moment in our life.[34]

A few weeks later, in September, in Warsaw, Alexander told Nicholas in the presence of Constantine:

I should tell you, my brother, that I want to abdicate; I am tired and no longer have the strength to bear the burden of government. I warn you so that you can reflect on what you should do in that case. When the time has come to abdicate, I will let you know and you will convey what I am thinking to our mother.[35]

Why precisely in 1819 did the emperor mention twice to his brothers his desire to abdicate? If his ever secretive personality does not allow a firm answer to this essential question, we may stress two factors. First, there is the role of his increasingly vibrant faith, which involved him in a quest for the "internal Church" that appeared less and less compatible with the exercise of absolute power over a land as huge as the Russian Empire. Then, a tragedy had struck the tsar in January 1819, from which he had not recovered: the terrible death of his favorite sister Catherine, carried off at age 30 by an erysipelas of the face. This death threw him into a depressive state, accentuating his distaste for any kind of activity.

Whatever the cause, the issue of abdication posed a dual dilemma to Alexander. First, there was the religious dilemma because, since the tsar took his power from God, he was not in a position to undo what Providence had decreed—unless, that is, his power was not by divine rights, but constitutional. As Sergey ronenko has stressed with finesse, it was the very moment when Alexander was reflecting seriously but still secretly about a possible constitutional reform that he allowed himself to confide his desire to abdicate to his family members.[36] It also posed a political dilemma, for in 1819 he had to find out who would truly be able to succeed him. In 1814, after the death of the two daughters born of his union with Elizabeth, the tsar could no longer hope for a direct heir. By the general act of succession to the throne adopted by Paul in 1797 and confirmed by Alexander at his ascension, Constantine was the first in line. But the latter, who had been separated since 1801 from his wife Princess Juliana of Saxe-Coburg, was childless and living with a Polish and Catholic countess, Jeanne Grudzinska; thus, he could not inherit the throne, to which he did not aspire anyway. In contrast, Nicholas was the irreproachable husband of Alexandra Feodorovna, born Charlotte of Prussia,[37] and father of a small Alexander born in 1818; he offered all the moral and religious guarantees. So when in September 1819 the sovereign visited Constantine, it was tacitly to authorize him to divorce and then marry morganatically Countess Grudzinska in exchange for renouncing the throne in favor of Nicholas. On April 2, 1820, a ukase reaffirmed a certain number of rules, including the requirement for any Russian sovereign to choose as wife a young woman of royal or princely blood who had converted to Orthodoxy. A few days later, Constantine thus broke his marriage and wed Countess Grudzinska.[38]

So, in short, the tsar was deeply transformed when he returned in 1815: however, increasingly absorbed by his faith and tempted to an abdication that would allow him to be totally devoted to the search for God, Alexander was still keen to conduct major reforms.

Reforms Implemented, Reforms Sketched

When he returned, Alexander got down to giving "his" Poland both its own status and constitution. For the tsar, Poland was a crucial gamble. Because Napoleon had bet on the nationalism of the Polish elites to win it over against the tsar and had made many fallacious promises, Alexander had obtained from the Congress of Vienna the reconstitution of the kingdom—and he dreamed of being that clement, liberal, and constitutional sovereign. It was here that he would make his reform aspirations concrete and give free rein to his taste for liberalism and his interest in constitutionalism. It was in the new Poland, transformed into a political laboratory, that he was going to experiment with the reality of a representative government.

He entered Poland on November 12, 1815, symbolically dressed in a Polish uniform; two weeks later he signed the charter that made him a constitutional king. This text was the fruit of deliberations begun long months before with Czartoryski on the one hand, and with Novosiltsev, Kochubey, and his diplomatic advisors Kapodistrias and Pozzo di Borgo on the other hand. It had not gone without difficulty: the tsar's plan to give "his" Poland a constitution had aroused much criticism.

In October 1814, while Alexander and his advisors were still at the Congress of Vienna, Pozzo di Borgo, although of liberal convictions, had composed a long memorandum[39] in which he explained the dangers of making Poland into "a separate state body," as he said. First, there was a diplomatic danger: as soon as rights had been conceded to the Polish subjects of the Russian Empire, the Polish subjects of the Prussian and Austrian monarchs would demand to be affiliated with Russia; "from the moment there exists a diet, a form of representation, a Polish army, it would be a flag summoning them to a rallying sign," which would cause tension, even conflicts with Prussia and Austria. There was also a political danger because "the title of King of Poland can never be compatible with that of autocratic emperor of all the Russias—these two titles can never go together." Moreover, Pozzo di Borgo was viscerally hostile to attaching the current Polish provinces of the Russian Empire to the new entity; he saw it as discrimination among the subjects of the empire and likely to engender frustration. In effect, the "Polish" lands that had been integrated into the empire for several decades would now be governed by a constitution, while the rest of the empire[40] would stay under an autocratic regime. Moreover, the "old" Polish provinces not attached to this new Poland would also escape reform—another source of tension. Finally, he stressed the danger represented by a sovereign Poland to the development and civilization of the Russian Empire.

> As soon as the mass of nine million formed as a nation exists between Russia and the rest of civilized Europe, then the reciprocal influence and communications that derive from immediate contact will diminish perceptibly. [...] The delay that this separation might bring to the development of [Russian] moral faculties, to [Russian] education, to the communication of enlightenment, arts and liberal ideas—is incalculable. It was in order to plunge Russia into barbarism and make it exclusively an Asiatic power that Napoleon imagined re-establishing Poland, as it was to make Russians take a distinguished rank among the most civilized nations of Europe that the predecessors of Your Majesty[41] planned conquests that would necessarily amalgamate with them.[42]

This passage is of fundamental importance: beyond the diplomatic and geopolitical situation, the whole stake of the Polish question was for Pozzo di Borgo actually about Russia's relation to Europe, the crucial issue of its belonging to "civilized" Europe. For the diplomat a Poland integrated into the empire was likely to serve as a lever to increase ties to Europe. But an independent Poland, by contrast, claiming its cultural superiority over Russia, would turn as soon as possible away from Russia and abandon her to her backwardness and Asiatic barbarity, because the "habitual hatred"[43] of the Pole for the Russian would take the upper hand over their gratitude. But the tsar dismissed Pozzo di Borgo's warnings, and the latter was not able to make himself heard. The sovereignty of a territorially enlarged Poland was for Alexander a moral imperative—in 1796 he had disapproved (like his father Paul) of the iniquitous partitions of which Poland had been victim—as well as a political one. Napoleon's having failed in his plan to reestablish Poland, it came down to him to succeed in this, while preserving Russia's security interests as best he could. This is what he told Czartoryski in 1813 and Kosciuszko in 1814. Finally, while he shared Pozzo di Borgo's conviction that Poland as a land of contact with western Europe was indispensable to the development and modernization of Russia, he was more optimistic than his diplomat. A Poland that was independent but dynastically tied to the Russian Empire might better than an annexed Poland play the role of "cultural intermediary" that both men assigned it, for it would infuse a liberalism propitious to trade and initiatives.

A few weeks after the treaty that set Poland's destiny in May 1815, Alexander decreed a ukase explaining his choices to the Russians. He affirmed that a sovereign Polish state, with its own institutions but linked to Russia, would be the best token of security. He then[44] announced to the Poles their new kingdom in the form of a constitutional state with its own army, and he signed a text called "Bases of the Constitution of the Kingdom of Poland." The fruit of a collaboration of several Polish nobles under the aegis of Czartoryski, this text decreed the outlines of the future constitution,[45] to be written by a commission. A charter would guarantee individual liberty; no arbitrary arrest would be authorized; the Catholic Church would enjoy special status, but all Christian religions would be tolerated without discrimination. All official posts would be occupied by subjects of the kingdom, and public debates would be conducted in Polish. The diet would have responsibility for the budget and finances. A Council of State presided over by the viceroy would prepare the new legislation. Judges appointed for life by the monarch would ensure the independence of justice. The army would be national; if Russian contingents should happen to be stationed in the kingdom, the Russian treasury would pay for their maintenance. Education would be national and free. Cities would administer themselves, peasants would keep individual freedom and the right to acquire land. Finally, the situation of the Jews would be improved.

On the basis of this working document, ambitious and generous, full of a liberal spirit and Enlightenment thinking, the definitive text of a constitutional charter was adopted by Alexander on November 27, 1815. He personally approved its 165 articles after having made some revisions to earlier versions,[46] so invested was he in this document.

The kingdom of Poland was "forever" united with the Russian Empire (article 1) and therefore was not the master of its foreign policy, not authorized to keep plenipotentiary agents abroad.[47] Its institutions were now based on a constitutional charter[48] that guaranteed all inhabitants their individual freedom and equality before the law; there was freedom of the press and of property, the use of the Polish language at all levels of administration and in the courts. A diet (Sejm) was formed, composed of the emperor and two chambers. The upper chamber (or senate) was composed of members appointed for life by the emperor; their number would never exceed half the number of representatives in the lower house. The latter, the deputy chamber, would be composed of 128 elected representatives. Voting rights were granted to all land-owning nobles aged over 21, to property owners who paid taxes, and to people of "merit" (teachers, artists)—i.e., the professions—which would result in an electoral body of almost 100,000 adults.[49] (In France at the time, the electoral body was only 80,000 persons, and it remained until 1848 completely closed to the professions, despite repeated demands from liberals.) The tsar as king of Poland held executive power, with the sole right to declare war and conclude treaties, and he appointed all administrative jobs; he was head of the army. He also benefited from wide prerogatives with respect to legislation: he alone could initiate it, and laws proposed by the diet required his approval. However, the diet also had a right to veto proposed laws emanating from the emperor.

The charter was therefore a major text that granted freedoms unique to Polish lands (neither Austria nor Prussia would respect the commitments made in Vienna), as well as compared to the Russian Empire; these rights went even beyond those enjoyed in Finland. It expressed Alexander's attachment to Enlightenment ideas and his concern to make Poland into an experimental laboratory for reforms to be conducted in the rest of the empire. However, this spirit of openness did not prevent Alexander from carefully preserving Russian interests: he made his brother Constantine the commander in chief of the 35,000 soldiers of the new Polish army; he named the malleable General Joseph Zajaczek as viceroy, depriving Adam Czartoryski of a post he coveted and that would normally have come to him, but in Alexander's eyes Czartoryski's strong personality and the renown of his family would have given this post too much prestige. Finally, Alexander named his friend Novosiltsev, a Russian, as the tsar's "personal commissioner" to the Polish government, charged with attending its meetings. So, while Poland was granted inalienable rights and freedoms, it still remained tightly linked to the Russian Empire and to the imperial family. For the tsar this link was meant to become even stronger because the constitutional experiment would serve as a model for the rest of the empire, "a first step on the road to the Russian constitution."[50]

* * *

Indeed Alexander's objective in this constitutional experiment was to generalize it eventually to all of his empire. Those close to him were convinced that this was his plan: in a letter of May 1818 to her brother Constantine, the young Grand Duchess Anna Pavlovna (now the Princess of Orange) said she was "seized with admiration" for the speech given by Alexander during the closing session of the diet, stressing that because she lived in a constitutional country, she was able to appreciate its full value.[51]

In November 1815, in a conversation with Mikhail Oginski, a Pole who continued to plead for attaching the western provinces of the empire to the Polish kingdom, Alexander confided that such a move, which he did not want because he intended to maintain strong links with "his" Polish lands, was even less justified on the political level because the constitutional model granted to the kingdom w ould in future be the norm throughout imperial territory.[52] But while this declaration seems very important, it remained private and therefore without consequences. By contrast, less than three years later, his public and solemn speech at the opening of the Polish diet on March 27, 1818, had a much more resonant impact. Alexander had written it himself in French, and although he had got advice from Kapodistrias, he scarcely followed it, preferring his own over the various versions prepared by his prudent diplomat. His was significantly more engaged on the political level and no doubt written after intense discussions with Novosiltsev.[53] A sign of the importance he gave this speech (pronounced in French)[54] was that he had the translation printed in several Russian newspapers in the two capitals.[55]

Representatives of the Kingdom of Poland!

Your hopes and my wishes are accomplished. The people you are called to represent finally enjoy a national existence, guaranteed by the institutions that time has ripened and sanctioned.

The most sincere forgetting of the past alone could produce your generation. It [the existence of the nation] was irrevocably decided upon in my mind, from the moment I could count on the means to realize it.

Jealous of my country's glory, my ambition was to have it gather a new distinction.

Russia after a disastrous war, by rendering good for evil according to the precepts of Christian morality, has extended its fraternal arms to you, and among the advantages that victory gave it, it has preferred one alone: the honor of lifting up and restoring a valiant and estimable nation.

And by contributing, I obeyed an internal conviction that has been powerfully seconded by events. [...]

The organization that was in vigor in your century permitted the immediate establishment of what I gave you, by putting into practice the principles of these liberal institutions that have always been the object of my solicitude, and I hope with God's help to extend their salutary influence over all the lands that Providence has entrusted to my care.

You have thus offered me the means to show my country what I have long been preparing for it, and which it will obtain, when the elements of such an important task have reached the necessary development.

Polish people! Recovering as you are from the harmful prejudices that caused you so much evil—it is up to you to consolidate our renaissance.

This is indissolubly linked to the destinies of Russia: all your effort should tend to fortifying our salutary and protective union.

Your restoration is defined by solemn treaties. It is sanctioned by the constitutional charter. The inviolability of these external commitments and this fundamental law now assure to Poland an honorable rank among the nations of Europe, a precious good it has long sought in vain amid the most cruel ordeals. [...]

The constitutional order is applied successively to all parts of the administration. The legal system is going to be organized. Drafts of civil and penal laws will be submitted to you. I am pleased to believe that in examining them with sustained attention, you will produce laws designed to guarantee the most precious benefits; the security of persons, that of your property, and the freedom of your opinions.

Despite my efforts, perhaps all the evils under which you have been groaning are not yet repaired. That is the nature of things: good is only grown slowly and perfection remains inaccessible to human weakness. [...] May God make our work prosper.[56]

In this text, Alexander publicly reaffirms his attachment to and his trust in the liberal principles that Napoleon had warped; for the first time he officially asserts his plan to extend to the whole empire what he had granted to the kingdom of Poland. Making a strong impression on Polish opinion, this speech aroused more varied reactions on the Russian side. For some skeptics a declaration of intention did not amount to action, and they wanted see what really became of it;[57] for others who were more enthusiastic—in the forefront the future Decembrists[58]—the speech announced a veritable political and social revolution; and for still others, including Karamzin, the text was dangerous. By calling implicitly for the abolition of serfdom, it could only destabilize the current political and social order in Russia. But Alexander ignored these mixed reactions because for him the real stakes were the *civilization* of the Russian Empire, as he confided in 1818 in a conversation with Borstell, a Prussian general:

> Poland is necessary to me for the civilization of my Empire, which is too vast to want to enlarge it any more. I gave it a constitution and I hope it will be worthy of this mark of confidence, *it is an attempt over which I will watch.*[59] The peace of the world and the civilization of Russia—that is my ambition, that is the purpose of my policy—and may lightning strike me if ever I fail these holy principles![60]

This desire to extend the Polish experiment for civilizing purposes can also be perceived in the status Alexander gave in April 1818 to Bessarabia, taken from the Ottoman Empire by the treaty of 1812. A large autonomy was handed over; legislative and executive powers were given to a higher council composed of five members named by the tsar and six deputies elected by the provincial nobility.[61]

In parallel, in the greatest secrecy, without the knowledge of Tsarevich Constantine, the emperor gave to Novosiltsev, the imperial commissioner in Warsaw, in June 1818 the task of preparing a comprehensive constitutional document.[62] The chancellery went to work. The poet Peter Viazemsky, who had entered the service of the state a year earlier, played a major role in writing the text, translating and adapting into Russian the political concepts borrowed from the French, with the help of the French jurist Péchard-Deschamps, secretary to Novosiltsev since 1799. In October 1819 the latter presented to Alexander (who was in Warsaw) a first draft of the constitution. But the tsar was not satisfied and allowed two more months for a new version.[63] Given the scope of the modifications demanded by the emperor and the brevity of the available time, it was an entirely new and shorter text, written in French and titled "Précis of the Constitutional Charter for the Russian Empire" that was offered to Alexander two months later. As regards the complete and final text, it was submitted to the emperor during his new stay in Warsaw in the fall of 1820; one copy was in French and the other in Russian.[64] Composed of 191 articles divided into six "titles" or headings, this work was largely inspired by the Polish charter, but also by the U.S. Constitution with respect to the federative organization of the empire.

In its preliminary provisions the constitution stressed the empire's administrative structure, now divided into major districts called lieutenancies, themselves subdivided into governments, cantons, towns, hamlets, and villages. Indivisible sovereignty resided in the person of the monarch (article 11); the crown was hereditary (article 9); article 12 defined the powers of the monarch: "The sovereign is the sole source of all powers—civil, political, legislative, and military—of the Empire. He exercises executive power in all its plenitude. Any administrative and judicial executive authority can only emanate from him." Yet article 13 provided that legislative power would be exercised "by the sovereign concurrently with the Diet of the Empire," and so his power was not absolute. The monarch did benefit from extremely extensive powers, and here we find many of the provisions contained in the Polish constitutional charter: he is the supreme head of the general administration; he watches over internal and external security; he alone has the right to declare war and to conclude treaties and conventions; he is chief of the army and appoints commanding generals and officers; he directs diplomacy and designates all ambassadors; he names all civil, administrative, and legal posts; he is the head of the Orthodox Church and names all the titles in the ecclesiastical hierarchy; finally, he has the sole right of pardon. He can adopt decrees, has the right to dissolve the chamber of deputies, but shares with the diet the responsibility for pronouncing laws. He is assisted by a Council of State (article 35) formed of ministers, advisors, and state secretaries and charged with preparing and editing all proposed laws concerned with the general administration of the empire (article 42). In each district the sovereign would be represented by a lieutenant assisted by a council (article 49). The Orthodox religion is proclaimed "the dominant religion of the state, of the sovereign, and of the imperial family," but freedom of worship is recognized; "the law protects all citizens with no distinction" (article 80), and nobody can be punished without having been informed beforehand of the crime of which he is accused, interrogated within three days of his arrest, and being judged in court (article 81); freedom of the press is guaranteed (article 89); any Russian subject has the right to live abroad and to take his fortune there (article 97). Finally, on a more purely political level, article 91 affirms that "the Russian nation will forever have a national representation" ensured by the diet. This would be formed of the sovereign and two chambers, high (senate) and low (deputies). This article is of capital importance since it is the legal basis for a representative form of government.

The general diet, convened by the sovereign (article 126) will meet every five years, and the diets of the lieutenancies every three years; so the diets are not a permanent organ, and this is the first limit on constitutionalism. But the general diet possesses wide legislative prerogatives and a right to veto proposals emanating from the emperor. The senate is composed of grand dukes and those of the imperial house aged more than 18, and of members named for life by the sovereign (article 136) who have fulfilled a number of conditions: to be aged over 35, to have passed exams for the lower grades, to benefit from a revenue in real estate of at least 1,000 rubles per year; the total number of senators should never exceed a quarter the number of deputies in the lower chamber. The deputies are to be chosen by the sovereign from among the elected of the diet of each lieutenancy, and to be elected a deputy, one has to be 30, enjoy civic rights, and pay a certain tax contribution determined by each lieutenancy according to local conditions.

At the community level, assemblies of all property owners will be held every three years in order to present to the government a "table of their needs." Jews[65] could not sit in any of these assemblies, and they could exercise no political rights (article 166). Finally, courts are to be composed of judges, some of whom are appointed by the sovereign and others are elected (article 176).

* * *

What can we conclude from this document? It concedes new rights and essential liberties, but nowhere mentions the issue of serfdom, which remains the great lacuna. It gives the monarch very wide prerogatives and makes him the exclusive depository of sovereignty. If the word "nation" does figure in the text, the idea of national sovereignty is absent. But despite these limits, it was a totally unprecedented attempt in Russia to circumscribe the absolutist power of the monarch with the establishment of an elected diet that enjoys powers of legislation; it attests to the undeniable will of the tsar to give the Russian Empire a constitutional government. However, although written under Alexander's leadership as begetter of its spirit and form, the fruit of rigorous work led by Novosiltsev and his chancellery, awaited by all those who in 1818 had seen the imperial speech given to the Warsaw diet as the promise of a peaceful political revolution, this text was never unveiled in Alexander's lifetime. It is almost by chance, thanks to Polish events in 1831, that the document was exhumed from the papers of Novosiltsev in Warsaw.

Why this decision? How can we explain what seems like a reversal?

Alexander never expressed himself on this point; and he was not likely to talk about a decision that remained secret, as had been the very preparation of a text written in Warsaw, far from St. Petersburg in order to limit the risk of indiscretion. The historian is reduced to formulating hypotheses that are buttressed by the chronology of domestic and foreign events. In 1818 the emperor still believed in the virtue of liberal ideas and of constitutionalism: the speech he gave to the Warsaw diet illustrates a sincere desire to advance along this road. But two years later, when the text was finally ready, its provisions had changed as the result of three lines of influence. First, conservatives at court (Karamzin, author of that Memoir on Ancient and Modern Russia presented to the emperor in 1811, Rostopchin, etc.) and in imperial administration had refused any evolution toward a constitutional government likely to destabilize the political and social order and weaken the empire. In 1803 Karamzin had written a monumental History of the Russian State; despite vicissitudes (in 1812 he lost his personal library in the Moscow fire), the work made him one of the most famous historians of the nineteenth century. Printed in eight volumes in 1816, the first editions sold 3,000 copies in barely a few months, and for Russia at that time, this represented a publishing success. Eight years later, in 1824, the work was finally complete and published in a dozen volumes. By the scope of its philosophical and political thinking, the fine analysis of Russian customs, the wealth of knowledge put to use, and the acuity and vivacity of the psychological portraits he drew (particularly of Ivan the Terrible and Boris Godunov), Karamzin raised history to the rank of an art, initiated Russian elites into their past, and allowed them to appropriate it with pride. But the work was also a vibrant plea for maintaining an autocratic and centralized regime, the only form of government possible, the author thought, for a country as large as Russia. In this sense, Karamzin's history weighed heavily in Alexander's gradual conversion toward conservative ideas. The second influence was that of Golitsyn and the mystics who surrounded the emperor, which we know had been growing from 1815 to 1820; for them, the ideas of the Enlightenment carried the germ of atheism, and as such they should be combated. Finally, the third influence came from outside: in 1818–1819 the international situation was marked by the rise of revolutionary movements in Europe and the ferment of destabilization in France, where the Duke de Berry was assassinated in 1820; in Germany, where Kotzebue, a writer and spy for the Russians, was killed by a student in 1819; in Portugal, in Spain, in Naples, and in Piedmont. All these movements entrained monarchs toward a conservative hardening that also had an effect on the tsar. In a symptomatic way the speech that Alexander gave in September 1820[66] to the Polish diet was quite different from the one he had given two years previously. The words "liberal" and "liberalism" no longer figure in the text, and while Alexander does not deny his constitutional effort, he insists on the need to combat the spirit of evil everywhere it arises, announcing that he will be inflexible on this point:

> I feel real satisfaction seeing myself for the second time among you; and I repeat with pleasure that in gathering you here, and calling on you to cooperate in maintaining and developing your national institutions, I am obeying an impulse of my heart, realizing one of my dearest wishes.
>
> Resulting from the confidence I placed in you, these institutions are made firmer by the confidence you place in me. […]
>
> Let us not forget that institutions are only the work of men. They need, like men, support against weakness, conscience against error, and like men they find this support, this conscience, only in Christian morality and its divine precepts.[…]
>
> Representatives of the Kingdom of Poland! Show your country that—strengthened by your experience, your principles, your sentiments—you have conserved under the auspices of your laws a calm independence and a pure freedom. […] Elsewhere, uses and abuses have been placed on the same level; *elsewhere, by exciting the factitious need for servile imitation, the genius of evil has tried to reassert his woeful empire, and already he floats over a part of Europe, already he accumulates forfeits and catastrophes.*
>
> Amid these calamities, my system of government will remain invariable. I have drawn its principles from the intimate sense of my duty. I will always fulfill this duty in good faith. Nevertheless, this good faith would not be complete if I misrecognized the great truths taught by experience.
>
> *The century in which we are living undoubtedly demands that the social order have tutelary laws as a base and guarantee. But this century imposes on governments the obligation to preserve these same laws from the fatal influence of passions, always restless, always blind.*
>
> Under this relation, a grave responsibility weighs on you, as on me. It orders you to follow faithfully the route that your wisdom and loyalty indicate. *It commands me to warn you frankly of the perils that might surround you and to*

guarantee your institutions: it requires me to judge the measures on which I will be called to pronounce, according to their real consequences and not how they are described, because party spirit either blackens or decorates them. It obliges me, in short, to prevent the birth of evil or the necessity of violent remedies, to extirpate the germs of disorganization as soon as they are perceived.[67]

These various influences all converged to make such an impact on Alexander that as of 1820 he could believe his empire in turn had been taken over by unrest and disturbances. One October night, when the tsar was absent to take part in the Congress of Troppau,[68] the Semenovsky Regiment, his preferred one, which we remember as supporting him during his accession to the throne, mutinied against a brutal colonel. There was no seditious political intent underlying this gesture of anger and even despair; it was the repeated and unjust mistreatment of his men by the colonel that was the cause. But, already shaken in his liberal convictions, the tsar became convinced that the regiment had been tainted by revolutionary propaganda. Even though a report written by Kochubey[69] gave credence to the thesis of a spontaneous revolt triggered by Colonel Schwarz's cruelty and that the incident had no link to any ideological premises, Alexander was stubbornly convinced that behind the soldiers' uprising lay something other than a desperate reaction against a cruel officer.

In Troppau Alexander told Metternich that revolutionaries had tried in his absence to destabilize the army, to weaken his authority, and to sap the foundations of the empire. Metternich was not convinced, but he, too, noticed how much the Russian emperor had changed in only a few months:

The tsar believes there is a reason why three thousand soldiers let themselves go in an act that is so unlike the national character. He goes so far as to figure that radicals did the deed in order to intimidate him and to make him come back to St. Petersburg. I am not of his opinion. It would be unlikely that in Russia radicals could already dispose of entire regiments. But this proves how much the emperor has changed.[70]

Fighting this "subversive" element, Alexander was pitiless: the mutineers each had to suffer 6,000 strokes of the rod, and those who survived were condemned to forced labor, while the regiment was entirely disbanded.

Similarly, in Poland after the great hopes born in 1815, political practice gradually toughened: the constitutional government was maintained, of course, but the powers with which the diet was theoretically endowed were not put into effect. Gradually, it started to function as a consultative body rather than a representative one: between 1815 and 1830, it was not authorized to debate the state budget. Bitterly, Adam Czartoryski, himself distanced from any real responsibility by the tsar—he was reduced to the rank of curator of the University of Vilnius—witnessed this hardening of the line.

Thus within five years the political hopes born in 1815 had evaporated. There was no question of giving the empire a constitutional government. The outlined reform campaign had been aborted. However, in this period not everything was in vain: on the periphery of the empire, reforms were underway on the agrarian question. But the benefits that could have resulted were not sufficient to counterbalance the utopia of the new military colonies that became a disastrous dystopia.

* * *

From the start of his reign, Alexander had a plan to put an end to the moral, religious, and social scandal of serfdom, as well as to its ineffectiveness on the economic level. This plan was accentuated by the war of 1812. The enormous human and material losses suffered in the countryside during the patriotic war and the courage displayed by peasants in the time of conflict called in effect for a strong gesture in exchange for their sacrifices. The tsar discussed this plan with several interlocutors. But unlike the political question that was the object of public declarations, this more sensitive terrain required acting with much discretion. When the emperor consented in 1816–1817 that freedom should be given to peasants in the Baltic provinces, it was in the shadows that he resumed reflection about the abolition of serfdom and the means to bring it about, while he was starting work on the first military colonies.

The reform of the peasantry in the Baltic provinces took effect from 1816 to 1819. It began in June 1816 with an imperial ukase that gave personal freedom to Estonian peasants, a decision requested by the local nobility, who had rallied to the example given by Prussia in 1807 and was convinced that serfdom was economic nonsense and that tax revenue would benefit from including free peasants. However, land ownership was not granted to the latter; and for many peasants, that individual freedom, while fundamental on a social and political level (it would be the source of deep changes that appeared over the decades and fostered the emergence of nationalist feelings within the peasantry),[71] did not, economically speaking, make any concrete improvement in their living conditions. A year later Alexander tried to enlarge this reform to Ukraine and other Baltic provinces. It failed in Ukraine for in fertile regions requiring manpower landowners were opposed to any change. But the nobility of Latvia and Livonia did support the proposal, and in these regions serfdom was abolished in 1817 and 1819, to the great satisfaction of Alexander, who publicly declared, "I am glad that the nobility has justified my expectations. Your example is worthy of being emulated. You have acted in the spirit of the times and understand that only liberal principles can be the basis of the people's happiness."[72] In parallel, as early as 1816 the emperor asked Kochubey to work on a general reform of serfdom; but the latter's conclusions, handed over in 1817, strongly disappointed the tsar's expectations.[73] The peasant condition was described accurately, but no concrete procedure was envisaged to relieve it. Alexander did not give up his plan, however, and a few months later he ordered 12 senior civil servants (among them Count Guriev, minister of finance, Admiral Mordvinov from the state council, Balugiansky, rector of the University of St. Petersburg, and more surprisingly, Arakcheev) to each draft a plan to liberate the serfs of Russia. Most of the plans advocated the principle of gradual emancipation of the serfs, which would be achieved with a compensation for owners; for example, in February 1818 Arakcheev proposed creating a commission that would have an annual subsidy of five million rubles to buy, partially or totally, the goods and serfs of owners who were ready to sell. By means of this commission, the government would adopt the premise of a buyback founded on the free decision by owners; here we find again an idea to which Alexander was very attached, i.e., reform based on voluntary action. Finally, Balugiansky's plan intended that peasants with state support should become owners of only a portion of the lands of the nobility.

The years from 1816 to 1819 were thus effervescent ones, in which the issue of abolition of serfdom was examined in a resolute way at the summit of the state. But these various projects led to nothing concrete: Alexander still maintained that reform should not be imposed on owners but rather negotiated with them and implemented with their agreement. But the vast majority of the nobility, impoverished by the destruction caused by the war of 1812, was incapable of consenting; even more than in 1801, it remained viscerally attached to the current socioeconomic order—and made this known when the first rumors of reform started to spread. It was this bitter realization that led Alexander to give up experimenting with these various projects and gradually to give priority to the organization of military colonies.

* * *

After the war the Russian army was numerically very reduced, and the state budget was considerably more meager—it seemed barely able to support its regiments. At the same time the tsar (who had rendered homage to his troops in his August 1814 ukase) wanted to shorten the duration of service (25 years at the time) by giving soldiers the prospect of a return to normal life. But how could this goal be achieved with the diminished financial means?

A plan for military colonies had appeared back in 1809–1810, but the war had interrupted any development, and by 1812 only one single colony had been established, located between Smolensk and Minsk. In the army's context of penury, the idea was reactivated in 1816 and would become the object of the tsar's attention, even obsession. Several influences were at work in this fascination. First, the more or less conscious model was the familiar example of the Cossacks of the Ukraine, who as peasant soldiers had been integrated into the empire in the seventeenth century. Then there was the tsar's reading of writings by the French General Servan, in particular a small work called Citizen Soldier, or Patriotic Views on the Best Way of Providing Defense of the Realm[74] that developed the idea of a "farmer-soldier." To support the costly maintenance of armies in peacetime, Servan said, soldiers had to be turned into farmers by combining work on the land with military training. Working the land would allow them to become self-sufficient—and no longer a drain on the state budget; once their years of service were over, older soldiers would receive bits of land and thus become landowners who could transmit their skills to their successors. This utopia had everything to seduce the tsar: in the short term it offered a solution to the cost of maintaining an army, and in the long term it proclaimed the generous goal of enabling veterans to provide for themselves. In the Russian context, this latter point assumed particular resonance: by giving bits of land to farmer-soldiers, the state would gradually transform into free and landowning peasants those who as serfs had enrolled in the army against their will. This avenue interested Alexander because it would contribute to liberating the serfs over time.

On top of this theoretical influence came the practical example provided by the Prussian General Scharnhorst. In order to overcome restrictions imposed on the Prussian army by the Treaty of Tilsit, he had established the Landwehr, a reserve army in disguise. Every soldier had to serve three years actively, and after that he became a farmer, while remaining subject to military obligations, which were heavy for five years and then lighter for seven more. Finally, a fourth source of inspiration was the military colonies set up in Austria that Alexander had visited in 1814 during his trip to Vienna. Fascinated by this mode of organization, in January 1815 he asked Arakcheev to develop a plan for military colonies. At first the latter was skeptical because he thought peasants were resistant to any change and would be hostile to the new system; he also stressed the need to offer guarantees to the military colonists, specifically the full ownership of their land and their homes, exemption from all taxes, and free education for their children guaranteed by the state.[75] Moreover, Barclay de Tolly in a memorandum dated 1817 thought such a system was inefficient for the army since the peasants would not be free to organize their working time as they should be to obtain maximum efficiency; moreover, soldiers in contact with villagers would be incapable of offering them effective help and would soon be considered parasites.[76] Alas, the tsar ignored the reservations of his war minister, and in August 1816 a thousand grenadiers taken from a regiment of Arakcheev were transferred to the Vysotsk district in the province of Novgorod to become the first military colony. In the requisitioned villages peasants were to divide their time between the farm work necessary to support their families and the military duties that they would practice alongside regimental soldiers settled there, at a rate of three days a week in winter and two in summer. Under the personal control of Arakcheev, who created a separate corps for military colonies, everything was codified to the smallest detail, from the dimensions and geometric arrangement of shops, depots, sawmills, flour mills, and the houses of colonists to the operation and furnishing of hospitals, nurseries, and schools, right down to everybody's use of time, programmed almost hour by hour. Everything in this utopia was subject to precise regulation, governed by the state. Cleanliness and hygiene were at the fore, and peasants were summoned to rise at four in the morning to work on the land before going to military exercises; after 1817 they even had a uniform to wear while working in the fields. In the months following this first experiment, the system of military colonies was extended to other provinces, and gradually almost 400,000 men were involved, or a third of the ranks of the Russian army. Everywhere the same scenario was produced: the establishment of any regiment in the district transformed all the peasants of the district into soldiers divided into companies, battalions, and squadrons; they formed reserve units that were supposed to work concurrently in the fields and devote themselves to military exercises. On the accounting level the military colonies were a great success: well administered and managed, by 1824 they had amassed a capital of 26 million rubles and were able to grant loans at low rates of interest to their officers;[77] this flourishing state contrasted with the army's deficit in 1815. But on the human level things were quite otherwise. The pernickety regulations made the life of the peasants, who were deprived of any privacy, almost unbearable. Marriages were imposed: at the age of seven, sons were enrolled in the battalions of road builders, where they remained until the age of 12, before working on the land until 18. As adults, they were in turn integrated into the regiment of their district—for service lasting 25 years! The modern and progressive institution of which Alexander had dreamed in order to relieve peasant conditions thus evolved into a terrible coercive institution that was hated by the people. Starting in 1817 desertions and complaints multiplied. Charlotte, the young wife of Grand Duke Nicholas, would later write in her memoirs:

> They talked a lot about the military colonies set up a year before. The emperor had the idea, but the execution was entrusted to Arakcheev, who did not do it gently but on the contrary with hard and cruel measures that made the poor peasants discontented. Going about, we found here and there the residents of some villages on their knees, imploring us that their traditional way of life not be changed.[78]

Two years later, in 1820, in a report sent to the French minister of foreign affairs, the Count de la Ferronnays, ambassador in St. Petersburg, was very severe about the military colony system, attacking the person he (wrongly) considered as the instigator in this affair—for Arakcheev was merely the overly zealous executor of Alexander's wishes:

> Full of haughtiness and pride toward everybody, treacherous and bilious, a despot by character, hard and false, with no regard for his subordinates, he is hated by all; the universal sentiment can only be held in check by the fear he inspires—such is the portrait of the author of the military colonizations. This plan itself bears the imprint of the despotic character of the person who conceived the idea.[79]

Highly unpopular both among the peasantry and in the army, the military colonies soon aroused unrest and revolts in the Ukrainian province of Sloboba in 1818 and in Chuguyev in southern Russia a year later. But Alexander, like Arakcheev, remained deaf to this manifest disaster. Uprisings were punished with unprecedented cruelty. In August 1819, after the rebellion in Chuguyev in which almost 28,000 peasants rose to demand the abolition of the colonies, a military tribunal made 2,003 arrests and condemned 363 people, including 275 to the death penalty.[80] These executions were commuted by the "magnanimity" of Arakcheev, but the 12,000 strokes in the gauntlet caused frightful suffering and killed 160 of those condemned. However, Alexander did not criticize this cruelty, so important was it to him that the enterprise be successful, whatever the human cost. In 1819 this terrible repression sounded the death knell of the aspirations and confidence of the people in their tsar. By this date his image was no longer that of a "blessed" emperor, but already like Paul I, that of a cruel and stubborn despot.

CHAPTER 14

Russian Diplomacy in the "European System"

1815–1825

In 1815 Alexander had been the indisputable vanquisher of Napoleon, and he aspired to a renovation of international relations. He thought if they were entrusted to divine Providence, they would bring forth fraternity and bestow upon the European continent a kind of development that would be harmonious and peaceful. As an idealist the tsar advocated a philosophy of history that made the various states and peoples of Europe the children of one single Christian family: he enjoined them to work for peace and solidarity in the name of divine commandment. Thus, beyond the strictly religious message he delivered, the tsar invited the European sovereigns in 1815 to radically new diplomatic practice, founded on law and morality. However, in barely a few years these aspirations collapsed and initial hopes evaporated. While the European theater was no longer the sole focus for Russian diplomacy and other horizons were appearing, the tsar's initial goal of erecting a Christian fraternity as a principle of government was undermined by the skepticism of other members of the European system. Little by little, the Holy Alliance was instead transmuted into an instrument of repression.

Toward an Enlargement of the Russian Diplomatic Sphere

While Alexander's personal participation in the Congress of Vienna illustrated the crucial importance of European issues in Russian diplomacy in 1814–1815, this predominance tended to give way in the following decade. Of course it was not challenged—Europe remained the main object of

Russian diplomatic preoccupations—but other centers of interest appeared, leading to organizational changes in the diplomatic apparatus.

The campaigns of 1813–1814, which had been disapproved of by Chancellor Rumyantsev (for reasons similar to those of Rostopchin and Kutuzov), put an end to the career of the minister of foreign affairs. For Rumyantsev, the interests of Russia did not mean pursuing any offensive beyond the imperial borders and the country should now return to its domestic concerns, should exploit the recently annexed territories, and should privilege its diplomatic relations with immediate neighbors: the Ottoman Empire, Persia, China. But in those years the tsar was focused on his dream of a European renovation and did not pay attention to this argument; he relieved Rumyantsev of his functions in August 1814 and replaced him with Count Nesselrode, already secretary of state at foreign affairs, who was promoted to full minister of foreign affairs in August 1816. He was assisted by Kapodistrias as secretary of state. The two men divided up the tasks: Nesselrode took the lead in Russian general diplomacy and European questions, while Kapodistrias was responsible for relations with the Ottoman Empire and the integration of Bessarabia into the empire. They each had a chancellery, and twice a week they made a joint report to the emperor. But in 1822 Kapodistrias would resign and Nesselrode would be sole master of foreign affairs.

May 1816 saw the creation of an "Asiatic department" on the site of the "college" founded by Paul I. Now directed by Constantine Rodofinikin, a specialist who would occupy the post until 1837, the department had two sections: one to deal with Ottoman, Persian, and Georgian affairs and relations with the mountain peoples of the north Caucasus, and the other to deal with the khanates of Khiva, Kokand, and Bukhara. Of modest size—about ten people worked there at most—the Asiatic department attests to the imperial will to know the Orient better and to increase the Russian presence there. This same goal motivated the foundation in 1820 of the Asiatic Committee, which included people from various ministries (finance, interior), the military chief of staff, and (after 1821) the new governor-general of Siberia, Mikhail Speransky, now back in favor. This Asiatic Committee was supposed to consider means of developing the Russian Empire's political and commercial relations with khanates of Khiva and Bukhara and the countries of the Far East, principally China. In June 1823 the Asiatic department created a section for teaching Oriental languages, designed to train future diplomats for the Ottoman Empire and Persia. To organize this school, the empire called on two well-known French Orientalists, Jean-François Demange and François Charmois, who began to teach six future diplomats the Turkish, Arabic, and Persian languages.

These institutional changes reflected a growing interest in the Caucasus and Central Asia, whether as strategic zones recently integrated into the Russian Empire or as regions situated on its immediate periphery.

Indeed, in the wake of the conquests between 1801 and 1804,[1] then of the wars conducted against the Ottoman Empire and Persia, the Russian Empire had consolidated its military and diplomatic presence in the Caucasus. By the Treaty of Bucharest with the Ottoman Empire in May 1812, Russia had annexed Georgia and also acquired Bessarabia, a region of 50,000 square kilometers (today Moldavia), predominantly populated by Rumanian speakers of Orthodox tradition, plus a minority of Christian Orthodox Turks. Finally, that same treaty confirmed previously acquired Russian rights over the Danube principalities of Moldavia and Walachia dating from 1774. This point is crucial: by giving Russia a specific right over Christian peoples of the Ottoman Empire, the treaty conferred on the Russian Empire a privilege that it shared with no other great power on the European continent. To better assure continuity of foreign policy toward the Ottoman Empire, the tsar counted on the stability of his personnel, and in fact, ambassadors there succeeded each other less often than in other capitals. In 24 years only two men directed the embassy in Istanbul: Andrey Italinsky (1801–1816), a doctor in medicine from the University of London, who entered a diplomatic career by chance and became a connoisseur of Ottoman domestic and foreign issues. He was succeeded by Gregory Stroganov, cousin of Paul Stroganov, who was a diplomat by training and had been a brilliant ambassador in Spain (1805–1810) and then in Sweden (1812–1816), where he played an important role as intermediary between Alexander and Bernadotte. In 1816 his talents and experience naturally raised him to succeed Italinsky.

In parallel, the Treaty of Gulistan with Persia (1813) confirmed Russian advances in the Caucasus; Persia recognized the annexation of Georgia, as well as the Russian takeover of Dagestan and the north of Azerbaijan, including several key towns such as Baku and Derbent. So the treaty effectively ended Persian influence over the region to the benefit of Russia. Moreover, there was a clear military dimension in Russian expansion. Named commander in chief of the Russian armies of the Caucasus and Georgia in 1816, General Ermolov was placed at the head of 50,000 well-armed men and led punitive expeditions against the northern Caucasian peoples who refused subjection to the Russian Empire and thus formed a pocket of resistance inside Russia. He erected several fortified bases—the most important was Grozny in 1818—and annexed the region of Sirvan[2] in 1820 and then Karabagh in 1822. Ermolov also held diplomatic roles:

in 1817 he was promoted to ambassador extraordinaire to the court of the Shah, charged with obtaining the agreement of Fath Ali Shah for the establishment of Russian consulates in frontier towns and winning him over into an alliance against the Ottoman Empire. He failed in both these missions, however.

The final decade of Alexander's reign was also marked by a significant growth in trade between the Russian Empire and the khanates of Central Asia; it was from there that Russia imported most of the silk and cotton it needed, exporting in return fabrics, sugar, tobacco, and metallurgic products. In parallel, efforts were made to try to stabilize political relations, which had suffered from the mutual absence of permanent representatives. But due to the distrust among the khans, contact remained irregular. Expeditions of exploration that were both political and military, and were launched with the tsar's support, had mixed results: in 1819–1820, Admiral Mordvinov gave Captain Muravyov the mission to prepare the installation of a Russian fortress on the eastern bank of the Caspian Sea and to develop trade with Khiva,[3] but contact with the khan resulted in nothing concrete. Three years later, Alexander sent from Orenburg to Bukhara a new diplomatic mission conducted by Negri: he had to obtain guarantees about the security of Russian trade caravans transiting through Bukhara, as well as an agreement to open a consulate there. But again, these first contacts petered out. Meanwhile, in the wake of the first attempts made by Catherine II, Russian diplomacy turned to China, trying to establish good neighbor relations that would enable Russian merchants to secure favorable conditions in the Chinese market and to gain access to resources and raw materials from that empire. This rapprochement proved very difficult: in October 1805 an embassy led by Senator Count Golovkin reached the Chinese border in Mongolia, where it was abruptly halted. Golovkin was obliged to abandon part of his escort—to which he agreed—in order to pursue his mission. In January 1806 he reached Urga,[4] where during a banquet given in his honor, the local authorities required him to submit to a religious ceremonial to the glory of the Son of Heaven. But because he refused to perform ten genuflections that he considered humiliating to his own emperor, he was forced to turn around and go back to St. Petersburg empty-handed.[5] Alexander approved of the ambassador's conduct, but he also drew a lesson from it: relations with China were by nature complex, due to the opposition between two quite different cultural systems of representations, and they required more professionalism and better mutual understanding—hence the creation of the Asiatic department. But the effects of this initiative on Russo-Chinese relations would be felt much later, in the 1830s–1840s. Lastly, Russian diplomacy in the last decade of Alexander's reign was also interested in the Pacific zone, where it soon ran into American interests.

It was during the period of alliance with France that the Russian Empire, while pursuing its policy of strategic expansion in the Pacific, got a foothold on the Californian coast. In 1812 Baranov, governor of the Kodiak Islands,[6] was behind an expedition that led to the construction of a small fort[7] 150 km north of San Francisco. For the Russians it was a matter of countering Spanish presence in a region considered strategic, which might become a "reservoir" able to supply vegetables and meat to Russian compatriots of the Pacific, those of Alaska principally. Thus, as early as the end of the 1810s, 300 Russians, Aleuts, and Californian Indians developed agricultural practices and hunted seals and sea lions, sending their products toward the Russian forward post on the island of Sitka, south of Alaska. But the dynamism of the Russian presence in these lands caused hostile reactions from both Spanish and American governments. In 1821 a ukase that extended Russian sovereignty to the south, to the fifty-first parallel, and forbade commerce with any ship other than Russian, caused a diplomatic crisis with the United States. In February 1822 a note from Secretary of State John Quincy Adams stated that "we should contest the right of Russia to any territorial establishment on this continent, and that we should assume distinctly the principle that the American continents are no longer subjects for any new European colonial establishments."[8] This note is the first formulation of the document to be adopted in December 1823 by President James Monroe and known thereafter as the "Monroe Doctrine." Henceforth the American continent could no longer be considered as a territory of colonization for European powers. In return, the United States would not interfere in European affairs. In this tense context the rivalry between Russia and America ended in a compromise. In April 1824 a bilateral treaty allowed the Americans to contain Russian expansionism to 54 degrees 40 minutes latitude north, in exchange for exclusive rights granted to Russian ships. As regards the Mexican government, its concern to counter the Russian installation in the area led it to support an intense activity of religious proselytism that resulted in the founding of Catholic missions, including that of Sonoma in 1823.

As these various directions of foreign activity attest, an expansion of spheres of presence and influence was witnessed in the aftermath of the Napoleonic Wars. Now the Russian Empire asserted its Euro-Asian duality and a new interest in America. However, this looking elsewhere should not make us forget the predominant weight of European issues.

Beginnings of a "Vienna System"

Once the final text of the Congress of Vienna was signed in 1815, Russian diplomats were forced to accept amendments demanded by Metternich, but they still wanted to believe in the Holy Alliance as a global framework likely to foster a lasting peace in Europe. However, Russia had to deal with the views of other signatory nations, as well as with Britain, which supported the Holy Alliance but had refused to sign it. Consequently Russian diplomacy constantly oscillated between idealism and pragmatism.

After the Congress, Russian diplomacy appeared at its zenith. Apart from Alexander's personal prestige, there was dynamism in the institution itself. The Russian Empire had "extraordinary" ambassadors with full powers in Paris and London, plenipotentiary ministers in Vienna, Berlin, Stockholm, Copenhagen, Dresden, Munich, Karlsruhe, Frankfurt, Rome, Madrid, Philadelphia, and Istanbul, plus ministers residing in Hamburg and Krakow, and chargés d'affaires in The Hague, Stuttgart, Florence, Bern, Lisbon, and Teheran. Thus, this active diplomacy benefited from a close network of representation in the known world.

But this influence, combined with the geopolitical power acquired by the Russian Empire during the negotiations in 1814–1815, ultimately aroused the distrust of other European governments, and sharp tension with Britain particularly, which became patent in the autumn of 1815. Along with the negotiation of the second treaty of Paris, Lord Castlereagh suggested the formation of a Quadruple Alliance that, in the event of a return of a Bonaparte to the French throne or of a new challenge to the French borders legalized in Vienna and Paris, would call for joint military action. He also suggested frequent meetings among sovereigns (or their representatives) in order to ensure the Alliance's smooth functioning. Here Castlereagh was somewhat the precursor of the summit conference; he saw such meetings as favorable for maintaining collective peace and security.[9] However, Castlereagh's Quadruple Alliance was not supposed either to constrain British diplomacy (many Britons aspired to a return to traditional isolationism) or to be prejudicial to its interests. Thus in October–November, throughout negotiations that autumn, British diplomats insisted that the prime function of the Quadruple Alliance was to keep France apart, while at the same time the Holy Alliance, conceived as an alliance of Christian thrones, intended to integrate France into the ranks of other nations. During the negotiations Alexander proposed that the new agreement should not take an anti-French line but should extend to other themes: the four powers would reciprocally guarantee all their possessions, they would mutually agree on oversight of the domestic affairs of member states, and they would have the right to intervene collectively against any revolutionary movement likely to destabilize the equilibrium obtained at the Congress of Vienna; finally, in order to coordinate their diplomatic positions, they would hold regular international conferences. But Castlereagh objected: while he was favorable to maintaining international security and to the concept of a balance of power,[10] he was also viscerally hostile to the idea of any intervention aiming to consolidate authoritarian monarchical regimes, as well as to any general pact to guarantee borders, both of which he knew would be rejected by the British Parliament. Consequently, Alexander's project was set aside, and instead, on November 20, 1815, they signed a Quadruple Alliance that was given an administrative body—a conference of ambassadors in Paris that would be a diplomatic and military instrument potentially directed against France. The four powers declared that they had formed "a permanent league" designed to ensure respect for the second treaty of Paris; they reaffirmed that Napoleon and the members of his family were forever excluded from the French throne and agreed that in the event that "revolutionary principles" again "split France" and threatened "the repose of other states," they would "cooperate with each other and with His Very Christian Majesty"[11] to "adopt measures they judged necessary for the security of their respective states and for the general tranquility of Europe."[12] The only concession to Alexander's plan—but one that also featured in Castlereagh's—was the idea of summit meetings to promote "European cooperation" founded on collective action, not purely bilateral actions. Seen from St. Petersburg, this concession was quite minor so the content of the treaty of November 1815 disappointed the tsar a great deal.

Meanwhile, more or less explicit subjects of tension appeared among the coalition powers. The Russians deplored the role played by the Austrians in German and Balkan matters, while the Bucharest treaty and Alexander's propensity to pose as a champion of the interests of the Christian peoples in the Ottoman Empire irritated the cabinet of St. James. And rivalries were not limited to the European sphere: Britons and Russians were both interested in Central Asia and Afghanistan, upon which they had identical aims.

In the months following the signature of the second Paris treaty, these disagreements among allies persisted. Views continued to diverge over the crucial issue of relations with France: for Alexander it was still imperative to develop good relations with Paris as guarantee of a counterweight to Vienna and London, and he constantly supported France's aspiration to resume its role as a great European power. In 1816 he insisted to the Count of Noailles (the French ambassador to Russia) on the need for a solid entente between

France and Russia "to guarantee the peace of Europe."[13] On the contrary, London (out of principle) and Vienna (to have a free hand in Italy) continued to want France kept apart from the rest of Europe.

The allies also diverged on France's political evolution. While Chancellor Metternich was supporting the ultraroyalists, advocating the revival of an absolute monarchy, Alexander I and his diplomats supported the Duke of Richelieu in his desire to safeguard the constitutional charter and to liberate the country as soon as possible from foreign occupation.

Finally, desiring to proceed to the renovation of the European system, its security in particular, the tsar sent a letter to Lord Castlereagh in April 1816 proposing that Great Britain, and through her the other members of the Quadruple Alliance (whom he thought would take the British line), make a "reduction in armed forces of any kind whose maintenance on war footing attenuates the credibility of existing treaties and can only be onerous to all peoples."[14] He saw this measure as a pledge of collective security, and he justified its importance:

> But this proof of mutual trust[15] and of perfect conformity in political views will still leave much to be desired if it is not followed by more effective and general measures to guarantee the durability of the new order of things and to encourage all peaceful nations to engage in it without fear for their complete security. This convincing and decisive measure would consist in the simultaneous reduction of armed forces of all kinds, which the powers would adopt for the salvation and independence of their peoples.
>
> If until now I have not proposed disarmament or executed it in my states, this is because the same motives that seem to dictate this measure, impose on sovereigns the duty to maturely consider all the circumstances and results in order to make its execution really salutary.[16]

For the first time in European history, there was a proposal to move to multilateral disarmament that would relieve nations of the cost of a defense rendered useless by the treaties of 1815. With this unprecedented proposal the tsar allied idealism and pragmatism: devastated when the war ended, Russia aspired to reduce the volume of its troops. Yet his idea remained no less strong and original—even if British diplomats continued to be deaf to it.

At the end of 1817 and the beginning of 1818, Russian diplomatic advances were still very modest, but the tsar remained attached to two major ideas: first, to resolve the fate of France quickly by liberating the troops occupying it, by giving it back its status as a grand power and integrating it into a Quintuple Alliance that would replace the Quadruple Alliance and offer

Russia the best guarantees of a balance of power; second, to advance the establishment of a European system of security founded on the principles of the Holy Alliance that he was trying to promote "not for me, not for Russia, but in the interest of the whole world."[17]

In July 1818, on the eve of the Congress of Aachen, Kapodistrias prepared for Alexander a report on the forthcoming meeting.[18] In this analytical text the diplomat recalled first that England and Austria were aiming to isolate Russia within the Quadruple Alliance and that other allies would have to be found. Then, according to a scheme given by Alexander, he developed the idea of a pan-European league that would respect the principles of the Holy Alliance, would integrate France, and would guarantee the peace of Europe by concrete measures. It would ensure the defense of small European states—including the German ones—against the appetites of the large ones and guarantee borders and political regimes, which would become as much as possible founded on constitutional monarchies. This last point should be stressed: in 1818, for both Kapodistrias and the tsar, the Holy Alliance was perceived as useful for security and for obtaining a balance of power in Europe—they did not yet perceive it as a weapon to be systematically turned against liberal ideas. But in both London and Vienna these plans were perceived as unacceptable. In August 1818, a few days before the opening of the Aachen Congress, an exasperated Metternich complained to Emperor Franz of the "moral and political proselytism of the terrible Emperor Alexander,"[19] and he would prove an implacable adversary to most of the ideas that Alexander advanced. As regards Castlereagh, in a memorandum dated October 19 he rejected the Holy Alliance principles being incorporated into "the ordinary diplomatic obligations that link state to state"[20] and virulently attacked the imperial project, arguing that "sustaining the state of succession, of government, and of possession in all other states against all violence or attack"[21] would amount to a supranational government that he absolutely rejected.

The Aachen Congress met from September 29 to November 21, 1818, gathering together representatives of the members of the Holy Alliance and of France: the three sovereigns (Alexander I, Franz I, and Frederick Wilhelm III) and their ministers (Metternich, Castlereagh, Nesselrode, and Kapodistrias), plus the Duke of Richelieu (the French prime minister) and the Duke of Wellington, commander of the allied occupation troops. The Congress held 47 plenary sessions, alternating working sessions and social receptions, in an atmosphere that was not always serene, so much did personalities and interests diverge. In one of his letters to the Countess of Lieven, Metternich admitted his relationship with Alexander:

There are not two more essentially different persons in the world than he and I. So in relations over thirteen years, we have had, as perhaps never before with two individuals placed as we are in direct and sustained contact, many highs and lows.[22]

Laborious and often strained, the work resulted in compromises both on the issue of how to treat France and on Alexander's proposals. On October 9 a convention was signed that set the date of November 30 for the departure of the occupation troops—upon payment of a contribution of 260 million francs. Due to Russian insistence, France was finally reintegrated into the European concert on November 18, which de facto transformed the Quadruple Alliance into the Quintuple Alliance. But the Russian plan for a pan-European union was blocked by intransigent opposition from both Castlereagh and Metternich. For the latter, Austria could not support (in writing) the least evolution toward constitutionalism; while Castlereagh did not want Great Britain to find itself forced to intervene—or to approve of intervention by the hypothetical league—in the domestic affairs of any European state. In this context it was a compromise document that was ultimately signed by the four countries on October 19; the obligations agreed in November 1815 when the Quadruple Alliance was founded were renewed but were only applicable in the event of war against France—in other words, they could not serve as the basis for any peaceful and lasting relations that should be established with a country now considered as a "member of the European system." This final point is important: torn by Russia from England and Austria, the agreement put an end to France's pariah status; to Alexander's great satisfaction, it opened the way to a normalization of relations between France and its former enemies. Moreover, the text stressed that the five powers "do not wish—and will not be able—to decide questions touching the interests of other states without a request from the affected countries,"[23] which implicitly sheltered France from any hostile and concerted action.

While Alexander had largely won on the French question, his project for a pan-European league did not see the light of day; the tsar's insistence on the need for allies to commit to precise obligations in order to guarantee the European order—that "the principle of the general coalition should be established and developed by rules"[24]—ran up against opposition from the other participants. A small consolation was offered: the protocol of the final declaration adopted at Aachen mentioned that "sovereigns recognize solemnly that their duties to God and toward the peoples they govern oblige them to give the world insofar as possible an example of justice, harmony, and moderation." The text stressed the monarchs' attachment to peace and domestic prosperity—another notion directly borrowed from the Holy Alliance. But Alexander was not duped by this symbolic mention; he remained extremely disappointed by the cautiousness of the coalition powers about his pan-European union plan.

The second problem tackled at the Aachen Congress concerned the question of potential European mediation in the conflict between Spain and its rebellious Latin American colonies. For Great Britain, persuaded that the Russian proposals merely camouflaged ambitions that could hurt its naval and commercial interests,[25] there was no question of exercising any pressure on the insurgents for mediation. On the contrary, Russian and French diplomacy were in solidarity with the Spanish Bourbons and considered that the conflict imperiled the existence of Spain, and so mediation was desirable. In November the Duke of Richelieu and Kapodistrias jointly proposed that negotiations, placed under Wellington's direction, in which the United States would participate, would be held in Madrid between the Spanish authorities and representatives of the rebelling colonies. In case of failure, commercial reprisals might be applied against them. But the British, Austrians, and Prussians refused this project and so the plan was abandoned. The result was another compromise: a declaration in favor of moral support for Spain was adopted, but the mediation of Wellington was postponed. Still, although it had no outcome, the Russian proposal has to be stressed: it attested to Alexander's growing political inflection to the right: in a conflict opposing a conservative regime and its colonies struggling for emancipation and liberalism, he officially took the part of the conservative state.

Finally, the issue of the treatment of slaves was also tackled at the Aachen Congress. And here the Russian and British positions were similar: both were favorable to the interdiction of the trade. But the other participants were hesitant, and no decision was taken.

* * *

Coming out of the congress, what had Russian diplomacy achieved? In a note to the tsar at the end of December 1818,[26] Kapodistrias offered an interesting analysis. Of course he was glad that all the participants had declared themselves concerned for European peace, but he stressed that at the same time each delegation remained attached to its own interests and that no collective vision had been proposed on which to build a peace. To him, England still remained the strongest and most resolute adversary of the Russian Empire, still desirous of playing a key role in Europe, while conserving its maritime hegemony. He also deplored the Austrian propensity to arrogate preeminence in German affairs and called on the imperial state to get closer to France and Spain to seek a counterweight.[27] This tells us that at the end of 1818 there was no longer any possibility of a harmonious entente among the former allies; the distrust that had arisen since 1813–1814 had quickly resurged. Still, despite his disillusion, Alexander in a voluntarist approach wanted to safeguard the spirit of the Holy Alliance; while he was still at the Aachen Congress, he wrote to Count Lieven, his ambassador to London, to say that "the results achieved by the Congress characterize the second period of the great political era that began from the moment when sovereigns became brothers for the cause of religion and good order, of justice and humanity."[28] In a meeting with the British Quaker Thomas Clarkson, he asserted his optimism, saying he was "sure that the spirit of Christianity is categorically peaceful." Two years later it was in the same pacifist and European spirit that he went to the Troppau Congress in 1820. But in the interval the international context and the tsar had both changed. In barely a few months, the Holy Alliance had become the favorite tool of a conservative European diplomacy.

The Holy Alliance as an Instrument of Conservatism

In the wake of the Congresses of Vienna and Aachen, those of Troppau in 1820, Laibach (Silesia) in 1821, and Verona in 1822 undoubtedly did secure the European accord born in 1815, while fostering among elites the emergence of a shared feeling of European belonging. But in an international context increasingly troubled by the nationalist and liberal aspirations that extended across Europe, Alexander's fraternal dream was rapidly being put into the service of the established order. Starting in 1819–1820, fearing that the contagion might reach "his" Poland, Tsar Alexander became convinced (to the point of obsession) that liberalism was merely an instrument of political destabilization and that the revolutions that were bursting out in various parts of Europe were the fruit of a global scheme run by secret societies that were closely linked to each other. In February 1821 he sent Alexander Golitsyn a long letter (written over the course of a week[29]) that attests to his preoccupations, both spiritual and political. For him, Europe was threatened by an anti-Christian revolutionary plague that had to be fought at all costs. The style of the letter, which astonishingly mixes geopolitical considerations and mystical passages, tells us much about Alexander's political and psychological evolution. He begins by attacking the "disorganizing principles that in less than six months have revolutionized three countries and threaten to extend to Europe as a whole," those principles that though "enemies of thrones, are directed even more against the Christian religion," and stressing that these principles are "targeting Christianity—thousands of authentic documents can be produced to show you. In a word, this is just putting into practice the doctrines preached by Voltaire, Mirabeau, Condorcet, and all those self-styled philosophers known under the name of Encyclopedists." The tsar drove the point home:

> I would say that the current evil is of an even more dangerous kind than was the devastating despotism of Napoleon, since the current doctrines are much more seductive for the multitude than the military yoke under which he held them.[30]

The danger seemed to him even greater because he saw these nationalist and revolutionary movements as part of a general conspiracy orchestrated against God:

> Have no illusions: there is a general conspiracy among all these societies; they confer and communicate with each other, and I have irrefutable proof in my hands. [...] All these sects are anti-Christian and are founded on the principles of the so-called philosophy of Voltaire and the like; they have sworn the fiercest vengeance upon all governments. We have seen some attempts in France, England, and Prussia, while in Spain, Naples, and Portugal they have already succeeded in toppling governments. But what they are really pursuing is less the governments than the religion of the Savior. Their motto is "Kill the Inf..."—I cannot even quote this horrible blasphemy, well known in the writings of Voltaire, Mirabeau, Condorcet, and suchlike.[31]

Guided by this extreme view verging on paranoia, imperial diplomats were now shifting toward increasingly conservative positions, where mysticism mingled with realpolitik.

✳ ✳ ✳

At Troppau and the following congresses there were no more festivities; the tsar proved increasingly solitary in his exercise of power. In December 1820 he wrote in a characteristic way to Alexander Golitsyn: "I live in complete retreat. My sister is the only distraction that I have, at dinner or when we have the possibility of going out to take the air together."[32]

In fact, in the small town of Troppau in Bohemia,[33] he was content to share moments of freedom with his young sister Maria and his brother Nicholas, who was attending an international conference for the first time. From now on, there were no more liberal reveries but, on the contrary, thoughts of defending the established order and its values. However, if the tsar gradually came around to Chancellor Metternich's arguments that the European entente should above all serve to maintain the existing order, he did keep some moderation due to the continuing influence of Kapodistrias. In October 1820, in a preparatory report written at Alexander's request, the latter reaffirmed the need to safeguard the moral principles that the Holy Alliance attempted to apply; but in Spanish and Neapolitan matters he was in favor of a diplomatic and not a military solution that would be negotiated by the coalition powers and would accept a certain amount of constitutionalism as long as the process remained moderate.

In November 1820 in Troppau, the uprisings underway focused everyone's attention. The first took place in Spain, where discontent was sharpened by both the newly returned king's reactionary policy and by his determination to send troops to the American colonies in revolt. On January 1, 1820, military units based in Cadiz that were supposed to leave for the colonies staged a mutiny, and in only a few days the military uprising reached Madrid, forcing the king to restore the liberal constitution of 1812. In July a related movement influenced by the Spanish example, and led by officers who had served under Murat, burst out in Naples, forcing the new sovereign to accept a constitution. Finally in August another military uprising arose in Portugal, and there again in October, the king had to accept the principle of a constitution. Thus, in many places on the continent, liberal and revolutionary ideas threatened the monarchical order reestablished in 1815 by the Congress of Vienna.

Faced with this situation, as soon as the Congress of Troppau opened, Metternich and Kapodistrias started a bitter fight to win Alexander over; the tsar remained on Austrian territory almost eight months. He did meet Metternich often; the two men had frequent tête-à-têtes after the official sessions without the knowledge of Nesselrode or his secretary of state.

When the summit began, Kapodistrias presented two plans in the name of the Russian Empire. The first was a general one that asked the five powers to pronounce in favor of a right to interfere in the domestic affairs of the coalition states. For Castlereagh, this proposal would transform the existing alliance into "a general government of Europe,"[34] struggling against revolutionary ferment, and this was unacceptable to the British. He had to deal with Parliament and British opinion, which were open to liberal ideas and not receptive to any idea of solidarity among European powers. So, although supported by Metternich, the Russian proposal was officially disavowed by British diplomats who (as at Aachen) refused to go down that path. The second proposal was to grant the smaller European states the right to proceed freely to domestic reforms provided that these were acceptable to the five coalition powers. But here it was Metternich's resolute opposition that blocked the plan; he could not tolerate the great European powers authorizing (and a fortiori supporting) the least liberal trend. Instead of sanction for political and moral interference, Metternich asked for outright power to intervene militarily in Naples. While until then Alexander had been hesitant about any military solution, the uprising of the Semenovsky Regiment,[35] which had been skillfully instrumentalized by Metternich, caused an abrupt reversal in the Russian sovereign's position, much to Kapodistrias's regret. Alexander now rallied to the Austrian proposal, even offering the support of 100,000 Russian soldiers.[36] Disturbed by this radicalization to the right, Kapodistrias tried to obtain some safeguards. In the new text he submitted to the congress in November, he stressed that they not consent to military intervention unless "friendly approaches" failed, and he insisted that the coalition powers should act collectively on the Naples issue. The provisos irritated Metternich, who wanted to obtain from the congress carte blanche to intervene militarily in Italy. But the tension did not last: in the following days Alexander dropped Kapodistrias and came around to Metternich's perspective, but not without first being assured that his crucial support would earn him Austrian acceptance of action in the Balkans. While the uprising of the Semenovsky Regiment played a patent role in his new position, the tsar had not lost sight of the empire's geopolitical interests.

In November 1820 Russia, Austria, and Prussia signed a preliminary protocol drafted by Kapodistrias and amended by Metternich, which would be published in the form of a circular on December 8. The text ratified the principle of armed intervention against the revolution in Naples and more generally the right of military interference by coalition states in the domestic affairs of other states as soon as they were confronted with revolutionary movements or uprisings. Laharpe devoted in his Correspondence a long commentary on this protocol, which he thought truly put an end to the pioneering role played by the Russian Empire in the construction of a liberal European order. Barely five years after having dreamed of a Europe that would rest on the values of peace, fraternity, and toleration that respected the principle of nationalities, Alexander I had come to support the maintenance of a conservative and monarchist Europe that was beating back national movements. Meanwhile, the British judged the protocol to be unacceptable as it was; in London parliamentary and public opinion attacked a text that turned the European concert into a tool of repression. In January Castlereagh sent the representatives of the signing countries a circular in which Great Britain expressly condemned this stance.

Suspended at the end of 1820, the work of the congress resumed a few weeks later, this time in Laibach,[37] again on Austrian territory. But while the British diplomats still hoped to obtain the annulment of the Troppau protocol, the Austrian government found support for its right to repress the Naples uprising, and in April 1821 Austrian troops annihilated the liberal government of Naples.

At the same time Alexander was increasingly desirous to support any regime in place, including in the Ottoman Empire.

For many Russians, most European diplomats, and Christian subjects of the Ottoman Empire, the signing of the Holy Alliance in 1815 had augured an alliance among Christian powers liable, when the time came, to turn against the Sublime Porte. In one of his dispatches to his sovereign,[38] written shortly after the Alliance was concluded, Gentz, Metternich's secretary, noted that in the eyes of many observers, Alexander's secret intention was to bind the Christian powers by a solemn oath to undertake a new crusade, like the one dreamt of by Catherine II and Potemkin as the "Greek project." Moreover, in the emperor's entourage some shared his interpretation or wished for it; for example, the Baroness of Krüdener and the tsar's secretary, Alexander Stourdza, wanted to see Alexander I as the benefactor of the Greek cause. At the same time a Greek diaspora converging on Odessa was very active; in 1814 the Philike Hetaireia (Society of Friends) was created, whose goal was to reconstitute the old Byzantine Empire, with Constantinople as capital. But if (like his grandmother) Alexander was attached to preserving in Ottoman lands the Orthodox rights inscribed back in 1774 in the Treaty of Kutchuk-Kaynardji,[39] and although he had obtained new rights for regions populated by Orthodox Christians by the Treaty of Bucharest (Walachia, most of Moldavia, and Serbia had autonomous principalities under Russian protection), he preferred to wait and see. Prudent about peoples' aspirations to be liberated from Ottoman rule, he was not certain that these aspirations would necessarily help him to accomplish Catherine's ambitious plan of annexing the Danube principalities and taking Constantinople. Thus, in March 1816 he asked his ambassador in London to tell the British government that the Holy Alliance had "no hostile intention with respect to people who are not sufficiently fortunate as to be Christians."[40]

In February 1822 Alexander Ypsilantis, a Greek general in the Russian army who thought he might benefit from the tsar's support, crossed the

Prut and provoked in Moldavia an anti-Ottoman uprising; he took Jassy without difficulty and called for a general insurrection against Ottoman rule. But the Balkan population did not respond to his appeal, and nine months later a beaten Ypsilantis was forced to recross the border and take refuge in Austria, where he was arrested and imprisoned. Nevertheless, an anti-Ottoman uprising began to gain ground in the Peloponnese; faced with the sultan's troops, the insurgents hoped that in the name of Orthodox solidarity, Russia would intervene militarily in their favor. But their hopes were quickly disappointed when Alexander disavowed the insurrection at the end of March. While those close to him, including Golitsyn (in the name of defending Orthodoxy) and Kapodistrias (in the name of liberal principles), pressed him to intervene, the tsar (who had in the interval symbolically stripped Ypsilantis of his Russian military titles) refused: to him, the Greek uprising was an act of insubordination that emanated from an international conspiracy that aimed only to destabilize the continent. As we recall, in his February letter to Golitsyn written from the Congress of Laibach, he tried to convince his friend of the existence of an organization that united "all liberal, leveling, radical revolutionaries and carbonari[41] from all corners of the world"[42]—including the Greek insurgents. Similarly, he wrote to the Princess Meshcherskaia, a fervent Orthodox believer who was begging him to engage Russia alongside the insurgents, that the sovereigns gathered at Laibach were reflecting on the means to combat "the devil's empire."[43] And ten days later he again justified his position in a new letter to Golitsyn, one full of paranoid overtones:

> There is not a doubt that the calls for this revolt were given by the same directing central committee in Paris in order to create a diversion for the benefit of Naples and to prevent us from destroying one of the synagogues of Satan, established for the sole purpose of preaching and diffusing his anti-Christian teaching. Ypsilantis himself writes in a letter to me that he belongs to a secret society founded for the liberation and renaissance of Greece. But all these secret societies are affiliated to the central committee in Paris. The revolutions in Piedmont have the same goal of establishing one more center for the same doctrine and of paralyzing the alliance of Christian authorities that profess the Holy Alliance.[44]

And so, to the great regret of Russian opinion, which remained in favor of Greek nationalism, Alexander allowed the sultan to crush the insurrection. Henceforth, upholding existing state structures and fighting any liberal expression (understood by the tsar as a natural element in the worldwide conspiracy) were the main priorities of his diplomacy. In the summer of 1821, however, his position did shift a little: when the Austrian and British governments took the sultan's side, for fear that Russia would take too much advantage of a possible destabilization of the Ottoman Empire and pursue its own expansionist policy there, the execution of the Greek Patriarch Gregory V, hanged in front of the door of his church on Easter Day 1821, the massacres of Orthodox Greeks perpetrated in Istanbul at the same time, as well as the pressure from elites and some of those close to him (like Baroness de Krüdener) led Alexander to reconsider his policy on Greece. On July 18, by the intermediary of his ambassador, he sent an ultimatum written by Kapodistrias to the Ottoman Empire that demanded reparations for the death of the patriarch, for the destruction of Orthodox churches, and the "repeated breaches" of the 1812 treaty;[45] he also began (through Ambassador de la Ferronays) to sound out the French government about a plan for the French and Russians to intervene in Turkey "in the name of Europe."[46] The emperor was concerned with respecting the functioning of the European system and avoiding any international crisis so he did not intend to act alone in any aggressive act against the Ottoman Empire—even when Kapodistrias, a fervent promoter of the Greek cause, pushed him in that direction. Still, the absence of any response from Paris, the tsar's growing fear of liberal movements, and warnings from Castlereagh about the consequences of a new Russian-Turkish war all led him to abandon his plan for intervention. At the end of 1821, the disgraced Baroness de Krüdener was forced to leave St. Petersburg. In July 1822, when Metternich proposed another international congress in the spirit of Laibach on the Greek issue, a bitterly disappointed Kapodistrias chose to retire from the Russian diplomatic service as well as to leave the empire, to the Austrian chancellor's great satisfaction. The modest congress in August 1822 in Vienna lasted only a few weeks; Metternich, assisted by British ambassador Lord Strangford (who replaced Castlereagh who had committed suicide), skillfully managed to convince Alexander to renounce any military plan in favor of a common diplomatic effort to force the Ottomans to extend more humane treatment to the Greeks and to withdraw their troops from the Danube principalities.

A few months later, during the international congress that took place in Verona from September to December 1822, the Greek issue was once again examined, and now the tsar joined the chorus of other monarchs to denounce the Greek revolt as "a criminal enterprise."[47] The congress also studied the Spanish problem: the Bourbon king was calling for French assistance in a looming civil war. Despite the opposition of the British government (now represented by Lord Canning), the powers decided on armed intervention and gave command of it to the French Bourbons. In April 1823 Ferdinand VII was consolidated in power; however, despite Alexander's insistence, the congress refused to support the Spanish king in his struggle to reconquer his American colonies.

Relations between the French and Russians were at their zenith during the Congress of Verona, which resulted in France's full integration into the European system by giving it the right to intervene militarily in Spain. There arose a veritable political and intellectual complicity between Alexander and Chateaubriand, the French minister of foreign affairs. In their exchanges, the tsar detailed his positions on the Greek question, arguing once again for the need to preserve the current political order in the face of revolutionary dangers:

> Would you believe, as our enemies say, that "alliance" is a word that merely camouflages ambitions? Possibly that might have been true in the former state of things, but today it is a matter of particular interests, when the civilized world is in peril.
>
> There can no longer be distinct English, French, Russian, Prussian, and Austrian policies; there is only a general policy that should, for the benefit of all, be accepted by peoples and by kings alike. It is up to me to be the first to demonstrate that I am convinced of the principles on which I founded the Alliance. An opportunity has presented itself: the uprising in Greece. Nothing might appear more in my interests, in those of my peoples, in my country's opinion, than a religious war against Turkey. But I believed I saw in the troubles of the Peloponnese a revolutionary sign and so I abstained. They did everything they possibly could to break the Alliance, but I resisted. People tried in turn to warn me and to wound my *amour-propre;* I was openly offended. They know me very badly, those who believe that my principles relate only to vanity or else might yield to resentment. No, I will never separate myself from the monarchs to whom I am united. Kings should be permitted to have public alliances to defend themselves against secret societies. What could tempt me? Why would I need to increase my empire? Providence has not placed 800,000 soldiers under my command in order to satisfy my ambition, but to protect religion, morality and justice, to make the principles of order prevail, those upon which human society is based.[48]

A few months after the Verona congress closed, the Greek issue came again to the fore of the international stage due to a spurt in the insurrection. Alexander proposed in 1824 holding a ministerial conference in St. Petersburg; in the circular he sent his European interlocutors, he proposed to reflect on the creation of three Greek principalities to be placed under

Ottoman protectorate. The plan was publicized in the French press and soon aroused objections from British diplomats, who refused to take part in a conference to which the Ottomans were not invited. Furious with this response, Alexander I persisted and organized a meeting in the spring of 1825, in the absence of any British delegation; the result was very disappointing to both Russian diplomacy and to the Greek liberals. In turn, Metternich, because he feared they would fall into the Russian orbit, was hostile to the creation of Greek principalities under Ottoman protection; so he advanced a counterproposal—the formation of an independent Greek state. But this suggestion ran up against Russian opposition. Alexander would not consider (as per his diplomatic credo mentioned above) touching the territorial sovereignty of the Ottoman Empire. So the conference ended in the summer of 1825 without any tangible decision. In the long term this failure would have a major impact on Russian diplomacy because it convinced the tsar—and later his successor—that the difficult question of the Orient could not be solved by European cooperation and that therefore Russia should resume its full and complete room for maneuver.

Ten years after the triumphal inauguration of the Holy Alliance, Alexander's diplomacy, on the eve of his demise, offered a mixed result. Admittedly, the tsar had managed to preserve Russian interests towards the Ottoman Empire, to reintegrate France into the European cooperation and thereby to counterbalance the influence of Great Britain and Austria, to reequilibrate the geopolitical order in Russia's favor. But none of his repeated proposals for the creation of a league of European nations and for disarmament had been adopted. Even more seriously, to the great regret of his main diplomatic advisors, Kapodistrias in the forefront, the Holy Alliance had mutated into a weapon in the service of conservative monarchies. On the diplomatic front, as on the domestic one, Alexander's utopian aims had failed.

CHAPTER 15

Twilight

1820–1825

On the domestic scene—with the final abandonment of the plan for a constitutional charter—well as on the international front—the Russian signing of the Troppau convention—the year 1820 marked a final turning point in the reign of Alexander I. From this date until the tsar's death in November 1825, his power evolved toward a repressive conservatism, while he appeared to have abandoned the empire to the tyrannical management of Arakcheev. Of course, the emperor still reigned as an autocrat and constantly proclaimed his personal authority by a growing intransigence, by his presence, by trips within his empire that became increasingly frequent and increasingly long. As Jean-Henri Schnitzler stressed as early as 1847, "If you can believe an idle calculation, Alexander during his lifetime travelled no less than 200,000 verstes [160,000 miles] and as these distant travels became more frequent, all the departures and arrivals and stays were minutely planned."[1]

But, at the same time, authoritarian crises that attest to a state of tension in his power alternated with phases of deep despondency that were not propitious for taking action. Tired, embittered by dissident movements that were cropping up across the country, and also bitter about his own political and diplomatic failures, miserable about the blows of fate that struck those close to him (which he saw, with almost pathological anguish, as punishment from God)—Alexander became more and more distant from his empire. Well before his actual death, increasingly indifferent to the world around him, he had already left it.

"I Almost Never Go Out"

Over the course of the years 1820 to 1825, even in the opinion of those close to him, the personality and behavior of Alexander I were becoming confused. The tsar was proving more and more shut off, suspicious, and even paranoid. In her memoirs Alexandra Feodorovna (wife of Grand Duke Nicholas) gave a perceptive account of the brutal changes over these years. Whereas in 1817 the imperial family still led a joyous lifestyle—she recalls agreeable promenades and boat excursions on a trip to Kronstadt—a year later, and still more after 1820, she remembers a totally different atmosphere, infinitely heavier and more tense. She lays responsibility for this degradation on the emperor's growing deafness:

> Without being precisely deaf, he had difficulty hearing those across from him at table, and preferred to speak one-on-one. He imagined seeing things that nobody would have thought of doing: that people were making fun of him, that they were comically imitating him, that people were making signs he was not supposed to notice. In a word, such foolishness that attests to a pettiness that was painful in a man so distinguished in heart and mind. I cried so much when he made such remarks and reproaches to me that I almost choked. But since then, there has never been a cloud between us, and he believes in my good faith, my friendship for him, which derives from adoration going so far as exaltation—and certainly not mockery.[2]

Alexander I led a solitary and retired life. While in the first years of his reign he enjoyed the theater and music, a noticeable narrowing of his foci of interest[3] marked the years 1820–1825. Dramatic and musical performances at the Hermitage had ceased; the emperor would read only works of piety or theology, had no literary correspondents abroad, and consented to exchange intellectual talk with only Karamzin and spiritual reflections with only Golitsyn, Koshelev, and some preachers. He who in the past particularly enjoyed salon discussions on all kinds of topics now went to visit others very sporadically. To the Countess of Nesselrode, the wife of the chancellor, who wrote that she was sad that he no longer came to see them, Alexander unambiguously replied in a letter dated April 1825:

> In my defense, I will tell you, Madame, that for some years I almost never go out, not having the leisure because of my occupations, which up to now have not diminished but rather augmented. This wrong on my part—if it is one— affects many people whom I frequented in the past, although very rarely, and now not at all.[4]

More and more strict, his daily schedule unfolded in an unvarying and persnickety order. In the fine season that he spent at Tsarskoye Selo, he rose at five, worked until eight, and then walked in the park, before returning to the castle for his frugal lunch. At midday, without escort, accompanied only by one or two servants, he set off by barouche for Pavlovsk, where he visited members of his family. Upon his return, he dined alone or in the company of Elizabeth and then disappeared into his apartments to hold audiences, to work, or else to read pious books. The Countess of Choiseul-Gouffier left a very precise description of her stay over several summer days in the intimacy of sovereigns in 1824:

> Emperor Alexander led in Czarskoye-Selo a kind of country lifestyle: there was no court, and in the absence of the Grand Marshal, it was the emperor himself who asked for the accounts of household expenses. He received only his ministers on specified days of the week. Ordinarily Alexander rose at five, performed his toilette, wrote, then descended into the park, or he visited his farm, viewed new constructions, gave audiences to persons who had memorandums to present to him, and who sometimes pursued him through the park, which was always open both night and day. The emperor walked alone there without any misgivings, though there were sentinels only in the chateau and palace. Obliged because of his health to observe a strict diet, Alexander dined alone in his apartment, and out of habit went to bed early. In this retreat, the guards played music under his windows, almost always melancholy airs, which I could hear from my apartment.
>
> Empress Elizabeth, for her part, lived in deep solitude; she had only one maid of honor with her, and received nobody at Czarskoye-Selo.[5]

In the poor season, the emperor resided in St. Petersburg at the Winter Palace, but his schedule varied little: rising at six, the sovereign spent the early morning on political matters, then at nine precisely he went to the exercise hall in the palace courtyard to witness the guards' parade. Around midday he left the palace by carriage or sleigh (with a team of only one horse) and visited his relatives. Returning about two o'clock, he had his meal and retired to work, to receive ministers, or to meditate. He showed himself seldom at court. Except for individual audiences he had requested from concerned ambassadors, the diplomatic corps saw the emperor only three or four times a year, during ceremonial appearances.

His obsession for order—his mania—grew constantly. An impeccable order reigned over his worktable; nothing could disturb the very symmetrical arrangement of objects, and the tsar required that papers brought for his signature should always have the same format.[6] A Frenchman, Dupré de Saint-Maur, who lived at the court of St. Petersburg from 1824 to 1829, stressed this obsessive attention to detail and to perfection:

His love of order and utmost neatness shows itself in the smallest things. All the tables, all the desks on which he writes are of an admirable cleanliness; he cannot bear the least disorder, not the slightest trace of dust, nor the smallest scrap of paper foreign to his work. He cleans up and puts back in place everything he uses. One sees on all his desks a folded cambric handkerchief, and ten newly trimmed pens, which are reshaped even if they have been used for only one signature. This daily upkeep was a real business: the pen trimmer, for this service, receives 3,000 rubles a year.

Would one believe it? Every time I happen to enter one of the emperor's apartments, I am never envious of him, of all his power—apart from these ten fine and clean pens that invite you to write, yet never give their master the anguish of the penknife.[7]

With age—and this point strikes historians—Alexander was coming to resemble more and more his father. He now had the latter's distrust, his obsession with order down to the most minor details, his fits of anger—and sometimes also of indifference, as shown by his intransigent attitude to the sufferings of peasants in revolt against the military colonies.

He loved to walk around his capital but also travelled a lot. In the summer of 1819, laid low by dejection due to the sudden death of his sister Catherine, he left on a long sojourn through the northern territories. Leaving St. Petersburg on August 4, he reached Arkhangelsk on August 9, then went to Finland, where he stayed until the end of August. At the beginning of September, he was back on the road to inspect the military colonies of the Novgorod government and then went to Warsaw before returning. A year later, in the spring of 1820, the tsar was again roaming, visiting Arakcheev in Gruzino, where he inspected the southern military colonies before reaching Warsaw on August 27 to participate in the session of the diet, staying there two months, then to Troppau in October. In the spring of 1821, he returned to spend a week in Gruzino, then back to St. Petersburg before going to Vitebsk in September. The following year he went to Vilnius and Gruzino, stayed again in Warsaw from August 1822 to January 1823. In the course of 1823, he stopped twice at Gruzino, in March and June, and then went on a voyage of two and a half months: first to Moscow, then on a journey that led him to Yaroslav, then to Rostov, where he stopped in a monastery, then the military colonies of the Mogilev government, and from there to Volhynia and Podolia. In the town of Czernowice, situated on the Austrian frontier, he met the emperor of Austria before leaving for Bessarabia, staying a long time to inspect his troops, and then returning to St. Petersburg by mid-November. The following year, he remained a month in Gruzino, before undertaking from August to October a new trip through his provinces to the southeast: Riazan, Tambov, Penza, Simbirsk, Orenburg, Ekaterinburg were all stops on his itinerary.[8]

This constant movement—which does not fit with his aspiration to meditation and retreat—has aroused a great deal of commentary from historians. For some, these repeated voyages are explained less by the tsar's concern for his empire than by his desire to flee the memory of parricide—and thereby to flee himself. For others, because he never trusted anybody, Alexander aimed by frenetically travelling thousands of miles to ensure the docility and trustworthiness of his local representatives, or perhaps the success of the military colonies. For still other historians, these tours through the empire were part of his insatiable quest for God—as the repeated halts at monasteries demonstrate. Whatever the cause, one can only be struck, observing this bulimic traveling, by the way in which the son, again, was imitating the father.

When he was not going to meditate in monasteries or to visit anchorites, Alexander continued to devote himself to deepening his faith; his whole spirituality tended to make him drop political activity for the sake of religious meditation. In his letter to Alexander Golitsyn in February 1821, he confessed of his relation to God:

> I abandon myself completely to His guidance, to His decisions, and it is He who brings and decides things. I merely follow in total abandon, persuaded as I am in my heart that this can only lead to that goal that His Economy has decided for the common good.[9]

He prayed fervently for hours, as his doctor Tarasov testified:

> The emperor was very religious and a sincere Christian. He said his prayers on his knees morning and night, and prolonged them so long that he formed large calluses on both knees that persisted until his death.[10]

At the end of his reign, the sovereign tended to detach himself from any material contingency. This penchant grew even more in 1824, due to two tragedies that struck him successively. On June 18 he lost Sophie, his last remaining daughter. Afflicted by tuberculosis, the young woman died at the age of 18, which was devastating for Alexander. This cruelty of fate was witnessed by the Countess of Choiseul-Gouffier, who was staying at Tsarskoye Selo at the time and left a moving account:

He had just lost his daughter, his daughter whom he had never recognized, and who bore her mother's name. [...] This interesting and young person, attacked in her chest,[11] was brought from Paris to Petersburg, against the advice of doctors but on a faith in some charlatans and magnetizers who had predicted for her long life, health, and marriage. Already dying, she was engaged to Count S., who had her magnetized according to the orders from the Paris clairvoyants; when the magnificent trousseau ordered in Paris arrived (it had cost 400,000 francs), the lovely child was no longer alive; the ornaments of the funeral procession and a deceased virgin's crown replaced the brilliant gowns and nuptial veil destined for marriage celebrations. The emperor learned of this cruel event during the parade. His face in an instant went extremely pale; yet he had the courage to not interrupt the exercise, and let slip only these striking words: "I receive punishment for all the errors of my ways." He often went alone to his daughter's tomb, and had a monument erected to her in the Church of the Holy Sergey in Petersburg.[12]

While Elizabeth, who liked the girl very much, tried hard to support Alexander in this terrible ordeal, others preached submission to God, referring him back, somewhat brutally, to his own culpability. In a letter he sent the sovereign in June 1824, Alexander Golitsyn, whose influence over the emperor was immense, made declarations of a psychological and moral violence that make us wonder:

God has miraculously torn you from sin, when You gave yourself to it; humanly you could not know how to deal with the rupture of a tie so solidly established and that produced the happiness (although illegitimate) of Your existence. God is faithful—at present He takes back to Himself the fruit of this tie, which should not, so to speak, have seen the light of day according to the Holy Will of God; by this call He corrects the fault of Your own will, which is sin. He takes back to his bosom this dear child—and in what estate? In the purest innocence and piety, an angel who instead of sinning in this base world and making you responsible before God, will pray for Your sins and those of her mother. This is a new call, Sire, that He is making to you to give him your whole heart. That part from which Sophie is torn, offer the bleeding whole to the Savior, for him to take and fill with his Divine Spirit.[13]

A few months later, a new catastrophe struck him. A violent flood on the Neva River caused the inundation of St. Petersburg; for four days, starting November 19 at 9:00 a.m., it sowed destruction and panic. Frequent in autumn, these floods had haunted the residents since the founding of

St. Petersburg. To try to protect the city, Alexander once had a canal constructed to divert the water, but it was ineffective against the great overflow. The flood of November 1824 was particularly devastating because almost the whole city was affected; at its center the water reached nine feet. Of course, help was quickly organized, and the tsar was very active during the catastrophe; he visited the inhabitants of Vasilevsky Island, ordered money distributed in front of churches, had shelters opened to feed and house those who had lost homes. He called for the solidarity of Moscow, which sent emergency help—15 troikas loaded with clothing and foodstuff were sent from the holy city. But nearly 500 people perished, and more than 300 homes were destroyed. The superstitious tsar could not prevent himself from seeing this plague as a new punishment from God—directed at him.

* * *

Less and less concerned to govern the empire himself, Alexander tended to rely on Arakcheev. This veritable vice emperor, often serving as intermediary between the emperor and his ministers, aggravated the tsar's isolation ever more. In 1820, in a dispatch to his minister, the French ambassador de la Ferronays severely criticized this isolation, the political dysfunction it was producing, and the harmful consequences for the empire:

> The silence that reigns around his throne, at the foot of which no demand or complaint can arrive except through the channel of a minister who is often interested in deception and always disposed to flatter his master, means that the emperor is ignorant of the cost of having his wishes fulfilled. When he rapidly visits his vast empire, everywhere he finds his orders executed. He sees only the governors of his military divisions, and consequently hears only flattering and comforting reports. He takes the results of force and violence for those of wisdom and good administration. He believes he is building, but he is disorganizing, because nowhere are there any institutions.[14]

In 1822–1823, at the height of his power, Arakcheev went so far as to name ministers and holders of the most important posts. Most faithful servants to the tsar were replaced by new arrivals—Campenhausen in the ministry of the interior, Tatishchev in the ministry of war, Kankrin in finance—who were not always competent but were devoted to Arakcheev, to whom they owed their appointment.[15] Meanwhile, some embittered friends of the emperor quit public service—sometimes even first performing an act of servility to the all-powerful minister. In May 1823, for example, Kochubey, who had just willingly given up his portfolio as minister of the interior, solicited financial rewards for the employees of his former administration by begging Arakcheev to intercede in his favor with Alexander:

> I have always avoided annoying anybody by solicitations, but, allowing myself to hope for the indulgence of Your Most Illustrious Excellency, I today decide to address one to You. During my direction of almost four years of the Ministry of the Interior, the employees of said ministry have not received a single bonus. They reproach me—and with reason, since comparisons can be made with other ministries. [...] My representations on this topic, presented to the Committee of Ministers in 1821, were examined; Your Illustrious Excellency would render me a great service if You could support this affair by obtaining the approval of His Majesty. I feel the need of some consolations in the sad destiny that was decreed for me by Divine Providence and it would be particularly agreeable to become on this occasion obliged to Your Illustrious Excellency.[16]

That so close a friend of Alexander as Kochubey should now be forced to pass through Count Arakcheev—and with such obsequiousness—in order to reach the emperor clearly demonstrates the drifting away of power after 1822–1823. Some could not bear it. This was the case with Pyotr Volkonsky, who gave up his post as chief of staff in April 1823, quickly replaced by General Dibich. From Paris where he was staying, Volkonsky, a longtime and faithful assistant of Alexander, sent a letter to his friend Zakrevsky, then governor-general of Finland, that was explicit about his motives for leaving:

> Adieu, dear friend, write me as often as possible via Bulgakov, every time you have the opportunity to send me a letter via someone, for probably our letters are censored in the post. [...] I only feel sorry for the emperor, who will one day learn of the acts of this maniac; an honest man cannot remain a witness to that, and such is the emperor's inexplicable blindness to this man, that there is no way of opening his eyes. In the meantime, he will lose many honest people, and abuses and disorder will return to what they were in olden times.[17]

A year later, in May 1824, the outcome of a cabal in which Arakcheev played a key role led to Alexander Golitsyn's being removed. Powerful and active, the Biblical Society over the years had eaten away at the prestige and prerogatives of the senior prelates in the Orthodox Church, which of course aroused their discontent. Arakcheev, attached to an Orthodoxy that he saw as the keystone of the regime, decided to profit from this ecclesiastical rebellion to end the "pietist heresy" and to defeat Golitsyn. To do so, he sought the support of the new Metropolitan of St. Petersburg, Seraphim, and even more so the help of the archimandrite Photius, former Hieronymite of Novgorod.

Then aged about 30, Photius had the reputation of a rigorous (if not fanatic) ascetic. He consumed only bread and water and wore the hair shirt and iron belt under his robe. In May 1822 Golitsyn asked to meet him, and fascinated by the ascetic, he presented him a month later to the emperor. The first meeting in June 1822 lasted two hours, during which Photius, "absorbed" by God, did not even greet the emperor and spent the time in prayer and meditation; in a trance he reproached the tsar for having left the holy path of Orthodoxy to stray away toward Protestantism and Illuminism. Seduced by the strength of his piety, Alexander soon made him a monk and then named him archimandrite of the St. Georgey Monastery, all within two months.

However, the meeting between the tsar and Photius had no direct impact on the status and recognition enjoyed at the time by the Biblical Society. The tsar continued to follow the Society's works closely, maintained tight links with various preachers who were more or less tolerated by the Church, and remained fully friends with Golitsyn. Thus this first attempt at destabilization by the Orthodox was not successful, but Arakcheev, Seraphim, and Photius decided to resume an offensive against the Pietists, and the "Gossner affair" gave them an opportunity.

At the start of 1824, the German preacher Johann Gossner, then in fashion throughout Europe, published an exegesis of the New Testament, *Der Geist des Lebens* (The Spirit of Living). The Russian Biblical Society had it translated into Russian, and Golitsyn had obtained from the tsar the sum of 18,000 rubles for the purchase of a building destined to host Gossner's sermons. But barely published, the work unleashed the anger of Photius; in two epistles sent to the emperor, he condemned the book in violent terms, denouncing this new religion "that is nothing other than the apostasy of the Christian, apostolic, and orthodox faith of our fathers. This new religion is faith in the advent of the Anti-Christ, which leads to bloodthirsty revolution inspired by the Satanic spirit of revolt and hatred. Its false prophets and apostles are Yung-Stilling, Eckartshausen, Madame Guyon, Boehm, Labzin, Gossner, Fessler, plus the Methodists and the Moravian Brothers."[18]

Meanwhile, Metropolitan Seraphim fulsomely criticized the book, which led Alexander, in a state of doubt, to ask the Committee of Ministers to look into the affair on April 17, 1824. In a few days, united around Arakcheev—naturally!—the committee pronounced for the expulsion of Gossner, the destruction of his book, and the legal conviction of the censors who had authorized its publication. Skillfully, they avoided attacking Golitsyn directly. It was Photius who delivered the final blow to him; received by the emperor in a tête-à-tête on April 20, he denounced the existing ties between the Biblical Society and European revolutionary movements; he convinced the tsar—whose psychological, moral, and nervous equilibrium appeared more and more fragile—that Golitsyn was to blame in the affair. Three weeks later, the imperial sanction fell; in May 1824 Alexander Golitsyn was reduced to the post of minister of the postal service. The Ministry of Spiritual Affairs and Public Education was dissolved; Metropolitan Seraphim became president of the Biblical Society. Photius demanded the dissolution of that society but did not win on this point; nevertheless, this campaign put a definite end to the pious readings and spiritual exercises in which the emperor had previously engaged with Golitsyn and Koshelev. By 1824, then, Arakcheev reigned as master over both the empire and the mind of Alexander I.

However—and this is fundamental—we should not overestimate the role of Arakcheev in the final years of the reign. Of course, as vice emperor and president of the Committee of Ministers, he held practically all power and could impose his tyrannical authority on the military colonies. But as regards the empire's general affairs, he was deprived of any vision of the whole or of a global strategy and so remained essentially an executor. Poorly educated, narrow-minded, not speaking French, ill at ease with political subtleties that he scarcely understood, incapable of the least abstract thought but wholly devoted to his emperor, Arakcheev had neither the capacity nor even the will to substitute himself for the sovereign. In the absence of directives from Alexander, he contented himself with administering the empire with an iron hand, in the most conservative spirit. The return of Speransky to the forefront—in 1819 he was appointed governor-general of Siberia and in 1821 authorized to come back to St. Petersburg as a member of the law department of the state council—for a while gave credit to the idea that the management of the empire would be improved. But nothing of the sort happened. Faithful to his qualities as an organizer and still of exemplary morality, Speransky did manage to reorganize the administration of a territory that had suffered considerably from the corrupt and arbitrary rule of his predecessor, Ivan Pestel.[19] A year later, in 1822, Siberia was endowed with a new administrative structure and a specific status inspired by the new governor. But despite this success, Speransky's star dwindled, and in those years he recovered neither the ear nor the trust of the tsar. Meanwhile public expectations were rising—as was the discontent of the elites.

Growing Opposition

While displeasure swelled among the elites, neither Alexander, buttressed in his conservatism and his obsession with a revolutionary plot, nor Arakcheev, blinkered by his certitude as a disciplined military man, was able to understand the expectations that were appearing in the country, let alone able to respond to them.

While the peasantry complained more and more openly about its conscription into the military colonies, the tsar, convinced that a system that governed the hygiene and lodging of the colonists, as well as the education of their children, was bringing undeniable social progress, instead wanted to multiply them on imperial territory. By 1822–1823, a million people were already enrolled in the colonies, but Alexander still demanded establishing more of them in the province of Yaroslavl, which made even Arakcheev hesitate, since he wanted to slow down the pace of these colonies.[20]

Upon his return from Troppau, the emperor, supported by Arakcheev and Balashov, whom he placed at the head of the state police, ordered (again as a result of the shock of the Semenovsky uprising) the tracking of the secret societies to which he attributed subversive activities. In the intellectual context of the time, it is true, a certain number of them, in revolt against imperial conservatism, were swarming. Several factors explain their appearance: first, we have to recall the crucial role played by the patriotic war of 1812, which enabled young officers from the nobility to get closer to the people and take a full measure of their suffering, then, the role of the campaigns of 1813–1814 that put them in direct contact with the situation in western Europe and suddenly allowed them to perceive the degree of Russia's political, economic, and social backwardness. The Masonic lodges, authorized in the Russian Empire until they were quashed in 1822, also played an essential role. Some of them, like the Astrée Grand Lodge, founded in 1815, preached respect for the current political order and aimed only at the moral perfecting of its members, but most of them were very influenced by European liberal ideas and advocated the abolition of serfdom and the advent of a liberal political order, thereby nourishing wider contestation of the autocratic regime. Finally, after 1820, the example of the uprisings in Spain, Italy, Portugal, and Greece contributed to popularizing liberal ideals among Russian elites.

At the same time, over the whole imperial territory, reestablishment of strict censorship, which began in 1815 and became more systematic in 1820, curbed the free diffusion of these ideas within civil society. Hence, small secret societies were emerging inside the army, whose structure and functioning were reminiscent of the Masonic lodges. A great similarity between these secret societies and the insurrectional groups of Spain and Portugal can be observed; in all these cases it was indeed the army that became the driving force of liberal ideas and the spokesmen for a muzzled society.

The first Soiuz Spasenia ("Society of Salvation") was created in St. Petersburg in February 1816, on the initiative of Nikita Muravyov, Prince Sergey Trubetskoy, Yakushkin, and brothers Matvei and Sergey Muravyov-Apostol, who all belonged to old and illustrious aristocratic families. These officers of the Guard had superior education and were open to western European culture; most of them had fought alongside the tsar in the French campaign of 1814, and some were part of the occupation troops stationed in France after the fighting. Later, these founding members would recruit other adepts, among whom were General Orlov, Mikhail Fonvizin, and Pavel Pestel, son of the Siberian governor and a valorous soldier during the Napoleonic wars, who had been promoted to colonel in 1821. He came back from western Europe firmly decided to struggle against the autocratic regime. Most of the members of this society aspired to the establishment of a constitutional regime and the abolition of serfdom. Some demanded that "foreigners" (meaning German-speaking subjects, who were judged to be overly docile to power) be removed from any administrative post. Finally, a minority of them were indeed more radical and envisaged an actual revolution—or even tsaricide—to bring down the autocracy by force. The last point should be stressed: it was through these few extremist members that collective violence, conceived as a political weapon that might even extend to killing the emperor, made its entry into Russian culture, a prelude to the emergence of the nihilistic revolutionary movements of the 1870s and 1880s.

In any case, these movements were heterogeneous in their political aspirations. In January 1817 the Society of Salvation took the name Union of Salvation (or "Union of the Authentic and Faithful Sons of the Homeland") in homage to the soldiers who had fought in 1812; a month later, it adopted relatively elaborate organizational rules that, like the Masonic lodges, set up different degrees of initiation. That same year, when the Imperial Guard received the order to accompany the emperor to Moscow, the secret society moved there. In the holy city it reorganized itself, accepted new members, and took the name Sojuz Blagodenstvija (Union of the Public Good). More structured than the previous society and larger (200 members), it adopted statutes known as the "green book," inspired largely by the Prussian Tugen-bund,[21] yet without proclaiming its loyalty (as did the German organization) to the current government.[22] Directed by six members, the society's essential tasks were philanthropic activities: the creation of hospitals, assistance for the poor, and advocacy of penitentiary reform. At first sight its horizon seemed more social than political, but actually, by advocating progress in education and justice, the society did indeed encroach on politics. In parallel, in 1820 some of its members started to demand the establishment of a government that was not just constitutional, but republican. This radicalization—and police surveillance—pushed it to dissolve at the end of that year.

After this dissolution two centers of conspiracy were established in Russia. The "Southern Society" was founded in 1821 with Pestel at the head; based in Tulchin in the Ukraine, it had affiliates in five regiments in five different towns. The "Northern Society" was created in St. Petersburg in 1823 and included a branch in Moscow. The two societies stayed in contact with each other and agreed on a certain number of points—political freedom and the ending of serfdom—but they were clearly distinct in their sociopolitical projects, as shown by two documents from them that have survived, a constitution for the Northern Society written by Nikita Muravyov and Russkaja Pravda (Russian Justice) written by Pavel Pestel for the Southern Society.[23]

Muravyov's constitution in its preamble stresses the rights of the Russian people. In the future the Russian people will be free and independent and constitute the source of supreme power. Therefore, serfdom will have to be abolished; freedom of association, thought, expression, and publication to be instituted; and the military colonies to be abolished. Inalienable civil rights will be granted to individuals under the law. Everyone will have the right to vote, but only those citizens owning property will be eligible. Transformed into the "supreme officer of the Russian government," the emperor would become like the American president. In fact, Muravyov's constitution was largely inspired by that of the United States. All the privileges of the imperial family would be abolished; the emperor would have an annual income allotted by the state, and like the American president he would have the right to veto legislation. The country would include 13 states, each having its capital, plus two provinces, Moscow and the Don. All 15 would be divided into 368 uezdi and subdivided into volosti of 360 to 1,500 inhabitants. Muravyov was obviously thinking of the Russian Empire as an administrative network on the model of a federation. Legislative power would be given to two chambers: the chamber of representatives of the people, and the supreme duma (much like the U.S. Senate). Members of the duma would be elected for six years, their mandate being renewed every second year. It would include 42 elected members, three per state, plus two from Moscow and one from the Don. The Chamber of Representatives would have 450 members elected for two years. At the level of each of the 13 states, the same structure would exist. Thus Muravyov's scheme made the people the depository of the law and the emperor their foremost public servant—he planned a constitutional and federal monarchy.

Pestel's plan for the Southern Society was much more radical. He abolished the monarchy, and legislative power was given to a "people's assembly," Narodnoe Veche, named in honor of the assemblies of the medieval principalities of Novgorod and Pskov. Unicameral and elected for five years, the assembly could not be dissolved. A fifth of its members would be elected every year. Executive power would belong to an executive duma (Derzhavnaja Duma) composed of five members. Elected for five years and renewed at the rate of one member every year, the duma would supervise ministerial activities and would be itself subject to supervision by an assembly of 120 bojary[24] charged with making sure all new laws respected the constitution. This meant that the country would be a centralized republic with no concession to federalism; no particular arrangement was made for the other nationalities that composed the empire. On the socioeconomic level, Pestel's plan promised liberty and equality, abolished serfdom, and guaranteed farming peasants that their land could not be sold, exchanged, or mortgaged against their will, in order to ensure that each peasant family had enough autonomy to survive. Obstacles to free commerce and enterprise were suppressed and merchant guilds dissolved.

Despite their political differences, the two societies quickly sought to establish contact with each other; in the course of 1823, Pestel sent emissaries to the Northern Society, and in 1824 he himself went to St. Petersburg to present his theses and try to establish close ties between the two organizations. But his plan failed due to opposition from Muravyov, who was hostile to any notion of violence, terror, or, of course, to killing an emperor to advance the cause. However, while the Southern Society could not make a pact with that of the Northern, it did not remain isolated. In 1823, thanks to Muravyov-Apostol and Bestuzhev-Riumin, it approached a quite recently created secret society in Poland, the Polish Patriotic Society.

Despite the country's constitutional charter and their special form of government, the Polish elites had not on the whole rallied to Russian authority, and their desire to reconstitute the old kingdom of Poland-Lithuania as an independent state had remained intact. Consequently, the end of the 1810s was marked by a rise in dissent among both students and soldiers. In 1819 Major Lukasinski was behind the founding of a Masonic lodge within the

Polish army that formed connections with Poles who had become Prussian subjects in 1815, such as General Uminski. In May 1821 a secret meeting between Lukasinski and Uminski led to the founding in Potock, near Warsaw, of the Polish Patriotic Society, whose goal was to spread its ideas not only in the kingdom of Poland, but also in Vilnius, Cracow, Poznan, and Lvov. However, in October 1820 Lukasinski was denounced to the Russian authorities; after a detailed inquiry conducted by Novosiltsev in Warsaw, he was arrested with seven others in May 1822 and in June 1824 condemned by a military tribunal to imprisonment. The society survived regardless; in Kiev representatives from the Polish and Southern Societies managed to meet in secret. Both sides promised support in case they proceeded to armed struggle; the Russian representatives recognized the independence of Poland, while leaving the question of borders rather vague. But these contacts remained limited, while the danger of police surveillance was large. In 1823 students at Vilnius University plotted vaguely to assassinate Grand Duke Constantine. Discovery of the affair triggered the arrest of several dozen students and the forced resignation of Czartoryski, obliged to leave his post as rector of the university. This shows how much the western provinces of the empire were under strict police surveillance. In this context contacts between these two societies were strained. On the contrary, the ties forged by Pestel with the Society of United Slavs were more substantial.

The Society of United Slavs was born in 1823, in southern Russia, on the initiative of the brothers Andrey and Peter Borisov and Julian Lublinski. Gathering together almost 35 middle-ranking officers, it presented a very different sociological profile than that of the two original Russian societies. Coming from the minor and medium nobility, lacking wealth—if not downright poor—the members of the Slavic Society proclaimed resolutely atheistic and humanitarian convictions. Fervent partisans of abolishing serfdom, favorable to a democratic and republican government, they aspired to end the autocratic regime. Beyond the imperial borders, they wanted to unify the Slavs in a pan-Slavic federation, privileging ethnic and linguistic criteria over religious ones—this kind of thinking was very innovative at the start of the nineteenth century. Unlike the Northern Society, members were ready to resort to revolutionary means, which made them closer to the Southern Society. In 1824 contacts were discreetly established via Muravyov-Apostol, and representatives met in September 1825 to coordinate plans. The force of convictions of the founders of the Southern Society and its higher degree of organization in comparison to the smaller Slavic one led the latter to transform itself into a branch of the former. Yet at the death of Alexander I, this absorption was not complete, perhaps due to the reticence of the Slavs to accept the authority of the larger society, reflecting in turn the minor nobility's distrust of the greater nobility.

In the course of the years from 1821 to 1825, the Southern Society sketched several plans for revolutionary activity: it proposed to kidnap the emperor when he was visiting Bobruisk; a year later it envisaged assassinating him during maneuvers in Belaya Tserkov and calling for an armed uprising, first in Kiev and then in Moscow; in 1825, a mutiny was planned when the Guard gathered in Leshchin. But these attempts were all aborted. It was only after Alexander's death, thanks to the confusion of the transmission of imperial power to Constantine and then to Nicholas, that in December 1825 the plotters made their entry into history. Under the name "Decembrists" the conspirators would attempt to overthrow the autocratic regime by force.

In the face of these subversive intrigues by various secret societies, the police services had not remained inactive. During the winter of 1820–1821, the imperial police managed to detect some of them, including the Union of Salvation, which was kept under surveillance by spies, causing it to dissolve, as we saw. In February the authorities were able to establish a list of the most active members, a list that in May General Vasilchikov, governor-general of St. Petersburg, passed to Alexander. But at the time the tsar had not completely shed his youthful ideals and so refused to punish the "unfortunates"—with whom he confessed sharing views in his youth. He told the general that it was not up to him to punish the conspirators.[25] But he did not close his eyes to them, setting up a secret police force designed to keep watch over troops stationed in and around St. Petersburg.

The following years showed a clear hardening. In August 1822 Alexander sent Kochubey, still minister of the interior, a ukase banning all secret societies and Masonic lodges and requiring all military men and civil servants to declare in writing that they did not adhere to them and promised never to join. In parallel, police surveillance increased. A dense and centralized police network was set up within the army, private correspondence was systematically opened, and denunciations were encouraged. The country was also closing down foreign influences: starting in 1822 Russian students were no longer authorized to attend foreign universities like Heidelberg or Iena, while certain disciplines like natural law and political science were forbidden to be taught on imperial territory. However, despite this strict surveillance and repressive measures, the state proved incapable of preventing new secret societies from emerging or the dissident movement from growing. In July 1825 Alexander was informed by a young subofficer of the Third Uhlans of the Ukraine, Sherwood (British by origin), that officers of several regiments of this province, with the aid of accomplices in St. Petersburg, were preparing a coup designed to overthrow the autocratic regime. Sherwood declared that he did not know any more but that he was ready to pursue his inquiry if so authorized by the tsar. Alexander consented, on condition that Arakcheev was kept personally informed of the result of the investigation. For the emperor, defense of the empire was incumbent on his minister, and without being completely uninterested in his own security or in that of his government, he chose to place his confidence in Arakcheev.

At the same time, more and more deaf to any criticism, tired of exercising power, and increasingly thirsty for mystical ideals, Alexander I was preparing his succession, while dreaming of a final grand political act, the reunification of the churches of East and West.

From the Desire to Abdicate to the Messianic Dream

As of 1820 Alexander I was making more mention of his possible retirement from the imperial throne; as we saw, he had begun to prepare his succession by removing his brother Constantine from the line, with his full agreement. But at the time knowledge of these preparations remained closely restricted to the family circle, and no written document was prepared. On the contrary, starting in 1822, at the emperor's specific request, the situation became more official. In a letter to the tsar on January 26, 1822, Constantine, who was in St. Petersburg to explain his position to the Dowager Empress Maria Feodorovna and his sister Maria, confirmed his renunciation of the throne:

> Not finding in myself either the genius or talents or strength necessary to be elevated forever to the sovereign dignity in which I would have had right by my birth, I beg Your Imperial Majesty to transfer this right to the one to whom it belongs after me, and to thereby ensure forever the stability of the empire. As for me, I add by this renunciation a new guarantee and new strength to the commitment to which I spontaneously and voluntarily contracted, on the occasion of my divorce from my first wife. All these circumstances of my current situation bring me even more to this measure, which will prove to the Empire and to the whole world the sincerity of my sentiments.[26]

In his response of February 14, Alexander took note of his brother's renunciation:

> Beloved brother, I read your letter with all the attention due to it. Always appreciating the elevated sentiments of your fine soul, I was not surprised.

It gave me new evidence of your sincere love for the Homeland and of your solicitude for its unshakeable peace. According to your desire, I submitted it to the attention of our dear mother. She read it with the same feeling of gratitude for the honorable sentiments that had guided you. It remains to us both only to take into consideration the reasons you explained, giving you full freedom to follow your firm decision, and praying All-Powerful God to bless the consequences of your pure and noble plan.[27]

Having taken Arakcheev and Golitsyn into his confidence, he entrusted to Metropolitan Philaret the task of preparing an official act establishing jointly Constantine's renunciation and the passing of power to Nicholas. At the start of 1823, Philaret sent his text to the emperor, and the final version, written and signed in Alexander's hand, was ratified on September 4.[28] The preamble explains why the emperor had delayed designating his successor.

We could not, like our predecessors, appoint him immediately, in the expectation we had that it did not please divine Providence to grant us an heir in direct line to the throne. But the more our years increase, the more we believe we ought to hasten to place our throne in a position so that it will not remain vacant, even for a moment.

Then, recalling Constantine's "sacrifice" because he felt unworthy to reign and had chosen to renounce the throne, he declared Nicholas heir of the Empire of All the Russias.

The spontaneous act by which our younger brother, the Tsarevich and Grand Duke Constantine, renounces his right to the throne of All the Russias, is and remains fixed and invariable. For knowledge of it to be ensured, said act of renunciation will be preserved in the Great Cathedral of the Assumption in Moscow, and in the three high administrations of Our Empire: in the Holy Synod, the Council of the Empire, and the governing Senate.

As a consequence of these provisions, and in conformity with the strict tenor of the act of succession to the throne, Our heir is to be recognized as Our second brother, the Grand Duke Nicholas.[29]

This document was placed in a sealed envelope on which the tsar took care to write "Preserve in the Cathedral of the Assumption, with the acts of State, until I require it; or in the case of my death, to be unsealed by the Archbishop of Moscow, before any other action, in the same Cathedral."[30] This done, the envelope was deposited by Philaret in the coffer of acts of the Cathedral of the Assumption. But even though Philaret, Golitsyn, Arakcheev, Maria Feodorovna, Constantine, and Grand Duchess Maria were all informed of the process, Grand Duke Nicholas himself was not told of the decision taken in his favor. Why did Alexander choose to leave his brother in ignorance? The answer is not easy. At least we should consider that in 1823 the question of his death appeared neither opportune nor imminent since he was only 46 years old and in good health. Hence, Alexander might have wanted to avoid his younger brother's[31] having to carry a heavy secret. But, in fact, this position would prove disastrous because it was precisely during the cacophonic interregnum that followed the announcement of the tsar's death that Nicholas, not having any assurance of Constantine's renunciation, would hesitate for several days to mount the throne in place of his brother, allowing the Decembrist plot to take place, threatening for several hours the foundations of the empire.

In 1825, ignorant of the intrigues within the Imperial Guard and considering his position assured by the act deposited in the cathedral, Alexander resumed his voyages at the start of the year. During his stops he regularly sent Elizabeth very short notes full of tenderness, which are evidence of a rapprochement between the spouses, as well as of his limited interest in political matters. Only the future of the military colonies and the Polish question still interested him. From Warsaw, where he came to witness the work of the Polish diet, he wrote on April 27:

> It is to tell you that I have happily arrived here, my dear, that I send you these lines. Thanks be to God, my trip was fine, and since Niesvige I have found a true summer. I tell you no more, not having a moment to myself. May God assist you and guide you in everything![32]

A month later, still in Warsaw, he sent her a letter where he notes his satisfaction at the development of "his" Poland:

> I was very satisfied with my little trip. As I did not take the major roads, making many zigzags to see better all that has been newly established in manufacturing, I had a real satisfaction in finding how much the country has gained in agriculture and in factories. Here are whole new towns that have been created, and the country presents a happy aspect that is a pleasure to see. Other ancient towns like Kalisch and Plotz have become very beautiful.[33]

Coming back to St. Petersburg by the end of June, the emperor found Elizabeth quite weak. A few weeks later her doctors, worried about her condition, advised the empress to go at the end of the summer to a more temperate climate. Alexander decided they would both go to Taganrog, a small town of 10,000 inhabitants situated on the Azov Sea. This choice appeared incongruous to many: the region was known to be very windy, which led Pyotr Volkonsky to say that he could not "conceive the idea of doctors who found nothing better in Russia as a climate than Taganrog."[34] In fact, it was Alexander who imposed this destination: he wanted to return to a region that he had visited in May 1818.

* * *

While his departure for Taganrog was imminent, the emperor received twice in St. Petersburg in the month of August his aide-de-camp General Alexander Michaud. From a family originating in Savoy, born in Nice, friend of Joseph de Maistre whom he frequented in Moscow, a fervent Catholic, Michaud had first served the king of Sardinia before entering the service of Russia. He was illustrious in the war against the Ottoman Empire, and during the 1812 campaign he served the tsar as colonel and aide-de-camp. A man of character—he had opposed part of the general staff by pushing for the abandonment of the Drissa camp because he considered it indefensible—it was he who was charged by Kutuzov with telling the emperor about the abandonment of Moscow. Finally, in the weeks following the catastrophe, he was one of those who persuaded Alexander not to yield and to continue to resist the enemy.

The dates and content of their conversations in August and September of 1825 cannot be known for certain. There is no mention of them in the Russian archives, but that is scarcely surprising since many documents linked to Alexander's reign, including some letters, Maria Feodorovna's diary, and part of Elizabeth's have all disappeared, no doubt destroyed at the request of Nicholas I.[35] But during these conversations the emperor may have asked the devoted General Michaud to perform a crucial mission: to go to Rome, meet Pope Leo XII discreetly, and share with him the imperial desire to see the Orthodox Church reintegrated into the pontifical bosom, and for this purpose to send to the Russian court a negotiator who spoke good French. With such a directive, Michaud may have gone to Rome in September.

This extraordinary mission, whose stakes were of crucial importance—it was no less than a matter of trying to end the schism of Christianity—has since the final third of the nineteenth century aroused a historiographic polemic. In 1877, relying on confidential sources, the Jesuit father Jean

Gagarin published a little work titled "The Russian Archives and the Conversion of Alexander I."[36] Formerly Prince Gagarin, he had converted to Catholicism at the age of 27 in 1841 and a year later entered the Society of Jesus. Banished since his conversion and then living in Paris, Gagarin had a plentiful correspondence[37] with major Russian and French intellectuals, serving as confessor to a number of the wellborn and receiving frequent visits from Russians, Catholic or not, who were visiting Paris. The little work published in 1877 described Alexander I's attraction to Catholicism and "revealed" his desire to see a fusion between churches of East and West. While Gagarin does not always mention his sources very precisely—as his detractors have remarked—his archives (which I have consulted) do include the documents on which he relied.[38] We find there an astonishing recollection (written in the hand of the Baroness de Ricci) from the duchess de Laval Montmorency[39] who, then very old, could only write these final lines, adding her signature to the bottom of the document. In this note, certified by Gagarin in 1877, we read:

> I certify having learned from the mouth of General Michaud that he, aide-de-camp of Emperor Alexander, had from this prince the secret mission of carrying to the reigning Pope (I think it was Leo XII) the homage of perfect submission to his spiritual authority. The general went on his knees to the Pope and recognized him in the name of the emperor as head of the Church.[40]

More than 40 years after the publication of this first assertion, Father Pierling, a Jesuit trained by Father Gagarin as an archivist and historian, took up his predecessor's study. In a first brochure published in 1901 under the provocative title "Did Emperor Alexander I Die a Catholic?"[41] he revived the hypothesis of a conversion by Alexander to Catholicism and a plan to unite the two churches, but this time Pierling delivered sources which, although independent one from another, nevertheless converged.[42] He reveals first that Michaud, well after the death of Alexander, confided his secret to two close friends: Constance de Maistre (here he accepts the assertion of Gagarin, whose archives he consulted) and the Count Toduti de l'Escarène (later a minister of the king of Sardinia), who reported the confidence to his sovereign in a little memorandum written in 1841, a few weeks after the death of Michaud.[43] In a roundabout way Michaud is said to have mentioned "a secret" to a member of his family, his niece, the Countess Paoletti de Rodoretto,[44] with whom he often stayed in Palermo in the last years of his life. In fact, in 1869 the Countess Paoletti de Rodoretto published in Turin a little book of a hundred pages titled "Glances at the life of S. E., Count Alexander Michaud de Beauretour, Lt. General, aide-de-camp of Their Majesties the Emperors of Russia, Alexander I and Nicholas I, and on the life of his brother Louis Michaud, engineer and aide-de-camp of His Majesty Emperor Alexander I"[45] that I found. She asserts that in 1825 Michaud had to go "on the emperor's orders" to Italy, with permission to go to Nice,"[46] that the emperor lent him one of his particular carriages and provided all the expenses of the trip,[47] and that Michaud had kept a secret linked to Alexander:

> Even when in the close intimacy of his family, where he thought he was able to give free reign to his effusions, one still noticed much reticence, causes of the regrettable lacuna that mar my book a bit.
>
> In effect it is accepted by us, his nieces, living close to him and almost never leaving him, that he had at the bottom of his heart many secrets, now buried with him in the silence of the tomb. How many times, for example, we heard him cry out, in speaking of the grandeur of the sentiments and actions of emperor Alexander: *Ah, if only it was permitted to me to say everything! But I promised to remain silent!*[48]—a final homage to the memory of this prince so favored by Heaven and so worthy of being loved.[49]

To these sources emanating from Catholics close to General Michaud, Pierling adds others coming from the Vatican: Mauro Cappellari, former abbot of a monastery, who became pope under the name Gregory XVI, confided to his personal secretary Gaetano Moroni (who noted it in his diary and then published it in his *Dizionario)* that he was once designated by Pope Leo XII to go to St. Petersburg at the tsar's request to prepare for the fusion of the churches; he declined this mission, though, in favor of father Orioli. The latter was getting ready to go when the tsar's sudden death in Taganrog put a stop to the plan.

Barely published, Pierling's brochure was forcefully denied by Grand Duke Nicholas Mikhailovich, Russian biographer of Alexander I but also a member of the imperial family, who refused to validate this thesis because no other Russian source attested to the stated facts and because nothing proved the existence of an interview between the aide-de-camp and the pope. But Pierling persisted (and in 1913 published) a revised edition of his previous brochure;[50] this time he refers very precisely to Vatican sources that prove that an interview did take place between Pope Leo XII and General Michaud on December 5, 1825,[51] without anything about its content having filtered through. This publication made Nicholas Mikhailovich waver, and in the posthumous edition of his biography of Alexander I, he supplied new details:

The fact is that Michaud [...] took a leave-of-absence to settle in Italy where he died in 1841, leaving for Emperor Nicholas I, then reigning, a sealed box, that Michaud's family delivered after his death to the emperor. We managed to discover receipts from Prince P. M. Volkonsky, proving that this box containing the papers was received, but these have disappeared, probably burnt by Emperor Nicholas.[52]

By 1913, then, there was no more trace in the Russian archives of the documents that could have been sent to Russia by Michaud's family; as for the pontifical sources that I have consulted, they are scarcely explicit, mentioning the request for an audience with the pope by Count Italinsky on November 25, 1825, the tsar's envoy to the Holy See, on behalf of Michaud and Rakiety, "secretary general of the Ministry of Religion and Education of the Kingdom of Poland,"[53] as well as on December 3, the response from Cardinal della Somaglia, fixing the audience with the pope for Monday, December 5. But there are no minutes, and so the Vatican archives permit only one established fact: at the request of Alexander I, General Michaud met with Pope Leo on that date.

What did they say to each other? In his investigation of 1913, Pierling stuck to the testimony left by those close to the general, while implying (a hypothesis confirmed by Grand Duke Nicholas Mikhailovich) that Michaud, haunted by his secret, had written an explanatory letter to Nicholas I, a letter that came to the tsar in 1841 by means of his brother Gaétan Michaud. In fact, in 1846, five years after having sent the document to Russia, Gaétan Michaud reported the affair to a friend, Father Bresciani, who consigned it in turn to his diary,[54] regretting that the plan to reconcile the churches had led to nothing. But in 1913, Pierling could go no farther in his investigation beyond a network of assumption. The written sources were lacking.

However, in 1932 the affair resurfaced: if the letter sent by Gaétan Michaud was indeed destroyed when it arrived in Russia, the draft of this letter had remained in the Michaud family archives in Nice, where a local scholar, Louis Cappatti,[55] found it this year. He then published an article titled "Count Michaud de Beauretour, Alexander I, and the Pope in 1825," which revealed that the draft of the letter written by Michaud in June 1835[56] when he was staying in Turin had been found in the archives of the deceased canon Augustin Michaud Beauretour, the general's nephew, and that this draft now belonged to Count Felix Michaud de Beauretour, the nephew of the latter, who agreed to show it to him. And in his article Cappatti reproduced the whole text of Michaud's extraordinary letter, of which these are the main passages:

I was in the service of His Majesty the terrible year of 1825, at Kaminskii-Ostrof where His Majesty arrived from Czarkoye-Selo to spend the day a few days before the Peterhof Party. (His Majesty received that day the ambassador of France, Count de la Feronais,[57] who excused himself to take the waters.) His Majesty did me the honor of calling me and ordering me to sit at his side, giving me orders in approximately these terms. [...]

To remove any suspicion by Your Imperial Majesty that my religion might be the cause of a story invited by false zeal, my religions teaches me, Sire, that I would be damned without recourse for all eternity if I dared use it for falseness, deception, and lying or betrayal, and if, in dying, I did not consign it to flames!

"Dear general," His Majesty said to me: "I want to give you a mark of the trust that I have in you, I am sending you to Rome, you will go to the Holy Father, you will tell him that long ago I formed the desire in my heart to see the two Churches reunited, that several reasons have prevented me from letting him know my intentions until now, that I am sending you to beg him to choose a reliable monk that you will bring back to me next year in the month of May. Tell him that the matter must be dealt with between he who is the Head of the Catholic Church and me who am [...] here." (His Majesty made a pose as if his modesty made it repugnant to give himself the title of the Head of the Greek Church [...]) I took over: "Yes, Sire, you represent here the head of your Church. [...]"

"You will say then that because this affair is between him and me, I regard the thing as easy to achieve with the help of divine Providence, but make him feel the importance of secrecy; first nothing ever in writing; when his confidant arrives here, we will understand each other easily, I hope. And I do not doubt that the Holy Father will put his goodwill into it, as I will do on my side, but he should not let his choice fall on some person of high rank, we must absolutely avoid anything to give warning. I would like (if possible) for him to choose among the mendicant orders of St. Francis, or the Camaldules [a branch of the Benedictines] or Capuchins. I have had occasion to know a good one in Verona, he was confessor to the king of Naples, but I do not mean to say that he should send me that one, for he would be too visible, having been in Verona. Moreover, tell him that I do not conceal to me the difficulties that we will encounter in bringing Russia to this great step!

But I have full confidence in God! So that we will succeed, I am well determined to do everything possible, the Holy Father will do the same, and God will do the rest, and if necessary we will die martyrs!

Do not forget to tell the Holy Father that I beg him to choose someone who knows French." [...]

I left for Nice where I let my relatives know of my desire to profit from the moment of jubilee to go see Rome. [...] Arriving in Rome we had the misfortune to find the Holy Father ill, so that I stayed almost 40 days without seeing him. [...] Finally [Minister Italinsky][58] presented me to the Holy Father on December 6 or 7.[59]

I seized this opportunity to procure an individual audience with His Holiness by begging him to allow me to present my brother [...] and the Holy Father assigned me the following Friday, December 9.

Here, Sire, are the means I used to make known to His Holiness that I had a secret to reveal to him: I warned my brother that [...] I needed as a military man to say a word of confession to the Holy Father and ask permission to put myself at his feet after the presentation, and that seeing me lay down my sword, he should withdraw.

In fact, after several minutes of conversation, I told the Holy Father that his moments were too precious to abuse his time, and I begged him to let me go down on my knees to tell him something in confession that pertained to resting my conscience.

The Holy Father said he was ready to listen to me and my brother went behind a curtain. Kneeling, I declared under the seal of confession to His Holiness the mission with which I was charged [...], at which the Holy Father marveled and gave me an accolade of tears in his eyes, telling me:

"Ah, general! What comfort you bring to my heart, what a beautiful message you have." Embracing me, he praised the emperor and thanked Heaven for the good news I had brought. He added that we had to see each other several times to arrange everything, and that he had an excellent subject to give me to bring to Russia, a Camaldule of highest merit and exemplary faith, he was man who would please His Majesty, in whom I could place total trust.

But when I remarked that His Majesty begged him to send someone who spoke French, there was a moment of embarrassment: "Ah, I don't think so, unfortunately my Camaldule is ignorant of this language, it is pity, but we will choose another one; I am even more annoyed because I want to make this Camaldule a Cardinal, and first I would have wanted him to perform this fine mission."

I think, Sire, that the current Holy Father is very probably the Camaldule of whom the Holy Father was speaking, since he made him Cardinal shortly afterward. His Holiness gave me a way of entering secretly in the evening, where I had several tête-à-tête discussions, always with the promise of the greatest secrecy, the importance of which he recognized. He had already chosen the monk and introduced me to him, I should plan for us to find ourselves together at the end of April in Piedmont, to arrive in Russia in

May. When the fatal news arrived of the death of His Majesty the emperor Alexander of always glorious and immortal memory, it made the Holy Father sick and he could only see me three days later, to mourn with me the loss we had just suffered, about which the Holy Father was desolate and inconsolable. I told him I was leaving right away to arrive in time to meet the funeral convoy and render my final duties to His Majesty, my august master.

I excused myself and left for Nice where I stopped only 24 hours.

Your Majesty will recall that I asked upon arriving in St. Petersburg, after my compliments and condolences, for permission to leave immediately to join the funeral convoy escort that was supposed to arrive in Moscow the same day.

I have just, Sire, freed my conscience of a weight that would have overcome me at my last moment, if I had carried with me a secret that I am depositing in the heart of Your Imperial Majesty, fully convinced by the profound esteem that Your Majesty had for his August brother, and being persuaded that he could form so delicate a plan only after much pure and holy reflection, and in the conviction of his Faith and fine conscience. Your Majesty will perhaps find it good one day to realize the holy project that his august brother had conceived, which by his prayers will attract heavenly blessings on his reign and on his enterprises, if Heaven has destined Your Majesty to receive the glory of such holy work.

I am, Sire, the faithful devoted and grateful servant, his Aide-de-Camp.[60]

Two major questions are posed by this document. First, is it authentic? Nothing permits me to doubt it. Why should the nephew of General Michaud (or his grand nephew), who had no ties with Russia (and later Russia became a communist regime)—why would they elaborate a forgery that no longer had any stakes? Still, to try to see more clearly, and out of concern for honesty and rigor, I tried to take up Cappatti's investigation. Alas, today, 55 years after the publication of the article, the document is nowhere to be found, either in the Michaud archives or in the Nice archives. However, in Cappatti's archives (conserved in a private library, the Cessole Library[61]) we find a typescript of Michaud's letter. As a good historian, Cappatti had taken care to type the document with which he had been entrusted for a while and kept a version. Without being determinative, this point is not negligible: for Cappatti, a serious scholar, there must have been no doubt that this was a genuine and authentic document. The second question is whether the document could be an older forgery, which returns us to the question of the trustworthiness of Michaud himself: might he have embellished (or even wholly invented) this mission—which would make it as fable?

My long investigation, full of pitfalls, enables me to be certain that Michaud did indeed meet Leo XII at least once in December 1825; in his letter to Nicholas I, he gives within two days (ten years after the fact) the exact date of the first conversation to which Vatican archives also attest; moreover, nothing in the background of this officer, who was deeply attached to Alexander I, brave on the front, and a fervent Catholic, would suggest the creation of a fable. So it appears that Michaud was indeed sent by Alexander on an exploratory mission for the rapprochement between, or even fusion of, the churches of East and West—toward which in fact Alexander's political and religious vision and psychology were tending. The messianic ecumenism of the Holy Alliance plan, Alexander's concept of an international church incarnated by the Biblical Society (which he never banned, even after Golitsyn's fall), the crucial importance he granted to the church within the soul, his tolerance[62] of other Christian faiths, and finally his lack of interest in the functioning of the Orthodox Church—all tend to confirm the credibility of this project. In addition, we know that during the Congress of Verona, Alexander and French foreign minister Chateaubriand frequently discussed religious matters. On this occasion the writer-diplomat Chateaubriand (who had written *The Genius of Christianity* in 1802) appears to have discerned in Alexander's convictions the desire to unite the churches of East and West:

> We touched on the reunion of the Greek and Latin Church: Alexander was inclined to it, but he did not think he was strong enough to attempt it; he wanted to make the trip to Rome, and he remained on the border of Italy; more timid than Caesar, he could not cross the sacred torrent because of the interpretations that would unfailingly have been made of his trip. These interior struggles did not occur without self-doubt: in the religious ideas with which the autocrat was dominated, he did not know if he was obeying the hidden will of God, or if he was not ceding to some inferior suggestions that made him a renegade and a sacrilege.[63]

The Vatican archives also contain an exchange of letters between the pope and Alexander in which the latter says he is ready to visit the pontiff as soon as he finds himself near Rome. Yet this trip did not take place, at the express demand of Maria Feodorovna, according to Grand Duke Nicholas Mikhailovich:

> The tendency of Emperor Alexander to Catholicism was suspected in the imperial family; the Empress Mother feared that a meeting with the Holy Father

would determine her son to enter the bosom of the Church, and she insistently begged him not to go to Rome. Emperor Alexander, always full of deference toward his mother, promised this and kept his word.[64]

Once again, this testimony shows Alexander's attraction to Catholicism. And—not the least of the arguments—is that this enterprise to fuse the churches had already been envisaged by Paul I, who had, as we recall, asked a Jesuit, Father Gruber, for a memorandum on this question that was on his worktable the very morning of his death. In this context could we advance the hypothesis that his son, in the grip of growing mysticism and remorse in 1824 and 1825 might have tried to redeem the original parricide? Whatever the case, this capital project that would no doubt have run into ferocious opposition from both the Orthodox Church and believers, would remain a dead letter due to the death of the emperor on the morning of November 19 (O.S.).

* * *

On the evening of September 13, two days before the empress's departure, Alexander surreptitiously left St. Petersburg at 4:00 in the morning; he stopped at the Saint Alexander Nevsky monastery, where he received the blessing of the metropolitan Seraphim and spoke at length with Father Alexis, an ascetic, before resuming his route. He was accompanied by a small retinue, his chief of staff and aide-de-camp General Dibich, his doctors Wylie and Tarasov, the boatswain, Colonel Solomko, and four junior officers and some valets. Throughout his voyage he was writing to Elizabeth, who was herself on the way to Taganrog. On September 17 he sent her a thoughtful note:

> I do not want to let this day pass, dear one, without offering you my felicitations and my best wishes. May God grant you all that I desire for you and may he make you enjoy all his blessings!
>
> I very much desire that you may travel as happily and as agreeable as we. The weather is ravishing and the roads perfect. I also hope that you will be tolerably satisfied with the inns. Adieu, dear one, may God accompany and guide you in all things.[65]

Arriving in Taganrog on September 25 in the evening, Alexander established himself in a very modest palace, where he spent a peaceful and retired life, alternating reviews of the troops, promenades, and prayers while waiting for Elizabeth's arrival. She joined him on October 5, accompanied by Pyotr Volkonsky,[66] Secretary of State Longinov, two maids of honor (Princesses Volkonskaia and Valueva), three doctors (Stoffregen, Dobbert, and Reinhold), and a pharmacist (Prott). For their domestic happiness the couple led a tranquil and unadorned life as simple individuals. Far from the court and the turbulence affecting the empire, Alexander and Elizabeth appeared to have renewed their ideal as adolescents—to live retired "in a little house" on the banks—not of the Rhine, but of the Azov Sea. In a letter to her mother dated October 5, the empress evokes her new life with evident joy:

> The town is really pretty and pleasant. One sees the sea from almost every street, and my house, of which the emperor has taken care in all its details with so much solicitude, is pretty and *heimlich*.[67]

Three days later, in a new letter to her mother, she described her new residence in detail:

> The emperor has arranged it very well, in part with things sent from Petersburg, in part with quite pretty furniture made here, and by his really touching care for me I am well and comfortably lodged. [...] The house has only a ground floor; it is up at the end of a street called "Greek street" and its longest side faces this street, and a garden with a courtyard is beside us. On the corner, the view is of the ramparts of this ancient citadel I told you about, but from the apartments that look out on the courtyard, one sees the sea through a little garden adjacent to the house. There is in a corner of this garden a terrace where the view is magnificent and I would want warmth to be able to come and dream lazily on this terrace. A room which as deep as the house, is the main room. From there one enters on the right to the emperor, who has given himself only two rooms, and on the left to my lounge; then comes my cabinet with a good comfortable divan, a piece of furniture precious to me, and it is from this cabinet that I am writing to you. After comes the bedroom, which by the arrangement of doors, windows and by proportion reminds me of your red bedroom in your house in Karlsruhe. From the little door at the back, one enters in a lovely little room with one window, which the emperor has destined for my dining room; from this room one sees on one side a very small bathroom and on the other a rather large chamber for the maids, which gives onto the courtyard. At the end there is another little cabinet that the emperor has had arranged as a library for me, so as to give me a view of the sea from at least one room.[68]

In October the emperor undertook a new trip that led him to Crimea on November 1. He lingered there, and again the desire to abdicate and end his imperial charge was felt to be pressing. To Pyotr Volkonsky he confided half-seriously, half-daydreaming:

> Soon I am going to move to the Crimea, I am going to live like a simple mortal. I have served twenty-five years and soldiers are given leave after this lapse of time. [...] And you, too, you will resign and you will be my librarian.[69]

This growing lassitude of power is also explained by two other factors: first, it was during his stay in Taganrog that he learned from General Dibich of the catastrophe that occurred in Gruzino on September 22: the assassination by servants of Anastasia Minkina, Arakcheev's mistress and the mother of his only son, which plunged Arakcheev into a deep depression to the point that he refused to serve the state anymore. The sympathetic emperor then invited him out of affection to spend a little time in Taganrog before going back to his post:

> Come to me, you have no friend who could love you more sincerely. We are in a very tranquil place. You will organize your life as you wish. But your pain will be softened by chatting with a friend who shares it deeply. But I swear to you by all that is most sacred to you, remember that the country needs you. I say that your services are indispensable to it and to me, who am inseparable from the fatherland.[70]

Although this letter says a lot about Alexander's affection for him, the count, lost in grief, did not even answer it; renouncing exercise of all of his functions, he named (without informing the tsar) one of his subordinates to replace him. So, after September 1825 the government of the empire was totally adrift. At the same time the investigation led by Sherwood culminated: around Pavel Pestel, commander of the Viarka infantry regiment, a secret society was indeed hatching a plot. Alongside Pestel figured a number of great Russian names: Ermolov, Orlov, Guriev, and several high-ranking officers were implicated in the plan. But despite the report submitted by Sherwood, Arakcheev, overcome by his family tragedy, took no preventive measures against the conspirators. On October 20 Alexander learned from a second source of the imminence of a conspiracy to depose him. He merely asked for more information and did not enact any repressive measure. This lack of a reaction from either Arakcheev or Alexander himself would undeniably facilitate the preparation and implementation of the Decembrist coup.

During his stay in Crimea, the tsar inspected the troops and naval installations and visited the great monasteries of the peninsula. But on November 8, while he was riding by horse to the abbey of St. Georgey near Sebastopol, he caught cold; despite a fever he pursued his Crimean tour, visiting barracks and military hospitals. Increasingly febrile, to the point that his doctors wondered whether if he might have contracted typhoid fever by contact with hospitalized soldiers, he refused to take care of himself for several days, until November 26, by which time his condition had seriously deteriorated. But the fever did not fall, and he weakened day to day: on November 27 he asked for an Orthodox priest, made confession, and received the last rites, before dying on December 1 (November 19 (O.S.) at 10:50 a.m., with Elizabeth at his side. That very day, she wrote to her mother to share the devastating news:

> Dear mama, our angel is in Heaven and I am on earth, of all those who mourn him, I am the most unhappy creature; if only I could soon join him! Oh, my God, it is almost beyond human strength but since he sent it, it must no doubt be borne. I do not understand, I don't know if I am dreaming, I cannot think out or understand my existence.[71]

A few weeks later, she wrote her mother again, expressing her suffering:

> All the earthly ties are broken between us… Friends from childhood, we walked together for thirty-two years. Together we traversed all the stages of life. Often distant, we always found each other again, in one way or another. Finally, on the true path, we tasted only the sweetness of our union. It was at this moment he was taken away from me.[72]

Exhausted and overwhelmed with grief, the empress was even incapable of setting off to accompany the funeral convoy; and it was only in the spring of 1826 that she started to come back to St. Petersburg. But on May 15, while she was stopping in Belev in the region of Tula, Elizabeth, aged 45, died suddenly of a heart attack. She had survived Alexander by less than six months.

* * *

In 1824, a year before Alexander's death, Count Langeron wrote to the contemporaries of Catherine II that they would not recognize their country if by chance they came back to earth because, he said, "between the Russia of 1790 and that of 1824, there is a distance of three hundred years."[73] Why this judgment? How had the 24 years of Alexander's reign transformed the Russian Empire?

On the international stage the country had become a major actor, not only due to the power of the army and the victories bitterly won over Napoleon but also due to the constant interest expressed by the tsar in European matters, his desire to make Russia a European power on a par with Great Britain or France. Alexander I had also contributed to modifying the image of Russia and Russians in western Europe: in 1801, and still more in 1812, due to the Napoleonic propaganda that played on this register, they had appeared as dangerous barbarians, living on the edge of the civilized world. But as of 1814–1815 these hostile impressions faded, ceding to a more nuanced, even complimentary, discourse. There is no doubt that the trip made by Alexander through western Europe in these two years was a determining stage in this evolution, so much did the tsar use his persona, his charm, and his seductiveness to convince the western European elites of Russia's full-fledged belonging to European civilization. It is within the same perspective that we should situate his attachment to the Holy Alliance: of course, after 1821–1822 it was transformed into an instrument of repression, designed to support authoritarian monarchies in their antirevolutionary combat, but as retrograde as this change was, it did not prevent the tsar from making himself—until his death—a promoter of a European cause that he wanted to advance in the name of a shared identity. Does this mean that Alexander, obsessed by European matters, might have neglected and even sacrificed national interests? A view spread by some nationalist Russian historians, this thesis does not resist examination of the facts. While European matters did occupy a predominant place in the tsar's diplomatic analyses, to the point that one can speak of his "European dream," the membership of Russia in European civilization was supposed to be a factor in its national power. In other words, for the emperor, the engagement in European questions was in turn to signify a growth in Russian power. For him, these two notions were closely connected.

Moreover, in the course of Alexander's reign, the empire had considerably expanded, both to the west and to the south; the annexation of Finland, the breakthrough realized in the Caucasus, the integration of Bessarabia and the creation of a Polish state under Russian control were the fruits of an expansionist dynamic that clearly placed Alexander in the lineage of Peter the Great and Catherine II.

On the other hand—crucially—Alexander's continuous engagement in the service of Russian power and geopolitical interests was largely accomplished to the detriment of the domestic scene and its development. The long wars against France proved terribly costly on the demographic, financial, and economic levels. Maintaining the imperial army seriously hurt the state budget, and after the 1812 invasion the cost of reconstructing territories was particularly high, given the heavy damage caused by the Grand Army's invasion. But the consequences were also political: as soon as diplomatic and strategic questions became more pressing in 1805, until they assumed vital importance in 1812, domestic affairs found themselves either conditioned by diplomatic priorities (it was because national union required a scapegoat that Speransky—a Francophile in the court's eyes—was removed from power in 1812) or completely dropped (in the hour of peril, there was no time to launch into hypothetical reforms). When the country finally acquired peace in 1812, the tsar, still dragged into the diplomatic scene, continued to invest a large part of his energy there—again at the expense of domestic politics. And this situation had major consequences.

With the exception of the first years of the reign, when the spirit was reformist and a certain number of concrete initiatives were taken (remaking the education system and the creation of new universities), and when the emperor was envisaging granting political liberties and even a constitution to his people, then with the exception of the "Speransky years" (1807–1812) that coincided with the return of peace and gave priority to domestic issues, the tsar's reforming activity remained, in fact, limited despite the hopes he had raised when he came to the throne. Overall, the country was more "administered" than truly "governed," since ultimately the initiatives taken at the top of the state were not numerous or very convincing.

On the economic and social levels the Russian Empire changed little: the urban population represented only four percent of the total population at the end of the eighteenth century; the demographic rise, despite the Napoleonic wars, that Russia enjoyed in these 25 years, did not change the ratio. While in the middle of the eighteenth century the Russian Empire was the first world producer of iron, at the end of that century it was joined by Great Britain, then largely outstripped in the first quarter of the nineteenth century. Finally, on the political level, while the tsar occasionally entertained ideas of constitutional reform and the abolition of serfdom, and even though they were materialized in some working documents, these ideas never passed the sketching stage. For this failure, some historians have blamed in turn a lack of courage on Alexander's part, his vacillating character, his adherence on the surface to reformism, his fear of being the victim of a plot woven by a reactionary aristocracy. But in reality none of these accusations sticks: he proved himself courageous and even stubborn in many circumstances. We remember his capacity to resist the pressure from a court bristling with rumors hostile to the Tilsit accords, his trip to Erfurt, and his conduct at the head of his Cossack regiments in the 1813 campaigns. Nor can we doubt his sincere attachment (at least until 1820–1821) to liberal ideas and reform projects.

On the other hand, despite his initial optimism and his efforts to modernize the imperial administration and to give the country, by means of educational reform, new elites emanating from widened social categories, Alexander was, throughout his reign, confronted with a major problem: the absence of auxiliaries and powerful supports able to accomplish a program to which a majority of the nobility remained aggressively hostile, well aware that constitutional plans would eventually lead to a questioning of the current order, notably of serfdom. This reality, the lack of relays, and the hostility of the nobility was, I believe, determinative in Alexander's renunciations. But other factors were at play, particularly his faith. The emperor whose absolute power was by nature sacred could also have hesitated, as his faith grew, to undo a mandate received from God and which he had to transmit, intangibly, to his successor.

However, despite these renunciations that seriously compromise an assessment of the reign, important changes were achieved during this quarter century; apart from an increase in Russian power and an opening toward Europe, we should stress the breadth of the rights granted to Finland and to Poland—both places for the apprenticeship of constitutionalism—the abolition of serfdom in Baltic lands, a prelude to an overall abolition, the creation of universities that later played the role of training grounds for new ideas. Finally, although the Russian nationalist movement was previously attached to exalting the popular roots of the Russian culture as much as demarcating itself from Western influences and touched only a small elite, after 1812 it was significantly enlarged. Moving between social differences, the war against Napoleon welded the nation against the invader and contributed to the emergence of a national consciousness and of a national identity going beyond the narrow circles of the intelligentsia. So, far from the immobility and conservatism of which historiography has often accused it, the reign of Alexander was in many respects a period of political, intellectual, and social germination that, beyond the reign of Nicholas I, would prepare minds for the great reforms of Alexander II.

By Way of Epilogue
The Feodor Kuzmich Mystery

In the autumn of 1836, the government police of Perm in the Urals arrested a man traveling on horseback who said he was called Feodor Kuzmich. Aged about 60, tall in height and large in shoulder, with blue eyes, deaf in one ear, educated and expressing himself with great ease, the man, who did not carry a domestic passport, refused to say more; he was condemned to 20 strokes of the whip and several months in prison. His punishment completed, still silent about his past, Kuzmich was sent to Tomsk to work in a state distillery. He stayed there five years, living in poverty among simple folk, but he was very active and interested in others: he delivered advice on hygiene, health, and agriculture to the peasantry, taught their children Holy Scripture, the elementary rules of spelling and arithmetic, history and geography. This strange man—he spoke French and seemed to know the Russian court and its customs—whose ascetic life was given to charity, soon was the subject of rumors. Already, he was spoken of as a nobleman fleeing his past.

Tired of the rumors, the starets[1] took up his peregrinations in 1842 across Siberia without really settling down anywhere. In 1858 he was welcomed by a merchant from Tomsk, Semyon Khromov, who lodged him in a small, isolated house away from town, where he lived permanently as a hermit. Dying in 1864, the old man was buried in the cemetery of the Tomsk monastery. On the tomb, which quickly became a place of pilgrimage, Khromov had inscribed, "Here lies the great hermit blessed by God,[2] Feodor Kuzmich, who died on January 20, 1864."[3]

The choice of the expression "blessed by God" is significant because it refers to the title with which the senate had honored Alexander I; in fact, after the death of Kuzmich, the rumor spread in Siberia and tongues wagged: Kuzmich and Alexander I were one and the same. Convinced of this,

Khromov wrote to Alexander II in 1866, hoping to meet him to give him notes and documents that had belonged to Kuzmich, but he got no answer.[4] He persisted and at the start of the reign of Alexander III, in the summer of 1881, he went to St. Petersburg, where he met the procurer of the Holy Synod, Constantine Pobedonostsev,[5] to explain the affair with notes he had clumsily drawn up and to ask him to pass on the to the new emperor the dead man's personal effects, including several icons and a portrait of the starets, which Alexander III did keep on his desk. Later—but written sources are lacking, and we are reduced to unverifiable oral testimony—Alexander III may have had the tomb of Alexander I in the Peter and Paul Fortress of St. Petersburg opened up, and Count Vorontsov-Dachkov, in charge of the operation, is said to have found that the tomb was empty.[6]

* * *

At the end of the nineteenth century, educated elites in turn appropriated the mystery. Convinced that Kuzmich and Alexander were mixed up with each other, Tolstoy devoted a work of fiction to the affair, titled Memoirs of the starets Feodor Kuzmich, who died on 20 January 1864 in Siberia, near Tomsk, in the hamlet of the Merchant Khromov. In the guise of writing Kuzmich's memoirs, Tolstoy imagines how the tsar organized a fake funeral after planning his flight. At the same time, in 1897–1898, in his enormous, four-volume biography of Emperor Alexander I, Shilder in turn gives credit to the idea that the emperor voluntarily disappeared, which was easier to perform in Taganrog, far from court, than in St. Petersburg. He stresses that at Kuzmich's death there were found in his cell several icons, including one dedicated to the Virgin that had under the protective glass the letter "A" with a crown over it.[7] Shilder's view was shared by several archivists of St. Petersburg[8] and more privately by some members of the imperial family, including Tsarevich Nicholas (the future Nicholas II), who went to the hermit's grave in 1891.[9] But Grand Duke Nicholas Mikhailovich (the biographer) contradicted these assertions at the end of the tsarist period; in a little book published in 1912, the official historian categorically denied Shilder's idea. For him, the initial under the icon's glass in no way proved that Kuzmich and Alexander I were the same person; moreover, the handwriting of the two men clearly differed from one another. Finally, to accept the thesis of a voluntary disappearance would amount to accepting that either the empress, when she wrote in her diary of the "illness" and agony of her husband, was participating in an enormous charade—which runs counter to her character—or that she was not taken into the confidence of the others. But such treachery—given the renewed affections between the couple and the empress's advancing tuberculosis—seems totally implausible.[10] However, his book did not put an end to the debate, and the Grand Duke himself, shortly before being executed by the Bolsheviks, is said to have seen new documents and to have changed his mind.[11]

The polemic resumed immediately before World War I. In a text published in St. Petersburg in 1913 and reprinted in Paris in 1929,[12] Prince Bariatinsky made himself the fervent advocate of the idea of Alexander I's having deliberately disappeared and staging his "death" in a Machiavellian fashion; the prince drew rigorously and convincingly on gross inconsistencies in the stories told by the various witnesses present in Taganrog.

After the victory of the Bolsheviks and the advent of the Communist regime, the Soviet authorities (in 1921) may have examined the remains of the Russian sovereigns buried in the Peter and Paul Fortress—and found, too, that Alexander I's tomb was empty.[13] But this assertion, discreetly circulating among archivists and historians at the very time that Soviet biographers were officially denigrating the "legend" of Feodor Kuzmich as a baseless story, could not be supported by written sources. And, unfortunately, the files referring to the opening of Alexander's grave have remained missing from the archives to the present day.

The "Kuzmich mystery" has given rise to interpretations that vary according to the political and cultural leanings of the biographers: while Soviet historians were resolute partisans of the tsar's natural death, in the West the thesis of a deliberate disappearance was supported, particularly in works by emigrant Russians. Today, in a spectacular turnaround, academic works recently published in Russia call the latter idea "very probable,"[14] if not "certain."[15]

* * *

If, at the end of this epilogue, I am reluctant to take a definitive position, I would like to note some important points. Of course, Russian history over the centuries has been full of myths that feature false tsars, or else imposters, and so the early death of Alexander (at age 47), out of sight, was likely to feed the most implausible rumors. In this legend there might be the more or less conscious desire to refuse this "abnormal" death, given Alexander's age. But this argument seems to be hard to believe: in 1825, the emperor had become extremely unpopular, due to the regimentation of people in the military colonies. Why would the little people of Siberia have wanted, years after the events, to "prolong" the tsar's life by this fiction, when the final years of his reign had brought them only suffering and desolation? The other argument advanced by the proponents of a natural death in Taganrog relates to the difficulty of conducting the affair of a disappearance to the end: for "rationalist" historians it was perhaps easy for the tsar to simulate illness, but to find a substitute cadaver and pass it off as the body of the deceased would imply complicity among those closest to the emperor, and sooner or later the secret would have come out. Finally, the delayed "reappearance" of the emperor also seems suspect. How could the tsar have lived for 11 years incognito in his own empire and resurface only in 1836? Where was he during those 11 "lost" years? And if the most plausible hypothesis is that the emperor was living in a monastery during this period, then how could word not have filtered out? In this context should we simply accept that Kuzmich, though strongly resembling Alexander and ending up strongly identifying with him, was not really the emperor?

These arguments confront equally plausible ones from the partisans of a voluntary disappearance. Foremost among these arguments are Alexander's weariness and oft-expressed desire to abdicate and the growing urgency of doing so. In the absence of any constitutional reform, the power he had inherited remained a sacred and absolute power from which only death—or the staging of this death—might deliver him. In the autumn of 1825, more and more tired of power, Alexander had already mentally left his empire, relying entirely on Arakcheev; the defection of Arakcheev after the personal tragedy he had suffered might have convinced the tsar to accelerate his plan of a disguised renunciation of the throne in order to devote himself to an anonymous life of prayer, to which he had long aspired. Finally, and most especially, how can we understand that the illness and death throes—if that is what they were—that involved the fate of the most important person in the empire (sacred, in principle) could give rise to so many contradictory stories among those closest to him, members of his family, friends, and doctors?[16] For—and this makes the affair troubling—these accounts do not correspond to one another at all. In the crucial week from the eleventh to the nineteenth of November (O.S.), versions differ: Pyotr Volkonsky, the emperor's aide-de-camp and friend, and the personal doctor Wylie disagree on the chronological description of the illness; as for the diary meticulously kept by Elizabeth since her arrival in Taganrog, it suddenly ends on the eleventh (O.S.). Was it destroyed, or did the empress prefer to keep silent? Both hypotheses remain. As regards the last hours of the tsar's life, the two doctors, Tarasov and Wylie, give completely contradictory accounts. While Tarasov writes that the emperor spent "a calm night," Wylie describes "a very agitated night," with the sovereign "getting worse and worse." Should we see these fluctuations as the result of "diaries" written after the fact, in a clumsy attempt to give an account of an event that did not take place? The autopsy results are themselves subject to caution: one document mentions cerebral lesions linked to syphilis—from which the tsar never suffered! And while in 1824 Alexander had suffered an erysipelas in his left leg, recorded in the medical register kept by Wylie, it was on the cadaver's right leg that the scars of an old wound were found! Finally, while the record of the autopsy was supposedly signed by nine doctors in the presence of General Chernyshev, Tarasov, who supposedly wrote it and whose name is at the bottom of the document, asserted in his memoirs that he had never signed it. Nor do the contradictions end there. For Tarasov, the work of embalming the body was perfectly executed; for Schonig, the body quickly became black, and many of the few who approached it found it unrecognizable. Finally, on the pretext that the sickness had disfigured the sovereign, during the funeral that took place on March 26 (O.S.), 1826, in St. Petersburg, the coffin, laid in the Cathedral of Our Lady of Kazan, was hidden from view, contrary to the Orthodox rite that required that the deceased be left in an open bier. Nobody was allowed to see the face of the emperor.

* * *

From these elements, the historian cannot draw any absolute conclusion—unless one could open the sovereign's tomb. But in either case—whether Alexander may have lived the life of a prayerful ascetic in Siberia in the guise of the starets Feodor Kuzmich, which finally allowed him to expiate the original parricide, or whether he died in Taganrog, far from the capital and the court, whether his death was simulated or natural—after December 1, 1825, whether rendered to anonymity or to the soil of his fathers, Alexander I no longer belongs to Russian history.

Notes

Introduction

1. "Our Angel is in Heaven," wrote Elizabeth to announce Alexander's death to her mother, in Taganrod on November 19, 1825.
2. Comtesse de Choiseul-Gouffier, *Mémoires historiques*, 15.
3. Talma was a famous French actor.
4. Napoleon to Caulaincourt.
5. For example, his mother and his beloved sister Catherine.
6. Quoted by K. Waliszewski in *La Russie*, 1: 25.
7. Ibid., I: 23.
8. Caulaincourt to French Foreign Minister, September 19, 1810, in Romanov, *Relations diplomatiques*, 5: 139.
9. The image is poet Viazemsky's.
10. See, in particular, Troubetskoy, *Imperial Legend*.
11. See Pypin, *Obshhestvennoe dvizhenie*.
12. The same idea is present in N. K. Shilder's analysis.
13. Waliszewski, *La Russie*, passim.
14. Platonov, *Polnyj kurs*.
15. Troyat, *Alexandre Ier*.
16. Paléologue, *Alexandre Ier*.
17. Grunwald, *Alexandre Ier*.
18. Arkhanguelski, *Alexandre Ier*.
19. Olivier, *Alexandre Ier*.
20. Rain, *Un tsar idéologue*.
21. Klimenko, *Tsar Alexander I*.
22. McConnell, *Tsar Alexander I*.
23. Fedorov, V., in *Emperors and Empresses*, 216.
24. Sakharov, *Aleksandr I*.
25. See, on a methodological level, Dosse, *Le pari biographique*.
26. This collection (fd n.679) is located in Moscow, at the GARF (Governmental Archives of the Russian Federation). But the Russian archives about Alexander's reign are partial because Nicholas I burned many valuable documents when he came into power. Among these lost documents were parts of the diaries of Maria Feodorovna and Elizabeth.
27. I consulted the Jesuit archives located in Rome (Italy) and in Vanves (France).
28. Only a part of this correspondence has been published. Many letters written by Alexander I, in French or in Russian and unpublished so far, are located in Moscow, either in the RGADA or in the GARF, where the personal archives of the tsar are preserved.

29. Napoleon to Las Cases, in Las Cases, *Mémorial de Sainte-Hélène*, March 10–12, 1816.

Prologue

1. Marquis de Sanglin, "Mémoires," *Russkaja Starina*, 38 (1883): 3.
2. A. Czartoryski, *Mémoires*, 1: 223.
3. Ibid., 1: 261.
4. See Suvorin *Careubijstvo*.
5. Comte de Langeron, *Mémoire sur la mort de Paul Ier*, manuscript with no page numbers. This manuscript is located in the Richelieu collection, Mémoires et Documents, Paris, Bibliothèque de la Sorbonne, ref MS 99. It was written in 1826, but Langeron mentions in the introduction that he gathered testimonies much earlier: Pahlen's testimony in 1804, Bennigsen's and Constantine's a bit later.
6. Langeron, *Mémoire*. Italics are mine.
7. Whitworth to Panin, manuscript letter, May 26 (June 7), 1800. The document is located in the Kent Archives Office (U 269 O 197/7). Quoted by Kenney in "Lord Whitworth," 214–15.
8. Ibid., 216–17.
9. Ibid.
10. Brian-Chaninov, *Alexandre Ier*, 20–21.
11. Meaning the officers of the Semenovsky and Preobrazhensky regiments.
12. Pahlen's testimony, quoted in Langeron, *Mémoire*.
13. Ibid.
14. Ibid.
15. Ibid.
16. This thesis is defended by Grand Duke Nicholas Mikhailovich in his biography of Tsar Alexander: *Le tsar Alexandre Ier*, 18. This biography was published twice: in two volumes in French and in Russian (with illustrations) in 1912 in St. Petersburg (Romanov, *Imperator Aleksandr I*); in one volume (with no illustrations) in 1931 in Paris after the Grand Duke's death (Romanov, *Le Tsar Alexandre Ier*). I will mostly refer to the latter edition.
17. This is the analysis of Waliszewski, *La Russie*, 1: 4.
18. Elizabeth to her mother, March 13 (25), 1801. Quoted by Romanov in *Imperatrica Elisaveta Alekseevna*, 271.
19. Quoted in Paléologue, *Alexandre Ier*, 1.
20. This image is Herzen's.

Chapter 1

1. Catherine II, *Sbornik*, letter n.46. The birthdate is by the old calendar (hereafter O.S.).

2. See Heller, *Histoire de la Russie*, 545–46.

3. *Raskol* in Russsian. The *raskol* took place in the seventeenth century when Patriarch Nikon decided to come back to the primitive texts of the Church, which required believers to change their rituals. But a large part of these believers rejected this return to the old liturgy. Called "raskolniki," that is, "schismatics," they had to face prosecutions, and many of them chose to perish rather than renounce their convictions.

4. Meaning peasants who did not belong to noblemen.

5. Elizabeth was Peter's daughter, and her reign lasted from 1741 to 1761. See Liechtenhan, *Elisabeth Ière*.

6. Indeed, Peter was infertile.

7. See Fedorov, in *Emperors and Empresses*, 181–82.

8. Golovkine, *La cour et le règne*, 100.

9. Ibid., 104.

10. He was expelled from Russia in 1797, one year after Paul came to power, and began to write his memoirs, the first volume of which was published in 1800.

11. Masson, *Mémoires secrets*, 179–181.

12. Fedorov, in *Emperors and Empresses*, 183.

13. Ragsdale, *Tsar Paul*, 8–9.

14. Sakharov, *Aleksandr I*, 27–28.

Chapter 2

1. The collection n.728, entitled "Kollekcija dokumentov rukopisnogo otdelenija biblioteki Zimnego Dvorca," which is located in the GARF, presents a very fine corpus of letters exchanged by Alexander and his mother during the years 1790–1794 and 1797–1800.

2. In these early letters, there are no syntax mistakes; words are well formed and lines are very regular. In the letters written after 1792, this will no longer be the case!

3. This expression, often used by Catherine in correspondence with Grimm, first appears in her letter of March 28, 1779.

4. For example, in her letter n.92, February 2, 1780, she asks her agent to provide her with a new edition of Rousseau's *Emile*, underlining that "this is an excellent book."

5. Catherine to Grimm, letter n.96, May 24, 1781.

6. Catherine to Grimm, letter n.79, May 30, 1779.

7. Catherine to Grimm, letter n.82, July 5, 1779.

8. A quite surprising assertion from an autocratic empress!

9. These maxims were all collected and published together in 1781 in St. Petersburg, under the title "Rossijskaja azbuka dlja obuchenija junoshestva."

10. Catherine to Grimm, letter n.93, end of May 1780 (no more precise date).

11. See, for example, Catherine's letter to Grimm, n.116, June 3, 1783.

12. Maria Feodorovna gave birth to six girls: Alexandra (on July 29, 1783);

Helen (on December 13, 1784); Marie (on February 4, 1786); Catherine (on May 10, 1788); then came Olga (on July 11, 1792) but she died on January 15, 1795; and finally Anne (on January 7, 1795).

13. Catherine to Grimm, letter n.117, August 16, 1783.

14. As reported in a letter to Grimm written on March 28, 1784.

15. "Instructions composées pour la gouverne de Nicolas Saltykov," text written in French by Catherine. The document is quoted *in extenso* in Laharpe, *Le gouverneur d'un prince*, 269–92. This book, published with no signature, is based on Russian documents and on Laharpe's private manuscripts that he donated after his death to the Lausanne Public Library.

16. Catherine to Grimm, letter n.122, March 28, 1784.

17. Later he would be the father and the uncle of three Decembrists (see chapter 15).

18. Masson, *Mémoires secrets*, 2: 157.

19. In order to prevent the boys' suffering from constipation! Masson, *Mémoires secrets*, 2: 163.

20. She will become later a very close friend of Empress Elizabeth.

21. Golovine, *Souvenirs*, 44.

22. A. Czartoryski, *Mémoires* 1: 118.

23. Masson, *Mémoires secrets*, 2: 163–64.

24. Ibid., 165.

25. This confession from Alexander I was collected and reported in Schnitzler, *Etudes sur l'empire*, 461–62.

26. Masson, *Mémoires secrets*, 2: 165.

27. Ibid., 166.

28. His name has been spelled La Harpe, Laharpe, and even LaHarpe. We chose here the spelling used by Catherine and Alexander and the one mentioned in the 1902 collection of manuscripts. This spelling is also the one used by his descendants today.

29. Alexander to his mother-in-law, the Princess of Baden, May 9, 1797, in collection n.658, (Imperatrica Elizaveta Alekseevna collection), GARF, delo 109.

30. Quoted by Brian-Chaninov in *Alexandre Ier*, 42–43.

31. Laharpe wrote a short autobiographical essay entitled *Mémoires de Frédéric-César Laharpe, concernant sa conduite comme directeur de la République Helvétique.* This biography is mostly based on this text.

32. Laharpe, *Mémoires*, 67.

33. Ibid., 73.

34. Catherine to Grimm, letter n.107, February 25, 1782.

35. Quoted in Laharpe, *Le gouverneur d'un prince*, 11.

36. Laharpe, *Mémoires*, 75–76.

37. Ibid., 82.

38. Including the Count of Artois, who settled in St. Petersburg in 1793.

39. Quoted in Masson, *Mémoires secrets*, 2: 159.

40. Letter to Stapfer, February 17, 1810, in Laharpe, *Le Gouverneur d'un Prince*, 19.

41. This document is reproduced in ibid., 23.

42. Letter to Favre, August 8, 1785, quoted in ibid., 16–17.

43. Ibid., 26.

44. Laharpe's course, in ibid., 116.

45. Ibid., 33.

46. Ibid.

47. As mentioned in the report he sent to Count Saltykov in December 1790. This report is reproduced in *Russkaja Starina*, 2: 256–57.

48. This document is preserved in the collection "Katalog sobranija rukopisej hranjashhihsja v biblioteke Zimnego Dvorca," collection n.728, delo 306, in GARF.

49. Ibid.

50. Ibid.

51. Catherine's letter to Grimm, September 18, 1790.

52. The two extracts are from Laharpe, *Le Gouverneur d'un Prince*, 46–48.

53. See Amacher, "Alexandre Ier," 46.

54. Waliszewski, *La Russie*, 8–9.

Chapter 3

1. Masson, *Mémoires secrets*, 2: 169.

2. On May 24, 1783, a discussion between Catherine and her son attests to differences in their viewpoints on this question, see Sorotkin, *Paul Ier*, 189.

3. Quoted in ibid., 193.

4. Masson, *Mémoires secrets*, 1: 308.

5. Quoted by M. Martin, *Maria Feodorovna*, 92.

6. Arkhanguelski, *Alexandre Ier*, 29.

7. He was born in October 1769, i.e., eight years before Alexander.

8. See Jenkins, *Arakcheev*.

9. Ibid., 43.

10. Sakharov, *Aleksandr I*, 50.

11. The grand dukes used to arrive at Gatchina on Friday to participate in maneuvers on Saturday and to get back to St. Petersburg on Sunday.

12. A. Czartoryski, *Mémoires*, 1: 107–8.

13. See Shilder, *Imperator Aleksandr I*, 1: 233.

14. Ibid., 235.

15. As Alexander explained it in a letter to Laharpe, March 12 (O.S.), 1796. Quoted in La Harpe, *Correspondance*, 1: 160.

16. Czartorsyki, *Mémoires*, 1: 108.

17. Quoted in Jenkins, *Arakcheev*, 51.

18. Quoted in Shilder, *Imperator Aleksandr I*, 1: 249.

19. They are preserved at GARF (Archives of the Russian Federation) fd n.728.

20. For example, Waliszewski in *La Russie*, 1: 18.

21. She was born in Karlsruhe on January 24, 1779.

22. Catherine to Grimm, October 31 (O.S.), 1792, letter n.214.

23. O.S.

24. Golovkine, *La Cour et le Règne,* 276–77.

25. Quoted in Heller, *Histoire de la Russie,* 626.

26. The expression is Catherine's. See ibid.

27. She wrote French with no mistakes and elegantly, while her written German was more awkward.

28. Quoted by Grand Duke Nicholas Mikhailovich in Romanov, *Imperatrica Elizaveta Alekseevna,* 1: 85.

29. Elizabeth to her mother, January 18 (O.S.), 1793; Romanov, *Imperatrica Elizaveta Alekseevna,* 1: 85.

30. GARF, fd n.728, opis' 1, delo 357, 1, 122.

31. Elizabeth to Alexander, August 27 (O.S.), 1793, GARF, fd 658, opis' 1, delo 48.

32. GARF, fd 658.

33. Alexander to Maria Feodorovna, probably at the end of 1792, no precise date. GARF, fd 728, opis'1, delo 357, 1, 104.

34. Alexander to Maria Feodorovna, fall 1793, undated, GARF, fd 728, opis' 1, delo 357, 2, 70.

35. Alexander to Maria Feodorovna, beginning of 1794, undated, GARF, fd 728, opis' 1, delo 357, 2, 52.

36. Alexander to Maria Feodorovna, fall 1794, undated, GARF, fd 728, delo 357, 118–19.

37. The precise date is not mentioned in the letter.

38. Alexander to Maria Feodorovna, end of 1793 or beginning of 1794, GARF, fd 728, opis' 1, delo 357, 1, 131.

39. Protasov to Count Vorontsov, May 1794 (undated), GARF, 658, delo 109.

40. Ibid.

41. I.e., Alexander. The passages in italics are underlined in the original letter.

42. This will lead some historians to assert that Alexander was a complacent husband. Elizabeth to Countess Golovina, December 12, 1794, in GARF, fd 658, opis' 1, delo 48.

43. We cannot be more precise for the date of the document, but in any case the letter was written after May 30, 1795.

44. Elizabeth to Countess Golovina, spring 1795, GARF, fd 658, opis' 1, delo 48.

45. Golovine, *Souvenirs.*

46. See Krylov "Prelestnaja Elizaveta."

47. Laharpe, *Le Gouverneur d'un Prince,* 48.

48. Protasov to Count Vorontsov, May 18 (O.S.), 1794, GARF, fd 658, opis' 1, delo 109.

49. As mentioned by Alexander himself in a letter to his mother, fall 1794, GARF, fd 728, opis' 1, delo 357, 2, 119.

50. Ibid.

51. Laharpe's instructions to Alexander, April 1795, in Laharpe, *Le Gouverneur d'un Prince*, 316–27.

52. Ibid.

53. The letter is quoted in ibid., 49.

54. Masson, *Mémoires secrets*, 1: 182–83.

55. Alexander to Laharpe, February 26, 1796, in La Harpe, *Correspondance*, 1: 159–60.

56. As early as 1793, a 74-page catalog listing all his paintings was published under the title *Catalogue raisonné des tableaux qui composent la collection du comte Stroganoff*.

57. A. Czartoryski, *Mémoires*, 1: 979.

58. That represented 3 million people and 250,000 square kilometers.

59. That represented 1.5 million people and 120,000 square kilometers.

60. Alexander to Maria Feodorovna, beginning of 1795, GARF, fd 728, opis' 1, delo 357, 2, 52.

61. A. Czartoryski, *Mémoires*, 1: 978–79.

62. Alexander to Kochubey, May 10 (O.S.), 1796, quoted in Laharpe, *Le gouverneur Gouverneur d'un Prince*, 336–37.

63. On October 30, 1793.

64. Quoted in Laharpe, *Le Gouverneur d'un Prince*, 50.

65. Tsar Nicholas I.

66. Quoted in M. Martin, *Maria Feodorovna*, 104.

67. This document was found after Catherine's death among Platon Zubov's personal papers. Quoted in Shilder, *Imperator Aleksandr I*, 1: 279.

68. Alexander to La Harpe, February 21, 1796. In La Harpe, *Correspondance*, 1: 157.

69. Alexander to Kochubey, May 10, 1796, quoted in LaHarpe, *Le Gouverneur d'un Prince*, 336–37.

70. Ibid.

Chapter 4

1. Among the few academic books on Paul, see Ragsdale, *Paul I* and his fascinating essay *Tsar Paul*. See also McGrew, *Paul I of Russia*.

2. He is, in fact, the hero of the short story written by Iuri Tynianov, *Podporuchik Kizhe*.

3. In particular, see Peskov, *Pavel I* and Obolenskii, *Imperator Pavel I*.

4. As Paul expressed it in conversation with the Count of Ségur in 1784.

5. Golovkine, *La Cour et le Règne*, 131.

6. These examples and the quotation come from Arkhanguelski, *Alexandre Ier*, 89–90.

7. Heller, *Histoire de la Russie*, 606.

8. This expression is Paul's and refers to his father's assassination.

9. Heller, *Histoire de la Russie*, 697.

10. Quoted by Andolenko, *L'armée russe*, 138–39.

11. Jenkins, *Arakcheev*, 60.

12. Andolenko, *L'armée russe*, 136.

13. As asserted by Suvorov, see ibid., 138.

14. In four and a half years, 2,600 officers suffered disciplinary punishment.

15. Sakharov, *Aleksandr I*, 79.

16. Ibid., 77.

17. On this question, the tsar issued not a ukase, but a recommendation that meant the owners were free to adopt it or not.

18. See Sorotkin, "Paul I," 204.

19. GARF, fd 728, opis' 1, delo 357, 2.

20. Sakharov, *Aleksandr I*, 80.

21. Golovkine, *La Cour et le Règne*, 124.

22. Eidel'man, *Gran Vekov*, 90–113.

23. Sorotkin, "Paul I," 209.

24. Golovkine, *La Cour et le Règne*, 152.

25. Ibid.

26. Jenkins, *Arakcheev*, 61–62.

27. See A. Czartoryski, *Mémoires*, 1: 144–45.

28. Quoted by Brian-Chaninov, *Alexandre Ier*, 13.

29. He was on his way to England.

30. Alexander to Laharpe, September 27 (O.S.), 1797, in La Harpe, *Correspondance*, 1: 214–17.

31. A. Czartoryski, *Mémoires*, 1: 156–58.

32. Alexander to Laharpe, September 27 (O.S.), 1797, in La Harpe, *Correspondance*, 1: 214–17.

33. Actually "Istanbul," but since the Russian elites always referred to Constantinople, this name is deliberately kept.

34. As shown by the letter she sent to her mother on the same day.

35. Quoted by Arkhanguelski, *Alexandre Ier*, 84–85.

36. As convincingly demonstrated by Ragsdale in his essay *Tsar Paul*.

37. Masson, *Mémoires secrets*, 1: 348.

38. Several contemporary diplomatic sources and rumors mentioned this project, but we lack evidence to be sure about it.

39. See Ratchinski, *Napoléon et Alexandre Ier*, 23.

40. On the activity of the Jesuits in Russia, see the Jesuit archives in Rome, fd Russia, n.1005, 1805–1814.

41. Paul's expression is mentioned in Ratchinski, *Napoléon et Alexandre Ier,* 26.

42. Ibid., 26–27.

43. Ibid., 28.

44. Quoted by Grunwald in *Trois siècles*, 137.

45. Andolenko, *L'armée russe,* 146–47.
46. Quoted in Heller, *Histoire de la Russie,* 615.
47. *Russkij Arhiv,* 1878, vol 1. Quoted in Grunwald, *Trois siècles,*140.

Chapter 5

1. Quoted in Heller, *Histoire de la Russie,* 623.
2. Edling, *Mémoires.*
3. Quoted in Heller, *Histoire de la Russie,* 616.
4. Golovkine, *La Cour et le Règne,* 376.
5. Rey, *Le dilemme russe,* chap. 4, passim.
6. Hartley, *Social History,* 2.
7. See Coquin, *Des pères du peuple,* 1–24.
8. Hartley, *Social History,* 9.
9. "Soslovie" in Russian.
10. Troitskij in *Rossija v XIX veke,* writes that at the end of the eighteenth century there were 225,000 nobles in the Russian Empire, (i.e., less than 1 percent of the total population), whereas Arkhanguelski asserts that there were 726,000. See Arkhanguelski, *Alexandre Ier,* 101.
11. The serfs represented 55 percent of all peasants.
12. It was indeed a recommendation, not a compulsory ukase.
13. Troitskij, *Rossija,* 9.
14. Hartley, *Social History,* 40.
15. Raeff, *Comprendre l'Ancien Régime,* 109.
16. By contrast, the Charter of the State Peasants would not be promulgated, see Raeff, ibid., 108.
17. Rey, *De la Russie.*
18. At that time, they were called Bolgari or Volga Bulgarians.
19. Called Cheremissians by the Russians.
20. The other Armenians remained within the Ottoman Empire.
21. Troitskij, *Rossija,* 10.
22. Savary, *Duc de Rovigo.*
23. M. Martin, *Maria Feodorovna,* 154–55.
24. Ibid., 156.
25. Quoted in Arkhanguelski, *Alexandre Ier,* 127–28.
26. A. Czartoryski, *Mémoires,* 1: 290–92.
27. My emphasis.
28. Laharpe to Alexandre, August 30, 1801, in La Harpe, *Correspondance,* 1: 243.
29. Maria Feodorovna to Alexander, April 18, 1806, in *Russkij Arhiv,* n.1, 1911, 140–42.
30. J. de Maistre, *Mémoires politiques,* 77.
31. Joseph de Maistre's letter of July 17, 1803. Ibid., 97.

32. The quai along the front of the Winter Palace.

33. Nicholas Mikhailovich, *Alexandre Ier,* 40.

34. Quoted by Troyat, *Alexandre Ier,* 157.

35. Panin, *Materialy,* vols. 6, 7–8.

36. The words in italics were in Russian in a letter written mainly in French. In Alexander, *Perepiska,* 3.

37. Ibid.

38. Ibid. The italics indicate that this part of the letter was in Russian.

39. *L'Hermite en Russie,* 2: 228.

40. Karlinsky, *Russian Drama.*

41. Quoted in Troyat, *Alexandre Ier,* 88.

42. Quoted in Arkhanguelski, *Alexandre Ier,* 108.

43. Ibid., 110.

44. As shown by Laharpe's law course of 1786, in GARF, fd 718, delo 306.

45. His interesting digression is quoted in Laharpe, *Le Gouverneur d'un Prince,* 116.

46. Hartley, *Social History,* 57.

47. The document was published by V. P. Semennikov in *Radishshev, ocherki i issledovanija* (Moskva: Gosudarstvennoe izdatel'stvo, 1923), 180–84. For an analysis, see Sakharov and Bertolissi, *Konstitucionnye proekty,* 312–32.

48. Simon was the Russian ambassador to Great Britain from 1784 to 1806.

49. See Grunwald, *Alexandre Ier,* 92.

50. A. Czartoryski, *Mémoires,* 1: 292–93.

51. This gave the senate some limited legislative power.

52. See Mironenko, *Samoderzhavie i reformy,* passim, and Mironenko, *Stranicy tajnoj,* passim.

53. McConnell, "Hundred Days," 373–93.

54. A. Czartoryski, *Mémoires,* 1: 248.

55. Duroc to Bonaparte, May 26, 1801, in *Sbornik,* 70.

56. Simon Vorontsov to Novosiltsev, May 18, 1801, in Vorontsov, *Arhiv,* 11: 391.

57. Sakharov, *Aleksandr I,* 127. Again Maria Feodorovna played a key role at a decisive moment in her son's life.

58. Viktor Kochubey to Simon Vorontsov, Dresden, April 8, 1801. In Vorontsov, *Arhiv,* 18: 236.

59. "Result of a conversation with the Emperor, April 23, 1801," notes by P. Stroganov, quoted by Romanov in *Stroganov,* 2: 1–3.

60. "Neglasnyj komitet" in Russian.

61. Mironenko, *Samoderzhavie i reformy,* 67.

62. A. Czartoryski, *Mémoires,* 1: 266.

63. Quoted in Shilder, *Imperator Aleksandr I,* 2: 335–36.

64. A. Czartoryski, *Mémoires,* 1: 269.

65. The reports on the committee sessions were written by Paul Stroganov and became part of the archives of the Stroganov family. They were used by Nicholas Mikhailovich Romanov in writing his biography of Count Stroganov and were partially published as an appendix to it.

66. Quoted by Romanov in *Stroganov*, 2: 61–62.

67. Ibid., 202–3.

68. Ibid.

69. McConnell, "Hundred Days," 386.

70. The report of the August 5 (17), 1801, session of the committee is quoted by Nicholas Mikhailovich in Romanov, *Stroganov*, 2: 85.

71. Alexander to Laharpe, 21 May 1801, in La Harpe, *Correspondance de Frédéric-César de La Harpe*, 1: 240–41.

72. As asserted by Alexander to Kochubey in August. See Kochubey to Vorontsov, August 6 (18), 1801, in Vorontsov, *Arhiv*, 14: 154.

73. Count Panin's expression was used in a letter to Simon Vorontsov, then repeated in a letter to Viktor Kochubey written in London on January 3, 1802, now located in Vorontsov, *Arhiv*, 11: 359.

74. A. Czartoryski, *Mémoires*, 1: 271–72.

75. See chapter 6.

76. See Laharpe to Alexander, April 17, 1801, in La Harpe, *Correspondance*, 1: 236.

77. Laharpe to Alexander, April 13, 1801, ibid., 229.

78. Laharpe to Alexander, October 16, 1801, ibid., 319.

79. Laharpe to Alexander, October 16, 1801, ibid., 317–18.

80. Simon Vorontsov to his brother Alexander, June 14, 1801, in Vorontsov, *Arhiv*, 10: 100.

Chapter 6

1. A. Czartoryski, *Mémoires*, 1: 269.

2. Quoted in Heller, *Histoire de la Russie*, 631.

3. Sakharov, *Aleksandr I*, passim, and Ragsdale, *Russian Tragedy*, 76.

4. Mironenko, *Samoderzhavie i reformy*, 67.

5. Safonov, *Problema reform*, 78.

6. In *Polnoe Sobranie*, vol. 27, doc. 20406.

7. See the previous chapter.

8. Seton-Watson, *Russian Empire*, 79.

9. Ibid., 80.

10. This would be particularly complicated to manage. On this new organization see *Polnoe Sobranie*, vol. 27, doc. 20406.

11. Raeff, *Comprendre l'Ancien Régime*, 125.

12. This privilege was granted by Peter the Great.

13. Ledonne, *Absolutism*, 107.

14. Raeff, *Comprendre l'Ancien Régime*, 125.

15. Czartoryski to the members of the secret committee, February 22, 1802, quoted by Grand Duke Nicholas Mikhailovich in Romanov, *Stroganov*, 104.

16. Seton-Watson, *Russian Empire*, 82.

17. Quoted by Shilder, *Imperator Aleksandr I,* 2: 345–46.

18. Alexander to Laharpe, October 26 (O.S.), 1802, in La Harpe, *Correspondance,* 1: 676.

19. Kochubey to Vorontsov, January 20 (O.S.), 1803, in Vorontsov, *Arhiv,* 18: 283.

20. Novosiltsev to Vorontsov, January 20 (O.S.), 1803, ibid., 18: 453.

21. As attested by his letters to Kochubey.

22. Cf. Alexander's letter to Laharpe, July 7 (O.S.), 1803.

23. Quoted in Hartley, *Alexander I,* 33.

24. Ibid.

25. Raeff, *Comprendre l'Ancien Régime,* 127.

26. Hartley, *Alexander I,* 50.

27. In the beginning of the nineteenth century, the Jews of the empire numbered about 30,000 to 35,000.

28. By this ban the state pretended to protect Russian peasants from being "exploited" by Jewish owners.

29. Mironenko, *Samoderzhavie i reformy,* 65–66.

30. Hartley, *Alexander I,* 46.

31. Quoted in Sakharov, *Aleksandr I,* 145.

32. Quoted by Grand Duke Nicholas Mikhailovich in Romanov, *Stroganov,* 63.

33. This approach was very important, and it was close to the one eventually adopted in 1861.

34. Only the male serfs were counted, but their liberation meant the liberation of their wives and children.

35. Mayor, *Economic History,* 1: 312.

36. Quoted in Romanov, *Tsar Alexandre Ier,* 168.

37. For the reforms adopted in the Baltic provinces, see Minaudier, *Histoire de l'Estonie,* 146–47.

38. The report was presented on March 16, 1801, to Paul by the Imperial Commission for School Affairs. It was requested by Laharpe because he wanted to use it as a basis for his own report on education dated March 16, 1802.

39. Alexander to Laharpe, January 1802 (the day is not mentioned) in La Harpe, *Correspondance,* 1: 478.

40. Alexander to Laharpe, July 19, 1803, ibid., 2: 46.

41. And presented to the National Assembly on the same day.

42. It was submitted to Alexander along with a detailed letter on educational questions by Laharpe on March 16, 1802. See La Harpe, *Correspondance,* 1: 495–505.

43. See Walker, "Enlightenment and Religion."

44. Where there was already a well-known Jesuit secondary school.

45. Hartley, *Alexander I,* 53–54.

46. Schakovskoy, *Saint-Pétersbourg et Paris,* 141.

47. Schmidt, "Restoration of Moscow."

48. Maybe due to Alexander's interest in Freemasonry.

49. He was probably the illegitimate son of Count Stroganov.

50. Ratchinski, *Napoléon et Alexandre Ier*, 56.

51. Edling, *Mémoires*, 60.

52. Quoted in *Sbornik*, 70: 180–81.

53. Edling, *Mémoires*, 60.

54. Archives of the Russian Federation, GARF, f 728, opis' 1, delo 1204.

55. Ibid., f 728, opis' 1, delo 120.

56. Edling, *Mémoires*, 198–99.

57. The illegitimate children all bore the name of Naryshkin.

58. GARF, f 728, opis' 1, 120.

59. Ibid., f 728, opis' 1, delo 961.

60. Edling, *Mémoires*, 57.

61. That is Maria Naryshkina.

62. Elizabeth to her mother, June 10 (O.S.), 1804, quoted by Grand Duke Nicholas Mikhailovich in Romanov, *Imperatrica Elizaveta Alekseevna*, 2: 133–34.

63. Ibid., 147–48.

64. It is impossible to be more precise. Elizabeth's diary, recently discovered, brings some answers, but most of the documents related to this affair disappeared on 1826, probably destroyed on the order of Tsar Nicholas I. Nicholas showed the letters to his wife, Alexandra Feodorovna, who alluded to them in her diary and condemned this affair because it was morally unacceptable to her.

Chapter 7

1. Quoted by Sokolov in *Austerlitz*, 85.

2. The text was published in *Vneshnjaja Politika Rossii*, I, 1: 28–34.

3. Sirotkin, *Napoleon i Aleksandr I*, 55.

4. "On the political system of the Russian Empire," memorandum written by Panin between March and July 1801 and given to Alexander I on July 28, 1801. *Vneshnjaja Politika Rossii*, I, 1: 62–67.

5. A. Czartoryski, *Mémoires*, 1: 284.

6. Quoted in *Sbornik*, 70: 178.

7. Alexander's instructions to Count Morkov, July 9, 1801, in Martens, *Sobranie traktatov i konvencij*, vol. 13.

8. Quoted by Sokolov in *Austerlitz*, 85.

9. *Sbornik*, 70: 705.

10. Kochubey to Vorontsov, November 27 (O.S.), 1801, quoted in Vorontsov, *Arhiv*, 14: 171–72.

11. Kochubey to Vorontsov, May 7 (O.S.), 1802, quoted in Vorontsov, *Arhiv*, 18: 271.

12. I.e., Queen Louise and her sister.

13. A. Czartoryski, *Mémoires*, 1: 296.

14. Ibid., 227.

15. On the question of the boundaries between the two structures, see *Ocherki ministerstva inostrannyh*, 1: 241–43.

16. See Jenkins, *Arakcheev*, 100.

17. Imeritia corresponds to the Kutaisi region; it is now located in Central Georgia.

18. Alexander to Laharpe, July 7 (23), 1803, quoted in La Harpe, *Correspondance*, 2: 44–45.

19. Quoted in Grunwald, *Alexandre Ier*, 99.

20. J. de Maistre, *Mémoires politiques*, quoted by Grand Duke Nicholas Mikhailovich in Romanov, *Tsar Alexandre Ier*, 40.

21. Sirotkin, *Napoleon i Aleksandr I*, 60.

22. Quoted by McConnell, "Hundred Days."

23. Sirotkin, *Napoleon i Aleksandr I*, 62,

24. Report from Alexander Vorontsov, November 12 (24), 1803, quoted by Sirotkin, *Napoleon i Aleksandr I*, 62.

25. Report from Adam Czartoryski, February 17 (O.S.), 1804, quoted by Sirotkin, *Napoleon i Aleksandr I*, 62.

26. Czartoryski to Simon Vorontsov, March 9 (O.S.), 1804, quoted by Sirotkin, *Napoleon i Aleksandr I*, 63.

27. Letter written on April 18 (30), 1804, in J. de Maistre, *Mémoires politiques*, 110–11.

28. On this meeting and on the discussions that took place, see A. Czartoryski, *Mémoires*, 1: 378–80. The verbatim of this session is reproduced *in extenso* in *Vneshnjaja Politika Rossii*, I, 1: 686–92.

29. A. Czartoryski, *Mémoires*, 1: 380.

30. Czartoryski's declaration, April 5 (17), 1805, quoted by Sokolov in *Austerlitz*, 135.

31. *Vneshnjaja Politika Rossii*, I, 1: 698.

32. Quoted in Tatischeff, *Alexandre Ier et Napoléon*, 79.

33. Quoted in Martens, *Sobranie traktatov i konvensij*, 13: 289–90.

34. On Piatoli and on his role in relation to Czartoryski, see Cartoryski, *Mémoires*, 1: 392–95 and Waliszewski, *La Russie*, 143–44.

35. The two documents are reproduced in A. Czartoryski, *Mémoires*, 2: 62–66.

36. On this key point, see Grimsted's analysis in *Foreign Ministers*, 115.

37. A. Czartoryski, *Mémoires*, 2: 62–66.

38. Ibid.

39. Ibid.

40. Alexander's instructions are reproduced *in extenso* in *Vneshnjaja Politika Rossii*, I, 2: 138–51 and in A. Czartoryski, *Mémoires*, 2: 27–45.

41. I.e., Russia and England.

42. A. Czartoryski, *Mémoires*, 2: 29.

43. Ibid., 28.

44. Ibid., 30.

45. Ibid., 29.
46. Ibid., 31.
47. Ibid., 32.
48. Ibid.
49. The expression is used by Alexander I, see A. Czartoryski, *Mémoires*, 2: 34.
50. Ibid., 2: 35.
51. Ibid., 2: 36.
52. Quoted by F. Vermale in *Joseph de Maistre*, published in 1927, in Mémoires et documents de la Société Savoisienne d'Histoire et d'Archéologie.
53. A. Czartoryski, *Mémoires*, 2: 37
54. A. Czartoryski, *Mémoires*, 1: 376.
55. Quoted in Martens, *Sobranie traktatov i konventsij*, 11: 88.
56. Quoted in ibid., 11: 94–95.
57. Quoted in ibid., 11: 104–5.
58. Quoted in *Vneshnjaja Politika Rossii*, I, 2: 246.
59. Quoted in Martens, *Sobranie traktatov i konventsij*, 11: 100.

Chapter 8

1. Quoted by Nicholas Mikhailovich in Romanov, *Imperatrica Elizaveta Alekseevna*, 2: 167–68.
2. S. Zhikharev, *Zapiski Sovremmenika* (Moskva: 2004), 137–38, quoted in Sokolov, *Austerlitz*, 152.
3. From 1803.
4. The word "treaty" is used in the text itself and it is reproduced in *Vneshnjaja Politika Rossii*, I, 2: 613–14.
5. See Andolenko, *L'armée russe*, 161.
6. Today Dürnstein.
7. Quoted in Troyat, *Alexandre Ier*, 120.
8. Quoted in Shilder, *Imperator Aleksandr I*, 2: 284.
9. Alexander to Napoleon, November 15 (27), 1805, quoted in ibid.
10. Napoleon to the elector of Württemberg, Austerlitz, December 5, 1805, in *Correspondance de Napoléon*, published on the Web site www.histoire.-empire.org.
11. Napoleon to Talleyrand, November 30, 1805, in *Correspondance de Napoléon*, ibid.
12. Napoleon to the elector of Württemberg, Austerlitz, December 5, 1805, in *Correspondance de Napoléon*, ibid.
13. Quoted by Mikhailovich-Danilevski, in *Première guerre*, 172–73.
14. On Austerliz, see the meticulous account of the battle in Sokolov, *Austerlitz*, 343–417.
15. Langeron's memoirs, quoted by Shilder in *Imperator Aleksandr I*, 2: 283.
16. Ibid.

17. See Sokolov, *Austerlitz*, 370.

18. Quoted by Mikhailovich-Danilevski, in *Première guerre*, 181–82.

19. However, in his study of the Austerlitz battle, O. Sokolov denied that these men drowned en masse. He sees this description as exaggerated and asserts that only a few men died (frozen and not drowned) in the Satchan pond.

20. General Marbot's memoirs, quoted by Mascilli Migliorini in *Napoléon*, 269.

21. On these losses, see Sokolov, *Austerlitz*, 420–21.

22. This expression is Talleyrand's. On his role and his vision of the Presburg peace, see Waresquiel, "Talleyrand."

23. Novosiltsev to Stroganov, January 6 (O.S.), 1806, quoted by Nicholas Mikhailovich in Romanov, *Stroganov*, 3: 106.

24. Czartoryski to Alexander, April 1806 (no more precise date), quoted in A. Czartoryski, *Mémoires*, 2: 121–23.

25. The text is reproduced in ibid., 2: 66.

26. Ibid.

27. Maria Feodorovna to Alexander, April 18, 1806, in *Russkij Arhiv*, 1911, n.1.

28. Quoted in Sirotkin, *Napoleon i Aleksandr I*, 96.

29. See *Vneshnjaja Politika Rossii*, 3: doc n.54, quoted in ibid.

30. The text is reproduced in *Vneshnjaja Politika Rossii*, I, 3: 226–28.

31. See Ratchinski, *Napoléon et Alexandre Ier*, 84–85.

32. Which was quite paradoxical!

33. This pseudonym was based on the Russian word *bogatyr*: in popular legend, the brave knights fighting for the Russian motherland.

34. Quoted in Jacoby, *Napoléon en Russie*, 35.

35. Then Mitau.

36. See Sirotkin, *Napoleon i Aleksandr I*, 125.

37. Then Pollangen.

38. On the psychological impact of the Eylau battle on Napoleon, see Englund, *Napoléon*, 356–57.

39. See Sirotkin, *Napoleon i Aleksandr I*, 109–13.

40. See ibid., 145.

41. Ibid., 144.

42. Quoted by Tatischeff in *Alexandre Ier et Napoléon*, 148–49.

43. This anonymous poem was composed in Paris, just after the Tilsit meetings. Quoted by Shilder in *Imperator Aleksandr I*, 2: 294.

44. Chateaubriand, *Mémoires*, 6: 2.

45. *Souvenirs du général baron Paulin* (Paris: 1895). Quoted by Shilder in *Imperator Aleksandr I*, 2: 293.

46. See Shilder in *Imperator Aleksandr I*, 2: 293.

47. As expressed by Alexander in his first meeting with Napoleon, quoted in ibid., 296.

48. As shown by his instructions to conclude peace, in *Vneshnjaja Politika Rossii*, I, 3: 754–57.

49. Declarations to Las Cases, made between Sunday, the 10th, and Tuesday, the 12th of March, 1816.

50. Edling, *Mémoires*, 83–86.

51. Quoted by Olivier in *Alexandre Ier*, 139.

52. Quoted by Englund in *Napoléon*, 359.

53. Alexander to his sister Catherine, written in Weimar, May 26 (O.S.), 1807, quoted in Alexander, *Perepiska*, 17.

54. Alexander to his sister Catherine, Tilsit, June 17 (29), 1807, quoted in ibid., 15.

55. Kurakin to Maria Feodorovna, Tilsi, June 22 (O.S.), 1807, quoted in Tatischeff in *Alexandre Ier et Napoléon*, 136–37.

56. The text is fully reproduced in *Vneshnjaja Politika Rossii*, I, 3: 631–37.

57. Some Greeks will not accept the French domination and will choose to serve Russia instead. This would be the case of J. Capo d'Istria who, born in Corfu, will then enter the Russian diplomatic service. As we will see below, he will play a key role during the Vienna Congress in 1814–1815.

58. Article 5 in the text.

59. *Vneshnjaja Politika Rossii*, I, 3: 632.

60. Frederick Wilhelm to Ambassador Finkenstein, June 30, 1807, quoted by Shilder in *Imperator Aleksandr I*, 2: 298.

61. Quoted in Méneval, *Mémoires*, 2: 105.

62. Quoted by Sirotkin, *Napoleon i Aleksandr I*, 181.

Chapter 9

1. Extract from Alexander's ukase, August 9 (21), 1807, quoted by Sirotkin, *Napoleon i Aleksandr I*, 197.

2. Count Stedingk to the Swedish king, October 10, 1807, in *Mémoires posthume*, 2: 355.

3. J. de Maistre, *Correspondance diplomatique*, 65.

4. Elizabeth to her mother, August 29 (O.S), 1807, quoted by Nicholas Mikhailovich in Romanov, *Imperatrica Elizaveta Alekseevna*, 2: 256–57.

5. Caulaincourt, *Mémoires*, 1: 94.

6. His official appointment began on February 12, 1808.

7. See Sirotkin, *Napoleon i Aleksandr I*, 198.

8. Elizabeth to Count Rumyantsev, October 7 (O.S.), 1807, quoted in Jacoby, *Napoléon en Russie*, 33.

9. Memoirs of the duke of Rovigo, quoted in Jacoby, *Napoléon en Russie*, 33.

10. Ibid.

11. Arkhanguelski, *Alexandre Ier*, 163.

12. Ratchinski, *Napoléon et Alexandre Ier*, 268.

13. He took part in the arrest of the duke but not in his death.

14. An allusion to the character of Ninette in the eponymous comic opera written by Charles-Simon Favart in 1757.

15. Quoted by H. Troyat in *Alexandre Ier, le sphinx du nord,* 160

16. Caulaincourt, *Mémoires,* 1: 96.

17. Quoted by Romanov in *Relations diplomatiques,* 1: introduction, xx.

18. Quoted by Paléologue, *Alexandre Ier,* 68.

19. Tolstoy was uncomfortable with his post in Paris and asked the tsar to relieve him and recall him to St. Petersburg. See Romanov *Relations diplomatiques,* 1: introduction, xxi.

20. See Sirotkin, *Napoleon i Aleksandr I,* 206–8.

21. Caulaincourt's report to Napoleon, June 12 (O.S.), 1808, quoted in Romanov, *Relations diplomatiques,* 201.

22. Maria Feodorovna to Alexander, August 13 (O.S.), 1808, in RGADA, fd 1, opis' 3(1).

23. Alexander to Maria Feodorovna, August 13 (O.S.), 1808, quoted by Olivier in *Alexandre Ier,* 183.

24. Vandal, *Napoléon et Alexandre Ier,* 1: 141–42.

25. This expression is Napoleon's.

26. Napoleon's instructions to Talleyrand, quoted by Waresquiel in *Prince immobile,* 692.

27. Caulaincourt, *Mémoires,* 1: 273.

28. Described by Caulaincourt in his memoirs, ibid., 273.

29. The economic and financial consequences of the alliance will be analyzed in chapter 10.

30. The text is fully reproduced in *Vneshnjaja Politika Rossii,* I, 4: 259–361.

31. Ibid., 4: 360.

32. Quoted by Waresquiel in *Prince immobile,* 390.

33. Quoted by Paléologue in *Alexandre Ier,* 83.

34. Waresquiel in *Prince immobile,* 391.

35. Ibid.

36. Talleyrand's memoirs, quoted by Waresquiel in *Prince immobile,* 392.

37. Ibid.

38. As we will see below.

39. Quoted by Paléologue in *Alexandre Ier,* 89–90.

40. She died on July 8, 1810, at the age of 34.

41. Quoted by Paléologue in ibid., 92. A copy of Louise's diary is located in the Russian National Archives (GARF).

42. Alexander to his sister Catherine, September 6 (O.S.), 1809, quoted in Alexander, *Perepiska,* 25.

43. See Laharpe's letter to Alexander on March 31, 1808, in La Harpe, *Correspondance,* 307.

44. Quoted by Vandal in *Napoléon et Alexandre Ier,* 2: 95–96.

45. Caulaincourt to Napoleon, August 19, 1809, entitled "It is said," quoted in ibid., 2: 112.

46. Ibid., 2: 284.

47. See the next chapter.

48. The duke was the father of Alexander's brother-in-law.

49. Quoted by Tatischeff in *Alexandre Ier et Napoléon*, 137–38.

50. See the next chapter.

51. Both letters are reproduced in L. Czartoryski, *Alexandre Ier*, 127–35.

52. Ibid.

53. Ibid.

54. Ibid.

55. Ibid.

56. Ibid.

57. Caulaincourt, *Mémoires*; Caulaincourt's meeting with Napoleon on June 5 appears on pages 1: 270–93.

58. Caulaincourt's letter to Champagny, September 19, 1810, in Romanov, *Relations diplomatiques*, 5: 139.

59. Quoted by Paléologue in *Alexandre Ier*, 137.

60. Ibid., 125–26.

61. Sirotkin, *Napoleon i Aleksandr I*, 324.

62. Ibid., 325.

Chapter 10

1. Alexander I to his sister Catherine, June 27 (O.S.), 1810, quoted by Nicholas Mikhailovich in Alexander, *Perepiska*, 33.

2. Seton-Watson, *Russian Empire*, 97.

3. See chapter 6.

4. See Maikoff, "Rozenkampf," 373.

5. Romanov, *Tsar Alexandre I*, 60.

6. The son of his sister.

7. For biographical details, see the anthology, *M.M Speranskij, zhizn'*, 16.

8. Or "departments."

9. *Speranskij, zhizn'*, 19.

10. See Mironenko, *Samoderzhavie i reformy*, 29.

11. As shown in his sermons, written when he was a student at the St. Petersburg seminary. See Raeff, "Political Philosophy," 3.

12. See Mironenko, *Samoderzhavie i reformy*, 29–30.

13. Raeff, "Political Philosophy," 6–7.

14. *Chin* in Russian.

15. There were 14 ranks in the civil table. Personal (and not hereditary) nobility was granted by the state from the ninth rank.

16. *Speranskij, zhizn'*, 22.

17. *Gubernjaja* in Russian.

18. *Okrug* in Russian.

19. *Volost'* in Russian.

20. *Oblast'* in Russian.

21. Abolition of serfdom was not on Minister Speransky's agenda.

22. Quoted by Vernadsky in *Charte constitutionnelle*, 18.

23. Quoted by Kappeler in *La Russie*, 96.

24. See Selovuori, *Le pouvoir*, 11.

25. See Tegner, *Armfelt*, 3: 294.

26. Kappeler, *La Russie*, 94.

27. Article 17 of the treaty, then called the Friedrichshamm treaty, signed on September 5 (O.S.), 1809. In *Vneshnjaja Politika Rossii*, I, 5: 218.

28. See the excellent biography by Josselson and Josselson, *Général Hiver*.

29. Mironenko, *Samoderzhavie i reformy*, 34.

30. Maria Feodorovna's notes, December 27 (O.S.), 1809, in GARF, fd 663 (Maria Feodorovna fond); opis' 1; delo 43.

31. Quoted in Arkhanguelski, *Alexandre Ier*, 165.

32. Ibid., 166–67.

33. See Jenkins, *Arakcheev*, 137.

34. See Richard Pipes's study in Karamzin, *Memoir*.

35. McConnell, *Tsar Alexander I*, 72–73.

36. *Speranskij, zhizn'*, 23.

37. McConnell, *Tsar Alexander I*, 74.

38. A sect defending the ideas of Louis Claude de Saint-Martin.

39. He will become a Freemason in April 1818. See Serkov, *Russkoe Masonstvo*.

40. Illuminism was the Russian version of Martinism. Speransky's letter to Alexander is quoted in *Speranskij, zhizn'*, 24.

41. See, for example, Sakharov, *Aleksandr I*, 132–35.

42. Speransky will eventually conduct this reform under Nicholas I.

43. Raeff, *Comprendre l'Ancien Régime*, 126.

44. The state council would have 42 members in 1825.

45. See the remarkable study by Mironenko in *Samoderzhavie i reformy*, 34–35.

46. Quoted in Alexander, *Perepiska*, 57.

47. Ibid.

48. Report by Barclay to Alexander, written between February 12 and 28 (O.S.), 1810, in *Vneshnjaja Politika Rossii*, I, 6: 379.

49. One verste was 1,067 meters, i.e., 66 miles.

50. Josselson and Josselson, *Général Hiver*, 136.

51. Ibid., 138.

52. Letter from Count Lieven to Barclay de Tolly, December 2 (O.S.), 1810, in *Vneshnjaja Politika Rossii*, I, 6: 635–37.

53. Quoted in Cate, *La campagne de Russie*, 79.

54. Ibid., 78–82, for a detailed analysis of the roles of Chernyshev and Michel.

55. He will later become Alexander's foreign minister.

56. Talleyrand to Alexander, September 15, 1810, in RGADA, fd 5, opis' 1, delo 210.

57. Dispatch from Count Loewenhielm, April 5 (O.S.), 1812, quoted in Vandal, *Napoléon et Alexandre Ier*, 2: 441–42.

58. Of the 30 million rubles' worth of merchandise exported in 1802 from St. Petersburg, England bought 17 million rubles' worth and France less than a half million.

59. Sirotkin, *Napoleon i Aleksandr I*, 237.

60. Ibid., 241.

61. Ibid., 243.

62. Ibid., 249.

63. Quoted in L. Czartoryski, *Alexandre Ier*, 170.

64. Quoted by Arkhanguelski in *Alexandre Ier*, 194.

65. Quoted in Olivier, *Alexandre Ier*, 213.

66. Quoted in L. Czartoryski, *Alexandre Ier*, 173–74.

Chapter 11

1. See Troickij, *Otechesvennaja vojna*, 3.

2. Key books were still produced during those years, including those by E. Tarlé.

3. See the numerous books written in France by Jean Tulard and my own book *L'effroyable tragédie*, which takes into account both Russian and French perspectives. For the Russian side, see Dominic Lieven's recent book, *Russia against Napoleon*, and in Russian Troickij, *Otechesvennaja vojna*, and *Aleksandr I*.

4. The word "duel" is frequently used by historians to describe the 1812 war.

5. Napoleon confessed several mistakes to Las Cases on St. Helena.

6. Quoted by Shilder in *Imperator Aleksandr I*, 3: 368.

7. Quoted by Cate, *La campagne de Russie*, 23.

8. Ibid., 62.

9. Ibid.

10. See Troickij, *Rossija*, 38.

11. Choiseul-Gouffier, *Mémoires historiques*, 75–77.

12. Later, 150,000 soldiers will cross the Niemen, so the total number of soldiers taking part in the Grande Armée will be about 600,000.

13. Troickij, *Rossija*, 37.

14. Napoléon Ier, *Correspondance*, 5: 535–36.

15. For more complete data, see Troickij, *Rossija*, 34.

16. Quoted by Josselson and Josselson in *Général Hiver*, 173.

17. Quoted by Tulard in *Dictionnaire Napoléon*, 356.

18. Troickij, *Rossija*, 37.

19. See D. Lieven's brilliant article "Defeat of Napoleon."

20. See Beauvois, "Les Français."

21. Boudon, *La France*, 264.

22. Vilnius was called Vilna at that time.

23. Caulaincourt's memoirs, quoted by Sokolov in "Campagne de Russie."

24. Tulard in *Dictionnaire Napoléon*, 356.

25. The great theoretician and strategist. Disapproving of the evolution of French-Prussian relations, Clausewitz decided to join the Russian army in 1812.

26. Quoted by Sokolov in "Campagne de Russie."

27. Quoted by Josselson and Josselson in *Général Hiver*, 181.

28. Quoted by Romanov in *Le Tsar Alexandre Ier*, 122–23.

29. Quoted by Sokolov in "Campagne de Russie."

30. Ibid.

31. Boudon, *La France*, 262.

32. Meaning a peasant insurrection like the one led by Pugachev under the reign of Catherine II.

33. See Parsamov, *Istorija Rossii*, 198.

34. Quoted in Alexander, *Perepiska*, 82.

35. Langeron's unedited memoirs, quoted in Tulard, *Dictionnaire Napoléon*, 1008.

36. See A. Martin, "Response," 473.

37. Quoted by Sokolov in "Campagne de Russie."

38. Quoted in Ségur, *Comte Rostopchine*, 207.

39. Paul Stroganov to his wife, September 13 (O.S.), 1812, quoted in Romanov, *Le Tsar Alexandre Ier*, 129.

40. Boudon, *La France*, 264.

41. By the Russian calendar.

42. Equivalent to 5 degrees F.

43. Extract from X. de Maistre, *La correspondance*, vol. 1.

44. J. de Maistre, *Correspondance diplomatique*, 246.

45. Imperial Library of St. Petersburg, Department of Manuscripts, fd n.152, opis' 1, delo 209.

46. Posharsky was the prince who led the Russian troops during the Polish invasion in 1611–1612.

47. Palitsyn was an orthodox monk who took an active part in the struggle against the Poles.

48. Minine was the butcher of Nizhni-Novgorod who organized Pozharsky's expedition against the Poles.

49. Imperial Library of St. Petersburg, Department of Manuscripts, fd n.152, opis' 1, delo 209.

50. Choiseul-Gouffier, *Mémoires historiques*, 134.

51. Jacquerie: a peasant insurrection, after the common first name often given to poor peasant boys.

52. Alexander's ukase, August 13 (O.S.), 1812, Imperial Library of St. Petersburg, Department of Manuscripts, fd n.152, opis' 1, delo 209.

53. Parsamov, *Istorija Rossii*, 198.

54. Elizabeth to her mother, August 26 (O.S.), 1812, quoted by Nicholas Mikhailovich in Romanov, *Imperatrica Elizaveta Alekseevna*, 2: 542–43.

55. The assertion is ironic. The supposedly civilized nation is France.

56. Elizabeth to her mother, August 28 (O.S.), 1812, quoted by Nicholas Mikhailovich in Romanov, *Imperatrica Elizaveta Alekseevna*, 2: 543.

57. Catherine to Alexander, September 3 (O.S.), 1812, quoted by Nicholas Mikhailovich in Alexander, *Perepiska*, 83.

58. Alexander to Catherine, September 7 (O.S.), 1812, ibid., 84.

59. Catherine to Alexander, September 6 (O.S.), 1812, ibid., 83–84.

60. Alexander to Catherine, September 7 (O.S.), 1812, ibid., 86–93.

61. Conversations with Abbot Eylert, in *Charakterzüge ans dem Leben Koenigs Friedrich-Wilhelms III*, 2: 246–48, quoted in Schnitzler, *Etudes sur l'empire*, 1: 461–62.

62. "Alexandre I" in Serkov, *Russkoje Masonstvo*.

63. Conversations with Abbot Eylert, Schnitzler, *Etudes sur l'empire*, 1: op. cit., 461–62.

64. *Russkij Arhiv* no. 4 (1886), 87.

Chapter 12

1. Quoted in Troickij, *Aleksandr I*, 219.

2. Lincoln, *Sunlight at Midnight*, 110.

3. Kalisch=Kalisz (Poland).

4. This text was written in 1812 and published in 1821 in *Douze années d'exil*, quoted in Grève, *Le Voyage en Russie*, 809–10.

5. See D. Lieven, "Defeat of Napoleon."

6. Alexander's ukase, November 11 (23), 1812, published in *Kazanskie Izvestija*, no. 48 (November 30, 1812).

7. Quoted by Ratchinski, *Napoléon et Alexandre Ier*, 319.

8. Ibid.

9. Quoted in *Alexandrana*, 18.

10. Quoted in Renouvin, *Histoire des relations internationales*, 2: 244.

11. Paléologue, *Alexandre Ier*, 177.

12. Troickij, *Rossija*, 56.

13. Hartley, *Alexander I*, 123.

14. Slightly more than a third of the engaged troops died at Leipzig.

15. Notice that the tsar was still using the expression "Supreme Being" after his 1812 mystical revelation.

16. Paléologue, *Alexandre Ier*, 178–79.

17. Quoted by Choiseul-Gouffier in *Mémoires historiques*, 162–63.

18. The Battle of Valmy (a northern village in Champagne-Ardennes) was the first major victory by the army of France during the French Revolution. It took place on September 20, 1792. When Prussian troops commanded by the Duke of Brunswick attempted to march on Paris, Generals Kellermann and Dumouriez defeated them at Valmy and stopped their advance.

19. Quoted by Romanov in *Imperator Alexandre Ier* (1912 ed.), 2: 7.

20. Ibid., 1: 530.

21. Alexander I to Alexander Golitsyn, February 26 (O.S.), 1812, in GARF, fd 728, opis' 1, delo 803.

22. Quoted in Romanov, *Imperator Alexandre Ier* (1912 ed.), 1: 531.

23. Ibid.

24. Quoted by Pingaud, *L'Empereur Alexandre Ier*, 15.

25. Choiseul-Gouffier, *Mémoires historiques*, 134–35.

26. Quoted in *Alexandrana*, 39–40.

27. Ibid., 40.

28. Choiseul-Gouffier, *Mémoires historiques*, 74–75.

29. Chateaubriand, *Mémoires*, 495.

30. Alexander's use of the Corsican family name of Buonaparte is interesting, implying that for Alexander Napoléon was no longer emperor of the French—and not even French by nationality!

31. Quoted in *Alexandrana*, 47.

32. Quoted in Troyat, *Alexandre Ier*, 265.

33. Aleksandr Mikhailovskij-Danilevskij's documentary sources and manuscript notes are preserved in the St. Petersburg Imperial Library, fd 488, where I consulted them.

34. This diary was partially published before 1917 and was republished in 2001. The years 1814–1815 were published as a book, see Mikhailovskij-Danilevskij, *Memuary*.

35. In the opinion of the Countess de Boigne!

36. Boigne, *Mémoires*, 1: 331.

37. Troyat, *Alexander of Russia*.

38. See Hantraye, *Les Cosaques*, 34.

39. Boigne, *Mémoires*, 324–25.

40. Hantraye, *Les Cosaques*, 225.

41. Ibid.

42. Ibid., 226–27.

43. In 1815 the Catholic Easter day was the same as the Orthodox one.

44. Quoted H. Valloton in *Le tsar Alexandre Ier*, 225.

45. *Alexandrana*, 75.

46. Choiseul-Gouffier, *Mémoires historiques*, 176.

47. *Alexandrana*, 76.

48. Ibid., 85.

49. Mikhailovskij-Danilevskij, *Memuary*, 47.

50. *Alexandrana*, 58.

51. Quoted in Martens, *Sobranie traktatov i konvencij*, 14: 237.

52. Ibid., 261.

53. Chateaubriand, *Mémoires*, 495–96.

54. Boigne, *Mémoires*, 359.

55. He was Louis XVIII's brother and will later become King Charles X.

56. Uvarov did not strangle Paul I, but he was among the small group of people who violently entered his room.

57. Boigne, *Mémoires*, 361–62.

58. Quoted by Paléologue, *Alexandre Ier*, 199.

59. According to Countess de Lieven (the wife of Count Lieven), Alexander's ambassador in London. See Comtesse de Lieven, *Mémoires*, 226.

60. Ibid., 228.

61. Allen, *Life of William Allen*, 1: 197–98.

62. Quoted by Hartley in *Alexander I*, 126.

63. Ibid.

64. No precise dating is possible.

65. Notice that the tsar alludes to 1801, the date of his first flirtation with Maria, and not 1803, when their affair began. This is probably to reinforce the value of his sacrifice and the extent of his pain.

66. Alexander to Catherine, Summer 1814, GARF, fd 728, opis' 1, delo 1336.

67. Alexander to Koshelev, 1817 (undated), GARF, fd 728, opis' 1, delo 860.

68. See Sedouy, *Congrès de Vienne*, 160–61.

69. See, for example, Kissinger, *Diplomatie*, which begins with a detailed analysis of the Congress.

70. GARF, fd 728, opis' 1, delo 972.

71. Quoted by Zawadski in *Man of Honour*, 252.

72. Renouvin, *Histoire des relations internationales*, 254.

73. This extract from his diary was published in *Russkaja Starina* (June 1899).

74. Mikhailovskij-Danilevskij, *Memuary*, 186.

75. Hartley, *Alexander I*, 130.

76. See Romanov, *Imperator Alexandre Ier* (1912 ed.), 1: 115.

77. However, this generous behavior did not prevent Russian troops in 1813–1814 from large-scale requisitions of occupied Polish lands, which led to violence against the local population and to some cases of starvation. See Zawadski, *Man of Honour*, 227.

78. Ibid., 231–32.

79. Quoted by Troickij, *Rossija*, 58.

80. See Zawadski, *Man of Honour*, 238–39.

81. Quoted by Waresquiel in *Prince immobile*, 485.

82. Quoted in M. Martin, *Maria Feodorovna*, 406–8.

83. The Plaine of Vertus is close to the small town of Aubervilliers.

84. Quoted in "Antonin Carême," 22.

85. Count Molé's memoirs, quoted by Grunwald in *Trois siècles*, 165.

86. Quoted by Ratchinski, *Napoléon et Alexandre Ier*, 346.

87. Moreover, Austria was given Illyria, Tyrol, Lombardia, and Venetia, thereby recovering her predominance in Italy.

88. Hartley, *Alexander I*, 133.

89. The expression is Castlereagh's.

90. Quoted by Renouvin, *Histoire des relations internationales*, 370.

91. The full text of the Holy Alliance is reproduced in *Vneshniaia Politika Rossii*, I, 8: 502–4.

92. Madame de Krüdener's first name.

93. Alexander to Catherine, May 22 (O.S.), 1815, quoted in Romanov, *Imperatritsa Elizaveta Alekseevna*, 194–95.

94. Boigne, *Mémoires*, 491.

95. A mistake, since Mme. de Krüdener was not a countess but a baroness.

96. Boigne, *Mémoires*, 491.

97. Quoted by Valloton, *Le Tsar Alexandre Ier*, 340.

98. Both texts, the initial draft written by Alexander and the final version as expurgated by the Austrians, are reproduced in *Vneshniaia Politika Rossii*, 8: 502–4.

Chapter 13

1. See his conversation with Mme. de Staël in December 1812 that she reported in *Douze années d'exil*, quoted by Grève in *Voyage en Russie*, 809–10.

2. Edling, *Mémoires*, 200–201.

3. Quoted by Shilder in *Imperator Aleksandr I*, 3: 394.

4. Alexander to P. V. Chichagov, March 21, 1806, quoted by Grimsted in *Foreign Ministers*, 28.

5. Arakcheev did not have any ministerial responsibilities.

6. This style was also called Classical-Romantic.

7. Schmidt, "Restoration of Moscow."

8. They were the symbols of patriotic resistance to the Polish invaders in 1612.

9. Schmidt, "Restoration of Moscow."

10. The Bolshoi Theater will open in 1825.

11. Quoted by Sokolov in "L'Eglise."

12. Ratchinski, *Napoléon et Alexandre Ier*, 57.

13. Golitzyn to Alexander, July 18 (O.S.), 1820 or 1821, in GARF, fd 728, delo 1109.

14. On Moravian Brothers, see Minaudier, *Histoire de l'Estonie*, 131–35.

15. Ratchinski, *Napoléon et Alexandre Ier*, 56.

16. GARF, fd 728, delo 1303.

17. The document is quoted in Alexander, *Perepiska*, 286–90.

18. I.e., Christianity.

19. Alexander spelled the name "Mallebranche," instead of "Malebranche."

20. Grellet, *Memoirs*, 1: 417; quoted by Hartley in *Alexander I*, 187.

21. Allen, *Life of William Allen*, 2: 265, quoted in J. Hartley, *Alexander I*, 187.

22. Alexander's conversation with Abbot Eylert, quoted by Schnitzler, *Etudes sur l'empire des tsar*, 463–64.

23. Ibid.

24. See J. de Maistre, *Oeuvres complètes*, 13: 282–88.

25. Ibid.

26. A theory presented in a document from Vienna, written by Mgr. the nuncio Severoli and sent to the papal secretary on January 27, 1816. It was taken up in a letter written by R. P. Desiderius Richardot, on February 14, 1844. In the archives of the Jesuit Order, Rome, doc Russ 6-VII, 31 box 1005, Russia, 1805–1814.

27. Joseph de Maistre to Severoli, St. Petersburg, December 1 (O.S.), 1815, ibid.

28. Note on the expulsion of the Jesuits, 1821, ibid.

29. The Old Believers separated after 1666 from the official Orthodox Church as a protest against reforms introduced by Patriarch Nikon between 1652–1666. They continued liturgical practices maintained by the Russian Orthodox Church before the implementation of these reforms and suffered severe persecution.

30. Pushkin stayed in Bessarabia until the spring of 1823, before being exiled to Odessa, then to the family estate of Mikhailovskoe, close to Pskov.

31. "Decrees of Providence" was an expression often used by the tsar.

32. Choiseul-Gouffier, *Mémoires historiques*, 134.

33. Quoted by Arkhanguelski, *Alexandre Ier*, 442.

34. *Russkaja Starina*, no. 88 (1896), 53–54.

35. Quoted by]Arkhanguelski, *Alexandre Ier*, 442.

36. See Mironenko, *Samoderzhavie i reformy*, 117.

37. Charlotte of Prussia was the daughter of Queen Louise.

38. See the letter written from Warsaw by Constantine to his younger sister Anne, Princess of Orange, on May 15 (O.S.), 1820, reproduced in Jackman, *Romanov Relations*, 80–81.

39. "Memorandum de Pozzo di Borgo sur la question polonaise" (in French), October 8 (O.S.), 1814, in GARF, fd 679, opis' 1, delo 47.

40. With the exception of Finland.

41. Particularly Catherine II.

42. "Memorandum de Pozzo di Borgo sur la question polonaise," GARF, fd 679, opis' 1, delo 47.

43. Ibid.

44. On May 25, 1815.

45. See Zawadski, *Man of Honour*, 256–57.

46. Mironenko, *Samoderzhavie i reformy*, 150.

47. Zawadski, *Man of Honour*, 261–62.

48. For a detailed analysis of this document, see Mironenko, *Samoderzhavie i reformy*, 150–54.

49. Only Polish men could vote.

50. Mironenko, *Samoderzhavie i reformy*, 153.

51. Anna Pavlovna to Constantine, May 21, 1818, quoted in Jackman, *Romanov Relations*, 76.

52. Mironenko, *Samoderzhavie i reformy*, 154.

53. Ibid., 156.

54. He did not want to offend the Poles by using the Russian language.

55. Mironenko, *Samoderzhavie i reformy*, 157.

56. Archives of the Jesuit Order, Library of the Ecole Normale Supérieure de Lyon, Manuscript Department, personal archives of Father Pierling, file BSL/PI, 9 no.5.

57. This was Mikhailovsky-Danilevsky's point of view. See Mironenko, *Samoderzhavie i reformy*, 158.

58. Or *Dekabristi*. These were the Russian revolutionaries who led an unsuccessful uprising on December 14 (O.S.), 1825, and through their martyrdom served as an example to succeeding generations of revolutionaries. They were primarily members of the upper classes who had military backgrounds; some had participated in the Russian occupation of France after the Napoleonic Wars and came back from France with revolutionary ideas.

59. Emphasis is mine.

60. Alexander's conversation with General Borstell, in GARF, fd 728, opis' 1, delo 633a.

61. Mironenko, *Samoderzhavie i reformy*, 163.

62. Ibid., 168.

63. Ibid., 173.

64. The Russian document is located in Moscow in RGADA, fd 3, razrjad III, delo 25. The French version is in St. Petersburg's Imperial Library, Manuscript Department, fd 37, delo 916.

65. The text does not say anything about the Muslims of the Russian Empire.

66. Alexander's speech to the Polish diet, September 1 (O.S.), 1820, in Archives of the Jesuit Order, Library of the Ecole Normale Supérieure de Lyon, Manuscript Department, personal archives of Father Pierling, file BSL/PI, 9 no.5.

67. Ibid. Italics are mine.

68. The Troppau Congress gathered the representatives of the Quintuple Alliance. See chapter 14.

69. Kochubey's report to Alexander, October 22 (O.S.), 1820; quoted in Shilder, *Imperator Aleksandr I*, IV: 540–41.

70. Quoted by Troyat in *Alexandre Ier*, 333.

71. See Minaudier, *Histoire de l'Estonie*, 145–57.

72. Quoted by M. Heller, *Histoire de la Russie*, 655–56.

73. Mironenko, *Samoderzhavie i reformy*, 96.

74. Servan, *Le soldat citoyen*.

75. Jenkins, *Arakcheev*, 185.

76. Ibid., 189. The text of Barclay's memorandum was published in *Voennyj Sbornik*, no. 6 (1861), 336–40.

77. Fedorov, *Speranskij i Arakcheev*, 185.

78. *Russkaja Starina*, no. 88 (1896), 36.

79. Report from Count de la Ferronays to Baron Pasquier, April 1820, in Archives du duc de Richelieu, fonds Richelieu, Ms99, Bibliothèque de la Sorbonne, Paris.

80. Fedorov, *Speranskij i Arakcheev*, 178.

Chapter 14

1. See chapter 7.
2. Today in Azerbaijan.
3. See RAN anthology *Istorija Vneshnej Politiki Rossii*, 245–46.
4. Then called Urga.
5. See *Ocherki ministerstva inostrannyh*, 285.
6. Today these islands are part of Alaska.
7. The place still exists and is called Fort Ross.
8. Quoted in Rey, *De la Russie*, 105.
9. Bridge and Bullen, *Great Powers*, 34.
10. On Castlereagh's positions, see Bartlett, *Peace, War*, 16.
11. Meaning the Restoration king, Louis XVIII.
12. Quoted in Renouvin, *Histoire des relations internationales*, 3: 372.
13. Quoted in Hartley, *Alexander I*, 142.
14. Alexander to Lord Castlereagh, March 21 (O.S.), 1816, in *Vneshnjaja Politika Rossii*, II, 1:(X), 108–11.
15. I.e., the creation of the Quadruple Alliance.
16. Alexander to Lord Castlereagh, March 21 (O.S.), 1816, in *Vneshnjaja Politika Rossii*, II, 1: (X), 108–11.
17. Hartley, *Alexander I*, 144.
18. Report of the foreign minister to Alexander, June 24 (O.S.), 1818, in *Vneshnjaja Politika Rossii*, II, 1: (X), 409–22.
19. Quoted in Ley, *Alexandre Ier*, 215.
20. Quoted in Renouvin, *Histoire des relations internationales*, 377.
21. Ibid.
22. Metternich, *Lettres*, 78.
23. *Istoriia Vneshnej Politiki Rossii*, 154.
24. Hartley, *Alexander I*, 144.
25. Bartlett, *Peace, War*, 18.
26. Note by the state secretary to Alexander, Vienna, December 19 (31), 1818, in *Vneshnjaja Politika Rossii*, II, 1: (X), 611–18.
27. *Istoriia Vneshnej Politiki Rossii*, 157.
28. Quoted by Shilder, *Imperator Aleksandr I*, 4: 497.
29. Alexander to Golitsyn, February 8–15, 1821, GARF, fd 728, opis' 1, delo 1113.
30. Ibid.
31. Ibid.
32. Alexander to Golitsyn, December 14 (O.S.), 1820, GARF, fd 728, opis' 1, delo 803.
33. Bohemia was then part of the Austrian Empire.
34. Quoted by Bartlett, *Peace, War*, 19.
35. See the previous chapter.
36. Seton-Watson, *Russian Empire*, 177.

37. Today Ljubljana.

38. See Ley, *Alexandre Ier*, 180.

39. Article 7 of the treaty forced the Ottoman Empire "to protect on a permanent basis Christianity and Christian churches" and article 16 gave Russia the right to interfere in domestic issues of Danubian principalities. See Bridge and Bullen, *Great Powers*, 50.

40. Quoted in Shilder, *Imperator Aleksandr I*, 3: 553.

41. The carbonari (coal-burners) were an influential revolutionary group, formed as a secret organization in southern Italy. Inspired by the principles of the French Revolution, they wanted to promote liberalism and the unification of Italy.

42. Alexander to Golitsyn, February 8–15, 1821, GARF, fd 728, opis' 1, delo 1113.

43. Quoted by Zorin in "Star of the East," 338.

44. Ibid.

45. Bridge and Bullen, *Great Powers*, 54.

46. McConnell, *Tsar Alexander I*, 163.

47. Bridge and Bullen, *Great Powers*, 56.

48. Chateaubriand, *Le Congrès de Vérone*.

Chapter 15

1. Schnitzler, *Etudes sur l'empire*, 1, 459.

2. *Russkaja Starina*, 1896.

3. See Dupré de Saint-Maur, *L'Hermite en Russie*, passim.

4. Alexander to Countess de Nesselrode, Warsaw, April 25 (O.S.), 1825, in Nesselrode, *Papiers et archives*, 5: 224–25.

5. Choiseul-Gouffier, *Mémoires historiques*, 292–93.

6. Schakovskoy, *Saint-Pétersbourg et Paris*, 44.

7. Dupré de Saint-Maur, *L'Hermite en Russie*, 230–31.

8. Arkhangelski, *Alexandre Ier*, 380–81.

9. Alexander to Golitsyn, February 8–15 (O.S.), 1821, GARF, fd 728, opis' 1, delo 1113.

10. Quoted in Romanov, *Imperator Aleksandr I* (1912 edition), 299.

11. Sophie was suffering from tuberculosis.

12. Choiseul-Gouffier, *Mémoires historiques*, 308–9.

13. Golitsyn to Alexander, June 1824 (no more precise date), GARF, fd 728, opis' 1, delo 120.

14. De la Ferronays to Pasquier, March 30 (April 10), 1820, quoted in McConnell, "Hundred Days," 393.

15. Of the three mentioned, only Kankrin was competent.

16. Kotchubey to Arakcheev, May 17 (O.S.), 1823, quoted by Romanov, *Imperator Aleksandr I* (1912 ed.), 312.

17. Volkonsky to Aleksey Zakrevsky, October 3 (O.S.), 1823, quoted ibid., 315–16.

18. Quoted ibid., 309.

19. Ivan Pestel was the father of the future Decembrist Pavel Pestel. On Speransky's contribution to the development of Siberia, see Hartley, *Alexander I*, 170.

20. See Jenkins, *Arakcheev*, 222.

21. This was a secret society created in Königsberg (Prussia) in 1808 that intended to regenerate Prussia through the diffusion of liberal ideas.

22. Seton-Watson, *Russian Empire*, 187.

23. Ibid., 187–92.

24. The term *bojyar* belongs to the history of medieval Russia, but it had a new meaning for Pestel: now *bojyary* would be chosen for their expertise and their wisdom, not for their aristocratic origin.

25. See Shilder, *Imperator Aleksandr I*, 4: 204.

26. Constantine to Alexander, January 14 (O.S.), 1822, GARF, fd 728, opis' 1, delo 67.

27. Alexander to Constantine, February 2 (O.S.), 1822, GARF, fd 728, opis' 1, delo 1144.

28. The final version of the document is dated August 23 (O.S.), 1823, GARF, fd 679, opis' 1 delo 68.

29. Ibid.

30. Quoted by Bariatinsky, *Le mystère*, 14.

31. Nicholas was born in 1796; he was almost 20 years younger than Alexander.

32. Alexander to Elizabeth, April 15 (O.S.), 1825, in GARF, fd 658, opis' 1, delo 96, 4.

33. Alexander to Elizabeth, May 12 (O.S.), 1825, in GARF, fd 658, opis' 1, delo 96, 5.

34. Volkonsky to Zakrevsky, quoted in Bariatinsky, *Le mystère*, 18.

35. As admitted by Nicholas Mikhailovich in 1913.

36. Gagarine, *Les archives russes*.

37. All this correspondence belongs to his personal papers that are preserved in the Jesuit archives in Vanves (a Paris suburb), where I consulted them.

38. Personal archives of Father Ivan Gagarin. Archives of the Jesuit order, Vanves. The file devoted to Alexander's conversion is BS GA L 11.

39. She was born Constance de Maistre and was Joseph de Maistre's daughter.

40. Father Gagarin's archives. Archives of the Jesuit order, Vanves, BS GA L 11.

41. Pierling, *L'Empereur Alexandre Ier* .

42. The personal papers of Father Pierling and his sources are preserved in the archives of the Jesuit order located in Lyon, Library of the Ecole Normale Supérieure, Manuscript fd, file BSL Pi 13, n.8.

43. This memorandum was published on November 4, 1876, in *La Civilta Cattolica*.

44. She was born Anastasie Michaud de Beauretour.

45. The book was published in 1869 in Italy (Turin: J. Baglione). A copy of this book is preserved in the collection of ancient and rare books of the Biblioteca Reale

di Torino. I express my gratitude to the directors of this library, in particular Clara Vitulo, who provided me with a copy of the text.

46. Paoletti de Rodoretto, *Coup d'oeil*, 117.

47. Ibid., 118.

48. The italics are in the original.

49. Paoletti de Rodoretto, *Coup d'oeil*, 131.

50. Pierling, *Problème d'histoire.*

51. That is, on November 23 in the Russian calendar.

52. Romanov, *Imperator Aleksandr I* (1912 ed.), 303.

53. Vatican Archives, Rome, Segretaria di Stato, 1825–1830, vol. 268.

54. The diary of Father Antonio Bresciani (Diario di Padre Bresciani) that I consulted is preserved in the archives of the Civilta Cattolica, Rome, Scaffale 24, Palchetto C. The report is mentioned on January 22, 1846.

55. Louis Cappatti did not have any links with Russia. But he was a specialist in the history of Nice. In cooperation with J. Eynaudi, he wrote a *Dictionnaire de la langue niçoise.* His article on Michaud, entitled "Le comte Michaud de Beauretour, Alexandre Ier et le pape en 1825," was published in 1932 in Nice, in *Annales du comté de Nice.*

56. I.e., six years before the letter was sent.

57. De la Ferronays.

58. Indeed, the Vatican archives attest to the fact that Italinsky served as an intermediary between the pope and Michaud.

59. Ten years after the fact, Michaud's memory was quite precise: the Vatican archives prove that the meeting took place on December 5.

60. This draft was written in 1835. The final version of the letter sent in 1841 might have been slightly different.

61. This document was communicated to me by Geneviève Chesneau, director of the Bibliothèque du Chevalier de Cessole, Masséna Palace, Nice. I am very grateful to her.

62. The Jesuit case apart.

63. Chateaubriand, *Le Congrès de Vérone*, chap. 32.

64. Romanov, *Imperator Aleksandr I* (1912 ed.), 302.

65. Alexander to Elizabeth, September 5 (O.S.), 1825, GARF, fd 658, opis' n.1, delo 96, 9.

66. After a long trip to France, Volkonsky came back in 1825 and reentered the imperial service to accompany Elizabeth in Taganrog. So Volkonsky, who was probably the closest and the most loyal friend to the tsar, would be present at his illness and death.

67. This means intimate or cozy.

68. Letter quoted by Romanov in *Imperatrica Elizaveta Alekseevna*, 3: 455.

69. Quoted in Arkhanguelski, *Alexandre Ier*, 452.

70. Quoted by Romanov in *Tsar Alexandre Ier*, 339.

71. Elizabeth to her mother, Taganrog, November 19 (December 1), 1825, quoted in Romanov, *Imperatrica Elizaveta Alekseevna*, 3: 469.

72. Elizabeth to her mother, Taganrog, December 31 (O.S.), 1825, quoted in ibid., 3: 488.

73. Quoted in McConnell, "Hundred Days," 187.

By Way of Epilogue

1. A spiritual adviser, often a monk or religious hermit, in the Orthodox Church, who was known for his great piety and his wisdom.

2. My emphasis.

3. Faybisovic, *Aleksandr I*, 13.

4. Gromyko, *Sviatoj pravednij starets*, 55.

5. The meetings between Khromov and Pobedonostsev that took place on July 31, August 11, and August 25 are documented in the Russian archives, RGALI, fd 487, opis' 1, delo 137.

6. Gromyko, *Sviatoj pravednij starets*, 200.

7. For a precise description of the icon, see Arkhanguelski, *Alexandre I*, 509.

8. And today in the inventories of the Department of Manuscripts of the Imperial Library in St. Petersburg, which were established before the October 1917 Revolution, documents related to Alexander I and Feodor Kuzmich are classified in the same place!

9. Gromyko, *Sviatoj pravednij starets*, 127.

10. Romanov, *Legenda o konchine*, 15.

11. Gromyko, *Sviatoj pravednij starets*, 123.

12. Bariatinsky, *Le mystère*.

13. See Arkhanguelski, *Alexandre Ier*, 482, and Gromyko, *Sviatoj pravednij starets*, 201.

14. This is the position taken by A. N. Sakharov in his biography of Alexander I, *Aleksandr I*, published in 1998.

15. This position is defended by Gromyko, *Sviatoj pravednij starets*, passim.

16. Most of these contradictions were meticulously reported in Bariatinsky, *Le mystère*, passim.

Sources

Primary Sources

Archives

RGADA (Rossijskij gosudarstvennyj arhiv drevnih aktov) (Russian State Archive of Early Acts, Moscow).

Fond n.1, Gosudarstvennyj arhiv rossijskoj imperii, razrjad I, sekretnye pakety, ser. XVIII v.–1830, opis' n.1. (Fd n.1, State Archive of the Russian Empire, section I, secret documents, 18th century–1830, opis' n.11)

   See, in particular, Semejnaja perepiska Aleksandra I, Marii Fedorovny, Elizavety Alekseevny, vel. Kn. Konstantina Pavlovicha, Aleksandry Pavlovny, Ekateriny Pavlovny, Eleny Pavlovny 1780–1825. (Family correspondence of Alexander I, Maria Fedorovna, Elizabeth Alekseevna, Grand Duke Constantine Pavlovich, Alexandra Pavlovna, Catherine Pavlovna, Elena Pavlovna, 1780–1825.)

Fond n.4, Perepiska lic imperatorskoj familii i drugih vysochajsih osob, opis' n.1. (Fd n.4, correspondence of the Imperial family members and other princes, opis' n.1)

Fond n.5, razrjad V—Perepiska vysochajsih osob s chastnymi licami 1682–1869 opis n.1. (Fd n.5, section V, correspondence of the princes with individuals, 1682–1869, opis' n.1)

   See in particular, Perepiska Aleksandra I s inostrannymi gosudarstvennymi dejateljami, 1808–1825, Kn. Sh.-M. Talejranom (kop.), 1808–1810, gercogom A. E. de Rishel'e 1820, kn. K.-V. Metternihom o revoljucionnom dvizhenii v Evrope 1820–1823, pisatelem N. Bergasom o politicheskih sobytijah v Ispanii i Francii 1820–1823, gercogom M.-Zh.-F. Monmoransi 1825. Pis'mo gercogu A.-U. Vellingtonu o polozhenii v Grecii (chern.) 1821 (Correspondence of Alexander I with foreign statesmen, 1808–1825, with Prince Ch.-M. Talleyrand (copy), 1808–1810, the duke de Richelieu 1820, Prince K.-W. Metternich on the revolutionary movement in Europe 1820–1823, the writer N. Bergas on political events in Spain and in France 1820–1823, the duke M.-J.-F. de Montmorency 1825. Letter to the Duke of Wellington on the situation in Greece (draft), 1821).

GARF, Gosudarstvennyi arhiv Rossijskoj Federacii (State Archive of the Russian Federation), Moskva.

Fond n.663, Imperatrica Marija Fedorovna (fd n.663), full fond.

Fond n.679, Imperator Aleksandr I (fd n.679), full fond.

Fond n.658, Imperatrica Elizaveta Alekseevna (fd n.658), full fond.

Fond n.728, Katalog sobranija rukopisej hranjashhihsja v biblioteke Zimnego

Dvorca (fd n.728, Collection of the Manuscript Department of the Winter Palace Library).

Rossijskaja nacional'naja Biblioteka (prezhde Imperatorskaja Publichnaja Biblioteka) Sankt-Peterburg, otdel rukopisej, fond Mikhajlovskogo-Danilevskogo.

(Russian National Library, former Imperial Public Library, St. Petersburg: Manuscript Department, fd Mikhailovskij-Danilevskij; fd n.37, delo n.916: text of the 1820 Constitutional Chart.)

Archives of the French Ministry of Foreign Affairs, Paris.

Correspondance diplomatique, Russie, dossiers n.140 à 167. (Diplomatic correspondence. For the years 1808–1812, this correspondence was partly edited by Grand Duke Nicholas Mikhailovich.)

Vatican Archives, Rome.

Secret Chancellery and Special Ecclesiastic Affairs.
Russia files, 1820–1825.

Collections of Published Russian Archives

F. F. Martens, ed., *Sobranie traktatov i konvencij, zakliuchennyh Rossiej s inostrannymi derzhavami* (New compendium of treaties signed by Russia with foreign countries since 1808).

Nicholas Mikhailovich Romanov, *Les relations diplomatiques de la Russie et de la France, d'après les rapports des ambassadeurs d'Alexandre et de Napoléon, 1808–1812* (St. Petersburg: Imprimerie Nationale, 1905–1907).

Russkaja Starina (Russian Antiquities), 1870.

Russkij Arhiv (Russian Archives), 1866, 1870, 1911.

Sbornik Imperatorskogo Russkogo Istoricheskogo Obshchestva, Collections of the Russian Imperial Historical Society, See, in particular, vols. 2, 6, 11, 54, 70, 77, 82, 89, 112, 119, and 127.

Vneshnjaja Politika Rossii XIXogo veka i nachala XXogo veka (Russian Foreign Policy in the 19th Century and in the Beginning of the 20th Century, edited by A. L. Narochnickij and others, first series 1815–1830, 8 volumes, Moscow, 1960–1972; 1815–1830, second series, 1816–December 1824, 5 volumes, Moscow, 1974–1982), Moscow: Gosudarstvennoe Izdatel'stvo Politicheskoj Literatury.

Collections of Private Russian Archives

Panin, *Materialy grafa Nikity Petrovicha Panina (*Materials of Count Panin*),* 1770–1837, 7 vols. (St. Petersburg: 1892).

Vorontsov, *Arhiv knjazja Voroncova* (Archives of Prince Vorontsov) 40 vols. (Moscow: 1860–1895).

Collections of Private Western Archives

Archives of the Jesuit Society.
In Rome (Italy): Dossiers sur la Russie.
In Vanves (France): Archives of Father Jean Gagarin: file about Alexander I's relation toward Catholicism.
In Lyon (France): (Library of the Ecole Normale Supérieure, ENS LSH): Archives of Father Pierling:
BSL/Pi 9, n.5: Alexander's speech at the Polish Assembly, Warsaw, 1818–1825.
BSL/Pi 13, n.8: On Alexander's death and his relation towards the Catholic Church: Documents communicated by Grand Duke Nicholas Mikhailovich.
Documents communicated by Cardinal Rampolla.
Archives of the Civiltà Cattolica:
Diario del Padre Bresciani. Scaffale 24, Palchetto C. (Father Bresciani's diary).
La Civiltà Cattolica, November 4, 1876, quad. 633.
Archives of Duke of Richelieu, Department of Manuscripts and Old Books, Sorbonne Library, Paris. Among them: Comte de Langeron, *Mémoire sur la mort de Paul Ier.* (manuscript in French).

Letters

Alexandre Ier et Napoléon d'après leur correspondance inédite, 1801–1812, edited and commented by Sergey Tatischeff (Paris: Perrin et Cie, 1891).
L. Czartoryski, *Alexandre Ier et le prince Czartoryski, correspondance et conversations particulières* (Paris: M. Lévy Frères, 1865).
Perepiska Imperatora Aleksandra I so sestroj Velikoj Knjaginej Ekaterinoj Pavlovnoj, princesoj Ol'denburgskoj, korolevoj Vjurtembergskoj, 1815–1818, St. Petersburg: Izd. Velikim knjazem Nikolaem Mikhajlovichem, Jekspedicija Zagotovelija gos.; Bumag, 1910) *Correspondence of Emperor Alexander I with his sister the Grand Duchesse Catherine, Princess of Oldenburg, then Queen of Wurtemberg, 1815–1818,* edited by the Grand Duke Nicholas Mikhailovich (Saint-Petersburg: 1910).
Chère Annette, Letters from Russia, 1820–1828, the Correspondence of the Empress Maria Feodorovna of Russia to her Daughter the Grand Duchesse Anna Pavlovna, the Princess of Orange, edited by S. W. Jackman (London: Alan Sutton Publishing, 1994).
Letters from Catherine II to Baron Grimm, 1774–1796, in *Sbornik Imperatorskogo Russkogo Istoricheskogo Obshchestva,* vol. 23 (St. Petersburg: 1878).
Correspondance de Frédéric-César de la Harpe et Alexandre Ier, suivie de la correspondance de F-C. de la Harpe avec les membres de la famille impériale de

Russie, 3 vols., edited by J. C. Biaudet and F. Nicod (Neuchatel: Editions de la Baconnière, 1978–1980).

Correspondance diplomatique de Joseph de Maistre, 1811–1817, edited by Albert Blanc (Paris: Michel Lévy Frères, 1860).

Œuvres inédites de Xavier de Maistre, Premiers essais, fragments et correspondance (Paris: Alphonse Lemerre, 1897).

Pis'ma Imperatricy Marii Fedorovny k Imperatoru Aleksandru I (Letters of the Empress Maria Feodorovna to the Emperor Alexander I) in *Russkij Arhiv*, no. 1 (1911), 132–72.

Xavier de Maistre, *La correspondance inédite de Xavier de Maistre*, edited by Eugène Reaume (Paris: Alphonse Lemerre, 1897).

Lettres de Metternich à la comtesse de Lieven, edited by Jean Hanoteau (Paris: Plon, 1909).

Correspondence of Napoleon, published on the website www.histoire-empire.org.

Lettres et papiers du chancelier comte de Nesselrode, 1760–1850, 6 vols. (Paris: Lahure, 1904).

Romanov Relations, the Private Correspondence of Tsars Alexander I, Nicholas I and the Grand Dukes Constantine and Michael with their Sister Queen Anna Pavlovna, 1817–1855. Edited by S. W. Jackman, assisted by B. Steel (London: Macmillan 1969).

Nikolay Mikhailovich Romanov, *Imperatrica Elizaveta Alekseevna, supruga Imperatora Aleksandra Pervogo*, 3 vols. (St. Petersburg: 1910) Grand Duke Nicholas Mikhailovich, Empress Elizabeth Alekseevna, spouse of Emperor Alexander I).

Memoirs and Diaries

Alexandrana ou bons mots et paroles remarquables d'Alexandre Ier, anonymous text (Paris: Imprimerie de D'Hautel, 1815).

Imperatrica Aleksandra Fedorovna v svoih vospominanijah (Empress Alexandra Feodorovna in her Memories), in *Russkaja Starina*, 88: 10–65 (1896).

Une année de l'Empereur Alexandre ou Résumé de ses principaux actes et tableau de la Russie pendant les quatre derniers mois de 1802 et les huit premiers mois de l'an 1803, anonymous text, written by a French man in 1803 (Paris: Nouzou, 1834).

Mémoires du général Bennigsen 3 vols. (Paris: Berger-Levrault, 1907–1908).

Mémoires de la comtesse de Boigne née d'Osmond, Récits d'une tante, presented and commented by Jean-Claude Berchet (Paris: Mercure de France, 1999, collection Le temps retrouvé, paperback, 1st vol. *Du règne de Louis XVI à 1820*).

Mémoires du général de Caulaincourt, duc de Vicence, grand écuyer de l'empereur, introduction and notes by Jean Hanoteau, 3 vols. (Paris: Plon, 1933).

François-René de Chateaubriand, *Mémoires d'Outre-Tombe* (Paris: Classiques Garnier), edition J.-C. Berchet, vols. 2 and 4, 1998).

Mémoires historiques sur l'empereur Alexandre et la cour de Russie publiés par Madame la comtesse de Choiseul-Gouffier née comtesse de Fisenhaus), ancienne demoiselle d'honneur à la Cour (Brussels: Auguste Wahlen, 1829).

Prince Adam Czartoryski, *Mémoires et correspondance avec l'empereur Alexandre Ier,* 2 vols. (Paris: Plon, 1887).

Emile Dupré de Saint-Maur, *L'Hermite en Russie, ou Observations sur les mœurs et les usages russes au commencement du XIXème siècle,* vol. 2, anonymous book (Paris: Pillet aîné, 1829).

Mémoires de la comtesse Edling, née Stourdza, demoiselle d'honneur de Sa Majesté Elisabeth Alexeievna (Moscow: Impr. du Saint-Synode, 1888).

Souvenirs de la comtesse Golovine, née princesse Golitsyne (Paris: Plon, 1910).

La Cour et le Règne de Paul Ier, Portraits, Souvenirs et Anecdotes, Count Fedor Golovkine, with an introduction and notes by S. Bonnet (Paris: Plon-Nourrit, 1905).

Une année mémorable de la vie d'Auguste de Kotzebue (Paris: Henrichs, 1802).

Frédéric-César de Laharpe, *Le Gouverneur d'un Prince, Frédéric-César de Laharpe et Alexandre Ier de Russie, d'après les manuscrits inédits de Laharpe et des sources russes* (Lausanne-Paris: Georges Bridel, 1902).

Mémoires de Frédéric-César Laharpe, concernant sa conduite comme Directeur de la République Hélvétique (Bern: Librairie de Joël Cherbuluz, 1864).

Mémoires de Langeron, général d'infanterie dans l'armée russe, campagnes de 1812, 1813, 1814, publiés d'après le manuscrit original (Paris: A. Picard et Fils, 1902).

Langeron, Louis-Alexandre-Audrault, comte de, *Journal inédit de la campagne de 1805: Austerlitz* (Paris: La Vouivre, 1998).

Las Cases, Emmanuel-Auguste-Dieudonné, comte de, *Mémorial de Sainte-Hélène* (Paris: Editions du Seuil, 1968).

Mémoires de la comtesse de Lieven (London: 1814).

Anecdotes recueillies à Saint-Pétersbourg par le comte de Maistre, published by Jean Gagarine in *Etudes religieuses, historiques et littéraires* (Anecdotes collected by Count de Maistre in St. Petersburg, edited by Jean Gagarine, vol. 2 (Paris: Joseph Albanel, November 1868).

Mémoires politiques et correspondance diplomatique de Joseph de Maistre, edited and commented by Albert Blanc (Paris: Librairie Nouvelle, 1858).

Charles François Philibert Masson, *Mémoires secrets sur la Russie, et particulièrement sur la fin du règne de Catherine II et le commencement de celui de Paul Ier, formant un tableau des mœurs de Saint-Pétersbourg à la fin du XVIIIème siècle, et contenant nombre d'anecdotes recueillies pendant un séjour de dix années* (Paris: Charles Pougens, 1800).

Baron C.F. de Méneval, *Mémoires pour servir à l'histoire de Napoléon Ier depuis 1802 jusqu'à 1815* (Paris: 1894).

Aleksandr Mikhailovskij-Danilevskij, *Memuary, 1814–1815 (Mémoires),* in collection *Rukopisnye Pamjatniki vypusk* 6 (St. Petersburg: Rossiiskaja Nacionalnaja Biblioteka, 2001).

Conversation de l'Empereur Napoléon avec le général russe Constantin Poltoratzky en 1814 après la bataille de Champaubert, abstract from *La Revue d'Alsace,* May 1855, 226.

Comtesse Paoletti de Rodoretto, *Coup d'œil sur la vie de S. E. le comte Alexandre Michaud de Beauretour lieutenant général, aide de camp de leurs Majestés les empereurs de Russie, Alexandre I et Nicolas I et sur la vie de son frère le chevalier Michaud Louis, colonel du génie, aide de camp de S. M. l'empereur Alexandre Ier* (Turin: J. Baglione, 1869).

A-J. M-R. Savary, *Mémoires du duc de Rovigo pour servir à l'histoire de l'empereur Napoléon*, 8 vols. (Paris: A. Bossange, 1828).

Comte Anatole Henri Philippe de Ségur, *Vie du comte Rostopchine, gouverneur de Moscou en 1812* (Paris: V. Retaux, 1893).

Jean-Henri Schnitzler, *Etudes sur l'empire des tsars: histoire intime de la Russie sous les empereurs Alexandre et Nicolas et particulièrement pendant la crise de 1825*, 2 vols. (Paris: Renouard, 1847).

Mémoires du prince de Talleyrand, 5 vols. (Paris: Calmann-Lévy, 1891–1892).

Dmitrij K. Tarasov, *Imperator Aleksandr I: poslednie gody carstvovanija, bolezn', konchina i pogrebenie. Po lichnym vospominanijam doktora Dmitrija K. Tarasova* (*The Emperor Alexander I, the Last Years of His Reign, His Illness, His Death and His Funerals. Based on Personal Memories of Dr. Dimitri K. Tarasov* (Petrograd: 1915).

General Bibliography

Some General Works Including Alexander I's Reign

Christopher John Bartlett, *Peace, War and the European Powers, 1811–1914* (London: Macmillan, 1996).

F. R. Bridge and Roger Bullen, *The Great Powers and the European States System, 1814–1914*, 2nd ed. (London: Pearson Longman, 2005).

Michel Heller, *Histoire de la Russie et de son empire* (Paris: Plon, 1997).

Andreas Kappeler, *La Russie, empire multiethnique* (Paris: Institut d'Etudes Slaves, 1994).

John P. Ledonne, *Absolutism and Ruling Class: The Formation of the Russian Political Order, 1700–1825* (New York: Oxford University Press, 1991).

Vadim S. Parsamov, *Istorija Rossija XVIII–nachalo XX veka* (*History of Russia, 18th Century*–Beginning *of the 20th Century*) (Moscow: Akademija, 2007).

Richard Pipes, *Russia under the Old Regime* (New York: Collier Books, 1992).

Marc Raeff, *Comprendre l'Ancien Régime russe: Etat et société en Russie imperial* (Paris: Seuil, 1982).

Hugh Ragsdale, *The Russian Tragedy: The Burden of History* (New York: M. E. Sharpe, 1996).

Hugh Seton-Watson, *The Russian Empire, 1801–1917* (Oxford: Clarendon Press, 1967).

Nikolaj A. Troitskij, *Rossija v XIX veke, kurs lekcij, ucheb.* (*Russia in the 19th Century, a Course.* (Moscow: Vysshaja Shkola, 2003).

Biographies of Alexander Published during the Tsarist Period

Modest I. Bogdnavovich, *Istorija carstvovanija Aleksandra I i Rossii v ego vremja (The History of Alexander's Reign and of Russia during His Reign)*, 6 vols. (St. Petersburg: Tip. F. Sushchinskago, 1869–1871).

Adrien Egron, *Vie d'Alexandre Ier, empereur de Russie, suivie de notices sur les grands-ducs Constantin, Nicolas et Michel et de fragments historiques, politiques, littéraires et géographiques propres à faire connaître l'empire russe depuis le commencement du 19ème siècle jusqu'à ce jour* (Paris: F. Denn, 1826).

A. Kizevetter, "Imperator Aleksandr I i Arakcheev" ("The Emperor Alexander I and Arakcheev"), in *Istoricheskie ocherki (Essais historiques)* (Moscow: 1912).

Hannibal E. Lloyd, *Alexander I, Emperor of Russia. A Sketch of His Life* (London: Treuffel and Würtz, 1826).

Konstantin Mel'gunov, *Dela i ljudi Aleksandrovskogo vremeni (Things and People during Alexander's Time)* (Berlin: Vataga, 1923).

Walter Alison Phillips, *Alexander I*, in *Encyclopedia Britannica*, 11th ed., 1:556–59, (1910).

Léonce Pingaud, *L'Empereur Alexandre Ier* (Paris: Plon, 1913).

A. Pypin, *Obshchestvennoe dvizhenie v Rossii pri Aleksandre I (The Social Movement in Russia during Alexander I)*, 3rd ed. (St. Petersburg: Tip. M. M. Stasiulevicha, 1900). *(Public opinion and major intellectual trends during the reign of Alexander I)*

Pierre Rain, *Un tsar idéologue, Alexandre Ier (1777–1825)* (Paris: Perrin, 1913).

Nikolay Mikhailovich Romanov, *Imperator Aleksandr I: opyt istoricheskogo issledovanija* (Grand Duke Nicholas Mikhailovich Romanov, *The Emperor Alexander I, an Historical Essay)*, 2 vols. (St. Petersburg: Jekspedicija zagotovlenija gosudarstvennyh bumag, 1912).

Nicholas Mikhailovich Romanov, *Le Tsar Alexandre Ier* (Paris: Payot, 1931).

V. Semevskij, *Krest'janskij vopros v Rossii v XVIII i pervoj polovine XIX veka (The Agrarian Question in the 18th Century and in the First Half of the 19th Century*, 2 vols. (St. Petersburg, 1888).

Nikolaj K. Shilder, *Imperator Aleksandr I: ego zhizn' i carstvovanie (The Emperor Alexander I, His Life and His Reign)*, 4 vols. (St. Petersburg: A. Suvorin, 1897–1898).

K. Waliszewski, *La Russie il y a cent ans: le règne d'Alexandre Ier*, 3 vols., vol. 1: *La Bastille russe et la révolution en marche, 1801–1812*, vol. 2: *La guerre patriotique et l'héritage de Napoléon, 1812–1816*, vol. 3: *La faillite d'un régime et le premier assaut révolutionnaire, 1818–1825* (Paris: Plon, 1923–1925).

Biographies of Alexander I Published during the Soviet Period

Edith M. Almedingen, *The Emperor Alexander I* (New York: Vanguard Press, 1964).

Boris Bashilov, *Aleksandr Pervyj i ego vremja: masonstvo i carstvovanie,(Alexander I and His Time: Masonry and the Reign)* (Villa Ballester, Argentina: Rus⊠, 1950).

Nicholas Brian-Chaninov, *Alexandre Ier* (Paris: Grasset, 1934).

M. K. Dziewanowski, *Alexander I: Russia's Mysterious Tsar* (New York: Hippocrene Books, 1990).

Francis H. Gribble, *Emperor and Mystic; The Life of Alexander I of Russia* (London: Nash & Grayson, 1931).

Constantin de Grunwald, *Alexandre Ier, le tsar mystique* (Paris: Amiot-Dumont, 1955).

Allen McConnell, *Tsar Alexander I: Paternalistic Reformer* (Chicago: AHM Publishing, 1970).

Daria Olivier, *Alexandre Ier, prince des illusions* (Paris: Fayard, collection Les grandes études historiques, 1973).

Maurice Paléologue, *Alexandre Ier, un tsar énigmatique* (Paris: Plon, 1937).

Alan W. Palmer, *Alexander I: Tsar of War and Peace* (London: Weidenfeld and Nicolson, 1974).

Henri Troyat, *Alexandre Ier: le sphynx du nord* (Paris: Flammarion, 1980).

Henri Troyat, *Alexander of Russia, Napoleon's Conqueror*, translated by Joan Pinkham (New York: Dutton, 1982).

Henry Vallotton, *Le Tsar Alexandre Ier* (Paris: Berger-Levrault, 1966).

Biographies of Alexander I Published after the Collapse of the USSR

Alexandre Arkhanguelski, *Alexandre Ier: le feu follet* (Paris: Fayard, 2000).

V. I. Baljazin, *Imperator Aleksandr I (Emperor Alexander I)* (Moscow: Prosveshshenie, 1999).

Janet M. Hartley, *Alexander I* (London: Longman, 1994).

Michael Klimenko, *Tsar Alexander I: Portrait of an Autocrat* (New York: Hermitage Publishers, 2002).

D. S. Merezhkovskij, *Aleksandr Pervyj (Alexander I)* (Moscow: Armada, 1998).

Paul Mourousy, *Alexandre Ier, tsar de Russie: un sphinx en Europe* (Paris: Editions du Rocher, 1999).

Donald J. Raleigh, (ed.), *The Emperors and Empresses of Russia: Rediscovering the Romanovs* compiled by A. A. Iskenderov, The New Russian History Series (London: M. E. Sharpe, 1996). Pages 216–55 are devoted to Alexander I's reign and were written by Vladimir Aleksandrovich Fedorov.

Aleksander N. Sakharov, *Aleksandr I (Alexander I)* (Moscow: Nauka, 1998).

Aleksander N. Sakharov, *Chelovek na trone (A Man on the Throne)* (Moscow: Nauka, 1992).

On the Reign of Paul I

Nathan I. Ejdel'ma, *Gran' Vekov politicheskaja bor'ba v Rossii, konec XVIII–nachalo XIX stoletija (The Political Life in Russia, the End of the 18th and Beginning of the 19th Century* (Moscow: Mysl', 1982).

Constantin de Grunwald, *L'assassinat de Paul Ier, tsar de Russie* (Paris: Hachette, 1960).

Mikhail Jenkins, *Arakcheev, Grand Vizier of the Russian Empire* (London: Faber and Faber, 1969).

M. V. Klochkov, *Ocherki pravitel'stvennoj dejaltel'nosti vremeni Pavla I (Essays on the Governmental Practices during the Time of Paul I)* (St. Petersburg: Senatskaja tipografija, 1916).

Roderick Macgrew, *Paul I of Russia, 1754–1801* (New York: Oxford University Press, 1992).

Marie Martin, *Maria Feodorovna en son temps, 1759–1828, contribution à l'histoire de la Russie et de l'Europe* (Paris: L'Harmattan, 2003).

Pierre Morane, *Paul I de Russie, avant l'avènement, 1754–1796* (Paris: Plon-Nourrit, 1907).

Gennadij Obolenskij, *Imperator Pavel I (Emperor Paul I)* (Moscow: Russkoe Slovo, 2000).

Aleksej M. Peskov, *Pavel I (Paul I)* (Moscow: Molodaja Gvardija, 1999).

Hugh Ragsdale, (ed.), *Paul I: A Reassessment of His Life and Reign* (Pittsburgh, PA: University Center for International Studies, University of Pittsburgh, 1979).

Hugh Ragsdale, *Tsar Paul and the Question of Madness: An Essay in History and Psychology* (New York: Greenwood Press, 1988).

Donald J. Raleigh, (ed.), *The Emperors and Empresses of Russia: Rediscovering the Romanovs* (compiled by A. A. Iskenderov), The New Russian History Series (London: M. E. Sharpe, 1996). Pages 177–215 are devoted to Paul I and were written by Yuri Alekseevich Sorokin.

Nikolay K. Shilder *Imperator Pavel I. Istoriko-biografičeskij ocherk (The Emperor Paul Ier. A Historical Biography)* (St. Petersburg: A. Suvarin, 1901).

A. Suvorin, (ed.), *Careubijstvo 11 marta 1801, zapiski uchastnikov i sovremennikov* (St. Petersburg: Vsja Moskva, 1907; new edition, St. Petersburg: Izdatel'skoe ob"edinenie "Kul'tura," 1990). (The March 11, 1801 murder of the tsar, narratives of actors and contemporaries).

On Domestic Aspects of the Reign of Alexander I

William L. Blackwell, *The Beginnings of Russian Industrialization, 1800–1860* (Princeton, NJ: Princeton University Press, 1968).

Jerome Blum, *Lord and Peasant in Russia from the Ninth to the Nineteenth Century* (Princeton, NJ: Princeton University Press, 1961).

A. Fedorov, *M. M. Speranskij i A. A. Arakcheev (M. M Speransky and A. A. Arakcheev)* (Moscow: Izadel'stvo Moskovskogo Universiteta, 1997).

Janet Hartley, *A Social History of the Russian Empire* (London: Faber and Faber, 1969).

Michael Jenkins, *Arakcheev, Grand Vizir of the Russian Empire* (London: Faber and Faber, 1969).

N. M. Karamzin, *A Memoir on Ancient and Modern Russia: A Translation and an Analysis,* edited by Richard Pipes (Cambridge: Harvard University Press, 1959).

S. V. Mironenko, *Samoderzhavie i reformy, Politcheskaja bor'ba v Rossii v nachale*

XIX v., *(Autocracy and Reforms, the Political Struggle in the Beginning of the 19th Century)* (Moscow: Nauka, 1989).

Marc Raeff, *The Decembrist Movement* (Englewood Cliffs, NJ: Prentice-Hall, 1966).

Marc Raeff, *Michael Speransky: Statesman of Imperial Russia, 1772–1839*, 2nd ed. (The Hague: Martinus Nijhoff, 1969).

Marc Raeff, *Plans for Political Reform in Imperial Russia, 1730–1905* (Englewood Cliffs, NJ: Prentice-Hall, 1966).

Marc Raeff, *Siberia and the Reforms of 1822* (Seattle: University of Washington Press, 1956).

Nicholas Mikhailovich Romanov, *Le Comte Paul Stroganov (1774–1817)*, 3 vols. (Paris: Imprimerie Nationale, 1905).

M. M. Safonov, *Problema reform v pravitel'stvennoj politike Rossii na rubezhe XVIII i XIX vv.* (*The Problem of Reforms in the Governmental Policy of Russia at the Turn of the 18th–19th Centuries* (Leningrad: Nauka, Leningradskoe otdelnie, 1988).

Aleksander N. Sakharov and S. Bertolissi, *Konstitucionnye proekty Rossii XVIII–nachalo XX veka* (*The Constitutional Projects in Russia, 18th–Beginning of the 20th Century)* (Moscow: RAN, 2000).

A.I. Serkov, *Russkoe Masonstvo, jensiklopedicheskij slovar* (*The Russian Free masonry, an encycopledic dictionary'* (Moskva: ROSSPEN, 2001).

M. M. Speranskij, *zhizn', tvorchestvo, gosudarstvennnaja dejatel'nost'* (*M. M. Speransky, His Life, His Work, His Governmental Activity* (St. Petersburg: Izdatel'stvo Nestor, 2000).

G. Vernadsky, *La Charte constitutionnelle de l'Empire russe de l'an 1820* (Paris: Sirey, 1938).

Kenneth R. Whiting, *A. A. Arakcheev*, doctoral thesis (Harvard: Harvard University Press, 1951).

On the Foreign Policy of Alexander I (French-Russian Relations Excepted)

Maurice Bourquin, *Histoire de la Sainte-Alliance* (Geneva: 1954).

Maurice Capefigue, *L'Empereur Alexandre Ier au Congrès de Vienne et les traités de 1815* (Paris: Amyot, 1866).

Patricia K. Grimsted, *The Foreign Ministers of Alexander I: Political Attitudes and the Conduct of Foreign Diplomacy* (Berkeley: University of California Press, 1969).

Istorija Vneshnej Politiki Rossii, pervaja polovina XIX veka, ot voyn Rossii protiv Napoleona do Parizhskogo mira 1856 g (History of Russian Foreign Policy in the first half of the 19th century, from Rusain wars against Napoleon to the Congress of Paris in 1856 (Moskva: Mezhdunarodnye Otnoshenija, 1999).

Barbara Jelavich, *A Century of Russian Foreign Policy, 1814–1914* (Philadelphia, PA: Lippincott, 1964).

Barbara Jelavich, *St. Petersburg and Moscow; Tsarist and Soviet Foreign Policy, 1814–1974* (Bloomington: Indiana University Press, 1974).

Marion Kukiel, *Czartoryski and European Unity: 1770–1861* (Princeton, NJ: Princeton University Press, 1955).

Francis Ley, *Alexandre Ier et sa Sainte-Alliance: 1811–1825, avec des documents inédits* (Paris: Fischbacher, 1975).

Boris Mouravieff, *L'alliance russo-turque au milieu des guerres napoléoniennes,* (Neuchatel: Éditions de la Baconnière, collection L'évolution du monde et des idées, 1954).

Vasilij K. Nadler, *Imperator Aleksandr I i ideja Svjashchennogo Sojuza (The Emperor Alexander I and the Idea of the Holy Alliance)* (Riga: Izd. knigoprodavca N. Kimmelja, 1886–92).

Ocherki ministerstva inostrannih del Rossii, 860-1917. (Essays on the Russian Ministry of Foreign Office), vol. 1, (Moscow: Olma-Press, 2002).

Henri Pirenne, *La Sainte-Alliance; organisation européenne de la paix mondiale* (Neuchatel: Éditions de la Baconnière, collection L'Évolution du monde et des idées, 1946).

Marie-Pierre Rey, *Le dilemme russe, la Russie et l'Europe occidentale d'Ivan le Terrible à Boris Eltsine* (Paris: Flammarion, 2002).

Jacques A. de Sedouy, *Le Congrès de Vienne, l'Europe contre la France, 1812–1815* (Paris: Perrin, 2003).

W. H. Zawadski, *A Man of Honour, Adam Czartoryski as a Statesman of Russia and Poland* (Oxford: Clarendon Press, 1993).

On the French-Russian Wars and the Relations between Napoleon and Alexander I

General Andolenko, *Histoire de l'armée russe* (Paris: Flammarion, 2007).

L. G. Beskrovnyj, *Otechestvennaja Vojna 1812 goda, (The Patriotic war of 1812)* (Moscow: 1962).

Napoléon Bonaparte, Correspondance générale, publiée par la Fondation Napoléon, volume XII, La Campagne de Russie, 1812 (Paris : Fayard, 2012).

Curtis Cate, *La campagne de Russie: 1812, le duel des deux empereurs* (Paris: Tallandier, 2006).

Curtis Cate, *The War of the Two Emperors: The Duel between Napoleon and Alexander* (New York: Random House, 1985).

Paul Gaulot, *Napoléon et l'Empereur de Russie, entrevue d'Erfurt,* in *Récits des grands Jours de l'Histoire* 20.

Hereford B. George, *Napoleon's Invasion of Russia* (London: Empiricus Books, 2002).

Constantin de Grunwald, *La campagne de Russie: 1812* (Paris, 1963).

Jacques Hantraye, *Les Cosaques aux Champs Elysées, l'occupation de la France après la chute de Napoléon* (Paris: Belin, 2005).

J. Jacoby, *Napoléon en Russie, nouveaux documents* (Paris: Les Libertés françaises, 1938).

Thomas Jones, *Alexander the Blessed, Conqueror of Napoleon* (1978).

Michael Josselson and Diane Josselson, *Le général Hiver, Michel Bogdanovitch Barclay de Tolly* (Paris: Editions Gérard Lebovici, 1986).

Dominic Lieven, *Russia against Napoleon, The Battle for Europe, 1807–1814* (London: Allen Lane, 2009).

A. Mikhailovich-Danilevski, *Description de la première guerre de l'empereur Alexandre contre Napoléon en 1805* (Saint-Pétersbourg: 1844).

Nigel Nicolson, *Napoleon: 1812* (London: Weidenfield and Nicolson, 1985).

Alexander C. Niven, *Napoleon and Alexander I: A Study in Franco-Russian Relations, 1807–1812* (Washington, D. C.: University Press of America, 1978).

Alan Palmer, *Napoleon in Russia* (London: Constable, 1997).

André Ratchinski, *Napoléon et Alexandre Ier: la guerre des idées* (Paris: B. Giovanangeli, 2002).

Marie-Pierre Rey, *L'effroyable tragédie, Une nouvelle histoire de la campagne de Russie* (Paris: Flammarion, 2012).

P. Renouvin, *Histoire des relations internationales*, vol. 2, 1789–1871 (Paris: Hachette, 1994).

Vladlen G. Sirotkin, *Napoleon i Aleksandr I: diplomatija i razvedka Napoleona i Aleksandra I v 1801–1812 gg.* (*Diplomacy and Intelligence under Napoleon and Alexander I in 1801–1812*) (Moscow: Algoritm, Eksmo, 2003).

Oleg Sokolov, *Austerlitz, Napoléon, l'Europe et la Russie* (Paris: Commios, 2006).

Leonid Strakhovsky, *Alexander I of Russia: The Man Who Defeated Napoleon* (New York: W.W. Norton, 1947).

Eugene Tarle, *Napoleon's Invasion of Russia, 1812* (New York: Oxford University Press, 1942).

J. Tulard, *Dictionnaire Napoléon* (Paris: Fayard, 1987).

Nikolaj A. Troickij, *Aleksandr I i Napoleon* (Moscow: "Vysshaja shkola," 1994).

Albert Vandal, *Napoléon et Alexandre Ier. L'alliance russe sous le premier empire*, 3 vols. (Paris: Ed. Plon, Nourrit, 1898–1903).

Emmanuel de Waresquiel, *Talleyrand, le prince immobile* (Paris: Fayard, 2003).

On Alexander's Interest in Catholicism and Rapprochement of the Churches

F.-R. de Chateaubriand, *Le Congrès de Vérone*, chap. 32, online on *gallica*, the website of the French National Library, www.bnf.fr/en/tools/lsp.site_map.html.

Father Gagarine, *Les archives russes et la conversion d'Alexandre Ier*, in *Etudes religieuses* (Lyon: Imprimerie Pitrat Aîné, 1877).

Father Pierling, *L'empereur Alexandre Ier, est-il mort catholique?* (Paris: Plon, 1901).

Father Pierling, *Problème d'histoire: L'empereur Alexandre Ier, est-il mort catholique?* (a new investigation), (Brussels: Gabriel Beauchesne, Publication de la bibliothèque slave, 1913).

On Alexander's Death: Hypotheses and Scenarios

Aleksandr I i starets Fedor Kuz'mich (*Alexander and the starets Fedor Kuzmich*), in *Brevi* (St. Petersburg: Gosudarstvennij Jermitazh, 2004).

V. Baljazin, *Sokrovennye istorii Doma Romanovyh (Secret Stories of the Romanov Dynasty)* (Moscow: Armada, 1996).

Vladimir V. Barjatinskij, *Carstvennyj mistik: imperator Aleksandr I–Fedor Kuz'mich,* (Reprintnoe Vosproizvedenie, 1990). Reedition of a text published in St. Petersburg in 1913 under the title: *The imperial mystic, the Emperor Alexander I–Fiodor Kuzmich.*

V. Bariatinsky, *Le mystère d'Alexandre Ier, le Tsar a-t-il survécu sous les traits de Fedor Kouzmitch?* (Paris: Payot, 1923).

Igor Bunich, *Dve smerti imperatora Aleksandra I: legendy i fakty (The Two Deaths of Emperor Alexander I: Tales and Facts)* (Saint Petersburg: Vita: Oblik, 1993).

V. B. Faybisovic, *Aleksandr I i starets Feodor Kuzmich: istorija odnoj legendy* (St. Petersburg: Brevi, Gos. Ermitazh, Izdatel'stvo Ermitazh, 2004).

V. I. Fedorov, *Aleksandr Blagoslovennyj–svjatoj starets Fedor Tomskij: istoricheskoe issledovanie (Alexandre le Béni—Saint Feodor de Tomsk: recherche historique* (Tomsk: Sibirskij izdatel'skij dom, 2001).

M. M. Gromyko, *Svjatoj pravednij starets Feodor Kuz'mich Tomskij–Aleksandr I Blagoslovennij, issledovanie i materialy (The Starets Fedor Kuzmitch from Tomsk and Alexander I the Blessed, Investigations and Materials)* (Moscow: Palomnik, 2007).

Lev D. Ljubimov, *Tajna imperatora Aleksandra I (The Secret of the Emperor Alexander I)* (Paris: Kn-vo "Vozrozhdenie," 1938).

Vsevolod Nikolaev, *Aleksandr Pervyj–Starets Fëdor Kuz'mich: istoricheskaja biografija, (Alexander I–The Starets Fiodor Kuzmich: Historical Biography)* (San Francisco, CA: Izd-vo "Globus," 1984).

Nikolay Mikhailovich Romanov, *Legenda o konchine imperatora Aleksandra I v Sibiri v obraze starca Fedora Kuz'micha (Tale of the Death of the Emperor Alexander I in Siberia under the Name of Starets Feodor Kuzmich* (St. Petersburg, 1907).

Nikolay Mikhailovich Romanov, *Nekotorye Novye Materialy k voprosu o konchine Imperatora Aleksandra I (Some New Documents on the Death of Alexander I)* (Saint Petersburg: 1914).

Alexis Troubetskoy, *Imperial Legend: The Mysterious Disappearance of Tsar Alexander I* (New York: Arcade Publishing, 2002).

Baron Wrangel, "B grobu lezhal dlinnoborodyj Starets," ("In the coffin was a starets with a long beard"), edited and commented by Irina Pushka, in *Istochnik* (1994): 64–67.

A Few Articles on Precise Points

D. Beauvois, "Les Français à Vilnius en 1812," *Annales historiques de la Révolution Française* no. 246 (October–December 1981), 560–71.

"Antonin Carême," *La France pittoresque* no. 10 (April–May–June, 2004).

James J. Kenney, "Lord Whitworth and the Conspiracy against Tsar Paul I: The New Evidence of the Kent Archive," *Slavic Review* 36, no. 2 (June 1977): 205–19.

Aleksandr Krylov, "Prelestnaja Elizaveta" ("The Charming Elizabeth"), *Novaja Junost'* 54, no. 3, 2002.

Dominic Lieven, "Russia and the Defeat of Napoleon, 1812–1914," *Kritika: Explorations in Russian and Eurasian History* 7, no. 2 (Spring 2006): 283–308.

Allen McConnell, "Alexander I's Hundred Days: The Politics of a Paternalist Reformer," *Slavic Review* 28 (September 1969): 373–93.

P. Maikoff, "Baron G.A. Rozenkampf," *Russkaja Starina* 12 (1904).

A. Martin, "The Response of the Population of Moscow to the Napoleonic Occupation of 1812," in *The Military and Society in Russia: 1450–1917*, edited by E. Lohr (Boston: Brill, 2002).

M. Raeff, "The Political Philosophy of Speranskiy," *American Slavic and East European Review* 12, no. 1 (February, 1953).

Elmo E. Roach, "The Origins of Alexander I's Unofficial Committee," *Russian Review* 28, no. 3 (July 1969): 315–26.

J. Schmidt, "The Restoration of Moscow after 1812," *Slavic Review* 40, no. 1.

O. Sokolov, "La campagne de Russie," *Napoléon Ier, la revue du Consulat et de l'Empire* (November 2000).

O. Sokolov, "L'Eglise orthodoxe et Napoléon," *Revue du Souvenir Napoléonien*, no.470–71 (May–June, 2007).

F. A. Walker, "Enlightenment and Religion in Russian Education in the Reign of Tsar Alexander I," *History of Education Quarterly* 32, no. 3 (Fall 1992): 343–60.

Emmanuel de Waresquiel, "Talleyrand et la paix de Presbourg," *Revue du Souvenir Napoléonien* (Paris, n.462).

A. Zorin, "Star of the East: The Holy Alliance and European Mysticism," *Kritika, Explorations in Russian and Eurasian History* 4, no. 2 (Spring 2003): 313–42.

Index